ESSAYS ON AMERICAN SOCIAL HISTORY

HRW Essays in American History Series
Paul Goodman, Editor

John Braeman	*Essays on the Progressive Era*
John Braeman	*Essays on Recent American History: The 1920s and 1930s*
John Braeman	*Essays on Contemporary America since 1945*
David Brody	*Essays on the Emergence of Modern America: 1870–1900*
Frank Otto Gatell	*Essays on Jacksonian America*
Lawrence E. Gelfand	*Essays on Diplomatic History*
Paul Goodman	*Essays in American Colonial History*
David L. Jacobson	*Essays on the American Revolution*
James Kindegren	*Essays on the History of the South*
John Lankford and David Reimers	*Essays on American Social History*
Leonard Levy	*Essays on the Early Republic: 1789–1820*
Stephen Salsbury	*Essays on the History of the American West*
Wilson Smith	*Essays on American Intellectual History*
Irwin Unger	*Essays on the Civil War and Reconstruction*

ESSAYS ON AMERICAN SOCIAL HISTORY

EDITED BY

JOHN LANKFORD

University of Missouri
Columbia, Missouri

DAVID REIMERS

New York University

HOLT, RINEHART AND WINSTON, INC.

New York · Chicago · San Francisco · Atlanta
Dallas · Montreal · Toronto · London · Sydney

for Merle Curti

Cover: Edward Hicks, "Peaceable Kingdom." Courtesy of The Brooklyn Museum.

Preface

This volume of readings in American social history is the first of its kind. The authors hope that it will stimulate the teachings of the subject in American colleges and universities. This anthology will also prove useful for those introductory American history courses organized around major problems and concepts rather than the older chronological approach. Accompanying each selection are suggestions for further reading; those available in paperback are marked with an asterisk.

In preparing this collection the editors had to make many choices. John Lankford is responsible for Part I, and David Reimers for Part II. John Lankford wishes to thank Nellie Homes, director of the History Section of the Kansas City Public Library and former director of the Division of Geography, History, and Philosophy, University of Missouri Library, and her successor there, Ned Kehde, and his staff. David Reimers wishes to thank David Konig of Harvard University, the staff of the library of New York University, and Jo McNally.

Both editors are indebted to Paul Goodman and, for all the usual reasons, their wives. George Alfred Schnoschneider was also of great assistance.

Columbia, Mo.
New York
February 1970

John Lankford
David Reimers

Contents

One / What Is Social History?

1 / The American Social Order: A Conservative Hypothesis

Rowland Berthoff

There is little argument about the content of American military, diplomatic, or economic history. These boundaries and guide lines are clearly defined. But what is American social history about? The answer is not simple, and several generations of scholars have quarreled over it. Rowland Berthoff traces these conflicting discussions and then develops a conception of social history that focuses on "the social order—the structure of society—and the functional interplay of various institutions and population groups that make it up." Within this context, he suggests mobility as the central theme of American social history. Finally, Berthoff presents an overview of the American experience to substantiate his position.

This essay marks an important step forward in the process of defining social history and clarifying the mission of social historians. Younger workers in the field, while agreeing with Berthoff, stress even more the need for an interdisciplinary approach based on the findings and methods of the social and behavioral sciences.

In addition to interdisciplinary approaches, social historians are beginning to exploit the insights of the comparative dimension by contrasting historical experiences in two or more countries or among different regions and social classes in a given country.

Yet this leads to an apparent contradiction. While historians stress the value of interdisciplinary and comparative analysis, there are a large number of case studies appearing which focus on well-defined situations and examine them in depth. This is especially true of recent quantitative work. In most instances, these are intended as building blocks for a more complete understanding of complex institutions, and can be used in a comparative manner.

At the risk of compressing, then, social history can be defined as the study of structure (institutions, groups, classes, populations), function (the workings of a given institution or class or group and/or the interrelations between them in the larger societal context), and process (change over time). These studies are interdisciplinary in nature and deeply indebted to the social and

American Historical Review, Vol. LXV (1960), 495–514. Reprinted by permission of the author. Copyright 1960 by Rowland Berthoff.

behavioral sciences (especially sociology, anthropology, social psychology, political science, and economics). Social historians strive for comparative understanding, but often turn to case studies in order to achieve maximum control of materials and depth of analysis.

For further reading: Mario S. DePillis, "Trends in American Social History and the Possibilities of Behavioral Approaches," *Journal of Social History*, I (1967), 37–60; Thomas C. Cochran, *The Inner Revolution: Essays on the Social Sciences in History* (1964); *Frederick J. Teggart, *Theory and Processes of History* (1962); Werner J. Cahnman and Alvin Boskoff (eds.), *Sociology and History: Theory and Research* (1964); Edward N. Saveth (ed.), *American History and the Social Sciences* (1964); *Seymour Martin Lipset and Richard Hofstadter (eds.), *Sociology and History: Methods* (1968); *Seymour Martin Lipset and Richard Hofstadter (eds.), *Turner and the Sociology of the Frontier* (1968); *C. Vann Woodward (ed.), *The Comparative Approach to American History* (1968); William O. Aydelotte, "Quantification in History," *American Historical Review*, LXXI (1966), 803–825; Robert F. Berkhofer, Jr., *A Behavioral Approach to Historical Analysis* (1969).

"We need," Samuel Eliot Morison advised us in his presidential address in 1950, "a United States history written from a sanely conservative point of view." [1] The subsequent decade of "dynamic conservatism" in politics and a "new conservatism" among intellectuals would seem a propitious time to attempt a conservative reinterpretation of the history of American society.

It is unlikely, however, that this essay will lead to a revival, sane or otherwise, of precisely the Federalist-Whig-Republican line of conservative history to which Professor Morison referred. That a modern equivalent to a Federalist interpretation is conceivable I hope to make clear, but the "line" connecting Federalists with Whigs and Republicans, although in its day a political reality, latterly has come to seem tortuous and disconnected. In particular, the common American usage of the word "conservative," for defenders of the doctrines of classical liberalism, already appears as the incongruous notion of a past era. This sort of conservatism is evidently a contradiction in terms: a conservatism that is devoted, to be sure, to maintaining existing institutions, but foremost among these a system of breaking down institutions; a conservatism that consistently resists change, but nowhere more than in perpetuating change itself as a way of life, and whose tradition is one of hostility to settled tradition. "It is not easy," Clinton Rossiter truly says, "to state the common principles of laissez-faire conservatism." [2] The habit of equating "conservative" with "laissez faire" has produced the odd but quite familiar political spectacle of self-styled conservatives who champion the economic freedom of rugged individuals against regimentation by a welfare state created by professed liberals. Lately the

[1] Samuel Eliot Morison, "Faith of a Historian," *American Historical Review*, LVI (Jan. 1951), 273.

[2] Clinton Rossiter, *Conservatism in America* (New York, 1955), 135.

politicians have begun to recognize the anomaly; many a faithful New Dealer now avows himself a new kind of conservative.

Historians have been less enterprising. Recently a few have broken away from commonly received definitions in reinterpreting particular episodes in American history, but as yet we have had no broad conservative synthesis. This inertia is due not only to the professed liberalism of scholars whose courses were charted during the Progressive and New Deal era, but also to the fact that the search for a new synthesis has not proceeded in the most likely direction, that of social history. The recent preoccupation with the history of ideas, although it has succeeded brilliantly in illuminating a whole new dimension of the past, has also had at least one unfortunate result. Rethinking the ideas of the past has perhaps unduly blinkered our vision of other aspects of the past. Although the ideas of a particular epoch, as part of the reality of that time, can never be left out of the account, they seldom serve as an adequate or accurate picture of that reality itself; if it were otherwise, the world would have little need for new interpretations by historians. Perhaps by laying aside briefly our concern with the ideas that Americans have held, of liberalism and conservatism for example, and by taking a fresh look at the humbler but fundamental history of the society that first gave rise to those ideas, we may find a way toward a new and yet a conservative interpretation of American history in general.

At the outset, this plan of attack threatens to bog us down in an all too familiar quagmire. In nearly eighty years of discussion since the time of McMaster and Eggleston we have not even managed to agree upon the proper subject matter of social history. Nor have we yet found an adequately "dynamic principle," or any "great synthetic principle," around which to organize this still amorphous material.[3] Social history remains the "synonym for miscellaneous or nondescript" which Dixon Ryan Fox found it to be in 1929 and the "big booming confusion" and "abyss of thought" which Charles A. Beard deplored in 1933, with no better a principle than the eclectic one, expressed by Roy F. Nichols in 1937, that America "has evolved because of, or in spite of, a series of forces let loose in helter-skelter fashion with no particular order of importance or sequence."[4] A recent survey of university courses bearing the label "social history" or "social and intellectual history" reconfirms these impressions. Virtually anything is apt to be found in such courses—" 'cultural and intellectual achievements,' education, religion, reform, science, and the fine arts, . . . population, immigration, minority groups, . . . 'daily life,' 'social trends,' or 'social ideas,' . . . 'the development of the American mind' "—anything, that is, as long as it is not conventionally classified as political history.[5] In this unsatisfactory situation, one may risk what Fox, taking the opposite tack, characterized as the social historian's "secret bias toward simplicity" in "seeking one principle of synthesis into which everything can be jammed."[6]

[3] *Approaches to American Social History,* ed. William E. Lingelbach (New York, 1937), 20, 79.

[4] Dixon Ryan Fox, "A Synthetic Principle in American Social History," *American Historical Review,* XXXV (Jan. 1930), 265; Charles A. Beard, review of Arthur M. Schlesinger, *The Rise of the City, ibid.,* XXXVIII (July 1933), 779–80; Roy F. Nichols, "A Political Historian Looks at Social History," *Approaches to American Social History,* ed. Lingelbach, 20.

[5] H. L. Swint, "Trends in the Teaching of Social and Intellectual History," *Social Studies,* XLVI (Nov. 1955), 244.

[6] Fox, "A Synthetic Principle," 261.

What is, first of all, the proper subject matter of social history? The history of society need not be, as it usually has been, a merely residual field, "left after every other group has defined the boundaries of its interests." [7] It pertains instead to a quite specific area of human affairs which, as it happens, has already been conveniently marked out for study by the sociologists: that is, the social order—the structure of society—and the functional interplay of the various institutions and population groups that make it up. In American society such groupings as local or regional communities, social and economic classes, ethnic groups, business corporations, trade-unions, political machines, voluntary associations of many kinds, and of course the family have all been conspicuous. The evolution of a society composed of such groups, and also, in America, of a large proportion of more or less unattached individuals, presents the appropriate subject for the social historian.

It would be difficult to say precisely where the boundary lies between social history so defined and cultural history, since the content of the life of the groups within the social order is their culture; a description of the organization of a group that did not advert to its mind or culture would be threadbare indeed. Yet social history and cultural history can differ in emphasis much as sociology differs from literary criticism. By the same token, social history and intellectual history are related to each other, most elementarily in the fact that social institutions are no more substantial than their members and others think they are. Furthermore, the intellectual pattern of a nation —certainly of America—derives in large part from its past and present social pattern. And yet ideas, whatever their social subsoil may have been, do come to have their own flowering, which the intellectual historian can clip and dissect. On an earthier level, the economic base, past or present, from which any social order is itself largely derived has an objective physical existence partly independent of human ideas and purposes, so that no argument is needed to justify economic history as a subject distinct from social or intellectual history.

All this is by no means to assert a simple economic or social determinism in history. Ideas, whatever their origins, do react upon the social order, and both ideas and social institutions together help to determine the uses to which we put the objective phenomena of the natural environment. But in examining the oft-praised seamless web of history, we can, without unduly straining a metaphor, distinguish, in terms of a carpet, economic history and social history as the basic warp and weft of the coarse backing, cultural history as the finer substance of the carpet, and intellectual history as the figure that both rests upon and gives form to the other materials. If the ultimate goal of historians no less than carpet weavers is to construct a whole fabric, still they must first perfect the elements of their carpets or of the grand historical synthesis.

As social historians we have, to be sure, included in our courses and books material relevant to the structure and functioning of the American social order, though it has been rather aimlessly tangled together with all manner of more or less extraneous things. What is evidently still needed today, no less than twenty or thirty years ago, is an adequate central theme around which to arrange this material, a synthetic rather than a merely eclectic principle. What I have to suggest may seem only to reflect the odd preoccupation of our time with problems of social status. I am en-

[7] John A. Krout, "Reflections of a Social Historian," *Approaches to American Social History,* ed. Lingelbach, 61.

couraged, however, by the number of perceptive recent studies by historians and social scientists which are essentially consistent with the assumption that the central and continuous factor throughout the history of American society is its characteristic mobility.

The concept of mobility does, it is clear, furnish us with a principle adequate at least to comprehend a number of conventional concerns of American historiography. The westward movement, which since Frederick Jackson Turner's time has figured as a special field claiming fundamental importance, had better be considered as only one of a number of kinds of physical and social movement. For that matter, along with the even more extensive movement of people to the cities, it proves to have been only one kind of internal migration. Immigration history has grown in recent years into another such primary field. A third, as yet only beginning to be developed by historians, is the occupational and social mobility—the constant vertical movement up and down the ladder of wealth and status—that characterizes any modern industrial country, England or Japan not less than the United States.[8]

Furthermore, each of these three well-known kinds of movement in our history has given rise to certain of our most characteristic social institutions and population groups. The process of settlement, whether westward or cityward, produced our regions and sections and our urban communities. The process of immigration successively introduced a great variety of ethnic and religious groups into the population. Social or vertical mobility, fostered both by the free land of the frontier and by opportunities in expanding commerce and industry, has been with us virtually since our beginnings and has created our characteristic structure of social classes. These three kinds of mobility, and likewise the three kinds of resultant social groupings, of course have always been closely interrelated. We expect to find a certain coincidence in the South, for example, of British ancestry, Protestant religion, and well-defined class distinctions; or in a northern coal-mining town of people of Slavic descent, Catholic or Orthodox religion, and the working class. While there have no doubt been individuals who incorporated in themselves every conceivable regional, ethnic, and social mixture, still our history has made some combinations of ancestry and religion, locale, and class more likely than others.

It is in fact this interrelationship between the different kinds of mobility that makes mobility a useful concept for our social history. And likewise it is the lack of such a concept that has misled many historians of the frontier or of immigration to claim too exclusive an importance for these special subjects—to suppose that egalitarian democracy came only out of the frontier forests, or that the end of both the frontier and of unrestricted immigration presaged the demise of economic opportunity in America. It will continue to be convenient to demarcate these fields of history for monographic research, but otherwise to isolate them is unlikely to produce work of general importance.

If the social order is agreed to be the proper concern of social history, and mobility the central theme in American social history, a general hypothesis can then be proposed for the peculiar evolution of the American social order. This evolution has followed a long cycle. The first phase comprised the seventeenth and eighteenth centuries, down to about 1815, and was characterized by relatively low mobility

[8] Seymour Martin Lipset and Reinhard Bendix, *Social Mobility in Industrial Society* (Berkeley, Calif., 1959), 11–75.

(though high by European standards) and the establishment of a fairly stable social order in the various colonies and new states.[9] The second phase, the nineteenth century, was an epoch of enormous migration, immigration, and social mobility, during which the recently established social order became badly disorganized and in fact disorderly. Finally, after a transitional period from about 1900 to 1930, during which free land and free immigration came to their end and a profound effort to reorganize American society began, we have in the past thirty years established a society which, although still highly mobile, is better integrated than that of the nineteenth century and is in this respect more comparable to that of the eighteenth.

How well does this hypothesis fit the familiar annals of frontier history? Well enough, I think, to confirm one of the main points of the Turner thesis. In so far as Turner's critics have denied the *exclusive* significance of the frontier, they have the better case; but free land, considered as one of several sources of mobility, by and large was the egalitarian social force that the frontier school has always maintained it was. By establishing this point statistically for an ordinary district in Wisconsin, Merle Curti's recent study of Trempealeau County has broken through the timeworn pattern of debate on the matter.[10] Some qualification of this is necessary; as Paul W. Gates has shown, the land laws permitted various speculators to monopolize vast tracts here and there throughout the West.[11] But as in Trempealeau County, so we may suppose elsewhere, if "the rich became somewhat richer, the poor became a good deal less poor." [12]

The leveling force of free land was, of course, already at work in the seventeenth and eighteenth centuries, so that almost everywhere there was established the self-reliant and comfortable yeomanry whom foreign observers thought so remarkable. And yet mobility and stability were still in balance. The process of settlement was relatively gradual before the Revolution, especially in New England, where until late in the colonial period it proceeded in organized groups of like-minded people strictly controlled by authority. In the South it took more than a century for the east-west migration of tobacco planters and farmers to cross the Blue Ridge, and then only to find back-country migrants already moving down from Pennsylvania. Even with these reinforcements, southern settlement did not pass west of the mountains in any great numbers until near the end of the eighteenth century. This low rate of migration presumably contributed to the stability and homogeneity of the society in which the class of self-made country squires figured so prominently among the generality of yeomen in both North and South. Another notable result was the strength of the local or regional attachments which these relatively stationary Americans evidently felt at that time. The more than a dozen distinct dialect areas which exactly mirror the pattern of colonial settlement between the seaboard and the mountains are telling evidence of this parochialism.[13]

In the nineteenth century, the westward migration which had been measured in

[9] The best description of this society, in its last days, is still Henry Adams, *History of the United States of America during the First Administration of Thomas Jefferson* (2 vols., New York, 1889), I, 1–184.

[10] Merle Curti, *The Making of an American Community: A Case Study of Democracy in a Frontier County* (Stanford, Calif., 1959), 140–221.

[11] Paul W. Gates, "Frontier Estate Builders and Farm Laborers," *The Frontier in Perspective*, eds. Walker D. Wyman and Clifton B. Kroeber (Madison, Wis., 1957), 143–63.

[12] Curti, *Making of an American Community*, 445.

[13] Hans Kurath, *A Word Geography of the Eastern United States* (Ann Arbor, Mich., 1949).

hundreds of miles rapidly preempted the remaining thousands. However admirable we have been accustomed to think the restless individualism of the westward migrants, the movement was a disorderly process. Although in general these individuals succeeded, as the Trempealeau study indicates, in their effort to maintain or improve their economic and social status, their migration tended to break down the social order which had been painfully attained in the East in the previous two hundred years. The rush for free land inhibited the development of any stable hierarchy of social and economic classes, except, of course, in those parts of the Old Southwest where the introduction of Negro slavery, which had been the most extreme class distinction in the eighteenth-century Tidewater, perpetuated an anachronism. The social and economic leveling of the frontier is still commonly applauded and indeed has become an essential part of our liberal tradition.

Besides social classes, however, other and less dubious forms of social organization, such as local communities, were likewise stunted. Although a score of new regions, from fertile prairie and rugged upland to arid plains and barren desert, were settled, the social differences that these physiographic conditions produced were hardly more remarkable than the social resemblances between the new regions.[14] Even the cattle kingdom of the Great Plains, which, as the last high-water mark of the westward movement, rightly lives on as a national legend, was much like the earlier livestock ranges of the savannas and canebrakes of the Old Southwest, although there it had often been hard to see the cowboys for the trees.[15] What these and almost all other parts of the nineteenth-century West had in common was a disorderly or at best a yet unordered society, whose population was too transient, and consequently too mixed in its origins, to permit the growth of integrated local communities. The townships, counties, and cities may have been "settled," but their inhabitants were not.

This tenuousness of local attachments had a result besides the undifferentiated nationalism for which Turner praised the West. Although western settlements did share a fairly homogeneous culture, to the extent that the folk customs of the Old Northwest and Southwest, the Plains and the Far West were in many particulars identical, this common culture was perforce rudimentary. It was as conservative as possible of the institutions and values of eastern society, but distance and the half-settled state of the New West were uncongenial. The rawness of the West is one of our great traditions, and rightly so; even the most careful listing of churches, newspapers, libraries, theaters, literary societies, and other infant amenities of the cultural frontier can hardly convince us that the West sprang into being as a highly developed or creative social order. It was not a seedbed of innovation and reform; it was merely unformed. The theology of the frontier camp meeting, for instance, was an old doctrine rudely preached. More thoroughgoing novelties in religion were the work of long-settled eastern communities which could afford to be liberal.[16]

[14] Obviously American history is full of sectional conflicts, but these have for the most part, and with the notable exception of the Civil War, arisen from economic rather than social differences. Even the incompatible societies of North and South, for that matter, went to war only after their social differences had been transmuted into antipathetic moral and ideological convictions.

[15] Compare Walter Prescott Webb, *The Great Plains* (New York, 1931), 205–69, with Frank Lawrence Owsley, *Plain Folk of the Old South* (Baton Rouge, La., 1949), 23–50.

[16] Compare, e.g., Owsley, *Plain Folk of the Old South,* 90–149; R. Carlyle Buley, *The Old Northwest: Pioneer Period, 1815–1840* (2 vols., Bloomington, Ind., 1951), I, 138–394; Everett

How the twentieth century removed the influence of the frontier from American society is an old story. As settlement approached its natural limits between 1890 and 1920, so did the egalitarian effect of free land. Class distinctions hardened, not only in western cities and towns, but on the land itself. Farm laborers and tenants no longer could confidently expect to rise into the class of landowning farmers. (The same thing in effect had happened long before in the Old Southwest, where the suitable cotton land had virtually all been entered before 1860.) Alarm over this situation, so novel in the West, was heightened around the turn of the century by the misconception, endorsed by Turner, that mobility had been due solely to the influence of the frontier. That perhaps a less restless western population, including an accepted upper class which in time could set a higher tone to western culture, might have a certain social value, was a possibility that nobody seemed to consider worth expressing.

In any case, it is clear that the end of the frontier movement was by no means the end of internal migration. This had long since started to turn toward the cities, in large part because of the other two factors mentioned above, immigration and social mobility.

Like the westward movement, of which indeed it was literally a part, immigration from the Old World was, in the seventeenth and eighteenth centuries, a relatively gradual process. Although it was the source of the entire white and Negro population of some four million in 1790, it had involved, in the course of nearly two hundred years, probably not as many as a million persons. Even that degree of movement was cut down during most of the forty years between, 1775 and 1815. More important (since numbers are only relative), the colonial immigration established, with only a few local exceptions, a homogeneous population of English origin and culture. Other European and African peoples came, but mostly in the eighteenth century, after the English had already set the pattern of colonial society. Even though some of the others managed to maintain their separate ethnic identities, in general the persistence of immigrant culture meant the persistence of a variant of English culture. Americans were Englishmen established in a new environment. The New World modified the social order that they established, but it was, in the circumstances, a remarkably orderly society which in many particulars approximated, often quite consciously, that of the mother country.

After 1815, however, and throughout the hundred-odd years down to the immigration restriction acts of the 1920's, the enormous influx of some 35,000,000 persons —numbering more than four times the entire American population of 1815 and coming from all the countries and cultures of Europe—contributed as much as any factor to the general disorder of nineteenth-century American society. Recent scholarship has made the essential facts of this migration as familiar as those of the westward movement.[17] It has already become a commonplace to remark on the uprooting of the immigrants, especially the peasants among them, out of their accustomed Old

---

Dick, *The Sod-House Frontier, 1854–1890: A Social History of the Northern Plains from the Creation of Kansas and Nebraska to the Admission of the Dakotas* (New York, 1937), *passim;* Louis B. Wright, *Culture on the Moving Frontier* (Bloomington, Ind., 1955), *passim.*

[17] William I. Thomas and Florian Znaniecki, *The Polish Peasant in Europe and America: Monograph of an Immigrant Group* (5 vols., Boston, 1918–20); Oscar Handlin, *Boston's Immigrants, 1790–1865: A Study in Acculturation* (Cambridge, Mass., 1941), and *The Uprooted: The Epic Story of the Great Migrations That Made the American People* (Boston, 1951).

World communities, and their equally abrupt transplanting as so many isolated individuals into the unfamiliar and often inhospitable American social climate. Like the westward movement, immigration was not effectively managed by society; in most cases it was undertaken voluntarily by individual families as their particular response to economic and social circumstances that endangered their accustomed status at home or promised a better one in America. But their quest for security, ironically enough, often had unwelcome results, when peasants found themselves piled on top of each other in urban slum tenements, where they were too crowded for their taste, or scattered across remote midwestern prairies on farms which were too isolated.

To be sure, the social confusion suffered by these people was somewhat relieved by the ethnic associations which they organized for themselves. But the immigrants' clubs, newspapers, singing societies, even their churches, were at best but fragile substitutes for the customary social order they had once known and feeble custodians of the old culture they had never intended to abandon. Most of these associations eventually dwindled and dissolved, unable to withstand the atomization to which American social mobility subjected the American-born second generation. (There was at least as great a cultural loss in this deracination as in the restless mobility of the frontiersmen.[18]) Moreover, even in so far as the ethnic group succeeded for a time in providing the warmth of community for the first-generation immigrants themselves, most of whom as workingmen were already isolated from Americans of other classes, it compounded the general lack of integration in American society. Our retrospective compassion for these "strangers in the land" may extend also to the Yankees who objected to them as disruptive intruders.

Within the span of the same early twentieth-century generation which saw the end of the frontier migration, free immigration likewise was brought to its end by the national-origins quota acts. The racial theory running through this legislation has since been exposed as pseudoscientific quackery, but the situation of social disorder which made so ill-considered a theory credible to Americans (especially to those anxious for their own status) was real enough.[19] To be sure, immigration was no more exclusively the cause of the disorder than were the westward movement and the Industrial Revolution, both of which most Americans considered salutary, but it was one cause. In the 1920's, as Nathan Glazer has put it, "America had decided to stop the kaleidoscope and find out what it had become." [20]

By that time the homogeneity of 1815 had been transformed into a wild complexity of peoples and cultures in various stages of assimilation. Although the immigration acts, by cutting off further additions from abroad to this mosaic, have tended to consolidate the myriad of ethnic groups into a single new American culture, somewhat as was intended, the new homogeneity is still incomplete. In place of an unstable cultural pluralism we now have simpler divisions between Protestants, Catholics, and Jews which seem likely to persist as a permanent social heritage from the nineteenth century.[21] For that matter, partly because of the crudity of the

[18] Nathan Glazer, "The Immigrant Groups and American Culture," *Yale Review,* XLVIII (Spring 1959), 382–97.
[19] John Higham, *Strangers in the Land: Patterns of American Nativism, 1860–1925* (New Brunswick, N. J., 1955).
[20] Nathan Glazer, "The Integration of American Immigrants," *Law and Contemporary Problems,* XXI (Spring 1956), 269.
[21] Will Herberg, *Protestant—Catholic—Jew: An Essay in American Religious Sociology* (New York, 1955), 18–58.

racial notions embedded in the immigration acts, they have in one notable way failed to accomplish even their sponsors' goal of ethnic homogeneity. Since the First World War, fresh waves of migrants have been set in motion within the United States, among them Puerto Ricans and poor southern Negroes and whites, who have come north to take the places now denied to Italian and Polish immigrants. But however imperfect from any point of view, the immigration acts of 1921 and 1924, and of 1952, are at least symptomatic of the twentieth-century impulse to reintegrate a shaken social order.

This impulse has been more consciously expressed, curiously enough, in this century's anxiety to maintain social mobility, the vertical movement of individuals from one class to another. Social mobility in America has been the product of an expanding economy, of which western settlement and immigration were parts no less than commercial expansion and the Industrial Revolution. In the seventeenth and eighteenth centuries the economy expanded at a slower rate than it was to do thereafter, industrialization having hardly begun here. It was commonly agreed at that time, furthermore, that in economic affairs there were certain narrow standards of fair dealing which limited private enterprise and which ought to be enforced by government.

The opportunity was at hand, however, in commerce and in land speculation or large-scale cultivation, for many a humble immigrant and his descendants—even for indentured servants after their time was up—to prosper and become gentlemen after the model of the merchants and gentry of England. Even in Pennsylvania and the New England colonies, which were settled for a less earthly purpose, society had its higher ranks, and it was not long before the foremost among these were the merchants of the ports and such landed magnates as the Connecticut Valley "river gods." [22] There and elsewhere—especially in South Carolina and the Chesapeake colonies after the mass importation of Negro slave labor—the social order consisted of this aristocracy and of various inferior social classes, distinct from each other and accepting the distinctions.[23] These distinctions were kept from becoming as extreme as in England by the availability of land, on which nearly everywhere the broad class of roughly equal yeoman freeholders established itself as the bulk of the population. As we may again surmise, however, this leveling was itself limited by the slow pace of settlement. Even after the political Revolution won independence from the mother country, in most of the new states society continued on the whole to acquiesce in domination by a class of "gentlemen freeholders." [24]

That after 1815 this social order was to be swept away nearly everywhere was not immediately apparent. It became plain in the early 1830's, the time of the great rush of settlers to the West, when in both East and West the rough equality of the class of yeoman farmers was transmuted into an egalitarian ideology. As recent studies of Jacksonianism have demonstrated, the new industrial entrepreneurs as well

[22] Bernard Bailyn, *The New England Merchants in the Seventeeth Century* (Cambridge, Mass., 1955); Frederick B. Tolles, *Meeting House and Counting House: The Quaker Merchants of Colonial Philadelphia, 1682–1763* (Chapel Hill, N.C., 1948); Robert J. Taylor, *Western Massachusetts in the Revolution* (Providence, R.I., 1954), 11–26.

[23] Thomas Jefferson Wertenbaker, *The Planters of Colonial Virginia* (Princeton, N.J., 1922), 134–61.

[24] Charles C. Sydnor, *Gentlemen Freeholders: Political Practices in Washington's Virginia* (Chapel Hill, N.C., 1952); Robert E. Brown, *Middle-Class Democracy and the Revolution in Massachusetts, 1691–1780* (Ithaca, N.Y., 1955).

as the small farmers and handicraft artisans adopted this ideology. These new and old groups alike hated privileged monopoly, though for opposite reasons. The yeoman farmers and artisans were looking backward, seeking to preserve the society of the eighteenth century, in which, even though there were class divisions, the lower classes had a kind of security that kept them from sinking too low. The new group of rising capitalists, on the contrary, looked forward to a liberal society in which none of their competitors would enjoy a monopoly established by government wherewith to block their own individual progress to success and fortune.[25]

From that time on, this ambiguous egalitarianism gave direction (or, rather, lack of direction) to both the industrial and the frontier expansion of the nineteenth century. Thus, just when industrialization opened a myriad of opportunities for individuals to rise in position, wealth, and status, the checkrein of governmental regulation was thrown off. The irony of the inadvertent result is another familiar fact: unregulated industrial expansion quickly produced both a glittering plutocracy and a depressed proletariat, far more widely divided in sentiment and interest than colonial social classes had ever been. The fact that the proletariat consisted largely of immigrants of foreign culture widened still further the social divisions. On the other hand, the egalitarian yeoman tradition was by no means dead, and indeed in so far as industrial expansion kept alive a semblance of equal opportunity for the individual, Americans tolerated the actual inequality of wealth and status at any given time within their society.

Well before the end of the century, it became abundantly clear that the industrial revolutionaries had produced an American social disorder almost without parallel in the modern world. A self-made plutocracy recognized little responsibility for the working classes, the latter repudiated whatever common interest they had once felt with their employers, ethnic groups regarded each other with little sympathy, the farming regions resented their exploitation by businessmen and bankers, and individuals in general acknowledged few social duties except to themselves, their families, and their narrow interest groups. Even so elemental an institution as the family, for that matter, was feared to be in a state of disintegration, as divorce became a common practice, women left the home to work, and each new generation of children, even those who did not have to work for a living, seemed to have less respect for parental authority.

The forces of social reintegration were feeble indeed. Symptomatic of the need for a new sense of community was the fraternal order. It is customary for historians to dismiss the lodges of Masons or Odd Fellows which sprang up everywhere as an unimportant eccentricity of a "nation of joiners," and yet they were highly significant of the lack of other forms of community in American society in their day.[26] Despite the extravagant flummery of these lodges and the evident lack of cultural taste among their millions of members, perhaps the invention and maintenance of any kind of social community was in itself a sufficient cultural achievement for their time. (Much the same might be said of the still ineffectual trade-union movement.) The American's habit, when taxed by a European visitor with the poverty of Amer-

[25] Marvin Meyers, The Jacksonian Persuasion: Politics and Belief (Stanford, Calif., 1957); Bray Hammond, Banks and Politics in America: From the Revolution to the Civil War (Princeton, N.J., 1957).

[26] Charles W. Ferguson, Fifty Million Brothers: A Panorama of American Lodges and Clubs (New York, 1937), 3–15.

ican culture, of pointing with pride to "our institutions"—meaning, of course, primarily political institutions—was not altogether irrelevant. Europeans might not value either political or social institutions among the higher forms of "culture," but in America the ever-present task of shoring up the social framework inevitably exhausted energies that might otherwise have been devoted to filling the structure with finer things. Like the contemporary English working-class culture, in the view of Raymond Williams, American popular culture in the nineteenth century created social institutions rather than art, literature, or science—in its context, a remarkable achievement indeed.[27]

Apart from such palliatives, however, the chief resistance to social disorder came from various old-fashioned groups, some of them numbered, to their eventual discomfiture, among Jackson's original supporters, who resented being superseded by the Industrial Revolution. It has recently been suggested that even the humanitarian reformers of the 1830's and 1840's, who have hitherto been ranked as the vanguard of liberalism, in fact included many whose concern for the downtrodden reflected their conservative anxiety over their own loss of prestige or influence in society. Thus a large proportion of the abolitionist leaders were genteel folk of the old order, and it might be added that at least a few, like Garrison himself, came from the class of artisans whose handicraft skills were already obsolescent.[28] If it is true that the impulse of these reformers was essentially conservative or even reactionary, this may account for their remarkable proneness, when endeavoring to liberate the individual from bondage to alcohol and other evils, ultimately to resort, with no consciousness of incongruity, to legal prohibition and other restrictions not at all welcome to the individual drinker.

The history of the second quarter of the nineteenth century abounds in similar examples of the reformer who resists change. The clearest is the labor movement, which, until the 1850's, was composed largely of preindustrial workingmen with a reactionary program.[29] Again, the most perceptive account of the "burned-over district" of upper New York State suggests that the susceptibility of the small farmers there to novel religious cults in this same period was in some degree the reaction of a settled rural backwater that had already been left behind by the march of progress.[30] Among these groups only the Mormons achieved their own kind of success, and it is significant that they did so by utterly repudiating liberal individualism when they built their own hierarchic social order in the western deserts.

In recent years the agrarian crusaders of the late nineteenth century have likewise been denied their reputation as radicals and demoted to the ranks of reactionaries. Populism, it now appears, was the unrealistic attempt of unsuccessful rural capitalists to take refuge in an outworn myth. It is true that, in Richard Hofstadter's words, "when times were persistently bad, the farmer tended to reject his business role and its failures [and] to withdraw into the role of the injured little yeoman." [31] But it should be noted that this yeoman tradition evoked nostalgia for a social order in

[27] Raymond Williams, *Culture and Society, 1780–1950* (London, 1958), 327.

[28] David Donald, *Lincoln Reconsidered: Essays on the Civil War Era* (New York, 1956), 19–36.

[29] Norman J. Ware, *The Industrial Worker, 1840–1860: The Reaction of American Industrial Society to the Advance of the Industrial Revolution* (Boston, 1924), 198–240.

[30] Whitney R. Cross, *The Burned-over District: The Social and Intellectual History of Enthusiastic Religion in Western New York, 1800–1850* (Ithaca, N. Y., 1950), 55–109.

[31] Richard Hofstadter, *The Age of Reform: From Bryan to F.D.R.* (New York, 1955), 47.

which the small farmer had enjoyed a more secure status. That is, it harked back to the pre-Jacksonian society of the eighteenth century rather more than to the individualistic disorder of the nineteenth in which these farmer-speculators themselves had injudiciously indulged. The Populists, in this sense, were double-dyed reactionaries, longing not merely for the past epoch, but for the epoch before that.

Nostalgia, however, is sometimes more than a perverse rejection of reality. All these so-called radicals of the nineteenth century, reminiscent as they are of various modern yet archaic European groups of "primitive rebels," may have been only reactionaries out of step with their progressive industrial age, but in the end they were not wholly ineffectual.[32] Their spirit has infused a good deal of the twentieth-century movement to reorder society, and in the process something that was obsolete in 1890 has in effect been restored.

This fundamental task of reintegrating the social order had hardly been begun by 1900, when Americans for the first time came seriously to grips with it. This, it may confidently be said, is the meaning of the Progressive movement for our social history. Politics from that point on no longer merely followed the lines of the underlying economic and social foundations of the country, but dug down and reshaped them by an act of will.

At the outset, a nineteenth-century habit of speech dictated that honest anxiety be expressed for the survival of equality of opportunity, that is, of social mobility, mortally wounded as it was supposed to be by the closing of the frontier and the spread of industrial monopoly. The trust movement no doubt had battened on the egalitarianism of liberal American democracy; still, the cure for the ills of democracy was said to be more democracy. But while it is true that the Progressive movement was literally "the complaint of the unorganized against the consequences of organization," in particular such organizations as trusts and political machines, nevertheless by force of circumstances Progressives themselves had to organize in order to control these institutions.[33] Thus the Progressive movement, though undertaken to liberate opportunity for the individual, tended rather to encase it in new regulatory institutions over and alongside the objectionable institutions. This proliferation of interlocked institutions was a conservative counterrevolution. In its course, the big business corporation eventually would shed its early reputation as a monopolistic monster and, in effect, become esteemed as the pioneer of modern institutional society, and the urban political machine would be affectionately recalled as the prototype of the welfare state.[34]

Americans of all classes after 1900 preached the Progressive gospel of mutual responsibility, even though we may suspect some of them, like some earlier reformers, of more anxiety over their own insecure economic and social status than over the general welfare.[35] Others, who still denied their social duties, had responsibility forced, at least gingerly, on them by the Progressive regulation of railroads, labor conditions, banks, food handling, natural resources, and so forth. The Progressive legislative record hardly amounted to a root-and-branch social revolution, but for a

[32] E. J. Hobsbawm, *Primitive Rebels: Studies in Archaic Forms of Social Movement in the 19th and 20th Centuries* (Manchester, Eng., 1959).

[33] Hofstadter, *Age of Reform*, 213–69.

[34] Samuel P. Hays, *The Response to Industrialism, 1885–1914* (Chicago, 1957), 48–70.

[35] Hofstadter, *Age of Reform*, 131–63; Robert Bremner, *From the Depths: The Discovery of Poverty in the United States* (New York, 1956).

time in the 1920's it appeared sufficient. The big business corporation, though still growing, seemed a beneficent monster to middle-class investors, and to many other Americans as well it appeared that social reform had been consummated by the legislation that ruthlessly cut back immigration and that thought to restore morality through the prohibition of drink.

After 1929 the Great Depression provoked the more thorough reforms of the New Deal, differing in detail from Progressivism, but directed more consciously than before at the same essential purpose of social reconstruction. For a time in the 1930's it seemed that the industrial depression would, like the closing of the frontier, be permanent, and that at best the old social mobility of the individual might be succeeded by the stability of a mature economy kept in balance by the government. Social security for all was to be the surrogate for the vanished equality of opportunity. The fear was mistaken; the renewal of industrial expansion since 1940 has also renewed social mobility, even in the absence of the frontier and of free immigration.

And yet the reorganization of society by the Progressives and New Dealers, which was part of the broad reaction against the general disorder, often miscalled the *status quo*, of the nineteenth century, has helped to impose a new social order. As suggested above, this twentieth-century revolution has in the long view been essentially a counterrevolution to reintegrate society somewhat as it was before 1815. True, the bulk of the population no longer consists of yeomen farmers, but the welfare state does secure a minimum subsistence as the family farm once did. (The Farm Security Administration for a time even endeavored to restore the yeoman farmer himself.) Likewise, since the depression the erstwhile proletariat, with a few still conspicuous exceptions, has climbed back to a comfortable standard of living, while the relative income of the erstwhile plutocracy has declined by about one third.[36] In a sense, the broad middle-class homogeneity of the eighteenth century has been restored. To complete the parallel, now that Roosevelts, Tafts, and Rockefellers not only accept the responsibility of their class to lead the common voter but are in turn accepted by him, it is evident that we once again have an established upper class with privileges and duties roughly equivalent to those of the eighteenth-century gentry.

There is more to our complex social order, of course, than classes, and it would take more confidence than present evidence warrants to assert that such institutions as the family and the local or regional community have as yet regained the stability of their eighteenth-century counterparts. On the other hand, just as vested economic interests were subject to public regulation in the eighteenth century, so are they now.[37] It is no longer doubted, for instance, that capital and labor bear a responsibility, however tentatively defined, to each other and to society at large; indeed, the responsibility is enjoined by law. There is no need to rehearse the familiar list of special economic interests, and also minority groups and other segments of the American population, whose social rights and duties now are or can be supervised in the common interest by government.

[36] Simon Kuznets, *Shares of Upper Income Groups in Income and Savings* (New York, 1953), xxxvii.

[37] That public regulation of economic affairs is no foreign "ism" but a return to an American precedent of great age and respectability is the discovery of the considerable body of recent research into such activity in the early nineteenth century. For a review of this literature, see Robert A. Lively, "The American System," *Business History Review*, XXIX (Mar. 1955), 81–96.

To the extent that, partly as the result of the New Deal, our economy is made up of a balance between such groups as big business, organized labor, the farmers' associations, and government itself, these "countervailing powers" are likewise components of the mid-twentieth-century social order.[38] Recently we have had a spate of professional and popular sociology lamenting the enmeshing of the individual in a network of institutions, from the mammoth business corporation with its uniformly clad executives and its ambitionless workingmen, both groups tied to the job by pension plans and seniority rights, all the way to the suburban family enslaved to its peer group. But the institutions and even the new elite of our social order, though they shock traditional liberals not only by their imperfections but by their very existence, would seem to be only the latest manifestations of the reordering of American society. The liberal critics of institutional society can take heart from the fact, exemplified by their own criticism, that the individualistic tradition of the nineteenth century does endure at least as a counterweight to the main trend of the twentieth, to no less a degree, certainly, than eighteenth-century conservatism lingered on in the liberal nineteenth. The individualist crying out against conformity plays a role in the 1950's like that of the status-conscious "reformers" of the 1830's or 1890's who resisted excessive individualism.

One can also speculate that the gradual decline since about 1920 of those make-shift communities, the fraternal lodges, is no less significant in our society than their rise was amid the social confusion of the nineteenth century. The psychic energy that Americans formerly expended on maintaining the jerry-built framework of such "institutions" as these has in our more assured institutional structure of recent years been freed, at least potentially, for the creation of more valuable kinds of "culture." The same end may likewise be served if the new social order can allay the kind of personal anxiety over one's social status which, as we have seen, pre-occupied the individual members of such varied groups as middle-class Progressives and agrarian Populists, Yankee nativists and peasant immigrants, yeomen and artisan Jacksonians and genteel humanitarian reformers, and presumably others whom historians have not yet reinvestigated. The evidence is already becoming plain that status striving is no latter-day degeneracy of Americans; rather, since such insecurity was a by-product of excessive mobility, it preoccupies the individual today not more but somewhat less than two or three generations ago. If so, the recent popular success of books deploring the unworthiness of status striving indicates that Americans are throwing off this obsession and making it, as in other societies, including pre-industrial America, merely one concern among many.

No doubt, in so far as Americans have gained a certain freedom to turn from these purely social problems to the task of evolving a cultural tradition for their new society, they have tended to be "other-directed"—unduly subservient to a still inchoate public opinion—as indeed they already were coming to be when Tocqueville observed their lack of "independence of mind and freedom of discussion" shortly after the start of the disorderly nineteenth century.[39] How else could an individualistic people be expected to evolve an indigenous cultural tradition out of social confusion

---

[38] John Kenneth Galbraith, *American Capitalism: The Concept of Countervailing Power* (Boston, 1952), 115–93.

[39] David Riesman, *The Lonely Crowd: A Study of the Changing American Character* (New Haven, Conn., 1950), 19–25; Alexis de Tocqueville, *Democracy in America,* tr. Henry Reeve (2 vols., New York, 1838), I, 244.

but by consulting, observing, and censuring each other? The result may turn out to be good or bad, but that the process has taken so long to approach a result is due to the ultraliberal nineteenth century, some of the cultural and intellectual effects of which still linger with us in the socially conservative twentieth.[40]

Today there are European traditionalists who lament the recent "Americanization" of the Old World, by which they mean the erosion of genteel manners, parental discipline, working-class subservience, and aristocratic patronage of art and literature of a certain standard. In the sense that the old European social order has about vanished, they are right. The American example, however, has been less important a cause of this than the continuing industrialization of Europe itself. In the nineteenth century, America, with far less of "feudal" tradition to restrain it, did succumb far more rapidly than Europe to the social mobility that accompanies industrialization—succumbed indeed almost at one blow, since the impact of modern industry here was multiplied by the coincidence of massive immigration and the westward movement.[41] But in a sense no less real, as we have seen, America in the present century has itself undergone a sort of Europeanization, though this did not proceed from Europe, as its opponents have suspected, any more than Americanization really went full-grown across the ocean to Europe. In either case the causes were essentially indigenous.

In effect, Western Europe has recently adopted a social pattern which, as early as the eighteenth century, already was distinctly American: orderly and adequately regulated, yet strongly infused with a robust egalitarianism. In the past, Europe has lacked the practical egalitarianism, and in the nineteenth century America temporarily lost its orderliness and regularity. Recently the Old and New Worlds have become more alike. Like Europe, America no longer has vast immigration or a frontier of free land, but both America and Europe are being continually transformed by the social mobility inherent in their industrial economies, a force that works, however, within the solid and coherent structure of a new institutional order. Whether an equally impressive Western popular culture will also arise on these social foundations is not yet so certain; a historian may be excused from outright prophecy.

[40] The way in which the recent preoccupation of historians with intellectual history has tended to obscure this essential social difference between the nineteeth and twentieth centuries should be evident. To the historian of ideas and culture, the nineteenth century appears, and rightly so, as a period of "formalism," characterized by abstract, deductive thought and derivative cultural standards, while the twentieth has been a time of pragmatic rebellion in the name of relativism in ideas and cultural norms. But in social history the term "formalism" can hardly be applied to the disorder of the nineteenth century. In fact, the "formal" ideas themselves— the Protestant ethic, classical economics, even the Malthusian inspiration for social Darwinism, with which apologists defended social disorder—were drawn largely from the previous, pre-industrial age and were already out of date as descriptions of contemporary reality. Likewise, when after 1880 certain intellectuals revolted against this formalism, their own ideas reflected the liberalism of a nineteenth-century society that was already about to pass away. This is in some degree an illustration of the usual lag with which social ideas follow behind social changes. On the other hand, since at the same time the foremost intellectual rebels, as preachers of what has been called "historicism" and "cultural organicism," were among the prophets of the new, more formally integrated social order, evidently the propriety of the usual characterization of twentieth-century America as an age of pragmatic disintegration needs to be reexamined. See Morton G. White, *Social Thought in America: The Revolt against Formalism* (New York, 1949), 11–31, 94–103.

[41] Louis Hartz, *The Liberal Tradition in America: An Interpretation of American Political Thought since the Revolution* (New York, 1955), 3–32.

Part I

ESSAYS IN EARLY AMERICAN SOCIAL HISTORY

American social history falls into four broad divisions. From the founding of the colony at Jamestown in 1607 to the end of the eighteenth century, America was an agrarian society. Cities were few, and over 90 percent of the population lived and worked on the land. As late as 1790 the largest single group in America (79 percent) came originally from England, Ireland, and Scotland. Trade and commerce took the form of exchange in overseas markets or in limited home markets. The bulk of Americans were virtually self-sufficient. A sense of American identity grew slowly, yet the national character was forming. The Revolution did not so much interrupt older social and political arrangements as it brought them to perfection.

After 1790, however, the new nation entered its preindustrial phase. Economic growth began. An urban frontier followed on the heels of migrating farmers. Between 1820 and the Civil War, five million immigrants swelled the population. Factories sprang up in the North and then the West, and those two regions became joined together by an increasingly complex communications and transportation network.

Industrial society developed rapidly after the Civil War and the foundations of American wealth shifted from agriculture to industry. Cities grew apace at the expense of farms and small towns and immigration swelled to a mighty stream.

After 1920 the final phase of American society became apparent: mass society. Based on automation, bureaucratization of government and industry, and the maturing welfare state, this new phase of social development is still unfolding before our eyes.

Part I of this anthology concerns the social development of America down to the beginnings of industrial society. The five sections into which this part is divided reflect the editor's conception of the mechanics and dynamics of American society through the mid-nineteenth century.

It is hoped that the reader will retain three major impressions after examining these materials on early American social history. The first is a sense of the structure of society: the institutions, groups, and classes that make up American civilization. Secondly, there is the pervasive sense of change: the nature of social dynamics and the process of social and cultural change. Finally, there is the qualitative dimension: the nature of life as experienced by individuals who lived in times past. At many points the reader will be able to catch glimpses of what it meant to live in other times amid different institutional settings. While the new social history tends toward the study of groups, classes, and institutions rather than individuals, it is ultimately concerned with human behavior in all its richness and complexity.

For further reading: Arthur M. Schlesinger, Sr., and Dixon R. Fox (eds.), *A History of American Life* (13 vols., 1927–1948); Harvey Wish, *Society and Thought in Early America: A Social and Intellectual History of the American People Through 1865* (1950); *Stuart Bruchey, *The Roots of American Economic Growth, 1607–1865: An Essay in Social Causation* (1965); John B. McMaster, *A History of the People of the United States from the Revolution to the Civil War* (8 vols., 1883–1913).

Two / The Social Order

2 / Notes on Life in Plymouth Colony

John Demos

In our times, nostalgia often takes the form of seeking the "good old days." Such dreams include the picture of an unhurried life lived in a home in which the family had lived for generations. What a very different view of those good old days is revealed here by John Demos. Social and geographic mobility, the profit motive, and anxiety all abounded in seventeenth-century Plymouth.

Based on wills, court records, and vital statistics found in church registers and churchyards, Demos paints a picture of life in early Plymouth that allows us to follow the lives of its inhabitants from birth to death. There we find the very bedrock of social history. We learn about population growth, life expectancy, marriage patterns, birthrates, child life, and even old age. We find that the citizens were mobile and followed opportunity to new frontiers. This pattern of mobility and restlessness bred anxiety in both those who left and those who remained behind. Old notions are challenged: the nuclear family rather than the extended family seems to have been the dominant form; marriage occurred later than was previously assumed. Clearly these early colonists were not as prim as their descendants have suggested; all too often the first child arrived within 6 months of the wedding ceremony.

In conclusion, the essay touches on a question that social historians have not fully clarified. A large number of children in seventeenth-century New England lived in families other than those into which they were born. In part this was due to the death of one parent and the subsequent remarriage of the other. It also relates to practices of apprenticeship. Some parents gave out their children in the hope that ersatz parents could more successfully discipline them. If Demos is correct, and one-third to one-half of the children in the colony did not live with their family of origin, then we may have some small clue to one source of American individualism. These children must have grown up quickly. Childhood was not prolonged as it would be at a later date. Attachment to persons and places must have been sharply reduced. These young people probably found it easy to follow the Western star of fortune to new frontiers.

William and Mary Quarterly, 3rd series, XXII (1965), 264–286. Footnotes have been omitted except where they are necessary for an understanding of the text.

For further reading: Darrett B. Rutman, *Winthrop's Boston: A Portrait of a Puritan Town, 1630–1649* (1965); *Sumner Chilton Powell, *Puritan Village: The Formation of a New England Town* (1963); *Philippe Ariès, *Centuries of Childhood: A Social History of Family Life* (1962); *Edmund S. Morgan, *The Puritan Family: Religion and Domestic Relations in Seventeenth-Century New England* (2nd ed., 1966); Philip J. Greven, Jr., "Family Structure in Seventeenth-Century Andover, Massachusetts," *William and Mary Quarterly*, 3rd series, XXIII (1966), 234–256; Philip J. Greven, Jr., "Historical Demography and Colonial America: A Review Article," *ibid.*, XXIV (1967), 438–454; John Demos, "Families in Colonial Bristol, Rhode Island: An Exercise in Historical Demography," *ibid.*, XXV (1968), 40–57.

Our traditional picture of the earliest New England communities is essentially a still life. By emphasizing the themes of steadfast piety, the practice of the old-fashioned virtues, measured forms of civil government, and a closely ordered social life, it suggests a placid, almost static kind of existence. We take for granted the moral and religious aims which inspired the founding of many of these communities; and we accept the assumption of the colonists themselves, that success in these aims depended on maintaining a high degree of compactness and closeness of settlement.

Yet, in the case of the Plymouth Colony at least, this picture is seriously misleading. It has served to obscure certain striking elements of movement and change—indeed, a kind of fluidity that is commonly associated with a much later phase of our national history. Individuals frequently transferred their residence from one house, or one town, to another. Land titles changed hands with astonishing rapidity. Families were rearranged by a wide variety of circumstances.

These tendencies can be traced back to the first years of the settlement at Plymouth. Some of the original townspeople began to take up lots across the river in Duxbury even before 1630; among them were such prominent figures as John Alden, Myles Standish, Jonathan Brewster, and Thomas Prence. The process was accelerated by the arrival to the north of the settlers at Massachusetts Bay. An important new market for cattle and corn was thereby opened up, and the compact town of Plymouth was not large enough to meet the demand for increased production. But the profits to be made from farming were probably not the only, or even the major, stimulus to expansion. The land beckoned because it was empty; the colonists were excited simply by the prospect of ownership for its own sake.

In any case, by the mid-1630's this pattern of geographical expansion had become well established. In 1636 the town of Scituate was officially incorporated and began to send its own representatives to the General Court. Duxbury achieved a similar status the following year; and by 1646 seven other new towns had been established. The direction of the earliest expansion was north and south along the coast; then a westerly thrust began, which led to the founding of such towns as Taunton, Rehoboth, Bridgewater, and Middleborough, all well inland. Still other groups of people pushed onto Cape Cod; indeed, in the early 1640's there was a move to abandon the original settlement at Plymouth altogether and relocate the town on the outer cape. This proposal was finally defeated after much discussion in the meetings of the freemen, but some families went anyway, on their own, and founded the town of Eastham. By 1691, the year that Plymouth ended its independent existence and joined with Massachusetts Bay, it contained no less than twenty-one recognized townships, and many smaller communities as well.

This steady dispersion of settlement caused considerable anxiety to some of the leaders of the colony, and sporadic efforts were made to keep it under control. On several occasions when new land was parceled out, the General Court directed that it be used only for actual settlement by the grantees themselves. Also, the Court criticized the unrestrained way in which lands were distributed by the freemen in certain of the newer townships. Grants were no longer confined to upright, religious-minded settlers. Towns accepted, with no questions asked, almost anyone who proposed to move in. Such was the charge leveled against the people of Sandwich, for example, in 1639. A similar situation seems to have prevailed in Yarmouth, for in 1640 the Court specifically directed the town elders there to require of each new arrival a "certificate from the places whence they come . . . of their religious and honest carriage."

William Bradford was one of those to whom the process of dispersion came as a great disappointment; it runs through much of his famous history of Plymouth as a kind of tragic refrain. "This I fear will be the ruin of New England, at least of the churches of God there," he wrote at one point, "and will provoke the Lord's displeasure against them." When the plan for moving the town to Eastham was debated, Bradford, and others of like mind, discerned the real motive behind the proposal: "Some were still for staying together in this place, alleging men might here live if they would be content with their condition, and that it was not for want or necessity so much that they removed as for the enriching of themselves." Finally, near the end of his work, with more and more of the original stock moving away, Bradford described Plymouth as being "like an ancient mother grown old and forsaken of her children, though not in their affections yet in regard of their bodily presence and personal helpfulness; her ancient members being most of them worn away by death, and these of later time being like children translated into other families, and she like a widow left only to trust in God. Thus, she that had made many rich became herself poor." He could hardly have chosen a better metaphor. It is extremely telling as a literary device, and—more than that—is highly suggestive from a historical standpoint. It describes an experience that must have been quite real, and quite painful, for many Plymouth settlers. The whole process of expansion had as one of its chief effects the scattering of families, to an extent probably inconceivable in the Old World communities from which the colonists had come. This was particularly hard upon elderly people; their anxiety that they should be properly cared for in their old age is readily apparent in the wills they wrote. The flow of men into new areas was inexorable, but it took a profound psychological toll, even among those who were most willingly a part of it.

Nearly every category of person—young and old, rich and poor, immigrant and old settler—was involved in the expansion of the Plymouth community. The careers of the four Winslow brothers who arrived at various times during the early years of the colony may be regarded as more or less typical. Kenelm Winslow came from England to Plymouth in 1629 and moved to Marshfield in 1641; Edward came in 1620 from Leyden and returned to England in 1646; John went from England to Leyden, to Plymouth, and in 1656 to Boston; and Josiah Winslow arrived in Plymouth from England in 1631, moved to Scituate in 1637, and then went from there to Marshfield. Although two of the sons of Kenelm Winslow remained in Marshfield on land that he bequeathed to them, another son moved to Yarmouth and the fourth one moved three times, to Swansea in 1666, to Rochester in 1678, and to Freetown in 1685. And third-generation Winslows could be found scattered among many different towns of Massachusetts and in other colonies as well. Nor did William Bradford's strong convictions on the matter of expansion prevent his own children from leaving Plymouth. His daughter married a Boston man; two sons moved to the neighboring settlement of Kingston; and a third led a large Bradford migration, mostly third generation, to Connecticut.

The movers were often young men, but not invariably so. Indeed there were many who moved in middle age and with a large family. Experience Mitchell and William Bassett, both of whom arrived in the early 1620's, were among the original proprietors—and residents—of three different towns. After several years in Plymouth they resettled in Duxbury (each one, by this time, with a wife and young children), and in the 1650's they went to Bridgewater.

For the most part, removals were arranged and carried out by individuals; they were not affairs of large groups and elaborate organization. Family ties were sometimes a factor, as in the case of the Connecticut Bradfords, but even here the pattern was rather loose. It was usually a matter of one man moving to a new community, and then several other members of his family following, separately and later on.

An obvious concomitant of such general mobility was a rapid rate of turnover in the ownership of land. In this connection the land deeds and proprietary lists that survive from the period become an important source. For example, there are two lists of proprietors for the town of Bridgewater, one made in 1645 at the time of its incorporation, and the other in 1682 when additional grants of land were being debated. Of the fifty-six names on the first list only twelve reappear thirty-seven years later. To the latter group should be added five sons of original proprietors who had died in the meantime, making a grand total of seventeen men who retained their interest in Bridgewater. But this means that thirty-nine relinquished their holdings altogether, fully 70 per cent of the initial group. It is probable that some of them never lived in Bridgewater at all, acquiring rights there only in order to sell.

This pattern of land turnover is further exemplified by the varied transactions of certain individuals, as noted in the *Colony Records*. Samuel Eddy, a good case in point, came to Plymouth in 1630 as a young man of twenty-two. In the next fifty years he was involved in at least eighteen transactions for land and housing. Presumably there were still more, of which no record remains, as in some cases we find him selling lands not previously identified as being in his possession. At least three times he seems to have moved his residence within Plymouth (selling one house in order to buy another), and as an old man he left the town altogether and went to Swansea in the western part of the colony. Two of his sons had already settled there, and he probably wished to be near them. A third son had gone to Martha's Vineyard; and a fourth, who seems to have been particularly restless, moved from Plymouth to Sandwich, to Middleborough, back to Plymouth, back to Middleborough, back to Plymouth, to Taunton, and back once more to Middleborough, over a period of some forty years.

Seven of Samuel Eddy's land transactions seem to have been directly connected with his changes of residence; the rest were for the purpose of enlarging his estate, or for profit. Eddy, incidentally, was a tailor by trade and not a rich man; most of the business in which he engaged was for relatively small amounts of land and money.

The profit motive was equally clear in the dealings of many other Plymouth residents. Perhaps one more example will suffice. In June 1639 John Barnes bought four acres of meadowland from John Winslow for eight pounds and a month later resold them to Robert Hicks for nine pounds, fifteen shillings. Soon afterwards he made a similar deal in which he bought a parcel of land for twelve pounds and sold it within a few months for eighteen.

It would be interesting to know more about the lives of these people, and the lives of their ancestors, before their migration to America. Perhaps there was more mobility among inhabitants of the English countryside than is commonly supposed. Perhaps the first colonists at Plymouth were conditioned for change by their prior attempt to establish themselves in Holland. It is hard to say. In any case, the settlers were doubtless predisposed to conceive of wealth in terms of land, and the circumstances of Plymouth, where currency was so scarce and land so plentiful, probably strengthened this instinct. It is clear from the wills they left that their desire to possess and to expand was usually satisfied. Even a man of relatively moderate means usually had several plots of land to deed away, and wealthy ones had as many as twelve, fifteen, or even twenty. In some cases these holdings were located in a number of different townships—showing that their owners could not always have thought in terms of actual settlement at the time of acquisition.

It would be interesting to know how many people lived in Plymouth Colony during these years. Three scholars have offered guesses based on varying kinds of evidence. Their findings do not agree, but suggest, when averaged together, that the total number of Plymouth residents was probably around 300 in 1630, and did not exceed 1,000 before the early 1640's. It had passed 3,000 by 1660, 5,000 by 1675, and by the time the colony had merged with Massachusetts probably stood somewhere between 12,000 and 15,000. The rate of growth, if not spectacular, was steady and fairly sharp; the population seems to have doubled about every fifteen years.

This growth was due, in part, to immigration but perhaps even more to certain characteristics of the people within the colony itself. For example, the popular impression today that colonial families were extremely large finds the strongest possible confirmation in the case of Plymouth. A sample of some ninety families about whom there is fairly reliable information, suggests that there was an average of seven to eight children per family who actually grew to adulthood. The number of live births was undoubtedly higher, although exactly how much higher we cannot be sure because no trace exists today of many who died in infancy and early childhood.[1]

[1] Various attempts to subject evidence to quantitative analysis have been an important part of my "method," such as it is. It is not possible to achieve anything approaching total accuracy in these computations; the sources simply are not that exact. I have not knowingly employed doubtful figures, but probably a small portion of those that I have used are incorrect. In certain cases I have accepted an approximate date (e.g., 1671, when it might as well be 1670 or 1672), but only where it would not prejudice the over-all result. In general, the numerical data that I shall present should be regarded as suggestive rather than conclusive in any sense. Above all, I have sought to keep my focus on individual lives and to build up my story from there. The people about whom I have assembled information total roughly 2,000. (It is very difficult even to estimate the total number of people who lived in Plymouth Colony between 1620-91, but it was probably between 25,000 and 50,000.) Only a part of these could be employed in the treatment of any particular question, since the data for most individuals are not complete. But a sample of several hundred should still be enough at least to outline certain general patterns.

With respect to the data on family size (Table I), I have used only families in which both parents lived at least to age 50, or else if one parent died, the other quickly remarried. That is,

TABLE I

SIZE OF FAMILIES IN PLYMOUTH

	Average Number of Children Born	Average Number Lived to Age 21
Sixteen First-Generation Families	7.8	7.2
Forty-seven Second-Generation Families	8.6	7.5
Thirty-three Third-Generation Families	9.3	7.9

Even allowing for the obvious likelihood that errors in the figures for the number born are somewhat greater than in the figures for those who grew to maturity, the rate of infant mortality in Plymouth seems to have been relatively low. In the case of a few families for which there are unusually complete records, only about one in five children seems to have died before the age of twenty-one. Furthermore, births in the sample come for the most part at roughly two-year intervals[2] with relatively few "gaps" which might indicate a baby who did not survive. All things considered, it appears that the rate of infant and child mortality in Plymouth was no more than 25 per cent[3]—less than half the rate in many parts of the world today.

These figures seem to indicate a suprising standard of health and physical vigor among Plymouth residents, and a study of their longevity—the average life expectancy in the colony—confirms this impression. Table II is based on a sample of more than six hundred people, who lived at least to the age of twenty-one and for whom the age at death was ascertainable.

The figures in II are really astonishingly high. Indeed, in the case of the men, they compare quite favorably with what obtains in this country today. (The life expectancy of an American male of twenty-one is now a fraction over seventy, and for a female of the same age, is approximately seventy-six.) It is at least possible that some selective bias, built into the data, may have distorted the results. For example, as between two men one of whom died at thirty and the other at ninety, it is more likely that the latter should leave some traces for the genealogist and historian to follow up. Still, I do not believe that this has been a serious problem in the above sample. A good part of the information on longevity has come from a few especially well-preserved grave-yards in the Plymouth area, and presumably these offer a fairly random selection of the adults in the community. Moreover, those families for which information is relatively complete—where we know the age at death of all the members—present

---

in all these families there were parents who lived up to, and past, the prime years for child-bearing.

[2] This spacing is quite interesting in itself, for it immediately raises questions as to how Plymouth parents avoided having even higher numbers of children. Probably the mothers nursed their babies for at least one year, but—contrary to popular belief—there is no proved biological impediment in this to further conception. Since effective contraceptive methods are a fairly recent development, it seems likely that Plymouth couples simply eschewed sexual contact over long periods of time. In many less advanced cultures of the world today there are taboos on sexual relations between husband and wife for one year or more following the birth of a child. It is just possible that a similar custom prevailed in Plymouth.

[3] It is impossible to estimate what proportion of these were infants (less than one year old) and what proportion were young children, for in most cases the records say only "died young."

a picture not very different from that of the total sample. And even if we do allow for a certain inflation of the figures, the outcome is still striking.

The difference in the results for men and women is mainly due to the dangers attendant on childbirth. A young woman's life expectancy was seven years less than a man's, whereas today, with childbirth hazards virtually eliminated by modern medicine, it is six years longer. The second table shows that 30 per cent of the women and only 12 per cent of the men in the sample died between ages twenty and fifty, the normal years of child bearing. If a woman survived these middle years, her prospects for long life became at least as good as those of a man, and indeed a little better. A majority of those who lived to a really very old age (ninety or more) seem to have been women.

TABLE II

LIFE EXPECTANCY IN PLYMOUTH *

Age	Men	Women	Age Group	Men (percentages)	Women (percentages)
21	69.2	62.4	22–29	1.6	5.9
30	70.0	64.7	30–39	3.6	12.0
40	71.2	69.7	40–49	7.8	12.0
50	73.7	73.4	50–59	10.2	10.9
60	76.3	76.8	60–69	18.0	14.9
70	79.9	80.7	70–79	30.5	20.7
80	85.1	86.7	80–89	22.4	16.0
			90 or over	5.9	7.6

* The figures on the left are the control points, i.e., a 21-year-old man might expect to live to age 69.2, a 30-year-old to 70.0, and so forth.

The figures on the right (columns two and three) represent the percentages of the men and women in the sample who died between the ages indicated in column one.

The records which reveal this pattern of growth and dispersion in the colony of Plymouth also provide much information about courtship, marriage, and family life. Courtships were usually initiated by the young people themselves, but as a relationship progressed toward something more permanent, the parents became directly involved. In fact, a requirement of parental consent was written into the colony's laws on marriage: "If any shall make any motion of marriage to any mans daughter . . . not having first obtayned leave and consent of the parents or master so to doe [he] shall be punished either by fine or corporall punishment or both, at the discretion of the bench and according to the nature of the offence." The attitude of parents toward a proposed match depended on a variety of spiritual and material considerations. Speaking very generally, it was desirable that both parties be of good moral and religious character. Beyond that, the couple would hopefully have enough land and possessions, given to them by both sets of parents, to establish a reasonably secure household.

But in a community as fluid as Plymouth it is unlikely that parental control over courtship and marriage could have been fully preserved. A few surviving pieces of evidence suggest that it was possibly quite an issue. In 1692 the widow Abigail Young died without leaving a will. The court moved to settle her estate on the basis of her intentions as revealed in several conversations held before her death. Two sons, Robert and Henry, were the prime candidates for the inheritance. Witnesses testified that "when shee dyed [she said] shee would Leave all the estate that shee had with Henry, if Robart had that gierl that there was a discourse about: but if he had her not I understood that the estate should be devided betwix them." A third son, Nathaniel, confirmed this. "My mother young," he reported, "told me that if Robirt had that gierl which there was a talke about shee would not give him a peny."

The first official step toward marriage was normally the betrothal or "pre-contract" —a ceremony before two witnesses at which the couple exchanged formal promises to wed in due time. A period of several weeks or months followed, during which these intentions were "published." A betrothed couple was considered to have a special status, not married but no longer unmarried either. They were required to be completely loyal each to the other; the adultery laws treated them no differently from husbands and wives. Sexual contact between them was forbidden; but the penalty for it was only a quarter of what was prescribed for single people. It may be that this actually encouraged premarital relations among betrothed couples because of its implication that fornication was much less reprehensible in their case than otherwise. The Court records show sixty-five convictions for misconduct of this kind, over a forty-five year period. (Note that this total comprises only those who were *caught,* and whose cases were recorded.) In some instances members of the most prominent families were involved: for example, Peregrine White, Thomas Delano, and Thomas Cushman, Jr. Occasionally the basis for conviction was the arrival of a child less than nine months after the wedding ceremony. Perhaps innocent couples were sometimes punished under this system; but the number of "early" babies was, in any event, extremely high.[4]

Once the betrothal was formalized, considerable thought had to be given to the economic future of the couple. In all but the poorest families each child could expect to receive from its parents a "portion"—a certain quantity of property or money with which to make an independent start in life. In most cases this occurred at the time of marriage, and its purpose was everywhere the same. A man was to use it to "be for himself" (in the graphic little phrase of the time); a woman would transfer it to her husband for the greater good of the household which they were starting together. To make special provision for the possibility that he might die while his children were still young, a man usually directed in his will that his "overseers" hold part of his estate intact to be distributed later as portions, at the appropriate time.

There was no set formula governing the actual substance of these portions. More often than not, however, a male child was given land, cattle, tools, and a house or a promise of help in the building of a house; a woman, for her part, usually received movable property, such as furniture or clothing and money. Occasionally the terms of these bequests were officially recorded in a "deed of gift"; more often they seem to have been arranged informally. Most parents hoped to have accumulated sufficient property by the time their children came of age to make these gifts without suffering undue hardship. Some had to buy land specifically for this purpose; others petitioned

---

[4] For example, a random sampling of fourth-generation Bradfords turned up nine couples whose first child arrived within eight months of their wedding and all but two of these within six months. Also, it appears that Thomas Cushman's first baby was not only conceived, but actually born, before his marriage.

the Court "to accommodate them for theire posterities," i.e., to give them a free grant. It appears that fathers sometimes retained the title to the lands which they gave as portions: there are many Plymouth wills which direct that a son shall inherit "the land wherein he now dwells," or use words to this effect. Perhaps this practice served to maintain some degree of parental authority beyond the years of childhood.

It is widely supposed that people married early in the colonial period. For Plymouth, however—and I suspect for most other communities of that time—this impression cannot be sustained. Indeed, the average age of both men and women at the time of their first marriage was considerably higher then than it is today—and quite possibly has never been exceeded at any subsequent point in our history.

TABLE III

FIRST MARRIAGES IN PLYMOUTH
(BASED ON A SAMPLE OF SOME 650 MEN AND WOMEN)

	Born Before 1600	Born 1600–25	Born 1625–50	Born 1650–75	Born 1675–1700
Mean age of men at time of 1st marriage	27.0	27.0	26.1	25.4	24.6
Mean age of women at time of 1st marriage	—*	20.6	20.2	21.3	22.3
Percentage of men married at age 23 or over	25%	18%	25%	26%	38%
Percentage of men married at age 30 or over	44%	23%	27%	18%	14%
Percentage of women married at age 25 or over	—*	9%	10%	20%	28%

* Insufficient data for women born before 1600.

This table is largely self-explanatory. Only one point requires additional comment: the steady, if unspectacular, narrowing of the age gap between the sexes at the time of marriage. At the start this gap averaged six and one-half years; by the end it was verging on two. Men were marrying earlier and women later. During the early years of the colony there was certainly a shortage of women; spinsters were a rarity, and marriageable girls, of whatever charm and property, must have received plenty of offers. At some point, however, new factors began to come into play, and this imbalance in the sex ratio was gradually corrected. Above all, the process of expansion removed substantial numbers of young men from the areas that had been settled first, and by the end of the century some towns may well have held a surplus of females. Wherever women outnumbered men, there were some who did not find husbands until relatively late and at least a few who never married at all. Conversely, the men had a larger and larger group to choose from and tended to marry somewhat earlier. By 1700 there were occasional marriages in which the woman was older than her husband, and for the first time the number of spinsters had become noticeable. The earliest official count of males and females in Plymouth that still survives comes from a census taken for all Massachusetts in 1765. At that time all of the eastern counties showed a substantial majority of women over men; the reverse was true for the western counties. In the towns which formerly belonged to Plymouth Colony the figures were 53.2 per cent female as against 46.8 per cent male. It is my guess that this surplus began as much as a century earlier.[5]

Marriage was conceived to be the normal estate for adults in colonial New England. When one spouse died, the other usually remarried within a year or two. Most were in their thirties and forties at the time of their remarriage, but some were much older. Robert Cushman, Jr., for instance, took a new wife at eighty! This pattern affected a very considerable portion of the community, as the following table shows.

TABLE IV

RATES OF REMARRIAGE IN PLYMOUTH COLONY *

Number of Marriages	Men		Women	
	Over 50	Over 70	Over 50	Over 70
1	60%	55%	74%	69%
2	34%	36%	25%	30%
3	6%	8%	1%	1%
4	—†	.5%	—	—
5	—†	.5%	—	—
Total married more than once	40%	45%	26%	31%

* The figures for men and women are separate, and in each case there is a percentage for all those who lived to be fifty or more, and another for those who lived to be seventy or more. The sample, comprising over seven hundred people, does not include anyone who died before the age of fifty.

† Less than one half of one per cent.

Generally speaking, the property of husband and wife was not merged in a second marriage to the extent customary for a first one. The main reason for this, of course, was to preserve the claims of the children by the first marriage to a just inheritance. In fact, wills were always framed with this point in mind. Often the bulk of a man's estate was transmitted at his death directly to his children, or if to his wife, only until she married again. The part that remained to herself alone was usually one third of the estate, and sometimes less. Widows in Plymouth did not control a large amount of property.

[5] See J. H. Benton, Jr., *Early Census Making in Massachusetts, 1643–1765* . . . (Boston, 1905). The dimensions of the problem, for Plymouth, can be further refined. The findings in the 1765 census are divided into two parts: people under 16, and people 16 and over. The 53.2 to 46.8 ratio, quoted above, is for the 16-and-over group. But, as almost all males remained single until age 21, a more significant ratio would be one for only those males and females who were 21 or over. We can assume, from a breakdown of other parts of the census, that the 16–21 grouping composed about 10 per cent of the total over 16. We also know from the census that the ratio of males under 16 to females under 16 was 51.2 males to 48.8 females. If this ratio of 51.2 to 48.8 is projected to the 16–21 age group for the purpose of eliminating those under 21 from the final ratio, we discover that the ratio of men 21 or older to women 21 or older becomes approximately 53.8 to 46.2. This means that for one out of every seven girls there was no man, at least in her own home area. In a few individual towns the situation was worse—as high as one in four.

When a marriage between a widow and widower was planned it was customary to make an explicit agreement as to terms. The man pledged a certain sum to his (new) wife in the event of his death, but it was often only a token amount, much less than the "thirds" that a first wife might expect. The woman, for her part, retained the right of "sole disposition" of any property she might possess; it never became part of her husband's estate.

A widow's children were placed in a doubtful position when their mother remarried. Sometimes the new husband agreed to take them into his household, but more often they were placed elsewhere. Occasionally the first husband had anticipated this problem before his death. Anthony Besse's will provided that should his widow remarry, "the five bigest [children] to bee put forth and theire Cattle with them according to the Descretion of the overseers." Another father,

> Lawrence Lichfeild lying on his Death bedd sent for John Allin and Ann his wife and Desired to give and bequeath unto them his youngest son Josias Lichfeild if they would accept of him and take him as theire Child; then they Desired to know how long they should have him and the said Lawrance said for ever; but the mother of the child was not willing then; but in a short time after willingly Concented to her husbands will in the thinge; if the said John and Ann would take the Child for theire adopted Child; whereunto they Assented . . . [The boy too] being asked by his owne mother . . . if hee Did Concent and Chuse to live with the said John and Ann as hitherto by the space of about nine yeares hee had Done; Willingly answered yea.

No doubt the boy was deeply attached to the Allens after having lived with them for so long. The agreement, then, imposed no particular hardship on anyone involved; it simply continued, and formalized, a previous arrangement.

If children did remain with their mother after her remarriage, their stepfather was not supposed to exercise normal parental authority over them. Although at the time of his marriage to the widow, Mary Foster, Jonathan Morey contracted to "bring up" her son Benjamin at his own expense, he also agreed not to interfere in any future plans for binding the boy out. A fairly common solution to the problem of stepchildren was to keep them with their mother for a few years and then as they grew older to "put them out." Ultimate responsibility for such children passed to some persons specially designated in their father's will—often to his overseers, occasionally to his own parents. When Jacob Mitchell and his wife were killed by Indians at Rehoboth in 1675, their small children went to live with Mitchell's father in Bridgewater. John Brown of Swansea wrote in his will: "Conserning all my five Children I Doe wholly leave them all to the ordering and Disposeing of my owne father . . . for him to bring them up not once questioning but that his love and Care for them wilbee as it hath bine for my selfe." Brown's wife survived him, and the children probably remained in her day-to-day care, or else were "bound out"; but over-all direction of their lives was henceforth in the hands of their grandfather.

It has been widely assumed that the "extended family" was characteristic of Western society everywhere until at least the eighteenth century, and that the change to our own "nuclear" pattern came only with the Industrial Revolution. The term "extended family" in its strict sense means a household consisting of several couples, related as siblings or cousins, and their children, and perhaps their children's children.

This pattern, of course, still prevails in many parts of the world. Its most striking results are a diffusion of affections and authority within the whole, or extended, family, and a sharing of economic responsibilities. The term is also applied, somewhat more loosely, to situations where the various family members do not form one household in the sense of living "under one roof" but still live close together and share loyalties and responsibilities which go beyond their own offspring or parents.

In colonial Plymouth, there were no extended families at all, in the sense of "under one roof." The wills show, beyond any doubt, that married brothers and sisters never lived together in the same house. As soon as a young man became betrothed, plans were made for the building, or purchase, of his own house. For example, when Joseph Buckland of Rehoboth married, his father promised "to build the said Joseph a Convenient house for his Comfortable liveing with three scores of acrees of land ajoyning to it." Some young men moved out of the family even before marrying, either to join in the expansion toward the interior or simply to "be for themselves" while remaining nearby. Girls stayed with their parents until they found a husband, but never beyond that time. I know of only one case in which there is documentary evidence suggesting that two couples shared a house, and it is truly the exception that proves the rule. The will of Thomas Bliss (Plymouth, 1647) contained this clause: "I give unto my soon Jonathan my house and home lot Conditionally that hee shall give unto my sonninlaw Thomas Willmore his lot which hee now hath and allso the one half of my broken up ground for two yeares and shall healp him to build him an house and let him peacably and quietly live in the house with him untell they shall bee able to set up an house for him."

In a true extended family the death of the father, or even of both parents, causes no radical change in living arrangements. The widow or the children, or both, continue their lives much as before, and the functions of the deceased are assumed by other relatives (uncles or cousins or grandparents). When a man died in Plymouth, however, his household usually broke up. If the children were still young, some might remain with their mother, but others were likely to be placed in new families. If the children were adult, the "homestead" was given to a certain designated one of them, who was then obliged to pay to each of his brothers and sisters an amount equivalent to some fair proportion of the property's value.

An unusually wealthy man in Plymouth Colony, and especially one who participated directly in the founding of new towns, could accumulate enough land to provide his sons with lots near or adjoining his own. Wills and land deeds show, for example, that John Washburn divided up his very large estate in Bridgewater with three sons, and that John Turner did the same kind of thing in Scituate. This sort of arrangement comes as close to being an extended family as anything found in and around Plymouth—and it is not very close at all. There is no evidence of shared economic activity, no mention in the wills of profits or crops to be divided up. Moreover, in both the Washburn and the Turner families there were other sons who do not seem to have remained nearby.

Among those who were less wealthy, the drive to expand and to increase their property proved more powerful than the bonds which might have held families together. Children left, when they came of age, to take up new holdings several towns and many miles away. The process of dispersion was, in fact, sometimes encouraged by the very system of portions described earlier. Often a father simply had no land to spare in the immediate vicinity of his own farm. He might, however, own property in one, or two, or three of the newer townships; and this was what he passed on to his children. The will of William Bradford, Jr., shows that he had sons living in Connecticut (on land which he had given them); and he made additional bequests, to his youngest children, in Plymouth and Duxbury. Similarly, when Benjamin Bartlett died he left his children a wide variety of lots in Duxbury, Middleborough, Little Compton, and Rochester. In some cases the recipients may have sold these gifts soon afterwards, but at least as often they went to make their homes on them.

What we would most like to know is something of the effect of this dispersion on a whole range of more intimate aspects of family life. A court case at Plymouth in 1679 throws some light on such matters. An elderly man named Samuel Ryder had just died and left his whole estate to two sons, Benjamin and John. A third son, Joseph, had been left nothing. What made this especially hard was the fact that Joseph had already built a house on a piece of land belonging to his father and had expected to receive title to it in the father's will. The Court approached the problem by taking a number of depositions from friends and family. Elizabeth Mathews was called first and gave the following testimony: "I being att the Raising of Joseph Riyders house; Joseph Ryders Mother Came into the house Joseph then lived in and Cryed and wrong her hands fearing that Joseph would Goe away; Josephs Mother then said that if you would beleive a woman beleive mee that youer father saith that you shall never be Molested; and you shall Never be Molested." Samuel Mathews verified this report and supplied additional details: "In the Morning before wee Raised the house old Goodman Ryder Joseph Ryders father Came out and marked out the Ground with his stick; and bid the said Joseph sett his house where it Now stands . . . the occation of the womans Lamenting as above said was fearing her son would Goe away; for shee said if hee went shee would Goe too."

There are several striking things about this episode: the mother's distress at the thought that her son might leave (even to the point of suggesting that she would follow him); the hint of hostility between father and son; the threat to go away used by the son as a means of forcing a gift from his father; and the implication that parents could, and did, use gifts of land to induce their children to stay nearby. Evidence bearing directly on the human dimension of life in Plymouth is extremely hard to come by, but something like the Ryder case does offer a glimpse of the enormous strain that the whole pattern of geographic mobility must have placed upon family ties and sanctions.

Land and property represented one advantage still possessed by most parents when they wished to rearrange their own lives and the lives of their children. They tried to use it in a variety of ways. Bequests to children were often hedged by a requirement of good behavior: "I give [my estate to] my two sonnes Daniell and Samuell [ages 15 and 17] upon this proviso that they bee Obeidient unto theire mother and carrye themselves as they ought . . . but if the one or both live otherwise then they ought and undewtyfully and unquietly with theire Mother . . . then hee that soe carryeth himselfe shall Disinherit himselfe of his parte of this land." Another legacy, this one to a daughter, was made conditional on her "pleas[ing] her mother in her match." In still another case a man left his widow to judge their child's behavior and reward him accordingly from out of his estate. And the reasoning behind this was made explicit: "I would have the boy beholding to my wife; and not my wife to the boy."

Sometimes portions were shaped in the same way. One of the rare letters that survives from seventeenth-century Plymouth describes a father bestowing upon his son "the full of his porshon except upon his sons better behaver [he] should desarve more."

It is likely, then, that rewards in the form of property were held out as an inducement to all sorts of "better behavior." But this was especially true in regard to the care of elderly couples and widows. Virtually every man who left a widow directed in his will that she be looked after by one of their children, and made a large bequest contingent thereupon. Usually the family homestead went to a particular child, with one room or more reserved for the widow. Often the instructions were spelled out in great detail: She would have full rights to the use of the "garden" and "orchard"; yearly payments of a certain specified amount must be made to her, wood must be brought to her door in wintertime, her cows milked, etc.

Some men made arrangements of this kind even before their deaths. John and Deborah Hurd of Barnstable, for example, deeded "all that our hom sted" to their daughter and son-in-law in exchange for "the whole and sole Care and charge of us . . . for and during the tarm of our Natural Lives." And Robert Sprout of Middleborough gave his farm to his sons Ebenezer and James, on condition that they "pay yearly for my support . . . the sum of forty pounds to that child which I live with and provides for me and looks after me." These conditions are nailed down so tightly in so many wills (and similar deeds) that it is tempting to infer some particular anxiety behind them. It clearly was the general custom for aged parents to live with one of their children who would provide the care and support they needed. Probably in the majority of cases this was managed without too much difficulty; but in a society as fluid as Plymouth there must have been some elderly fathers and mothers who were more or less neglected. One recalls Bradford's vivid image of the "ancient mother, grown old and forsaken of her children, though not in their affections, yet in regard of their bodily presence and personal helpfulness."

Although one set of parents with their own children always formed the core of a Plymouth household, this nuclear pattern was, as we have seen, sometimes modified by the inclusion of one or more aged grandparents. It was often further modified by servants and apprentices, who lived in the houses of their masters. Among such people were at least a few Negroes and Indians whose service was normally for life. The vast majority, however, were young boys and girls, "bound out" for a specified term of years. Some of them were orphans but many others had both parents living. Often, in fact, the parents had made all the arrangements and signed a formal contract with the couple whom their child served. In 1660 "An agreement appointed to bee Recorded" stated that "Richard Berry of yarmouth with his wifes Concent; and other frinds; hath given unto Gorge Crispe of Eastham and his; wife theire son Samuell Berry; to bee att the ordering and Disposing of the said Gorge and his wife as if hee were theire owne Child, untill hee shall accomplish the age of twenty one yeares; and in the meane time to provide for the said Samuell in all thinges as theire owne Child; and afterwards if hee live to marry or to goe away from them; to Doe for him as if hee were theire own Child." It is noteworthy that the Crispes took full responsibility for young Samuel—even to the point of promising him a portion. This is, then, a virtual deed of adoption.

No age was indicated for Samuel Berry, but it is clear from other cases that the children involved were often very young. John Smith and his wife gave their four-year-old son to Thomas Whitney "to have the full and sole disposing of him . . . without annoyance or disturbance from the said John Smith or Bennit his wife." Samuel Eddy arranged apprenticeships for three of his sons, at ages six, seven, and nine. Two of them went to the same man, Mr. John Brown of Rehoboth. Upon reaching maturity, they both received property from Brown, and, in addition, were given modest portions by their father. It appears from this that Eddy continued to take a direct interest in his children even after they had left his household.

The most difficult question these arrangements raise is, what purpose lay behind them? No answer that would serve in all cases suggests itself. In some, poverty was obviously a factor. For example, Samuel Eddy, in the apprenticeship papers for his sons, pleaded his "many children" and "many wants." On the other hand, George Soule of Duxbury bound out his daughter to John Winslow, and Soule was a wealthy man. In certain cases, learning a trade was mentioned, but in a perfunctory manner. When young Benjamin Savory was bound out to Jonathan Shaw in 1653, the papers directed that he be taught "whatsoever trad[e] the said Jonathan Shaw can Doe." Something must have gone amiss with this arrangement, because four years later the child was placed with still another family. The terms were only slightly less vague: his new master, Stephen Bryant, was to "teach him in learning that is to say to read and write and to Intruct him in husbandry."

Another possible motive was to improve a child's educational opportunities. Instruction in reading and writing was often included among the conditions of the contract, as in the case of Benjamin Savory above. Finally, Edmund Morgan has suggested in his *The Puritan Family* that "Puritan parents did not trust themselves with their own children . . . and were afraid of spoiling them by too great affection"; it was for this reason, he argues, that so many children were placed in families other than their own. It is an interesting thought, but there is simply no explicit proof for it. At least Morgan found none, and I have had no better luck with the materials for Plymouth.

The household of Samuel Fuller seems to have been about as varied as any in Plymouth, and is worth mentioning in this connection. When Fuller died in 1633 it included nine people, six of whom were not of his own immediate family. There were, besides himself, his wife, and his son, a nephew, two servants, a ward, and two "additional children." The last of these had been sent to him for education, from families in Charlestown and Sagos. The ward was the daughter of a close friend who had died some years before. Meanwhile, Fuller's own daughter was living with "goodwife Wallen." Fuller was obliged to leave instructions about all these people in his will. His daughter was to continue where she was for the time being. The children from Charlestown and Sagos should be returned to their former homes. The ward was committed to his brother-in-law, and passed thereby into her third family. Fuller's son should continue to live in the "homestead" and one day would inherit it; but the same brother-in-law was to take charge of his education. Fuller's wife would have the day-to-day care of the youth until she died or remarried. She would also take charge of the servants for the remainder of their contracted term.

Fuller's household was hardly typical, however. A close reading of hundreds of Plymouth wills has turned up no other family as complicated as this one. In many there were one or two people not of the immediate family—aged grandparents, servants, wards, or additional children—but rarely more. The basic unit remained one set of parents and their children or stepchildren, living apart from all other relatives.

Clearly children in seventeenth-century Plymouth often found themselves growing up in a household other than that of their parents. The records are so scattered that it is impossible to calculate how many this category actually included. It must, however, have been a considerable number; my own guess is somewhere between a third and a half of all the children. This figure does not seem too high when it is remembered that one in three of the parents in the colony married twice or more, and that some children were placed in new homes even when their own father and mother were living.

The impact of these situations on the children cannot be proved—only imagined. But a hint of what they could mean comes to us in the story of a rather sad little episode, which by a lucky chance has been preserved in the *Colony Records*. Christian (Penn) Eaton and Francis Billington, widow and widower, were married in Plymouth in 1635. Christian's son, Benjamin Eaton, was "put forth" into another family immediately thereafter. The couple began to have children of their own: first, Elizabeth, and then, Joseph—both of whom were also placed in other families. But little Joseph apparently did not take to this arrangement very well, for in 1643 the Court was obliged to issue the following order:

> Whereas Joseph, the sonn of Francis Billington . . . was . . . placed with John Cooke the younger, and hath since beene inveagled, and did oft departe his said masters service, the Court, upon longe heareing of all that can be said or alleadged by his parents, doth order and appoynt that the said Joseph shalbe returned to his said master againe immediately, and shall so remaine with him during his terme; and that if either the said Francis, or Christian, his wyfe, do receive him, if he shall againe depart from his said master without his lycence, that the said Francis, and Christian, his wyfe, shalbe sett in the stocks . . . as often as he or shee shall so receive him, untill the Court shall take a further course with them.

Joseph Billington was five years old.

3 / Foundations of Political Power in the Virginia House of Burgesses, 1720–1776

Jack P. Greene

Since the pioneering work of the German sociologist Max Weber (1864–1920), scholars have approached the problem of power in society in an increasingly sophisticated manner. Weber insisted that it was necessary to know who exercised power and in what kind of institutional and cultural context that power was exercised. Following this approach, students of American political development have subjected such institutions as the Virginia House of Burgesses to detailed inquiry. The following essay analyzes the foundations of power in the Burgesses in the eighteenth century. It goes far beyond older approaches, which concentrated on legal or constitutional aspects.

Jack P. Greene provides a profile of the men who controlled the Virginia lower house in the 50 odd years preceding the Revolution. Wealthy, well-educated, connected by marriage, versed in the arts of local politics, Anglican in religion, and of British origins, this small group dominated the major committees of the House. There they controlled the flow of legislation and the political decision-making process. Such an empirical examination removes the study of power from the realm of impression and conjecture, and allows the historian to form a profile of a political elite. Only against such a background can questions of political strategy and ideology be fully understood. It is a step toward a fuller understanding of the origins and nature of the American political system.

For further reading: *Reinhard Bendix, *Max Weber: An Intellectual Portrait* (1960), 285–494; *Robert A. Dahl, *Who Governs? Democracy and Power in an American City* (1961); Jack P. Greene, *The Quest for Power: The Lower Houses of Assembly in the Southern Royal Colonies, 1689–1776* (1963); Bernard Bailyn, "Politics and Social Structure in Virginia," in * James Morton Smith (ed.), *Seventeenth-Century America: Essays on Colonial His-*

William and Mary Quarterly, 3rd series, XVI (1959), 485–492. Reprinted by permission of the author. Copyright © 1967 by Jack P. Greene. Footnotes and tables have been omitted.

tory (1959), 90–115; *Charles S. Sydnor, *Gentlemen Freeholders: Political Practices in Washington's Virginia* (1952); *Jackson Turner Main, *The Social Structure of Revolutionary America* (1965).

Historians have devoted more attention to the Virginia House of Burgesses than to any other lower house in the continental colonies. They have treated its internal development, its part in royal government, its procedure, and its personnel. They have assessed its role in developing the leaders of the Revolutionary generation and traced its part in the "struggle for liberty." Yet, no one has attempted to analyze the structure of power within the Burgesses in the half century before the American Revolution.

The first question to be asked in such an analysis is how was power distributed in the house? Was it spread more or less equally among all members, or was it generally concentrated in the hands of a few? The answer to this question lies in the committees where the work of the house was done and where the real decisions were made. The only way one can hope to determine the pattern of the distribution of power in the eighteenth-century house is by a qualitative analysis of committee posts—that is, by a study which takes into account not only the number of committee posts held by each member but also the varying degrees of importance of the committees themselves.

I have undertaken such an analysis and used my findings as a yardstick to measure the influence or power of individual burgesses. The results indicate that relatively few members played significant roles in the proceedings of the house: of the 630 men who sat in that body between 1720 and 1776, some 520 can safely be eliminated from consideration, because only 110 members belonged at one time or another to the select few who dominated the proceedings of the house. Of these few, some, of course, were more powerful than others. In fact, the leaders as a whole may be divided into two groups, those of the first rank and those of the second. In any given session, the top level was composed of the speaker, who made appointments to all committees, and from two to perhaps seven or eight others, including, as a rule, the chairmen of the standing committees. Men of somewhat less importance, usually five to ten in number, constituted the second level. For example, in the 1736 session five men at the top level handled about a third of the committee assignments while seven others at the second level handled another fourth. Altogether these twelve burgesses—one-sixth of the total membership—occupied more than half of the committee seats. Until 1742 it was not uncommon for as many as one-third to one-half of the burgesses to serve on no committees at all; then, for reasons that are not now entirely clear, the size of the standing committees was enlarged and nearly three-fourths of the members were given assignments on these committees. Beginning in 1748, the speaker adopted the practice of giving each member at least one post on a standing committee, but this diffusion of assignments does not appear to have affected the structure of power in the house; in 1752 somewhat less than one-fifth of the members handled over half of the business of the house, with the six most powerful men occupying a fourth of the committee posts and eleven others holding another fourth. This pattern did not change significantly for the rest of the colonial period. It was modified slightly after 1766, when Peyton Randolph succeeded John Robinson as speaker. Randolph further increased the size of the standing committees and, more important, sprinkled the major assignments among a greater number of members, with the result that the number of men at both levels of power increased slightly.

These men of power provided the house with a certain continuity of leadership from 1720 until well after the Declaration of Independence. Some of them died, some retired, some were defeated at the polls, but never at any time was there any wholesale turnover in leadership. This continuity plus the lack of evidence of any major dissatisfaction with the leadership or of the existence of any group intent upon challenging it emphasizes the fact that organized political parties did not exist in colonial Virginia. There was often disagreement on specific issues, but, as St. George Tucker later suggested to William Wirt when the latter was preparing his biography of Patrick Henry, the disagreements were "only such as different men, coming from different parts of our extensive Country might well be expected to entertain." Tucker had never witnessed anything in the House of Burgesses "that bore the appearance of *party spirit.*"

The discovery of the fact that the House of Burgesses was dominated by the few rather than the many immediately raises some important questions about the leaders. What were their professional and economic interests, their social and family backgrounds and connections, their political experience and education, their national origins and religious affiliations, and their geographical distribution?

Most of these men were comparatively wealthy. Unfortunately, it is usually impossible to determine the extent of a man's wealth at any given time, but at least a general idea of the land and slave holdings of most of the 110 may be culled from existing wills, inventories, tithable and tax lists, and personal records. Information on land holdings is available for all but ten. Slightly less than three-fourths of them had large holdings—that is, holdings in excess of ten thousand acres. Seven of the 110, and perhaps three others, owned more than forty thousand acres; and the holdings of forty-six, certainly, and perhaps as many as sixty-four, exceeded ten thousand acres. A dozen possessed from one to five thousand acres. Only one man is thought to have owned fewer than five hundred acres. Records of slaveholdings are more difficult to find, but reasonably exact information is available for over half of the 110, and most of the others are known to have possessed some slaves. Quite naturally, the larger landowners—men like John Robinson, Charles and Landon Carter, Benjamin Harrison, and Archibald Cary—also owned the greater number of slaves. Eleven of those for whom records are available owned more than three hundred slaves—a staggering number for the times. Twenty-five possessed from fifty to three hundred slaves; twenty-two others had more than ten. Land and slaves were, of course, not the only assets of these burgesses. Livestock, plantation dwellings and outbuildings, farm equipment, and town houses must be added to their riches. Some men, like the Nelsons and Richard Adams, had large mercantile establishments; and a few dabbled in mining and manufacturing.

Most of the 110 leaders of the house were, of course, planters. Indeed, at least ninety-one were directly involved in planting and raising tobacco, although a third of these engaged in planting only as a secondary occupation. The lawyers—most of whom were planters on the side—were the next most numerous professional or occupational group. Thirty-nine of the 110 were practicing lawyers, but they were far more significant than their number would indicate. The services of trained lawyers were invaluable to the house. They had precisely those talents required in framing legislation and carrying on the business of the Burgesses; and throughout the period under consideration, they were conspicuous by their presence at the top level of power. Of the four men who served as speaker, three—John Holloway, Sir John Randolph, and Peyton Randolph—were lawyers. Other occupational groups were less prominent. Of the thirteen men not accounted for above, ten were merchants, two were physicians, and one was a teacher.

Nearly all of the leaders of the house had secondary economic interests. It has already been pointed out that the majority of the lawyers were planters too. So also were the merchants, one of the physicians, and the teacher. Similarly, most of those who were primarily planters had other interests. Their most important secondary occupation was land speculation. Over two-fifths, and perhaps more, speculated in Western lands—a profitable avocation. A dozen participated in some form of mercantile activity. Three were engaged in mining; four were part-time surveyors; four were part-time soldiers; and one was a part-time teacher. Archibald Cary might even be classed a manufacturer, for one of his many secondary interests was an iron works.

Historians from the time of William Wirt to the present have considered family an important ingredient of political power in eighteenth-century Virginia. Bernard Bailyn has recently put forward the provocative thesis that a new ruling class emerged out of an immigration to Virginia that began in the late 1630's or early 1640's and continued through the 1660's. According to Bailyn, this ruling class supplanted the leaders of the earlier immigrants, secured more or less permanent control first of the county institutions and then of the House of Burgesses, and supplied much of the political leadership of the eighteenth century. My own investigations of the family backgrounds of the Burgesses' leaders indicate that this thesis is only partly valid. Certainly, the generation that came to Virginia between 1635 and 1670 contributed more leaders than any other generation. Forty-nine of the 110 were descendants of that generation. Only seven derived from the pre-1635 immigrants. However, fifty others—nearly half of the leaders who dominated the Burgesses from 1720 to 1776— descended from the several generations that came to the colony after 1670. This fact is significant, for it indicates that the earlier immigrants did not have a monopoly on political power or a very tight control over the House of Burgesses. In fact, families still comparatively new on the Virginia scene in 1720 supplied a significant proportion of the Burgesses' leadership during the fifty years preceding the Revolution. Nearly one-fifth of the 110 were drawn from families that arrived in Virginia between 1690 and 1720, and another tenth from those that came after 1720. Some of the newcomers, of course, found marriage into an established family a convenient avenue to social and political power, but many, like Speaker John Holloway, John Clayton, and James Power, acquired wealth, position, and political power without the advantages of connections with older families—an indication that social lines were still fluid and that a political power was still attainable for the ambitious and gifted among the newly arrived.

It should not be inferred, however, that family connections were unimportant. Over half of the leaders were connected either through blood or marriage to one of the great eighteenth-century families, and only a conspicuous few reached the top level of power without such a connection. Indeed, certain families—notably the Randolphs, Carters, Beverleys, and Lees—supplied an unusually large proportion of the leaders of the house. Including descendants through both male and female lines, the Randolphs provided eleven, the Carters nine, the Beverleys eight, and the Lees six. The Blands, Burwells, and Corbins each furnished four, and the Blairs, Harrisons, Ludwells, and Nelsons three; these families were connected through marriage with other leading burgesses: six had marriage ties with the Carters, five with the Randolphs, and four with the Beverleys. Membership in, or alliance with, one of these families was certainly an important political asset, although, to keep the matter in proper perspective, from one-third to one-half of the leaders were not related to any of these families and not every member so related attained political power.

In religion and nationality the leaders were remarkably homogeneous. Of the 80 per cent ascertainable, all were Anglicans. It seems likely that those about whom information is not available were also Anglican, although it is entirely possible that several adhered to other Protestant faiths. In national origins the vast majority were English, and, if there were a few Scots, some Welsh, and even an occasional Irishman, still they all were Britons.

The educational level of the 110 leading burgesses appears to have been remarkably high. At least fifty had some education at the college or university level. Some forty attended the College of William and Mary, but others journeyed to England for at least a part of their formal schooling. Richard Henry Lee and Robert Munford studied at Wakefield Academy in Leeds; Charles and Landon Carter at Solomon Low's School, near London; Gabriel Jones at the Blue Coat School in Christ's Hospital, London; and four others at unknown schools in the British Isles. Ten others read law at the Inns of Court—for whatever that may or may not have been worth. A few matriculated at the universities; two at Oxford, another at Cambridge, and one, possibly two, at Edinburgh. Of those who had neither the benefits of an English education nor study at William and Mary, many, like Francis Lightfoot Lee, were taught at home by a private tutor. Others, like George Washington, got their education in parish schools conducted by local clergymen. No fewer than seventeen of those without university training successfully undertook the study of law; they proceeded either, like Edmund Pendleton and Paul Carrington, under the watchful eye of a practicing attorney or, like Patrick Henry, on their own. From the records at hand it is impossible to determine if the educational attainments of the leaders were higher than those of their fellow burgesses or just how much higher their educational level was than the general level in Virginia. In all likelihood, however, they were at least as well educated as any men in the colony.

The leaders' formal education was supplemented by practical experience at the county and parish levels. In fact, a record of active county and parish service was in the background of almost every burgess. The late Charles S. Sydnor, in his study of eighteenth-century Virginia politics, found that posts on the county courts, the parish vestry, and the county militia were important milestones on the pathway to political power. My own investigation amply supports his findings. Either before or during their service in the house, well over four-fifths of the Burgesses' men of power between 1720 and 1776 served as gentlemen justices of the peace. Over half were vestrymen, and nearly two-fifths were officers of the county militia. A few had also been clerks, king's attorneys, sheriffs, surveyors, and coroners in the counties. Some had served as town officials; no fewer than five had been mayors of Williamsburg. Five others combined burgessing with the colony's attorney generalship. Each of these posts—military, judicial, civil, and ecclesiastical—gave the prospective burgess an opportunity to develop the sort of leadership that would prove useful in the house, to gain an intimate knowledge of his future constituents, and to learn something of the obligations and responsibilities of political office and political power.

An analysis of the geographical distribution of the leaders shows that no one section had a monopoly on political power within the house. Neither does there appear to have been any attempt by representatives from the older counties in the Tidewater to exclude from places of importance those burgesses who came from the newer areas. On the other hand, it appears that leadership and geographical origins were not unrelated, for leaders were rarely drawn from sections settled for less than a generation. During the period under consideration, more leaders came from the Tidewater, in particular from the region extending from the south side of the James River northward to the Rappahannock and from the western rim of Chesapeake Bay westward to the fall line, than from any other section; in fact, until 1730 most of the leaders were Tidewater men. However, from 1705 on, representatives from the Northern Neck, that area lying between the Rappahannock and Potomac Rivers and stretching westward to the mountains, played an increasingly important role in the affairs of the house and by 1730 equaled the Tidewater in supplying the house with leaders. In the 1730's, the counties around the fall line also began to contribute a significant number of leaders. This development was, after all, a logical one, especially since the social and economic patterns of the Tidewater were extended not only to the Northern Neck and the fall line area but also into the Piedmont, and since family ties cut across geographical lines. From 1689 to the end of the colonial period, there appears to have been an almost continuous shift of the geographical center of power northward and westward, following the frontier by about a generation. Thus, the house did not draw leaders from the Piedmont until the late 1740's, nearly twenty-five years after the first settlement of that region. Similarly, although the occupation of the Shenandoah Valley and mountain area further west began in the 1740's, none of its representatives rose to positions of power until the late 1760's.

Why these particular 110 rose to positions of power rather than their colleagues is a question of fundamental importance. As individuals they exhibit most of the "qualifications" I have discussed. They were wealthy, derived part of their income from planting, were often related to the great Virginia families, were Anglicans, were of English (or at least of British) origin, had attained a high educational level for the time and place, were experienced in local politics, and came from areas settled for at least a generation. These were the tangibles upon which political power was based, although the lack of any one, two, or even three of these qualifications might not necessarily bar a man from a position of power. The more essential elements were wealth, family, and education; but even a generous helping of all three would not guarantee a position among the leaders of the house. Otherwise William Byrd III, Robert Wormeley Carter, Charles Carter, Jr., Richard Bland, Jr., and others would have been assured of such a place. In the long run the capacity to put these elements to effective use—call it political acumen, sagacity, the quality of political leadership—was probably decisive, although it is not susceptible of analysis in a study of this nature. But to secure the support of the electorate and the confidence of his colleagues and to exercise leadership in the Virginia House of Burgesses, 1720–76, a man had to have some measure of the tangible "qualifications" as well as the capacity to use them.

4 / The Sect to Denomination Process in America: The Freewill Baptist Experience

Ruth B. Bordin

Denominations do not appear full-grown on the religious scene. As with other institutions in society, they change over time and these changes are of great interest. Which classes in the community do they serve at a given period? What are the social origins and training of the preachers and church leaders? How do the activities and constituencies of these institutions change over time?

These questions have been discussed by sociologists and students of the history of religion. Ruth B. Bordin provides a detailed case study to test previous hypotheses and theories. The Freewill Baptists emerged in New England toward the end of the eighteenth century. The first preachers and leaders were humble people who lacked formal education, and their followers came from the lower strata of society. Informality, patterns of voluntary association, and spontaneity marked the early years. Only later, as the sect moved toward denominational status, did these patterns change. As the sons of the founders tended to move up the social ladder, spontaneity gave way to formalism and routine. A professional ministry replaced spirit-moved laymen, and theological schools emerged. Thus, the sect matured into a denomination.

Much of the data for this study is quantitative. By the use of simple statistical techniques and the arrangement of findings in tabular form, new light is shed on the past. It is in the context established by such research that fuller understanding of theology and ecclesiology will be gained.

For further reading: Henry F. May, "The Recovery of American Religious History," *American Historical Review*, LXX (1964), 79–92; John Lankford, "The Contemporary Revolution in Historiography and the History of the Episcopal Church: Observations and Reflections," *Historical Magazine of the Protestant Episcopal Church*, XXXVI (1967), 11–34; A. Leland Jamison, "Religions of the Christian Perimeter," in James Ward Smith and A. Leland Jamison (eds.), *Religion in American Life: The Shaping of American Religion* (1961), 162–231; *Sidney E. Mead, *The Lively Experiment:*

Church History, XXXIV (1965), 77–93. Footnotes have been omitted.

The Shaping of Christianity in America (1963); Robert W. Doherty, *The Hicksite Separation: A Sociological Analysis of Religious Schism in Early Nineteenth Century America* (1967); Elwyn A. Smith, *The Presbyterian Ministry in American Culture: A Study in Changing Concepts, 1700–1900* (1962).

Shortly after the turn of the century Ernst Troeltsch joined Max Weber in examining the history of religious organizations from the point of view of the newly evolving discipline of sociology. Of the contributions Troeltsch made in his monumental study, *The Social Teaching of the Christian Churches*, the one which has proved most stimulating when applied to American church history was his differentiation of sect-type from church-type religious organization. In 1929, H. Richard Niebuhr in his *Social Sources of Denominationalism* elaborated Troeltsch's ideas, especially as they related to American developments, suggesting that in the American environment the denomination occupied a midway position between church and sect. While Troeltsch hints at the tendency of the sect to acquire churchly characteristics in time, Niebuhr spells out the steps in the process of transformation from sect to denomination which he sees as following inevitably, arguing that each generation's sects must become denominations in the next generation. These in turn leave behind a new group of disinherited whose needs are unmet and from which spring the next sect movement.

The main points in the Troeltsch-Niebuhr thesis are well-known and there is no need to repeat them here. Everyone working in American church or religious history since Niebuhr published his *Social Sources* has been influenced by his ideas in the sense of describing the long-term trends in various religious bodies which corroborate his thesis. No one, however, has attempted to demonstrate empirically in the dimension of time, this transformation from sect to denomination or test statistically any characteristics of the process. North America has seen the birth of dozens of sect-type religious organizations in the last three centuries and they are still being generated. For our purposes, the Freewill Baptists, founded by Benjamin Randall on the New England frontier in the late 1770's and 1780's, are clearly identifiable as such a sect, and their institutional life-cycle will be used in this paper to show what, if any, quantitative changes took place in their first hundred years to substantiate their transformation from sect to denomination.

The Freewill Baptist movement had its origins in the reaction against Calvinism which had infiltrated the New England Baptist churches largely as a result of the Great Awakening. In the period following the Whitefield revivals, many of the Separatists or New Lights who left the old churches moved to the Maine, New Hampshire, and Vermont frontiers, where within a few years most of the churches they organized had embraced Baptist principles. Although the Separatists found the practice of adult baptism congenial, they clung to other Calvinist doctrines and brought them with them into the Baptist churches. Before the Awakening New England Baptist churches had almost all been Arminian, but by 1780 the large influx of Calvinist Separatists into the denomination, plus the closer association with Calvinist Baptists of the Middle Colonies, had changed their picture completely, and most New England Baptist churches were firmly committed to Calvinist principles.

Benjamin Randall, then a young sailmaker's apprentice in New Castle, N.H., had heard George Whitefield preach three times when the great evangelist visited Portsmouth in September of 1770, was converted on hearing the news of Whitefield's death, and formally joined (with his young bride) the Congregational church he had attended all his life. But orthodox Congregationalism did not satisfy him. What Randall saw as its immoralities and hypocricies soon drove him toward identification with the Separatists. He became convinced of the need for adult baptism, himself was immersed, and joined the Berwick Baptist church. Even before taking this step he had begun to hold meetings and eventually preached to small groups in his home, and when he cast his lot with the Baptists his preaching activities greatly increased. Again he found himself in conflict, this time with his new allegiance, when he refused to preach the doctrine of predestination, so in 1778 he moved to New Durham, N.H., where he plied the trade of tailor and preached to a small group of followers. Dissension with other Baptist clergy continued, and when his views were formally challenged at a two-day confrontation by Baptist clergy at Gilmanton, he formally separated himself from his Baptist association and with a small group of seven followers signed the covenant which made them a new independent religious community.

The organization of this new body very consciously was patterned on primitive Christianity. As was typical of sects, they saw themselves returning to the simple faith of Christ's early followers. They "laboured to reconstruct the apostolic platform," they eschewed doctrine, including of course election, and saw the Bible as their only rule of faith and practice. Ritual and outward forms of worship concerned them not at all, and government of the group rested with its lay members, led by an elected teaching elder who preached, a ruling elder who took care of the church's business affairs, and a deacon who administered to the poor. Randall continued to work at his tailor's bench and did his preaching and evangelizing only at great personal sacrifice of time and money. Free communion was practiced. A true moving of the spirit in each individual was a prerequisite of full fellowship, and a deeply experienced call such as the one with which Randall himself had struggled, was the only criterion for beginning to preach. Ordination followed the call and was conferred by the fellowship group.

By the end of 1781 there were fourteen tiny congregations stemming from Randall's evangelistic activities in Maine and New Hampshire which were associated with the New Durham congregation. In 1783 they bound themselves together in a formal organization known as the Quarterly Meeting, which assumed some of the functions of the local Meeting, but remained a congregation of all present rather than a delegate body. At first growth was slow and concentrated in New Hampshire and Maine. By 1810 there were 98 congregations in those states and two in Vermont. And it is not until 1830 that the movement reached any considerable size, when it could boast 466 churches embracing 21,499 members and had spread throughout New England, New York state, Ohio and western Pennsylvania.

Two of the characteristics which Niebuhr uses to differentiate the sect from the denomination are examined in this paper in the light of Freewill Baptist experience: first, Niebuhr's emphasis on the commitment to democratic organization on the part of all sect groups, including the election of preachers and church officials by local congregations and the consciously lay character of all pastoral and preaching offices; and secondly, the emphasis on the religious society as a voluntary fellowship of truly converted believers, requiring a personal religious experience as a requisite of fellowship. If the Freewill Baptists follow the expected developmental pattern and move from sect to denomination in these areas, we would expect to find them in their early years with untrained, self-supporting lay preachers, who would take to sermonizing and exhorting at any time of life when they felt the call to preach. Later as the sect matures and becomes a denomination it would develop a trained professional clergy, financially supported by the lay membership and ordained at a conventional age with the sanction of a church hierarchy or leadership at the end of a formal training period. We should also expect to find that as the sect becomes a denomination, the original commitment to a voluntary association of true believers would have been modified in practice (if not theory) by a conventionalization of the conversion experience, permitting the second generation to be absorbed into full fellowship in a regularized and relatively automatic fashion.

However to test Niebuhr's hypothesis that the sect is viable as a sect for only a single generation, some criteria must be arrived at for deciding what constitutes a generation in the life of a religious movement. Unfortunately Niebuhr himself does not make this clear. Actually during the first years at least of this new sect, member-ship was so small that it could only grow (or possibly even maintain itself) through conversion. Inevitably most of its members for several decades after 1780 were as individuals the first generation of the movement. To some extent this is always true of individuals in any voluntary religious association, although in decreasing propor-tion as the group matures.

However, one can also think of the group as a whole having a life apart from its individual members. At least it should be possible to ascertain that time at which a religious group is sufficiently institutionalized so that its majority and particularly its leadership will view it as an on-going movement with a life of its own which must be safeguarded. Certainly the Freewill Baptists were approaching this stage by the 1830's. In 1827 they had formed their state and local associations into a delegate body known as the General Conference, which although it was expressly denied judicial or legislative functions did exercise considerable moral suasion over both individuals and churches and certainly acted as the official mouthpiece for the group as a whole. Surely it was of great significance that one of its first acts was to authorize the drawing up of a formal statement of beliefs, published in 1834, *Treatise on the Faith of the Freewill Baptists, with a summary of their usages in church government.*

Another way to view the problem is to recognize that one cannot expect those factors which act to change the group in its second generation to become operable until there is a body of members of sufficient size to constitute a first generation. Along the New Hampshire-Maine border, where membership was then concentrated, this phase was probably reached by 1810. It came at least a decade later in Vermont and upper New York state, and still later in the old Northwest. Thus one would expect the characteristics of maturity which we have singled out to be reached earlier in some parts of the country than in others. Nonetheless there seems to be ample evidence that the group as a whole was large and strong enough by 1820 to be viable, and that both as group and as individuals the first generation was well under way.

To test these assumptions, an attempt was made to analyze biographical data on the 1,945 Freewill Baptist ministers ordained between 1780 and 1890. Sufficient in-formation for the purposes of this study was obtainable on 1,478 of these ministers.

Date and place of birth, date of conversion, date of ordination, amount and kind of education, and place of ministerial service were collected and analyzed to determine the relationships between the length of time the Freewill Baptists had been in existence and several other factors: first, the range of age of its ministers at the time of their ordination; second, the educational equipment and professional training of the ministers being ordained; and third, the range of age at time of conversion. The data were also analyzed by geographical region to see if sect characteristics were modified more quickly in those areas where the group had been in existence longest.

Amount and kind of education and training were used as the primary criteria for evaluating the degree to which the ordained ministers were becoming a professional group. Individuals were divided into three groups for classification purposes. Group 1 consists of those with no formal education of any kind or with formal schooling which did not advance beyond the common schools. Group 3 is composed of those who had formal theological training obtained in an educational institution and designed specifically to fit them for the ministry. Group 2 is a miscellany of ministers with secondary or higher education of a general nature or education designed to train them for some other profession such as law or school teaching, and also includes a few men who received formal private theological tutoring from ordained ministers.

As can be seen from Table I, there is a steady decrease, as would be expected, in the percentage of ministers ordained in each decade who had little or no education, although after a hundred years and two full generations after 1820, forty percent of the men being ordained were still untrained and relatively uneducated. Concomitantly the percentage with formal theological training steadily rose after the 1830's when the first ministers with theological educations appear, but at the end of the century still represented only half of those being ordained.

In the first years of the movement the lay character of the ministry is indisputable. The first sixty-four ordinations by Freewill Baptists were all unlettered farmers or craftsmen, called to preach at ages ranging from 19 to 61, and before 1800 none of those ordained had even been converted until they were fully mature men. It is most likely that among the Free Baptist membership at that time, few if any possessed more education than those called to preach. In this sense they truly exemplify Niebuhr and Troeltsch's definition of the sect member as coming from among the poor and disinherited. When Timothy Dwight visited the area around Maine's Lake Winnepesaukee in 1813, he described it as inhabited by "Baptists, of the class generally known as *Free-Willers,* who are generally extremely ignorant. It is a very great evil to these settlements, and many others in New Hampshire, that they are . . . destitute of well educated ministers of the Gospel." And a Congregationalist minister in Gorham, characterizing the Freewill Baptists in his locality said, "They glory in an ignorant ministry. Many of their ministers have scarce ability to read the Scriptures. . . ."

The emphasis was not on training or education but on a moving of the spirit. The call was the important thing and it was resisted until a man was fully convinced of its genuineness. After all it was not really he who preached, but the Holy Spirit who preached through him. John Colby, one of their early ministers, phrased his feelings in the introduction to his journal, in explaining the depression and unworthiness he felt when he first began to experience the call, "For I viewed it to be a great and solemn thing to be mouth for God. . . ." And this inner urge to

TABLE I

PERCENTAGE OF MEN ORDAINED AT EACH EDUCATIONAL
LEVEL BY DECADE

Date of ordination	1780–99	1800–09	1810–19	1820–29	1830–39	1840–49	1850–59	1860–69	1870–79	1880–89
Number of men ordained	20	44	60	107	175	280	163	197	226	206
Percentage in Group 1	100%	100%	98%	93%	85%	69%	58%	48%	47%	40%
Percentage in Group 2			2%	6%	6%	9%	12%	16%	14%	10%
Percentage in Group 3				1%	9%	22%	29%	36%	39%	50%

preach was needful each time they rose to speak as preacher to their fellows. There is a story told that when John Buzzell, another of their early leaders, was to preach the chief sermon of a Sunday morning during Yearly Meeting, he rose but was not moved to preach, and after a few words admitted, "Brethren, I have not got the word; if anyone has it let him stand forth." Hearing this, sixteen-year-old Jonathan Woodman who had been caring for the horses during meeting time, "trembling and with the burden of God upon his soul, arose to his feet and began to deliver the message." So great was his eloquence that strong men wept and sinners trembled.

This anecdote shows clearly the spontaneous expression required of all who preached. All through the literature and personal papers of the clergy, evidence abounds of how important they felt this to be. Ministers, in speaking of their own performances, referred to this quality as "freedom" or "liberty," and without it on any given occasion the would-be preacher had no recourse but to remain silent. Preparation for preaching, other than Bible reading and praying for the aid of the Holy Spirit, was considered unnecessary and unwarranted and could only interfere with the free flow of the spirit by way of the preacher to the congregation.

The anecdote about Woodman illustrates another characteristic of the early Freewill Baptist ministry. Preaching always preceded ordination. Frequently the time interval between conversion and preaching was almost non-existent, but a man's call to preach had to be exercised for a reasonable length of time before he could be considered a candidate for ordination. He must have proved by much preaching and exhorting that he was a vehicle through which the Spirit could work. Randall himself had held meetings for seven years and preached for four years before he was ordained. Later this period became shortened in most cases to less than a year, and eventually was formalized into a licensing system, similar to that used by the Methodists and some Presbyterians. A man was "licensed to exhort" or to "practice his gifts"; in brief he was formally given permission by the Elders' Conference of the Quarterly Meeting, composed of preachers, deacons, and ruling elders, to indulge his call to preach. Although this committee of elders had the power to examine the candidate requesting ordination on the genuineness of his conversion and his call, the request for either licensing or ordination always came from the local church which also assumed the ultimate responsibility of conferring ordination on him.

Granted that the attitude of the Freewill Baptists towards ministerial functions for the first forty years of the movement possesses all the characteristics which testify to sect status, are Freewill Baptist clergy for that period really very different from the clergy of other more mature religious groups cohabiting with them in time and place? During the colonial period the Congregational and Presbyterian clergy were almost all college trained. Of the 1586 Congregational ministers ordained in New England, only seventy-nine were not college graduates. The Presbyterians ordained 250 ministers between 1758 and 1789, and of these 120 were trained at Princeton, twenty at Yale, and others at small colleges in New Jersey, Pennsylvania, and elsewhere. At the time Randall first organized his movement and set the patterns it followed in its early years, clearly the clergy of New England's mature Protestant denominations were very different in terms of educational status from those of the Freewill Baptists.

In the decade of the twenties, the first theologically trained minister, a graduate of Brown University, appears among the Freewillers, but he was originally a Calvinist Baptist, ordained by them, and joined the Freewill connection after his training had been completed. By this time a very few of the ministers differ from the rest in that they had been educated in secondary schools and academies. But education was still no recommendation for a minister. During this decade the first Freewill Baptist General Conference met at Tunbridge, Vt., and affirmed that the call was all-important:

> He must be led by the Spirit into the sanctuary of God, see the end of the wicked, and be so impressed with a sense of their awful situation while uncon-verted, that he shall absolutely feel like Paul—Woe is me if I preach not the Gospel.

Not a word was yet said about any other qualifications.

In the next decade, a period in which the denomination experienced considerable growth, real changes begin to take place. Although 85 per cent of the ministers or-dained are still untrained, fifteen of the new recruits have received professional edu-cations. Most of these attended the first Freewill Baptist school at Parsonfield, founded in 1832, but one was actually a graduate of Yale Theological School. Another dozen received some kind of further schooling which set them apart from their fellows. For the first time education was sanctioned as a desirable prelude to ministerial service. The circular letter which followed the General Conference of 1835 stated, "The importance of an intelligent and well-informed ministry is beginning to be appreciated by many of our brethren," and "seminaries of learning have been estab-lished in different parts of our connection." Parsonfield was joined by Strafford Academy in 1834 and Randalian Seminary in 1835, and by 1837 the Conference was hoping that the time was not far distant when "in point of learning as well as piety and usefulness, we shall compare with other Christian denominations."

The lay status of the clergy was being eroded in still other ways. As early as 1831 John Buzzell was urging that congregations should provide financial support for their preachers. And only six years later, in 1837, the Conference went unequivocally on record as believing that it was the "duty of every church that engages a preacher to give him a reasonable and suitable compensation for his labors." As the ministry takes on the prerequisites of an occupation, what happens to the Spirit whose instru-ment the preacher had been? Some ministers were obviously preparing for their Sunday duties, rather than waiting for the Spirit to work in them, and some of them must have been delivering sermons from notes. In fact, the question of the appro-priateness of sermon preparation was characterized at the time as the warmest issue of the Conference of 1837. The formal statement, on which that body eventually agreed, hedged, recommending that the ministry

> avoid the use of skeletons [outlines], notes, or written discourses in preaching the gospel, as general practice, believing that extemporaneous discourses are more scriptural, interesting, and useful. Notwithstanding, we think that every minister should follow that method in his preaching which he conscientiously believes or finds by experience to be most conducive to his own spiritual interest and the ad-vancement of the Redeemer's kingdom.

The many who were still strongly committed to the earlier view of the ministry inter-preted this as encouraging sermon preparation. They marshalled their forces, which must still have represented a majority, for in 1839 a resolution was passed which stated unequivocal disapproval of the use of "skeletons, notes or written discourses."

In the first few decades little value was placed on a settled ministry. Once licensed and ordained, a man preached where the Lord sent him rather than exercising pastoral care over a specific group. Although most of his preaching might be done to a single meeting, the one to which he belonged and where he resided, he alone was the judge of when he was called elsewhere and he often preached in nearby churches. The young men especially would hear and follow a call to wander from place to place almost without plan, living on long journeys off the charity of those with whom they worked. By the 1830's some regulation of this practice was attempted. In 1832 the Conference resolved: "Every travelling preacher of our order, ought to be able to show that he is properly authorized to travel and preach, and that he is a regular member of some one of our churches." The next year a salaried itinerant ministry, much like the Methodist circuit system, received formal support as the proper way to regularly serve those churches not having a settled minister. These preachers were "to keep a true account of the time they labor and of all they receive, and to report this to the next Yearly Meeting. . . ." But the plan was never really put into practice.

While in the decade of the 1830's the range of age when ordination took place remains as great as it had in the previous fifty years, fewer men of over forty (only 26 out of 175) were being ordained, which would seem to indicate that the ministry was being viewed as a life-long occupation whether one specifically prepared for it or not. And those who sought professional education were all ordained as young men.

In the forties these trends were accelerated. There is an abrupt drop of 16 percentage points in the number entering the ministry with no educational background, and the group who have obtained some measure of formal training has risen to nearly a quarter of those ordained. These figures reflect the policies toward which the group was inexorably moving. In 1840 an Education Society had been organized whose first task was devising means to support the Biblical School at Parsonfield. Education of ministers was the great Conference issue of the early 1840's. An attempt was made to alleviate the fears of the conservatives by resolutions which admitted that "some of our beloved brethren entertain fears, that a certain course of study or amount of knowledge will ultimately be required of candidates for admission to the gospel ministry in this denomination," promising no such test should ever be required for ordination. But three years later the Conference was cautioning that men had "no right to neglect the cultivation of their talents" and recommending that all ministers "pursue a regular course of study, even if they should be unable to study more than one hour per day." A committee was appointed with the specific task of recommending books and a course of reading suitable for young preachers.

However it was still necessary to justify these innovations and it was emphasized that those attending the Biblical School were assiduously studying the Bible, a task to which there could surely be no objection. Also there were no regulations on how long they should attend school, anywhere from three years to a few months was acceptable, and the trainees were not forced to suspend preaching. The "Biblical School was never intended to dispense with a call from God," and the Conference regretted that there were those who so misrepresented its purposes.

The question of ministers accepting support from their congregations was also being argued. The General Conference fully accepted the desirability of support, and ministers who still earned their livings by manual labor were seen as indulging "the penuriousness of their hearers." But not all ministers and members were convinced that this was the proper view. One of the disgruntled complained that "the majority of the people do not like such innovations as Missions, effective Sabbath Schools, paying preachers a salary, ministers living off the gospel, etc., etc.," and the tendency of ministers to forsake the struggling churches of the west "for the sake of a better salery [sic]" in the East. And these two dissenters were not alone, for although the articulate leadership of the group, in this its second generation, clearly supported both training and a steady income for the clergy, the lay minister in the old tradition was not disappearing as quickly as they might hope.

Typically a man who sees the ministry as a life-long profession is ordained in early manhood. We assumed for purposes of this study that a conventional age at ordination would be 23 to 33. It is clear from Table II that less than half of Group 1 fall within that category in the 1840's, or over a third of the total number being ordained.

TABLE II

PERCENTAGE ORDAINED BETWEEN 23 AND 33 YEARS OF AGE

	1780– 99	1800– 09	1810– 19	1820– 29	1830– 39	1840– 49	1850– 59	1860– 69	1870– 79	1880– 89
Group 1	35%	43%	59%	51%	48%	48%	31%	40%	31%	39%
Group 2				66%	83%	90%	50%	72%	61%	20%
Group 3					93%	92%	75%	82%	78%	86%
Total	35%	43%	59%	52%	64%	62%	46%	60%	53%	60%

When we look at the figures for range of age at ordination in Table III, the same picture confronts us.

TABLE III

RANGE OF AGE IN YEARS AT ORDINATION

	1780– 99	1800– 09	1810– 19	1820– 29	1830– 39	1840– 49	1850– 59	1860– 69	1870– 79	1880– 89
Group 1	23–54	19–61	20–55	16–65	16–68	19–67	21–62	21–69	20–65	21–59
Group 2				22–26	21–38	22–48	19–43	21–43	22–62	21–47
Group 3					22–31	21–42	21–45	20–39	18–47	21–48

In the 1840's, twelve men who were over fifty, certainly elderly men by mid-nineteenth century standards, were ordained. All were members of Group 1. At the same time only two of those receiving professional education were ordained after reaching age thirty-three, and the fact that even two older men felt the need of training for their ministerial duties seems to indicate wider acceptance by the group as a whole of the role formal theological education should play. The ordaining of the very young almost disappears in this decade. Only five or less than 2 per cent of the 280 ordained in the 1840's were twenty or under, and none of these were in the group receiving any theological education.

As the tables indicate, these trends continue in the 1850's, with fewer and fewer young men seeking ordination unless they also acquire an education. Only three of Group 1 are under 23 and only 20 per cent under thirty. In contrast, twenty-eight, or nearly a third of Group 1 were over forty and almost another third (25) were between thirty-five and forty, which would suggest that a man feeling a call to preach in middle-life was still fully acceptable with only lay qualifications. But the range of age when a ministerial candidate sought professional training is also rising. In the thirties and forties nearly all of those who attended theological school were young men, over 90 per cent being ordained before they reached thirty-three. But this drops abruptly to 75 per cent in the 1850's, probably because even the older man in increasing numbers was feeling pressures which sent him to the seminaries to improve his gifts.

Official encouragement was all in the direction of professionalization by the 1850's. As early as 1850, the General Conference resolved that it was the "duty of every man who is thus called of God, to seek the best education in his power," and recommended the establishment of more permanent settled relationships between pastors and churches. By 1856, Conference commitment to a full-time ministry was complete, when they urged that even "feeble churches [should] unite, as far as practicable, by organization or otherwise, in securing pastors who shall devote their entire time to the ministry."

By the end of the decade the General Conference advised those entering the ministry to go to the Biblical School if possible and stipulated that it was the "duty of licensing and ordaining bodies to examine candidates . . . in respect to their literary attainments as well as in doctrine and piety." Those whose "circumstances" would not allow their attendance at "our Biblical School or any other theological institution" were to pursue a course of independent study in which they could be examined. Even older ministers were seeking learning. Ministerial associations organized conventions which met once a year for a week or two to study "logic and rhetoric, theology, [and to] examine sermons and sketches." The prejudice against prepared sermons was fast disappearing, and as early as 1850 there is evidence of the occasional publication of sermons by the Freewill Baptist publishing house. They could hardly have been extemporaneous.

All of these efforts bore fruit, if slowly, for the percentage of uneducated pastors being ordained drops sharply again in the sixties, and only three of these were under twenty-five. Several members of Group 2 had received excellent general educations, although they lacked professional theological training, and all of those attending theological schools were ordained as relatively young men in their twenties and thirties, 82 per cent of them between 23 and 33 as shown in Table II. Eleven additional educational institutions (three of which gave theological training) had been founded by 1860, and the next decade saw the beginnings of nine more. The profits of the Freewill Baptist Printing establishment were being used to endow theological professorships, although not without opposition from those who thought they might better be used for missions and proselytizing. The Ministerial Associations continued their programs of self-education, and even the elderly and unlettered who experienced a call considered attending theological school.

In the last half of the sixties there was a partial retreat from this strong commitment to full professional education. Actually there was no real hope at that time of obtaining a large enough body of educated ministers to serve every congregation. The number of ordinations drops sharply in the sixties, and because of the needs of the new Negro churches in the south and the many unserved smaller churches in the north and west, the General Conference of 1865 asked that "all who are called by God to the ministry leave . . . their secular callings" and assume the duties of an active ministry regardless of their educational qualifications. The admonition to churches in want of pastors to turn to that "class of ministers, who, in consequence of the want of educational advantages or for other reasons are laid aside from the work" was repeated in 1868. And the special skills of the lay evangelist were treasured again, for the Conference deeply deplored "the almost entire disuse among us of this effective and Scriptural method of preaching Christ, so generally employed by the fathers of the Denomination" and strongly recommended its revival. While circumstances required the compromise of educational standards, there was no real return to a lay ministry. The Conference position that a minister should give full time to his calling, be supported by his congregation or congregations, and eschew secular pursuits was not modified.

While there is no reversal of trends during the 1870's, the changes which had been going on for the last forty years almost come to a halt. The percentage of ordinations of the uneducated remains almost the same as in the previous decade, and 41 per cent of these were forty years or over. The one case of a minister, theologically trained, who was ordained in his teens, appears in this decade, but he was a Virginia ex-slave, ordained long before he attended theological school. Otherwise the boy preacher, once popular and accepted (if relatively infrequent), had completely disappeared.

In the next decade for the first time half the ordinations were of men with formal theological educations. Bates Theological Seminary had been founded in 1870, and by the '80's, was in a position to give a relatively rigorous and complete theological training. Thirty-one of these men were its graduates, another fifteen were trained at Cobb Divinity School, two came from Union Theological Seminary, and one each from Andover and Yale. The rest were educated at the theological department of Hillsdale College in Michigan or the smaller and less rigorous Bible schools and seminaries. This is in marked contrast to the 1840's, when theological education was dispensed at the Biblical schools of Parsonfield, Whitestown, or New Hampton without prior college training, and only four men had been educated at Oberlin and one at Andover. Thus not only did numbers and percentages increase but the quality of education for those able to acquire it was significantly higher. While in the earlier years ordination almost invariably came first and training followed, over half of the men in Group 3 in the 1880's were ordained after their education was completed. Even those without formal training were required to pass an examination in theology and church history.

The function of the local congregation or fellowship group as the ordaining body had lost all its force. While the local group was still allowed to call and give one of its members a certificate as a lay preacher in its midst, it was warned that this was in no case equivalent to ordination, for it was neither wise nor safe for one church alone to be advisor and director in the matter of ordination, and the approval of the Quarterly Meeting and a ministerial council was necessary. It would seem that this phase of the cycle from sect to denomination was complete after a full century.

Was this professionalization of the Freewill Baptist clergy really a function of the sect to denomination process or did it merely reflect the rising level of professional training typical of several occupations in the middle decades of the 19th century? Lawyers, physicians, and dentists were also receiving professional educations in increasing numbers and were setting higher and higher standards of training and competence for entrance into their professions. Had the high educational standards of the colonial clergy been maintained in the early 19th century by the older denominations when they lost, as did the Congregationalists in New England, the prerequisites of an established church?

TABLE IV

EDUCATIONAL STATUS OF CONGREGATIONAL MINISTERS

Date of Ordination	before	1829	1830–39	1840–49	1850–59	1860–69	1870–79	1880–89
Number in Sample		72	106	100	80	95	72	43
Percent College Trained		78%	70%	80%	86%	80%	82%	65%
Percentage with Theological Training		60%	72%	84%	70%	72%	76%	60%

Table IV shows that while the percentage of Congregational ministers who received college educations fluctuates from 65 to 86 per cent during the several decades under study, the low point oddly enough is reached in the 1880's, rather than earlier in the century. Andover Theological Seminary was not founded until 1808, and prior to that time a post-college period of two or three years of privately reading theology under the guidance of an ordained minister was the normal course of professional training. This accounts for the relatively small number of theological school graduates in the group ordained before 1830. The sudden drop in the 1880's which parallels a similar drop in college graduates cannot be explained and probably merits further investigation in its own right, but does not detract from the obvious conclusion that Freewill Baptist trends are not mere duplications of general patterns and do not parallel the experience of fully mature denominations. Certainly the sect to denomination theory seems to offer a more meaningful explanation.

The hypothesis that conversion becomes a conventionalized experience as a religious group matures is less easily demonstrable, at least with the Freewill Baptists as a case in point.

TABLE V

RANGE OF AGE IN YEARS AT TIME OF CONVERSION

Date of Ordination	1780–99	1800–09	1810–19	1820–29	1830–39	1840–49	1850–59	1860–69	1870–79	1880–89
Group 1	23–39	12–37	12–36	9–35	8–43	12–40	9–36	10–43	10–38	10–48
Group 2				15–21	14–27	9–29	14–24	8–32	8–26	13–38
Group 3					9–24	11–31	10–26	5–33	10–32	6–31

TABLE VI

PERCENTAGE CONVERTED BETWEEN AGE 12 AND 20

Date of Ordination	1780–99	1800–09	1810–19	1820–29	1830–39	1840–49	1850–59	1860–69	1870–79	1880–89
Group 1	0%	38%	65%	54%	44%	61%	61%	59%	36%	43%
Group 2				83%	55%	76%	82%	75%	68%	54%
Group 3					60%	76%	67%	70%	70%	69%
Percentage of Total	0%	38%	65%	55%	47%	66%	66%	65%	58%	57%

It is clear enough from Tables V and VI that in the very early years of the sect's existence, age at conversion was relatively random, and up to 1810 only about a third were being converted between the ages of 12 and 20. After that period a high percentage of conversions fall during those years when pressure to conform would be greatest for a second generation, the age when a child is maturing into an adult and assuming his responsibilities as a full member of society. In every decade the percentage whose conversions fall in the years we have assumed to be conventional is greater in the case of the professionally trained ordination candidates, suggesting they were more likely to belong to a second generation (as individuals) than their uneducated brethren. A closer look at the data shows a high percentage of conversions of men in their twenties, and it seemed possible that the maximum age at which conversions could be viewed as part of a coming of age pattern had been set too low. Only 4 per cent of the professionally trained ministers were converted after their thirtieth year, which shows much more clearly that relatively early conversion was characteristic of those who felt a need for education. However, only 12 per cent of those with at most a common school education were converted after reaching thirty during the period 1840–49, a noticeably larger proportion than in Group 3, but certainly again indicating that conversion was typically an experience of youth rather than middle age, regardless of educational status, and that this general convention may be fully as operative as any conventionalization accompanying the transformation from sect to denomination. Only forty-six or 4 per cent of the 1,052 ministers whose age at conversion is known were under twelve at the time they made their commitment, indicating that conversion of young children was always rare. All this tells us something about conversion but provides relatively little evidence that conversion was becoming increasingly conventionalized as sect characteristics were transformed into denominational patterns. Perhaps conventionalization of conversion takes place much earlier in the sect to denomination process than professionalization of the clergy. Only when compared to the years before 1810, when numbers were so small as to scarcely constitute a generation in the life of the movement, is the evidence of change clear cut.

The relationship between geography and sect status is clearly demonstrable. Sect characteristics were retained longest in those areas where the Freewill Baptist movement had come most recently.

TABLE VII

GEOGRAPHICAL DISTRIBUTION OF UNEDUCATED (GROUP 1) MINISTERS BY AREA WHERE THEY SPENT OVER HALF OF THEIR MINISTRIES

	Total No. Uneducated Ministers	New England and New Brunswick	New York, Pennsylvania and Quebec	Ohio, Mich., Ill., Wis., Ind., Iowa and Ontario	Trans-Mississippi West	South
1820–29	74	65%	22%	14%		
1830–39	123	67%	19%	15%		
1840–49	155	45%	25%	29%	.7%	
1850–59	74	41%	16%	36%	7%	
1860–69	77	31%	12%	33%	13%	12%
1870–79	90	20%	11%	26%	21%	22%
1880–89	67	19%	8%	19%	25%	28%

Table VII shows the geographical distribution of the ministries of those clergy with at most a common school education who were ordained from 1820 through the

1880's. In the twenties the figures really show the distribution for the whole body of Freewill Baptist clergy since almost all fell into Group 1 during that period. However, Freewill Baptist strenth was heavily concentrated in New England throughout the period under study, so the proportion of uneducated clergy who served there in later years in relation to the number of churches is much smaller than this table would indicate. In the 1880's 44 per cent of the total membership was in New England, but only 19 per cent of the untrained clergy ordained in that decade were to serve there. Over 50 per cent, or seven and one half times as many as their 7 per cent of the total membership would entitle them to, were to serve in the churches of the trans-Mississippi west (mostly Missouri, Kansas, and Minnesota) and in the South, where many small Freewill Baptist churches served by one of their own members had been gathered among the ex-slaves.

Upper New York state, Quebec, and western Pennsylvania were the first areas outside New England into which the young Freewill Baptist movement expanded after 1800, and for a while many lay ministers were absorbed here, usually farmer-preachers who frequently organized the church which they served. But as the 19th century wore on these churches took fewer and fewer in terms of their total membership, although they never came as close to a completely professional clergy as did New England. In the eighties the New York-Pennsylvania churches absorbed 8 per cent of the uneducated preachers into 15 per cent of the total membership of the denomination. The middle west took its largest share of uneducated clergy from those ordained a decade later. By the end of the '80's while 34 per cent of the Freewill Baptists lived in this region, only 19 per cent of the uneducated among the newly ordained worked among them. This uneven geographical distribution makes the trends shown in Table I on professional education much more dramatic. When the West and South with their really insignificant contribution to total membership are eliminated, the professionalization of Freewill Baptist clergy is easily comparable to that of their Congregationalist brethren by 1890.

The trends we have demonstrated for the Freewill Baptists unquestionably bear out the Troeltsch-Niebuhr thesis. While the transformation from sectarian to denominational characteristics never becomes absolute, this is probably true of almost all religious groups (except the rigidly authoritarian) in a society which permits only voluntary religious associations. If conversion becomes conventionalized, it happens very early in the total process. Professionalization of the clergy comes later, and is certainly not accomplished by the second generation, although total commitment to the principle by the leadership of the group was reached before the end of that period. Sectarian characteristics also disappear most rapidly where the group has been in existence longest, and prove most persistent on both class (i.e., the newly freed Negro) and geographical frontiers. And finally, these patterns of change seem to appear only in those groups in the process of evolving from sect to denomination and are not typical of the life-cycle of mature religious organizations.

5 / The Social Order
of the Anthracite Region, 1825-1902

Rowland Berthoff

This essay is a study of social disorganization. The impact of rapid economic growth, immigration from Europe and migration out of the region by those who either succeeded or failed, the lack of responsible leadership or of a traditional upper class—all contributed to the creation of an incomplete and dysfunctional social order.

As John Demos probed seventeenth-century Plymouth, Rowland Berthoff subjects the Pennsylvania anthracite region to a microscopic examination. The time span allows us to follow the changes from the beginning of coal mining in the area through the maturation of the industrial economy. In human terms this is not a pleasant story; indeed, it is as grim as the slate heaps and unpainted houses that dominate the landscape. Yet, without an understanding of the truncated nature of the class system and the great gulfs that separated one ethnic group from another, the political and labor history of the region can never really be understood.

For further reading: *W. Lloyd Warner (ed.), *Yankee City* (abridged ed., 1963); *Allan G. Bogue, *From Prairie to Corn Belt: Farming on the Illinois and Iowa Prairies in the Nineteenth Century* (1963); Merle Curti, *The Making of an American Community: A Case Study of Democracy in a Frontier County* (1959).

The place of the Pennsylvania anthracite region in American history has been fixed for nearly a century. The Molly Maguire conspiracy, the miners' strikes of the 1870's and 1902, the Lattimer massacre, a railroad president who believed himself one of "the Christian men to whom God in His infinite wisdom has given control of the property interests of the country," and, looming behind all these, the anthracite coal trust have become stock types of nineteenth-century capitalistic oppression and labor resistance. A region of company towns and stores, child labor and mine

Pennsylvania Magazine of History and Biography, LXXXIX (1965), 261–291. Footnotes have been omitted.

disasters, starvation wages and squalor, race wars between successive waves of immigrants; they are all familiar enough.

From the perspective of the mid-twentieth century, however, things that were *not* present in the society of the anthracite region appear no less significant than things that were. Instead of a simple melodrama of ruthless bosses and embattled workingmen, the story is one of groups, classes, institutions, and individuals so equivocally related as to be mutually unintelligible and quite heedless of each other. The region had plenty of groups, classes, institutions, and notable personages, to be sure, but it is hard to find among them any functional design of reciprocal rights and duties, the nuts and bolts which pin together a stable social order.

Geology was partly to blame. The anthracite region is an irregular area or discontinuous series of areas broken by mountain ridges and coalless farming valleys, altogether some four hundred square miles scattered over eight counties, reaching from a wide southern base north of the Blue Mountain, between the Susquehanna and Lehigh rivers, nearly a hundred miles northeastward along the broad Wyoming and narrow Lackawanna valleys. In 1825, the whole region was still wilderness, broken only by upland farms and a few market villages and hamlets. In the course of the nineteenth century these quiet communities were overrun by industry as drifts and shafts were drilled into the coal outcrops and underlying seams. Some two hundred new settlements, from remote mine patches to the metropolis of Scranton, with "its newness and its roughness—its helter-skelter way of doing things—its ups and downs—its push and enterprise—its rapid growth and busy hum—its work-a-day dress—its grime and smut and business air," sprang up among the hills. Carbondale, the first coal town of the northern field, had only fifty people in 1828, five years later some 2,500 lived there, and by 1850 nearly 5,000. Pottsville, a hamlet of a few houses and taverns in 1825, by 1831 numbered more than five hundred houses among "the stumps in the street showing that but yesterday a dense forest and impassible swamps existed"; by 1845 it was the southern anthracite metropolis with more than 5,000 inhabitants. And here and there, in no regular order, new clusters of houses and shanties kept appearing. Nanticoke grew from a village to "a full blown town" within the five years after 1868 and, as soon as the depression of 1873–1880 was over, shot up from 3,000 to 8,000 people in another three years. By 1900, the population of the entire region approached one million.

Since coal mining caused almost all this growth, the villages and towns were strewn, by the caprice of the worn and upended strata, between the barren ridges and along the narrow valleys: the Schuylkill and Little Schuylkill rivers; Nesquehoning, Mauch Chunk, Mahanoy, Shenandoah, Shamokin, Swatara, and Wiconisco creeks; Warrior Run, Sugar Notch Run, Nanticoke Run and Laurel Run; Locust Creek, Mill Creek, Norwegian Creek, Silver and Black, Beaver, Wolf, and Panther creeks; Roaring Brook, Lost Creek; and the broad Susquehanna itself. It would have been difficult to impose a tidy human plan had anyone tried to do so.

In time each of the disconnected coal fields of the region came to be economically unified within the sphere of influence of one or another of the half-dozen anthracite-carrying railroads. This produced only a slightly broader localism, however, within what colloquially remained the anthracite *regions*: Schuylkill and Lehigh to the south, Wyoming and Lackawanna to the north. The north-south grouping had begun, in fact, as early as the original settlements of "wild Yankee" farmers from Connecticut and New York, and "Pennamites" and Pennsylvania "Dutch" from the south, a distinction long marked in dialect, folk customs, and domestic architecture. Industrialization perpetuated the division as the southern fields looked to Philadelphia for capital and a market; to Schuylkill and Lehigh operators and miners alike, the Wyoming-Lackawanna field, with its New York orientation, was a remote and unfamiliar place at best and a cutthroat competitor at worst. Even the anthracite coal combination, the trust which after 1873 imposed an uneasy cooperation on the whole industry, never quite touched this petty regionalism.

Community ties were weak, even within towns and villages. Apart from a nucleus of shopkeepers, professional men, and what passed for old families in the few places in the Wyoming Valley that dated from the eighteenth century, the population of most mining towns was too mobile, too transient, too quickly gathered and easily scattered again. The burning of a coal breaker, exhaustion of a mine or abandonment of an unprofitable one, the bankruptcy of a company could at any time disperse a settlement of several hundred. In 1855, two shafts were sunk at the new village of Jessup; halted by the panic of 1857, Jessup fifteen years later was described as one of the deserted villages of the Lackawanna Valley, with two crumbling buildings where once had been "depots, machine and repair shops, stores, hotels, new dwellings, extensive coal crackers, etc." Jessup later revived, declined, and revived again, but each time it underwent a permanent turnover of much of its population. Frequent depressions in the anthracite market reduced not only the wage rate but work itself to "short time" of so few days each month that, unless the work was carefully spaced, the working force at a mine was apt to lose heart and move away. "Short stoppages are best for men & mules," a mining official advised; "in long ones they get demoralized and scatter." In Schuylkill County in the depressed year of 1850, it was estimated that almost half the mineworkers had left, some for the Wyoming or Wiconisco valleys, others for Maryland or even California. A generation later, one could observe in the Lackawanna Valley the same hard-times derangement:

> The slack time at the mines is causing quite an exodus of people. . . . A feeling of unrest pervades the minds of many, and the shorter the time at the mines the stronger the fever for travel. Before resumption takes place a fair percentage of those now here will emigrate wherever the best inducement is offered.

The great strikes or suspensions of the late 1860's and early 1870's, and again in the late 1880's and in 1900 and 1902, had the same effect; if some strikers went only to the next county, perhaps more sought out the bituminous regions of the Midwest and Far West, or returned to the Old Country. Even a small local strike could nearly depopulate villages such as Glen Lyon and Wanamie in 1899, when hundreds of miners cleared out for the West and other distant places. This was crippling for communities no less than for employers, who sometimes lamented that "the best men have of course gone" while the poorest and least reliable sullenly hung on.

Strikes and depressions merely intensified a continual movement in and out of the region. Skilled men left to try their luck in western, southern, or South American mines or ironworks, perhaps as foremen, superintendents, or even owners; hundreds of Welsh Mormon converts from the Lackawanna Valley went to Utah in the 1870's and 1880's; ordinary men took several years' savings back to Europe or out to a western farm, some of them returning after a time; and fresh immigrants arrived, even during hard times, to join friends in the region. On occasion, such as when mine operators looking for labor at the end of a suspension found the skeptical miners continuing to depart, the tides of migration caused concern. But ordinarily the unsettled state of society in the region—in a clergyman's words, "restless, migratory, and sometimes violent"—was too familiar to be remarkable. Indeed, even within the towns of the region, since housing leases customarily expired on April 1, a yearly "flitting" of "about every tenth family in town"—so it was estimated in Scranton in 1884—occurred on that day. One could never be quite sure in that hill country whether wagons or sleighs would be needed for the move. For conservative German immigrants it was "the dreadful ordeal of 'moving day'"; if some Americans and Irishmen were "never so happy as when they are . . . preparing to move" to a better house, others saw only a barbaric restlessness fatal to "the spirit of contentment of the poorer people." But, for the most part, no more attention was paid to the incessant coming and going, except that of the "detestable" Gypsies or "menacing" tramps, than to the occasional vertical movement of somebody's house down into an old, caved-in mine.

It was also taken for granted that most of the people in almost every locality were immigrants. Welsh and English miners, Irish laborers, and Germans of various occupations entered the region at the start of mining in the 1820's, and continued to come, along with Italians, Poles, Slovaks, and other Eastern Europeans—colloquially "Hungarians"—after 1870. The coexistence of several ethnic groups in even the smallest mine patches seemed less noteworthy than the occasional altercations among them. Competition between unskilled Irish laborers and skilled Welsh or English miners for work, German and Irish militiamen brawling at a muster, barroom fights between Welshmen and Germans or Irishmen and Italians, one-day "race wars" between Magyars and Slovaks, gangs of Irish or Welsh boys beating a hapless "Hungarian" or hooting at a Chinese laundryman, Slavic peasants-turned-laborers stoning a Jewish peddler, the dynamiting of a "Hungarian" boarding house, German or Italian "carousing" on the Yankee Sabbath, American constables arresting the riotous celebrants of a Polish wedding or christening—only on such occasions, which were frequent enough, and of course on the exposure of Molly Maguire or Mafia conspiracies, did relations between ethnic groups seem to pose a problem for society.

Intergroup conflict was nevertheless rarer than newspaper accounts suggested. In fact, native Americans sometimes congratulated themselves that most of the turbulence of this poorly policed region occurred *within* particular ethnic groups, and that the foreigners were "respectful and often polite" toward "their superiors." The Molly Maguire episode of 1859–1875, in which Irish laborers were convicted of murdering British and American miners and superintendents, was quite exceptional. In the early years it was more usual for Irish navvies—"the Far-downs and the Connaught men"—to riot on payday among themselves, or, after 1895, for the Black Hand to be reported extorting money from its Italian countrymen. Americans or Welshmen or Germans of course reprobated such behavior, but they were slow to take responsibility for it—after all, as a mine operator said in 1867, "Every man . . . must take care of himself"—unless the safety of "the better class of citizens" was threatened, business was disrupted, or law enforcement became a burden to the taxpayers. It was enough to prosecute or perhaps mob a few foreigners—the usual "hue and cry to hang some one"—in order to teach American decorum to the others. But all too often immigrants who were harassed by reckless or predatory countrymen had no one to turn to for protection but their own ethnic spokesmen or arbitrators, perhaps some figure known to Americans only as a rather sinister "King of the Huns" who might be hardly better than an extortionist himself.

Members of ethnic outgroups were all too apt to be "beyond the reach of law and lawlessness alike."

If intergroup conflict was not the rule, neither was the melting pot. The usual social relationship between ethnic groups in the region could better be described as a state of mutual ignorance and indifference, shading off to ignorance and contempt. A harmless cultural trait like the Welsh immigrants' circuitous manner of speaking, for example, was misunderstood by blunter Americans. To one of their employers, Welshmen seemed "apt to be a little tricky, & to lie a little more or less gently, as it suited their purposes." They were accused in the 1870's of "bearing malice, and of being clannish, or of 'keeping together.' 'I think,' [said] a Scotsman, 'that that is why they keep up the Welsh language.'" A generation later, when they all spoke English and had American manners, a friendly observer still saw little prospect of their merging with American society. For their part, the evangelical Welsh never lost their old-country scorn of the Catholic Irish, "the most barbarous people on the continent." Similarly, the "real Germans" considered the native Pennsylvania Dutch, whom they could admire for still speaking German, to be, perhaps by the same token, lamentably unprogressive and illiberal. In their turn, after 1900, Polish-American children derided the Orthodox Russians, "the so-called Huns," however timid and inoffensive, as people who "do not worship God." Such misapprehensions went as deep as the everyday humor of the region, in tales like that of the Scotch-man indignant at a "Dutchman" he had been set to work with: "I tell't tae gang awa' wi' the barrow an' spill thae stanes, an' the creature just glowered at me."

Men of different groups did work together: the Welsh miner with an Irish "butty" or laborer or, later, the Irish miner with a Slavic laborer (whom he perhaps called Mike O'Brimsky, Matthew Morecabbage, or simply "No. 1198") were familiar types. Even in the mines, however, the earlier or more skilled nationalities were generally separated in occupational status from those who came later or lacked useful skills, and they sought to perpetuate their advantage. As a mining official observed, the Welsh "are clannish and the best places at their disposal are given to their friends." In time, the older groups tended to leave the mines altogether. Many American-born children of immigrant miners went into more promising occupations —learning another trade, seeking "a broader field of operations in the West, or else crowding into the professions or engaging in mercantile pursuits"—and thereby lost acquaintance with the later arrivals among the mineworkers. Furthermore, a minority of the Germans, almost no Italians, and hardly a single Jew ever worked underground in the mines at all; in their other occupations they lived in different social compartments from the British, Irish, and Slavic mineworkers. The usual pattern of settlement within towns and cities—the Welsh and Irish of Hyde Park in Scranton and the Germans of the South Side, the neighborhoods called Scotch Hill, Welshtown, Shanty Hill or Cork Lane or Paddy's Land, Nigger Hill, Dutch Hollow, *Hessestadel*, Little Italy, Hungarian Hill, Polander Street—embodied this vertical division of local society into ethnic fragments. The population might shift, Italians filling up the Scranton Little England, and Shenandoah changing from heavily Welsh in the 1860's to "that great Polish city" only twenty years later, but the peoples did not mix.

The immigrants maintained a great array of societies—Hibernians, Sons of St. George, True Ivorites, Caledonians, Harugari, Liederkranz, Grütli Verein, Mazzini or Vittorio Emanuele societies, Polish Alliance, Slovak Union, and so forth—carrying on the customs peculiar to their respective homelands, or rather to similar communities of their fellow countrymen elsewhere in America. One might commend them for, as a German said in the 1850's, "breaking up the uniformity of American life," but they also compartmentalized American society even on the Fourth of July, when everyone paraded, from the Father Mathew Temperance and Benevolent Society and the Turnverein to, at a suitable interval, the Patriotic Order of Sons of America and the American Protestant Association. If St. Patrick's Day was a favorite time for a Welsh eisteddfod, it was only because the Irish holiday forced the mines to stand idle each year. Both the Welsh and the Germans went in for singing societies, but until the 1890's Germans hardly ever attended an eisteddfod—what would they have made of the long-winded adjudications of Welsh poetry in the strict meters?— nor did Welshmen take part in what some of them considered the "Bacchanalian feast" of a Sängerfest, except when a William Watkins called himself Conrad Lutz for the day. Even this *sotto-voce* harmony began only two or three generations after the German and Welsh communities of the region were established, by which time, presumably, many of the choristers were American-born.

The lack of social intermixture can be measured in the county marriage records beginning in 1886. Of the Welshmen who got married in Lackawanna County in 1886, about 80 percent married women born in Wales or of Welsh parentage; among the Irish the proportion marrying with their own ethnic group was at least 94 and probably nearer 100 percent; among the Germans about 92 percent; and even among English immigrants at least 40 percent and perhaps considerably more. Twenty-five years later, in 1910, there were no longer many persons born in these countries getting married in Lackawanna County, but immigrants from Austria, Hungary, Poland, Italy, and Russia were marrying almost without exception within their respective groups. These distinctions carried over almost intact into the next generation. Schoolteachers and employers alike tended to classify the American-born by their parents' nationalities.

Virtually no effort was made to bridge the ethnic chasms in society. The most notable exception was a certain cordiality shown the small German-Jewish communities, in such forms as frequent newspaper articles explaining Jewish holidays and customs to Americans; often enough written by the local rabbi, to be sure, they became something of a tradition in their own right. Anti-Semitism troubled the region hardly at all, except perhaps in the 1870's and 1880's when Polish Jews began peddling there.

Until well after 1900, however, newspaper editors were oblivious of any need to promote assimilation of immigrants, and even then their comments seem inspired more by the stock editorials in their metropolitan exchanges than by the situation around them. Certainly no practical means were suggested. Not until about 1905 did the public school boards or teachers assume that Americanizing children of diverse cultures was part of their task. In the 1890's, several free private kindergartens set about teaching foreign children "English and cleanliness" and "a clearer citizenship and identification with our American people." Visitors were gratified to see the pupils, for all their "intense marks of race peculiarities," becoming as "handsome and sweet" as American children. But not until school attendance was made compulsory in Pennsylvania, some years after the first law on the subject in 1895, did children of many of the ethnic groups even attend school, either public or parochial, after they came of working age—say nine or ten years old. Although between the late 1870's and early 1900's some public-school boards conducted elementary night schools for working children, the coal-breaker and mine boys were often so boisterous and inattentive that the authorities thought the schools "dismal failures." During prolonged depressions or strikes, the regular day schools were thronged by idle slatepickers and youthful muledrivers, who disrupted the recitations perhaps oftener than they learned anything themselves.

Consequently, the schools, which the few educated foreigners found inferior in any case, lacked even the merit of social egalitarianism. In the city of Scranton hardly one per cent of the number of children who started public school in 1880 managed to graduate twelve years later; most of the few high school graduates there and elsewhere were girls. In the elementary schools, children of foreign parents might heavily outnumber those of American parentage, but the proportions were reversed among the minority who proceeded to the grammar and high schools. The Catholic parochial schools and several private academies—the latter mostly for boys—by no means closed the educational and social gap between the children of the local "aristocracy" and those the latter were said to scorn as "the dirty Irish and Welsh." At a time when as many as a quarter to a half of the immigrant workingmen could not so much as sign their names to a payroll—even among the English and Welsh, though the Germans and Scots did better—the schools had hardly begun to improve their children's chance for integration into American society.

Nor were the churches very useful in this social mission. In the anthracite region as elsewhere in America, the principal *social* function of a church was the exact opposite of integration; it provided as stable an institutional nucleus as possible for a discrete ethnic community. Even this was difficult enough in view of what a Welshman called "the unsettledness of the members, the great amount of movement, and failure of business enterprises." Exceptions to the general lack of social communion between ethnic groups, like exceptions to other rules, attracted undue notice at the time. County Bible societies, for instance, reported at length the travails of distributing the King James version among poor but ungrateful Catholic immigrants, and in the 1890's Presbyterian home missionaries converted a few score Italians and Chinese and sought out Protestant Hungarians. But the main tendency was anything but ecumenical. Even within the Catholic church separate parishes were established for each nationality as soon as possible after the start of its immigration, and yet riots and lawsuits over parish property set Poles against Lithuanians, Galicians against Slovaks, and Uniate Greek against Roman Catholics, culminating in the secession, which started at Scranton in 1897, of the independent Polish National Church.

Since none of the local or regional anthracite-miners' unions of the nineteenth century managed to survive more than a few years, they too failed to harmonize ethnic differences as they would have had to do in order to introduce collective bargaining, and thereby help stabilize the economy and society of the region. Although the Workingmen's (or Miners' and Laborers') Benevolent Association of 1869–1875 transcended ethnic mistrust—and the economic rivalry of the several "regions"—with mounting success, the men had to be appealed to as members of English, Welsh, Irish, and German blocs no less than as fellow workers at particular mines. Ultimately, the union's strike of 1875 collapsed amid bitter recriminations by the "hungry, foolish dupes" of each nationality against the others. Even after 1900, when the United Mine Workers of America brought "old" and "new" immigrants together, once again each local was a carefully arranged alliance of distrustful ethnic groups.

The alliance of certain groups within one or the other political party was also more a source of friction than of amalgamation. The Democratic party maintained a running squabble between its Irish and German factions for what each considered its due share of city and county nominations, on the principle that "if Germans refuse to support Irishmen, of course Irishmen will refuse to support Germans, and . . . neither will be elected." The Republicans balanced the claims of a solid Welsh bloc against an uncertain German contingent after the Civil War. As early as 1874, Poles dominated a ticket in Mahanoy City, and by the 1890's the older party leaders everywhere had to admit Italians, Lithuanians, and other new-immigrant politicians, "garlic councilmen" though the latter might be. This sort of politics and local government had even less relevance to solving the economic and social problems of the region than to harmonizing ethnic factions. In 1874, Welsh mineworkers might desert a Republican candidate who happened to have commanded the militia during their strike three years before, and in 1878 Terence V. Powderly of the Knights of Labor was elected mayor of Scranton on the Greenback-Labor ticket in a general working-class reaction—Irish, Welsh, and Germans together—against the armed suppression of the railroad and mine strike of 1877. Powderly, however, proposed no more thoroughgoing local reform than appointment of "friends of labor" to the police force; his re-election in 1882 represented merely an opportunity for one of the Democratic factions, recently under the cloud of embezzlement convictions, to return to city hall. The politics of the region seldom came closer to a stand upon important principles than when local "taxpayers' associations" sought to "secure the county from the burden of taxation" for schools, bridges, poor relief, pay raises for firemen, and other projects whereby politicians might be plotting to defraud the public.

Distinctions between social classes were much less precise than those between ethnic groups. To a great degree, of course, social classes *were* ethnic groups. Most obviously, the working class in or about the mines and other industries was composed of certain immigrant nationalities and their children. Among them there were individuals who got rich as contractors, or as wholesale liquor dealers, or as bankers handling foreign remittances, businesses in which they enjoyed the advantage of dealing with laborers or customers of their own group. But even such persons did not thereby gain entry into the upper social class of Scranton, Wilkes-Barre, or Pottsville. Andrew Casey, Frank Carlucci, and Michael Bosak might be recognized as leaders of the Irish, Italian, and Slovak communities of Scranton, but their credentials were evidently not valid across ethnic lines. Foreign origins were somewhat less of a social barrier for immigrant Welsh mine operators and German brewers and lawyers, and no bar at all to the rise of notable English, Scottish, Canadian, and even Irish immigrants like John Jermyn, Thomas Dickson, William Connell, and John Handley from working-class beginnings to millionaires' fortunes and social status in the American community of Scranton. Such individuals apart, the upper class was virtually limited to native Americans.

This class shared, as far as it was able, the manners and customs fashionable elsewhere at the time. As early as 1851, the "wit, beauty and grace" of Pottsville were arrayed at cotillions; in 1869, the Pittston Social Union, made up of "the *elite* of East and West Pittston," achieved a "thoroughly select and brilliant" Dress Soiree; the gifts displayed at a Scranton society wedding in 1870 were said to be worth $12,000; and there were resolutely exclusive men's clubs as early as the 1870's in Wilkes-Barre, Scranton, Pottsville, Pittston, and Carbondale, and plebeian imitators even in overgrown mining patches like Mahanoy City. By the mid-1880's these towns had their regular annual seasons of balls, masquerades, concerts (well attended for their "social tone"), art lectures and exhibits, "brilliant private parties" for boys and girls home from college or finishing school, and numerous "at homes" in the mansions along the River Common in Wilkes-Barre, on "Quality Hill" in Scranton, or on Mahantango Street in Pottsville.

Although to those involved, and no doubt to the envious or uncomprehending masses, all this activity signified great éclat, the resident upper class of the region was, even by American standards, severely middle class. It numbered some of the independent mine operators, foundry, shop, and store owners, the resident corporation superintendents, canny retired farmers and land speculators drawing tonnage royalties from the lease of their "coal estates," local bankers, real-estate developers, leading lawyers and doctors, and the like. There were indeed millionaires among them by the late nineteenth century. But, in a sense, the uppermost social class of the anthracite region did not live there, infrequently visited it, and played no part in its high society. They were the capitalists, chiefly New York and Philadelphia men, who controlled the dominant railroad and mining corporations of the region. None of the highest officials of the Delaware, Lackawanna & Western, the Erie, the Central of New Jersey, the Lehigh Valley, the Reading, or (except in 1869–1884 when Thomas Dickson was president) the Delaware & Hudson graced local society. The family of William R. Storrs, the general coal agent of the Lackawanna, might be seen at the annual New Years' balls of the Scranton Bachelors' Club, but not the line's president, Samuel Sloan, nor such directors and major stockholders as the New York merchants, bankers, and entrepreneurs Moses Taylor, Percy R. Pyne, William E. Dodge, and John I. Blair, for whom mine shafts were named but who had greater economic interests and social concerns far from the coal region.

This headless society misled itself on that score as it may still mislead readers of novels set in the region. In Scranton from the era of the miners' strikes of 1871 and 1877 down to 1916, no name was more portentous of economic and social eminence than that of William W. Scranton, son and nephew of the founders of the Lackawanna Iron and Coal Company for whom the city itself had been named. He was the incarnation of the gentleman vigilant for social order—or, from the opposite point of view, of the "local tycoon"—when he led the citizens' posse which fired on a mob—or a strikers' march—in 1877. His mansion, when his father Joseph H. Scranton built it in 1869, was called "the most remarkable structure in this part of Pennsylvania. . . . It overlooks the vast iron works of the town, and will serve for centuries to illustrate to future generations the make and style of the men whose successes under difficulties have been the greatest and most striking of the age. . . ." So it continued to do, but rather deceptively. Joseph Scranton, though president of the company, had been subordinate, since the panic of 1857, to the New York City Bank group which also controlled the Lackawanna Railroad. After his death in 1872, his son did not succeed him, as he supposed his experience in the mills had prepared him to do, but perforce accepted the superintendency under a president in New York who was not a technological expert. William Scranton's faded letterbooks still glow with his pride in steelmaking, but, although he resigned and started his own Scranton Steel Company in 1881, within ten years the older company bought this out; he had no choice thereafter but to confine himself to managing the local waterworks, begun as only a subsidiary family interest. In fact, neither "Scranton of Scranton" nor anyone else in the "Barony of Scranton" was able to keep the merged Lackawanna Iron and Steel Company itself from moving away to Buffalo in 1901, though it seemed "the end of the world for this community."

Exceptions to the rule of outside control, as to other rules, have been more memorable. There were self-made coal magnates who were fairly free of railroad control even in the Wyoming and Lackawanna valleys, men such as Charles Parrish of Wilkes-Barre, John Jermyn of Jermyn, and Orlando Johnson of Priceburg. In the Schuylkill region, many smaller operators maintained a proud though usually poor independence until the Philadelphia & Reading Coal and Iron Company assumed control in the 1870's. The Lehigh operators kept their sovereignty longest, most notably Ario Pardee of Hazleton and Eckley B. Coxe of Drifton. Coxe, profiting from the land speculation of his grandfather Tench Coxe, was the one-man upper class of the isolated and, by his edict, saloonless village of Drifton, where he lived as an industrial feudatory, and leading Democrat, with his wife, as lady of the manor, visiting the sick and poor among their working people, who, it was said, "fairly worshipped" them. But in more typical mining villages, like nearby Eckley—in 1863 "a vast collection of shanties"—or in such larger towns as Shenandoah, inhabited almost wholly by men working for absentee corporations, the "uppermost social strata," so a visitor noted, "are yet to be formed." Even in the more urbane Pottsville, the tendency in the 1870's, as the Reading moved into mining, was to lose what upper class there had been; many of "the most wealthy inhabitants have removed," an editor observed, "and few new ones have come to take their place."

Neither absent capitalists nor the resident élite displayed much noblesse toward other classes in the community. This is not to rehearse the well-worn story of ruthless exploitation of labor in the anthracite region, which is overdrawn in most particulars, although not in all—the story of child labor, especially of the mine and breaker boys from the 1850's until after 1900, still horrifies the reader of old newspapers. But the ruthlessness of indifference and economic expediency was more to blame than the "rapacious greed" with which employers were sometimes charged. By the 1850's, the market required that any slate in the mined coal be removed at the breaker after the coal was crushed. Until late in the century, there was no practicable way to pick slate except by hand. Around any coal breaker, plenty of boys between five and twelve years of age could be hired for this task. Now and again, a local editor might deplore the plight of small children perched for ten hours a day astride the moving coal "ways," scrabbling for sharp bits of slate, beclouded with coal dust, and stumping home after dark "like little old men," but their fathers' unsteady wages of $1.50 or $2 a day—or was it their "bestial" thriftlessness and cupidity?—made the boys' daily earning of thirty-five or forty-five cents necessary to their families. And then many breaker boys were "sons of fathers who were killed in the mines, and their scanty earnings are frequently the support of a widowed mother or of brothers and sisters younger than themselves, so that their employment has more of kindness than of cruelty in it." If a breaker boy fell into the rolls or a "nipper" was run down by a trip of loaded cars in the mine and was crushed to a gruesome death, it could usually be shown that he had been "out of his place in disobedience of positive orders, and that the injury was the result of the boy's recklessness."

Who was to concern himself with such obscure cases of misfortune and how? "During the past week," it was reported at Wilkes-Barre in 1876, "nearly one boy a day has been killed, and the public has become so familiar with these calamities, that no attention is given them after the first announcement through a newspaper or neighbor." When the delegates to a Sunday School convention at Scranton in 1874 visited a mine, they watched "with much interest" the "barefooted, black-faced urchins . . . picking slate from the dusky diamonds," and then went down into the mine to hear a lecture on "the wonders of the Great Creator," namely fossils of extinct plants and animals which the discerning might find in a lump of coal. At any rate, most of the working boys were only foreigners' children. Effective reform finally came after 1903, when Pennsylvania prohibited breaker work by boys under fourteen and mine work under sixteen; within a few years, slate picking was perforce mechanized.

Other abuses likewise crept in somewhat inadvertently. Company stores and houses were relatively few except in the early years, when both miners and operators lacked credit or cash, and in isolated places where mine labor would not go unless houses and stores were provided. The large corporations generally avoided them as a nuisance, necessary to attract poor new immigrants and in such case perhaps useful to the company as well: "Living in Co Houses we control the labor," a Lackawanna official suggested in 1882. But he also believed that home ownership made their older hands "the best workers and best citizens, and . . . the last to go into strikes" more surely than would the threat of eviction from a company house or debt to a company store. Although the Reading Company in the 1880's rented some 3,000 houses, it also provided miners' trains at low fares so that its men and boys working at remote shafts could live, as many of them preferred, in larger communities like St. Clair or Minersville. "It makes better people," an official said, "to live with the schools and churches." It was the independent operators, such as Pardee, Coxe, and G. B. Markle in the Lehigh region, who customarily rented houses to their men and kept company stores —with their habitual "confusion and rattletebang, and above all, the dirt"—and often enough took advantage of their monopoly. "I am fully aware of the importance & justice of getting the hands to spend their money at the stores of those who employ them," a mining superintendent assured one operator in the early years. "The *cash* system was proved here long enough . . . to show that the Employer had no advantage from it." But at corporation mines such abuses seem to have been the doing of foremen who had a storekeeper in the family, a situation which from time to time the corporations tried to stamp out in their own interest as well as that of the men. Over the years, the cry for abolition of company stores came oftener perhaps from small private shopkeepers than from the workingmen.

In general, the labor policy of the major mining companies was the product of a genuine spirit of autocratic benevolence—a desire on the part of the owner to protect his own view of the common interest in which he felt his employees should share— rather than the product of an embattled tyranny. Given the fierce competition among the mine owners themselves, they assumed that they had no choice but to resist collective bargaining (except with the W.B.A. in 1869–1873), keep control over wages, and even employ small boys in the mines and breakers. But their letters show them also quite conscious of a need to foster the morale of their employees by at least listening graciously to their grievances and sometimes even granting "their requests—*not demands*"—as long as it could be done without compromising company authority. They also recognized that a low wage rate and "short time" would drive away their best men. In fact, the large corporations, though directed from New York or Philadelphia, were probably freer from petty strikes than the less efficient independent operators, who were more apt to try to balance their books by squeezing wages from time to time. It was indeed fortunate for the region that control by a few outside corporations led to the further step of their combining in 1873 to check competition and thereby maintain some minimum level of coal prices and wages. After 1898, the dominance of J. Pierpont Morgan over the combination both strengthened it and in 1902 induced its members to accept collective bargaining with the United Mine Workers, to the reasonable satisfaction of both capital and labor thereafter. Trust control was, notwithstanding local individuals who had been grumbling about it since the 1830's, the first practical step toward solving the basic economic problems of the region and, as a byproduct, stabilizing its society.

The communities of the region failed miserably to cope with matters left to their own resources and initiative. The hazards of the mines cast up an annual burden of hundreds of crippled men or destitute widows and orphans, and frequent depressions in the coal trade made massive unemployment almost as troublesome. Neither the private charity of the fortunate classes of each locality nor the public relief disbursed by the local poor boards, nor yet the rudimentary welfare arrangements of mine operators and other employers, could cope with poverty on this scale.

Public relief consisted basically of herding chronic paupers, including children and the insane, more or less promiscuously together at the county or city poor farms, some of which, in spite of sporadic reform, were so filthy and verminous as to be officially condemned as a "scandal" and "a disgrace to the state," where "the most cheerful sight . . . was a store room full of coffins." Casual outdoor relief, though restricted by state law, was also doled out at the monthly open meetings of the poor boards, but in such tiny amounts—two, three, four, or five dollars a month to an aged couple or a widow with several children—as to be hardly worth the trouble and shame of applying for it. Of twenty-one applicants at one poor-board meeting in the desperate depression winter of 1877–1878, eleven were rejected, though unemployed and destitute, for being abled-bodied or having relatives somewhere who, if found, might conceivably support them, or for refusing to go to the poor farm. Some suppliants were clearly more worthy, like Bridget Ruane of Scranton, widowed by a mine accident and left with seven children, the oldest a one-legged boy of fourteen, surely "one of the most deserving cases that had been reported"; she was allowed four dollars a month. Few miners or other skilled workingmen with the least hope of ever finding a job would "beg for such a paltry piece of charity."

Private charity was hardly more munificent. "Where are the charitable ladies," a Wilkes-Barre paper asked in 1861, who should take charge of the "squallid, ill-clad children" seen begging on almost every corner? In 1874 a "soup house" operated by the ladies did offer "a nutritious meal to the poor, free from all temptations of alcoholic drinks," namely "a plate of soup or cup of coffee and a roll of bread for the very moderate sum of TEN CENTS." Dorcas Societies repaired old clothing for the poor, carriages distributed provisions for "a bountiful Christmas dinner" to penniless families "known to be deserving," and in the 1870's Congressman Hendrick B. Wright gave away "nice fresh bread . . . piled up like ranks of cordwood" to all comers each Christmas. In the pit of depression the ordinary unemployed might be helped by some combination of private and public relief funds raised for the occasion. The first of these, at Pottsville in 1842–1843, distributed $156.53 among 130 families; twenty-five years later the Benevolent Association of Pottsville spent $632.55 to relieve sixty-seven families. In the winter of 1855, Scranton philanthropists dispensed

$702.55 to the "suffering poor," and managed to balance the account by recovering $124.86 from them later in the year. In 1877, after delegations of the unemployed virtually threatened the Scranton city council with looting if they were not given "Work or Bread," a more elaborate scheme of city work relief, supported by private subscription, was hastily improvised by ninety-three "leading men."

Usually the charitable were so fearful of "impositions" by the undeserving, who might "beg for a cake of soap, and . . . pawn it for a glass of whiskey," that they gave as little as possible—seven cents an hour for work relief at Wilkes-Barre in 1877 and only *one* dole of flour, beans, and pork per family at Scranton—and returned as soon as they could to the poorhouse system. Poor boards sometimes spent a lump sum to send a needy immigrant family back to the Old Country, though some tax-payers grumbled that nobody lavished free cruises on *them*. Private citizens made it their business to ferret out "all who are unworthy of support," such as one Mary Lawlor of Shenandoah, "an able-bodied woman" who during three months of 1882 had been given a total of $16.25 in relief—"an expensive luxury," as a taxpayer put it. At Scranton in the 1890's, a private Board of Associated Charities took over aspects of relief with which the public authorities could not cope under Pennsylvania law, but this Board, too, emphasized the unmasking of "monstrous impositions" by persons "not entitled to relief" almost as much as actual aid to the deserving. What was even more important than niggardly charity in the cities was the fact that few of the small towns and villages where most of the working class lived had any organized private charity at all. The only certain "poor man's friend" in the region was the culm heap, "picturesque" when swarming with men, women, and children gleaning bits of refuse coal.

"Why do bands always play '[Down in a] Coal Mine' returning from a funeral?" an editor mused in 1872. Death in the mines was an everyday matter. For the scores of families suddenly bereft of husbands and fathers by a major mine disaster, beginning with that at Avondale in 1869, special funds were raised from both within and without the region. In its six years of operation, the Avondale Relief Association distributed $170,000 among 73 widows, 156 children, and a few others. To these funds some of the corporations judiciously contributed "for the sake of the moral effect upon the men." (The companies likewise gave land and occasional small sums to orphanages, populated largely by children of mine casualties, and to workingmen's churches, hoping thereby to effect "a good feeling between Employers and Employed . . . so that as well as being humane, it will pay.") But most mine accidents happened one at a time; the odd victim could expect nothing as of right from his employer, who in practice paid, if anything, only the one hundred dollars or so that would avoid a law suit, local juries being certain to decide against a corporation. "So far I do not recollect," the Reading Coal and Iron Company's general manager wrote in 1886, "a single case in which we have finally been compelled to pay damages." During the quarter century after Avondale, however, the Reading and several other large corporations set up their own modest benefit funds for accident victims, to which both they and their employees regularly contributed. The annual cost of the fund to the Reading was "undoubtedly less," it estimated, "than the costs of suits and payments for damages . . . if no such provision had been made." Injured men might also be given a pass over their employer's railroad to go to a city hospital, and in 1882 Moses Taylor of the Lackawanna Railroad made the bequest (unfortunately unique in the region) of a hospital, opened ten years later, for injured miners of his company. But the benefactions of corporation directors were more likely to go elsewhere, notably to colleges like Lafayette, Lehigh, and Princeton.

Domination of the principal industries of the region by New York and Philadelphia corporations, however, ground the faces of the poor no more harshly than exclusive control by the sort of local magnate who was content not to "pose as a philanthropist" would have done. Beginning in the 1870's, a few small hospitals were organized by local doctors with rather meager private funds and intermittent state aid to care for injured miners and others. The only other charitable institutions were a few private and Catholic orphanages—an early one established at Scranton in 1871 was expressively named "The Home for the Friendless"—refuges for "misguided women" and their infants, evangelical "rescue missions" for drunkards and derelicts, the YM and YWCA and the Salvation Army, Eckley B. Coxe's Drifton School of Industry (1879), and Boys' Industrial Associations at Scranton and Wilkes-Barre in the 1890's for the self-improvement of poor working boys. But local men of property, organized in taxpayers' associations, systematically opposed public support of such projects. Although corporation officials were among the leaders of the associations, they seem not to have wrung every possible advantage from their economic overlordship of the region. The corporations periodically discouraged their employees, especially their foremen, from serving on borough and city councils and school boards, as in 1899 the Lackawanna found some forty employees of its mining department were doing; they feared loss of working time would cost the company more than any tax relief it might gain through this channel of political influence.

In the anthracite region as elsewhere, the poor were usually left to their own devices. The benefit concert for a crippled miner was a familiar institution among the Welsh. In the 1880's and 1890's, miners organized their own mutual-relief associations, or "keg funds" (originally supported from the ten cents refunded the miner for his empty powder kegs). The same secret fraternal lodges as elsewhere, from the Odd Fellows to the peculiarly ethnic orders, provided their members with a little insurance. And of course in each ethnic community the church mustered what charity it could through benefit bazaars, fairs, *Kirchen-Picnics,* and other money-raising ventures characteristic of most American churches. But toward the end of the nineteenth century the pitiful inadequacy of self-help only grew more evident among the thousands of single men from Eastern Europe who worked in the region. Intent upon saving every possible penny, huddled into filthy boarding houses, and eating the cheapest food even at the risk of scurvy, the "Hungarians" got a reputation for heartless inhumanity for refusing to take responsibility for a sick countryman or one killed in the mines. "Dead man no good" was the only reputedly Slavic folksaying known to American newspaper readers of the 1890's.

That the integrity of the family decayed any faster in the anthracite region than elsewhere in America can hardly be asserted. During the early years of any ethnic group in the region, when most of the immigrants were men, many a family's ties had to stretch across the ocean for a time, not infrequently ending in bigamy or a husband who had vanished when wife and children arrived. Looking after a houseful of male boarders strained the patience and sometimes the fidelity of some immigrant wives. Here the wife of a crippled Welsh miner was tempted to elope with a sounder bread-winner; there a Polish girl, after rebuffing thirty-six proposals, married a countryman with six hundred dollars which it turned out he had borrowed. The Slavic immigrants of the 1880's and 1890's were notorious for odd cases of wife-selling and near-polyandry, which got into the courts and the newspapers. But once the customary family life which all groups had known in the old country became possible, even for "the Poles and Huns," the family, like the church which supported it, was as conservative as any social institution could be in the circumstances. Immigrant husbands might discover that "in this country a man is not a woman's boss; she can do as she chooses"; still their families were large—as late as 1900, about nine children was the average in one district, even among English, Welsh, and Irish immigrants of long residence—and the divorce rate was below the national average. Desertion was "appallingly frequent" by the 1890's, so the poor boards complained, though they were quick to suspect collusion between "wife deserters and fake relief applicants."

The children of immigrants and native Americans alike provoked wider concern. For youths of 16 to 20 to be hanging about the street-corners nightly until 10 o'clock was *"rowdyismus von nichtsnutzigen jungen Bengeln,"* to German eyes in the 1860's. In Pittston, the gangs of juveniles aged eight to sixteen were known as the " 'Irish boys,' or boys of Irish parents," who *"often-times beat peaceable boys,"* made rude remarks to ladies, and stole from farmers' wagons. In Scranton, where even schoolboys carried revolvers, they disturbed the peace with "yelling and hooting—throwing stones —firing pistols—insulting residents of [the] neighborhood—beating children—challenging the boys of the German school to come out and fight." "Little girls with long dresses" were also on the streets after dark, "assuming all the airs of finished flirts" and presumably going from bad to worse at "ten cent hops." By the 1890's, it seemed ever more certain that "the tendency is toward hoodlumism" among the "boys and girls who nightly promenade the streets." Some children, it was said, were started on their downward path by over-indulgent parents whose solicitude led them arrogantly to assume their own superiority; others no older than infants roamed the streets, neglected while "mamma is at the festival and papa is at the saloon"; some parents of "wayward roughs" even egged them on in their neighborhood "factional fights" waged with stones and clubs. "The coming generation," whether because of lax discipline or "the modern boy literature," promised to be no better than "a community of robbers."

No doubt, the cry "what has become of parental authority?" was not peculiar to the anthracite region nor to the generation of the late nineteenth century. But unruly youths were an obvious case of the general social disorder toward which the economically successful were more complacent. If a local industrialist in the 1860's blamed "the great difficulty to secure just the right man for an important trust" upon a mysterious mania among modern young men for "fast horses, fine wines, good Liquors, Choice segars," at least occasionally a preacher or editor—perhaps an immigrant from a more conservative tradition—saw the industrial America of the nineteenth century as in "an anomalous condition of society," where employers and public officials took no more responsibility for the lives of workmen than for so many horses or mules. But even clergymen and editors seldom paused to formulate theoretical justifications for the prevailing economic individualism, like those which occupied a few intellectuals elsewhere. Abstract encomiums for selfishness as the source of "all the improvements of the present age"—or, for that matter, criticism of individualism as subversive of brotherhood—can be turned up by the diligent historian, but the divine-right theory of property imputed to President George F. Baer of the Reading in 1902 was seldom put any more coherently than in an 1894 commencement orator's text: "faith, hope, charity . . . and the greatest of these is business." A few in these valleys lamented that "progress has swallowed an independent agricultural people," whose only vestige was a weak local government, perhaps suited to farmers but incompetent now even to police "the drunken men who monopolize the public highway" on payday. It was in this context of near-anarchy that vigilantes, sheriff's posses, the corporations' "coal and iron police," the militia, or even the army were so often called upon to impose a desperate, eleventh-hour order, as at Lattimer in the Lehigh region in 1897 when sixty-five deputies shot down fifty-five of a crowd of unarmed strikers; one could easily blame the trouble on "aliens who are out of sympathy with our laws," and ignore the impotence of law itself.

The dominant note was, of course, optimistic in spite of present disorders: "Our people are not acclimated yet in the new order of things, and the old habits and moralities fail to fit the new situations." "The wonder is that . . . it is not ten times rougher, ten fold more crude in all the amenities of life. . . . These come in their own good time." Fortunately for the job of getting coal to market, even the classes hardest pressed usually endured submissively. "What a spectacle is offered," an editor remarked in the dark year of 1878, "by the quietness and perfect good order of people, thrown out of work and all but starving, . . . patiently waiting during the past summer. . . . The chief influences of American life are wholesome and vital, and tend to national prosperity." Faith in individual success, too, was always possible when an occasional breaker boy managed to rise to the dignity of schoolteacher, priest, mechanical engineer, mine superintendent or operator, Congressman, or even, in the case of Joseph Jermyn, millionaire's heir, so fast were some fortunes made. That a boy's ambition for a skilled miner's "plenty of work and good wages" was more likely to bring him back at last, old, asthmatic, and perhaps half-crippled, to end his days slate-picking in the breaker once more, was simply one of the vicissitudes of life.

The mobility of a liberal economy was never lacking in the anthracite region—immigration and emigration, settlement and unsettling of communities, the climb to better jobs, property, and social standing for many individuals. Headlong industrialization, damped by depression and then rekindled again, kept the people on the move for a century. But such mobility was hardly conducive to an organic social structure. The instability of the local community, the cultural discontinuities between ethnic groups, the failure of social classes to accept reciprocal responsibilities—in such ways unbridled economic progress undermined social order. Some of the parts of a social structure were present, but not the structure itself. No institution or group dominated society: neither an arrogant élite; nor imperious corporations ruling by the Winchesters of the coal and iron police; nor domineering labor unions; nor purposeful voluntary associations; nor insidious Molly Maguire conspiracies; nor the constituted authority of mayors or sheriffs; nor yet a vigorous church, school, or family, although in one way or another all groups from time to time attempted to impose an order satisfactory at least to their own interests. But this voluntarism, in failing to achieve any encompassing order, only furthered the social disorganization which the Industrial Revolution wrought in the anthracite region and elsewhere in nineteenth-century America.

6 / The Slave South:
An Interpretation

Eugene D. Genovese

This controversial essay deserves close and thoughtful reading. Employing the approach of political economy—an understanding of the interrelationships between economic, political, and social institutions as they are woven together to form the fabric of a civilization—Eugene D. Genovese explores a series of fundamental questions. Why did slavery become the central theme and institution in Southern life? What were the economic, social, and political consequences of the slave system? How do the answers to these questions throw light on the coming of the Civil War? Using a comparative analysis, Genovese explores the basic differences between the South and the remainder of the United States.

For further reading: The footnotes provide an introduction to the literature on this subject. * Eugene D. Genovese, *The Political Economy of Slavery: Studies in the Economy and Society of the Slave South* (1965); * Richard C. Wade, *Slavery in the Cities: The South, 1820–1860* (1964).

THE PROBLEM

Two interpretations of antebellum Southern society have, for some years, contended in a perplexing and unreal battle. The first considers the Old South an agrarian society fighting against the encroachments of industrial capitalism; the second considers the slave plantation merely a form of capitalist enterprise and suggests that the differences between Northern and Southern capitalism were more apparent than real. These two views, which one would think contradictory, are sometimes combined in the thesis that the agrarian nature of planter capitalism, for some reason, made coexistence with industrial capitalism difficult. None of these interpretations is convincing. Slavery and the rule of a special type of agrarians, the

Science and Society, XXV (1961), 320–337.

planters, characterized Southern society, which despite superficial resemblances to Northern was anti-bourgeois in structure and outlook.[1]

The first view cannot explain why some agrarian societies give rise to industrialization and some do not. A prosperous agricultural hinterland has generally served as a basis for industrial development by providing a home market for manufactures and a source of capital accumulation; and the prosperity of farmers has largely depended on the rise of industrial centers as markets for foodstuffs. In a capitalist society, agriculture is one industry among many, and its conflict with manufacturing is one of many competitive rivalries. There must have been something unusual about an agriculture that generated violent opposition to the agrarian West as well as to the industrial Northeast.

The second view, which is the more widely held, stresses that the plantation system produced for a distant market, responded to supply and demand, invested capital in land and slaves, and operated with funds borrowed from banks and factors. This, the more serious of the two interpretations, cannot begin to explain the origins of the conflict with the North and is intrinsically unsatisfactory. The reply to it will be the burden of this article.

SLAVERY AND THE EXPANSION OF CAPITALISM

The proponents of the idea of "planter capitalism" draw heavily, wittingly or not, on Lewis C. Gray's theory of the genesis of the plantation system. Gray defines the plantation as a "capitalistic type of agricultural organization in which a considerable number of unfree laborers were employed under a unified direction and control in the production of a staple crop."[2] The plantation system is here considered inseparably linked with the international development of capitalism. Gray notes the plantation's need for large outlays of capital, its strong tendency toward specialization in a single crop, and its commercialism; and he argues that these are features that appeared with the industrial revolution.

In modern times the plantation often arose under bourgeois auspices to provide industry with cheap raw materials, but the consequences were not always harmonious with bourgeois society. Colonial expansion produced three diverse patterns: (1) the capitalists of the advanced country simply invested in colonial land—as illustrated by the recent practice of the United Fruit Company in the Caribbean; (2) the colonial planters were largely subservient to the advanced country—as illustrated by the British West Indies early in the nineteenth century; and (3) the planters were able to win independence and build a society under their own direction—as illustrated by the Southern United States.

In alliance with the North, the planter-dominated South broke away from England, and political conditions in the new republic allowed it considerable freedom for self-

[1] For a succinct statement of the first view see Frank L. Owsley, "The Irrepressible Conflict," in Twelve Southerners, *I'll Take My Stand* (New York, 1930), p. 74. One of the clearest statements of the second position is that of Thomas P. Govan, "Was the Old South Different?" *Journal of Southern History*, XXI (Nov., 1955), p. 448.

[2] *History of Agriculture in the Southern United States to 1860* (2 Vols.; Gloucester, 1958), I, p. 302.

development. The plantation society that had begun as an appendage of British capitalism ended as a powerful, largely autonomous, aristocratic civilization, although it was tied to the capitalistic world by bonds of commodity production. The essential element in this distinct civilization was the planter domination made possible by the command of slave labor. Slavery provided the basis for a special Southern economic and social life, special problems and tensions, and special laws of development.

THE RATIONALITY AND IRRATIONALITY OF SLAVE SOCIETY

Slave economies manifest irrational tendencies that inhibit economic development and endanger social stability. Max Weber, for one, has noted four important irrational features.[3] First, the master cannot adjust the size of his labor force in accordance with business fluctuations. In particular, efficiency cannot readily be achieved through the manipulation of the labor force if sentiment, custom, or community pressure makes separation of families difficult. Secondly, the capital outlay is much greater and riskier for slave labor than for free.[4] Thirdly, the domination of a planter class increases the risk of political influence in the market. Fourthly, the sources of cheap slave labor are usually exhausted rather quickly, and beyond a certain point, costs become excessively burdensome. Weber's remarks could be extended. For example, planters have little opportunity to select specifically trained workers for special tasks as they arise.

There are other telling aspects of this economic irrationality. Under capitalism the pressure of the competitive struggle and the bourgeois spirit of accumulation direct the greater part of profits back into production. The competitive side of Southern slavery produced a similar result but one that was modified by the pronounced tendency to heavy consumption. Economic historians and sociologists have long noted the high propensity to consume among landed aristocracies. No doubt this difference is one of degree, and the greater part of slavery's profits also find their way back into production; but the method of reinvestment in the two systems is substantially different. Under capitalism profits are largely directed into an expansion of plant and equipment, not labor; in a word, economic progress is qualitative. In slave societies, for economic reasons as well as for those of social prestige, reinvestment of funds takes place along the same lines as the original investment—in land and slaves; that is, economic progress is quantitative.

In the South this weakness was fatal for the slaveholding planters. They found themselves engaged in a growing conflict with Northern farmers and businessmen

[3] The Theory of Social and Economic Organization (New York, 1947), pp. 276 ff. The term "rational" is used in its strictly economic sense to indicate that production is proceeding in accordance with the most advanced methods to maximize profits.

[4] This simple observation has come under curious attack. Kenneth M. Stampp, for example, insists that the cost of purchasing a slave forms the equivalent of the free worker's wage bill. See The Peculiar Institution (New York, 1956), pp. 403 ff. That equivalent, however, is to be found only in the cost of maintaining the slave through the year. The initial outlay is the equivalent of part of the capitalist's investment in fixed capital and constitutes what U. B. Phillips called the "over-capitalization" of labor under slavery. Surely, the cost of maintaining a slave is only a small part of the free worker's wage bill; but the difference in their productivity is probably much greater than the difference in their cost.

over tariffs, homesteads, internal improvements, and the decisive question of the balance of political power in the Union. The slow pace of their economic progress, in contrast to the long strides of the North, threatened to undermine their political parity and result in a Southern defeat on all major issues of the day. The qualitative leaps in the Northern economy were manifested in a rapidly increasing population, an expanding productive plant, and growing political, ideological, and social boldness. The South's voice grew shriller and harsher as it contemplated the impending disaster and sought solace in complaints of Northern aggression and exploitation.

Just as Southern slavery directed reinvestment along a path that led to economic stagnation, so too did it limit the volume of capital accumulated for investment of any kind. We need not reopen the tedious argument about which came first—the plantation, the one-crop system, or slavery. It should be clear that while slavery existed, the South had to be bound to a plantation system and an agricultural economy based on a few crops. The resultant dependence on Northern and British markets and on outside credit facilities and the inevitably mounting middleman's charges are well known. Perhaps less obvious was the capital drain occasioned by the importation of industrial goods. While the home market was retarded, Southern manufacturers had a difficult time producing in sufficient quantities to keep costs and prices at levels competitive with Northerners. The attendant dependence on Northern and British imports intensified the outward flow of badly needed funds.

Yet, many of the elements of irrationality were irrational only from a bourgeois standpoint. The high propensity to consume luxuries, for example, has always been functional (i.e., socially if not economically rational) in aristocratic societies, for it has provided the ruling class with the façade necessary to overawe the middle and lower classes. We may speak of the slave system's irrationality only in a strictly economic sense and then only to indicate the inability of the South to compete with Northern capitalism on the latter's grounds. The planters, fighting for political power in an essentially capitalist Union, had to do just that.

BOURGEOIS AND PSEUDO-BOURGEOIS FEATURES OF THE SLAVE ECONOMY

The slave economy had close relations with, and was in a sense exploited by, the capitalist world market; consequently, slavery developed many ostensibly capitalist features, such as banking, commerce, and credit. These features were not *per se* capitalist and played a different role in the South than in the North. Capitalism has absorbed and even encouraged many kinds of precapitalist social systems: serfdom, slavery, oriental state enterprises, and others. It has introduced credit, finance, banking, and similar institutions where they did not previously exist. It is pointless to suggest that therefore nineteenth-century India or twentieth-century Saudi Arabia are to be classified as capitalist countries. Our task is to analyze a few of the more important bourgeois and pseudo-bourgeois features and, in particular, to review the barriers to industrialization, for only by so doing can we appreciate the peculiar qualities of the slave economy.[5]

[5] This colonial dependence on the British and Northern markets was not ended when slavery ended. Share-cropping and tenantry produced similar results. Moreover, slavery at least offered the South a measure of political independence under planter hegemony. Since abolition occurred

The defenders of the "planter capitalism" thesis have noted the extensive commercial links between the plantation and the world market and the modest commercial bourgeoisie in the South and have concluded that there is no good reason to predicate an antagonism between cotton producers and cotton merchants. However valid as a reply to the naive arguments of the proponents of the agrarianism-versus-industrialism thesis, this criticism has unjustifiably been twisted to suggest that the presence of commercial activity proves the presence of capitalism.[6] Many precapitalist economic systems had well developed commercial relations, but if every commercial society is to be considered "capitalist," the word loses all meaning. In general, commercial classes have supported the existing system of production. As Maurice Dobb observes, their fortunes are bound up with those of the dominant producers, and merchants are more likely to seek an extension of their middlemen's profit than to try to reshape the economic order.[7]

In the Old South extensive and complicated commercial relations with the world market permitted the growth of a small commercial bourgeoisie. The resulting fortunes flowed into slaveholding, which offered prestige and was economically and politically secure in a planter-dominated society. Independent merchants found their businesses dependent on the patronage of the slaveholders. The merchants either became planters themselves or assumed a servile attitude toward the planters. The commercial bourgeoisie, such as it was, was tied to the slaveholding interest, had little desire or opportunity to invest capital in industrial expansion, and adopted the prevailing aristocratic attitudes.

The Southern industrialists were in an analogous situation, although one that was potentially subversive of the political power and ideological unity of the planters. Since the Southern countryside was dominated by large planters and slaves, the home market was retarded. The Southern yeomanry, unlike the Western, lacked the purchasing power to sustain rapid industrial development.[8] The planters spent much of their money abroad for luxuries. The plantation market consisted primarily of the demand for cheap slave clothing and cheap agricultural implements for use or misuse by the slaves. Southern industrialism needed a sweeping agrarian revolution to provide it with cheap labor and a substantial rural market, but the Southern industrialists were dependent on the existing, limited, plantation market. Leading industrialists like William Gregg and Daniel Pratt were plantation-oriented and pro-slavery. They could hardly have been otherwise.

The banking system of the South serves as an excellent illustration of an ostensibly capitalist institution that worked to augment the power of the planters and retard the development of the bourgeoisie. Southern banks functioned much as did those which

---

under Northern guns and under the program of a victorious, predatory, outside bourgeoisie, instead of under internal bourgeois auspices, the colonial bondage of the economy was preserved, but the South's political independence was lost.

[6] Govan, *op. cit.,* p. 448.

[7] *Studies in the Development of Capitalism* (New York, 1947), pp. 17 f.; cf. Gunnar Myrdal, *Rich Lands and Poor* (New York, 1957), pp. 52 ff.

[8] Twenty years ago an attempt was made by Frank L. Owsley and his students to prove that the Southern yeomanry was prosperous and strong. See *Plain Folk of the Old South* (Baton Rouge, 1949). This view was convincingly refuted by Fabian Linden, "Economic Democracy in the Slave South: An Appraisal of Some Recent Views," *Journal of Negro History,* XXI (Jan., 1946), pp. 140–89. Cf., Eugene D. Genovese, "The Limits of Agrarian Reform in the Slave South," unpublished doctoral dissertation, Columbia University, 1959, pp. 117–21.

the British introduced into Latin America, India, and Egypt during the nineteenth century. Although the British banks fostered dependence on British capital, they did not directly and willingly generate internal capitalist development. They were not sources of industrial capital but "large-scale clearing houses of mercantile finance vying in their interest charges with the local usurers." [9]

The difference between the banking practices of the South and those of the West reflects the difference between slavery and agrarian capitalism. In the West, as in the Northeast, banks and credit facilities promoted a vigorous economic expansion. During the period of irresponsible Western banking (1830–1844) credit was extended liberally for industrial development as well as for land purchases and internal improvements. Manufacturers and merchants dominated the boards of directors of Western banks, and landowners played a minor role. Undoubtedly, many urban businessmen speculated in land and were particularly interested in underwriting agricultural exports; but they gave attention to building up agricultural processing industries and urban enterprises, which guaranteed the region a many-sided economy.[10]

The slave states paid considerable attention to the development of a conservative, stable banking system, which could guarantee the movement of staple crops and the extension of credit to the planters. Southern banks were primarily designed to lend the planters money for outlays that were economically feasible and socially acceptable in a slave society: the movement of crops, the purchase of land and slaves, and little else.

Whenever easy credit policies were pursued in the South, the damage done outweighed the advantages of increased production. This imbalance probably did not occur in the West, for easy credit made possible agricultural and industrial expansion of a diverse nature and, despite acute crises, established a firm basis for long-range prosperity. Easy credit in the South led to expansion of cotton production with concomitant overproduction and low prices; simultaneously, it increased the price of slaves.

Planters wanted their banks only to facilitate cotton shipments and maintain sound money. They purchased large quantities of foodstuffs from the West and, since they shipped little in return, had to pay in bank notes. For five years following the New Orleans bank failures of 1837, the city's bank notes were at a discount of from ten to twenty-five per cent. This condition could not be allowed to recur. Sound banking and sound money became the cries of the planters as a class.

Southern banking tied the planters to the banks but, more important, tied the bankers to the plantations. The banks often found it necessary to add prominent planters to their boards of directors and were, in any case, closely supervised by the planter-dominated state legislatures. In this relationship the bankers could not emerge as a middle-class counterweight to the planters but could only serve as their auxiliaries.[11]

[9] Paul A. Baran, *The Political Economy of Growth* (New York, 1957), p. 194.

[10] The best introduction to this period of Western banking is the unpublished doctoral dissertation of Carter H. Golembe, "State Banks and the Economic Development of the West, 1830–1844," Columbia University, 1952, esp. pp. 10, 82–91. Cf. also Bray Hammond, "Long and Short Term Credit in Early American Banking," *Quarterly Journal of Economics*, XLIX (Nov., 1934), esp. p. 87.

[11] The bankers of the free states were also closely allied with the dominant producers, but society and economy took on a bourgeois quality provided by the rising industrialists, the urban middle classes, and the farmers who were increasingly dependent on urban markets. The ex-

The proponents of the "planter capitalism" thesis describe the planters and their society as bourgeois. Although this description is confusing and can serve no useful purpose, let us grant it for the moment. We are then confronted with a bourgeois society that impedes the development of every normal feature of capitalism; but when we realize that the planters were not bourgeois and that their society represented the antithesis of capitalism, these difficulties disappear. The fact of slaveownership is central to our problem. The seemingly formal question of whether the owners of the means of production command labor or purchase the labor power of free workers contains in itself the entire content of Southern life. All the essential features of Southern particularity and of Southern backwardness can be traced to the relationship of master to slave.

THE BARRIERS TO INDUSTRIALIZATION

If the planters were losing their economic and political cold war with the Northern bourgeoisie, the failure of the South to develop sufficient industry was the most striking immediate cause. Its inability to develop adequate manufactures is usually attributed to the inefficiency of the labor force. No doubt, slaves did not easily adjust to industrial employment, and the indirect effects of the slave system impeded the employment of whites.[12] Slaves were used effectively in hemp, tobacco, iron, and cotton factories but only under socially dangerous conditions. They were given a wide variety of privileges and elevated to an elite status. Planters generally appreciated the potentially subversive quality of these arrangements and were hostile to their extension.

There were other, and perhaps more important, impediments to industrialization. Slavery concentrated economic and political power in the hands of a slaveholding class hostile to industrialism. The planters feared a strong urban bourgeoisie, which might make common cause with its Northern counterpart. They feared a white urban working class of unpredictable social tendencies. In general, they distrusted the city and saw in it something incongruous with their local power and status arrangements. The planters were unwilling to assume a heavy tax burden to assist manufacturers, and as the South fell further and further behind the North in industrial development, increasing state aid was required to help industry offset the Northerners' advantages of scale, efficiency, credit relations, and business reputation.

Slavery led to the rapid concentration of land and wealth and prevented the expansion of a Southern home market. Instead of providing a basis for industrial growth, the Southern countryside, economically dominated by a few large estates,

---

pansion of credit, which in the West financed mining, manufacturing, transport, agricultural diversification, and the numerous branches of a capitalist economy, in the South bolstered the economic position of the planters, prevented the rise of alternative industries, and guaranteed the extension and consolidation of the plantation system.

[12] Slavery impeded white immigration by presenting Europeans with an aristocratic, caste-ridden society that scarcely disguised its contempt for the working classes. The economic opportunities in the North were, in most respects, far greater. When white labor was used in Southern factories, it was not always superior to urban slave labor. The incentives offered by the Northern economic and social system were largely missing; opportunities for acquiring skills were fewer; and in general, productivity was much lower than in the North.

provided only a limited market for industry. Data on the cotton textile factories almost always reveal that Southern producers aimed at supplying slaves with the cheapest and coarsest kind of cotton goods. Even so, local industry had to compete with Northern firms, which sometimes shipped direct and sometimes established Southern branches.

William Gregg, the South's foremost industrialist, was aware of the modest proportions of the Southern market and warned manufacturers against trying to produce exclusively for their local areas. His own company at Graniteville, South Carolina, produced fine cotton goods that sold much better in the North than in the South. Gregg was an unusually able man, and his success in selling to the North was a personal triumph. When he had to evaluate the general situation confronting Southern manufacturers, he asserted that he was willing to stake his reputation on their ability to compete with Northerners in the production of *"coarse cotton fabrics."* [13]

Some Southern businessmen, especially those in the border states, did good business in the North. Louisville tobacco and hemp manufacturers sold much of their output in Ohio. Some producers of iron and agricultural implements sold in nearby Northern cities. This kind of business was precarious. As Northern competitiors arose and the market shrank, Southern producers had to rely on the narrow and undependable Southern market.[14] Well before 1840 iron manufacturing establishments in the Northwest provided local farmers with excellent markets for grain, vegetables, molasses, and work animals. During the ante-bellum period, and after, the grain growers of America found their market at home. America's rapid industrial development offered farmers a magnificently expanding urban market, and not until much later did they come to depend to any important extent on exports.

To a small degree the South benefited in this way. By 1840 the tobacco manufacturing industry began to absorb more tobacco than was being exported, and the South's few industrial centers provided markets for local grain and vegetable growers. Since the South could not undertake a general industrialization, few urban centers arose to provide substantial markets for farmers and planters. Apart from Baltimore and New Orleans, the slave states had no large cities, and few reached the size of 15,000. Southern grain growers, except for those close to the cities of the free states, had to be content with the market offered by planters who preferred to specialize in cotton or sugar and buy foodstuffs. This market was limited by the restricted rations of the slaves and was further narrowed by limited transportation. It did not pay the planters to appropriate state funds to build a transportation system into the back country, and any measure to increase the economic strength of the back-country farmers was politically dangerous to the aristocracy of the Black Belt. The farmers of the back country remained isolated, self-sufficient, and politically, economically, and socially backward. Those grain-growing farmers who could compete with producers in the Upper South and Northwest for the plantation market were in the Black Belt itself. Since the planters did not have to buy from these local

[13] William Gregg, *Essays on Domestic Industry* (first published 1845; Graniteville, S. C., 1941), p. 4. Original emphasis.

[14] Consider the experience of locomotive, paper, and cotton manufacturers as reported in: Carrol H. Quenzel, "The Manufacture of Locomotives and Cars in Alexandria in the 1850's," *Virginia Magazine of History and Biography*, LXII (April, 1954), pp. 182 ff.; Ernest M. Lander, Jr., "Paper Manufacturing in South Carolina Before the Civil War," *North Carolina Historical Review*, XXIX (April, 1952), pp. 225 ff.; Adelaide L. Fries, "One Hundred Years of Textiles in Salem," *North Carolina Historical Review*, XXVII (Jan., 1950), p. 13.

producers, the economic relationship greatly strengthened the political hand of the planters.

THE GENERAL FEATURES
OF SOUTHERN AGRICULTURE

The South's greatest economic weakness was the low productivity of its labor force.[15] The slaves worked indifferently. They could be made to work reasonably well under close supervision in the cotton fields, but the cost of supervising them in more than one or two operations at a time was prohibitive. Without significant technological progress productivity could not be raised substantially, and slavery prevented such progress. Of greatest relevance, the impediments to technological progress damaged Southern agriculture, for improved implements and machines were largely responsible for the dramatic increases in crop yields per acre in Northern states during the nineteenth century.

Although slavery and the plantation system led to agricultural methods that depleted the soil, the frontier methods of the free states yielded similar results; but slavery forced the South into continued dependence upon exploitative methods after the frontier had been pushed further west and prevented reclamation of worn-out lands. The plantations were much too large to be fertilized easily. Lack of markets and poor care of animals by slaves made it impossible to accumulate sufficient manure. The low level of capital accumulation made the purchase of adequate quantities of commercial fertilizer unthinkable. Proper crop rotation could not be practiced, for the pressure of the credit system kept most available land in cotton, and the labor force could not easily be assigned to the required tasks without prohibitive costs of supervision. The general inefficiency of labor thwarted most attempts at improvement of agricultural methods.[16]

[15] Contemporary evidence points overwhelmingly to the conclusion that the productivity of slave labor was low. For a discussion of the relevant problems see my "Limits of Agrarian Reform in the Slave South," loc. cit., chapters I and II. Exact measurement of slave productivity is not possible, for the data necessary for the calculations are not available. Nevertheless, from time to time someone tries to measure it anyway. Algie Simons and Lewis C. Gray made unsuccessful attempts earlier in the century, and recently, two Harvard economists, Alfred H. Conrad and John R. Meyers, rediscovered their method (apparently without knowing it) and presented an elaborate and thoroughly useless paper: "The Economics of Slavery in the Ante-Bellum South," Journal of Political Economy, LXVI (April, 1958), pp. 95–130. This is not the place to subject their views to detailed criticism, but one or two observations may suffice. They measure productivity by dividing the cotton crop by the number of slaves within certain age limits. To begin with, I think they use the wrong age and price data, but let that pass. There are two troubles right at the start. This method assumes that the proportion of the cotton crop raised by white farmers in 1830, 1840, 1850, etc., was constant. There is not a shred of evidence for this; it is doubtful, and it cannot be verified. Secondly, it is well known that when cotton prices fell, some slaves were diverted to non-staple production. Thus, the assumption that in any two years the same proportion of slave force worked in the cotton fields is simply wrong. In addition, the authors use a great many statistical tricks, such as "rounding off" figures. In one key instance rounding off makes a 4 per cent increase look like a 20 per cent increase. But these matters must be pursued elsewhere and at another time.

[16] For a more detailed treatment of the problem of soil exhaustion see Eugene D. Genovese, "Cotton, Slavery and Soil Exhaustion in the Old South," Cotton History Review, II (Jan., 1961), pp. 3–17; for a more extensive treatment of the attempts of the South to improve its agriculture in general see my "Limits of Agrarian Reform in the Slave South," loc. cit.

The South, unable to feed itself, was caught in a series of dilemmas in its attempts to increase production of nonstaple crops and to improve its livestock. An inefficient labor force and the backward business practices of its ruling planter aristocracy were among the greatest difficulties. When planters did succeed in raising their own food, they also succeeded in depriving local livestock raisers and grain growers of whatever market they had. The stock raisers of the back country could not market their produce in the North because of the high costs of transportation.

The planters had little capital with which to buy improved breeds and could not guarantee the care necessary to make such investments worthwhile. Stock raisers too lacked the capital, and if they could get it, the investments would have been foolhardy without adequate urban markets.

Thoughtful Southerners, deeply distressed by the condition of their agriculture, made a determined effort to remedy it. In Maryland and Virginia significant progress was made in crop diversification and livestock improvement, but this progress was contingent on the sale of surplus slaves to the Black Belt. These sales provided an income that offset agricultural losses and made possible investments in fertilizers, equipment, and livestock. The concomitant reduction in the size of the slave force facilitated the problem of supervision and increased labor productivity and versatility. Even so, the income from slave sales remained an important part of the gross income of the planters of the Upper South. In other words, the reform was incomplete and could not free agriculture from the destructive effects of the continued reliance on slave labor.

The reform process had several contradictions, the most important of which was the dependence on slave sales. Surplus slaves could be sold only while gang-labor methods continued to be used in other areas. By the 1850's the deficiencies of slavery that had forced innovations in the Upper South were felt in the Lower South. Increasingly, planters in the Lower South were exploring the possibilities of reform. If the deterioration of agriculture in the Cotton Belt had proceeded much further, the planters would have had to stop buying the slaves of Maryland and Virginia. They would have had to look for markets for their own surplus slaves. Without the acquisition of fresh cotton lands there could be no general reform of Southern agriculture. The entire Southern economy was moving steadily into an insoluble crisis.

THE IDEOLOGY OF THE MASTER CLASS

The planters commanded Southern politics and set the tone of social life. Theirs was an aristocratic, antibourgeois spirit with values and mores that emphasized family and status, had its code of honor, aspired to luxury, leisure and accomplishment. In the planters' community paternalism was the standard of human relationships, and politics and statecraft were the duties and responsibilities of gentlemen. The gentleman was expected to live for politics and not, like the bourgeois politician, off politics.

The planter typically recoiled at the notions that profit is the goal of life; that the approach to production and exchange should be internally rational and uncomplicated by social values; that thrift and hard work are the great virtues; and that the test of the wholesomeness of a community is the vigor with which its citizens expand the economy.

The planter was certainly no less acquisitive than the bourgeois, but an acquisitive spirit is compatible with values antithetical to capitalism. The aristocratic
spirit of the planters absorbed acquisitiveness and directed it into channels that were
socially desirable to a slave society: the accumulation of land and slaves and the
achievement of military and political honors. Whereas in the North people were
impelled by the lure of business and money for their own sake, in the South specific
forms of property carried with them the badges of honor, prestige, and power. Even
the rough parvenu planters of the Southwestern frontier—the "Southern Yankees"—
strove to accumulate wealth in the modes acceptable to plantation society. Only in
their crudeness and naked avarice did they differ from the Virginia gentlemen. That
is, they were a generation removed from the refinement that follows successful primitive accumulation.

The basis of the planter's position and power was his slaveownership. It measured
his affluence, marked his status, and supplied leisure for social graces and aristocratic
duties. The older New England bourgeoisie, in its own way, struck an aristocratic
pose, but its wealth was rooted in commercial and industrial enterprises that were
being pushed into the background by the newer heavy industries arising in the
West, where bourgeois upstarts took advantage of the newer, more lucrative ventures
like the iron industry. In the South few such opportunities were opening. The
parvenu differed from the established planter only in being cruder and perhaps
sharper in his business dealings. The road to power was via the plantation. The older
aristocracy kept its leadership or made room for men in the same enterprises.

Many travelers commented on the difference in material conditions from one side
of the Ohio River to the other, but the difference in sentiment was seen most clearly
by de Tocqueville. Writing before the slavery issue had inflamed the nation, he
remarked that slavery was attacking the Union "indirectly in its manners." The
Ohioan "was tormented by the desire of wealth," and would turn to any kind of
enterprise or endeavor to make a fortune. The Kentuckian coveted wealth "much
less than pleasure or excitement," and money had "lost a portion of its value in his
eyes." [17]

Achille Murat joined de Tocqueville in admiration for Southern ways. Compared
with Northerners, Southerners were found to be more impulsive, frank, clever, charm-
ing, generous, and liberal.[18] The planters paid a price for these advantages. As one
Southerner put it, the North led the South in almost everything because the Yankees
had quiet perseverance over the long haul, whereas the Southerners had talent and
brilliance but no taste for sustained labor. Southern projects came with a flash and
died just as suddenly.[19] Despite such criticisms from within the ranks, the leaders
of the Old South clung to their ideals, their faults, and their conviction of superiority.
Farmers, said Edmund Ruffin, could not expect to achieve a cultural level above that
of the "boors who reap rich harvests from the fat soil of Belgium." In the Northern
states, he added with some justification, a farmer could rarely achieve the ease, culture, intellect, and refinement that slavery made possible.[20] The prevailing attitude of
the aristocratic South toward itself and its Northern rival was ably summed up by

[17] *Democracy in America* (2 Vols.; New York, 1948), I, p. 395.
[18] *America and the Americans* (Buffalo, 1851), pp. 19, 75.
[19] J. W. D. in the *Southern Eclectic*, II (Sept., 1853), pp. 63–66.
[20] *Address to the Virginia State Agricultural Society* (Richmond, 1853), p. 9.

William Henry Holcombe of Natchez: "The Northerner loves to make money, the Southerner to spend it." [21]

At their best Southern ideals constituted a rejection of the crass, vulgar, inhumane elements of capitalist society. The planter simply could not accept the idea that the cash nexus was a permissible basis for human relations. Even the vulgar parvenu of the Southwest embraced the plantation myth and refused to make a virtue of necessity by glorifying the competitive side of slavery as civilization's highest achievement. The planters did identify their own ideals with the essence of civilization and, given their sense of honor, were prepared to defend them at any cost.

This civilization and its ideals were profoundly antinational in a double sense. The plantation was virtually the only market for the small nonstaple-producing farmers and was the center of necessary services for the small cotton growers; thus, the paternalism of the planters toward their slaves was reinforced by a semi-paternal relationship between the planters and their neighbors. The planters were, in truth, the closest thing to feudal lords imaginable in a nineteenth-century bourgeois republic. The planters' protestations of love for the Union were not so much a desire to use the Union to protect slave property as a strong commitment to localism as the highest form of liberty. They genuinely loved the Union so long as it alone among the great states of the world recognized that localism had a wide variety of rights. The Southerners' source of pride was not the Union as such, nor the nonexistent Southern nation; it was the plantation, which they raised to a political principle.[22]

THE GENERAL CRISIS OF THE SLAVE SOUTH

The South's slave civilization could not forever coexist with an increasingly hostile, powerful, and aggressive Northern capitalism. On the one hand, the special economic conditions arising from the dependence on slave labor bound the South, in the colonial manner, to the world capitalist market. The concentration of landholding and slaveholding prevented the rise of a prosperous yeomanry and of urban centers. The inability to build urban centers, in turn, restricted the market for agricultural produce, weakened the rural producers, and dimmed hopes for agricultural diversification. On the other hand, the same concentration of wealth, the isolated, rural nature of the plantation system, the special social psychology engendered by slaveownership, and the political opportunity presented by the separation from England, converged to give the South considerable political and social independence. This independence was primarily the contribution of the slaveholding class, and especially of the planters. Slavery, while it bound the South economically, granted it the privilege of developing an aristocratic tradition, a disciplined and cohesive ruling class, and a mythology of its own.

Aristocratic tradition and ideology intensified the South's attachment to economic

[21] Diary dated Aug. 25, 1855 but apparently written later. MS in the University of North Carolina Southern Historical Collection, Chapel Hill.

[22] No genuine Southern nationalism was possible, for the bonds of commodity production did not link every part of the region with every other part. Each state's transportation system was designed to connect the Cotton Belt with the export centers. The back country was largely closed, and the typically capitalist road-railroad network was missing even in the Cotton Belt.

backwardness. Paternalism and the habit of command made the slaveholders tough stock determined to defend their Southern heritage. The more economically debilitating their way of life, the more they clung to it. It was this side of things—the political hegemony and aristocratic ideology of the ruling class—rather than economic factors that prevented the South from relinquishing slavery voluntarily.

As the free states stepped up their industrialization and as the westward movement assumed its remarkable momentum, the South's economic and political allies in the North were steadily isolated. Years of abolitionist and free soil agitation bore fruit as the South's opposition to homestead legislation, tariffs and the like clashed more and more dangerously with Northern needs. To protect their institutions and to try to lessen their economic bondage the slaveholders slid into violent collision with Northern interests and sentiments. The economic deficiencies of slavery threatened to undermine the planters' wealth and power. Such relief measures as cheap labor and more land for slave states (reopening the slave trade and territorial expansion) conflicted with Northern material needs, aspirations, and morality.[23] The planters faced a steady deterioration of their political and social power. Even if the relative prosperity of the 1850's had continued indefinitely, the slave states would have been at the mercy of the free, for the South could not compete with the capitalist North in population growth, capital accumulation, and economic development. Any economic slump threatened to bring with it an internal political disaster, for the planters could not rely on their middle and lower classes to remain permanently loyal.[24]

When we understand that the slave South was neither a strange form of capitalism nor an indefinable agrarianism but a special civilization built on the relationship of master to slave, the root of its conflict with the North is exposed. The internal contradictions in the South and the external conflict with the North placed the slaveholders hopelessly on the defensive with little to look forward to except slow strangulation. The only hope was a bold stroke to complete their political independence and to use it to provide an expansionist solution for their economic and social problems. The ideology and social psychology of the proud planter class made surrender or resignation to gradual defeat unthinkable, for its entire civilization was at stake.

[23] These measures were opposed by powerful sections of the planter class itself for reasons that cannot be discussed here. The independence of the South would only have brought the latent intra-class antagonisms to the surface.

[24] The loyalty of these classes was real enough but unstable. For our present purposes let us merely note that Lincoln's election and federal patronage would—if Southern fears were justified —have led to the formation of an anti-planter party in the South.

Three / Mobility: Social and Geographic

7 / The Maryland Gentry and Social Mobility, 1637-1676

William A. Reavis

One of the most striking characteristics of American society is its social mobility. Getting ahead has long been part of the American experience, and foreign travelers seldom fail to comment on it. Alexis de Tocqueville, a French visitor in the 1830's, remarked that "Everyone is tugging, trying, scheming to advance—to get ahead. It is a great scramble, in which all are troubled and none are satisfied." There were many avenues by which men could improve their social standing. The fluid years of the seventeenth century, the acceleration of economic growth after 1790 with the attendant industrialization and urbanization, the continuing lure of the frontier—all provided alternatives and strategies for advancement.

Geographic mobility is closely linked to social mobility. Men moved across mountains and rivers to seek new advantages—to follow the main chance. The man who could not or would not cut his ties with the old home was often at a great disadvantage in the race for wealth, power, and position. This scrambling across the landscape and up the social ladder introduced a frenetic quality into American life. As de Tocqueville stated: "In the United States a man builds a house to spend his latter years in it, and he sells it before the roof is on: he plants a garden, and lets it just as the trees are coming into bearing: he brings a field into tillage, and leaves other men to gather the crops: he embraces a profession, and gives it up: he settles in a place, which he soon afterwards leaves to carry his changeable longings elsewhere."

By the beginning of the nineteenth century, the American value system had enshrined achievement, and its social consequence—mobility—became the very core of the American dream. As de Tocqueville concluded, "Every other little ragged boy dreams of being President or a millionaire." While few made it to the White House or to Wall Street, a great many entered the ranks of the most remarkable middle class the world has ever known.

William A. Reavis focuses on the formative period in Maryland's history and convincingly demonstrates that most of the seventeenth-century gentry grew up with the land. As the population increased and the colony ex-

William and Mary Quarterly, 3rd series, XIV (1957), 418–428.

panded, more and more opportunities opened for public service. Tobacco production, shipping, commercial activities, and the like offered the inhabitants of the colony economic opportunity. However, by the last quarter of the century, the social structure became more rigid and opportunities for advancement diminished.

For further reading: Reinhard Bendix and Seymour Martin Lipset (eds.), *Class, Status, and Power: A Reader in Social Stratification* (1966); *Reinhard Bendix and Seymour Martin Lipset, *Social Mobility in Industrial Society* (1962); Pitirim A. Sorokin, *Social and Cultural Mobility* (1959); Aubrey C. Land, "Economic Behavior in a Planting Society: The Eighteenth-Century Chesapeake," *Journal of Southern History*, XXXIII (1967), 469–485.

The study of social structure is a nebulous thing at best, and it has suffered from the tendency of historians to rely almost exclusively upon diaries and memoirs, leaving the quantitative approach to the sociologists. But man in the mass *is* accessible even to the historian, and court records provide one of our best sources in this regard, particularly in the colonial period, when a man's social status was generally made a part of the public record.[1]

The *Archives of Maryland* contain seven volumes devoted to the records of the Maryland Provincial Court from 1637 until 1676.[2] In those years, 330 men who may be described as gentlemen appeared in the court. When labeled at all, they were called *Esq., Gent., Mr.,* or they were given a military or naval rank. Esquire was used almost exclusively for the Calvert inner circle. Of the entire group, 275 (83 per cent) were recognized as gentlemen from their first entry in the records, and have thus been dubbed "immigrant" gentlemen,[3] while 55 (17 per cent) rose from the ranks of the Maryland commoners,[4] and have been labeled "indigenous" gentlemen. With the exception of the inner circle, the immigrant gentleman was usually identified as *Gent.* from 1637 to 1650, while the indigenous gentleman was labeled *Mr.* From 1650 to 1665 both groups were usually labeled as *Mr.* and from 1665 to 1676 as *Gent.* The accompanying table lists the first appearance of immigrant and indigenous gentry in the Maryland Provincial Court, the latter group in their first appearance as gentlemen.[5]

[1] For a study based partly on New England court records, see Norman H. Dawes, "Titles as Symbols of Prestige in Seventeenth-Century New England," *William and Mary Quarterly*, 3d Ser., VI (1949), 69–83.

[2] *Archives of Maryland*, ed. William H. Brown and others (Baltimore, 1883-in process), IV, X, XLI, XLIX, LVII, LXV, and LXVI. There is a gap in the records for the period 1645–46. These seven volumes also contain many records of the St. Mary's and Calvert County courts, and a few records of other counties. Several volumes in the *Archives* are devoted exclusively to county court records.

[3] A few of the so-called "immigrant" gentlemen were actually born in the New World, either coming from other colonies or being the elder sons of Maryland gentry.

[4] The word "commoner" is used here as a convenient way to categorize all Marylanders who were not members of the gentry class. The court records contain no such term.

[5] Gentry markings were profuse during the first half of the period but tended to fall off in the last years, even in the case of the Calverts. They were always used, however, in formal legal papers, such as land sale agreements. But the only solution to this problem was to trace the entries

Year	Immigrant Gentry	Indigenous Gentry	Total
1637	25	0	25
1638	3	0	3
1639	6	0	6
1640	0	0	0
1641	0	0	0
1642	11	0	11
1643	4	0	4
1644	2	0	2
records destroyed, 1645–46			
1647	4	3	7
1648	3	2	5
1649	2	3	5
1650	6	6	12
1651	21	2	23
1652	13	1	14
1653	9	1	10
1654	13	0	13
1655	13	3	16
1656	5	1	6
1657	11	1	12
1658	13	7	20
1659	3	3	6
1660	5	0	5
1661	11	2	13
1662	0	2	2
1663	8	5	13
1664	12	2	14
1665	3	0	3
1666	7	0	7
1667	3	0	3
1668	8	1	9
1669	10	0	10
1670	9	1	10
1671	1	1	2
1672	4	0	4
1673	9	3	12
1674	9	2	11
1675	5	1	6
1676	4	2	6
Totals	275	55	330

Considering the immigrant gentlemen first, it is important to ask just what proportion of this group had been, or would have qualified as, gentlemen in England.

of each possible gentleman through many volumes; fortunately Marylanders were a litigious people, particularly if they were members of the upper commoner or gentry class, and there was no dearth of entries to compare.

The clerks of the Provincial Court were themselves gentlemen, and their decisions as to social status have been accepted throughout. Occasionally succeeding clerks disagreed as to borderline individuals, and an average had to be taken. But the clerks were very catholic in their designation of gentlemen: William Claiborne, Richard Bennett, William Fuller, William Bretton, Josias Fendall, and Nathaniel Utye, all of whom openly opposed the Calvert government at one time or another, were consistently marked as gentlemen by Calvert's own court clerks.

It has been observed that the English gentleman had the "prestige of birth . . . acquired in three generations of wealth or achievement leading to exemption from gainful labor. . . ."[6] Accepting this definition, it is obvious that few genuine English gentlemen of the early seventeenth century would have migrated to the New World simply to plant tobacco. For what reasons, then, and in what numbers did the gentry come?

Those who emigrated mainly to participate in the rewards of Maryland officialdom were probably all valid English gentlemen. The Calverts had a huge grant of land from the King, but this grant would do the family little good unless colonists could be moved to the New World in large numbers. To staff such a project the Calverts had to recruit a trusted "inner circle" of gentlemen of means and position who could be enticed to America by the promise of a share in the Calvert largess. As Donnell M. Owings has shown very clearly, this largess was distributed through the grant of provincial offices, in the form of salaries and fees of a princely nature.[7]

But this Calvert inner circle was never large: if the four Calverts are excepted, only thirteen of the 275 immigrant gentry held positions on the Provincial Council during periods of Calvert hegemony for as long as five years. They were Robert Clarke, Thomas Greene, Thomas Gerard, John Lewger, Giles Brent, Henry Coursey, Thomas Trueman, Baker Brooke, Jerome White, Jesse Wharton, William Evans, Edward Lloyd, and Thomas Hatton.[8] Only five of these men were included among the twenty-eight gentry who appear in the records in 1637–38. It can certainly be argued that a higher proportion of the original colonists were Calvert retainers who either returned to England or died or became alienated from the Calvert rule, and who thus had no opportunity to serve on the Provincial Council for as long a period as five years. Even so, the group of genuine English gentlemen, who were primarily attracted to America by a promise of a part of the Calvert largess, was small.

Those English gentlemen who came to Maryland mainly in the pursuit of adventure were even smaller in number. The records suggest that practically all who came for this reason, like Francis Trafford Esq. and William Talbott Esq., stayed but a year or two and then returned to England. The American wilderness held little continuing attraction for gentlemen assured in England of economic, political, and social standing; once the aura of adventure had worn off they were eager to return to remembered comforts.

English gentlemen who migrated primarily because of religious discrimination probably included most of the original group of Catholic gentry and some of the Puritans who came up from Virginia. But the fact that the estates of deceased Maryland gentlemen contained so little of value besides the lands given out by the Calverts indicates that this group could not have been very large; for if they had been gentlemen of means, it is reasonable to assume they would have managed to bring a good portion of their wealth with them.

Examination of the records of the Provincial Court shows that not more than fifty, and possibly fewer, of the 275 immigrant gentry can be placed in one of the above groups. That means that at least 225 members (82 per cent) of the Maryland immigrant gentry had not been real English gentlemen at all; they were either "gentle-

---

[6] *Encyclopaedia of the Social Sciences* (New York, 1930–34), VI, 617.

[7] Donnell M. Owings, *His Lordship's Patronage* (Baltimore, 1953).

[8] The *Archives of Maryland* have excellent indexes; where examples in the text can be easily traced they will not be footnoted.

men" of the fringe variety (those whose fortunes were on the wane, or possibly the younger sons of gentlemen, who found themselves with nothing but a famous name), or, more probably, they were English middling sort who filled the void in the Maryland upper stratum caused by the shortage of true English gentlemen. Thus it seems likely that the trip from England to America allowed scores of men to step a notch upward in the social scale without even having to serve an apprenticeship as commoners in the New World. This "shipboard mobility" has been generally ignored by historians, but it is an important phenomenon of the period of settlement on any frontier. In seventeenth-century Maryland it was far more significant numerically than was the "coming up through the ranks" by commoners, although both were based upon the same lack of valid gentry and the same frontier emphasis upon individual initiative and ability. The latter required a certain period of economic and social growth made possible by cheap lands and frontier opportunities for individual initiative; the former required only an air of distinction as one debarked from the ship.

Turning to the indigenous gentry, it is apparent from the above table that the accession of Maryland commoners to the status of gentleman was relatively constant after the first eight years. As we have seen, 17 per cent of the 330 Maryland gentlemen appearing in the Provincial Court were of this type.[9] These fifty-five gentlemen averaged twenty-five entries each in the Provincial Court records during an average of twelve years as commoners. They ranged all the way from Nicholas Gwither, who took four years to move from commoner to gentleman (sixteen entries as a commoner), to William Hatton, who spent twenty-six years as a commoner before he became accepted as a gentleman (thirty-two entries as a commoner).

While there was considerable social mobility in Maryland throughout the seventeenth century, it is easier to gauge it than to determine just how it took place. Certainly one factor to be considered would be the accumulation of riches. A considerable gulf existed between the average net worth of commoners and gentlemen in seventeenth-century Maryland: out of the fifty-five itemized and evaluated estates listed in the records of the Provincial Court,[10] the thirty-nine commoner estates had an average valuation of 3,695 pounds of tobacco, while the eighteen gentry estates

[9] This is, of course, a relative figure, based on the assumption that all of the immigrant gentry were bona fide residents of Maryland. There is good reason to believe that the actual percentage of indigenous gentry was much higher, perhaps as great as 25 or 33 per cent: 1) Many transients are included among the immigrant gentry. The records provide incomplete data on departures from the colony, and many of the immigrant gentry maintained little or no residence in Maryland. Among these were such mariners as Capt. Richard Husbands, Capt. Samuel Tilghman; Virginia gentry who were in and out of Maryland, such as Mr. John Hanceford, Mr. John Trussell, and Mr. Thomas Thornborough; and the English gentlemen-adventurers. All these men (and probably others who could not be identified as transients) have to be included in the immigrant gentry totals because the information on the extent of their activities in Maryland is so sketchy. 2) Some men who may have been indigenous gentry were placed in the category of immigrant gentry: those for whom the period of time between the first entry and first gentry entry was short, and those for whom too few entries intervened between first appearance in the records and first appearance as gentry.

For the above reasons, the table contains a higher proportion of immigrant gentry and a consequent lower proportion of indigenous gentry than was actually the case. It should be emphasized that all indigenous gentry were Maryland residents over a long period of time.

[10] The listing of the estates in the records of the Provincial Court is incomplete, even in the early period when there were no county courts. In addition, only about half of the estates listed contain appraisals of value.

averaged slightly over five times as much.[11] This was primarily because of the great differences in landholdings between the two classes: while Lord Calvert was rather liberal in his grants to many of the immigrant gentry, his policies toward the lower classes were much more restrictive, and many were kept in a state of semitenancy for at least a generation. This situation did not remain static: after 1660 there was a considerable inflation in land values,[12] and there were numerous sales of land to commoners, both by the proprietor and by individual gentlemen. The credit structure of provincial finance, based on the annual crop of tobacco, made it easy for commoners with little capital to buy as much land as they could profitably farm, and many others simply drifted off to the frontier and squatted. In either case, land was available which the commoners could not have dreamed of possessing in England, and by tradition the ownership of land has always carried with it the aura of gentility.

But there are many indications that the division between the two classes was not entirely economic. Many gentry estates had lower valuations than some commoners': the estate of Mr. Zachary Mottershead was virtually worthless after debts and death expenses were deducted, while James Jolly, a commoner planter and mariner, left an estate worth 37,367 pounds of tobacco, larger than most of the gentry estates. Both classes owned indentured servants about equally, and it is interesting to note that the commoner John Grammar owned more indentured servants (ten) than did any gentleman whose estate is listed in the records. Moreover, "wealthy" Marylanders were in reality land-poor; besides their indentured servants, livestock, boats, and an occasional slave, their personal property was of such a limited and frontier nature (even in the case of the Calverts) that it was almost negligible.

The main route upward for commoners lay in public service. In 67 per cent of the cases, accession to a higher social status was preceded by appointment to an office identified with the gentry class: all provincial posts, county commissioners, county sheriffs, county surveyors, commissioned ranks in the militia, ship captains, and professional attorneys. It can be argued that officeholding had some relationship to economic standing since the county offices, at least, paid very little and had to be supplemented by planting. But the relationship of wealth to officeholding was at best only secondary.

In the rural areas of England the gentry had always held the local offices, so it is not surprising that officeholding was the main avenue to gentility in Maryland. What is significant is the fact that only 52 per cent of the immigrant gentry ever held *any* provincial or county office. This fact, coupled with the constant formation of new counties, gave many commoners the chance to fill important local offices, an opportunity which would have been practically nonexistent in England. Thus in the newer counties of Baltimore, Dorchester, Somerset, and Cecil, all of which had

[11] During the seventeenth century in Maryland, pounds of tobacco were used as the unit of exchange because of the lack of coin. In 1639 one pound of tobacco was valued at three pence sterling (80 lbs. tobacco = 1£), and by 1665 the value of one pound of tobacco had depreciated exactly half, being equal to three halfpence sterling (160 lbs. tobacco = 1£). The pound of tobacco did, however, effectively measure the amount of labor necessary to purchase goods. *Archives of Maryland,* IV, 102–103, and XLIX, 388.

[12] The value of average tobacco lands increased from an average of 5–6 pounds of tobacco per acre in the period 1637–58, to 10 pounds in 1666, to 13 pounds in 1673, and to 17–20 pounds in 1675. *Archives of Maryland,* IV, 15, XLI, 103, 143, LVII, 45–54, LXV, 118, 501–502, 504–505.

only a few hundred inhabitants each in 1675, many commoners made the transition to gentry status.

The same thing was happening in the older counties, where just as many openings seem to have existed despite the greater number of immigrant gentry available to fill them. In 1668 George Beckwith became the Calvert County coroner and was recognized as a gentleman; in 1664 the commoner William Marshall was appointed Charles County commissioner after twenty years in Maryland, as Zachary Wade had been the year before. In 1663 Thomas Leitchworth and Tobias Norton became Calvert County commissioners after six years and seven years, respectively, as commoners. Apparently, because of the rough work involved in frontier planting, many of the immigrant gentlemen had little time for officeholding, and their apathy gave many new men their chance.

Very often commoners worked their way up through a succession of minor offices. Robert Vaughan, who had been a sergeant in the militia, was appointed a captain in 1647, and thus became a gentleman automatically. Philip Land served as the undersheriff of St. Mary's County while a commoner, but when he was appointed sheriff in 1650 he became a gentleman. Edward Packer served on juries constantly from 1638 to 1652; in the latter year he was appointed jury foreman, and the clerk inscribed a *Mr.* before his name from then on. Richard Smith served as a lay attorney for some years, and he became a gentleman when he was appointed attorney general in 1657. In 1651 Miles Cooke was mate for Captain Richard Husbands aboard the *Hopeful Adventure*; in 1659 Cooke obtained command of the *Baltimore* and assumed gentry status. James Thompson, while still a commoner, served as clerk of the orphans' court and the Calvert County court. Finally, in 1664, he was made clerk of the Provincial Court and accorded himself the rank of gentleman.

Some members of the indigenous gentry exhibited amazing progress in the social scale; while the majority probably came from among the upper commoners, there are some significant exceptions. James Langworth and James Linsey came to Maryland as indentured servants; Langworth rose in time to be a commissioner of St. Mary's County, a lay attorney, and a captain in the militia, while Linsey was appointed a Charles County commissioner sixteen years after achieving his freedom. John Jarbo, Henry Adams, and William Marshall all began as laborers; in time Jarbo became a lieutenant colonel in the militia and a St. Mary's County commissioner, while Adams and Marshall became Charles County commissioners and sheriffs within twenty years after their first appearance in the records. Other indigenous gentry started higher in the commoner group, but they climbed higher too: Samuel Chew, Edward Packer, John Hatch, Richard Banks, Robert Vaughan, and John Price all served on the Provincial Court for short periods.

As might be expected, many commoners came close to achieving the status of gentleman but were never quite accepted. Daniel Clocker was a significant example of this group. He first appeared in the Provincial Court in 1648 as a newly freed servant who acquired enough "freedom land" to get started as a planter. He was illiterate, but he served as a juror and lay attorney, and in 1655 was appointed a commissioner of St. Mary's County, serving for a year in that capacity. In 1661 he was appointed as executor for the estate of Colonel John Price, and in 1669 he became overseer of the highways in St. Mary's County. In the 1670's he was regularly a juryman until his death in 1676. The importance of the relationship between social status and political office is suggested by the fact that at no time other than the year he spent as a St. Mary's County commissioner was he marked as a gentleman; the fact that he was not so marked thereafter prevented him from being classed in the indigenous gentry.

The effect of family ties on social status was mixed: sometimes they helped and at other times they had no apparent influence. James Johnson married the daughter of Mr. Thomas Hatton in 1650, and in 1655 he was appointed a commissioner of St. Mary's County, becoming a gentleman after fourteen years as a commoner. Thomas Courtney, on the other hand, married the daughter of Mr. Thomas Taylor in 1664 and received one hundred acres of land as his wife's dowry. Although Court-ney was very active in the courts and as constable for St. Mary's Hundred, he was never accepted as a gentleman.

Only about one third of the sons of gentry were accorded the rank of gentleman as soon as they appeared in the records. It is difficult to distinguish between elder and younger sons, but it appears that most of the latter began as commoners, al-though some eventually achieved the status of gentleman. The Hatton family had three males who were immediately accepted as gentlemen and one who took twenty-six years to achieve that status. Three members of the Thompson family were marked as gentlemen immediately and three had to work up through the ranks of the com-moners. The Adams, Browne, Hall, Mitchell, Morgan, Price, Smith, Taylor, Thomas, and Wade families all had one male who was accorded gentry status on first appear-ance in the records, one who served a period of time as a commoner before becoming a gentleman, and others who remained commoners all their lives. Thus, while mar-riage and blood relationship, as well as riches, were factors in determining the gentry status, the big factor, as we have seen, was officeholding.

The upward movement of commoners was facilitated by the failure of the Calverts to enforce class distinctions in legal and property matters that existed in Old Eng-land. In a frontier environment and under the pressures of simultaneous struggles for control with democratic elements and with the Puritans, the Calverts simply could not allow special privileges in court for the gentry. It is true that by statute gentlemen were excluded, for at least a few years, from such debasing punishment as whipping,[13] but in all other matters the Provincial Court tended to be firm, yet fair, with both classes. In 1658, for example, both Mr. Henry Hooper and the com-moner John Cornelius were found guilty of swearing in court, and they were fined ten pounds of tobacco each. In 1648 Edward Cummings and in 1650 Mr. Luke Gardiner were found guilty of slander, and both fines were remitted upon apology in open court. In 1675 Thomas Taylor, commoner, complained to the court that Thomas Taylor, Gent., "an assault did make and him did beate wound and evill han-dle and him imprisoned and so imprisoned a long time deteined and other enormities." The jury found for the commoner, and the court awarded damages of 2000 pounds of tobacco. In 1653 Henry Hyde testified that Mr. Lawrence Starkey had threatened to make him a perpetual servant; the court ordered Hyde released at the end of his term with freedom dues as agreed.

The value of a gentleman's word in court actually declined considerably during the seventeenth century, possibly as a reflection of the changed nature of the gentry. Two cases may be cited to illustrate this trend. In 1642 Mr. Thomas Gerard was able to win a suit concerning a sow by assuring the court that he had never

---

[13] Ibid., I, 158, 184 (1642). However, the Provincial Court records indicate that there was very little whipping of freemen except during the years of Puritan domination.

promised the animal as was charged by a commoner. By contrast, in 1661 Mr. Thomas Mathews was sued for £10 wages by Thomas Walker, his former indentured servant, and although Mathews swore that the money had never been promised, the court awarded the £10 to Walker. It was not unusual for a commoner to administer the estate of a gentleman, as Joseph Edlowe did for the estate of Mr. Robert Wiseman in 1651. In 1658 Mr. William Eltonhead's estate was appraised by four commoners, and in 1650 Mr. Thomas Hatton and Captain William Mitchell agreed to arbitration of their suit by two men, a gentleman and a commoner.

From 1637 to 1643 all cases in the Provincial Court were decided by gentlemen sitting as judges; however, after that time almost all of the cases were decided by jury. Out of fifty-five jury cases examined, 16 per cent had all-commoner juries, even though most of the cases involved a gentleman either as plaintiff or defendant. When, in 1672, Mr. James Neale and his son were tried for hog stealing, both were found guilty by commoner juries. When Mr. John Blomfield, in 1675, sued Philip Russell for failing to live up to a contract, the all-commoner jury found for Blomfield.

In the mixed juries a gentleman was generally chosen as foreman, but in 15 per cent of those cases a commoner was chosen instead. Almost half of the mixed juries contained only one gentleman, and seldom were more than two or three assigned. The few juries which contained 50 per cent gentry or more seem to have been in trials of more than usual interest, such as that in 1652 when Captain William Mitchell was tried for adultery, blasphemy, and murder, and that in 1653 when two Indians were tried for murder.[14] Gentlemen did, at times, demand a place in the jury box, but it was more an effort to get a front row seat than to control the administration of justice.

By 1676 Maryland had grown from about 200 inhabitants to over 20,000,[15] and the colony's transition from frontier to settled, rural status meant that it would be more and more difficult for a new arrival to make the transition from commoner to gentleman. Only by moving westward, or by migrating to the unsettled frontier areas of South Carolina and Georgia, could he hope to match the mobility which had characterized the first settlers who established the Maryland social structure from 1637 to 1676. The heritage of an individualistic frontier tradition would always allow more social mobility in Maryland than had been possible in England,[16] but the days of free-wheeling social ascent were over.

[14] The trial of the Indians can be found in *Archives of Maryland*, X, 295.

[15] For more detailed population figures see E. B. Greene and Virginia D. Harrington, *American Population Before the Federal Census of 1790* (New York, 1932), pp. 123–124.

[16] For an excellent contemporary description of the English gentry, see Sir Thomas Smith, "De Republica Angolorum" (1565), in *Complaint and Reform in England, 1436–1714*, eds. W. H. Dunham and Stanley Pargellis (New York, 1938), p. 212. This source indicates that although there was some social mobility in England, not many men could look forward to such a transition in their own lifetimes; rather they worked to ease the progress of their sons.

8 / A Virginian Moves to Kentucky, 1793

Lowell H. Harrison

This essay, based on the Breckinridge family papers in the Library of Congress, is rich in human drama. It illustrates the interrelationship between social and geographic mobility. John Breckinridge left Virginia for Kentucky because he believed his law practice would thrive there and that he could build a valuable estate based on rich lands in the Bluegrass country. Muddy roads and late winter snows, Indian dangers, his wife and his slaves saddened and depressed at leaving the old home, optimistic land speculations, friends and relations in the West urging Breckinridge on—all these illuminate the dramatic elements of the story and make clear that the process of mobility touched all aspects of human existence.

For further reading: John D. Barnhart, *Valley of Democracy: The Frontier Versus the Plantation in the Ohio Valley, 1775–1818* (1953); *Francis S. Philbrick, *The Rise of the West, 1754–1830* (1965); *David M. Potter, *People of Plenty: Economic Abundance and the American Character* (1954); Frederick Jackson Turner, *The Frontier in American History* (1920).

John Breckinridge of Virginia moved to the Bluegrass region of Kentucky in the spring of 1793. For the next few years, until his death in 1806, he was to play an important role in Kentucky and national politics, but it is his decision to leave Virginia that will concern us here. Breckinridge was not a buckskin-clad pioneer who fought off Indians with one hand while erecting a crude log cabin with the other. Nor was he a member of the great planter-businessman group which later set the tone of the ante-bellum Bluegrass. As a second-generation pioneer of moderate means, he was a bridge between his Indian-fighting predecessor and his aristocratic successors. As such, Breckinridge was perhaps typical of a small but important group whose part in the development of the Old West is all too neglected.

It was not the lure of adventure which drew Breckinridge westward. Kentucky's great attraction for him was the economic advantage it promised over his Virginia prospects. "I am satisfied with this Country better than the old, for two substantial reasons," he wrote his wife's brother a few weeks after his arrival in Kentucky. "1. Be-

William and Mary Quarterly, 3rd series, XV (1958), 201–213. Footnotes have been omitted.

cause my profession is more profitable; and 2ndly. Because I can provide *good* lands here for my children, & insure them from *want,* which I was not certain of in the old Country, any longer than I lived."

In 1785, soon after opening a law practice, Breckinridge married Mary Hopkins (Polly) Cabell. Within the next eight years four children were born to the young couple, and Breckinridge experienced growing economic pressure. His efforts to secure financial independence led him to undertake the dual role of farmer and lawyer. The Glebe, his 400-acre farm in Albemarle County, Virginia, presented to him by his father-in-law, may possibly have paid its way; it certainly did little more. Similarly, while he had a good legal reputation, few places have ever boasted as illustrious and crowded a bar as Virginia's in the 1780's, and competition was keen. Many clients were unable or reluctant to pay their fees. In 1787 Breckinridge employed an agent, Arthur Hopkins, to collect fifty-four delinquent accounts. Other clients were able to make payments only in produce, and at various times the young lawyer received a horse worth £20, flour, pasture for his horses, brandy, and a slave—the last becoming his only if he won the case.

All in all, Breckinridge made a moderately comfortable living for himself and his family at the expense of considerable personal exertion. Yet, because of the growing demands of his family, he had little opportunity to build up an estate. It was thus natural that his attention should be drawn across the blue-hazed mountains to Kentucky where prospects were rumored to be bright for men of vision and enterprise. For over a decade his desire to enter that land was whetted by reports from friends and relatives who had already made the move: year after year they entreated him to join them.

Alexander and Robert Breckinridge, John's half brothers, headed the westward advance of their family, both of them moving to Kentucky soon after their release from British prison ships in Charleston harbor in 1781. The magic of the new land enthralled them, and they made only occasional trips back East. Alexander wrote John in the summer of 1784 that Kentucky had more money in circulation than Virginia, that the already sizable amount of legal business was sure to inc_ease, and that Walker Daniels, the attorney general, had spoken highly of him, expressing the hope that he would come to Kentucky. But John never had an opportunity to thank the kindly Daniels, for Alexander, writing again within the week, informed him that the lawyer had been killed by a band of Indians. John might secure the now vacant office, Alexander suggested, if he cared to come to Kentucky immediately.

Another brother, William Breckinridge, migrated in 1783 and sent back glowing reports of innumerable lawsuits, a scarcity of attorneys, and the deep satisfaction of living on one's own soil in the "rich and extensive country." He, too, hoped that John would join the Kentucky members of the family and that their mother could then be persuaded to leave Virginia.

It was not until 1788, however, that John Breckinridge finally decided to make the move. "I have it in Contemplation, (indeed firmly fixed on it)," he wrote his brother James, "to become an Inhabitant one day or other not far Distant of Kentucky." He would leave on a two months' inspection trip the following March to see for himself the possibilities of the new country. While few persons had been told of his ultimate intention, he had secured the consent of the people whose happiness was his greatest concern. The news came as an agreeable surprise to James, then at college in Williamsburg: "I always knew you had a great propensity for it yourself but was always apprehensive your own assent was all that could be had. I hope when you come to explore Kentucky you become more fixed and determined in your design. That being the country in which I at present design *burying my bones,* makes me the more anxious that you and some more of the family should move out; your going will no doubt be a means of taking others. . . ."

Thanks to several adventures in land speculation with his brothers, Breckinridge already owned a number of tracts in the West. His chief role in these transactions had been to procure military and treasury land warrants for his Kentucky associates, who in turn made the necessary entries. William Breckinridge, undeterred by strong Indian raids in the fall of 1784, wrote from Kentucky requesting enough warrants to cover 60,000 acres of entries. Always sanguine of his prospects, he predicted that he would be able to sell at £5 per hundred acres and would clear nearly £3000. Brother James, also in Kentucky at that time, showed even less concern for Indian danger when a chance for profit presented itself, for he planned to buy military warrants for use on the northern side of the Ohio. He would hire two or three Indians to guide him, being careful not to reveal his purpose to them. Although Alexander carried warrants for 200,000 acres with him when he went to Kentucky, he had not received his warrants for Revolutionary service, and he asked John to see why they had not been issued. John himself was always on the lookout for good Kentucky lands owned by nonresidents who might not know their true value and who might therefore be persuaded to sell at an advantageous price. By 1789, when he first visited Kentucky, he had made total entries there of nearly 30,000 acres, the individual entries ranging from 400 to 5,662 acres, and dating back to the spring of 1780 when he secured 1,000 acres on Beargrass Creek near the Falls of the Ohio. Besides new lands to consider, he thus had extensive properties of his own to choose from in selecting a site for the home and plantation he expected to build.

During the winter of 1788–89 Breckinridge made active preparations for his inspection trip while awaiting the adjournment of the courts in which he practiced. Robert Breckinridge, then in Virginia on a visit, was to accompany him, as was a cousin, John Preston. Part of his preparation, undoubtedly, was to convince his wife that he ought to go. Polly Breckinridge had labored under the hopeful delusion that the intended journey was only talk. When she finally realized her husband was actually going, every conceivable misfortune that could befall him came to mind. She worried all the more because attendance at the winter courts had left him feeling weak, with a terrible cough. Once he had left, her troubles and fears increased, and when the children became violently ill a few days after their father rode away, she longed for his return. "I was in hopes to of had the pleasure of receiving a letter From you before this time," she wrote on April 12. "It would give me more satisfaction To here from you than any thing in this world except your Return and I know that is a happiness I cannot promis my Self at least for some time: I am in hopes my Dear Husband this will Find you safe in Kentucky and hope the God that carried you safe there will bring you back to your little Family who laments your absence more than you can conceive. . . . pray my Dear Mr. Breckinridge be very caucious in comeing home expecially in comeing through the Wilderness; as my whole happiness or misery as to this life depends on your return I would wish you to have a large company."

The company with which Breckinridge traveled arrived safely in Kentucky by April 15, 1789, without encountering any danger, although rumors drifted back to

Virginia that John Breckinridge had been killed by Indians. He traveled widely over the central and northern parts of the country, searching for the exact location he wanted. With land cheap and money scarce, he had no desire to embarrass his future unnecessarily by plunging too deeply into debt at the very outset. Several spots met his specifications, but he had not fixed definitely upon any of them before he returned through the Wilderness to Virginia in June. Not until 1790 did he purchase, for £360 current money of Virginia, the six hundred acres of gently rolling land in the heart of the Bluegrass that became the nucleus of his Kentucky plantation. Lying on the North Elkhorn watercourse, the land was only six miles from Lexington, where Breckinridge would have his best prospects for an extensive law practice. Colonel Samuel Meredith, Sr., who sold him the land, was the father-in-law of his only sister, Betsy, and one of Breckinridge's purposes in selecting that particular site was to be near his sister, whose family was moving to an adjacent tract in the spring of 1790.

Back in 1788, when Breckinridge had broached the possibilities of moving to Kentucky, his brother James advised him to defer the actual move for two or three years, until the growth of the settlements north of the Ohio River would place a safe barrier between Kentucky and the Indian tribes. This was reasonable advice which he could appreciate, and so many bonds tied him to Virginia that a swift move would have been difficult even had he desired it. Since he had to delay his going, there were measures which could be taken to ease his ultimate removal. The first of these was the preparation of his lands. This task was entrusted to Colonel William Russell, a friend who had already settled in the neighborhood where Breckinridge planned to make his home. Almost as soon as he purchased the land from Meredith, Breckinridge wrote to Russell and asked him to place two or three tenants on the tract where immediate improvements were to be made. Russell wrote late in June that seven families had settled on the Meredith purchase and that they had agreed to clear one hundred acres. Other families had agreed to settle upon another piece of Breckinridge land nearby. The Colonel desired more information about Breckinridge's wishes before he drew up an instrument of agreement, but he suggested that the tenants should not be allowed to destroy timber outside of their improvements, that they should clear their acres in good form, get out the stumps, and leave fences in good repair and of good height. These suggestions were accepted, and by the following March Russell was able to report that the tenants had agreed in writing to the conditions specified. Russell was not completely satisfied with the caliber of the tenants, but there was little choice: the frontier afforded men opportunity to secure farms of their own. Enough were settled on one piece of land, however, to clear seventy to eighty acres, and the six tenants on the other tract would clear sixty acres.

The Breckinridges continued to receive glowing reports of the marvels of the land. Sam Meredith, Jr., the ever-optimistic husband of Betsy, told of corn which reached the amazing height of sixteen feet and reported the discovery of rich lead deposits just forty feet from their boundary line. He found no words adequate to describe the wonders of Kentucky. "To borrow Lewis Craig's phrase in comparing the Kingdom of Heaven he says it is a mere Kentucky of a place." Another friend who had been in Kentucky for nearly eight months sent back a report which must have delighted the heart of anyone interested in acquiring a large family in the shortest possible time: "female Animals of every sort are very prolifeck, its frequent for ewes to bear 3 Lambs at a time, and women and cows to have Twins at a time."

Besides having his land settled, Breckinridge also decided to send to Kentucky the bulk of his slaves, along with some other possessions, in advance of his own move. If they could be hired out upon their arrival, he would receive a welcome addition to his income at the time when his purse would be most strained by extraordinary expenses, and the trip for his immediate family would not be encumbered and slowed by his having to supervise and care for Negroes en route. Moreover, he was concerned about the future policy of Kentucky toward slavery, and he felt it advisable to get his slaves within the boundaries of the new state as soon as possible. Fortunately, George Thompson, another friend of Breckinridge's, was planning to go west in the spring of 1792 and would take the Negroes, while Sam Meredith and William Russell were already available to lend assistance in placing the slaves upon their arrival in Kentucky.

Preliminary arrangements were made by March 1792, and Breckinridge sent $20.25 to Thompson to cover the expenses of taking the twenty slaves with him. Thompson planned to leave for Kentucky by the end of the month if winter was broken, and he requested that those who were to make the journey be at his place with tent linen and a shotgun by the twenty-fifth or twenty-sixth. Snow lingered in the mountains, and the roads were quagmires at the time designated, so the party did not start its journey until April 3. The rest of that month was consumed in struggling through the mud to Red Stone, a small river port on the banks of the Monongahela some sixty miles south of Pittsburgh. It was a miserable trip, rain or snow slashing daily from the leaden skies, and high waters raging in every creek or river that had to be crossed. The cart which Breckinridge sent along to carry supplies had to be abandoned in the slush of the mountains.

Already depressed by their enforced departure and oppressed by the dismal conditions under which they traveled, the Negroes lost heart. Their fare of bacon, bread, and molasses failed to keep up their spirits, so Colonel Thompson had to resort to other means. When the slaves appeared about ready to quit, the Colonel came forward with his "good friend whiskey" and gave them a portion each waking hour. Thus stimulated, they completed the journey without trouble. Once the party arrived at Red Stone the worst of the trek was over. The trip down the Monongahela and the Ohio presented few problems, and on May 17 Colonel Thompson turned the slaves over to Colonel Russell in Kentucky. They were allowed to go on to Meredith's for a short visit with their Virginia friends and relatives.

Despite a severe drought which was cutting sharply into anticipated crop yields, the Breckinridge Negroes were all hired out at prices pleasing to their owner and in situations not unpleasing to themselves. Two prime hands were hired out until the first of December for £5.10.0 each, while each of the young women without children brought £3 for the same period. Women with children were placed for fifty shillings, and two youths were hired out for three shillings per month. All slaves were to be clothed by their employers, the garments for each man consisting of two strong shirts, a warm coat and breeches, and a good pair of shoes and stockings, all the articles being due at the end of their service, unless requested sooner by Colonel Russell. Breckinridge probably received at least £30 from the employment of his slaves in 1792, despite the lateness of the season when the transactions were made.

Other preparations for the move to Kentucky had to be made in addition to the purchase of a home site and the transportation of the slaves. One of the more important, from Breckinridge's viewpoint, was the collection of an adequate library for his future home. Books had been fairly hard to obtain in the back country of Virginia, and until the rawness of the frontier disappeared, they would be even scarcer west of the mountains. The major book purchase Breckinridge made consisted of a lot obtained from Donald and Burton of London, some 150 volumes, valued at £53.5.6. Their variety reveals a reader whose interests were not confined within the narrow limits of the legal profession. There was a strong emphasis upon history and biography; Rollin's *Ancient History*, Plutarch's *Lives*, Gibbon's *Roman Empire*, and Hume's *History of America* were all included. Treatises on government were also plentiful, the list being headed by Locke, *On Government*, Priestley, *On Government*, Burke's *Speeches*, a two-volume set of the *Letters of Junius*, and thirteen volumes of the *Debates in Parliament*. The lot also included ten volumes of Shakespeare, the *Works* of Swift, Milton's *Paradise Lost* and *Paradise Regained*, Johnson's *Lives of the Poets*, fifteen volumes of Rousseau's *Works*, and Adam Smith's *Wealth of Nations*. Several volumes which he ordered were out of print, but Breckinridge made additional attempts to secure them before he left Virginia, being especially careful to increase his law library.

New public responsibilities threatened for a time to delay Breckinridge still longer. On February 14, 1792, a miserable winter day, he wrote his good friend Archibald Stuart: "I run the Gauntlet in this District as a Candidate for Congress. You may judge of my anxiety in the business by referring to the date of this letter! This is the date of Election, & I snugly by a good fire at Home. . . . The People appearing willing to elect, I could have no objection to serve them one Winter in Congress. . . ." Breckinridge was elected, but before the close of 1792 he resigned the seat he had never occupied. An appointment as special state prosecutor in suits against delinquent tax collectors was also terminated before the spring of 1793 as he finally saw his way clear to leave Virginia.

Obstructions were thus overcome, one by one, until Breckinridge could at last write, "I am fixing fast for Kentucky; and shall be in perfect readiness by the time appointed. The opposition here is great; but I have reflected too long on the subject and am too firmly persuaded of its propriety to be shaken by any terrestrial mandate." Even his wife seemed somewhat more willing to move. She had not been elated over the opportunities open to them in Kentucky, but the presence there of her husband's mother and sister made the prospect of moving less distasteful than it had been before.

The Breckinridges started for Kentucky late in March 1793, carrying with them the few slaves who had not been sent out the preceding year. The overland journey through the Wilderness was rough and dangerous, so Breckinridge decided upon the Ohio River route, which promised to be speedier and more comfortable. After saying good-bys to a multitude of friends, they headed for Red Stone, or Brownsville, as it was sometimes called. This first leg of the journey, presumably made by horse and wagon, was more than 150 miles over rough, muddy roads, which did nothing to arouse Polly Breckinridge from the despondency caused by separation from family and friends. Her husband confided to a gentleman they met a day's journey from Red Stone that she had not smiled once since the start of the trip.

Red Stone's importance as a river port was hardly evident from its small size and crude facilities. Its population then numbered only a couple of hundred, yet it was the general embarkation point for the Monongahela River. Flatboats were turned out there on an almost assembly-line basis by the industrious Germans and Pennsylvania Dutch who constituted the bulk of the inhabitants. The vessels which

Breckinridge secured for the river portion of the journey were probably typical Kentucky flatboats, made of whipsawed oak and selling for about five shillings per ton, with forty tons being about average size. Usual dimensions ran to forty feet by twelve feet. From the pegged floor pieces, six-foot uprights provided means of attaching planks which enclosed the ends and sides. Many boats were covered over completely except for hatchways, while others were fitted only with a cabin at one end. Windows were sometimes cut and a chimney built to carry away the smoke from the cooking fire, but these were luxuries that could be omitted. Portholes were usually provided for oars, and a large sweep balanced on a pivot acted as rudder for the unwieldy craft.

When a sufficient number of flatboats were gathered to provide security against Indian attack, and cattle, horses, and household goods had been loaded, the little flotilla would shove off into the current and sweep downwards toward Pittsburgh and the Ohio. The river trip was faster and probably more comfortable than the slow overland route along wilderness trails, but water travel had perils of its own, the most serious being the constant danger of Indian raids. Boats offered rich stores of plunder, in goods as well as scalps, and warriors exercised their ingenuity and made skeptics of voyagers by a score of wiles designed to lure them from the comparative safety of mid-channel. A favorite trick was to force a white captive to plead for rescue from the bank until sympathetic but unwary travelers would veer inshore to destruction. Stories of such incidents were still common in 1793, although the frequency of actual attacks had perhaps diminished from a peak in the late 1780's. A group of six boats which preceded the Breckinridges by about three weeks had been fired upon by a large band of Indians, but the only damage was one horse killed. Other groups had not been so fortunate: time and again, bullet-pocked craft swung out of the current and into the bank at Limestone with dead and wounded lying on the decks and blood staining the planks.

Luck rode with the Breckinridges, however. They were comfortably fixed with the necessities for the trip, and since the party was strong they had little to fear. Hostile eyes may have watched from the northern shore as the cumbersome fleet drifted downstream, but the voyagers saw no Indians, and the keen-eyed guards searching endlessly for enemy signs found little to arouse apprehension. Day after day slipped away with the miles as the Ohio current carried them past Irwin's Island, Yellow Creek, Big Grave Creek, Devil's Hole, Twelve Pole Creek, the Little Sandy, and other landmarks. The older children may well have amused themselves by chanting a currently popular jingle:

> Where are you from? Redstone.
> What is your lading? Millstone.
> What's your captain's name? Whetstone.
> Where are you bound? Limestone.

On the eighth day aboard, near the end of April, eager eyes caught the first glimpse of greenness that marked Three Islands and the near proximity of Limestone where the craft were to be abandoned. A few hours later the Breckinridge boats were steered out of the Ohio current and turned into Limestone Creek, whose quiet waters made that hamlet the most important landing place in Kentucky short of Louisville. Only sixty-five miles from Lexington, Limestone had already become that city's main port. Polly Breckinridge could not have been overly impressed with the first real glimpse she had of the country that was to be her home. Limestone was crowded against the river and creek by a ring of steep hills which seemed on the verge of pushing the few dozen log cabins into the water. In rainy weather it became "a muddy hole of a place," and travelers found little inducement to stay there aside from the refreshments available at Kenny's Tavern. Prices were high, and the inhabitants took advantage of their position to wring every possible penny from those who passed through the port.

John Breckinridge, anxious to reach his new home, stopped in Limestone only long enough to make the arrangements necessary for the transshipment of his goods. Then he and his family climbed the hills back of the town and took the rough road which stretched toward Lexington. They rode much of the way between walls of cane twice the height of a man. A few years earlier, bands of warriors might have been hidden there, but in 1793 the way was safe and the journey uneventful. Three days after their boat tied up at Limestone, they rode into the yard at Samuel Meredith's. The way had been long, but at last John Breckinridge was a Kentuckian.

Four / Conflict and Change

9 / The American Revolution as a Colonial War for Independence

Thomas C. Barrow

In a stable democratic society without revolutionary traditions, the relationships between conflict and change are difficult to clarify. Some argue that consensus is the most obvious fact about the American social system. Others suggest that conflict is the hallmark of the American experience. The truth lies somewhere in between. Any analysis, however, will rest in part on the student's ideological commitments. Young radicals of the late 1960's argue, for example, that violence and direct action are the only ways to achieve meaningful social change in America.

The two following selections give some insight into the way previous generations viewed and dealt with conflict and change. They also probe some of the mechanisms of change.

Thomas C. Barrow cuts through obscuring myths and offers a comprehensive and exciting interpretation of the American Revolution. Revealing an understanding of the work done by sociologists and political scientists as well as a rich knowledge of comparative history, Barrow places the revolutionary struggle and the period to 1789 in a new context. If the Revolution is seen as a colonial war for independence, then many hitherto incongruous events assume a logical pattern. Frustrated by instability in all spheres of colonial life—an instability that flowed from their status as English colonies—Americans revolted to achieve stability by cutting ties with the mother country. Only in this way could the complete development of American institutions and society be achieved. Political and economic stability after 1781 were sought through political decentralization under the Articles of Confederation. This approach did not work, and in 1787 a new generation of Americans moved to create a more centralized form of government. By developing the comparative dimension, the American Revolution is more clearly understood in contrast to the French Revolution of 1789 or the colonial wars that followed World War II.

Barrow's notes provide an introduction to the literature on the subject. The suggestions below are on the larger topic of change.

William and Mary Quarterly, 3rd series, XXV (1968), 452–464.

111

For further reading: John Higham, "Beyond Consensus: The Historian As Moral Critic," *American Historical Review,* LXVII (1962), 609–625; Seymour Martin Lipset, "A Changing American Character?" in *Michael McGiffert (ed.), *The Character of Americans: A Book of Readings* (1964), 302–330; *Ralf Dahrendorf, *Class and Class Conflict in Industrial Society* (1959); Amitai and Eva Etzioni (eds.), *Social Change: Sources, Patterns and Consequences* (1964); Don Martindale, *Social Life and Cultural Change* (1962).

The current historiographical controversies over the American Revolution owe much to Carl Becker. From Becker's day to the present, historians have debated the question of the existence or non-existence of an "internal revolution" in American society. Some historians, following Becker's lead, search for traces of internal social or political turmoil. Others, disagreeing with Becker, stress the continuity of institutions and traditions during the Revolution. At issue is the basic question of just "how revolutionary was the American Revolution," and in the failure of historians to agree on an answer to that question lies the source of controversy. And so the great debate continues.[1]

[1] The major statements of the Becker-Beard approach are well known: Carl L. Becker, *The History of Political Parties in the Province of New York, 1760–1776* (Madison, 1909); Charles Beard, *An Economic Interpretation of the Constitution of the United States* (New York, 1913); J. Franklin Jameson, *The American Revolution Considered as a Social Movement* (Princeton, 1926). Arthur M. Schlesinger's interpretation is summarized in his article, "The American Revolution Reconsidered," *Political Science Quarterly,* XXXIV (1919), 61–78. Jameson's views are re-evaluated in Frederick B. Tolles, "The American Revolution Considered as a Social Movement: A Re-evaluation," *American Historical Review,* LX (1954–55), 1–12. The Becker-Beard approach is currently carried on most sophisticatedly in the work of Merrill Jensen, particularly in *The Articles of Confederation: An Interpretation of the Social-Constitutional History of the American Revolution, 1774–1781* (Madison, 1948). For an interesting later review of his earlier position by Jensen himself see his article, "Democracy and the American Revolution," *Huntington Library Quarterly,* XX (1956–57), 321–341. Elisha P. Douglass, *Rebels and Democrats: The Struggle for Equal Political Rights and Majority Rule During the American Revolution* (Chapel Hill, 1955), summarizes many of the points of controversy and offers his own arguments for an "abortive" internal revolution. On the other side is Clinton L. Rossiter, *Seedtime of the Republic: The Origin of the American Tradition of Political Liberty* (New York, 1953). See also the treatment of the Revolution in Daniel J. Boorstin, *The Genius of American Politics* (Chicago, 1953). But the single work which most directly challenges the Becker-Beard approach is Robert E. Brown, *Middle-Class Democracy and the Revolution in Massachusetts, 1691–1780* (Ithaca, 1955). A convenient summary of the "Brown thesis" is in his article, "Democracy in Colonial Massachusetts," *New England Quarterly,* XXV (1952), 291–313. Bernard Bailyn, "Political Experience and Enlightenment Ideas in Eighteenth-Century America," *Amer. Hist. Rev.,* LXVII (1962–63), 339–351, accepts the argument that there was no internal political or social "revolution" but suggests that the true revolution lay in the Americans' intellectual acceptance of the "revolutionary" implications of their previous experiences concerning government and society. Some recent publications indicate a renewed emphasis on the radical social and political aspects of the American Revolution. See, for example, Gordon S. Wood, "A Note on Mobs in the American Revolution," *William and Mary Quarterly,* 3d Ser., XXIII (1966), 635–642. Of interest, too, is Wood's effort to graft Bernard Bailyn's "intellectual" view of the Revolution onto the older socio-economic approach in "Rhetoric and Reality in the American Revolution," *ibid.,* 3–32. For another approach, see Jackson T. Main, "Government by the People: The American Revolution and the Democratization of the Legislatures," *ibid.,* 391–407; also Staughton Lynd, *Anti-Federalism in Dutchess County, New York* (Chicago, 1962).

Unfortunately, there is no adequate definition of a "revolution." The dictionary description of a revolution as a "total or radical change" certainly provides no effective guideline. Since history is the study of change in human society, locating a revolution according to that formula becomes a matter of appraising just how much change is involved in a given event, which inevitably comes down to a question of where one wants to place the emphasis. In any case, precise definitions are somewhat beside the point. When the word *revolution* is used today in connection with a political system, its meaning, if not its precise definition, is abundantly clear. The image called to mind is inescapably that of the French and Russian revolutions, which have provided us with our classic formulas for revolutionary re-structurings of society. A revolution in these terms represents the replacement of an archaic, repressive regime or regimes with something new, something more open, more flexible, more adaptable. In effect, in the interests of "progress," within the political system stability is replaced by in-stability until some new synthesis is achieved. Only then is stability restored, at which point the revolutionary drama is closed.

For generations now American historians have struggled to fit their "revolution" into this classic mold.[2] The difficulties they have encountered in doing so are reflected in the present historiographical impasse. It is a problem that might have been avoided had we remembered that the American people were, until 1776, colonials. By its very nature, a colonial society must be, in certain vital ways, unstable. Unable to exercise complete political control, subject to continual external intervention and negative interference, a colonial society cannot achieve effective "maturity"—that is, cannot create and control a political system that will be suited to the requirements of the interests indigenous to that society. A colonial society is an "incomplete" society, and consequently an inherently unstable society. This was as true of American society prior to 1776 as it is today of the colonial societies left in our world.[3] And, conse-quently, if instability is the given fact in American society at the beginning of the imperial crisis, it is hard to see how the classic pattern of "stability replaced by in-stability" can be imposed upon it. The answer, of course, is that it cannot, that in fact colonial wars for independence or "liberation" are generically different from revolutions of the French or Russian variety. And, after all, the American Revolution was just that—a colonial war of liberation. Given the widespread existence of such wars in today's world, it is odd that for so long a time we have overlooked the full implications of this fact.

[2] The classic statement of the process of "revolution" and its application is Crane Brinton, *The Anatomy of Revolution,* rev. ed. (New York, 1952). See also the formula as worked out in Alfred Meusel, "Revolution and Counter-Revolution," Edwin R. A. Seligman, ed., *Encyclopedia of the Social Sciences* (New York, 1934), XIII, 367–375. But the work that has been most influential in relating the American Revolution to the European revolutionary tradition is Robert R. Palmer, *The Age of the Democratic Revolution: A Political History of Europe and America, 1760–1800,* I (Princeton, 1959).

[3] An example of the relationship between colonial status and instability in colonial America is the Regulator movement in South Carolina. As Richard M. Brown points out in *The South Carolina Regulators* (Cambridge, Mass., 1963), the coastal inhabitants were willing to adjust themselves to the needs of the interior sections but were prevented from doing so by English policy decisions and intervention. The result was social and sectional cleavage and controversy. Another more general example, common to all colonies, is that of the currency problem. Any American attempts to solve the riddle of how to obtain and maintain an adequate currency were frustrated by English intervention, so that the problem remained as a continuous source of friction and instability.

Colonial wars for independence have an inner logic of their own. The first problem is to achieve self-determination. Once that is accomplished, it then becomes a matter of organization, about which, naturally, there always will be fundamental disagreement. What course this disagreement will take, and how bitter it will be, will be determined by the nature of the particular society. In former colonies which have emerged into nationhood in this century, the determining factor has largely been the heterogeneous nature of their societies; with little internal unity or coherence, these new nations generally have fallen back at first on authoritarian centralism. When this has proved incapable of solving the complex problems confronting the society, it has been replaced usually by some kind of collective leadership, often based on the only effective national organization in existence, the military.[4] It is at this point that many of the emergent nations of today find themselves.

Americans were more fortunate in their escape from colonialism. Thanks to the nature of the First British Empire, with its emphasis on commercial growth rather than on imperial efficiency, its loose organization, and the high degree of self-government allowed to the colonists, Americans had developed effective political units which commanded the allegiance of most inhabitants and served as adequate vehicles for the transition from colonial status to nationhood. Given a common English inheritance and a common struggle against British "tyranny," these states made the transition with a minimum of disagreement and dissension. In effect, by 1760 self-government in America, while still incomplete, had gone far. A tightening of English imperial authority after the last war with France brought about a reaction within the colonies toward complete self-determination, which was achieved finally through military success.

Yet, whatever the difference of the American experience from other colonial wars of liberation, certain elements were of necessity shared in common. Within any colonial society there exists an establishment, a group of men whose interests and situation tie them to the existing structure and whose orientation is towards the preservation of the colonial status. When the issue of independence or self-determination begins to be debated, these men are caught in powerful crosscurrents. As natives to the society, they identify to some degree with its problems. At the same time, as beneficiaries of their privileged position within the existing colonial structure, they are not enthusiastic for change. Such men fall back on arguments of moderation, particularly stressing the economic benefits of association with the dominant country and also emphasizing the immaturity of their own society. The gains associated with independence are outweighed for them by the prospects of social and political disorganization. So these men cast their lot with their colonial rulers. Such a man was Thomas Hutchinson. So, too, were many of his Tory associates.

And men like Hutchinson found much to disturb them within American society. Actually, not only was American colonial society subjected to the instability normally inherent in colonial status but there were certain peculiar circumstances which complicated matters further. The melting-pot aspects of American society, the diversity of ethnic, religious, and cultural backgrounds to be found within it, created problems of communication.[5] And, of equal importance, American colonial society was, after

---

[4] For example, such has been the course of Ghana during and after Nkrumah, of Algiers during and after Ben Bella, and of Indonesia during and after Sukarno.

[5] The best case study of the melting-pot aspect of colonial America is Dietmar Rothermund, *The Layman's Progress* (Philadelphia, 1961). Rothermund's reference to "indirection" as the key

all, an artificial creation. Unlike most other historic colonial episodes, the American case was not a matter of an indigenous native society being expropriated and exploited by outsiders. In such instances, the pre-existing patterns of such native societies provide a degree of internal continuity and stability. But the English colonies in North America had at their disposal no such pre-existence. They were created specifically and artificially to perform certain functions in relation to the mother country. Most particularly, from the very beginning their economy was geared to production for distant markets over which they had no control and little influence.

At the same time, while there were sizeable non-English elements within the colonial population which created special problems, nevertheless the majority of the colonists were of the same national origin as their "rulers." It was not an instance of a conquered native population forced to bow fatalistically before the superior skills and power of an alien culture. Rather, it was a case in large part of Englishmen being governed and exploited by Englishmen. The result was a high degree of friction between governed and governors—an insistence by the colonists on their rights as Englishmen—that gave a special flavor and complexity to colonial politics.

Thoughtful colonials were well aware of and influenced by these problems. Thomas Hutchinson and John Adams—Tory and Whig—disagreed not so much on the question of the eventual independence of the American colonies as on the question of timing. Hutchinson's toryism sprang in part from his conviction that American society was too immature, too unstable, to stand alone. External force and authority, it seemed to him, would be required for many years to maintain internal order and stability in America. Realistically, he understood that eventually independence was probable: "It is not likely that the American Colonies will remain part of the Dominions of Great Britain another Century." [6] But, Hutchinson added, until then, "as we cannot otherwise subsist I am consulting the best interest of my country when I propose measures for maintaining this subjection [to England]." [7] What particularly disturbed Hutchinson about the changes in English policy after 1760 was that they tended to increase the instability and disorder inherent within American society: "Sieur Montesquieu is right in supposing men good or bad according to the Climate where they live. In less than two centuries Englishmen by change of country are become more barbarous and fierce than the Savages who inhabited the country before they extirpated them, the Indians themselves." [8]

John Adams viewed American development in a different way. Contrasting the New World with the Old, he found the former far superior. The settlement of America had produced men who "knew that government was a plain, simple, intelligible thing, founded in nature and reason, and quite comprehensible by common sense. They detested all the base services and servile dependencies of the feudal system . . . and they thought all such slavish subordinations were equally incon-

---

to political success is particularly suggestive. *Ibid.*, 93, 134, 140. Interestingly, Rothermund views the Great Awakening as at least partially an effort to use religion to create a bridge, to form a common ground, between the various groups; when religion failed to accomplish this, logically the next development was the use of "patriotism," a "lay religion" acceptable on rational grounds, to fill the same need. *Ibid.*, 59, 62, 134.

[6] Thomas Hutchinson to John Healy Hutchinson, Feb. 14, 1772, Hutchinson Letterbooks (transcripts), XXVII, 296–300, Massachusetts Historical Society, Boston.

[7] Hutchinson to Richard Jackson, Apr. 21, 1766, *ibid.*, XXVI, 227–228.

[8] Hutchinson to [?], Dec. 30, 1773, *ibid.*, XXVII, 608.

sistent with the constitution of human nature and that religious liberty with which Jesus had made them free." [9] The problem was that this purity of mind and behavior was always threatened by contact with the corruption of the Old World. Specifically, subordination of Americans to a distant Parliament which knew little of their needs and desires was not only frustrating but dangerous to the American experiment: "A legislature that has so often discovered a want of information concerning us and our country; a legislature interested to lay burdens upon us; a legislature, two branches of which, I mean the lords and commons, neither love nor fear us! Every American of fortune and common sense, must look upon his property to be sunk downright one half of its value, the moment such an absolute subjection to parliament is established." [10] Independence was a logical capstone to such reasoning, although it took Adams some time to take that final step.

The differences between Hutchinson and Adams suggest that the divisions in American society between conservatives and radicals on the question of separation from Great Britain were related in part to a disagreement over the means to achieve coherence or stability within American society. For one side, continued tutelage under English authority was a necessity until such a time as maturity was achieved. For the other, it seemed that the major roadblock to maturity, to internal harmony and unity, was that self-same English authority. In effect, it was a disagreement on means, not ends. And disagreements similar to that between Hutchinson and Adams can be found within any society—whether in the eighteenth or twentieth century—which is in the process of tearing itself loose from its colonial ties.

It is possible, too, to suggest certain similarities between American intellectual development in these years and the experience of other colonial peoples. From his study of politics in eighteenth-century America, and particularly from his analysis of the pamphlet literature of the Revolutionary years, Bernard Bailyn has concluded that the "configuration of ideas and attitudes" which comprised the "Revolutionary ideology could be found intact—completely formed—as far back as the 1730's" and that these ideas had their origin in the "transmission from England to America of the literature of political opposition that furnished the substance of the ideology of the Revolution." [11] Colonial societies are both fascinated and yet antagonized by the culture of the dominant exploiting nation. They tend to borrow much from their rulers. The English background of a majority of the American colonists in their case made such borrowing a natural and easy process, particularly for those who, for one reason or another, identified themselves with British rule.

However, in colonial societies even many of those who are anxious to assert, or preserve, their native interests or culture cannot resist that fascination exerted by the dominant "mother country." These "patriots" borrow, too, but they are likely to borrow from the dissenting tradition within the dominant culture, from the literature of "opposition," to utilize in their own defense the language and literature of those elements within the ruling society which are critical, or subversive, of the governing traditions. In this way the prestige of the "superior" society can be used against that society itself. On the evidence of Bailyn's research, it seems that the Americans

[9] "A Dissertation on the Canon and Feudal Law" (1765), John Adams, *Works of John Adams,* ed. Charles F. Adams (Boston, 1850–56), III, 454.

[10] "Novanglus," *ibid.,* IV, 131.

[11] Bernard Bailyn, *The Ideological Origins of the American Revolution* (Cambridge, Mass., 1967), xi.

followed just such a line of development, fitting the "opposition" tradition into the framework of their own evolving institutions and traditions—a process which was facilitated by the natural connections between the American religious dissenting traditions and the "opposition" traditions of eighteenth-century English society.

Again, once the movement for independence enters its final phase within a colonial society and becomes an open contest of strength, other divisions tend to become obscured. The most determined supporters of the colonial rule are silenced or forced to rely increasingly on the military strength of their rulers to maintain their position. On the other side, the advocates of independence submerge momentarily whatever differences they may have and present a common front. It is a time of common effort, of mutual support within the forces interested in achieving self-determination. At the same time the "patriot" groups develop special organizations capable of coercing those elements within society, often a majority of the population, which are inclined towards neutrality or moderation. Such were the Sons of Liberty in the American Revolution, and the evidence suggests that they performed their work effectively. Partly because of their efforts, and more generally because of the peculiar character of American colonial society and the nature of the imperial conflict, American society weathered the crisis with relative stability and harmony. As John Adams put it, "The zeal and ardor of the people during the revolutionary war, supplying the place of government, commanded a degree of order, sufficient at least for the temporary preservation of society." [12]

With independence come altered circumstances for a former colonial society. Victorious patriots, confronted with the task of creating a permanent political structure, gradually begin to disagree among themselves as to how it can best be done. Since the only effective central direction came previously from the colonial rulers, the problem in each newly independent society is to fit the surviving local units into some coherent national structure. Here the forces of localism and centralism come into conflict. Those men or interests firmly entrenched in their positions at the local level see in increased centralism a threat to their existence and power. On the other hand, those men or interests of a more cosmopolitan nature, geared to extra-local activities and contacts, can see the benefits that would accrue to them through the introduction of the smoother flow of communications and transactions that effective centralization would bring. [13] The disagreement pits the particularism of the entrenched local interests and individuals against the nationalism of the cosmopolitan interests and individuals. In most contemporary emergent societies these latter groups are by far the weaker. Fortunately, in America the cosmopolitan groups were stronger and more effective, partly again because of the unusual origin and nature of American colonial society. From the beginning the English colonies had been geared to production for European markets; it was the reason for their existence. The result was

[12] Speech to Congress, Mar. 4, 1797, Adams, *Works,* ed. Adams, IX, 105. During the Revolution itself Adams had written that "there has been more of this tranquility and contentment, and fewer riots, insurrections, and seditions throughout the whole war, and in the periods of its greatest distress, than there was for seven years before the war broke out." Letter to Mr. Calkoen, Oct. 26, 1780, *ibid.,* VII, 305.

[13] The distinguishing characteristics of "cosmopolitan" and "local" elites as developed by Robert K. Merton, *Social Theory and Social Structure* (Glencoe, 1957), chap. 10, "Patterns of Influence: Local and Cosmopolitan Influentials," are useful. See also, Alvin W. Gouldner, "Cosmopolitans and Locals: Towards an Analysis of Latent Social Roles," *Administrative Science Quarterly,* II (1957–58), 281–306, 444–480.

the development of an economy which had geographical variations but a common external orientation. Merchants and large-scale producers of items for export dominated this society. In the period after independence was achieved, these men provided a firm base for the construction of an effective national political system. Their success came with the substitution of the Constitution of 1787 for the Articles of Confederation.

Historians following the Becker-Beard approach put a different interpretation on the period following the achievement of de facto independence. For them, it was the moment of the triumph of radical democratic elements within American society. The wording of the Declaration of Independence, the constitutions of the new state governments, and particularly the drawing up of the Articles of Confederation represent for these historians the influence of a form of "radicalism." Yet, as Elisha Douglass has noted, in the formation of the governments for the new states, rather puzzlingly the one political reorganization that was subjected to the most democratic method of discussion and adoption—that of Massachusetts—turned out to be not only the most conservative of all the state constitutions but more conservative, in fact, than the previous system.[14] Somehow in Massachusetts, at least, an excess of democracy seems to have led to an enthronement of conservatism. And, indeed, the new constitutions or systems adopted in all the states were remarkable generally for their adherence to known and familiar forms and institutions.

Obviously, given the disruption of the traditional ties to England, the interruption of the natural economic dependence on English markets, the division of American society into opposing Whig and Tory camps, and the presence on American soil of enemy troops (which occupied at different moments the most important commercial centers), some confusion and dissension was inevitable within American society. What is remarkable is how little upheaval and disagreement there actually was. Had American society been ripe for a social upheaval, had it been comprised of oppressing and oppressed classes, no better opportunity could have been offered. The conservative nature of the American response suggests that something other than a radical re-structuring of society was what was debated or desired.

Again, some historians have interpreted the decentralized political system created under the Articles of Confederation as a "triumph" of radical democracy. However, if instability, associated with colonial status and with the peculiar character of American colonial society, was a recurrent problem, and if inability to achieve positive control of their own political system was a major irritant, then the decentralization of the Articles was a logical development. In effect, if home rule was the issue and the cure, it was only natural that each local unit should seek as much autonomy within the national framework as possible. Seemingly, decentralization was the best method to bring coherence and stability, or maturity, to American society. Each local unit could look to its own needs, could arrange for the effective solution of its own special problems, could work to create that internal balance and harmony of conflicting interests that are the earmark of stability and maturity.

The problem with the Articles was not an excess of democracy. What brought

[14] "It is paradoxical that the first constitution formed by democratic processes should be one of the most undemocratic of its time. Although drafted by a convention elected by manhood suffrage, it was not only one of the most aristocratic of the Revolutionary period but also more thoroughly ensured government by the upper classes than the constitution of 1778 rejected by the same electorate." Douglass, *Rebels and Democrats*, 211.

about an effective opposition to them was their failure to achieve their purpose. The history of the states under the Articles, at least in the eyes of many contemporaries, suggested that decentralization, rather than being a source of stability, was a source of confusion and turmoil. James Madison explained the nature of the mistake in his Tenth Federalist. In spite of independence, under the system created by the Articles, wrote Madison, "complaints are everywhere heard from our most considerate and virtuous citizens . . . that our governments are too unstable." The problem, for Madison, was to control faction within society, and the most dangerous type of faction is that which includes a majority. Unfortunately, the "smaller the society, the fewer probably will be the distinct parties and interests composing it; the fewer the distinct parties and interests, the more frequently will a majority be found of the same party; and the smaller the number of individuals composing a majority, and the smaller the compass within which they are placed, the more easily will they concert and execute their plans of oppression." The solution is to enlarge the sphere, because if "you take in a greater variety of parties and interests," then "you make it less probable that a majority of the whole will have a common motive to invade the rights of other citizens. . . . The influence of factious leaders may kindle a flame within their particular States, but will be unable to spread a general conflagration through the other States." [15]

Nor was the opposition to the Constitution less concerned than Madison about order and stability within society. Again, disagreement was fundamentally over means, not ends. The anti-Federalists clung to the former ideas of local autonomy. They were, in fact, not more democratic than their opponents but more conservative. They were afraid of change: "If it were not for the stability and attachment which time and habit gives to forms of government, it would be in the power of the enlightened and aspiring few, if they should combine, at any time to destroy the best establishments, and even make the people the instruments of their own subjugation." The trouble was that the system created under the Articles was not yet sanctified by time: "The late revolution having effaced in a great measure all former habits, and the present institutions are so recent, that there exists not that great reluctance to innovation, so remarkable in old communities . . . it is the genius of the common law to resist innovation." [16] George Clinton agreed with Madison on the dangers of faction: "The people, when wearied with their distresses, will in the moment of frenzy, be guilty of the most imprudent and desperate measures. . . . I know the people are too apt to vibrate from one extreme to another. The effects of this disposition are what I wish to guard against." [17] It was on the solution to the problem, not on the nature of the problem, that Clinton differed from Madison. For Clinton, the powerful central government created by the Constitution might too easily become a vehicle for popular tyranny. It was this same sentiment which led eventually to the adoption of the first ten amendments, the Bill of Rights, with their reservations of basic rights and powers to local units and individuals.

[15] Jacob E. Cooke, ed., *The Federalist* (Middletown, Conn., 1961), 56–65. Madison considered the question of the appropriate size for political units further in Federalist 14, *ibid.,* 83–89.

[16] Quoted in Cecelia M. Kenyon, *The Antifederalists* (Indianapolis, 1966), xci–xcii. Miss Kenyon's introduction to this collection is an expansion of her provocative article, "Men of Little Faith: The Anti-Federalists on the Nature of Representative Government," *Wm. and Mary Qtly.,* 3d Ser., XII (1955), 2–43. See also Stanley Elkins and Eric McKitrick, "The Founding Fathers: Young Men of the Revolution," *Pol. Sci. Qtly.,* LXXVI (1961), 200–216.

[17] Quoted in Kenyon, *Antifederalists,* xcii.

It would not do to carry the comparison between the American Revolution and other colonial wars of liberation, particularly those of the twentieth century, too far. But there is enough evidence to suggest certain basic similarities between the American experience and that of other emergent colonial peoples—enough evidence, at least, to suggest that the efforts of historians to impose on the American Revolution the classic pattern of the French and Russian revolutions have led to a distorted view of our national beginnings. A French Revolution is the product of unbearable tensions within a society. The purpose of such a revolution is to destroy society as it exists, or at least to destroy its most objectionable aspects, and to replace the old with something new. In contrast, a colonial "revolution" or war of liberation has as its purpose the achievement of self-determination, the "completion" or fulfillment of an existing society, rather than its destruction. A French Revolution is first of all destructive; a colonial revolution, first of all constructive. In either case the process may not be completed. In the instance of the French Revolution, the re-constructed society may contain more of the old than the original revolutionaries desired. And in the case of the colonial revolution, the process of winning independence and the difficulties of organizing an effective national political structure may open the gates to change, may create a radicalism that carries the original society far from its former course; the result may be more destruction than was originally envisaged. Yet, the goals of these two revolutions are fundamentally different, and their different goals determine a different process of fulfillment. The unfolding of the revolutionary drama, the "stages" of revolution, will be quite different, if not opposite.

For John Adams, the American Revolution was an epochal event, a moment of wonder for the world to behold and consider. At times his rhetoric carried him beyond the confines of his innate caution, and he sounded like a typical revolutionary: "The progress of society will be accelerated by centuries by this revolution. . . . Light spreads from the dayspring in the west, and may it shine more and more until the perfect day." [18] But, as Edward Handler has noted, "The truth is that if Adams was a revolutionary, he was so in a sense very different than that produced by the other great modern revolutions." [19] Adams did indeed feel that his revolution had a meaning for the world but it was not related to the violent re-structurings of society. Rather its message, for Adams, was that free men can decide voluntarily to limit their freedom in the interests of mutual association, that rational men can devise a system that can at once create order and preserve liberty. The American success was in contrast to the traditional authoritarian systems of the Old World: "Can authority be more amiable or respectable, when it descends from accidents or institutions established in remote antiquity, than when it springs fresh from the hearts and judgments of an honest and enlightened people?" [20]

Most wars of liberation are not so orderly as that of the American Revolution. Most, at least in this century, have led to increasing radicalism and division within the liberated society. National unity has not been easily achieved. That the American

[18] Quoted in Edward Handler, *America and Europe in the Political Thought of John Adams* (Cambridge, Mass., 1964), 102.

[19] *Ibid.*, 101. Elsewhere Handler comments that "Adams' experience had nothing in common with the concept of revolution as a total renovation of existing institutions previously condemned as denials and perversions of the natural order" and that "nothing affords more certain indication that the Americans underwent a special kind of revolution than the peculiar breed of revolutionary typified by Adams who carried it through." *Ibid.*, 106–107.

[20] Speech to Congress, Mar. 4, 1797, Adams, *Works*, ed. Adams, IX, 107.

emergence from colonialism had a different ending is significant. A firm basis for unity obviously existed within American society, which, naturally, suggests that the reverse, too, was true—that such tensions and divisions as did exist within American society were relatively minor and harmless. It is no wonder that historians determined to find an internal social or political revolution of the French variety within the American Revolution have encountered such difficulties. Nor is it a wonder that the Revolution has become so beclouded with historiographical debates and arguments. The problem has been in our approach. We have been studying, it would seem, the wrong revolution.

10 / A Crusade to Extend Yankee Culture

Richard Lyle Power

This essay concerns cultural imperialism. The New England way, with its emphasis on orthodox piety, education, sound morals, and good government, was a commodity exported from western Massachusetts to California. Especially in the Middle West—from Ohio to Wisconsin and eastern Kansas—Yankees dug in and left an indelible imprint on the society that was formed there. To these "Yankee Crusaders," there was only one kind of American culture—that manufactured and distributed by New Englanders. The conflicts that resulted when these cultural missionaries met men and women from other parts of the nation are an important aspect of nineteenth-century social history.

For further reading: Richard Lyle Power, *Planting Corn Belt Culture: The Impress of the Upland Southerner and Yankee in the Old Northwest* (1953); Lois K. Mathews, *The Expansion of New England* (1909); R. Carlyle Buley, *The Old Northwest: Pioneer Period, 1815–1840* (2 vols., 1950); John J. Murray (ed.), *The Heritage of the Middle West* (1958).

Among the "clerical schemes and pompous undertakings of the present day under the pretense of religion" which *The Reformer,* a small, tightly-printed Philadelphia periodical of the early 1820's, aimed to expose and "show that they were irreconcilable with the spirit and principle of the Gospel" was a "plot" allegedly being fostered by certain New England religionists, notably the Reverend Lyman Beecher, to fashion the culture of the rising American nation entirely after the Yankee image.

The ire of *The Reformer*'s editors had been aroused by a passage in one of Beecher's tracts which in its cultural implications at large appeared to transcend ordinary and justifiable doctrinal controversy:

> The integrity of the Union demands special exertions to produce in the nation a more homogeneous character, and bind us together by firmer bonds. . . . A remedy must be applied to this vital defect of our national organization. But what shall that remedy be? There can be but one. The consolidation of the State Governments would make a despotism. But the prevalence of pious, intel-

New England Quarterly, XIII (1940), 638–653. Footnotes have been omitted.

ligent, enterprising ministers through the nation, at the ratio of one for 1000, would establish schools, and academies, and colleges, and habits, and institutions of homogeneous influence. These would produce a sameness of views, and feelings, and interests, which would lay the foundation of our empire upon a rock.

To Beecher's term "homogeneous influence" the editors of *The Reformer* rejoined:

These ministers to produce this *homogeneous influence* must, of course, be all of one religious persuasion . . . his own. . . . From such a *homogeneous influence* as *they* might effect, it becomes us to pray from the bottom of our hearts *"good Lord deliver us."* The fate to which it might doom us, we fear, would not be much better than that of Old Spain some time since. Four pious persons, we remember, were once hung at Boston by reason of such *homogeneous influence.*

To argue a large intrinsic importance for this particular bit of controversy is not intended. Worthy of remark, however, is the point that Beecher had with precision designated something which appeared to him to be a weakness in the national cultural structure, and with similar precision had prescribed a remedy in terms of a nation-wide program. Equally interesting is the fact that the editors of *The Reformer* recognized with alarm the far-reaching implications of the suggestion and lavished their wrath upon it. Leaving aside any personal and doctrinal animosities involved, one may profitably call attention to the implications for the development of a national culture, in the words, deeds, and hopes of those fervent Yankee souls who believed with Beecher that theirs was the only culture the rising nation could safely embrace; and to suggest certain other phases of cultural adjustment which derive their character and interest from the vigor of the Yankee thrust.

Whatever reticence Yankees may have felt about discussing the "plan," especially after it had been publicly discussed and challenged, it is still possible to trace with certainty its persistence, through occasional frank pronouncements of those who had the cause in their hearts. Even if evidence for the intervening period were lacking, the flow of uninhibited statements released by the War between the States would demonstrate that the idea of a cultural assimilation of the West by the Yankees—"a thirty years war," one writer called it—had never been suffered to lapse.

Among the principal motivations of this cultural imperialism one discovers impulses of an evangelical, economic, and political sort; also a persistent consciousness of the need of preventing New England's achievements from being submerged and lost in the disordered process which was giving birth to national institutions and culture—lest, as many must have felt, the "refluent wave" of frontier ignorance, skepticism, and sin rise higher and higher, until "it rolls over the beautiful monuments of Puritan intelligence and piety." Sometimes one, sometimes another motive or combination of motives appeared to be uppermost in the minds of those who urged or applauded the progress of the crusade.

Nor should one forget that perhaps no other age in man's experience ever entertained grander visions of the rewards of efforts directed at self-betterment. A zealot could write:

Who knows but the millennium sun is just behind the mountains, restraining its impatient course, and drawing in its effulgent rays, until honored and exalted man is fully prepared to bear the brighter glory which is now ready to burst upon his astonished vision.

Under the conviction that America was rushing to a mighty destiny, and that her phenomenal—"almost terribly sublime"—increase in population was God's way of bestowing duty and opportunity, reformers of many sorts believed that the American nation and even the world were so much plastic material to be correctly molded by strong, sanctified hands. "We purify California in the streets of Canton, and the year Nineteen Hundred in the year Eighteen Hundred and Fifty-five," wrote an enthusiast, revealing the scope of his thoughts in time and in earthly space.

Examination of economic arguments in favor of directing the growth of the national *mores* in accordance with a Yankee pattern seems to demonstrate that this line of reasoning was of no slight aggregate importance in maintaining the movement. Such economic arguments represented in general only an elaboration of the familiar principle that Lyman Beecher, for example, had expounded about 1820 in a sermon urging alms-giving in behalf of the poor of New Haven: educate the poor and stop the contagion of vice, else they will "pilfer from you ten times the amount you would need to give to render them useful and happy. . . . Give, then, if thou hast no bowels of compassion, upon principles of covetousness. In self-defense, give a pittance to promote industry and virtue."

Although articles on such a theme as "a stated ministry essential to American prosperity" were not uncommon, not all writers went so directly to the heart of the matter as did the author of a piece entitled "A Thought for Business Men," which appealed to the "city dealer" who frequently had "a large amount of his fortune in the hands of country customers." Since the laws, he pointed out, were altogether inadequate to protect creditors, it was only religious restraints that kept their losses from being much greater than they were. This condition was, moreover, "particularly true in relation to the new states." "Business men, therefore, *owe it to their own interests to aid this enterprise*," since "the very wealth . . . which adorns our cities, and gives the means of influence to its possessors, they owe, in some measure, to the operation of Christian principles diffused through the community by Christian teachers."

A variant argument besought the "opulent merchant" to "give nobly," insisting that it was "Far better . . . to give his money, not to say his prayers, to make the *people good*, where he entrusts millions of property, than to spend it upon bailiffs, to apprehend his runaway creditors, or to collect his debts among a dissolute people, without either responsibility or principle." The Reverend H. B. Hooker, in 1864, acknowledged the solicitude of Massachusetts for her heavy financial commitments in the West as well as for her sons and daughters who had gone thither. Fifty million dollars had gone, mostly from Massachusetts, into western railroads, he said; fifty millions into western lands, manufacturers, and loans; and another twenty-five millions into mining. His conclusion was that men shrewd enough to make money were shrewd enough to see that they had better create a good moral atmosphere in the communities where they had made investments. "They know that bonds and stocks and mortgages are all the more valuable for being within the sound of the *church-going bell.*" But it is at once evident that Mr. Hooker was only ringing the changes on an old theme. In fact, nothing essential remained to be said on the topic after the Reverend G. Crawford had written from Wisconsin Territory, in 1839: "*The Gospel is the most economical police on earth.*"

Turning now to the spread of the New England way of life, one must await the emotionally supercharged years of the Civil War to hear the diffusion of Yankee culture, faithfully propagated by generations of colonists, teachers, ministers, and enterprisers, most extravagantly praised as a national benefit, especially in its political phase. While there were of necessity differing versions as to how the process had actually operated, one conclusion was held in common by those who expressed opinions: Eastern patriotism and piety had enabled the Union to endure. *"All within that belt is loyal,"* declared the Reverend W. W. Patton, in alluding to the area of missions activity; "All south of it is either openly treasonable, or largely in sympathy with the rebellion." Yet the most pleasing aspect of the Yankee triumph was doubtless the belief that New England's pattern of life had been extended into a "greater New England," a cultural expansion which in addition to giving Western communities shade-trees, colleges, good morals, and temperance had "poured a stream of Puritan theology across the West." New England, in a favorite way of saying it, had at last made good the great sea-to-sea patent of 1620; and the process had harmonized discordant elements, "given character" to States such as Iowa and Kansas, and even bound to the Union "by a telegraphic and moral sympathy" the "chaotic mass" of California's population. Perhaps the Chilean cleric, Melchior Martínez, was correct when years before he referred to the United States as "the Boston republic!"

But it was Henry Ward Beecher who most magnificently proclaimed the political lessons which Yankee Northerners imputed to their own cultural dominance. "It is the Gospel that has saved the West and Northwest to this nation," thundered Beecher the summer of the battle of Gettysburg; he was himself a witness, he declared, that it was Eastern missionaries "who had carried with them Puritan ideas of human rights to the West." It was a fearful duty that God was laying upon the victorious North, he confessed, as he proceeded with words which forecast the psychology of radical reconstruction. That the war was impoverishing the South at the same time the North was engrossing wealth was God's way of preparing the North for the work before it.

> We are to have charge of this continent. The South has been proved, and has been found wanting. She is not worthy to bear rule. She has lost the scepter in the States themselves; and this continent is to be from this time forth governed by Northern men, with Northern ideas, and with a Northern gospel.

> "Is this sectional?" No, because Christ was not born all over the world. "There must be a nest somewhere from out of which the bird, the eagle, can fly."

> We hold the vitalizing principles of national life; and the nation is to be given to us because we have the bosom by which to nourish it. As a child feeds at the breast of its mother, so the nation is to feed upon us . . . . Our diocese will be little less than the whole continent.

That the analysis of certain observers penetrated to a much deeper level than that of alleged political benefits is demonstrated by the reasoning of the Reverend George F. Magoun of Iowa. "When Washington feared Western parties he did not foresee Home Missions," he declared, conventionally enough. But certain of his other observations reveal a conception of social process that would do credit to a theorist of the present century. "Your pioneer evangelism carries nationality along every parallel of latitude," he assured the public. That there were "century-long processes of society and history" which would eventually bind divisive elements into nationality he did not doubt. "But we cannot wait for these. Under the ministry of your missionaries, the thing is often done suddenly, as it were in the twinkling of an eye." Therefore, his reasoning proceeded, "Let missions, like freedom, follow the flag everywhere. The cannon of Fremont and Halleck will set before them many an open door. So, but gently and silently, will the Homestead Bill, the Pacific Railroad . . . set before them many more."

Concerning the exact nature of the "acculturative" process which they believed to have worked so miraculously, one is fortunately not left to mere conjecture. The Reverend H. D. Kitchel, of Detroit, described the "New England zone" as representing "Puritanized Saxon Blood, as pure as that which flows in the veins of Boston," and, taken in its direct and indirect contributions, "by far the most operative and influential, wherever it goes."

> It is the plastic and organizing force. It is not number, but weight, that tells in the formative process of a colonial state. A single family of genuine Puritan substance . . . is a germ, around which a whole flood of miscellaneous population will take form, and serve as nutriment. More than by its numbers, the innate validity of this element molds the rising communities of the West, and unconsciously fashions all after the ideas with which it comes charged.

Even non-Christian New England families were influential; they knew what a school, a church, a town meeting was, "and the subtle presence has a mastery. . . . It works dimly for a time, amid the colonial chaos; but presently, as the social web turns right side up, the figure appears—it's the New England pattern."

One would expect the individual worker who was closely attached to a great organization to entertain a high sense of the seriousness of his work, as did the one who wrote from Illinois:

> When I look upon the vast and beautiful prairie surrounding our town, and think that in a few years it will be covered with cultivated fields, and inhabited by thousands, I feel a most intense desire that the right kind of moral institutions should grow up with the increasing population.

But it is a little surprising to find that individual teachers from New England, presumably not attached to an organization, entertained a similar feeling as to the high import of their work. Writing from the village of Ontario, Lagrange County, Indiana, a teacher who signed himself "H. V. W." told how several Yankee teachers from various towns in Massachusetts had by chance settled near that Indiana village. Teaching he considered a promising and significant calling, especially since ". . . you cannot serve your country better than by assisting to lay well (after New England style) the foundations of the institutions of learning that are springing up throughout this western land."

Although the preponderance of materials cited thus far are religious or educational in their bearing, it would doubtless be possible to match them with similar views expressed by men of the world. In a secular idiom, but to the same relentless effect, was the letter of an unnamed layman written from the "Valley of San Joaquin, California Alta," dated October 2, 1848. Recovering from a pang of misgiving at the breathtaking growth of his country, he proceeded:

> Yet, why should I regret? Louisiana, Florida, Texas, were once, and but a few years since, the territories of France and Spain. Ultra foreigners in language, birth, race, habits, manners, and religion! but now naturalized, fraternized —incorporated with that all-pervading solvent and amalgam, the universal Yankee nation. . . . Thus push we the bark of enterprise, adventure, conquest and

commerce along, till we are fairly installed on the mountain heights that overlook the broad Pacific. Here am I, a confirmed emigrant, one of the foremost of that pioneer, pilgrim band, that starting from the north Atlantic shore, pursue the setting sun in his course. . . . This looks to me as the destiny of the Saxon, or Anglo-American race. If they fail to carry it out, it will be from their losing a part of that roving, restless (and if it were not for the alliteration, I would say) resistlessly-reforming principle, that has hitherto impelled them to come in contact with everything, and renovate everything they touched. So operative will be these national characteristics, that California will soon be California no longer. The hordes of emigrants and adventurers, now or soon to be on their way here, will speedily convert this wild, cattle-breeding, lasso-throwing, idle, bigoted, bull-baiting race, into an industrious, shrewd, trafficking, Protestant set of thorough-going Yankees.

Less willing to await the delayed fruits of preaching, teaching, and commerce were certain other Eastern workers in the West whose method might cause them to be classed as community "re-builders." While there must have been Yankees by the hundreds in the West who longed for a regeneration of their communities by the migration thither of congenial and desirable people, certain impatient workers went the length of suggesting in their correspondence the specific callings and financial ratings of those who might be induced to migrate from the East. Thus Samuel Merriwether, of Jeffersonville, Indiana, wrote on July 31, 1833, to Absalom Peters in New York City, suggesting that a cabinet maker, "a young Brother in the Lord," might migrate to that town and take over the Sunday School.

More importunate and detailed was the appeal of the Reverend Moses H. Wilder, writing from China, in southern Indiana:

> We want 3 intelligent Pious Farmers who love souls to emigrate and settle among us. One could buy a farm now owned by a Baptist Universalist drin[king?] Preacher who is a deadly enemy to everything like improvement price say 500$ Another could in another neighborhood purchase a farm now owned by a *campbelite* and when he moves away their strength is gone in the neighborhood— 660$
>
> A third could purchase a valuable farm now owned by the Elder which we have just dismissed to go to *Mr. R's* ch[urch] in Madison and with him Mr. R[ussell] would leave the neighborhood for he would have no one to hold up his hands—price 800$. In each of these places such a man would be able to sustain a Sabbath School . . . and . . . would soon relieve your Society from further aid to us. Can you not send us these men?

To every action there is a reaction. A profitable type of research would be a study of the specific and earthy character of the opposition encountered in the West by the Yankee colonists, ministers, editors, teachers, tradesmen, and enterprisers, and their ideas and ways. For this phase of development was in essence a magnificent struggle or adjustment of cultures. It is unfortunate that much of the story of the actual opposition to Yankees in the West has the unsubstantial quality of folklore. Had their Western opponents been of a more literary tradition, the present age would undoubtedly have a better picture of the Yankee plan in action. Even when written evidence of the contest fortunately exists one often suspects that it represents "good" reasons rather than "real" reasons for opposing the Easterners.

Thus, to accept at face value certain resolutions passed by the Indianapolis Pres-

bytery would lead to the erroneous belief that Eastern ministers were finding themselves in difficulties merely because they had failed to join a presbytery before taking
up ministerial duties in the West. But study of private correspondence of the time
causes the matter to take on a different face, as when the Reverend Eliphalet Kent
wrote from Shelbyville, Indiana, "It is a trying time for ministers from the east." A
few months later, May 1, 1833, he was again explaining to the New York headquarters the general impression that a few of the brethren of the Presbytery were
resolved on the removal of every American Home Missionary Society man from the
presbytery—"Is it best for me to remain on the ground?" Six months later still, he
reported his resignation, on account of this opposition, from the Shelbyville church.

Similarly harassed was the Reverend Moody Chase of Orleans, in southern Indiana.
In his early reports he had criticized his Indiana friends in a "pretty severe" manner,
he acknowledged to headquarters, July, 1833; but he still insisted, "They are afraid
of the reports of a Presbyterian preacher; especially if he be an *Eastern* man." Thirteen months later the unhappy Chase, who reckoned Quakers along with infidels and
Methodists as standing in his way, was acknowledging partial failure. At Paoli he
wrote, "I could not keep a S. School in operation. And some of our people had
heard that I was a new-school-man and under the H. M. S. away off to the East
there. And it seemed to me that it was not best to fish where there were so few fish
and they among so many rocks."

In the same state, in his posts at Connersville, Liberty, and Brownstown, the Reverend John Morrill was also having his difficulties. Chief among the partisans who
stirred up the trouble, he thought, were those "who learned that [he] was from
N. E., & acting on the principle that 'no good can come from thence,' with much
apparent kindness warned the good people of this place of their danger." His letter
written three months later from Laporte, where he had re-established himself, expressed the hope that in northern Indiana he would not find the same difficulties:
"They seem to be more acquainted with N. E. people, & consequently not so afraid of
them."

More interesting than any of the foregoing is the case of the Reverend J. R.
Wheelock, an Eastern minister who in 1831 settled at Greensburg, in southeastern
Indiana, where, he noted, "As many as two thirds of the inhabitants of this country
are from Kentucky." He had taken up his work enthusiastically and was "treated,
without a single exception, with much kindness and hospitality." In the same early
report he mentioned the organizing of a lyceum and the presence of certain exemplary
Christians in his congregation as well as "many men of intelligence" in the region.
All told, Pastor Wheelock's first estimate of Greensburg was decidedly a favorable
one, with the exception of the quality of the public instruction of youth, of which
he wrote:

> . . . as it respects the qualifications of teachers, and character of school books
> and mode of instruction they are far in the rear. In relation to this subject much
> is to be done. I have, today, given one of our merchants a list of the most approved
> N. E. school books which he has promised to obtain in Philadelphia. My wife
> has thought there is no way in which she could do so much good as she might
> by opening a School of 20 or 30 scholars and introducing those books. This she
> expects to do soon.

Three months later he described Mrs. Wheelock's school as consisting of forty or
fifty scholars; also he mentioned classes of "20 in Olney's Geography" and "3 in

Comstock's Nat. Philosophy." "She makes defining a distinct branch of study and this gives her a very favorable opp^y of correcting the children & thro' them, the parents of '*a heap*' of Kentuckyisms."

It would be extremely interesting to know how it came about that fifteen months later, everything was in a tangle for the Wheelocks. Perhaps he now regretted having written in an early letter, "Common sense teaches even us Kentuckians that '*a living dog is better than a dead lion.*'" Unremitted effort on the part of certain old-school church members to inflame feeling against "N. E. men & 'N. E. divinity'" had been too successful, Wheelock admitted, as he railed against "this ignorant self righteous Kentucky presbyterianism. . . ." He had not been "a man of war," he insisted; he had merely preached as he had in New England. There is no reason to doubt Wheelock's sincerity in believing that his "New England divinity" had caused the trouble. One suspects, however, that too many children had become aware of being corrected, "& thro' them, the parents of '*a heap*' of Kentuckyisms."

The foregoing evidence suggests that a precise appraisal of the motives, means, and practical success of this great Yankee crusade is highly desirable, as a prologue to the study of cultural development in the Old Northwest and other regions, as well as for the information it would afford concerning pioneering phenomena in general. Much remains to be learned about the various forces which played upon specific communities: for instance, the degree to which easy achievement of cultural dominance meant favorable publicity in the East for such communities; the effect upon the colonizing process of ties of consanguinity; and the degree to which Yankees tended to migrate to communities where Yankees were already numerous. Delay or failure of Yankees to dominate the culture of regions such as "Egypt" in southern Illinois, most of Indiana, and northwestern Ohio should also be studied. It may be suggested that, from a combination of causes, the Yankees found it hard going, and the result was, in part, a sort of publicity that shadowed the repute of these regions. The possible bearing of the cultural crusade upon the coming of the Civil War and the character of Reconstruction policy have been pointed out.

Interesting too is the division of sentiment which prevailed in New England on the matter of emigration. Early in the nineteenth century, spokesmen were pleading earnestly that the bleeding of the region by migration be stanched. "For more reasons than I have time to assign," insisted one advocate, "New England is the place in which to live and to die." Yet others urged migration *en masse* in order to make certain the "New Englandizing" of Western communities. Whether or not mass migrations were ever prevalent enough to please the most zealous, anxiety was felt lest the region pay too heavily for its role of "*seminarium heroum.*" But even if the worst were true, sectional decline could have its glories. Said one periodical in summarizing this chronically disturbing topic:

> New England has declined only because she has been translated. We go back and look in the old nest and find nothing there but shells; on the trees, all through the forests, are the winged ones that rose from the house of straw to fill the whole land with beauty and music. New England has declined—into America. Plymouth Rock is only the doorstep of a house that reaches to the Golden Gate.

Deliberate, calculating, even scientific, the engineers of this cultural movement were perfectly aware of the implications of their words and acts. Often their language attained a poetic level as they spoke of their task as they conceived it—the task of fashioning diverse materials, "like those of the image which was of gold, silver, brass, iron, and clay," into the symmetry of one body. One wonders whether any other essay in the propagation of a culture was ever undertaken on a similar scale with a fuller consciousness of the ends to be achieved and the agencies employed, or in a spirit of more militant sincerity.

11 / Epilogue from "The Liberator"

John L. Thomas

The antislavery movement of the nineteenth century stands as a high-water mark in the history of American reform. A conflict developed at that time that helped precipitate the Civil War. These reformers were at least indirectly responsible for changing the entire basis of Southern life by ending the institution of slavery. John L. Thomas sums up the motives that impelled antislavery men and examines the tensions between radical social movements and the fundamental stability of the democratic system. Whether in the 1840's or 1960's, these tensions and contradictions are of vital interest and importance to citizens of the Republic.

For further reading: *Alice Felt Tyler, *Freedom's Ferment: Phases of American Social History from the Colonial Period to the Outbreak of the Civil War* (1962); *Martin Duberman (ed.), *The Antislavery Vanguard: New Essays on the Abolitionists* (1965); *Stanley M. Elkins, *Slavery: A Problem in Institutional and Intellectual Life* (1963); C. S. Griffin, *Their Brother's Keepers: Moral Stewardship in the United States, 1800–1865* (1960).

When Garrison died in 1879, Reconstruction had already ended with Northern assent to the subordination of the Southern Negro. Slavery was dead, but racial inequality and the belief in the inferiority of the black man lived on. The Civil War had proved a limited victory that preserved the Union but intensified race conflict, freed the slaves but returned them to the management of their former masters. Beset by the new doubts of a Darwinian age, the postwar generation began to reassess the idea of human perfectibility and the message of liberation it had taught. Gradually the simple, buoyant faith in the perfectibility of man was giving way to a more sophisticated theory of evolution. Yet it was this belief in natural moral goodness—perfectionism—which had formed the credo of ante-bellum America, provided the driving force of the anti-slavery movement, and sustained the pitch of Garrison's reform. It had also caused a war.

All Americans before the Civil War shared in the perfectionist dream in some way, for perfectionism promised the country a perpetually renewable innocence and vigor. Perfectionism meant freedom—freedom from sin and guilt, freedom from the past and the burdens of history, freedom from institutions and power. What had Europe with its decadence and corruption to teach a young America? Left alone to flourish, the New World would produce a new race of men strong in their natural goodness and their commitment to total freedom. Perfectionism verified the American belief in the second chance.

The signs of this perfectionist faith were everywhere in ante-bellum America: in the physical fact of the frontier; in the Jacksonian bias against institutions and corporate power; in the pervasive sense of the civilizing mission of Americans; in the concept of nature as a regenerative experience; in the legends and folklore of the people. There were two principal sources of American perfectionism: the Enlightenment tradition of the American Revolution and the pietism of evangelical religion, the first a secular belief in progress transplanted from Europe, the second a millennial expectation at the heart of American revivalism. Combined, these two powerful ideals of infinite progress and the equality of souls made an explosive compound of moral idealism. It was this idealism which the abolitionists discovered they shared with the people and which gave their argument its peculiarly effective appeal.

The anti-slavery movement itself sprang from a religious impulse and advanced with the Second Great Awakening; that is, it originated in a religious revival and remained primarily a religious crusade. Since it was chiefly Christian in its emphasis, it was subject to the two great polar forces in Christian thought—the pull of pietism and the stress of social ethics. Pietism emphasizes the devotional ideal of religion, the desire for salvation and the achievement of holiness. Christian ethics, on the contrary, postulates a community and the good life to be lived within it. Pietism tends to be sectarian, mystical, perfectionist. It concentrates on the regenerative relation between God and the individual, on the inner experience of divine power. Thus it tends to be anti-institutional and ascetic. By stressing the role of the individual conscience and making obedience to it the highest form of duty, it gives the true believer a new freedom from the rules and regulations of the world; but in stressing the idea of purity it is apt to be rigoristic and exclusive. The idea of a social ethic is in many ways its exact opposite—adaptable, humanistic, inclusive, an ideal of Christian life that takes account of organization and power.

Both of these forces were at work within the anti-slavery movement from the beginning. The abolitionists knew very little about the institution of slavery. They approached the problem from the direction of regenerative experience through the avenue of conversion. Their strong Protestant individualism led them to treat slavery not simply as an inefficient labor system but as a betrayal of Christian values. They believed that slavery was inhuman because it denied God to the black man. They viewed slavery as a moral problem. It was not long, however, before some of them discovered the institutional complexities of the slavery problem. There were those like Garrison and his followers who persistently ignored these questions, but there were also those abolitionists like Birney, Stanton, and Leavitt who recognized the need for organization and policy. As the anti-slavery enterprise grew it was exposed to the same tension between piety and ethics as its parent Christianity.

The original American Anti-Slavery Society was both a sect and a church, a closed society of faithful saints and a wider community embracing all the people. Garrison's

Declaration of Sentiments exemplified the underlying ambiguity of the anti-slavery program: it promised political action but enjoined moral reform; it demanded immediate emancipation but failed to define it; it preached pacifism but appealed to passion. Within a decade these twin forces had produced divergent strains of anti-slavery, one based on political action, the other on moral preaching. Both groups of abolitionists claimed that their program was the only true one, and each accused the other of abandoning the slave. Both were wrong. In reality, each group embodied an aspect of the abolitionist temperament and the religious mind, and each in its own way illustrated the problems of religious idealism and defined the limits of Christian reform.

Both of these Christian strains found expression in William Lloyd Garrison. He wanted to abolish slavery and make a better world, but even more he wanted to avoid contamination by keeping his own hands clean. In the face of mounting evidence to the contrary he clung to the illusion that anti-slavery and pacifism were not merely compatible but complementary. Most of the abolitionists had indulged in this hope in the beginning, but it did not take long to undeceive them. Garrison, however, refused to give up the fiction of peaceful revolution. Until the actual outbreak of war he declined to admit that a situation might arise which would require him to choose between peace and freedom for the slave. The Civil War may not have been inevitable, but after the Compromise of 1850 a peaceful solution to slavery grew less likely each day. It was just this fact that his critics tried to tell him —that the pressure of events operating independently of the will of the majority of Americans was dividing the country and making his prophecy of disunion come true. Garrison failed to understand the very forces he had let loose. For thirty years he cried havoc, and when it came, he refused to credit it and contented himself with his prophet's role, rousing the emotion of Northerners and Southerners yet disavowing their actions, creating an atmosphere of unreason and ignoring the consequences. In his uncompromising stand against both slavery and politics he personifies the great strength and the equally great weakness of radical reform.

The radical reformer in American politics has been something of a split personality, a nonconformist with authoritarian leanings who presents the community with a dilemma by recalling it to its ideals and rejecting its arguments for order and stability. In the strength of his nonconformity Garrison contributed significantly to an American tradition concerned with the integrity of minorities and the protection of civil liberties. His anti-slavery career illustrates the importance of minorities in a free society, the need to withstand the pressure for conformity exerted by society and the willingness to be beaten rather than give hostages to majority opinion. Garrison believed that in the long run respect for law mattered less than concern for right. He considered politics dirty business and looked on the man of average goodness as an enemy in disguise. With his convictions of racial equality, his iron determination in the face of overwhelming opposition, and his insistence on the right to hold and preach unpopular opinions he has a strong claim on the American liberal tradition.

Nonconformity, however, is only one aspect of the radical temperament, and it was only a part of Garrison's mind. The other was distinctly authoritarian. Impulsive yet distrustful, seeking support but rejecting it when given, aggressive and undisciplined, demanding obedience but unable to accept it, he lacked the knowledge of men and the world that makes for leadership. His organization suffered grievously from his failings. When he did not try to do everything himself, he grudgingly delegated a task to a follower and then treated him as a threat to his ascendancy. His societies remained small because he refused to share power and tolerate possible rivals. Because he also lacked any administrative sense he convinced himself that it was unnecessary. His meetings and conventions were like religious revivals, spontaneous and disorganized, and the *Liberator* especially suffered from his lack of method. The man who demanded order and authority in the new world he was making could not find it in his own life. His view of the world as a vast arena for the struggle between God and the devil, his tenacious anti-intellectualism, and above all, his vision of a perfect and self-regulating society of saints disclosed the longings of an authoritarian mind concerned with getting and using power over others.

Inevitably the contradiction in Garrison's personality colored the cause to which he gave himself. Orestes Brownson, a tireless joiner of causes in his own right but also a shrewd observer, identified this contradiction when he noted that Garrison and the anti-slavery men had no just claim to the American civil rights tradition. "Moreover," he added, "the abolitionists do not, properly speaking, discuss the subject of slavery. Nay, it is not their object to discuss it. Their object is not to enlighten the community on the subject, but to agitate it. . . . *When men have made up their minds,* when the epoch for deliberation has gone by, and that for action has come, when their object is less to convince than it is to rouse, to quicken, to inflame; then proceedings like those of the abolitionists are very appropriate."

The abolitionists *had* made up their minds; they never doubted for a moment that slavery was wrong. Despite the complaints of Brownson and other critics, they succeeded in identifying their cause with the life of free society. They were the carriers, however unworthy at times, of perfectionism and the ideals of democracy. They invoked the freedoms guaranteed by the Constitution and demanded that the people honor them and listen to their arguments. Yet their arguments, as Brownson quite rightly pointed out, were not the kind that could be discussed dispassionately. Their ideas were packed with high explosive and eventually destroyed a community based on slavery. The abolitionists found the majority wrong and demanded the liberty to say so. The liberty that Garrison and his followers dreamed of, however, was an absolute liberty, a freedom that was neither brotherly nor Christian. It was this subversive ideal of liberty which, despite their professions of peace and Christian love, led logically to war and the overthrow of slavery.

This contradiction in the anti-slavery attitude was expressed on a higher level in the changes Garrison and the abolitionists made in the doctrine of natural law. As they received it from the Declaration of Independence and first invoked it in self-defense, natural law meant a body of rights pragmatically determined and consonant with what was believed to be the nature of man. In the course of their fight against slavery the abolitionists changed the content while keeping the concept. Natural law, as Garrison came to use it, meant metaphysical truth, a divine spirit hovering over humanity. For the pragmatic Aristotelian they substituted a Christian faith in a universally valid spiritual criterion. Drained of its pragmatic content, natural law came to mean, as Justice Holmes once observed, anything that people are willing to fight for. The Civil War proved that the American people were willing to fight over slavery.

The anti-slavery persuasion was marked by a final contradiction which was the source of the abolitionists' great strength and tragic weakness. Their courage and their fierce sense of freedom blinded them to the realities of the power struggle and the consequences of freeing the slave. The very intensity of their belief prevented them from understanding fully what it lay in their power to do for the Negro. They welcomed emancipation, but they were not ready for it and did not know how to use it. With the actual freeing of the slave their lack of understanding became increasingly apparent until finally anti-slavery radicalism broke down.

If Garrison personifies the contradictions of American radical reform, his anti-slavery career illustrates the continuing problem of moral absolutes in a democracy. A free society needs radicals with their moral absolutes just as ante-bellum Americans needed the abolitionists to tell them that slavery was wrong. But perfectionism —the dream of a perfect society of regenerate men—which sustained Garrison and his followers, rejected democratic politics and the idea of compromise, ignored programs and plans. By concentrating almost exclusively on the moral issue, appealing directly to individuals, and demanding immediate and wholesale change, it eliminated the very possibility of controlled change. Without radicals to criticize it a democracy is not really free; with them it maintains a precarious existence. If it cannot afford to silence its critics, neither can American democracy ignore the dangers to its stability inherent in their insistent demand for a better world.

"In every great fluctuation that takes place in human society," John Jay Chapman wrote of Garrison and the Civil War, "—whether it be a moral, a political, or even an industrial phenomenon,—force converges upon some one man, and makes him the metaphysical center and thought-focus of the movement." Chapman was not equipped to probe the collective mind of ante-bellum America: the grandson of an abolitionist, he was too close temporally and temperamentally to the Emersonian Representative Man to see Garrison as he was. Garrison was not a heroic figure but, rather, Emerson's sufficient man, "an officer equal to his task." He knew the contradictions of his age experientially, which is to say that his weakness was in a sense an American weakness. He lacked the power of a leader and the sureness to shape his feelings and give direction to his beliefs. Not a Representative Man, he was yet a representative figure of American society before the Civil War whose single great achievement and equally great failure testify to the tragic meaning of history.

Five / Race and Nationality

12 / The Significance
of the African Background

E. Franklin Frazier

America is a nation of immigrants. For three hundred years after the first Englishman scrambled ashore at Jamestown, Europeans, Asians, and Africans flocked to America. Some were attracted by the advantages and promises of life in the New World; others were simply pushed out of their old homes by war, famine, or economic dislocation. One significant group, however, did not immigrate voluntarily; the Negro was shipped to America in chains.

What happened to the Negro once he arrived in the New World? How did he adjust to his new environment? These questions can only be answered by understanding the fate of the Negro's African heritage. The late E. Franklin Frazier, dean of black social scientists, suggests that Negro immigrants were stripped of their African heritage and exposed to the new environment without any social or psychological protection. The transition from African freedom to American slavery was violent, swift, and devastating. There was nothing similar to the halfway house of the urban ghetto that eased the transition for eighteenth- and nineteenth-century European or Asian immigrants. A more complete knowledge of the beginnings of slavery and what cultural shock did to black people will aid in understanding the position of the Negro in American society.

For further reading: Eugene D. Genovese, "Materialism and Idealism in the History of Negro Slavery in the Americas," *Journal of Social History,* I (1968), 371–394; David Brion Davis, *The Problem of Slavery in Western Culture* (1966); Herbert S. Klein, *Slavery in the Americas: A Comparative Study of Cuba and Virginia* (1967); Winthrop D. Jordan, *White Over Black: American Attitudes toward the Negro, 1550–1812* (1968); *Laura Foner and Eugene D. Genovese (eds.), *Slavery in the New World: A Reader in Comparative History* (1969).

Among the "twenty Negers" who were brought in "a dutch man of warre" to Virginia in 1619, there were some whose names indicated that they had been baptized by the Spaniards.[1] But to what extent baptism and a new name were an indication that these slaves had lost their African cultural heritage or had acquired Spanish culture, the records do not inform us. Baptism and the acquisition of a Spanish name might have been artificial ceremonies, as they often were, when at the port of embarkation in Africa three or four hundred slaves were baptized and given a slip of paper in order that they might not forget their Spanish names.[2]

The manner in which young slaves were captured and sold on slave markets and confined in the slave pens in African ports had a more important effect upon the integrity of their cultural heritage. Such experiences, however, as well as the ordeal of the journey to the West Indies—the "middle passage"—did not destroy completely their African heritage. Individual slaves brought to America memories of their homeland and certain patterns of behavior and attitudes toward their fellow men and the physical world. It was in the New World, particularly in what became the United States, that new conditions of life destroyed the significance of their African heritage and caused new habits and attitudes to develop to meet new situations. Despite fresh importations from Africa, the process of sloughing off African culture continued. Since Emancipation this process has been so thoroughgoing that at the present time only in certain isolated areas can one discover what might be justly called African cultural survivals.[3]

OUR KNOWLEDGE
CONCERNING AFRICAN BACKGROUNDS

Only recently have we begun to secure sufficiently exact knowledge of the origin of the slaves brought to America to be in a position to identify African survivals. In the West Indies, the planters had some knowledge of the tribal backgrounds of the slaves; while in Brazil terms were used by the planters to indicate vaguely the area in Africa from which the slaves came. Recent investigations by Brazilian scholars have shown that "three great Negro peoples entered Brazil." "At the beginning of the slave trade," as pointed out by Ramos, "the largest number of those imported into Brazil were from Angola, the Congo and Guinea. When more active communication began with Bahia, the leading source of supply was Guinea and the western Sudan. There began a remarkable influx of Yorubas, Minas from the Gold Coast, Dahomans and various Islamized tribes such as the Hausas, Tapas, Mandingos, and Fulahs." [4] In the United States it has generally been assumed by scholars that throughout the slave trade slaves were drawn from far in the interior of Africa.[5] This assumption has

---

[1] Helen T. Catterall (ed.), *Judicial Cases Concerning American Slavery and the Negro* (Washington, D. C., 1926), Vol. I, pp. 55–56.

[2] Enrique de Gandia, *Francisco de Alfaro y la Condición Social de los Indios* (Buenos Aires, 1939), p. 38.

[3] The most comprehensive and systematic study of the problem of African cultural survivals is to be found in Melville J. Herskovits, *The Myth of the Negro Past* (New York, 1942). Throughout this chapter there will be occasion to refer to this work, though our discussion will often be in disagreement with the conclusions of Herskovits, who attempts to show that African survivals can be discovered in practically every phase of Negro life in the United States.

[4] *The Negro in Brazil*, by Arthur Ramos, p. 11. Copyright 1939 by The Associated Publishers, Inc.

[5] See for example U. B. Phillips, *American Negro Slavery* (New York, 1936), p. 31; Robert E. Park, "The Conflict and Fusion of Cultures," *Journal of Negro History*, Vol. IV, p. 117; and Edward Byron Reuter, *The American Race Problem* (New York, 1938), p. 123.

been challenged recently by Herskovits who has studied the documents bearing on the slave trade, especially those collected and analyzed by Miss Donnan.[6] By analyzing the data found "in manifests recorded from Virginia between the years 1710 and 1769" he was able to determine the specific areas from which came approximately 25,000 of the 45,000 slaves imported directly from Africa. The areas that figured most prominently were Guinea, "which means the west coast of Africa from the Ivory Coast to western Nigeria, Calabar, which represents the Niger Delta region, Angola, or the area about the lower Congo, and the Gambia."[7] As in the case of slaves imported into other states, only a few of these slaves—1,011 out of a total of 52,504—were from Madagascar. During the last half of the eighteenth century, the vast majority of the slaves imported into the American colonies came from the areas described above; but toward the close of the century the number of slave ships coming from the Congo increased.[8] In the nineteenth century when efforts were made by the United States, England, and France to outlaw the slave trade in those parts of Africa under the control of the latter two powers, the Congo, which was under Portuguese control, became the chief source of slaves for the illegal trade to the United States as well as to Brazil.

This more precise knowledge of the areas from which the slaves came has not, however, enabled investigators to refer African survivals in the United States to a specific tribe or a definite area.[9] In fact, students of the Negro are agreed that there were fewer African survivals in the United States than in other areas of the New World.[10] This was due, first, to differences in the character of slavery and the plantation system in the United States and in other parts of the New World. In the West Indies and Brazil, large numbers of African slaves were concentrated on vast plantations for the production of sugar. Under such conditions it was possible for the slaves to reestablish their African ways of life and keep alive their traditions. But in the United States the slaves were scattered in relatively small numbers on plantations and farms over a large area. In 1860 in the South as a whole, three-fourths of the farms and plantations had less than fifty slaves.[11] Even in the lower South, where the slaveholdings were larger on the average, two-thirds of the holdings were less than

[6] Herskovits, The Myth of the Negro Past, pp. 35–53. See also Elizabeth Donnan, Documents Illustrative of the Slave Trade to America, Vols. I–IV (Washington, D. C., 1930–1935).

[7] The Myth of the Negro Past, by Melville J. Herskovits, p. 41. Copyright 1941 by Harper & Brothers.

[8] Ibid., pp. 52–53. According to Herskovits' analysis of Miss Donnan's sources, approximately 22,000 of the 65,466 slaves imported into South Carolina between 1733 and 1738 came from Angola and the Congo. Ibid., p. 48.

[9] ". . . one can set off the United States from the rest of the New World as a region where departure from African modes of life was greatest, and where such Africanisms as persisted were carried through in generalized form, almost never directly referable to a specific tribe or a definite area." Ibid., p. 122.

[10] See ibid., p. 16, where Herskovits arranges areas of Negro concentration in the New World on a scale according to the intensity of African survivals. The area of most intensive survivals is in Suriname (the Bush Negroes) while next to the last group at the other end of the scale appear isolated groups of Negroes on the coast of Georgia and South Carolina. "Finally," writes Herskovits, "we should come to a group where, to all intents and purposes, there is nothing of the African tradition left, and which consists of people of varying degrees of Negroid physical type, who only differ from their white neighbors in the fact that they have more pigmentation in their skins." Ibid., p. 16.

[11] Lewis C. Gray, History of Agriculture in the Southern United States to 1860 (New York, 1941), Vol. I, p. 529.

fifty slaves. Only in Arkansas, Georgia, Louisiana, Mississippi, and South Carolina were there holdings with more than 500 slaves and such holdings constituted less than 1 per cent of the holdings in all these states except South Carolina.

SIZE OF PLANTATION
AND AFRICAN SURVIVALS

The size of the slaveholdings on the farms and plantations significantly influenced both the extent and nature of the contacts between the slaves and the whites. There was little contact between the great body of field slaves and the whites on the large sugar and cotton plantations in the southern states, as was true also on the large sugar plantations in Brazil and in the West Indies. Concerning the situation in South Carolina, Mrs. Johnson writes: "On St. Helena Island, where there were some two thousand slaves to little more than two hundred whites, the Negroes learned very slowly the ways of the whites. Their mastery of English was far less advanced than that of the Piedmont slaves." [12] However, as we have seen, the majority of the slaves in the United States were on small farms and plantations. In some of the upland cotton regions of Alabama, Mississippi, Louisiana, and Arkansas the median number of slaves per holding did not reach twenty; while in regions of general farming based mainly upon slave labor in Kentucky, Maryland, Missouri, North Carolina, South Carolina, and Tennessee the median holdings were even less. [13] In some of these latter regions the close contacts between the slaves and whites extended to working together on the smaller farms.

Slaves freshly imported from Africa usually had to be "broken in" to the plantation regime. A traveler in Louisiana described the process as follows:

> Negroes bought from the importers and carried home by the purchasers are ordinarily treated differently from the old ones. They are only gradually accustomed to work. They are made to bathe often, to take walks from time to time, and especially to dance; they are distributed in small numbers among old slaves in order to dispose them better to acquire their habits. These attentions are not usually due to sentiments of humanity. Interest requires them. It happens too often that poor masters, who have not other slaves, or are too greedy, require hard labor of these fresh negroes, exhaust them quickly, lose them by sickness and more often by grief. Often they hasten their own death; some wound themselves, others stifle themselves by drawing in the tongue so as to close the breathing passage, others take poison, or flee and perish of misery and hunger. [14]

It is likely that these new slaves with their African ways and memories of Africa had to face the disdain, if not the hostility, of Negroes who had become accommodated to the slave regime and had acquired a new conception of themselves. [15] They were

[12] Reprinted from *A Social History of the Sea Islands*, by Guion Griffis Johnson, p. 127, by permission of The University of North Carolina Press. Copyright 1930 by The University of North Carolina Press.

[13] Gray, *op. cit.*, Vol. I, pp. 534–35.

[14] "Voyages . . . de la Louisiane," vol. iii, 169–70, by C. C. Robin, from *Plantation and Frontier: Documents: 1649–1863*, Vol. II, p. 31, by Ulrich B. Phillips. Copyright 1909 by A. H. Clark Company.

[15] The following newspaper account of the reception of four native Africans on a Georgia plantation, except for the inferred detail concerning the delight of the newcomers, is probably

most likely to meet such an attitude on the part of the household slaves, who because of their intimate association with the whites had taken over the culture of the latter.[16]

ADJUSTMENT OF SLAVES TO NEW ENVIRONMENT

Because of the fact that the manner of the Negro's enslavement tended to destroy so completely his African culture, some scholars have been inclined to dismiss the influence of the African culture on the Negro's behavior. They have recognized, to be sure, that the speech of the Negro folk as well as their religious practices and family life differ from the behavior and customs of the whites; but these differences have been attributed to their isolation and incomplete assimilation.[17] On the other hand, there has been much speculation on the influence of African culture as a cause of these differences. In some instances this speculation has betrayed an ignorance of African cultures or has simply reflected popular prejudices in regard to "primitive" people or so-called "savages." But there has also been speculation of a nature that has led to fantastic conclusions concerning the influence of African survivals on the behavior of Negroes in the United States.[18] Only recently have competent scholars with a knowledge of the culture of the African areas from which the Negroes came attempted to identify definite African survivals.[19]

The first adjustment which the transported Negroes had to make in their new environment was to acquire some knowledge of the language of the whites for communication. Where the slaves, sometimes from childhood, were in close contact with the whites, they took over completely the speech and language of their masters. On the other hand, the great masses of isolated slaves, as in the case of the slaves on St. Helena Island, acquired the speech and language of the whites more slowly. The peculiar speech of Negroes in such isolated places has generally been attributed to

---

indicative of the general attitude of the slaves toward their African background: "Our common darkies treat them with sovereign contempt walking around them with a decided aristocratic air. But the Africans are docile and very industrious and are represented as being perfectly delighted with new homes and improved conditions. The stories that they are brutes and savages is all stuff and nonsense. It was put in the papers by men who do not know what they are talking about. As to their corrupting our common negroes, we venture the assertion would come nearer the truth if stated the other way." *Atlanta* (Ga.) *Daily Intelligencer*, March 9, 1859, from Phillips, *op. cit.*, 54–55.

[16] See Chapter III of *The Negro in the United States* by E. Franklin Frazier.

[17] See Reuter, *op. cit.*, pp. 129–31; and Park, *op. cit.*, pp. 115–17.

[18] For example, see Woodson, *The African Background Outlined or Handbook for the Study of the Negro*, pp. 168–75, where the author, among other equally untenable conjectures, states: "The industry of the Negro in the United States may be partly explained as an African survival. The Negro is born a worker. In the African social order work is well organized. Everybody is supposed to make some contribution to the production of food and clothing necessary for the whole community" (*The African Background Outlined or Handbook for the Study of the Negro* by Carter G. Woodson, p. 171. Copyright 1936 by Association for the Study of Negro Life and History. Reprinted by permission of The Associated Publishers, Inc.). The claim of a social worker (Corinne Sherman, "Racial Factors in Desertion," *Family*, III, 224) that she was not able to understand "the conjugal habits of colored clients" until she had gained a knowledge of African customs shows to what fantastic conclusions speculations about African survivals in America may lead one.

[19] See pp. 140ff. above.

their isolation, their lack of appreciation of grammatical rules, or to the fact that they had preserved the characteristics of English as spoken at an earlier period. But Lorenzo D. Turner has discovered approximately four thousand words of West African origin in the Gullah vocabulary of Negroes on the coast of South Carolina and Georgia.[20] Moreover, he found numerous African given names and African phrases that had been translated into English. In view of Turner's researches, the current notion that African words have completely disappeared from the vocabulary of Negroes in all sections of the United States must be modified.[21]

DESTRUCTION OF AFRICAN FAMILY

In contrast to such concrete data on linguistic survivals, there is scarcely any evidence that recognizable elements of the African social organization have survived in the United States. This has been especially true in regard to those phases of the African social organization which had a political character.[22] A rare instance of such a survival may be found in the early history of New England, where it was customary for the Negroes to elect a "governor," who exercised an almost despotic discipline over local groups of slaves.[23] In regard to the African family organization there have been from time to time reports of survivals.[24] For example, in the autobiography of an ex-slave the following incident is related:

> I assisted her and her husband to inter the infant—which was a little boy— and its father buried with it, a small bow and several arrows; a little bag of parched meal; a miniature canoe, about a foot long, and a little paddle (with which he said it would cross the ocean to his own country), a small stick, with an iron nail, sharpened, and fastened into one end of it; and a piece of white muslin, with several curious and strange figures painted on it in blue and red, by which, he said, his relations and countrymen would know the infant to be his son, and would receive it accordingly, on its arrival amongst them. . . . He cut a lock of hair from his head, threw it upon the dead infant, and closed the grave with

[20] See Herskovits, op. cit., pp. 276–79.

[21] In the West Indies and Suriname, it has been easier to trace many words in the language of the Negroes to their African sources. See Melville J. Herskovits, "On the Provenience of New World Negroes," Social Forces, XII, 252–59. In Brazil, the Islamized Negroes who maintained connections with Africa not only continued to speak Arabic but also conducted schools. Among the non-Islamized Negroes, Yoruba was the chief means of communication, this language being preserved today in the religious practices of Brazilian Negroes about Bahia. See Arthur Ramos, O Negro Brasileiro (Rio de Janeiro, 1940) and Nina Rodrigues, Os Africanos (2a Edição, São Paulo, 1935).

[22] In the West Indies and in Brazil, there were numerous instances where free Negroes and especially slaves that had revolted or escaped revived features of the traditional African political organization.

[23] H. S. Aimes, "African Institutions in America," Journal of American Folklore, Vol. XVIII, pp. 15–17.

[24] W. E. B. DuBois, who believed that careful research would reveal traces, but traces only, "of the African family in America" since "the effectiveness of the slave system meant the practically complete crushing out of the African clan and family life," nevertheless gives as an example of survival the case of a Negro country wedding in Lowndes County, Alabama, in 1892, in which the bride was chased "after the ceremony in a manner very similar to the Zulu ceremony." The Negro Family (Atlanta, 1908), p. 21.

his own hands. He then told us the God of his country was looking at him, and was pleased with what what he had done.[25]

If we can rely on the account of an old Negro woman that "a slave who married a girl from a group of native Africans just received on the plantation" was required "to obtain the consent of every member of the girl's group before he was allowed to marry her," [26] we have what might be an instance of the continued control of the extended family or clan organization. In his researches concerning linguistic survivals, Turner found that in isolated areas on the coast of Georgia and South Carolina, the Gullahs who often confine the use of African words to the intimate circle of the family reveal the influence of African traditions in the naming of their children. He writes:

> Even though the Gullahs may not know the meaning of many African words they use for proper names, in their use of English words they follow a custom common in West Africa of giving their children names which suggest the time of birth, or the conditions surrounding it, or the temperament or appearance of the child. All twelve months of the year and the seven days of the week are used freely. In some cases the name indicates the time of day at which the birth occurs.[27]

These rare and isolated instances of survivals associated with the Negro family only indicate how completely the African social organization was wiped out by slavery.

Although Herskovits agrees with other students of the Negro that the plantation system destroyed African family types as well as their underlying moral and supernatural sanctions, he nevertheless thinks that a diluted form of the African family continued to exist.[28] A diluted form of the African family may be recognized, he thinks, in the so-called common-law marriages among Negroes. "We . . . must recognize," he writes, "that the elasticity of the marriage concept among Negroes derives in a measure, largely unrecognized, from the need to adjust a polygynous family form to patterns based on a convention of monogamy, in a situation where this has been made the more difficult by economic and psychological complications resulting from the nature of the historical situation." [29] Likewise, he sees in the so-called "matriarchal" or "maternal" family among Negroes, in which the mother and grandmother play important rôles, evidence of the continuation in a diluted form of African traditions. "It cannot be regarded only as coincidence," he maintains, "that such specialized features of Negro family life in the United States as the rôle of women in focusing the sentiment that gives the family unit its psychological coherence, or their place in maintaining the economic stability essential to survival, correspond closely to similar facets of West African social structure." [30]

[25] Charles Ball, *Slavery in the United States: A Narrative of the Life and Adventures of Charles Ball, A Black Man* (Lewistown, Pa., 1836), pp. 203–5.

[26] Reprinted from *Folk Beliefs of the Southern Negro* by Newbell Niles Puckett, p. 24, by permission of The University of North Carolina Press. Copyright 1926 by The University of North Carolina Press.

[27] *The Myth of the Negro Past* by Melville J. Herskovits, p. 192. Copyright 1941 by Harper & Brothers.

[28] "It goes without saying," writes Herskovits, "that the plantation system rendered the survival of African family types impossible, as it did their underlying moral and supernatural sanctions, except in dilute form." *Ibid.*, p. 139.

[29] *The Myth of the Negro Past* by Melville J. Herskovits, p. 170. Copyright 1941 by Harper & Brothers.

[30] *Ibid.*, p. 180.

These statements concerning the continuation in a diluted form of the African family in the United States are not based upon any data showing continuity between African traditions and the familial behavior of American Negroes. They are only an ingenious attempt to show similarity between certain customs and practices of Negroes in the United States and in Africa in regard to sex and family behavior. However, the supposed similarities in attitudes and behavior are not real similarities in a cultural sense. When loose and unregulated sex behavior is encountered among American Negroes, it is not the same as the polygynous customs and practices of African Negroes. The latter are regulated by custom and tradition while the former lack the sanction of traditions and customs. Although in some areas "common-law" matings occur on a large scale among certain classes of Negroes, such behavior can be explained in terms of practices which sometimes have become customary as the result of social and economic forces in the American environment.[31] Moreover, such behavior is often recognized as being in conflict with the mores of the larger society.

The same fallacies appear in the attempt to explain illegitimacy among Negroes and the important position of the woman in the Negro family as a diluted form of African cultural survival. The argument that the impulsive and uncontrolled sex behavior of foot-loose Negro women which often results in illegitimacy has a basis in African traditions may be dismissed simply as unwarranted speculation. On the other hand, the statement concerning the survival of African customs in regard to the woman's place in the family deserves some consideration. It is probably true that the situation under the slave regime might have given support to those African traditions supporting the woman's important position in the family. But African traditions supporting male dominance were just as likely to survive in the New World. For example, even today it appears that the African pattern of family life is perpetuated in the patriarchal family organization of the West Indian Negroes.[32]

In the United States it is neither possible nor is it necessary to seek an explanation of the dominance of the male or the female in the family organization of Negroes in supposed survivals of the African social organization. The important position of the mother in the Negro family in the United States has developed out of the exigencies of life in the new environment. In the absence of institutional controls, the relationship between mother and child has become the essential social bond in the family and the woman's economic position has developed in her those qualities which are associated with a "matriarchal" organization. On the other hand, the Negro family has developed as a patriarchal organization or similar to the American family as the male has acquired property and an interest in his family and as the assimilation of American attitudes and patterns of behavior has been accelerated by the breaking down of social

[31] See E. Franklin Frazier, *The Negro Family in the United States* (Chicago, 1939), Part II, "The House of the Mother."

[32] Martha W. Beckwith, *Black Roadways: A Study of Jamaican Folk Life* (Chapel Hill, 1929), p. 54. In the following observations of a visitor to the French West Indies about the year 1700 we have, doubtless, an example of this patriarchal authority which had its roots in Africa. Labat says: "I have often taken pleasure in watching a negro carpenter at Guadaloupe when he ate his meals. His wife and children gathered around him, and served him with as much respect as the best drilled domestics serve their masters; and if it was a fete day or Sunday, his sons-in-law and daughters did not fail to be present, and bring him some small gifts. They formed a circle about him, and conversed with him while he was eating. When he had finished, his pipe was brought to him, and then he bade them eat. They paid him their reverences, and passed into another room, where they all eat together with their mother." Pere Labat, *Voyage aux isles francoises*, II, 54, cited in Aimes, *loc. cit.*, pp. 24–25.

isolation, sometimes through physical amalgamation.[33] Herskovits sees even in such well integrated patriarchal families, with a secure economic basis and traditions extending over several generations, evidence of the survival of the African ancestral cult in their family reunions when they praise the accomplishments of their ancestors or visit the family burying ground. Yet he admits that the overt manifestations of the ancestral cult have been obliterated and European religious beliefs have been taken over, and that only the "spirit" of ancestral culture has remained.[34] This simply means that the existence of such survivals cannot be validated on scientific grounds.

AFRICAN RELIGIOUS SURVIVALS

There can be no question about the survival of African religious ceremonies and rituals in some parts of the New World. In Brazil at the present time African religious survivals are easily recognized in the religious cults of the Negroes and people of Negro descent. The *macumbas* of the Negroes in the region about Rio de Janeiro are true African religious survivals that have become greatly "adulterated in contact with an elaborate and complicated urban civilization." [35] On the other hand, such religious cults as the *candomblés* of Bahia and some of the *shangôs* of the northeast have preserved many African elements. In these religious cults, formerly concealed from the whites, the worship of Yoruban deities was carried on for centuries; but at the present time African deities are becoming identified with Catholic saints and beliefs are becoming fused with spiritualism.[36] Likewise, in Haiti one may find African survivals in the religious beliefs and rituals of the peasantry.[37]

In the United States it has been more difficult to discover African survivals in the religious behavior of the Negroes. During slavery there were reports of the dancing and singing of the slaves which indicated that African religious ceremonies had been carried over. Moreover, there were reports of slaves praying in a manner that indicated that they had been converted to Mohammedanism.[38] Since the emancipation of the slaves, we have had accounts of authentic religious practices which were undoubtedly of African origin.[39] Then, too, on the Sea Islands, where the isolated unmixed Negroes speak a distinct dialect, the "praise house" probably represents a fusion of African culture traits and Christian practices.[40] However, except for such instances, generally occurring among isolated groups of Negroes, it has been difficult to identify religious traits that could correctly be called African survivals.

Despite the general absence of African beliefs and rituals in the religious behavior of the Negroes in the United States, there has been some speculation on the existence of less obvious African survivals. For example, the fact that the majority of the

[33] See Frazier, *op. cit.,* Part III, "In the House of the Father."
[34] See Herskovits, *op. cit.,* p. 199.
[35] *The Negro in Brazil* by Arthur Ramos, p. 81. Copyright 1939 by The Associated Publishers, Inc.
[36] *Ibid.,* pp. 82–93. See also Arthur Ramos, *O Negro Brasileiro;* Nina Rodrigues, *Os Africanos;* and Edison Carneiro, *Religioes Negras* (Rio de Janeiro, 1936).
[37] See Melville J. Herskovits, *Life in a Haitian Valley* (New York, 1937), pp. 139–248.
[38] See, for example, Ball, *op. cit.,* p. 127, where he tells of a slave "who prayed five times every day, always turning his face to the east."
[39] See George W. Cable, "Creole Slave Songs," *Century Magazine,* Vol. XXI, pp. 807–27.
[40] Guion G. Johnson, *A Social History of the Sea Islands* (Chapel Hill, 1930), pp. 147–53.

Negroes in the United States are affiliated with the Baptist churches seems to Herskovits to be due primarily to certain features in the Negro's African heritage. His first statement of this viewpoint was that

> The importance of baptism in the ritual practices of Negro Christians has often been commented upon. It is not unreasonable to relate the strength of adherence to this practice to the great importance of the river-cults in West Africa, particularly in view of the fact that, as has been observed, river-cult priests were sold into slavery in great numbers.[41]

Evidently after Herskovits became acquainted with the "aggressive proselytizing activities of Protestantism" and the fact that white Baptists emphasized total immersion, he revised the statement of his position so as to include these facts.[42] He, nevertheless, maintains his position with reference to the rôle of priests of river-cults who were sold to rich Dahomean "conquerors of troublesome leaders." His most recent statement is as follows:

> In the New World, where the aggressive proselytizing activities of Protestantism made the retention of the inner forms of African religion as difficult as its outer manifestations, the most logical adaptation for the slaves to make to the new situation, and the simplest, was to give their adherence to that Christian sect which in its ritualism most resembled the types of worship known to them. As we have seen, the Baptist churches had an autonomous organization that was in line with the tradition of local self-direction congenial to African practice. In these churches the slaves were also permitted less restrained behavior than in the more sedate denominations. And such factors only tended to reinforce an initial predisposition of these Africans toward a cult which, in emphasizing baptism by total immersion, made possible the worship of the new supernatural powers in ways that at least contained elements not entirely unfamiliar.[43]

The proselytizing activities of the Baptists and Methodists provide an adequate explanation of the fact that the majority of the Negroes are members of the Baptist church. Moreover, they provide an adequate explanation of the fact that about a third of the Negroes are members of Methodist churches, which do not practice baptism by immersion, a fact which the speculation about the influence of African river-cults fails to explain. The Negro slaves seemingly from the beginning of their residence in the United States took over the religious beliefs and rituals to which they were exposed. During the eighteenth century the Society for the Propagation of the Gospel in Foreign Parts operating through the ministers of the Established Church of England converted many slaves to Christianity. For example, in the Goose Creek Parish in South Carolina in 1705, a Reverend Samuel Thomas had given religious instruction to a thousand slaves, "many of whom could read the Bible distinctly and great numbers of them were engaged in learning the scriptures."[44]

---

[41] Melville J. Herskovits, "Social History of the Negro," in Carl Murchison, *A Handbook of Social Psychology* (Worcester, 1935), pp. 256–57.

[42] The backwoods preacher, Peter Cartwright, wrote as follows concerning the activities of the white Baptist preachers in Tennessee during the early years of the nineteenth century: ". . . indeed, they made so much ado about baptism by immersion, that the uninformed would suppose that heaven was an island, and that there was no way to get there but by diving or swimming." *Autobiography of Peter Cartwright*, edited by W. P. Strickland (New York, 1857), p. 134.

[43] Herskovits, *The Myth of the Negro Past*, p. 233.

[44] *The History of the Negro Church* by Carter G. Woodson, p. 7. Copyright 1921 by The Associated Publishers, Inc.

Then came the revivals during the latter half of the eighteenth century which drew vast numbers of the slaves into the Methodist and Baptist churches. Around the opening of the nineteenth century appeared the camp meeting revivals that tended to revive and enforce the effects of the religious awakening of the preceding century.[45] The Methodist and Baptist preachers carried the "gospel of salvation" to the black slave as well as to the poor and ignorant white.[46] In King William County, Virginia, in 1789 the sheriff appealed to the Governor because the Baptists and Methodists were meeting with slaves several times a week and had ejected the patrollers from their meetings.[47] In fact, when the Methodists and Baptists began their proselytizing among the slaves and poor whites they were outspoken against slavery. When they ceased to oppose slavery openly, they continued to present Christianity as an escape for the enslaved blacks from their earthly condition.

Although the Methodists made the same appeal as the Baptists, there were certain features in the Baptist church organization and in their policy with reference to the Negroes that caused the latter to enter the Baptist organization more freely than the Methodist church. The Baptists encouraged a form of local self-government that favored the growth of Negro congregations. Then, too, they permitted and encouraged Negroes to become preachers, at first to whites as well as Negroes, and later as leaders of Negro congregations. Because of these features of the Baptist church policy, the enslaved and free Negro was given an opportunity for self-expression not provided by the Methodist church.[48] Under the Methodist church organization he was not only subject to the control emanating from the bishops but he was generally under white leadership in churches.[49]

One may reasonably assume that among the Negroes who received the "call to preach," there were some who had been influenced by African traditions and that others cherishing memories of their African background found in the emotionalism and the ecstatic form of worship that characterized the Methodist and Baptist revivals an opportunity for self-expression. But such assumptions provide no proof for Herskovits' assertion that the emotionalism and ecstatic behavior that characterized the Great Awakening and the camp meetings were largely due to African influences and that contrary to usual accounts the whites took over the behavior of the Negroes.[50] In support of this view he cites Davenport's observation on the difference between the automatisms of the Kentucky and the Ulster revivalists, the former, he thinks, having been influenced by the Negroes.[51] This reasoning is in line with Herskovits'

[45] See Frederick M. Davenport, *Primitive Traits in Religious Revivals* (New York, 1917), pp. 60ff.
[46] The Presbyterian revivalists were also active at this time among the slaves.
[47] Luther P. Jackson, "Religious Development of the Negro in Virginia from 1760 to 1860." *The Journal of Negro History*, Vol. XVI, pp. 172–73.
[48] See Chapter XIII of *The Negro in the United States* by E. Franklin Frazier.
[49] See Jackson, *loc. cit.*, p. 147.
[50] Herskovits, *op. cit.*, pp. 227–32.
[51] Herskovits gives the following quotation from Davenport, *op. cit.*, p. 92: "I wish in closing to call attention to the difference in type of the automatisms of Kentucky and Ulster. In Kentucky the motor automatisms, the voluntary muscles in violent action, were the prevailing type, although there were many of the sensory. On the other hand, in Ulster the sensory automatisms, trance, vision, the physical disability and the sinking of muscular energy were the prevailing type, although there were many of the motor. I do not mean that I can explain it. It may be that as the Charcot and Nancy schools of hypnosis brought out by chance, each in its own field, different kinds of hypnotic phenomena which, when known, spread by imitation in the respective

general belief in the "toughness of culture," which enables it to survive under the most unfavorable conditions. However, such an argument fails to take into account the rôle of spontaneous impulses in human behavior, which probably account for the differences between the behavior of the Kentucky revivalists and those in Ulster. Likewise, much of the behavior of the Negroes was spontaneous and expressive and was not rigidly controlled by traditional patterns of behavior. It is significant that their religious behavior in the United States is similar to that of whites, while it differs markedly from that of Brazilian Negroes who have preserved African rituals and beliefs in their religious organizations.[52]

OTHER PHASES OF CULTURE

Herskovits' belief in the "toughness of culture" has led him to speculate upon the influence of African traditions upon various phases of Negro life. He thinks that economic cooperation among Negroes in the United States has been influenced by African traditions. Of the cooperation found in the lodges he writes:

> Cooperation among the Negroes of this country is principally found in such institutions as lodges and other benevolent societies, which in themselves are directly in line with the tradition underlying similar African organizations.[53]

Even in the fraternal organization among Negroes in cities, he sees "deep-seated drives in Negro life; drives so strong, indeed, that it is difficult, if not impossible, to account for them satisfactorily except in terms of a tradition which reaches further than merely to the period of slavery." [54] In regard to such speculation, one can only say that historical data concerning the leadership, the needs of an isolated group laboring under economic disadvantages, and the manner in which these organizations developed provide an adequate explanation of such phenomena. The "deep-seated" drives, which are referred to, are strong because they represent general human needs and, as we shall see [in a later chapter], they are provided for in a manner consistent with the resources and the experiences of the people involved.

In some of the magic and folk beliefs of the rural Negroes in the United States, some African elements have probably been retained. But it is recognized by even Herskovits that "magic and other types of folk belief" originating in Africa and Europe have become amalgamated.[55] Therefore, the problem of the student seeking African survivals is to disentangle African from other elements in such beliefs and practices. On the basis of his knowledge of African cultures, Herskovits has attempted to show that unsuspected African elements have survived.[56] Puckett, who has de-

---

localities and under the respective influences, so in Kentucky and the north of Ireland by chance there appeared different types of physical manifestation which were then imitated in the respective countries." *The Myth of the Negro Past* by Melville J. Herskovits, pp. 230–31. Copyright 1941 by Harper & Brothers.

[52] This statement is based upon the writer's uncontrolled observations as well as the accounts of others. See, for example, Arthur Ramos, *O Negro Brasileiro,* passim.

[53] *The Myth of the Negro Past* by Melville J. Herskovits, p. 161. Copyright 1941 by Harper & Brothers.

[54] *Ibid.,* p. 164.

[55] *Ibid.,* p. 235.

[56] *Ibid.,* pp. 235–51.

voted himself to the same task, concludes that the Negro has taken "over English practices in regard to the direct maintenance and perpetuation of life, while in things relating to pleasure, his customs seemingly have more of an African turn." [57] However, he adds that the African influence has been least where the Negro has had the most contact with the whites and that there are beliefs among Negroes "which seem to have no direct European or African parallels, and may represent independent Afro-American developments." [58]

The latter statement by Puckett concerning the appearance of new ways of thinking and acting applies to all aspects of Negro life in the United States. African patterns of thought and behavior could survive only where the Negroes were isolated and where there was sufficient common understanding among them to give significance to African survivals. But the isolation of the Negro from the whites was always limited by the fact that the majority of the slaves were scattered over a vast territory on small farms and plantations. Their isolation was further broken down by the organization of slave labor and the internal slave trade which created some mobility among the slave population. More important still was the fact that the African family system, the chief means of cultural transmission, was destroyed. Under such circumstances African languages were lost and the African social organization could not be reconstituted in the new environment. Consequently, Negroes acquired new habits and modes of thought, and whatever elements of African culture were retained lost their original meaning in becoming fused with their experiences in the New World. Beginning with emancipation Negroes have from time to time been uprooted from their customary ways of life and have gradually escaped from their isolation. As they have emerged from the world of the folk, they have been affected by the modes of thought and behavior characteristic of civilized or urbanized societies. This has constantly resulted in considerable social disorganization; but at the same time it has led to reorganization of life, at least among certain elements, on a pattern consistent with civilized modes of behavior. During this process of adjusting themselves to American civilization, the majority of the Negroes have sloughed off completely the African heritage.

[57] Reprinted from *Folk Beliefs of the Southern Negro* by Newbell Niles Puckett, p. 78, by permission of The University of North Carolina Press. Copyright 1926 by The University of North Carolina Press.
[58] *Ibid.*

13 / Consciousness of Kind

Robert Ernst

Between 1820 and the Civil War, 5 million immigrants arrived in the United States. Ireland contributed almost 2 million of these newcomers, and 1½ million came from Germany. Some moved westward to St. Louis and the thriving new cities of the Ohio River Valley, others sought out the rich farm lands in Wisconsin and Minnesota, and a few even went to the South. The majority of the immigrants, however, remained on the Eastern seaboard. In the growing urban centers, they settled in close-knit communities and re-created the culture and institutions of their homeland. From these urban ghettos, the foreign born looked out upon America, but the view was colored by the language, thought, and habit patterns of their non-American past. It remained for the children of these immigrants—the first American-born generation—to discover an America unhampered by memories of another life.

Robert Ernst describes in detail the way in which the immigrants surrounded themselves with European institutions to ease the shock of being uprooted from one world to another.

For further reading: *Marcus Lee Hansen, *The Atlantic Migration, 1607–1860* (1940); *Marcus Lee Hansen, *The Immigrant in American History* (1940); Oscar Handlin, *Boston's Immigrants: A Study in Acculturation* (rev. ed., 1959); Rowland Berthoff, *British Immigrants in Industrial America, 1789–1950* (1953); Theodore C. Blegen, *Norwegian Migration to America, 1825–1860* (1931); William V. Shannon, *The American Irish* (1963).

When immigrants set foot upon Manhattan Island, they brought with them memories of their old homeland. Past associations and sentimental feeling for the Old Country, involving attachments to region, church, and family, were cohesive elements in the new land to which they had come. Immigrants' letters were filled with intensely personal matters, of births, marriages, illnesses, and deaths in families, news of friends, employment conditions, and local gossip. Homesickness was unashamedly expressed

Immigrant Life in New York City, 1825–1863 (New York: Columbia University Press, Kings Crown Press, 1949). Reprinted by permission of the author. Copyright 1949 by Robert Ernst. The book was reissued by Ira J. Friedman, Inc., Fort Washington, New York (1965). Footnotes have been omitted.

in correspondence and in the press, as amateur poets burst forth with songs of longing for the Fatherland. Stationers and book-sellers offered inexpensive views of European towns, and museums exhibited bas-reliefs and miniature models of mountains, lakes, and cities, which refreshed the foreigners' memories of beloved birthplaces and scenes of childhood experiences. Among the Irish and the Germans, regional loyalties were sustained in New York by social and fraternal clubs like the Sligo Young Men's Association, the *Mecklenburger Mandschiens-Club*, and the *Norddeutsche Gemüt-lichkeit*. Military organizations were formed by natives of Baden, Bavaria, and the Palatinate, and the more ignorant Irishmen clanned together in secret societies representing Cork, Connaught, Down, and other counties.

When misfortune overtook those who remained in Europe, the national sympathies of immigrants in New York superseded local loyalties. The Irish gave spontaneously and generously to their kinfolk in the Green Isle, sending whatever they could afford —usually small drafts of a few dollars at a time—to stave off starvation in years of lean harvests. During the famine year of 1846, the Irish of New York City transmitted over $800,000 by every packet to every parish in Ireland. Others helped, too: Christians and Jews, natives, Germans, and Frenchmen contributed to a central relief committee in New York, which received over $170,000 in cash, and foodstuffs valued at $70,000. The Irish in America, however, were the most concerned, and for a decade following the famine they sent $19,680,000 to Ireland. When Scottish weavers, carpenters, and dock workers "depended upon human sympathy for their existence" during the depression of 1841–1842, the Scots in New York held public meetings and solicited contributions. The French collected over $2,000 to aid the families of the dead and wounded in the July Revolution and in the forties and fifties sent relief funds to the victims of floods in France. Italian merchants and intellectuals were responsible for raising a fund of $10,000 to relieve wives and children of Italian soldiers who were crippled or killed in the war with Austria in 1859.

Patriotic feelings were aroused by the arrival of royal personalities, as when the French tendered a reception to the Prince de Joinville upon his arrival in New York in 1838, or by the death of national figures like Lafayette, the Duke of Orleans, and the Duke of Wellington. National anniversary celebrations were likewise observed at New York. Every year the Scots met to observe the birthday of Robert Burns, amid poetry, songs, toasts, and speeches, and a number of Burns clubs were formed during the fifties. Wealthy Englishmen celebrated Queen Victoria's birthday, but the Irish commemorated instead the American Fourth of July. In 1859 the Germans held an elaborate *Schillerfeier*, honoring the great German poet with dramatics, concerts, speeches, dances, and illuminations.

The patriotic ferment which pervaded the Continent of Europe after the Napoleonic Wars, like the simmering Irish restiveness under British domination, mingled in the melting pot of New York. The Empire City was the American focal point of the political exiles of Europe. When the influential Professor Sylvester Jordan, of the University of Giessen, was imprisoned for freethinking and reform agitation, New York Germans collected some $600 for the relief of his family. Mazzini's Young Italy movement was spread among the Italians of the New World by Felice Foresti, who in 1841 organized its New York branch, the *Congrega Centrale*, as a center of Italian republican propaganda. Polish exiles in the city agitated for the liberation of Poland, Hungarians sought recruits to fight Austrian despotism, and a small band of Cubans formed juntas to free their island from Spanish rule. Stimulated by political refugees from abroad, the Germans held mass meetings, attended benefits, and joined societies for the collection of money and the dispatch of republican *émigrés* to aid the German revolutionists of 1848–1852. Themes of nationalism, republicanism, and—among the left-wing elements—the unity of the working classes drew together the French, Germans, Italians, Latin Americans, Poles, Hungarians, Irish, and Americans in mass meetings, processions, and dinners celebrating the cause of liberals all over Europe.

The common nationalistic fervor in 1848 heartened the champions of Irish freedom, who nevertheless deplored the anticlericalism of the Continental revolutionists. Indeed, Irish political freedom was closely related to the unhindered operation of the Catholic hierarchy in Ireland. When the Catholic emancipation movement gathered momentum in the twenties, Friends of Ireland associations sprang up in American cities; and the New York group, led by William J. Macneven and Robert Emmet, among others, kept up a vigorous agitation for Irish religious and political liberties. The Friends of Civil and Religious Liberty celebrated the Catholic Emancipation Act in 1829, and thereafter for fifteen years, the Irish in New York supported O'Connell's movement for the repeal of the legislative union of Ireland with England. In 1843 a mammoth Repeal Convention met for three days in the Empire City and planned to organize each state of the Union in a supreme effort to raise money for Repeal. The Irish had complete confidence in Daniel O'Connell, and many of the poorest immigrants eagerly donated their mite of twelve and one half cents or twenty-five cents, but the collapse of the Repeal movement and the appearance of the radical Young Ireland Party divided the loyalties of Irish-Americans. By 1848, the Irish had ceased contributing to Repeal; the more radical turned to the leadership of John Mitchel and T. F. Meagher and established "Directories" in several cities, the New York Directory receiving in a few weeks over $40,000. However, famine in the Green Isle drew from the immigrant Irish the funds which might have sustained the rebellion of 1848, the failure of which ended widespread support of movements to free Ireland.

These nationalistic activities, however, sprang from sources external to the lives of the immigrants. In not a few instances the embers of patriotism were fanned by refugees whose primary interest was in Europe, not America. Genuine immigrants, planning to spend their entire lives in the United States, were more deeply concerned about their everyday existence, the welfare of their families, the future of their children in the new world of opportunity. To satisfy their social and material needs, they founded a wide variety of institutions forming an intricate pattern of group activities which eased the adjustment of Europeans to American conditions.

Man craves companionship and associates with people of similar interests. So it was with the alien, who looked for friends in a friendless new home, social approval in the midst of the contempt of native Americans, and material well-being in a fiercely competitive, materialistic, young nation. In the saloon, the grocery, and the liquor shop, he associated with his fellow foreigners in pursuit of relaxation and the enjoyment of simple pleasures. Hundreds of restaurants, oyster cellars, and "pensions" offered opportunities for business and professional contacts as well. Love of liquor, fostered by the harshness of life in the Green Isle, led Irishmen to the myriads of barrooms of New York or to the more respectable Ivy Green Tavern of Malachi Fallon, Daniel Sweeny's House of Refreshment, or John Keefe's restaurant. Accustomed to the frivolity of the village *Wirtshaus*, the Germans flocked to the beer gardens in New York. One of the largest, and a favorite, was the Atlantic Garden on the Bowery, where both sexes of all ages congregated "amid dense clouds of tobacco-smoke, and hurry of waiters, and banging of glasses, and calling for beer." Like other big German beer halls, the Atlantic contained several bars, a shooting gallery, billiard tables and bowling alleys, and an orchestra. During the forties, the Atlantic catered exclusively to Germans, but by the late sixties it was patronized by crowds of French, Irish, English, Italians, Portuguese, and even Asiatics. The English gravitated to such places as the Richard the Third House, the Brown Jug Tavern, and the Albion Hotel; the Scots gathered at the Blue Bonnet, the Wallace, and the Burns houses; the French, Swiss, and Italians, at the Café de Mille Colonnes, the Restaurant Lafayette, and scores of other eating and drinking places.

At the larger restaurants, "assembly rooms," and hotels, immigrant groups held banquets, parties, balls, and anniversary celebrations. During the summer months, however, they deserted lower Manhattan for the coffee houses of Bloomingdale, Staten Island, Hoboken, and the north shore of Long Island. Excursions and picnics were popular among all nationalities, the Germans developing the habit into an inclusive group activity.

For closer and more permanent associations, the newcomers founded or joined a huge number of fraternal and benevolent societies. In their simplest and most typical form, these were mutual aid societies, much like those already existing in Europe and America. Their members usually were tradesmen, artisans, and laborers, whose meager earnings induced them to band together for protection against the uncertainties of life in an era which saw only the beginnings of life insurance. The mutual aid society provided sickness benefits to its members and paid the funeral expenses of those who died. Although the earliest of these associations appeared in colonial times, the surge of immigration in the nineteenth century greatly increased their size and number. In the twenties, the Irish formed a Hibernian Universal Benevolent Society and a St. Patrick Friendly Society, which were among the first of many similar groups appearing in the next three decades.

Daily occupational contacts led to the formation of mutual aid societies in various trades. Tailors, shipwrights and caulkers, painters, masons, quarrymen, and longshoremen were only a few of those who created benevolent associations, which sometimes increased their bargaining strength with employers. One of the largest of these societies was the Laborers' Union Benevolent Association, formed in 1843. By 1850 its 2,500 to 4,000 members paid monthly dues of twelve and a half cents, the sick received $2.00 per week, and families of deceased members were granted $15.00 for funeral expenses.

Other groups were formed under religious auspices. Catholic churches sometimes organized them for the benefit of their members, and all the earlier Jewish societies developed within the synagogues. Because of the secessions resulting from intra-synagogue controversies in the forties, many Jewish mutual aid societies severed their religious connections as the only means of preserving their membership. Meanwhile, newly formed independent societies appealed to Jews who were unaffiliated with any synagogue and, therefore, ordinarily ineligible for burial privileges.

The functions of some mutual aid associations expanded to include the relief of families of deceased members, and new groups were founded exclusively for the support of widows and orphans. All such organizations were by their very nature exclusive. Because of their limited means, they extended protection only to members and their families; and while they were of little aid to the charitable efforts of the community at large, they nevertheless performed a vital function in giving their members a sense of security and well-being.

Most of the larger benevolent associations, like the St. George's and St. Andrew's societies, and the Friendly Sons of St. Patrick, were composed of wealthy merchants and professional men. Thus it was customary for these groups to help the poor of their own nationalities, but their charity relieved only a minute proportion of the needy, and new societies attempted futilely to accomplish the same ends. In the thirties a few Scotch journeymen bakers formed the Thistle Benevolent Association and by a wise policy of admitting rich Scotsmen increased their membership to nearly two hundred in 1841. By the close of the Civil War virtually every nationality in New York claimed at least one benevolent society.

Fraternal lodges, combining sociability and mutual aid with features of secrecy and the ritualism of oaths, passwords and grips, attracted immigrants from all walks of life. The newcomers created their own orders and also organized chapters of existing fraternities like the Masons and the Odd Fellows. St. Andrew's Lodge, No. 169, under the jurisdiction of the Grand Lodge of Scotland, was active in New York Masonry before 1830, and during the following decades the Germans, the French, and later the Italians established Masonic lodges. The French and Germans organized branches of the Odd Fellows, the Swiss had their Helvetia Lodge, and the Germans formed lodges of the Brothers of Hermann, the Sons of Hermann, the Order of Templars, the Druids, and others. In 1843 German Jews established their first independent fraternal order, the B'nai B'rith, and six years later a similar order, the Free Sons of Israel.

Fraternal association and national consciousness were united in the myriads of sporting and athletic clubs founded by the foreigners. On the waters of New York Harbor, the Hudson and East rivers, and Long Island Sound, immigrants indulged in the popular pastimes of fishing and boating. As early as 1833 an East River Fishing Club was organized by Irishmen, and in 1844 English rowing enthusiasts formed a boat club. On the meadows of Manhattan and Long Island, and at the Elysian Fields in Hoboken across the Hudson, groups of newcomers introduced to New York the national games of Europe. German gymnasts performed as the "Jefferson Tumbling Company" in 1840, a number of Scotsmen created the St. Andrew's Curling Club in 1845, and an Irish hurling and football club was formed to revive that "truly Irish national sport." During the forties and fifties the St. George Cricket Club afforded Englishmen a chance to challenge such "brother amateurs" as the Toronto and the New York cricket clubs.

Some organizations enabled individuals to build and maintain their social position in the foreign community. To be a soldier or a fireman heightened one's prestige among the less favored inhabitants. After mid-century, a number of the city's volunteer fire companies were completely dominated by immigrants, usually Irish but also English and Germans, who formed with the natives innumerable chowder clubs and target companies. For the Germans, at least, the fire companies were not new. Both in Europe and in America, the German *Turnvereine*, or gymnastic societies, acted as volunteer fire companies. Feasting and drinking were an integral part of the fireman's life, and until the temperance movement crept into the firehouses, a barrel of liquor was frequently hauled along with the engine to each fire for the resuscitation of exhausted fire laddies.

More popular than the fire laddies were the glamorous, uniformed militia and target companies composed of workers, shopkeepers, and clerks, both native and foreign. Despite names and appearances, these organizations were really social clubs which afforded recreation and companionship. They lent dignity and prestige to their members, transforming them from forgotten men into proud patriots who displayed their prowess at target excursions and shooting matches, funeral processions, civic ceremonies, Fourth of July and St. Patrick's Day parades. When the men of the Napper Tandy Light Artillery Company marched in their green jackets with yellow braid, light blue trousers with scarlet stripe, and blue caps with braid and tassel, they never failed to win the admiring applause of the Irish onlookers, especially the ladies.

Irish immigrants banded together, frequently naming their companies after Emmet, Mitchel, Meagher, or other national heroes, while the Germans preferred to honor Washington and Jefferson, the French their Lafayette, the Italians their Garibaldi. Some units revealed the regional origin of their members, such as the Bavarian Military Club and the Kilkenny Volunteers, or their occupations, such as the companies of Irish shipwrights and caulkers and the German shoemakers, bakers, brewers, and coopers.

A compelling reason for the establishment of "foreign" military companies was the unwillingness of the native companies to admit immigrants. Thus in 1836, when the New York Cadets resolved to prohibit foreigners from joining the corps, ten Irish members immediately declared their independence and organized an Irish company, the Montgomery Guard. Because the newcomers were rarely admitted to the native units of the state militia, scores of Irish and German companies soon were organized, and although they bought their own uniforms, the state supplied them with arms and equipment. In 1850 some seven hundred men of the Irish Dragoons, Guyon Cadets, Felon Guards, Carroll Light Guard, Sarsfield Guard, Erina Guard, and other Irish companies combined as the "Irish Volunteers" to form the Ninth Regiment of the New York State Militia, the first Irish regiment in America. During the next ten years the Irish companies appeared in such profusion that they dominated the 69th and 75th regiments and were included in the 10th, 11th, 14th, and 70th regiments, while several maintained their independence of the state militia. The galaxy of Irish units, motivated partly by desire to fight a future war for Irish independence, contrasted strangely with the failure of the English to organize a single military body during the entire period.

The colorful uniforms, martial displays, and companionship provided by the militia also attracted hundreds of Germans, Frenchmen, Scots, and Italians, Christians and Jews. Four German companies, averaging eighty men apiece in 1840, included a cavalry troop, artillery, and grenadiers. The oldest of these companies was the Jefferson Riflemen, 38th Regiment of the New York State artillery and formerly the Jefferson Guard, founded in 1835 by a group of Germans headed by the politician Captain Francis Lassak. In the fifties the 3d and 5th regiments were completely German, as were units of the 2d, 4th, 6th, 11th, and 12th regiments. Toward the middle of the century the French and the Scots organized several companies. The Frenchmen formed the *Gardes Lafayette* in 1847, soon absorbed by the 12th and later the 55th regiments of the state militia. The Scottish Guard and the Highland Guards were created in the mid-forties, followed by the Scottish Fusilier Guards and the New York Scottish Highlanders; the latter, organized in 1859, became the 79th New York Highland Regiment. While revolution flared in Italy in 1848, the first Italian unit was organized; led by Captain M. G. Lenghi and the politician Charles Del Vecchio, the company presented a ceremonial sword to the valiant General Giuseppe Avezzana upon his arrival in New York. In 1858 the Italians created a *Guardia Nazionale Italiana,* and a Portuguese company was formed in the following year. Jewish military units, appearing in the fifties, included Troop K—Empire Hussars, the Joseph A. Jackson Guards, the Young Men's Lafayette Association, and the Asmonean Guard, which, however, included Christians. The significance of the immigrant military companies is evident in the fact that in 1853 more than 4,000 of the 6,000 uniformed militia in New York City were of foreign birth. Of these, 2,600 were Irish, 1,700 were German.

Less strenuous but no less effective as a cohesive force were the many social clubs established by foreigners. Most of the benevolent societies, such as the Friendly Sons of St. Patrick, the St. George's, St. Andrew's, and St. David's societies, the French Benevolent Society, and to some extent the German Society, were wining and dining clubs with limited charitable functions. The New York Caledonian Club, founded in 1856, was similar to the older societies but somewhat more democratic. Other groups were completely recreational and had no philanthropic motives, like the Mallow Social Club formed by Irishmen, a society of baldheaded Germans, a Welsh body known as the "Young Cambrians," the Jewish "Harmonie" society, the *Société Lyrique Française,* which gave quarterly banquets, and the *Amis de Gâité,* which conducted annual balls. In the thirties the wealthy English modeled their Albion Club after the fashionable clubs of London, and at their clubhouse in Park Place they gathered for mealtime sociability, billiards, whist, chess, and checkers, gambling only for limited stakes and allowing no games on Sundays. The Germans, with contempt for this austere attitude toward the Sabbath, organized countless singing and dramatic societies which gave performances on Sundays, the Germans' traditional time for jollity.

The social life of the Germans revolved around their innumerable *Vereine,* some of which fostered music, literature, dramatics, or gymnastics, but all of which gave vent to the time-honored Teutonic love of *Gemütlichkeit.* This was the initial impulse of many occupational *Vereine* of shoemakers, painters, turners, cabinetmakers, upholsterers, piano makers, butchers, confectioners, brewers, cigar makers, barbers, waiters, and members of other trades which flourished with the high tide of German immigration in the fifties. It likewise motivated the professional associations formed by German physicians and surgeons in 1846 and 1855, a German pharmacists' reading club in 1851, and two chess clubs which appeared several years later. German amateur dramatic clubs, first treading the boards in New York about 1840, provided the nucleus of the professional German theater. During the fifties several of these theatrical societies performed comedies and vaudeville acts in hotels and beer gardens, and occasionally in theaters, where "a strictly German audience, which if not very elegant was yet of a perfectly respectable stamp." A German amateur vaudeville performance at the Olympic Theater impressed the sophisticated *Albion* with its "very Germanesque acting, strongly characteristic of low life in the old Vaterland, and full of fun and drollery. The jokes, though rather broad perhaps, were still exceedingly good."

More characteristic of the Germans were singing societies, which presented regular concerts, performed on public occasions, serenaded popular stage and opera stars, and gave benefits for charitable causes. Patterned after the familiar *Liedertafel* of

Germany, they appeared first in the thirties but were small, informal, and ephemeral for a full decade until the increasing German population supported larger and permanent *Vereine*. All classes of society enjoyed this form of recreation, the singing club of the impoverished social reformers rivaling in musical attainments the aristocratic and wealthy *Liederkranz,* which gave its first concert in 1847. During the fifties the *Rheinischer Sängerbund,* the *Arion,* the *Yorkville Männerchor,* the *Sänger-runde,* and the *Concordia* were among the leading singing societies; and by 1858 at least seventeen well-known *Vereine* were vocalizing in Manhattan, Brooklyn, Williamsburg, and Hoboken.

More politically minded were the *Turnvereine,* gymnastic societies introduced to New York in 1848 and 1850 by political refugees who had been members of *Turnvereine* in Germany. Organized originally during the dark days of Napoleonic conquest, the turner groups emphasized bodily strength and vigor as a means of creating a united and liberal, republican Germany. In America their interest in German regeneration was paralleled by their forceful propaganda for free soil and the abolition of slavery. Although the turners' early leaders were intellectuals, the rank and file were skilled artisans, for whom social activities were perhaps more vital than political partisanship: the turners gave gymnastic exhibitions, held fencing and shooting matches, sang as glee clubs, acted in plays, listened to lectures, debated, and drank beer.

The societies of several nationalities in New York organized periodic large-scale social gatherings. The German *Folksfeste,* reminiscent of festive occasions in villages and towns of the Old Country, became a German-American institution in the decade of the fifties. German target companies marched to their *Schützenfeste,* and civic groups celebrated the memory of national heroes with popular gatherings on the outskirts of town. The various *Turnvereine* of New York held their first *Turnfest* in 1853; and a thousand turners, including hundreds from Washington, Baltimore, Philadelphia, Albany, Bridgeport, New Haven, and Boston, gathered for a series of processions, picnics, and performances. In these same years the German musical societies of scattered communities assembled every summer for their *Sängerfest.* The first took place in Philadelphia in 1850, the next in Baltimore, and in 1852 scores of *Vereine* including hundreds of singers participated in a gala four-day festival in the Empire City. New York played host again in 1855 and in 1858, when 278 musicians and 300 singers presented Beethoven's Ninth Symphony at the Academy of Music on a Sunday evening, paraded through the streets the next morning, and topped the festivities with a picnic at Jones' Wood along the East River north of 60th Street.

Like the Germans, other nationalities maintained in colorful ceremonies their time-hallowed traditions. "Clad in the garb of the ancient Gael," the Scots held annual games on Long Island or at the Elysian Fields in Hoboken, where members of the Highland Society or the Caledonian Club played shinty and competed at racing, leaping, throwing, and other tests of strength and skill. These events were climaxed with a banquet amid songs, recitations, and highland dances. On St. David's Day, the "National Cambrians" sang Welsh songs, heard the harp of the Cymri, and watched the Welsh Druids in ancient costume. The Irish celebrated St. Patrick's Day with dinners, dances, and parades led by the Irish military companies in full regalia. During the fifties, however, the enthusiasm of the Irish benevolent and trade societies for marching on St. Patrick's Day was dimmed by the American condemnation of foreign-born militia as fostering divided loyalties and standing in the way of assimilation of adopted citizens.

In the mid-century years, immigrants, like the natives, indulged in speculative ventures, some catching the gold rush fever and forming societies for group migration to California, others investing in land, steamships, railroads, mines, and industrial plants. The less fortunate newcomers, however, sank their savings into the treasuries of building and loan associations, which mushroomed in the New York area. The almost irresistible appeal of these enterprises during the fifties lay in the widespread desire of the poor to secure homes cheaply and conveniently. Following the pattern already in use in England, they banded together, raised funds by subscription, and loaned money to members paying the highest premiums. So great was the demand for money that would-be homeowners sometimes borrowed from several different associations, and in the heat of competition interest rates soared; borrowers were known to have paid discounts of 33.33 per cent in the early phases of building operations. In 1850 a group of French and Swiss planned, apparently without success, to found a little village for workingmen; and two years later a number of Irishmen formed a Village Homestead and Savings Fund Association through purchase of $100.00 shares in monthly installments of $2.00. Land was to be bought and laid out in lots; individual members would obtain land at cost, and as the property was expected to "quadruple in value," the owner had "all the advantage of the specula-tion." The Germans took part in "a thousand and one" speculations, of which the more important were the German Building Association, the First German Building Loan and Accumulating Fund Association, the German Building Association—Con-cordia, and the German Building Association in the City of New York.

These immigrant projects looked better on paper than they were in actuality. The difficulty of withdrawing funds and the fines for nonpayment of dues led to frequent charges of mismanagement. Promises of individual purchasers to pay promptly for land were based upon hopes never fulfilled. Sickness, unemployment, and rising living costs completed the ruin of many families who had made partial payments; and by 1856 these ventures, through lack of caution and unsound financing, had lifted $5,000,000 from the pockets of the working classes. Among the building and loan schemes, some were nothing but speculative frauds which, by humanitarian appeals, offered for $20 (or less) lots which turned out to be "a good place for catching fish" or "a bottomless marsh inhabited only by frogs."

After 1850 the wiser immigrants found better places for their money. Ignorance, suspicion, lack of interest, and insufficient funds had prevented the establishment of savings banks until in the winter of 1850–1851 the untiring efforts of the Irish Emi-gration Society secured a charter for an Emigrant Industrial Savings Bank. Most of the bank's depositors, numbering about 2,300, were servants and laborers, but some were well-to-do; their accounts in 1856 averaged $238.56 and ranged from $1.00 to $10,000.00. The Germans were the only other immigrant group to follow the Irish example. For years they talked about a bank, and countless schemes were advanced, but it was not until 1859 that a *Deutsche Sparbank* was opened. Although some of its 3,500 depositors were Americans and Irish, the great majority were Germans, among them a large number of tailors, shoemakers, cabinetmakers, and grocers. By 1860 the combined resources of these two banks amounted to nearly $2,500,000 be-longing to more than 10,000 depositors, and four years later they held $6,056,600 belonging to 24,151 persons and organizations, clear evidence of the necessity and the popularity of these institutions.

The group activities of businessmen were not limited to the founding of banks; insurance and shipping were of great concern to them. Early in 1859 the *Germania* life insurance company was formed, and three years later it showed an $18,000 surplus on a capitalization of $200,000. As late as 1865 the *Germania* was the only German life insurance company in the United States, and it busily insured the lives of Germans in all parts of the country. The German demand for other types of insurance was met by the creation in 1852 of an association for the insurance of horses and a $200,000 fire insurance company in 1857. With the development of commerce in the forties and fifties, foreign-born merchants considered the establishment of exclusive shipping services. Several attempts by Frenchmen in New York to create a permanent French steamship line ended in failure, and early Irish plans for a direct steamship service to Galway came to naught; however, in 1858 a Galway and New York Steamship Company was successfully launched; and in the meantime German merchants had fathered two lines, the Hamburg America in 1856 and the North German Lloyd, whose ships began their runs between Bremen and New York in 1858.

Except perhaps the business associations and the military companies, the group activities of the immigrant were necessary tools of adjustment to life in America. In some instances the newcomer adopted or joined institutions already familiar to Americans, such as the militia, the fire companies, building and loan associations, professional and commercial organizations, benevolent and mutual aid societies. These were foreign only in membership. Other immigrant associational activities, like the Scottish games, the English pursuit of cricket, and the German theatrical, musical, and gymnastic *Vereine*, were deeply rooted in the national cultures of these peoples. The foreigners freely accepted elements of American social and economic life which were compatible with their European experience, but when they found no satisfactory substitute for their own social groupings, they attempted proudly, even defiantly, to preserve their cultural heritage.

Six / Values and Beliefs

14 / Ethics and Enterprise:
The Values of a Boston Elite, 1800-1860

Paul Goodman

In conjunction with religious and political ideologies, societal and class values are powerful factors in determining patterns of human action. The isolation and examination of value patterns and systems is an important task for social historians.

Paul Goodman introduces us to the Boston business elite of the first half of the nineteenth century. There, in response to threats posed by an increasing rate of social change, a tightly knit group developed conceptions of responsibility that gave a special flavor to Boston life. This ethic of responsibility took three forms: to the family, the public, and the individual. Rapaciousness was sharply limited, and surplus wealth found socially useful outlets in endowments for education, the arts, and a building program that transformed the face of Boston. Individuals cultivated an interest in art and in science. It would be a mistake to see this group of business and commercial leaders in terms of the robber baron stereotype.

For further reading: Donald N. Barrett (ed.), *Values in America* (1961); Clyde Kluckhohn, "Have There Been Discernible Shifts in American Values During the Past Generation?" in Elting Morison (ed.), *The American Style* (1958), 142–217; John G. Cawelti, *Apostles of the Self-Made Man: Changing Concepts of Success in America* (1965); *Cleveland Amory, *The Proper Bostonians* (1947); *Seymour Martin Lipset, *The First New Nation: The United States in Historical and Comparative Perspective* (1963), 99–204.

By the early nineteenth century, the group of prominent families which had emerged in Boston by accumulating wealth in commerce later invested in the newer financial, transportation and manufacturing enterprises that transformed the face of nineteenth-century New England. At the same time that the group in its entrepreneurial role promoted and welcomed urbanization, industrialization and heavy immigration, it feared that rapid social change threatened stability by unleashing a

American Quarterly, XVIII (1966), 437–451. Copyright 1966 by the Trustees of the University of Pennsylvania. Footnotes have been omitted.

chaotic individualism which rewarded those unrestrained by standards of appropriate behavior. To resist this, the Bostonians utilized an elaborate web of kinship ties which made the family a potent institution that gave them cohesion, continuity and stability so they might perpetuate their power, prominence and way of life. In addition to ties of blood, the elite shared a common set of values which defined proper behavior, transmitted goals to the young and provided a measure by which to judge and punish deviance. "Close and hard, consolidated, with a uniform stamp on all and opinion running in grooves," the Boston elite formulated a set of beliefs that constituted a personal ethic and also defined its role in society as a republican aristocracy which stabilized as it transformed.

Believing in the gospel of progress, Boston's leading families saw themselves as agents of improvement. The Boston merchant was a "prince" with unique power and responsibilities. His claim to superiority in a republic stemmed not from hereditary privilege but from personal achievement. Endowed with wealth, honor, virtue and wisdom, he was also a patron of culture and innumerable charities, an exemplar of republican simplicity, and a leader of the nation. Men such as John A. Lowell, it was urged, gave "wisdom and stability to the methods by which the vast transition has been made in Massachusetts . . . from foreign commerce and agriculture to a great manufacturing and business commonwealth." The merchant was an architect of social progress because commerce liberalized peoples, pierced barriers among nations, diffused civilization and the arts, increased wealth and promoted the division of labor which equalized conditions among men. In a world governed by peaceful commercial ties, war would disappear, republican polities would replace monarchical ones, and businessmen would exercise power once monopolized by kings and aristocrats. Theodore Parker proclaimed the gospel:

> But the Saint of the Nineteenth century is the Good Merchant; he is wisdom for the foolish, strength for the weak. . . . Build him a shrine in a Bank and Church, in the Market and the Exchange or build it not; no Saint stands higher than this Saint of Trade. There are such men, rich and poor, young and old; such men in Boston.

While the image of the businessman as an apostle of progress located his public role, it did not entirely define his personal ambitions. The acquisition of wealth was necessary and desirable but it was only one of life's goals and its importance was shaped by its relations to other aims. The great danger was that one might become too greatly absorbed in the quest for treasure, neglect other proper pursuits and stain one's character. "The man who labors simply for the accumulation of property," George Hillard told the Boston Mercantile Library Association, "and with no higher aims, surely is unworthy of a day such as ours; he has mistaken his calling." "The truth is," insisted Nathan Appleton, "that my mind has always been devoted to many other things rather than money-making."

Men might agree that life should not be confined to the countinghouse but it was difficult to resolve the tensions between the claims of enterprise and the demands of conscience. The poignant diary of William Appleton reveals a man torn between the irresistible temptations of trade and the nagging conviction that cultivating the spirit was more important. Secretly and repeatedly he confessed that while sitting in church, his mind flew "from City to City, from Ship to Ship and from Speculation to Speculation." Yet though he longed for the life of the spirit, Appleton opted for the life of trade because only in it could he fulfill himself. Men of Appleton's generation no longer found the Calvinist ethic adequate justification for devotion to work and profit-seeking. Success in enterprise brought its own reward; no longer was it chiefly a sign of God's grace.

But the tension was too great for some. Youthful retirements were common among the successful. Since men often entered trade very young and acquired fortunes before they reached thirty, it was possible at an early age to retire from the marketplace and cultivate another world. P. C. Brooks, reputedly New England's richest man in the 1840s, "retired" at thirty-six; George Ticknor's father, Elisha, left trade after less than twenty years' labor; T. H. Perkins' son, Thomas, entered his father's business, and after a few very successful ventures, spent the rest of his life in affluence and enjoying leisure. Even Nathan Appleton intended to retire in 1815 on $200,000, claiming that "it was altogether accidental that I have ever gone further."

While some retired prematurely, others could not. Their calling had become a personal challenge that could not be declined. By the 1820s, the growing use of the corporation made investments less risky and gave businesses greater institutional longevity than the old-fashioned commercial partnership had enjoyed. Numerous banks, insurance companies, textile factories and railroads offered stable and prudent outlets for savings. Yet investing in these enterprises had still another attraction. P. T. Jackson preferred manufacturing because, it was urged, "he loved to take the raw material and by the skillful treatment of it to add to its value, by which the capitalist and the operative were profited; and the public were gainers if he could produce a useful article." John Murray Forbes, according to a partner, "never seemed to me a man of acquisitiveness, but very distinctly one of constructiveness." He shifted from trade to railroads, rescuing a road in difficulty, and while his investments were often profitable, he was governed by a "dominant passion for building up things." Success in one's calling yielded a sense of power and the satisfaction of creative accomplishment. Nor could one ever stop. "I must be busy," wrote William Appleton, "I don't know how to stop. I love best to do that which is most difficult. . . . That which others would not undertake pleases me most." When he was rich, honored and old, Appleton insisted that he remained in business not from love of gain but from "the pleasure of doing what others cannot do, and to get applause for so doing; not a high motive, but better than a sordid one."

Yet despite its rewards, the life of enterprise did not exhaust the limits of aspiration. Material accomplishment was a means of attaining other goals, particularly "ease of mind." Men sought personal independence and desired to live gracefully with honor and dignity. But the highest prize was character. Trade was honorable because it sharpened one's faculties and trained one's character. Though William Appleton had accepted a bank presidency with trepidation, years later he noted that his successful management had elevated his moral qualities. Samuel Eliot advised his son to pursue "those paths that will best conduce to the establishment of your character as a gentleman, a man of honour, the moralist, and the Christian."

The greatest threat to character was avarice, for it warped values, hardened hearts and led men into schemes which often destroyed both reputation and independence. But business was also one of the best schools of virtue. Character was the product of "wide and varied intercourse with men, and of large experience in the chances of life." In the world of trade, men believed, virtue was rewarded; one's credit was only as good as one's character. In the long run, Edward Everett observed, only those communities prosper "where virtuous principle is revered as the rule of conduct."

The center of the commercial ethic was personal responsibility. A man became what he made himself. The successful businessman was supposed to come from humble beginnings. He was born in rural isolation, migrated to Boston and entered a countinghouse as a lowly clerk or went to sea and rose from cabin boy to captain. Those born into established families were at a disadvantage because they had to overcome the temptations of leisure and indulgence. The development of personal responsibility was strengthened by mercantile experience. Youths not barely twenty sailed as first mates, captains and supercargoes entrusted with the success or failure of a voyage. Those performing their jobs well were handsomely rewarded, acquiring capital with which to enter business on their own. Clearly fixing individual responsibility, J. M. Forbes believed, was an article of sound business practice: "I have a great horror of a divided responsibility, preferring one common man, who has got to take all the credit or blame, to half a dozen geniuses, who put it off on somebody else."

The world of business rested on a complex tangle of human relationships. In Boston, unlike London, men were not lost in the crowd. Their virtues and vices could be closely observed and their characters judged. Men did not live in isolation but in a highly articulated social order which not only set standards but encouraged and enforced right conduct. Boston society with its elaborate web of family ties and its strong sense of personal responsibility deprived men of the cloak of anonymity. Since colonial times kinship ties had been important in New England's commercial development and in the advancement of individual and family fortunes. Separated by thousands of miles of ocean, lacking rapid means of communication, living in periods of international instability, traders throughout the Atlantic world built their business activities around personal, often blood relationships. One was never alone for successful traders often owed much to helpful kin and friends. The organization of overseas trade rested on trust. Houses preferred to send out younger men whom they knew and could rely on to shepherd and guard cargoes faithfully.

Investigating kin ties of prominent Massachusetts families, Kenneth Porter found that family connections shaped business relationships, influencing the selection of apprentices and captains, commission merchants and partners. A trader felt "bound not to go outside his circle of kinship, so long as there was in it any one desirous of employment." Commission merchants and supercargoes likewise believed "they had a moral if not a legal claim to the business of their mercantile relatives." Such practices had disadvantages. Some relatives lacked business skills and were indolent; others were uninterested in trade. Henry Lee charged that tight family control of certain textile mills led to nepotism, excessive salaries, stodgy management and low dividends. But despite these risks, businessmen felt safer delegating authority to those they knew intimately and trusted implicitly. Kinship ties and high standards of personal responsibility reduced the riskiness of overseas trade and the commercial partnership. Yet even after incorporation and limited liability offered safer institutional forms for the conduct of business, certain families, usually prominent in the firm's founding, remained identified with the enterprise. During its first sixty years, the Massachusetts Bank, N. S. B. Gras suggests, might have been called the Phillips' Bank: William Phillips (1722–1804) was second president and a director; his son, William Jr., was sixth president; his wife was a daughter of the third president; and a grandson became eighth president. Similarly, generations of Bowditches, Sargents and Lowells managed the Massachusetts Hospital Life Insurance Company.

The elite entrepreneur was thus not a free agent but a morally responsible person answerable to family and friends as well as to community and conscience. By deviating from expected norms, individuals not only risked censure but they also might injure the clan materially and morally. "You should place your standard of action so high," Amos Lawrence advised his brother Abbott, "as to require great vigilance in living up to it." The ideal businessman would risk his property for his honor and for the good of others. Though not legally obligated, J. M. Forbes repaid his father's needy creditors as soon as he had provided a competence for his mother. When friends in textile manufacturing were threatened by ruin during the panic of 1857, William Appleton saved them at considerable personal risk.

The honest trader must be truthful, fair and honest. "There is no class with whom the Christian rule of doing to others what we expect or require in return, is more strictly demanded than amongst merchants" proclaimed Nathaniel Appleton. Because mercantile honor was as delicate as woman's, the slightest stain or equivocation marked one as morally deficient and doomed to failure. The eulogists' proudest boast was that despite the temptations of gain, the character of an Appleton or a Lawrence remained unsullied. In these ways, the ethic of individual responsibility married moral duty to the calling of trade: the dead merchant prince "was one of those men who helped to raise the name 'Boston merchant' to the honor it has acquired." P. C. Brooks' career summarized the experience of a generation. Starting with small means he rose to great affluence, always guided by prudence, moderation and honor. In similar ways, an entire stratum of businessmen had been formed "in whom energy, moral courage, caution, and liberality were all remarkably combined."

While the family cultivated and enforced personal responsibility, it was also the hub of the domestic universe, defining a style of life and manners appropriate to a princely calling. Desiring a suitable physical environment in which to live, Bostonians commissioned architects such as Charles Bulfinch and Samuel McIntire to create homes and countinghouses of charm, dignity and taste. Bulfinch's Colonnade Row joined nineteen façades facing Boston Common while Franklin Crescent formed sixteen houses on a gentle curve shaded in a semi-oval park, giving these areas a refinement reminiscent of parts of London. John Lowell's house, remarked a French traveler, "breathes that air of magnificence accompanied by simplicity which is only to be found among merchants." Public architecture was also transformed. According to Timothy Dwight, the reconstruction of stores and wharves in the port of Boston lent "a magnificence to commerce, which it can boast of on no other spot of North America."

Architecture expressed the desire to adorn life with elegance and beauty appropriate to a world inhabited by gentlemen. The essence of gentlemanly behavior was devotion to virtue. "The merchant's life is a genteel and elegant profession," wrote George Hillard, "because it is consistent with the true character of a gentleman, and it admits of the indulgence of elegant and intellectual tastes." While a gentleman was a man of honor and integrity, responsibility and trust, he must also possess urbanity, culture, easy manners and dignified deportment. Though he prized beauty, the gentleman avoided ostentation, always seeking to achieve balance. Men must accumulate wealth but eschew avarice, work diligently but cherish domestic responsibilities, master the challenges of trade and finance but also pay due regard to culture and charity. The model was Thomas H. Perkins, whose "life was marked by self-control . . . an innate purity and love of order that made excess distasteful to him."

The gentleman's pursuit of balance together with the merchant prince's sense of social responsibility shaped the Boston elite's relationship to culture. "A country in which all men are engaged in acquisition of property," George Hillard told the Mercantile Library Association, ". . . without books, without scholars, without ideas . . . contains within itself the element of destruction." Governed exclusively by the passions, corrupted by selfishness, society would split apart. By pursuing culture, the businessman might broaden his sympathies, refine his sensibilities and escape the moral dangers of a consuming thirst for gain. Culture and learning shielded one from the "hardening influence of worldly pursuits," gave one "a new sense of the capacities and dignity of human nature" and taught "lessons of humility, patience, and submission." Because culture built character, it was one's duty to encourage arts and sciences, "without which, no fortune however ample, will bring contentment."

Love of learning and especially bibliophilia became a hallmark of the Boston elite. Samuel Eliot "had a great value and feeling for books themselves" (he owned four thousand volumes), William Sturgis possessed "a love of letters," Samuel Shaw never let commerce "seduce him from a love of science," while John Lowell, Jr., who owned ten thousand books, let "few subjects in science or literature" escape his attention. No layman knew more "of the standard or sound current literature of our language" than Peter C. Brooks. J. M. Forbes, like Brooks, surrounded himself with intellectuals such as Emerson, who observed: "How little this man suspects, with his sympathy for men and his respect for lettered and scientific people, that he is not likely ever to meet a man who is superior to himself."

While culture counteracted the harshness of the acquisitive life, it also afforded opportunities to serve the community. During the first half of the nineteenth century, Boston earned a reputation as the Athens of America, the republic's foremost patron of the arts, renowned for an extraordinary number of intellectuals, poets, novelists, historians, scientists, preachers and educators. The values of the arts and sciences penetrated Brahmin society. Scholarship and culture attracted many of the merchants' ablest sons, who dabbled in artistic efforts and gave only half-hearted attention to their professions and businesses. Commerce subsidized the careers of Prescott and Ticknor while the Lowells produced poets and educators, and the Eliots gave America a great nineteenth-century college president. William H. Channing, Professor Andrews Norton, Edward Everett and countless others married daughters of well-known merchants, thus personally uniting wealth with learning. By patronizing culture, men were creating a city which Emerson predicted would "lead the civilization of North America," a place such as was Renaissance Florence where "the desire for glory and honour is powerfully generated by the air in men of every profession. . . ." "All history and all experience show," said T. H. Perkins' eulogist, "that literature, science, art, all that ennobles and refines humanity, are intimately connected with the prosperity of commerce; and it is our intimate conviction that that prosperity is dependent upon, and inseparable from, those qualities for which Col. Perkins was so eminently distinguished." Thus culture, like virtue, was not its own reward.

Patronage took many forms. One was an endowment by John Lowell, Jr., of a series of lectures. Because "the prosperity of my native land, New England," Lowell said, "which is sterile and unproductive, must depend hereafter, as it has heretofore depended, first on the moral qualities, and second on the intelligence and information of its inhabitants," he sponsored a pioneering adventure in adult education designed to promote those moral principles essential to happiness. The Boston Athenaeum was established in 1807 as a private library, limited to those buying shares at $300 apiece, located in the heart of Boston where "the higher classes of society" might instruct "their taste in the fine and pleasing arts" and thus become better "patrons and judges of what is excellent." The Athenaeum was also a means of cultivating a balanced personality. It provided a place where people could find refuge from work and could cultivate the mind. Affluence excited the desire for pleasure and amusement and still greater wealth but the Athenaeum offered to substitute "mental occupation for sensual indulgence." Thus the library's founders applied "wealth to its noblest uses" by joining "to a spirit of commercial enterprise a just estimate of the value of letters and arts."

The spirit of patronage was closely linked to charitable and philanthropic enterprise and both were expressions of the businessman's role as steward of wealth. Those worried that the active life bred a lust for gain found solace in the ethic of stewardship. The merchant did not work for himself but for the race; commerce, progress and Christianity went hand in hand. "We must keep in mind," Amos Lawrence confided to his diary, "that we are to render an account of the use of those talents which are committed to us; . . . As our stewardship has been faithful or otherwise, will be the sentence pronounced upon us." Amos did more than talk, and besides innumerable donations to other causes made a large gift to Harvard to establish a scientific school. This gift, brother Abbott assured him, was the "last best work ever done by one of our name, which will prove a better title to true nobility than any from the potentates of the world. . . . It enriches your descendants in a way that mere money can never do and is a better investment than any you have ever made." Good works, like culture, were a means of countering an excessively acquisitive spirit.

Boston charities and philanthropies proliferated in the first half of the nineteenth century. Relatively few were founded during the colonial period but the desire to serve and improve, coupled with growing material resources, made Boston rich in public spirit. From 26 incorporated philanthropic, charitable and educational societies in 1830, the number increased to almost 160 by 1850. Between 1828–52 Amos Lawrence, who kept exact accounts of everything, gave away $639,000; he also set aside two rooms of his house for the accumulation of useful articles for the poor. Worried that he was getting too rich, Samuel Appleton decided one year to devote his income to charity, personal amusements and public needs. Merchants gave liberally to a galaxy of causes, educating the blind, succoring the poor and rescuing the orphan but they often gave quietly and anonymously. Public display that one had done one's duty cheapened the spirit of liberality and substituted greed for fame for love of money.

Unitarians boasted that they had "started every one of" the "best secular charities" in Boston. Though they may have exaggerated, Unitarians probably dominated philanthropy because so many leading businessmen flocked to the new denomination. Unitarianism flourished in New England because it suited the taste and needs of those who no longer accepted Calvinism. In its place, Unitarianism offered a faith refreshed by the winds of rationalism, confident of man's capacity for moral action. The good merchant attended church regularly, lived his faith by performing good works, and deplored denominational rivalry and bigotry. As the faith of the elite, Unitarianism was thus one more sign that the Boston merchant was an agent of progress who encouraged "whatever tended to exalt humanity."

Churchman, philanthropist, patron of the arts and man of family, the Proper Bostonian's range of responsibilities extended beyond his business and city to encompass the public affairs of the entire nation. In a republic, business enterprise was appropriately the chief means of acquiring great wealth because virtue and talent were rewarded, giving every citizen the same opportunity to prosper. Those who accumulated riches did so, it was argued, because they possessed personal merit, not hereditary advantage. The successful were obligated to serve the community in which they had prospered. Amos Lawrence expected his son to devote his talents "to the advancement of the moral and political influence of New England. New England I say; for here is to be the stronghold of liberty, and the seat of influence to the vast multitude of millions who are to people this republic." Abbott Lawrence went to Congress and later served as ambassador to Great Britain; William Appleton and his brother, Samuel, both served in Congress. Salem's Nathaniel Silsbee sat in the United States Senate and Benjamin Crowninshild was Secretary of the Navy.

As men of enterprise, Boston's elite professed standards of business conduct which were supposed to harmonize everyday practices with life's larger purpose. These expectations do not describe the way men behaved, yet their attitudes toward competition, speculation, profit and interest rates help further to delineate their values.

As the economy grew in complexity, men with a talent for managing and multiplying funds found themselves increasingly involved in a web of fiduciary relationships. Merchants engaged in overseas trade had permitted friends and relatives to send along small adventures in their vessels. Also, traders frequently loaned money, insured others, endorsed notes and helped out younger members of the family. Even when business became more institutionalized, high standards of personal responsibility were insisted upon. J. M. Forbes believed that those entrusted with funds of others must never recommend investments in which they had an interest. Trustees and directors were expected to take their obligations seriously. Ebenezer Francis insisted on mastering a knowledge of whatever enterprise he served as a director. When appointed to the Columbian Bank's committee of finance, William Appleton promised "to give much time to the business, and in all transactions for the institution, to pursue such a course as will bear the strictest examination."

The greatest test of one's probity came at moments of personal difficulty. P. T. Jackson was said to show more concern for the care of "interests consigned to his charge than of his own." He would sacrifice his own interests rather than jeopardize property entrusted to him and occasionally he bought and sold shares because of concern for a corporation's welfare. When the Massachusetts Bank loaned $31,000 to the Boston Brick Manufacturing Company and it failed, the bank's president, John James Dixwell, a graduate of the China trade, reimbursed the institution for $20,000. Though a bitter foe of slavery and one of John Brown's financial angels, J. M. Forbes felt that his obligations to the stockholders of the Hannibal and St. Joseph Railroad, running through proslavery country in Missouri, prevented him from publicly proclaiming his hatred of the peculiar institution. The fiduciary's deep sense of individual responsibility fitted well with the closeness of kin ties and the ethic of personal obligation.

The milieu bred cautiousness which informed a whole range of attitudes. The greatest sin was speculation for it violated all the values of the mercantile ideal. Eulogists boasted that P. C. Brooks' fortune did not come from "great speculative profits" but from "persevering attention to his regular business." Robert G. Shaw never ventured too boldly lest he be unable to meet promptly all demands made upon him; early in his career he paid his notes before they fell due. He was exact and upright and preferred to lose business rather than deal with those whose standards did not match his own.

The evils of speculation were many. It undermined the ethic of success which held that virtue and hard work were rewarded and it substituted the belief that financial magic was the way to wealth. Speculative gain was chance gain, not a reward for meritorious personal effort. Speculation was not only financially risky, according to Amos Lawrence, but it inevitably placed one's "honor in imminent peril." A desire to get rich quickly and easily was a sign of avarice. "The good merchant is not in haste to be rich," said Alexander Young. Besides threatening the purity of character, speculation jeopardized another prized goal, independence. Rash ventures did not pay; more men failed than succeeded. Believing the value of wealth was the personal independence it afforded, P. C. Brooks preferred moderate returns and avoided hazardous investments, including unproductive real estate, railroads and manufacturing which was vulnerable to "fluctuating political influence" and required entrusting "immense capitals to persons not trained to the business carried on." The only natural and elevating gains came from the individual's own prudent efforts in affairs he understood and in which he had some personal interest.

Enjoined not to hazard his fortune, the businessman had to be content with a moderate return on his investment. One should seek neither excessive profits nor interest since such returns usually required one to take advantage of another's necessity. Alexander Young condemned such practices as loss leaders and monopolistic combinations. Novices in trade should not cut prices too low since that would reveal an overeagerness for custom, and well-established houses should shun overly high and stodgy prices. Moderation not only formed character but was sound business because "fair" profits increased the consumers' purchasing power. Interest rates particularly should not exceed 6 per cent. "I have never taken more," claimed William Sturgis. Usury, John Jacob Astor had once told him, " 'narrered the mind and 'ardened the 'art.' " Interest over 6 per cent was unjust, P. C. Brooks believed, because money was not worth more. The capitalist who demanded excessive rates claimed "the benefit of the borrower's skill . . . his courage and energy . . ." and was taking "advantage of his neighbor's need."

During the first half of the nineteenth century, as a group of Boston businessmen were transforming their region's economy, they were also elaborating a value system whose leitmotif was an insistence on stable and conservative modes of behavior in an era of rapid change. Though American society was becoming increasingly impersonal, these Bostonians sought to create and preserve a tightly knit social order through the cohesive force of family and an ethic of personal responsibility. Rejecting the singleminded pursuit of wealth, Bostonians claimed to prefer the balanced personality that tempered the quest for wealth with standards of gentlemanly decorum and the purifying influences of culture and stewardship. "Boston is the only place in America," E. L. Godkin observed, "where wealth and the knowledge how to use it are apt to coincide." Writing a generation earlier, Charles Dickens observed: "The golden calf they worship at Boston is a pigmy compared with the giant effigies set up in the other parts of that vast counting-house which lies across the Atlantic, and the almighty dollar sinks into something comparatively insignificant, amidst a whole Pantheon of better gods."

Yet while Bostonians might take pride, many New Englanders were skeptical. Powerful forces challenged the Brahmin ideal. Despite the region's prosperity and the opportunities it afforded ambitious young men, many left for other communities, notably New York. Here people found a milieu quite different from the ordered ideal of the Yankee self-image. A New England businessman warned his venturesome son that Gotham's habits of extravagance "border on insanity. It is at war with general health, morals, and prosperity. It is, indeed, nearly allied to, if not the fruitful parent of, the mighty frauds, peculation, forgeries which are almost daily uncovered in that great city." But still the youth went.

The challenge was never entirely external, for possibilities within New England inspired ambitious schemers and daring adventurers who never accepted the sobering values of elite society. Moreover, even the genteel world of elite business alienated souls who thought that economic change was undermining New England's moral foundations. "What are his machines? Of steel, brass, leather, oak and ivory?" asked Emerson of the New England capitalist. He changed the world, no doubt, with his mills, telegraph, propeller, insurance company and democratic politics, but Emerson challenged, "Now let him make a harp!" Dismay was not confined to a few sensitive souls residing near Concord. Within Brahmin society sons of merchants turned their backs on the life of trade. Revolted by a growing commercialism, they watched newcomers acquire wealth without character or sensibility and challenge elite standards. "Commercial prosperity," George W. Curtis warned, "is only a curse if it be not subservient to moral and intellectual progress, and our prosperity will conquer us if we do not conquer our prosperity." One solution was to form a way of life governed by a cultural elite in which the social hero was not the self-made businessman but the idle man whose virtue was a "devotion to general literature" combined with "a diffuse, wide-ranging outlook governed by the imagination." By postulating an ideal of cultural aristocracy, one could exclude the parvenus lacking elegance and taste, and thereby surround life "with an aura of unshakable permanence." Failing to impose their standards on society, some withdrew to Brook Farm seeking to re-establish a pre-commercial order where gentleman farmers asserted that moral leadership denied them elsewhere.

From all sides the conservative values of Boston's elite were challenged, from those who thought the compromise of the successful was a sellout to materialism and from the ambitious, enterprising newcomers who scorned to play by the rules governing gentlemen. De Tocqueville noted that the rich in America were ceaselessly driven by a desire for material gratification. Opportunity beckoned everywhere and "the wealthy . . . never form a body which has manners and regulations of its own." The Boston elite tried to infuse their lives with standards of caution, personal responsibility and public duty. The model was P. C. Brooks who opposed "the modest and unconscious resistance of sound principles and virtuous example to those elements of instability, which are put in motion by the ambitious, the reckless, the visionary, and the corrupt." The governing guide of his life was moderation; never hazarding what he had for excessive gain, never risking independence or sullying character in the pursuit of wealth.

The articulation of a set of values to guide one's professional and personal lives defined aspiration. How well men integrated ideals and behavior is another matter. Future studies of elite-controlled businesses should reveal to what extent the group's values influenced men's performances as entrepreneurs, shaping the objectives and policies of their firms. Moreover, the experience of long-lived elite enterprises should reveal how successful the group was in competing with others who did not share their values and who threatened those dissenting from the prevailing ethics of enterprise that flourished in the late nineteenth century.

15 / Ethics, Folklore, and Morality on the Middle Border

Lewis Atherton

One of the curious anomalies of American social history is the persistence after 1850 of a cluster of values and beliefs that did not correspond to institutional reality. The rural conception of a proper social order resting on the family, the church, and the school, and a pervading belief in the unwholesomeness of cities were embodied in the pages of the McGuffey readers, and innumerable young Americans imbibed them. Thrift, sobriety, absolute honesty, fidelity to duty, piety, virtue and its manifest rewards: these might do in a simpler preindustrial world, but they appear naive in a complex society. How far they were functional for the growing urban middle class is open to question. These values and beliefs did help to justify small-town America and provided a rationalization for it as the great cities moved ahead in the race for wealth and power. These values have persisted in only slightly altered form well into the twentieth century in places remote from the influences of cities, mass communication, and welfare capitalism.

For further reading: *Merle Curti, *The Social Ideas of American Educators* (1935); Richard D. Mosier, *Making the American Mind: Social and Moral Ideas in the McGuffey Readers* (1947); Ruth Elson, *Guardians of Tradition: American Schoolbooks of the Nineteenth Century* (1964).

CHURCH, SCHOOL, AND HOME

Between 1850 and 1900 Americans bought one hundred million copies of William Holmes McGuffey's school readers. Though well received virtually everywhere, they appealed particularly to the Middle Border. As an apostle of religion, morality, and education, McGuffey wanted to bolster midwestern civilization against the dangers inherent in pioneering new frontiers. Since his Readers were directed to a supposedly classless society, they were all-inclusive in their appeal, and from them came a set of principles which remained unchallenged in the minds of common people until the turn of the century.

McGuffey worried so much about frontier dangers that he overlooked the revolutionary changes in transportation, manufacturing, and management which were then taking place. The 1857 revision of his Readers, which most Midwesterners studied, barely mentioned steamboats, and railroads received no attention at all. Pupils learned about horse-drawn transportation, about merchant rather than manufacturer, about artisan in place of factory laborer, of the outdoors, of birds and farm animals, of gossipy barbers, of Longfellow's "Village Blacksmith," and of town pumps, watering troughs, and village greens:

> *Then contented with my State,*
> *Let me envy not the great;*
> *Since true pleasures may be seen,*
> *On a cheerful village green.*

Moreover, children learned that village and country life surpassed that in cities. As a rule, McGuffey simply ignored urban ways or used them as examples of corruption. The story, "Mysterious Stranger," described the unhappiness of a man from another planet when he learned that city pleasures in our world were accompanied with the penalty of death. Still another story told of "Old Tom Smith," the drunkard, whose downfall came from city life. Through a clerkship in a city store, he became acquainted with bad company. Instead of spending his evenings reading, he went to theatres, balls, and suppers. Drinking and card playing followed next, and soon thereafter his saintly mother had to pay large gambling debts for him. Although his mother and wife grieved themselves to death over his city vices, nothing could stop his drinking. The story ended with reception of the news that he had received a ten-year prison sentence for stealing. Village boys often misbehaved in McGuffey's stories but they seldom fell prey to major vices.

McGuffey's emphasis on rural and village life pleased an agrarian age. His environmental picture squared with physical facts, and people knew just enough of the outside world to share his doubts about cities. His Readers thus gained strength by applying the eternal verities to a simple culture, uncomplicated by urban and industrial problems. This very strength, however, became a source of weakness as village and farm gave way to city and factory.

McGuffey ideals retreated slowly. Rural America believed in a classless society, which helped enforce still other pressures toward conformity. In the 1830's Tocqueville commented on the tyranny of the majority in making Americans conform to a common pattern. Although disagreeing with Tocqueville's analysis, James Bryce said much the same in the 1880's. According to him, American public opinion was not stated along class lines; it applied to all. In Bryce's estimation, Americans believed that common sense resided in the minds of the majority, with a consequent "fatalism of the multitude" evident in much of American life. Ed Howe commented that city people would behave better if they knew one another as well as did villagers who heard gossip about their sins on the way home from committing them, thus implying that conformity was even greater in small towns.

Perhaps also an emphasis on the immediately useful and the practical contributed to the survival of current moral values. An Iowa lawyer who spent his youth in a small town commented that most pioneers were of the earth, earthy. They knew practical things—weather, rains, common plants and animals, good livestock. But they were not philosophers. Whatever the explanation, small-town beliefs changed slowly, and this characteristic gave village life an impression of stability and permanence.

The God-centered, small-town code emphasized man's immortality. School and home both paid obeisance to God's plan and God's laws, for everything fell within His master plan. From McGuffey's Readers the pupil learned that Jesus was above Plato, Socrates, and all the philosophers, for He was a God. Evidences of His power and wisdom existed on every hand. McGuffey proved this with simple stories. Washington's father, for instance, secretly planted seeds in a design which spelled out George's name when they sprouted. Although George was surprised, he refused to accept his father's suggestion that chance explained the phenomenon. His father now admitted that he had planted the seeds to teach George a lesson, and urged the boy to look around him at God's planning on every hand. And thus, said McGuffey, driving home his point as usual, from that day George never doubted the existence of a God who was the creator and owner of all things.

Even the problem of evil in a universe governed by divine law was explained to school boys through simple stories. Everything happened for the best and every object had a purpose in the great plan of things. When one of two boys caught in a thunderstorm remarked that he hated the evil lightning, the other explained that lightning was necessary to purify the air of bad vapors, a greater good thus offsetting a lesser evil. Understanding would always clarify the appearance of evil. An observant boy asked his father to help him cut down thorn bushes and thistles which were snagging wool from the sides of passing sheep. Since parents in McGuffey's Readers were always wiser than children, the boy profited by taking his father's advice to wait until morning. In doing so, he discovered that birds used the wool to build their nests, and that God indeed was wise and good and had made everything for the best.

A former resident of Hillsboro, Iowa, described the operation of this philosophy in his childhood days. Belief in God was universal. People wondered why certain things occurred, chiefly the deaths of children and very good people, but no one doubted God's existence and His fatherly care. If a death occurred, the Lord willed it. The Lord sent affliction to punish sin and disbelief. The Lord could be prevailed upon to help His people out of difficulties. If the corn needed rain, the churches set a day of prayer. If success accompanied this, it had been the proper thing to do; if intercession failed, the people had not prayed with sufficient faith. The heavenly books were balanced daily by an omniscient bookkeeper who recorded every act. The idea of universal and impersonal law was displeasing. These people wisely turned to something warmer, something more directly personal in which man played the central part. He participated in a drama which included sky and earth, which began with Adam, and which would end only when the heavens were rolled up as a scroll.

McGuffey taught that society depended on religion. Christianity was conducive to national prosperity. It raised the poor from want, brought rich and poor together on a common level for an hour of prayer, and promoted good order and harmony. Self-respect and elevation of character, softness and civility of manners came from religious teaching. Christianity strengthened the family circle as a source of instruction, comfort, and happiness. Moreover,

> If you can induce a community to doubt the genuineness and authenticity of the Scriptures; to question the reality and obligations of religion; to hesitate, undeciding, whether there be any such thing as virtue or vice; whether there be an eternal state of retribution beyond the grave; or whether there exists any such being as God, you have broken down the barriers of moral virtue, and hoisted the floodgates of immorality and crime.

Insofar as school books are concerned, small-town Mid-America now reads of miracles of science. God, church, and even human death are generally ignored. Separation of church and state and a desire to shield children from morbid thoughts help explain this marked change. Perhaps, however, it would not have occurred had science not become the god of so many people, for gods are too important to be omitted in formal education of the young.

In the second half of the nineteenth century grade schools commonly opened the day with brief devotional exercises. Lessons also had a religious slant. McGuffey's *First Reader* pictured a little girl kneeling in prayer and asking God to protect her from sin. A poem in the *Second Reader* stressed the blessings of immortality:

> *A little child who loves to pray,*
> *And read his Bible too,*
> *Shall rise above the sky one day,*
> *And sing as angels do;*
> *Shall live in Heaven, that world above,*
> *Where all is joy, and peace, and love.*

These simple stories and poems in public-school readers document the tremendous shift in faith between the nineteenth and twentieth centuries, from a man-centered and God-centered universe on the one hand to an impersonal and science-centered universe on the other.

McGuffey also stressed the need for public schools. "We must educate!" Literary as well as religious institutions must keep pace with the headlong rush of western settlement. If the Middle Border expected to preserve republican institutions and universal suffrage, both *head* and *heart* must be trained. McGuffey thus urged pupils to feverish activity:

> *Haste thee, school boy, haste away,*
> *While thy youth is bright and gay;*
> *Seek the place with knowledge blest;*
> *It will guide to endless rest;*
> *Haste thee, school boy, haste away,*
> *While thy youth is bright and gay.*

Newspapers expressed the same ideas. Parents supposedly could do nothing finer for their children than to educate them. Although children often attended school only irregularly and quit at an early age, and less than half the adult population were formal church members, citizens generally believed that churches and schools made communities "decent places" in which to live. Even real-estate promotion—the most absorbing interest of all—stressed the presence of churches and schools as selling points.

McGuffey ranked family life with church and school as a third major conservator of ideals. Families were like a bundle of twigs; the strength of all far surpassed that of the individual:

> *We are all here!*
> *Father, Mother,*
> *Sister, Brother,*
> *All who hold each other dear.*

McGuffey stressed love of brother and sister in a nature poem which Theodore Roosevelt later was to criticize for its ignorance of birds:

> *Birds in their little nests agree;*
> *And 'tis a shameful sight,*
> *When children of one family*
> *Fall out, and chide, and fight.*

Idealization of motherhood and the mother's central position in family life was a frequent theme. One poem referred to the mother's voice:

> *It always makes me happy, too,*
> *To hear its gentle tone;*
> *I know it is the voice of love*
> *From a heart that is my own.*

Mutual interdependence was illustrated in simple stories. In one, grandfather sat in his easy chair before the fire, smoking his pipe. The family dog reclined nearby, and grandmother was busy at her spinning wheel. A granddaughter sat on the man's knee. As he thought about the death of the child's mother, tears rolled down his cheeks. Although the innocent child had not yet realized her loss, she was already repaying her grandparents for their care by catching the flies which buzzed around grandpa's head.

McGuffey stressed complete obedience to parental direction and parental ideals in return for the love and care lavished on younger members of the family. The poem "Casabianca" told of a boy burning to death on the deck of a naval vessel in obedience to his father's order to await his return, which was prevented by the father's death during the naval battle then under way. While such Spartan obedience may seem unduly severe to modern-day parents, it obviously was better to die than to suffer the intense remorse of a daughter who returned to her mother's grave in the village cemetery thirteen years after the funeral. Grief overwhelmed her at the memory of how unwillingly she had brought a glass of water at her mother's request the night of the latter's death. True, she had planned to ask forgiveness the following morning, but her mother was then cold in death. "Meddlesome Matty" received her just deserts in McGuffey's stories, as did a group of curious boys who applied to a rich old squire's advertisement for a youth to wait on him at table. To test the applicants, he filled his reception room with appealing items. The first boy could not resist eating a luscious-appearing cherry, only to find it filled with cayenne pepper, and others received equally just rewards for their curiosity. The one applicant who sat in the room for twenty minutes without yielding to temptation got the job, and ultimately a legacy from the rich old squire. Obedience paid off in many ways in McGuffey's stories, as the disobedient little fish learned after being pulled from the water on a hook:

> *And as he faint and fainter grew,*
> *With hollow voice he cried,*
> *Dear mother, had I minded you,*
> *I need not thus have died.*

At company dinners, McGuffey-trained parents made children eat at the second table and also expected them to be seen and not heard. Elders were always addressed as "Mr." and "Mrs." by properly reared children. At the same time, parents wanted their offspring to have every advantage of religion and education, if they really had taken the McGuffey lessons to heart.

MIDDLE-CLASS IDEALS

The dominant, middle-class code of McGuffey and his followers held that life was a serious business. In selections like Longfellow's "Psalm of Life" readers were urged to make the most of their opportunities:

> *Tell me not in mournful numbers,*
> *Life is but an empty dream!*
>
> .   .   .   .   .   .
>
> *Life is real! Life is earnest!*
>
> .   .   .   .   .   .
>
> *Footprints on the sands of time.*
>
> .   .   .   .   .   .
>
> *Let us, then, be up and doing,*
>   *With a heart for any fate;*
> *Still achieving, still pursuing,*
>   *Learn to labor and to wait.*

Even the ancients were cited to the same effect. Hercules turned away from the siren called "Pleasure" to follow a maiden whose path to happiness involved both pain and labor. In this selection, and others like "Hugh Idle and Mr. Toil," McGuffey stressed the virtues of labor. Youngsters who took him seriously could not indulge in leisurely enjoyment of wealth later on without a sense of guilt. Moreover, perseverance was highly recommended:

> *Once or twice though you should fail,*
>   *Try, Try, Again;*
> *If you would at last prevail,*
>   *Try, Try, Again;*
> *If we strive, 'tis no disgrace,*
> *Though we may not win the race;*
> *What should you do in that case?*
>   *Try, Try, Again.*

Truth, honesty, and courage belonged to the cluster of desirable traits. Washington's father so loved truth that nailing George in a coffin and following him to the grave would have been less painful than hearing a lie from the boy's lips. When George cut down the cherry tree, he manfully told his father "I can't tell a *lie*, father. You know I can't tell a *lie*." And his father in turn joyfully cried, "Come to my arms, my dearest boy. . . ." Common people could be equally noble. Susan's widowed mother made the family living by taking in washing, and Susan helped by making deliveries. On one occasion, Farmer Thompson gave her two bills in payment by mistake. She was severely tempted. The additional money would mean a new coat for mother, and little sister could have the old one to wear to Sunday School. Little brother could have a new pair of shoes. In spite of such desperate need, Susan corrected the mistake, and, sobbing with anguish, refused a shilling's reward on the grounds that she did not want to be paid for honesty. In this case, she received only a lightened heart, but McGuffey's heroines usually gained financially as well. McGuffey also stressed courage, even at the risk of ridicule. A boy who snowballed the schoolhouse to avoid the taunts of others, when he knew the act was wrong, was pictured as lacking in true courage.

Contentment, modesty, and kindness were praised. One story told of Jupiter permitting unhappy people to exchange burdens with others. One man discarded his modesty instead of his ignorance; another his memory rather than his crimes. An old man threw off his gout in favor of a male heir, only to obtain an undutiful son discarded by an angry father. All begged Jupiter to restore their old afflictions. Patience stood by as they resumed their old troubles and automatically reduced their loads by a third. The moral was plain, according to McGuffey. One should never repine over his own problems or envy another, since no man could rightly judge his neighbor's misfortune. A beauty who tossed her glove into a ring with lions to prove her lover's devotion, only to have him throw it in her face after regaining it, showed the silliness of vanity. A poem about Mary's lamb demonstrated the rewards for kindness to animals. When it followed her to school one day, and the children marvelled at its affection, the teacher commented:

> And you each gentle animal
> To you, for life may bind,
> And make it follow at your call,
> If you are always kind.

Greed, revenge, and selfishness toward others were castigated in stories which made plain the moral involved. "The Tricky Boy," for instance, was mean and given to teasing others. When a tired little girl asked help in shifting a jug of milk to her head in order to rest her weary arms, he purposely let it fall to the ground and break. He thought it was fun to see her cry until he slipped on the ground, made slick by the spilled milk, and was laid up for three months with a broken leg.

While McGuffey's code has been ridiculed for its emphasis on material rewards for virtue and unremitting labor—and a hasty reading of his stories may seem to bear this out—he offered a nicely balanced philosophy in which life's purpose and rewards transcended material gains. In his own life and in his Readers, McGuffey preached against the foolishness of material ambition alone, to which so many of his pupils turned:

> Praise—when the ear has grown too dull to hear;
> Gold—when the senses it should please are dead;
> Wreaths—when the hair they cover has grown gray;
> Fame—when the heart it should have thrill'd is numb.

Newspapers and preachers supported McGuffey's scheme of values. In 1870, the Centreville, Michigan, paper published a letter addressed to "My Dear Obadiah," urging young men to attend church, to act and dress modestly, to be ambitious, and to abhor drinking, smoking, and chewing. A companion letter to "My Dear Dorinda" encouraged girls to be sober and thoughtful in preparation for marriage and motherhood. Many were interested only in clothes, and their vocabulary was studded with vapid expressions like, "I thought I should die," "O my," "What are you going to wear," "O ain't that pretty," "Now you're real mean," "You think you're smart, don't you," and "Well I don't care, there now." The writer asked what such girls could do in the kitchen or sick room. A Chatfield, Minnesota, sermon on the "Fast Young Man" in 1896 pictured various types—"the Dude," "the Softie," "the Lazy," "the Dissipate." Young men, said the preacher, should adopt habits of personal cleanliness, avoid bad company, retire early at night, and practice modesty.

Protestant pulpit and press also generally supported McGuffey's views on Sabbath observance. At Monroe, Wisconsin, in 1896, the local Presbyterian preacher asked bicycle riders to discontinue the practice of visiting neighboring towns in groups on Sunday. Another local preacher used the bicycle problem as a springboard for discussing the relation of Sabbath observance to morals as a whole. Granting that times had changed and that the Sabbath was made for man, he insisted that people still must square their actions with their consciences. In developing this theme, he offered a number of observations paralleling McGuffey's ideals. Gambling at church affairs was as evil as gambling in saloons. Card playing wasted time that could be better employed. A man should feel just as free to encircle the waist of his neighbor's wife in a round dance as he would on the way home from prayer meeting. And there was no more harm in a bicycle "spin" on Sunday than in a drive with horse and carriage; less, as a matter of fact, if the horse was tired. People winked at bigger sins on weekdays, liquor drinking for example.

McGuffey firmly believed in private property and in its blessings to society. He quoted Blackstone to prove that necessity begat property and recourse was had to civil society to insure it. Private property had enabled a part of society to provide subsistence for all. It had insured leisure to cultivate the mind, invent useful arts, and to promote science. Simple stories again drove home the lesson. Although a little chimney sweep wanted more than anything else a beautiful, tune-playing watch which he saw in a lady's boudoir, he did not touch it because of his aversion to stealing. Fortunately for him, the lady saw him resist the temptation and took him as her ward. Education and success naturally followed. If he had stolen the watch, said McGuffey, he would have gone to jail. One could not steal the smallest thing without sin, and children should remember that God's eye saw all that transpired.

McGuffey also recognized an obligation of the rich to aid the unfortunate. "Grateful Julian" set the standard. Beyond old rags for clothing and a straw pallet, he possessed nothing but a rabbit which he dearly loved. When he fell ill, a rich and good man took him in and cured his sickness. In return, Julian wished to present the rabbit to his benefactor, an act which so touched the latter that he sent the boy to school. Julian naturally grew up into a bright and honest lad. Moreover, people were expected to give according to their means, as illustrated in a poem called "The Philosopher's Scales":

> A long row of alms-houses, amply endow'd
> By a well-esteem'd Pharisee, busy and proud,
> Next loaded one scale; while the other was prest
> By those mites the poor widow dropp'd into the chest;
> Up flew the endowment, not weighing an ounce,
> And down, down the farthing-worth came with a bounce.

Apart from illness and misfortune, no man needed to be poor. As one McGuffey story put the matter, all could find employment and there was no place for idlers and vagrants. Of course, one should be frugal, as the famous story of the string-saving boy proved, and labor was essential to success:

>*Shall birds, and bees, and ants, be wise,*
> *While I my moments waste?*
>*O let me with the morning rise,*
> *And to my duty haste.*

Henry, the orphan boy, illustrated the fruits of rugged individualism. In need of a new grammar book, he shoveled snow to earn the price, thus proving "Where There's a Will, There is a Way."

Newspapers elaborated the same theme. In 1867 the editor of the Algona, Iowa, paper replied sharply to a letter from a local citizen who objected to raising money for foreign missions when Algona had poor and destitute families of its own. The editor doubted if any Algonans were too poor to deny themselves at least one luxury, like owning a worthless cur, smoking or chewing at a cost of twenty-five to fifty dollars a year, or the inordinate use of tea or coffee. A man had recently told a local storekeeper a pitiful tale of hard times and no job, and had been given a sack of flour on credit. Having obtained this, he immediately produced twenty-five cents in cash to buy tobacco. With that style of poverty the editor had no sympathy. Furthermore, he had no sympathy with thievery, since any healthy man could "earn a living in this land of plenty."

Preachers and newspaper editors agreed with McGuffey that individuals could rise in the world through their own efforts. A Centreville, Michigan, preacher in 1869 affirmed that his community had no rich, no poor, no ignorant citizens save as each individual's own vice or virtue, own energy or indolence had made him so. When former Senator John J. Ingalls of Kansas expressed similar sentiments in 1893, the editor of the Gallatin, Missouri, paper devoted virtually a whole column to summarizing his remarks. According to Ingalls, all men were self-made; even chance and circumstance were made by men and not the other way round. He who was born poor was fortunate. Future leaders of thought, business, and society would not come from the gilded youth of 1893 but from ambitious sons of farmers and laborers.

Near the turn of the century, Markham's famous poem, "The Man with the Hoe," disturbed defenders of the old order because it seemingly condemned the economic system for injuring the common man. Businessmen offered prizes for poetical rebuttals, and William Jennings Bryan lectured on the implications of the poem. Small-town Mid-America was also disturbed. A "goodly contingent" of Brookfield, Missouri, businessmen gathered at the local Congregational church in the fall of 1899 to hear the pastor discuss the poem. According to him, the idea that the hoe could debase mankind was utterly un-American, degenerate, and unpatriotic. The man with the hoe was the man with opportunity; one needed only to keep an eye on the individual who refused to grasp its handle. Our mightiest leaders had been the products of lives of toil with the hoe, axe, crucible, mallet, and saw.

According to McGuffey, the inferior animals made no mistakes and no improvements; man made both. People were inclined to agree, although they accepted progress as so natural as to need no proof or analysis. And, of course, American standards were the measuring sticks. When John E. Young summarized world events in his diary at the close of 1868, he concluded that China was making rapid progress toward civilization and political greatness. American influence was given as the reason. Political revolution in Japan, moreover, gave hope that civilization and human progress would find a lodgment there. Even Abyssinia had been compelled to bow before the prowess of English civilization and Christianity.

Progress was most generally interpreted as growth in material things. When the historian of Kossuth County, Iowa, came to the subject of progress, he followed a very common pattern in telling the story in terms of *growth*—growth of population, of property values, of roads, of the butter and cream industry. Although the editor of a Kossuth County paper was inclined to agree with such measurements, he expressed some doubts in an article published in 1896. After pointing out the great growth in population, fine homes, wealth, and railroads in the short interval since Algona's first New Year's celebration in 1859, he raised the question of whether people locally were any happier. How much, he asked, had such externals added to the zest for life of those pioneers still present? Even town boosters could be sentimental about the good old days, but sentiment was not allowed to interfere with the constant itch for bigness, growth, and numbers—in short, with progress.

Part II

ESSAYS IN
MODERN
SOCIAL HISTORY

The main aspects of social development characterizing early American history—immigration, migration, social mobility, and economic expansion—continued in the late nineteenth and twentieth centuries. Old institutions persisted and yet the last century and a half has witnessed tremendous social changes. The Civil War destroyed slavery, thus fundamentally altering the status of black Americans, even though their emancipation was only half completed. Technology, industrialization, and urbanization have especially changed American life. Large cities and organizations, radio, television, and other familiar features of midtwentieth-century America were unknown in the world of 1800. In the essays that follow, the impact of modern social change on some aspects of American history will be explored.

For further reading: Harvey Wish, *Society and Thought in Modern America* (1966); *Philip Olson ed.), *America as a Mass Society* (1963); *B. Rosenberg and D. M. White, *Mass Culture* (1957).

Seven / The Social Order

16 / The Family and Its Functions

William Ogburn/Clark Tibbitts

Although the family has been a major social institution in the shaping of American behavior and is important for an understanding of American character, it has generally been neglected by historians. The nature of the family underwent many changes after the colonial era. Education moved from the home to the school and economic tasks previously performed in the home were moved to factories, shops, and offices. In the following essay William Ogburn and Clark Tibbitts discuss some of the changing functions of the family. In the last 50 years these changes have become more pronounced as the pace of technological innovation has increased. The status of children and child-rearing practices in particular have been modified. The decline of the family's importance in defining standards of behavior and the emergence of a youth culture in the twentieth century are only two manifestations of these changes. Clearly the parental role has declined as the mass media, peer groups, the schools, and a host of public and private organizations compete with the parents. Yet the full meaning of these changes in family life are only vaguely understood and need further examination.

For further reading: *Arthur Calhoun, *A Social History of the American Family*, 3 vols. (1917–1918); Bernard Wishy, *The Child and the Republic* (1968); *Edmund Morgan, *The Puritan Family* (1944); *Edmund Morgan, *Virginians at Home* (1952); John Serjamaki, *The American Family in the 20th Century* (1953); *Kenneth Keniston, *The Uncommitted* (1965); *Erik Erikson, *Childhood and Society* (1950).

The institution of the family has been attacked and defended with unusual vigor in recent years. The present chapter discusses changes in the family as an economic institution, its protective, religious, recreational and educational functions, trends in the way in which families are organized, the extent of broken homes and problems

From *Recent Social Trends in the United States*, I, 661–679, by the President's Research Committee on Social Trends. Copyright 1933 by the President's Research Committee on Social Trends, Inc. Used with permission of McGraw-Hill Book Company. Footnotes have been omitted.

arising in connection with them, relations of parents and children and of husbands and wives, and finally, the efforts to deal with family problems.

Two outstanding conclusions are indicated by the data on changes in family life. One is the decline of the institutional functions of the family, as for example, its economic functions. Thus the family now produces less food and clothing than it did formerly. The teaching functions of the family also have been largely shifted to another institution, the school. Industry and the state have both grown at the family's expense. The significance of this diminution in the activities of the family as a group is far reaching.

The other outstanding conclusion is the resulting predominant importance of the personality functions of the family—that is, those which provide for the mutual adjustments among husbands, wives, parents and children and for the adaptation of each member of the family to the outside world. The family has always been responsible to a large degree for the formation of character. It has furnished social contacts and group life. With the decline of its institutional functions these personality functions have come to be its most important contribution to society. The chief concern over the family nowadays is not how strong it may be as an economic organization but how well it performs services for the personalities of its members.

In colonial times in America the family was a very important economic organization. Not infrequently it produced substantially all that it consumed, with the exception of such things as metal tools, utensils, salt and certain luxuries. The home was, in short, a factory. Civilization was based on a domestic system of production of which the family was the center.

The economic power of the family produced certain corresponding social conditions. In marrying, a man sought not only a mate and companion but a business partner. Husband and wife each had specialized skills and contributed definite services to the partnership. Children were regarded, as the laws of the time showed, not only as objects of affection but as productive agents. The age of marriage, the birth rate and the attitude toward divorce were all affected by the fact that the home was an economic institution. Divorce or separation not only broke a personal relationship but a business one as well.

Other institutional functions of the family were at the same time strongly developed. It furnished protection to its own members, with less aid from the community than is expected today; it might even, as in the case of feuds, carry on private wars. The authority of the father and husband was sufficient to settle within the family many of the problems of conduct. Religious instruction and ritual were a part of family life. For a successful marriage it was considered important that couples should hold the same faith. In general the home was the gathering place for play activities though there were some community festivities. Educationally, the farm and home duties constituted a larger part of learning than did formal instruction in schools. Farm life furnished what we now call manual training, physical education, domestic science instruction and vocational guidance. The individual spent much of the daily cycle in the family setting, occupied in ways set by the family pattern. Kinship was part of the structure and family status meant much.

Such was the family in colonial days and with slight variations such it has been during much of our history. But changes set in as manufacturing technique evolved, as economic division of labor progressed and as trade developed. More people lived in towns, where they produced less of the food they consumed. Manufacturing first became specialized in the urban household, but with the introduction of steam power and the growth of mechanical invention it went into the factory. Markets and railroads stimulated the growth of cities. The making of furniture, thread, cloth, medicines and leather early left the household. At varying intervals other productive operations have been similarly transferred wholly or in part. This loss of economic functions has been a factor in many social questions, including the position of women in society, the stability of the family and the birth rate.

The family has been losing other functions as well. The government is assuming a larger protective role with its policing forces, its enormously expanded schools, its courts and its social legislation. Religious observances within the home are said to be declining. Opportunities for recreation can be sold for a profit and the existence of theaters, dance halls and ball parks indicates that members of families find more recreation than formerly outside the home. A child or adult is regarded more as an individual and less as a bearer of the family name.

These historical changes in family functions have not been accomplished without corresponding changes in structure. The household of today is about a quarter smaller than that of the colonial family. Marriage occurs probably somewhat later in life now than in earlier times, especially for women. There are many more families without children. The American home is broken much more frequently by separation and divorce than in colonial times. Children are an economic burden for a longer time and an economic asset for a shorter time, although in this respect there is still a difference between the city and the country. Wives, except when they work outside the home for pay, contribute proportionately less to the family support. The organization of the family is becoming diversified. The rural family differs from the city family, and the family in the village from both. Families in cities vary according to economic level, cultural status and occupation.

The personality functions of the family have suffered somewhat by the decline in the number of children in the average family and by the increase in the relative number of families with no children at all; by the growing demands of the schools; and perhaps also by the fact that the modern city makes possible a wider range of contacts beyond the limits of the family circle. Men in particular seem less dependent on the family for social contacts than was formerly the case.

Nevertheless, it may be said that the affectional function is still centered in the family circle and that no evidence is recorded of any extensive transfer elsewhere. The evidence of increased separations and divorces does not prove that husbands and wives now find marriage less agreeable than their ancestors did. It may mean only that certain functions and traditions which once operated to hold even an inharmonious family together have now weakened or disappeared.

If the personality functions have undergone a slight positive decline they have risen in relative importance because of the much greater decline of the institutional functions. To express it differently, the family is thought of much less as an economic institution than as an organization for rearing children and providing happiness. There is thus a greater individualization of the members of the family.

The changes in the family outlined in the preceding paragraphs have taken place over a long period of time. Although this chapter is primarily concerned with changes during recent years, it is essential to bear in mind the long time trends. For example, in interpreting data on the recent growth in the number of restaurants and delicatessens it is important to know whether such a development indicates a continuation at a slower or faster rate of a long time trend in the transfer of economic functions from the home. In other words, is cooking about to follow manufacturing out of the home? Or will the departure of economic functions from the home be retarded by the increased use of electrical appliances and other mechanical aids? These questions and others relating to the shift in emphasis in the functions of the family will be discussed in the later sections of this chapter.

I. THE FAMILY AS
AN ECONOMIC INSTITUTION

The economic functions which have been taken from the family were not all lost at once. Some, such as the making of metals, implements and furniture, began to decline early. Spinning and weaving, a more sudden and spectacular loss, followed somewhat later, the making of clothing later still. The loss of some of the functions, as, for instance, the making of medicines and soaps, extended over a long period. The loss extends only to a part of all the families. Thus there are still families who use the muzzle loading gun as a means of adding to the food supply. Not all families have given up baking and canning and sewing. All but a very small proportion of families do some cooking. Recent trends will be shown by considering one at a time some of the economic functions of the household that appear to be in transition.

Household Economic Activities

The production of bread has already been transferred in large part from the home to the bakery. In a sample study of over 1,000 homes in 1930 it was found that two-thirds of the farm households used baker's bread only. There is of course variation by regions. Three-fourths of the village homes and nine-tenths of the city homes used baker's bread only. One-fifth of the farmers' households used home made bread only, while only about 1 percent of the urban homes did.

The transfer of baking from the home was still going on during the decade preceding 1929, as is shown by the increase in bakery products manufactured outside the home. The quantity of bakery products is not available, but when their value in dollars is divided by the index number of retail prices of bread of the U.S. Bureau of Labor Statistics, the result is a fair index of the quantity of production, which is very near the index of consumption. The per capita production of bakery goods made outside the home increased 27 percent from 1919 to 1929, whereas the per capita consumption of wheat flour both inside and outside the home decreased about 10 percent.

Since 1929, however, this transfer of baking from the home may have been somewhat retarded, for during the Depression years there is scattered evidence of a slight revival of some of the earlier economic activities of the household. As to the future, it is difficult to predict whether or not the village and rural homes will become as dependent upon the outside bakery as the city home is now.

The evidence indicates also that canning is leaving the home. Certainly during the decade 1919–1929 it has developed rapidly outside of the sphere of the household. The per capita quantity of vegetables, fruits and soups canned outside the home approximately doubled during the decade. These products comprise about 70 percent of all canned and preserved products. The year 1919, the year following the war, may not be a good one from which to measure the change. If 1921, a depression year, and hence not a good base year either, be taken the quantity nearly tripled. Only a small portion of this great increase could be due to a change in dietary habits. The increase in per capita consumption of fresh fruits and vegetables seems to have been around 25 percent for this decade. The growth of canning and preserving outside the home is so rapid that a continuance may be expected in the future with a consequent lessening of time required in the household preparation of food.

Laundering has not left the household to the extent that baking has. In the special study referred to in presenting evidence on baking, the data show that 88 percent of farm homes and 33 percent of the city homes have no laundry done outside. Only 3 percent of the urban families sent all of their laundry out. The indications for the decade 1919–1929 are that an increasing proportion of laundering was being done away from home, but the data may not be wholly conclusive. The expenditures for work done in power laundries increased 110 percent from 1919 to 1929, when expressed in terms of dollars of equal purchasing power, while the total population increased 16 percent and the urban population 26 percent. The horse power of machinery installed in laundries increased 111 percent and the number of wage earners 79 percent. These changes are so great in a decade that it hardly seems reasonable that they could be explained on the basis of changes in standards of consumption or the increase of laundry prices above general prices, which sample opinion indicates is probably negligible. The sale of home washing machines has somewhat slowed up the transfer of laundering from the home.

In cleaning and dyeing the number of wage earners increased 220 percent from 1919 to 1929 and the machine horse power 274 percent. The growth of this industry may represent a rise in the standard of living and the resulting increased emphasis on cleanliness, as well as a transfer of an industry from the home.

As to sewing, the making of men's clothing seems to have left the home in earlier decades. The per capita production shows little significant change during the decade under discussion. With regard to the clothing of women and children, the evidence indicates a possible increase in per capita production, although perhaps not much more, save in the case of dresses, than might be explained by a not unlikely change in the standard of living or a decline in seamstresses not in the employ of manufacturers. The per capita production of domestic and factory sewing machines has shown a slight decline during the decade. The increases in the outside manufacture of knit goods and shirts occurred prior to the post-war period.

Losses in the Occupations
of Women at Home

These shifts of occupations from the home to the factory must obviously reduce the economic importance of the woman in the home. The tendency is, therefore, for her to seek outside employment or activities. This phase of the subject is discussed later in the book, but it is interesting to observe here that the entry of women into outside occupations has been rapid in the decade 1920 to 1930. The number of married women working outside the home increased 60 percent while the total number of married women increased only 23 percent, and the number of married women in the urban population increased 34 percent. The increase of all employed females over ten years old was 26 percent. Where both husband and wife work outside the home its economic functions become small indeed, but the housework of the married woman who works out is a double burden, since in many cases she does some work at home after business hours.

The contrast between present day conditions and those when the household was an economic unit may be visualized by a contemporary description of households in the isolated mountain regions of Kentucky. Churning is still done in 96 percent of these mountain homes, fruit canning in 99 percent, fruit drying in 86 percent, the pickling of fruits and vegetables in 94 percent, hog butchering in 85 percent, sausage making in 35 percent, lard making in 82 percent, the salting of meat in 57 percent, the smoking of meat in 17 percent, shoe making in 1 percent, shoe repairing in 48 percent, spinning in 8 percent, dyeing in 7 percent, weaving in 1 percent, knitting in 15 percent, quilting in 67 percent, broom making in 22 percent, furniture making in 4 percent and soap making in 76 percent. There are many household tasks other than these listed. The occupations of these mountain farm homes are somewhat like those of the typical home of earlier times.

The family dwelling tells something as to the economic functions carried on within. Thus the heating in the multi-family dwelling is often attended to by a janitor who is, of course, outside the family circle, and many other services are handled by outsiders. In addition, the individual family usually has less space to care for. Later in the book the extent of construction of multi-family dwellings in comparison with one-family dwellings is shown by years. The data indicate that since the war the number of homes provided for in multi-family dwellings in cities has increased, until in recent years about 50 percent of the new homes were in apartment buildings and only about one-third in one-family houses. There has been, however, a recession of this tendency since the depression hit building construction. The tendency toward multi-family dwellings has been much greater in large urban centers than in rural areas.

Data of dwelling construction in Chicago show that the new apartments constructed are smaller. In the five-year period from 1913 to 1917 inclusive, 45 percent of all new apartments approved by the Board of Health were less than five rooms, while from 1927 to 1931 new apartments of these sizes were 75 percent of the total. New apartments of more than five rooms were 25 percent of the construction in the earlier period and 8 percent in the latter period. In a study of 18,000 apartments in 1,000 buildings in 26 cities, 4 out of 10 had kitchenettes as contrasted with full kitchens. These data show nothing, of course, about the extent to which a room is used.

The Use of Power
in Household Production

The use of gas and electricity for cooking and other household tasks lessens somewhat the labor which was previously involved in the use of coal, wood or oil. The home becomes at the same time more dependent upon an outside industry. The number of domestic consumers of manufactured and natural gas increased 41 percent from 1920 to 1930 while the number of families increased 23 percent. The domestic users of electricity increased 135 percent during the same period. Gas and electricity are used largely for lighting, cooking and heating. It is interesting to inquire as to other uses of these sources of energy. Steam as a source of energy and power was not very practicable for home units. Its adaptation to larger units and the fact that energy thus generated could not be transported far from its source led to the transfer of production from the household to the factory. Electricity, however, can be transported to the household and there applied to machines for domestic production. One such machine is the refrigerator for preserving food and making ice. The large number of refrigerators that have been sold suggests a reversal of the usual movement, for with regard to ice we have a type of production that seems to be leaving the factory for the home. Many electrical machines for home use have to do with cooking, as for instance toasters, grills, waffle irons and percolators. The per capita production of these increased from 50 percent to 600 percent from 1923 to 1929, though declines are noted for the depression years since 1929. The manufacture of electrical washing and ironing machines per capita as measured in deflated dollars increased 65 percent, 1919–1929; the number of vacuum cleaners per capita 20 percent; and electric flatirons 50 percent. Great increases in production have also occurred for electric curling irons, heating pads, fireless cookers and radios.

Despite the service of electricity for cooking, the kitchen seems to be less used. The number of restaurant and lunch room keepers increased 88 percent from 1920 to 1930, whereas the urban population increased only 26 percent and the total population 16 percent. The number of waiters and waitresses increased for the same period by 72 percent. The increase in restaurants might be explained by the decline of boarding houses (if it were known that they have declined) but that would hardly explain the fact that waiters increased in numbers faster than did the number of families. Prior to 1920 delicatessen dealers increased about three times as fast as the population—since 1920 the statistics have not been collected.

The growth of traveling, commuting and hotel life is no doubt a part of the background of this movement. If data are used which exclude these factors the results are somewhat different. In a study that was made of the amount of time spent on the different household tasks, in which all individuals eating at home were included (with the exception of babies), it was found that in farm homes each person ate an average of 20.2 meals per week at home. This means that each person had an average of less than one meal a week away from home. In the homes in large cities each person took an average of 2.0 meals per week away from home. This does not mean, however, that only 19 meals per week were served in the city homes, for not all of the members were absent at the same time. In fact the actual number of meals served per week averaged 20.4.

While there may be somewhat less cooking at home than formerly, it seems probable that the use of electricity is slowing up the rate of decline. The very rapid growth in the manufacture of electric appliances suggests that the use of electricity in the home is only in its beginning. It is used now for lighting, cooking, washing, ironing, sewing, housecleaning, refrigeration, ventilation, projection of motion pictures and many other purposes.

Women's Present Housekeeping Duties

The outward movement of duties previously performed in the home arouses curiosity as to just how much time is spent in household work. Fortunately data are available on which a reply to this question can be based. Hildegarde Kneeland of the U.S. Bureau of Home Economics has collected and analyzed time records kept by housewives showing how much time is spent in different types of homes on such various duties as preparing meals, washing and ironing and the like.

One group of homes studied was in cities of over 50,000 inhabitants and another group was on farms. The city group consisted of the homes of college alumnae from whom the data were obtained by correspondence. The farm group was reached through the aid of the extension divisions of agricultural colleges. By comparing homes where less than 7 hours per week of outside paid help was employed, probable income differences were lessened somewhat. When thus restricted the sample for cities was only 82, since most of these homes employed outside help; for the farms it was 336. In the average of the city homes 66 hours and 48 minutes per week were spent on home making duties, while in the average of the farm homes the time was 63 hours and 32 minutes. Evidently keeping the home still requires many hours per week although many occupations have left it. Not all these hours of work were done by the home maker, however. Her time was 56 hours and 39 minutes in the city homes and 53 hours and 50 minutes on the farms. Most of the help given by others in these homes came from members of the family, only 1 hour and 50 minutes coming from paid help in the city homes and 14 minutes, on the average, in the farm home.

How this time was distributed among the different household tasks will next be shown, but comparisons here, as above, are further complicated by the fact that the average size of the farm homes, 4.8 persons, was 23 percent larger than that of the city homes, 3.9 individuals. Comparisons of the time spent on the specific duties may thus best be made in terms of proportions of the total time spent on various house-keeping tasks.

The percent of time spent on preparing meals and washing dishes was less in the city homes than on the farms, 33 percent as compared with 43 percent. The allotment for house cleaning was about the same for both, 13 and 14 percent respectively. But washing and ironing required a smaller proportion of the time in the city than in the farm homes, 8 and 10 percent. Only 23 percent of the city homes did all washing at home, as compared with 70 percent of the farm homes. Mending and sewing also occupied a smaller proportion of the time of the city household than of the farm household, 6 percent and 9 percent respectively. On "other care" of the house, which included the tending of fires, the proportion of time in the city (3 percent) was about one-half as large as in the rural households.

For the tasks just named which comprise roughly a large part of the labor spent on the production of essential economic goods and services, the city homes spent 63 percent of all the time required on home duties while the farm homes spent 82 percent. The remaining time was spent on the care of children, purchasing and management, going back and forth and other home making activities. It is interesting to compare city and country in regard to the time spent on the care of children. This duty took 24 percent of the time in the city homes but only 10 percent in the farm homes. It would be an interesting generalization if it could be said that the home maker of the city spends more time with her children than does the farmer's wife. But it is doubtful whether such an inference can be made, for in these samples one-half of the city homes had a youngest child under 3 years old as compared with only one-fifth of the farm homes. On the other hand, there were fewer children in the city homes to care for. Of the city homes 21 percent had 3 or more children as compared with 38 percent of the farm homes.

The homes just discussed all had children under 15 years of age. In other cases where the household consists of home maker and husband only and where paid help was employed for less than seven hours a week, the time spent on household duties, 43 or 44 hours a week, was about two-thirds of what it was in the city and farm homes where there were children. The one-child households of the cities called for about 45 percent more hours of home work than did the households of husbands and wives only and about 80 percent more for those households where there was considerable help employed. A first child adds from 45 to nearly 80 percent to the household duties but the latter figure for the one-child family households had on the average one additional person for every four families.

Household duties took less time for those living in apartments than for those living in houses, especially those duties having to do with meals and the cleaning and care of the house; the difference was nearly 30 percent in the city group (but the size of the apartment household was about 30 percent smaller). In the families where there were only husbands and wives these duties were 24 percent less in the apartment. Also fewer meals (per person) were served at home in the apartments than in the houses, the difference being a little less than 6 percent.

On the whole, despite the inroads which the factory has made on home occupations, the average family still spends a great deal of time in cooking meals, cleaning house, laundering, sewing and mending. Since we have no comparable earlier data it is difficult to make any inferences from the material presented as to trends. If, however, the domestic economy of the farm is thought of as containing a larger element of survival from an earlier cultural situation the differences between the rural household and the city household, assuming the economic level to be the same, might be taken to indicate the line of evolution.

Housekeeping still remains one of the major industries and home management is one of its most important occupations. The housewife still makes her contribution to the family's support through the production of goods and services in the home. There are 26 million housewives, though not all of them have full time jobs, as against 14 millions engaged in the manufacturing and mechanical industries. The home is a consumption unit, largely supported by the money earnings of the males, supplemented with increasing frequency by those of the wife and probably with decreasing frequency by those of the children. A summary of 20 studies shows that 53 percent of women working outside of their homes for money contributed all their earnings to the family and 39 percent contributed a part. In a study of sons and daughters in Manchester, New Hampshire, three-fourths of the girls and two-thirds of the boys contributed half or more of their earnings to the family.

But the shifting of home occupations to industry has created many problems other than economic. Some of the old ideals and standards for the prospective home maker are gone with the conditions which gave rise to them. Woman's duties and responsibilities are no longer as rigidly defined as they were. There is uncertainty about having children, about their care and education if it is decided to have them, about the relative advantages of housework and work outside the home, about the proper apportionment of the family income to the various necessities and luxuries. The many inventions of household equipment, contemporary experiments in new forms of housing and more scientific methods of purchasing all hold out possibilities for raising the quality of home service and perhaps giving it a genuinely professional status.

II. OTHER INSTITUTIONAL FUNCTIONS OF THE FAMILY

Economic functions are always important in the scheme of life, but there are other activities which are equally important. Some of these are closely correlated with the economic factors, others are not. Thus the changing protective and recreational activities of the family are closely related to its economic organization. Its educational and religious activities are less so. Under these headings the trend of the other institutional functions of the family will be presented.

The Protective Functions

Throughout history the family has afforded protection to its members. The marriage contract that comes down from earlier times carries the promise to protect. The family has traditionally guarded its members against bodily harm from enemies and against economic insecurity in infancy, illness and old age.

In recent times, the state has assumed important duties in protecting health. The budgets for public health and sanitation in cities of 30,000 and over have increased about twice as fast as urban families since 1903. The care for health has also passed in part to hospitals, many of which are non-governmental. The number of beds in hospitals increased 115 percent in the 20 years from 1909 to 1929. Nearly one-third of all babies are born outside the home. Hospitals have a capitalization exceeded only by 4 groups of manufacturing industries: iron and steel, textiles, chemicals and food.

The protection of the very old members of the family was formerly rendered almost exclusively by their offspring. With smaller families and greater mobility of the population they are less often so protected. In some countries, the care of the aged has been assumed in part by the state today. Within the decade preceding 1932, 17 states of the United States have legalized or adopted some form of old age insurance, either enabling counties to pass enactments, or being mandatory. In a sample study of families [discussed in a later section], there are shown to be fewer families in 1930 with three generations in one home than in 1900. In the sample of farm families 10.7 percent were three-generation families in 1900 and 6.2 percent in 1930. In the metropolitan area the percentages of three-generation families were 9.9 percent in 1900 and 7.3 percent in 1930. The number of endowment insurance policies, largely a protection against old age, increased 800 percent from 1899 to 1929. But equally rapid has been the growth of other forms of life insurance which may be viewed as a protection for the family through the aid of an outside institution. Many relatives are cared for by the family and in so far as the family does not do so, there is a tendency for this duty to fall to philanthropy or to the state.

The care of the feeble minded and the insane in public institutions is an assumption by the state of protective functions formerly belonging to the family and still exercised by many families, particularly outside the cities. Patients in state hospitals for mental disease increased 110 percent from 1904 to 1929, while the number of families increased 67 percent. The feeble minded and epileptics in special state institutions for such cases increased 45 percent in the seven years from 1922 to 1929, while the number of families increased but 15 percent. These figures, however, may have been augmented somewhat by an actual increase in the number of insane in society, by the transfer of feeble minded from other types of institutions and by a broader definition of feeble mindedness.

The extent to which the family is delegating the protection of life and property, or at least the extent to which such protection is growing up outside the family, is suggested by the fact that the total number of policemen, guards, watchmen, detectives, probation officers, sheriffs, marshalls and firemen increased 40 percent from 1920 to 1930, while the number of families increased only 23 percent. The recorded expenditures for protection to persons and property in cities of over 30,000 inhabitants in the United States have increased since 1903 somewhat more rapidly than have families. Of course the property to be protected has increased also and much of it lies outside the family habitation.

Some of the protective functions recently assumed by the state are designed to safeguard the family as a unit rather than as individuals. The state steps in to arrest what might otherwise be a process of disintegration. Thus provision for mothers' aid out of public funds, spreading rapidly over most of the states since 1911, enables mothers, though the allowances are small, to stay at home with their children. Child labor legislation and juvenile courts [discussed in other chapters], illustrate protective functions developed by the state to care for interests that were formerly thought of as family matters. Compulsory education, truancy laws and the provision for visiting teachers also represent an assumption of family functions by government agencies. If the provision and control of income is thought of as a protective activity, however, the family, at least in the United States, is still the primary guardian of its members' interests.

Religious Functions

Certain religious functions have traditionally been performed by the family and its role is significant in the inculcation and maintenance of ethical standards. Marriage is held by many to be a sacrament and some consider it desirable that a family be formed by mates with the same church affiliation. Family prayers are apparently a declining practice. In a study made of parents and children in 1930, including samples of school children in rural areas, villages, and in cities of various sizes, about 1 in 8 white American born school children of the seventh, eighth and ninth grades was found to participate in family prayers. There was not much difference in the practice of this custom between the city and the country, though in the very large city the proportion of children participating was slightly smaller.

The same study shows that family attendance at church is much more widespread than family prayers. In the rural area, 85 percent of the children went to church with their families (in the month preceding the study) while in the large city group only 40 percent went together to church. Family reading of the Bible was reported by 22 percent of the rural white children and 10 percent of the city children. Grace at meals was the practice in 30 percent of the samples from the large city and in 38 percent from the rural area. It should be observed that these data are for family rather than individual activities. Data for earlier years are not available for indicating the trends. Trends may possibly be indicated, however, by these comparisons between country and city at the same period or year, for the farm preceded the city in point of time and the city is often the center of cultural diffusion for the country.

The trend in the religious functions of the family is affected by trends in religion as truly as it is by trends in the family. There is variation in this regard between the different religions as well as different areas.

Recreational Functions

The great growth in commercialized amusements and the recreational programs of industry, church and state show that much recreation is provided by other institutions than the family. But this growth is not due solely to a transfer of function. Recreation has itself grown in institutions outside the home, thus affecting the relative position of the home in comparison with outside agencies. The reduction of 15 percent in hours of labor between 1890 and 1926 has made possible more leisure for recreation.

The subject of recreation and leisure time activities is presented later in the book. In general, the material there reveals that nearly all lines of recreational activity for which comparable data are available show increases much greater than the growth in the population. The growth in recreational facilities has been particularly large since the World War. Thus . . . it is shown that municipal parks expanded in acreage 240 percent from 1907 to 1930; public playgrounds increased 450 percent from 1910 to 1930; golf courses increased 207 percent from 1923 to 1930, and tennis clubs increased 170 percent from 1920 to 1930. Baseball attendance at the big league games was only 10 percent greater in 1930 than in 1920, but football attendance more than doubled, as did the receipts from social and athletic clubs. It is known that the moving picture audience has grown enormously, though the attendance declined during the depression following 1929. Municipal expenditures for recreation have been increasing two and a half times as fast as the number of families. Factories, too, are providing recreation, 430 of them having been enumerated as so doing in 1928.

While most of these facts indicate an overshadowing growth of outside recreational agencies, it should be remembered that the home is still the center of much recreation. A recent survey of 908 families from four different sections of Indianapolis shows that 90 percent of the homes had back yards, 60 percent were equipped with phonographs, 55 percent had pianos or pianolas, 60 percent subscribed to magazines and 365 husbands or wives played musical instruments.

In the study of the home activities of parents and children previously referred to, it was found that reading aloud was practiced in the families of 33 percent of the American born white children in the rural samples, but of only 13 percent of the children in the large city. The family played games together in about half the cases in the country and in about 40 percent of the cases in the city. The same percentages held true for singing or playing music together. Attendance of the family together at the moving picture was about twice as great in the city (65 percent) as in the country. Family visits were as numerous in the city as in the country; and walking together was twice as frequent among the city families.

Budgetary studies show a growing proportion of family expenditures for things other than food, household equipment, rent, fuel and light. Much of this increase is undoubtedly for recreation. Certainly the large expenditure for radios accounts for a portion of it; it has been estimated that there were some 16,000,000 sets in use in January, 1932. A far larger share has gone for expenditures on the family automobile which is said to have displaced maid service in the home as an item in the family budget.

Educational Functions

The school teacher may be viewed as a substitute parent in regard to the function of training the child. The teacher is reaching into the home earlier and taking the child at a younger age for part of the day. In 1910, 17 percent of all five-year-old children were in school. By 1930, the proportion had increased to 20 percent. Education is discussed later, but a few of the developments which throw light on the family will be noted here.

That the teacher is a competitor of the parent (without a feeling of rivalry, of course) for influence over the child is not readily recognized, for the teacher aids both child and parent and is in this sense a cooperator also. Yet the school performs many services which were once the function of the home. Thus the duties on the farm give some experience in manual training not found in city homes. The schools tend to develop this function. The development of manual training in the school may not, however, exactly balance its decline in the home. Manual training courses contain new practices not found in household life.

The same generalization may be applied to the whole system of modern education. The schools teach subjects never taught at home and so would have added to their functions even though the family had relinquished none. Farmers' daughters find much that is new in domestic science courses, even though they also learn much at home. But the evidence indicates that formal education has grown not only by developing new methods and new subjects but to some extent also by a transfer of functions from the home. No conclusion is here attempted as to the relative qualities of education in the home and education in the school. It is apparent, however, that the city child is on a different footing in regard to his opportunities for extra-mural education in the household arts than is the country child. Presumably young women might learn in the modern city home to do what they will need to do in their adult life as truly as the farmers' daughters learn in the rural home. Presumably, also, the city girl's home instruction is far from adequate and her school instruction in domestic science is not wholly a substitute but also a better type of training.

In a study of 35 high schools in 1929–1930, compared with an earlier study of 60 high schools in 1906–1911 and 1915–1918 in the middle west there was a 700 percent increase from 1906–1911 to 1929–1930 in the average number of courses offered in the industrial arts, which includes such subjects as manual training, mechanical drawing, woodwork and automobile mechanics, and a 500 percent increase in the household arts courses. There were no courses in physical education in 1906–1911, but 27 schools offered such courses in 1929–1930.

When society was based on a land economy most of the occupations had to do with farming and allied activities and were learned at home. There was then no need of schools for vocational training. Under a capital economy, with expanding varieties of occupations, the home is handing over the task of vocational training to specialized schools. The pupils enrolled in vocational courses of federally aided schools increased 270 percent from 1920 to 1930.

The number of children in schools is still increasing a little faster than the number of children in the population. In 1900, 59 percent of the children 5–17 years old were in the public elementary and secondary schools and in 1928, 80 percent. The average number of days these schools were in session increased from 144 in 1900 to 172 in 1928. The schools thus kept children away from home about 28 more school days in 1928 than at the beginning of the century. The number of teachers has doubled since 1900 which is not true of the number of parents. Married persons increased about 88 percent but the increase of parents was somewhat less.

It should also be recalled, in thinking of the educational function of the family, that with the increase of childless families, this function has correspondingly diminished. The fact that the schools are so universally desired and that they perform specific functions never performed by the family has obscured this relationship of institutional functions between the family and the school.

Family Status

Another function which the family performs is to confer upon its members a social status which as individuals they might not possess. In binding them together in a group it enables them to deal as they otherwise could not with other groups and agencies. In setting forth this concept more fully, it may be noted that this function is highly developed in China, where, it is said, loyalty to family has precedence over loyalty to state. In many countries marriages are often primarily arrangements between families rather than between the young couples on the basis of a love impulse, although even under such conditions the desires of the young may be more often respected than the traditions of romantic fiction would lead a casual reader to believe. The family name, at any rate, tends to overshadow the individual. Family *esprit de corps* and the family impulse toward mutual protection extend to all the members. A break between two members of different families often means a break between all the members of the two families and difficulties are frequently settled by the families rather than by the courts. The family feeling extends to relatives, between whom there is felt to exist an altogether special tie which implies hospitality and financial aid. To be born into or to marry into a particular family is all important in giving prestige to an individual. Such is the concept of family status.

That this family function of determining status is changing is obvious, though it is impossible to find data that can be presented in brief compass to establish a trend. The evidence is largely to be found in analyses of social conditions and in case histories of individuals. Certain theories of the factors causing such changes may, however, be briefly presented. Property holdings in land are very likely to help to fix family status, especially in small communities where everybody knows everybody else. Permanence of tenure also seems to be a supporting factor. Clearly it is difficult to maintain family status in a high degree when there is much mobility of population. The growth of large cities, in which the effectiveness of gossip and other forms of non-legal social control is diminished, tends also to diminish family prestige. With a few exceptions the personality of the individual family is lost in the crowd. The very phenomenon of rapid change makes the difference between generations appear greater than the differences between families.

For these reasons it is thought that family status as such has been declining in importance, though to what degree in recent years can only be inferred. Loyalty to the club, the school, the city, the team, the state, competes with loyalty to the family, yet no one of these groups absorbs the individual as fully as the family did historically. As the forces determining family status weaken, therefore, the individualization of the members of the family is accentuated. The knowledge and application of the facts of heredity might conceivably aid in restoring family status at some future time, but this development can not be anticipated in any predictable future.

The individualization of the members of the family finds recognition in changes in the law, particularly with regard to the wife. In very early times the law barely admitted the individuality of the wife. The common law held that "the legal existence of the woman is suspended during marriage." By marriage she lost the right to control her property; as a married woman she could not sue or be sued in her own name; and she could not make a will. Her earnings and the earnings of the children went to the husband as symbol of family authority. These and other laws illustrate the submergence of the personalities of the wife and children in that of the family, though in practice there was undoubtedly much freedom.

The laws, however, have undergone fundamental changes. Before 1900, all states had given married women the right to make a will. Eight states of the southwest and far west did not follow the ancient common law but adopted the system of "community property" rights. But while the property acquired after marriage belongs to both husband and wife, the husband still controls it. The other states before the close of the last century modified the common law by permitting married women to own property separately. Since 1900 there have been some amendments, particularly regarding real estate and court decrees in a few states. In nine states in 1930 there were still such reservations on the wife's property rights. Equal guardianship laws were not so early adopted. In 1900, 14 states had passed co-guardianship laws and by 1930 there were 39. In regard to citizenship there have been significant changes. The wife's citizenship followed that of her husband (for foreign born women since 1855 and for American born women since 1907), but in 1922 independent citizenship was given to married women.

The question of domicile becomes more important in an age when people move about freely. The recognition of separate domicile of the wife, largely for purposes of voting, holding office, or serving on juries, has been accorded by laws passed in eight states since the World War.

In other family laws there are still some states which do not accord the same rights to a married woman that they do to a single woman. Though in general married women can make contracts, in perhaps half of the states there are some restrictions, however slight, on this right. In one state a wife's earnings are her own only if she is living apart from her husband; and in one state the father can will away from the mother the custody of the child. There are still other evidences of the fact that the individualization of the married woman is not complete under the law.

17 / Revolution without Ideology: The Changing Place of Women in America

Carl N. Degler

From the founding of the colonies, American women have generally occupied a higher status than their European counterparts. The shortage of women along the frontier and the experimental nature of American society accounted for many of the differences. Yet the American woman still lacked certain basic rights at the beginning of the nineteenth century. Excluded from higher education and most occupations, denied political rights, and given only limited civil rights, American women were second-class citizens. The first feminist movement prior to the Civil War achieved a few gains, but it was not until after the Civil War that women made their greatest strides toward full equality. In spite of the improvements in the last century, women still face barriers to full equality.

Although egalitarian ideology helped bring reform, industrialization was in large measure responsible for the improvement of the position of women in America. This economic transformation affected women in two ways. First, new employment opportunities drew women out of the home and into the labor market, and second, household tasks, which were often difficult and time-consuming, became easier and gave women new freedom and more time to participate in society. Clothing, for example, which had formerly been made at home, could now be bought ready-made at the store. The emancipation of women from domestic drudgery was especially marked for the married women who increasingly spent less time at home and more time at work or in community activities. The role of the twentieth-century woman became more complex; she was no longer just a worker and housewife, but a citizen, a patron of the arts, and a doer of good works.

As Carl Degler points out in the following article, the change in status did not necessarily alter feminist ideology. The different roles occupied by women were not always clearly defined. A job did not necessarily mean a career. The new status, like the old, still left women, as well as men, uncertain about the role of women in American society. That uncertainty is even greater today than in the past as a younger generation challenges con-

"The Woman in America," *Daedalus*, XCIII (Spring 1964), 653–670. Reprinted by permission of *Daedalus*, Journal of the American Academy of Arts and Sciences, Boston, Mass.

ventional notions about the roles of the sexes and experiments with new relationships between men and women. If the emancipation of women continues, the functional lines separating the sexes will become even more blurred.

For further reading: Robert Smuts, *Women and Work in America* (1959); *Eleanor Flexner, *A Century of Struggle* (1959); *Andrew Sinclair, *The Better Half* (1965); Elizabeth Baker, *Technology and Woman's Work* (1964); *Simone de Beauvoir, *The Second Sex* (1953); Aileen Kraditor, *Ideas of the Woman Suffrage Movement, 1890–1920* (1965); President's Commission on the Status of Women, *American Women* (1963); Mabel Newcomer, *A Century of Higher Education for American Women* (1959); *Betty Friedan, *The Feminine Mystique* (1963).

If feminism is defined as the belief that women are human beings and entitled to the same opportunities for self-expression as men, then America has harbored a feminist bias from the beginning. In both the eighteenth and nineteenth centuries foreign travelers remarked on the freedom for women in America. "A paradise for women," one eighteenth-century German called America, and toward the close of the nineteenth century Lord Bryce wrote that in the United States "it is easier for women to find a career, to obtain work of an intellectual as of a commercial kind, than in any part of Europe."

Certainly the long history of a frontier in America helps to account for this feminist bias. In a society being carved out of a wilderness, women were active and important contributors to the process of settlement and civilization. Moreover, because women have been scarce in America they have been highly valued. During almost the whole of the colonial period men outnumbered women, and even in the nineteenth century women remained scarce in the West. As late as 1865, for example, there were three men for each woman in California; in Colorado the ratio was as high as 20 to 1. Such disparities in the sex ratio undoubtedly account for the West's favorable attitude toward women as in an Oregon law of 1850 that granted land to single women and, even more significant for the time, to married women; or in the willingness of western territories like Wyoming (1869) and Utah (1870) to grant the suffrage to women long before other regions where the sex ratio was more nearly equal.

Another measure of women's high esteem in American society was the rapidity with which the doors of higher education opened to women. Even without counting forerunners like Oberlin College, which admitted women in 1837, the bars against women came down faster and earlier in America than anywhere. The breakthrough came during the Civil War era, when women's colleges like Elmira, Vassar and Smith were founded, and universities like Michigan and Cornell became coeducational. The process was later and slower in Europe. Girton College, Cambridge, for example, which opened in 1869, was the sole English institution of higher education available to women until London University accorded women full privileges in 1879. Heidelberg, which was the first German university to accept women, did not do so until 1900. More striking was the fact that at its opening Girton provided six places for young women; Vassar alone, when it opened in 1865, counted some 350 students in residence. Another indication of the American feminist bias was that at the end of the century girls outnumbered boys among high school graduates.

But if the frontier experience of America helped to create a vague feminist bias that accorded women more privileges than in settled Europe, the really potent force changing women's place had little to do with the frontier or the newness of the country. It was the industrial revolution that provided the impetus to women's aspirations for equality of opportunity; it was the industrial revolution that carried through the first stage in the changing position of women—the removal of legal and customary barriers to women's full participation in the activities of the world.

Today it is axiomatic that men work outside the home. But before the industrial revolution of the nineteenth century, the great majority of men and women were co-workers on the land and in the home. Women worked in the fields when the chores of the home and child-rearing permitted, so that there was not only close association between work and home for both sexes, but even a certain amount of overlap in the sexual division of labor. The coming of machine production changed all that. For a time, it is true, many unmarried women and children—the surplus labor of the day—were the mainstay of the new factory system, but that was only temporary. By the middle of the nineteenth century the bulk of industrial labor was male. The coming of the factory and the city thus wholly changed the nature of men's work. For the first time in history, work for most men was something done outside the family, psychologically as well as physically separated from the home.

The same industrial process that separated work and home also provided the opportunities for women to follow men out of the home. For that reason the feminist movement, both socially and intellectually, was a direct consequence of the industrial changes of the nineteenth century. Furthermore, just as the new industrial system was reshaping the rural men who came under its influence, so it reshaped the nature of women.

The process began with the home, which, in the early years of industrialization, was still the site of most women's work. Because of high land values, the city home was smaller than the farm house, and with less work for children, the size of the urban family was smaller than the rural. Moreover, in the city work in the home changed. Machines in factories now performed many of the tasks that had long been women's. In truth, the feminist movement began not when women felt a desire for men's jobs, but when men in factories began to take away women's traditional work. Factory-produced clothing, commerical laundries, prepared foods (e.g., prepared cereals, canned vegetables, condensed milk, bakery bread) were already available in the years after the Civil War. Toward the end of the century an advanced feminist like Charlotte Perkins Gilman, impressed by the accelerating exodus of women's chores from the middle-class home, predicted that the whole kitchen would soon be gone. She was wrong there, but even today the flight continues with pre-cooked and frozen foods, TV dinners, cake mixes, special packaging for easy disposal, diaper services and the like.

Middle-class women were the main beneficiaries of the lightening of the chores of the home; few working-class or immigrant women could as yet take advantage of the new services and products. These middle-class women became the bone and sinew of the feminist movement, which was almost entirely an urban affair. They joined the women's clubs, organized the temperance crusades and marched in the suffrage parades. With an increasing amount of time available to them in the city, and imbued with the historic American value of work, they sought to do good. And there was much to be done in the raw, sometimes savage, urban environment of the late nineteenth century. For example, public playgrounds in the United States began in Boston only in the 1880's, when two public-spirited middle-class women caused a cartload of sand to be piled on an empty lot and set the neighborhood children loose upon it. Many a city and small town at the turn of the century owed its public library or its park to the dedicated work of women's clubs. The venerable giant redwood trees of northern California survive today because clubwomen of San Francisco and nearby towns successfully campaigned in 1900 to save them from being cut down for lumber. The saloon and prostitution were two other prevalent urban blights that prompted study and action by women's organizations.

More important than women's opposition to social evils was the widening of women's knowledge and concerns that inevitably accompanied it. What began as a simple effort to rid the community of a threat to its purity often turned into a discovery of the economic exploitation that drove young working girls into brothels and harried working men into saloons. Frances Willard, for example, while head of the Women's Christian Temperance Union, broadened the WCTU's reform interests far beyond the liquor question, causing it to advocate protective legislation for working women, kindergartens and training programs for young working girls. Jane Addams, at Hull-House in Chicago's slums, quickly learned what historians have only recently discovered, that it was the urban boss's undeniable services to the immigrants that were the true sources of his great political power and the real secret of his successful survival of municipal reform campaigns.

The most direct way in which industrialization altered the social function of women was by providing work for women outside the home. Production by machine, of course, widened enormously the uses to which women's labor could be put once physical strength was no longer a consideration. And toward the end of the century, as business enterprises grew and record-keeping, communications and public relations expanded, new opportunities for women opened up in business offices. The telephone operator, the typist, the clerical worker and the stenographer now took places beside the seamstress, the cotton mill operator and the teacher.

As workers outside the home, women buried the Victorian stereotype of the lady under a mountain of reality. After all, it was difficult to argue that women as a sex were weak, timid, incompetent, fragile vessels of spirituality when thousands of them could be seen trudging to work in the early hours of the day in any city of the nation. Nor could a girl who worked in a factory or office help but become more worldly. A young woman new to a shop might have been embarrassed to ask a male foreman for the ladies' room, as some working girls' autobiographies report, but such maidenly reticence could hardly survive very long. Even gentle, naïve farm girls soon found out how to handle the inevitable, improper advances of foremen. They also learned the discipline of the clock, the managing of their own money, the excitement of life outside the home, the exhilaration of financial independence along with the drudgery of machine labor. Having learned something of the ways of the world, women could not be treated then, nor later in marriage, as the hopeless dependents Victorian ideals prescribed.

In time work transformed the outer woman, too. First to go were the hobbling, trailing skirts, which in a factory were a hazard and a nuisance. Even before the

Civil War, Amelia Bloomer and other feminists had pointed out that women, if they were to work in the world as human beings, needed looser and lighter garments than those then in fashion. Until working women were numbered in the millions, no change took place. After 1890 women's skirts gradually crept up from the floor, and the neat and simple shirtwaist became the uniform of the working girl. A costume very like the original bloomer was widely worn by women factory workers during the First World War. Later the overall and the coverall continued the adaptation of women's clothes to the machine.

The most dramatic alteration in the image of woman came after the First World War, when there was a new upsurge in women's employment. The twenties witnessed the emergence of the white-collar class, and women were a large part of it. Over twice as many women entered the labor force that decade as in the previous one; the number of typists alone in 1930 was three-quarters of a million, a tenfold increase since 1900. And woman's appearance reflected the requirements of work. Except for some of the extreme flapper fashions, which were transient, the contemporary woman still dresses much as the woman of the 1920's did. In the 1920's women threw out the corset and the numerous petticoats in favor of light undergarments, a single slip, silk or rayon stockings, short skirts and bobbed hair. So rapid and widespread was the change that an investigation in the 1920's revealed that even most working-class girls no longer wore corsets, and the new interest in bobbed hair resulted between 1920 and 1930 in an increase of 400 per cent in the number of women hair dressers.

The physical freedom of dress that women acquired during the 1920's was but the superficial mark of a new social equality. The social forces behind this new equality are several. Some of these forces, like the growing number of college-trained women and the increasing number of women in the working force, go back far into the past; others, like the impact of the war and the arduous campaign for women's suffrage, were more recent. But whatever the causes, the consequences were obvious. Indeed, what is generally spoken of as the revolution in morals of the 1920's is more accurately a revolution in the position of women. Within a few short years a spectrum of taboos was shed. For the first time women began to smoke and drink in public; cigarette manufacturers discovered and exploited in advertising a virtually untouched market. As recently as 1918 it was considered daring for a New York hotel to permit women to sit at a bar. In the twenties, despite prohibition, both sexes drank in public.

Perhaps most significant, as well as symbolic, of the new stage in the position of women was their new sexual freedom. The twenties have long been associated with the discovery of Freud and a fresh, publicly acknowledged interest in sex. But insofar as these attitudes were new they represented changes in women, particularly those of the middle and upper classes. Premarital and extramarital sexuality by men had never been severely criticized, and discussion of sexual matters was commonplace wherever men gathered. Now, though, middle-class women also enjoyed that freedom. For the first time, it has been said, middle-class men carried on their extramarital affairs with women of their own social class instead of with cooks, maids and prostitutes.

An easier sexuality outside of marriage was only the most sensational side of the revolution in morals; more important, if only because more broadly based, was a new, informal, equal relationship between the sexes, culminating in a new conception of marriage. The day was long since past when Jennie June Croly could be barred, as she was in 1868, from a dinner in honor of Charles Dickens at a men's club even though her husband was a member and she was a professional writer. (Indeed, so thoroughly has such separation of the sexes been abandoned that the new Princeton Club in New York City has closed all but one of its public rooms to any man who is not accompanied by a woman!) And at least in the gatherings of the educated middle class, talk between the sexes was often free, frank and wide-ranging. The same mutual acceptance of the sexes was visible in the prevalent talk about the "new marriage," in which the woman was a partner and a companion, not simply a mother, social convenience and a housekeeper.

The reality of the new conception of marriage was reflected in the sharp increase in the divorce rate. Because marriage, legally as well as socially, in the nineteenth century was more confining for women than for men, the early feminists had often advocated more liberal divorce laws. And even though divorce in the nineteenth century was more common in the United States than in any European country, the divorce rate in the 1920's shot up 50 per cent over what it had been only ten years before. One sign that women in the 1920's were seeking freedom from marriage if they could not secure equality in marriage was that two thirds of the divorces in that decade were instituted by women.

By the close of the twenties the ordinary woman in America was closer to a man in the social behavior expected of her, in the economic opportunities open to her and in the intellectual freedom enjoyed by her than at any time in history. To be sure there still was a double standard, but now its existence was neither taken for granted nor confidently asserted by men.

In truth, the years since the twenties have witnessed few alterations in the position of women that were not first evident in that crucial decade. The changes have penetrated more deeply and spread more widely through the social structure, but their central tendency was then already spelled out. Even the upsurge in women's employment, which was so striking in the twenties, continued in subsequent years. Each decade thereafter has counted a larger number of working women than the previous one. During the depression decade of the 1930's, even, half a million more women entered the labor force than in the prosperous twenties. By 1960 some 38 per cent of all women of working age—almost two out of five women—were employed outside the home.

The movement of women out of the home into remunerative work, however, has been neither steady nor unopposed. Undoubtedly one of the underlying conditions is an expanding economy's need for labor. But something more than that is needed to break society's traditional habits of mind about the proper work for women. Certainly here the feminist demands for equality for women played a part. But a social factor of equal importance was war. By their very disruption of the steady pulse of everyday living, wars break the cake of custom, shake up society and compel people to look afresh at old habits and attitudes. It is not accidental, for instance, that women's suffrage in England, Russia and Germany, as well as the United States, was achieved immediately after the First World War and in France and Italy after the Second.

At the very least, by making large and new demands upon the established work force, war draws hitherto unused labor into the economic process. During the Civil War, for example, young women assumed new roles in the economy as workers in metal and munitions factories, as clerks in the expanded bureaucracy in Washington and as nurses in war hospitals. Moreover, when the war was over women had permanently replaced men as the dominant sex in the teaching profession. Furthermore, since many women found a new usefulness in the Sanitary Fairs and other volunteer work, the end of hostilities left many women unwilling to slip back into the seclusion of the Victorian home. It is not simply coincidental that the women's club movement began very soon after the war.

When the First World War came to the United States, feminist leaders, perhaps recalling the gains of the Civil War, anticipated new and broad advances for their sex. And the demand for labor, especially after the United States entered the war, did open many jobs to women, just as it was doing in contemporary Great Britain and Germany. All over the United States during the war customary and legal restrictions on the employment of women fell away. Women could be seen doing everything from laying railroad ties to working in airplane factories. The war also brought to a successful climax the struggle for the suffrage. Pointedly women had argued that a war for democracy abroad should at least remedy the deficiencies of democracy at home.

If politically the war was a boon to women, economically it failed to live up to feminist anticipations. The First World War, unlike the Civil War, did not result in a large permanent increase in the number of working women. Indeed, by 1920 there were only 800,000 more women working than in 1910. But as a result of wartime demands, women did get permanent places in new job categories, like elevator operators and theater ushers. (But women street car conductors disappeared soon after the armistice.) Certain traditional professions for women, like music teaching, lost members between 1910 and 1920, while professions that required more training and provided steadier income, like library and social work and college teaching, doubled or tripled their numbers in the same period.

The Second World War, with its even more massive demands for labor and skills, brought almost four million new women workers into the nation's factories and offices. Once again jobs usually not filled by women were opened to them. For example, the number of women bank officers rose 40 per cent during the four years of the war and the number of women employees in finance has continued to rise ever since. Furthermore, unlike the situation after the First World War, the female work force after 1945 not only stayed up but then went higher.

Measured in the number of women working, the changes in the economic position of women add up to a feminist success. Twenty-four million working women cannot be ignored. But weighed in the scales of quality instead of quantity, the change in women's economic status is not so striking. It is true that women now work in virtually every job listed by the Bureau of the Census. Moreover, the popular press repeatedly tells of the inroads women are making into what used to be thought of as men's jobs. Three years ago, for example, a woman won a prize as the mutual fund salesman of the year. Women are widely represented in advertising and in real estate, and even women taxicab drivers are no longer rare. Yet the fact remains that the occupations in which the vast majority of women actually engage are remarkably similar to those historically held by women. In 1950 almost three quarters of all employed women fell into twenty occupational categories, of which the largest was stenographers, typists and secretaries—a category that first became prominent as a woman's occupation over a half century ago. Other occupations which have traditionally been women's, like domestic service, teaching, clerical work, nursing and telephone service, are also conspicuous among the twenty categories. Further than that, the great majority of women are employed in occupations in which they predominate. This sexual division of labor is clearly evident in the professions, even though women are only a small proportion of total professional workers. Two thirds of all professional women are either nurses or teachers; and even in teaching there is a division between the sexes. Most women teach in the primary grades; most men teach in high school. Women are notoriously underrepresented in the top professions like law, medicine, engineering and scientific research. No more than 7 per cent of all professional women in 1950 were in the four of these categories together. Only 6 per cent of medical doctors and 4 per cent of lawyers and judges were women. In contrast, almost three quarters of medical doctors are women in the Soviet Union; in England the figure is 16 per cent. In both France and Sweden women make up a high proportion of pharmacists and dentists; neither of those professions attracts many women in the United States.

One consequence as well as manifestation of the sexual division of labor in the United States has been the differences in pay for men and women. That difference has been a historical complaint of feminist leaders. In 1900 one study found women's wages to be, on the average, only 53 per cent of men's. The reason was, of course, that women were concentrated in the poorer paying jobs and industries of the economy. The disparity in pay between the sexes has been somewhat reduced today, but not very much. In 1955 among full-time women workers of all types the median wage was about two thirds of that for men. In short, women are still supplying the low-paid labor in the economy just as they were in the last century. (In substance, women workers and Negroes of both sexes perform a similar function in the economy.) The willingness of women to supply cheap labor may well account for their getting the large number of jobs they do; men often will not work for the wages that women will accept.

Today, there does not seem to be very much disparity between men's and women's wages for the same work, though the sexual division of labor is so nearly complete that it is difficult to find comparable jobs of the two sexes to make a definitive study.

There has been no improvement in women's position in higher education; indeed, it can be argued that women have failed to maintain the place reached much earlier. As we have seen, the United States led the world in opening higher education to women. This country also led in broadening the social base of education for women. No other country educated such a large proportion of women in its universities and colleges as did the United States. At the close of the nineteenth century, one third of American college students were women; by 1937 women made up almost 40 per cent of the students in American institutions of higher learning. In Germany, just before Hitler took power, no more than one out of ten university students was a woman; in Swedish universities in 1937 only 17 per cent of the students were women; in British universities the ratio was 22 per cent.

But since the Second World War the gap between American and European proportions of women in higher education has narrowed considerably. In 1952–1953 women constituted only 35 per cent of the American college population, while France counted women as 36 per cent of its university students and Sweden 26 per cent. The *number* of women in American colleges, of course, is considerably greater than it was in the 1920's and 1930's, but in proportion to men, women have lost ground in America while gaining it in Europe.

A further sign of the regression in the educational position of women in the United States is that in the early 1950's women earned about 10 per cent of the doctoral degrees in this country as compared with almost 15 per cent in the 1920's.

How is one to explain this uneven, almost contradictory record of women in America? How does it happen that a country with a kind of built-in feminism from the frontier falls behind more traditional countries in its training of college women; that a country with one of the highest proportions of working women in the world ends up with such a small proportion of its women in medicine, in law and in the sciences? Perhaps the correct answer is that the question should not be asked—at least not by Americans. For like so much else in American society, such contradictions are a manifestation of the national avoidance of any ideological principle, whether it be in feminist reform or in anything else. To be sure there has been no lack of feminist argument or rationale for women's work outside the home, for women's education and for other activities by women. But American women, like American society in general, have been more concerned with individual practice than with a consistent feminist ideology. If women have entered the labor force or taken jobs during a war they have done so for reasons related to the immediate individual or social circumstances and not for reasons of feminist ideology. The women who have been concerned about showing that women's capabilities can match men's have been the exception. As the limited, and low-paying, kinds of jobs women occupy demonstrate, there is not now and never has been any strong feminist push behind the massive and continuing movement of women into jobs. Most American women have been interested in jobs, not careers. To say, as many feminists have, that men have opposed and resisted the opening of opportunities to women is to utter only a half truth. The whole truth is that American society in general, which includes women, shuns like a disease any feminist ideology.

Another way of showing that the historical changes in the status of women in America bear little relation to a feminist ideology is to examine one of those rare instances when women did effect a social improvement through an appeal to ideology, for instance, the struggle for the suffrage. By the early twentieth century the feminist demand for the vote overrode every other feminist goal. Once women achieved the vote, it was argued, the evils of society would be routed, for women, because of their peculiar attributes, would bring a fresh, needed and wholesome element into political life. In form, and in the minds of many women leaders, the arguments for the suffrage came close to being a full-blown ideology of feminism.

In point of fact, of course, the Nineteenth Amendment ushered in no millennium. But that fact is of less importance than the reason why it did not. When American women obtained the vote they simply did not use it ideologically; they voted not as women but as individuals. Evidence of this was the failure of many women to vote at all. At the end of the first decade of national suffrage women still did not exercise the franchise to the extent that men did. Nor did many women run for or hold political offices. The first woman to serve in Congress was elected in 1916; in 1920, the first year of national women's suffrage, four women were elected to Congress, but until 1940 no more than nine women served at one time in the House of Representatives and the Senate together. That we are here observing an American and not simply a sexual phenomenon is shown by a comparison with European countries. In nonfeminist Germany, where the ballot came to women at about the same time as in the United States, the first Reichstag after suffrage counted forty-one women as members. In 1951 seventeen women sat in the British House of Commons as compared with ten in the United States House of Representatives. Twice the number of women have served as cabinet ministers in Britain between 1928 and 1951 as have served in the United States down to the present.

Another instance in which social change was effected by feminist ideology was prohibition. The achievement of national prohibition ran second only to the suffrage movement as a prime goal of the organized women's movement; the Eighteenth Amendment was as much a product of feminist ideology as the Nineteenth. Yet like the suffrage movement, prohibition, despite its feminist backing, failed to receive the support of women. It was *after* prohibition was enacted, after all, that women drank in public.

In the cases of both suffrage and prohibition, women acted as individuals, not as members of a sex. And so they have continued to act. It is not without relevance that the women's political organization that is most respected—the League of Women Voters—is not only nonpartisan but studiously avoids questions pertaining only to women. To do otherwise would be feminist and therefore ideological.

One further conclusion might be drawn from this examination of the non-ideological character of American women. That the changes that have come to the position of women have been devoid of ideological intent may well explain why there has been so little opposition to them. The most successful of American reforms have always been those of an impromptu and practical nature. The great revolution of the New Deal is a classic example. The American people, like F. D. R. himself, simply tried one thing after another, looking for something—anything—that would get the nation out of the depression. If lasting reforms took place too, so much the better. On the other hand, reforms that have been justified by an elaborate rationale or ideology, like abolition, have aroused strong and long-drawn-out opposition. By the same token, when women became ideological in support of suffrage and prohibition, they faced their greatest opposition and scored their most disappointing triumphs.

The achievement of the suffrage in 1920 is a convenient date for marking the end of the first phase in the changing position of women, for by then women were accorded virtually the same rights as men even if they did not always exercise them. The second phase began at about the same time. It was the participation of married women in the work force. During the nineteenth century few married women worked; when they did it was because they were childless or because their husbands were inadequate providers. Even among the poor, married women normally did not work. A survey of the slum districts in five large cities in 1893 revealed that no more than 5 per cent of the wives were employed. Only Negro wives in the South and immigrant wives in big northern cities provided any significant exceptions to this generalization.

Before the First World War, the movement of wives into the working force was barely noticeable. During the 1920's there was an acceleration, but as late as 1940 less than 17 per cent of all married women were working. Among working women in 1940, 48 per cent were single and only 31 per cent were married. The Second World War dramatically reversed these proportions—another instance of the influence of war on the position of women. By 1950 the proportion of married women living with their husbands had risen to 48 per cent of all working women while that of single women had fallen to 32 per cent. In 1960 the Census reported that almost 32 per cent of all married women were employed outside the home and that they comprised

54 per cent of all working women. No industrial country of Europe, with the exception of the Soviet Union, counted such a high proportion. Today, married women are the greatest source of new labor in the American economy. Between 1949 and 1959, for example, over four million married women entered the labor force, some 60 per cent of *all* additions, male and female.

Such a massive movement of married women out of the home was a development few of the early feminists could have anticipated. That it has taken place is at once a sign and a yardstick of the enormous change in women's position in society and in the family. In the nineteenth century work outside the home was unthinkable for the married woman. Not only were there children to care for, but there were objections from husbands and society to consider. That is why the convinced feminist of the nineteenth century often spurned marriage. Indeed, it is often forgotten that the feminist movement was a form of revolt against marriage. For it was through marriage, with the legal and social dominance of the husband, that women were most obviously denied opportunities for self-expression. Even after the legal superiority of the husband had been largely eliminated from the law, middle-class social conventions could still scarcely accommodate the working wife. To the woman interested in realizing her human capabilities, marriage in the nineteenth century was not an opportunity but a dead end. And it was indeed a minor scandal of the time that many of the "new women" did in fact reject marriage. The tendency was most pronounced, as was to be expected, among highly educated women, many of whom felt strongly their obligation to serve society through careers. Around 1900 more than one fourth of women who graduated from college never married; more than half of the women medical doctors in 1890 were single.

Like other changes in the position of women, the movement of married women into the work force—the reconciliation of marriage and work—must be related to the social changes of the last three decades. One of these social changes was the increase in contraceptive knowledge, for until married women could limit their families they could not become steady and reliable industrial workers. Information about contraceptive techniques which had been known for a generation or more to educated middle-class women did not seep down to the working class until the years of the Great Depression. In 1931, for instance, there were only 81 clinics disseminating birth control information in the United States; in 1943 there were 549, of which 166 were under public auspices. As the number of public clinics suggest, by the end of the 1930's birth control was both socially and religiously acceptable, at least among Protestants. And a method was also available then to Roman Catholics, since it was in the same decade that the rhythm method, the only one acceptable to the Roman Catholic Church, was first brought to popular attention with the approval of ecclesiastical authorities.

Another social force underlying the movement of wives and mothers in the work force was the growing affluence of an industrial society, especially after 1940. Higher health standards, enlarged incomes of husbands and a better standard of living in general permitted a marked alteration in the temporal cycle of women's lives. Women now lived longer, stayed in school later and married earlier. In 1890 half the girls left school at 14 or before—that is, when they finished grammar school; in 1957 the median age was 18—after graduation from high school. The girl of 1890, typically, did not marry until she was 22; the age of her counterpart in 1957 was 20, leaving no more than two years for work between the end of school and marriage. Among other things this fact explains the fall in the proportion of single women in the work force in the United States as compared with other industrial societies. Few other countries have such an early median age of marriage for girls.

Early marriages for women produce another effect. With knowledge of contraceptive techniques providing a measure of control over child-bearing, women are now having their children early and rapidly. When this tendency is combined with a younger age of marriage, the result is an early end to child-bearing. In 1890 the median age of a mother when her last child was born was 32; in 1957 it was 26. A modern mother thus has her children off to school by the time she is in her middle thirties, leaving her as much as thirty-five years free for work outside the home. And the fact is that almost half of working women today are over forty years of age. Put another way, 34 per cent of married women between the ages of thirty-five and forty-four years are gainfully employed.

Unquestionably, as the practical character of the woman's movement would lead us to expect, an important force behind the influx of married women into the work force is economic need. But simple poverty is not the only force. Several studies, for example, have documented the conclusion that many women who work are married to men who earn salaries in the upper income brackets, suggesting that poverty is not the controlling factor in the wife's decision to work. A similar conclusion is to be drawn from the positive correlation between education and work for married women. The more education a wife has (and therefore the better salary her husband is likely to earn) the more likely she is to be working herself. Many of these women work undoubtedly in order to raise an adequate standard of living to a comfortable one. Many others work probably because they want to realize their potentialities in the world. But that women are so poorly represented in the professions and other careers suggests that most married women who work are realizing their full capabilities neither for themselves nor for society.

Over sixty years ago, in *Women and Economics*, the feminist Charlotte Perkins Gilman cogently traced the connection between work and the fulfillment of women as human beings. In subsequent writings she grappled with the problem of how this aim might be realized for married women. As a mother herself, raising a child under the trying circumstances of divorce, Gilman knew first hand that work outside the home and child-rearing constituted *two* full-time jobs. No man, she knew, was expected or required to shoulder such a double burden. Gilman's remedies of professional domestic service and kitchenless apartments never received much of a hearing, and considering the utopian if not bizarre character of her solutions, that is not surprising. Yet the problem she raised remained without any solution other than the eminently individualistic and inadequate one of permitting a woman to assume the double burden if she was so minded. Meanwhile, as the economy has grown, the problem has entered the lives of an ever increasing number of women. Unlike most of her feminist contemporaries, who were mainly concerned with the suffrage and the final elimination of legal and customary barriers to women's opportunities, Gilman recognized that the logic of feminism led unavoidably to the working mother as the typical woman. For if women were to be free to express themselves, then they should be able to marry as well as to work. Women should not have to make a choice any more than men. To make that possible, though, would require that some way be found to mitigate the double burden which biology and society had combined to place only on women.

As women moved into the second stage of their development—the reconciliation of work and marriage—the problem which Gilman saw so early was increasingly recognized as the central issue. Virginia Collier, for example, in a book *Marriage and Careers*, published in 1926, wrote that since so many married women were working, "The question therefore is no longer should women combine marriage with careers, but how do they manage it and how does it work." Interestingly enough, her study shows that what today Betty Friedan, in *The Feminine Mystique*, has called the "problem that has no name," was already apparent in the 1920's. One working wife explained her reasons for taking a job in these words, "I am burning up with energy and it is rather hard on the family to use it up in angry frustration." Another said, "I had done everything for Polly for six years. Suddenly she was in school all day and I had nothing to do. My engine was running just as hard as ever, but my car was standing still." A year after Collier's book appeared, President William A. Neilson of Smith College observed "that the outstanding problem confronting women is how to reconcile a normal life of marriage and motherhood with intellectual activity such as her college education has fitted her for." That the issue was taken seriously is attested by an action of the Board of Trustees of Barnard College in 1932. The board voted to grant six months' maternity leave with pay to members of the staff and faculty. In announcing the decision, Dean Virginia Gildersleeve clearly voiced its import. "Neither the men nor the women of our staff," she said, "should be forced into celibacy, and cut off from that great source of experience of joy, sorrow and wisdom which marriage and parenthood offer."

With one out of three married women working today, the problem of reconciling marriage and work for women is of a social dimension considerably larger than in the days of Charlotte Gilman or even in the 1930's. But the fundamental issue is still the same: how to make it possible, as Dean Gildersleeve said, to pursue a career or hold a job while enjoying the "experience . . . joy, sorrow and wisdom" of marriage and parenthood. The practical solutions to this central problem of the second stage in the changing position of women seem mainly collective or governmental, not individual. Child-care centers, efficient and readily available house-keeping services, and emergency child-care service such as the Swedes have instituted are obviously a minimal requirement if women are to have the double burdens of homemaking and employment lightened. The individual working woman cannot be expected to compensate for the temporary disabilities consequent upon her role as mother any more than the individual farmer or industrial worker can be expected single-handedly to overcome the imbalance between himself and the market. Today both farmers and workers have government and their own organizations to assist them in righting the balance.

But as the history of farmers and industrial labor makes evident, to enact legislation or to change mores requires persuasion of those who do not appreciate the necessity for change. Those who would do so must organize the like-minded and mobilize power, which is to say they need a rationale, an ideology. And here is the rub; in pragmatic America, as we have seen, any ideology must leap high hurdles. And one in support of working wives is additionally handicapped because women themselves, despite the profound changes in their status in the last century, do not acknowledge such an ideology. Most American women simply do not want work outside the home to be justified as a normal activity for married women. Despite the counter-argument of overwhelming numbers of working wives, they like to think of it as special and exceptional. And so long as they do not advance such an ideology, American society surely will not do so, though other societies, like Israel's and the Soviet Union's, which are more ideological than ours, obviously have.

Perhaps the kind of gradual, piecemeal advance toward a feminist ideology that Mrs. Rossi proposes in other pages of this book* may contain the seeds of change. But a reading of the past reminds us forcefully that in America the soil is thin and the climate uncongenial for the growth of any seedlings of ideology.

* "The Woman in America," *Daedalus* (Spring 1964).

18 / Religion and Culture in Present-Day America

Will Herberg

From the founding of the first American settlements, Protestant churches have had a profound influence on American culture. But at the same time that religious institutions and values flourished and were powerful social forces, they were being undermined. The churches were disestablished during and after the Revolution, and they accepted the principle and practice of voluntarism as the American way. Protestant sectarianism also lessened. The public schools, colleges, and universities originally founded by church groups became increasingly secular. The Enlightenment, higher criticism, and especially modern science eroded established religious beliefs. Shifting patterns of immigration in the nineteenth and twentieth centuries, which brought millions of Catholics and Jews to American shores, also threatened the Protestant influence.

In spite of growing secularism, religion apparently underwent a revival following World War II. Some critics have viewed with skepticism the statistical evidence of a return to religion, but, however exaggerated, there was some movement back to the churches. Will Herberg's essay attempts to explain why a revival occurred in a period of secularism. He suggests that American religion has taken on a new role—that of giving the individual social identification, as either Protestant, Catholic, or Jew. This thesis should be compared to that of Milton Gordon on assimilation of ethnic groups. Herberg wrote this article before the religious revival had leveled off and before the ecumenical movement of the 1960's. His discussion should be read with these two developments in mind.

For further reading: *Gerhard Lenski, *The Religious Factor* (1961); *Frank H. Littell, *From State Church to Pluralism* (1962); *Will Herberg,

Thomas McAvoy (ed.), *Roman Catholicism and the American Way of Life* (South Bend, Indiana: University of Notre Dame Press, 1960), 4–19. Reprinted without footnotes by permission of the University of Notre Dame Press.

Protestant-Catholic-Jew (1960); Edwin Scott Gaustad, *A Religious History of America* (1966); *Sidney Mead, *The Lively Experiment* (1963); *Milton Gordon, *Assimilation in American Life* (1964).

I

Whatever may be true about the religious situation, it certainly cannot be doubted that religion is enjoying a boom of unprecedented proportions in America today. Well over 95 per cent of the American people identify themselves religiously, as Protestants, Catholics, or Jews—an incredibly high figure by all available standards of comparison. The proportion of Americans who are church members—that is, actually on the rolls of the churches—has nearly doubled in the past half century; in the last twenty years indeed, church membership has been increasing twice as fast as population. Church and synagogue attendance is rising rapidly, Sunday school enrollment is rising even more rapidly, and religious giving has reached a formidable figure, even allowing for the inflationary devaluation of the dollar. Interest in religion and religious thinking is widespread on all cultural levels. Whatever the criterion of religiousness we take—and by religiousness I mean the "externals" of religion, using this term in a neutral sense, without prejudice—we cannot escape the conclusion that we are today witnessing an upsurge of religion without precedent in recent times.

But it is a curious kind of religion. The very same people who are so unanimous in identifying themselves religiously, who are joining churches at an accelerating rate, and who take it for granted that religion is a "very important" thing, do not hesitate to acknowledge that religion is quite peripheral to their everyday lives: more than half of them quite frankly admit that their religious beliefs have no influence whatever on their ideas in economics and politics, and a good proportion of the remainder are obviously uncertain. The very same people who distribute the Bible in vast quantities, largely by voluntary effort, are unable in their majority to give the name of one single book of the New Testament, and the showing is not very different when you take the Bible as a whole. The very same people who, four out of five, say they regard Jesus as divine, when asked to name the most important event in all universal history, place the Christ-event—the birth or crucifixion of Christ—fourteenth on the list, tied with the Wright brothers' invention of the airplane: the Number 1 event, almost without exception, is given as Columbus' discovery of America.

This is the problem: America is in the grip of a great religious boom, that is obvious; yet equally obvious, though not so easy to establish by facts and figures, is the continuing "trend toward secularism in ideas," to use Professor Handlin's phrase —it is really a trend toward secularism not only in ideas, but in attitudes and values as well. This is the problem: the religiousness of a secularist society, the "strengthening of the religious structure in spite of increasing secularization." Thinking through this paradox will take us a long way toward understanding the present religious situation in this country.

II

The best approach to the problem, I think, is to try to understand something of the role that religious belonging plays in the social structure and functioning of contemporary America. I well recognize that religion has its transcendent dimension, which escapes all external scrutiny and analysis; but I am deliberately limiting my inquiry at this point to those aspects that are subject to such scrutiny and analysis, and I think that these aspects are significant in the total picture. What, then, is it that strikes one about the new function of religion in the life of the American people today? It is, I think, that religion, in its tripartite form of Protestant-Catholic-Jew, is rapidly becoming the primary context of self-identification and social location in present-day America. Let us see what this really means.

By and large, since the latter part of the nineteenth century at any rate, Americans have tended to identify and locate themselves in terms of race, ethnicity, and religion. "When asked the simple question, 'What are you?,'" Gordon W. Allport has noted, referring to certain recent researches, "only ten per cent of four-year-olds answer in terms of racial, ethnic, or religious membership, but 75 per cent of nine-year-olds do so"—and the percentage is even higher for adults. "Race" in America today means color, white *vs.* non-white, and racial stigmatization has introduced an element of caste-like stratification into American life. For white Americans, ethnicity (immigrant origin) and religion have been, and remain, the major sources of pluralistic diversity, and therefore the major forms of self-identification and social location. But the relation between the two has changed drastically in the course of the past generation, and it is this change that provides a clue to the new role of religion in American life.

As long as large-scale immigration continued, and America was predominantly a land of immigrants, in the days when "the immigrants were American history," as Handlin puts it, the dominant form of diversity, and therefore the dominant form of self-identification, was immigrant ethnicity. The always interesting question about a new family moving into the neighborhood—"What are they?"—was regularly answered in terms of ethnic-immigrant origin. Religion was felt to be an aspect of ethnicity, a part of the ethnic heritage, recent or remote. The enthusiasts of the "melting pot" were eager to eliminate these diverse heritages as quickly as possible; the "cultural pluralists" were determined to perpetuate them; but both alike moved within a pluralism based substantially on ethnicity, ethnic culture, and ethnic religion.

Within the past generation, the picture has been radically transformed. The stoppage of mass immigration during the First World War, followed by the anti-immigration legislation of the 1920's, undermined the foundations of immigrant ethnicity and the immigrant ethnic group with amazing rapidity; what it did was to facilitate the emergence of third and post-third generations, with their characteristic responses and attitudes, as a decisive influence on American life, no longer threatened with submergence by the next new wave of immigration. Within the threefold American scheme of race, ethnicity, and religion, a shift took place, a shift is taking place, from ethnicity to religion as the dominant form of self-identification—as the dominant way of answering the question, "What am I? How do I differ from 'one man's family'? Where do I fit in in the totality of American society?" Ethnic identifications and traditions have not disappeared; on the contrary, with the third generation, they are enjoying a lively popularity as symbols of "heritage." But now the relation between ethnicity and religion has been reversed: religion is no longer an aspect of ethnicity; it is ethnicity, or rather what remains of it, that is taken up, redefined, and expressed through religious identifications and institutions. Religion, or at least the tripartite differentiation of Protestant, Catholic, and Jew has (aside from race) become the prevailing form of defining one's identity as an American in contemporary American society.

Keeping this in mind, we can begin to understand one of the most striking facts in the religious history of this country during the past half century—the transformation of America from a *Protestant* country into a *three-religion* country.

Writing just thirty years ago, André Siegfried described Protestantism as America's "national religion," and he was largely right, despite the ban on religious establishment in the Constitution. Normally, to be born an American meant to be a Protestant; this was the religious identification that in the American mind quite naturally went along with being an American. Non-Protestants felt the force of this conviction almost as strongly as did the Protestants; Catholics and Jews, despite their vastly increasing numbers, experienced their non-Protestant religion as a problem, even as an obstacle, to their becoming full-fledged Americans: it was a mark of their foreignness. (This was true despite the much esteemed colonial heritage of both Jews and Catholics, since it was not the "old American" elements in these two groups that influenced American attitudes, but the newer immigrant masses.) In the familiar Troeltschean sense, Protestantism—not any one of the multiplying denominations, but Protestantism as a whole—constituted America's "established church."

This is no longer the case. Today, to be born an American is no longer taken to mean that one is necessarily a Protestant; Protestantism is no longer the obvious and "natural" religious identification of the American. Today, the evidence strongly indicates, America has become a three-religion country: the normal religious implication of being an American today is that one is either a Protestant, a Catholic, or a Jew. These three are felt to be, by and large, three different forms of being religious in the American way; they are the three "religions of democracy," the "three great faiths" of America. Today, unlike fifty years ago, not only Protestants, but increasingly Catholics and Jews as well, feel themselves, and are recognized to be, Americans not apart from, or in spite of, their religion, but because of it. If America today possesses a "church" in the Troeltschean sense—that is, a form of religious belonging which is felt to be involved in one's belonging to the national community—it is the tripartite religious system of Protestant-Catholic-Jew.

This transformation of America from a Protestant into a three-religion country has come about not because of any marked increase in Catholics or Jews—the Protestant-Catholic ratio has remained pretty well the same for the past thirty years, and the proportion of Jews in the general population has probably been declining. It has come about, as I have suggested, through the emergence of a stabilized American third generation, which is able to set its mark on American life because it is no longer threatened with dissolution by recurrent waves of mass immigration.

The immigrant generation, and this is true of all immigrant nationalities, established itself in America as an ethnic group with an ethnic culture, of which the ethnic language and the ethnic religion were generally the most significant elements.

For the first, the immigrant generation, religion was part of ethnicity; for the Italian immigrant, in other words, his Catholicness was part of his Italianness; for the Jewish immigrant, his Judaism, his Jewish religion, was part of his *Yiddishkait,* his ethnic culture. You remember the movie "Marty." You remember how Marty brings home the girl Clara to introduce her to his mother. His mother is a good church-going Catholic, but what is the question she asks about Clara? Not "Is she Catholic?," but "Is she Italian?" Why? Because to the mother, the first-generation immigrant, if she's Italian, then she's Catholic, and if she's Catholic without being Italian, it doesn't do any good anyway! This is the outlook on ethnicity and religion characteristic of the immigrant generation.

The second generation is in a very different position. The second generation is marginal—"too American for the home and too foreign for the school," in Marcus Hansen's celebrated phrase. It is doubly alienated, belonging to two communities but at home in neither, torn away from the old moorings and not yet anchored in the new reality. The second generation responds to its marginality in a number of ways, but by and large it may be said that what the second generation wants most of all is to get rid of its foreignness and become American. This obviously influences its attitude to religion. Just because in the immigrant home, in which the second generation grows up, religion is understood to be a part of ethnicity, to be a part of the immigrant foreignness, the second generation takes a negative view of religion, sometimes breaking with it entirely, usually retaining an uneasy connection, mixed with hostility and embarrassment. The second generation—and that holds true for every immigrant group in America—is characteristically the least religious of American generations.

But now comes the third generation. The third generation—and with it we must include the post-third generations that have arisen on American soil—is again in a very different position. It is at last American, securely American, secure as any American is in his Americanness. But it is faced with a new problem, the problem of defining its identity. Ethnic identifications will no longer serve, as in one way or another they served the first and second generations. What then?—how is the third generation to answer the question, "What am I? How do I differ from 'one man's family'? Where do I fit in the totality of American society?" In an effort to define its social identity—without which no tolerable life is possible—the American third generation goes in search of a "heritage." In a sensational reversal of earlier attitudes, the third generation seeks a "return." Some two decades ago, Marcus Lee Hansen, studying not Italians or Jews on the east coast, but Scandinavian Lutherans in the Midwest in the twenties and thirties, expressed this reversal in a classic formula: "What the son wishes to forget, the grandson wishes to remember." The "son," constituting the second generation, wishes to "forget" because he wants so passionately to get rid of his foreignness; the "grandson," belonging to the third generation, wishes to "remember" because he needs a "heritage." But what of the grandfather can the grandson "remember"?—what of his grandfather's legacy can he take over and use for the purpose of giving himself a "heritage" and defining his identity? Not his grandfather's nationality, language, or culture; the American pattern of assimilative acculturation obviously makes that impossible. But the grandfather's religion is a very different thing: America not only permits, it even encourages, the perpetuation of one's religious diversity and distinctiveness without danger to one's Americanness. Of course, it is not the grandfather's religion as the grandfather would have recognized it; it is the grandfather's religion brought up to date and Americanized. But it serves; and so religion becomes the characteristic symbol of "heritage" for the third generation, and its return to its heritage becomes a return to religion. With Catholics and Jews, the process, however complex, is relatively unambiguous. With Protestants, however, there is a double movement: on the one side, a return to ethnically associated religion, as among Lutherans; on the other side, because of the confusion, blurring, and growing meaninglessness of denominational lines, a "return" to Protestantism rather than to any particular group within it as a form of religious identification. William H. Whyte's account, in *The Organization Man*, of the emergence of the United Protestant Church in Park Forest, Ill., a story which could be duplicated in so many other suburban communities, well illustrates this pattern of development; but even where denominational affiliations are still maintained, the basic identification is still Protestant, especially among the younger people. And so a three-religion America has emerged, an America in which being a Protestant, being a Catholic, and being a Jew are the three recognized alternative ways of being an American.

A word of caution is necessary. It should not be imagined that just because America has become, or is becoming, a three-religion country, all ethnic or religious group tensions are at an end. Anti-Semitism runs deeper than any merely sociological analysis can penetrate, and even on the sociological level, the new tripartite system would, for the time being at least, seem to make almost as much for the exacerbation as for the alleviation of intergroup tensions. Anti-Jewish manifestations are, for the moment, at a low ebb, but Protestant-Catholic antagonisms appear to be growing sharper. This accentuation of Protestant-Catholic tensions seems to me to be very largely a reflection of the painful transition period through which we are passing; there is every reason to hope that with the stabilization of the new situation, these hostilities too will abate. Yet we should not overlook the fact that the new system of tripartite coexistence is bound to raise its own problems and breed its own tensions with which we will have to cope in the time to come.

III

What has the transformation of America from an ethnic into a religious pluralism, and concomitantly from a Protestant into a three-religion country, meant so far as the status and character of religion in this country are concerned?

Very obviously, it has made for a boom in religious belonging. To have a "name" in American society today—to have an identity, to be able to answer the question "What am I? Where do I belong?"—means increasingly to identify oneself in religious terms, as Protestant, Catholic, or Jew. These are three alternative ways of being an American. This is eminently true of the burgeoning suburban sector of American society, least true in the rural areas, and measurably true in the older urban centers. It is certainly the over-all pattern of American life. Obviously, such self-identification in religious terms engenders a new sense of belonging to one's community; obviously, too, it impels to institutional affiliation, characteristically expressed in terms of concern for the children: "We have to join a church (or a temple) for the sake of the children." There is profound sociological wisdom in this remark, though its theological implications may be dubious. "The church," Oscar

Handlin points out, "supplies a place where the children come to learn what they are"—what kind of Americans they are. The mechanisms of other-directed conformity to which David Riesman has called attention serve to give religious belonging the compelling power it is acquiring in the pattern of suburban "sociability," but the new role of religion in this process is the result of the more basic factors I have tried to indicate in my remarks on the third generation and the transformation of America into a three-religion country.

Just as Americans are coming more and more to think of being a Protestant, being a Catholic, and being a Jew as three alternative ways of being an American, so they are coming to regard Protestantism, Catholicism, and Judaism, the "three great faiths," as three alternative (though not necessarily equal) expressions of a great overarching commitment which they all share by virtue of being Americans. This commitment is, of course, democracy or the American Way of Life. It is the common allegiance which (to use Professor Williams' phrase) provides Americans with the "common set of ideas, rituals, and symbols" through which an "overarching sense of unity" is achieved amidst diversity and conflict. It is, in a sense far more real than John Dewey ever dreamed of, the "common religion" of Americans.

Let me illustrate this point with two texts borrowed from President Eisenhower, who may, I think, be taken as a representative American really serious about religion. "Our government," Mr. Eisenhower declared shortly after his election in 1952, "makes no sense unless it is founded in a deeply felt religious faith, *and I don't care what it is*." It is the last phrase which I have emphasized—"and I don't care what it is"—to which I want to call your attention. Of course, President Eisenhower did not mean that literally; he would have been much disturbed had any sizable proportion of Americans become Buddhists, or Shintoists, or Confucianists—but of course that never entered his mind. When he said "I don't care what it is," he obviously meant "I don't care which of the three it is—Protestantism, Catholicism, or Judaism." And why didn't he care which it was? Because, in his view, as in the view of all normal Americans, they "all say the same thing." And what is the "same thing" which they all say? The answer is given to us from the current vocabulary: "the moral and spiritual values of democracy." These, for the typical American, are in a real sense final and ultimate; the three conventional religions are approved of and validated primarily because they embody and express these "moral and spiritual values of democracy."

Let me drive this home with the second text from President Eisenhower. In 1948, four years before his election, just before he became president of Columbia, Mr. Eisenhower made another important pronouncement on religion. "I am the most intensely religious man I know," he declared. "Nobody goes through six years of war without faith. That does not mean that I adhere to any sect. [Incidentally, following the way of all flesh, he was soon to join a "sect," the Presbyterian.] A democracy cannot exist without a religious base. I believe in democracy." Here we have the entire story in a single phrase: I believe in religion because I believe in democracy! Precisely the same conviction, though expressed in a rather more sophisticated manner, was affirmed by an eminent New York rabbi not long ago. "The spiritual meaning of American democracy," he declared, "is realized in its three great faiths." Similar statements, I assure you, could be found in the pronouncements of spokesmen of the other two religious groups.

What I am describing is essentially the "Americanization" of religion in America, and therefore also its thorough-going secularization. This process is not a recent one.

It began for Protestantism some time after the Civil War and proceeded apace in the latter decades of the nineteenth century. Sidney Mead's brilliant description of this trend is particularly relevant.

> What was not so obvious at the time [he writes] was that the United States, in effect, had two religions, or at least two different forms of the same religion, and that the prevailing Protestant ideology represented a syncretistic mingling of the two. The first was the religion of the [Protestant] denominations which was commonly articulated in terms of scholastic Protestant orthodoxy and almost universally practised in terms of the experimental religion of pietistic revivalism. . . . The second was the religion of the democratic society and nation. This . . . was articulated in terms of the destiny of America, under God, to be fulfilled by perfecting the democratic way of life for the example and betterment of mankind.

With remarkably little change—something would have to be said about the waning of scholastic orthodoxy and the new forms of pietistic revivalism—these words could stand as a description of the current situation. What is new, what is crucially new, is that this is no longer true merely of Protestantism; it is becoming more and more true of Catholicism and Judaism as well, precisely because Catholicism and Judaism have become American, integral parts of the three-religion America. In this, as in so many other respects, their Americanization has meant their "Protestantization," using this term to describe the American Protestant ethos, so at variance with classical Protestant Christian faith. With the loss of their foreignness, of their immigrant marginality, these two religious groups seem to be losing their capacity to resist dissolution in the culture. In becoming American, they have apparently become American all the way.

We are now, I think, in a position to penetrate the apparent paradox with which we initiated this discussion, the paradox of the religiousness of a secularist society. How can Americans be so religious and so secularistic at the same time? The answer is that for increasing numbers of Americans religion serves a function largely unrelated to the content of faith, the function of defining their identity and providing them with a context of belonging in the great wilderness of a mobile American society. Indeed, for such a purpose, the authentic content of faith may even prove a serious handicap, for if it is Jewish or Christian faith, it carries a prophetic impact which serves rather to unadjust than to adjust, to emphasize the ambiguity of every earthly form of belonging rather than to let the individual rest secure in his "sociability." For this reason, the typical American has developed a remarkable capacity for being serious about religion without taking religion seriously—in which respect he is not unlike sinful human beings of all ages. His ideas, values, and standards he takes from what is so often really his ultimate commitment, the American Way of Life. He combines the two—his religion and his culture—by making the former an expression of the latter, his religion an expression of the "moral and spiritual values of democracy." Hence his puzzling proreligious secularism, his secularistic religionism, which, looked at more closely, does not seem so puzzling after all. . . .

19 / Crime as an American Way of Life

Daniel Bell

Most studies of social mobility in America have regarded legitimate business as a source of opportunity for people on their way up. In the following essay, Daniel Bell suggests that disadvantaged ethnic groups, finding the legitimate upward paths blocked or filled with obstacles, have turned to crime to achieve success. For similar reasons, some ethnic groups have gravitated to certain businesses and occupations where they have better opportunities. Bell also probes the relationship between organized crime and politics, since some ethnic groups had greater political than economic power and used one to advance the other. The increasing tendency for American society to become more organized and bureaucratized has affected crime as well as legitimate business. The communications revolution has made its mark on gambling, and organized crime has sought to rationalize its business, to control competition, and to achieve greater stability just as other businessmen have done. Bell also suggests that American society is pluralistic, with some groups more likely than others to use criminal methods to achieve the American dream of wealth and status.

For further reading: *Andrew Sinclair, *Era of Excess* (1962); *Max Lerner, *America as a Civilization* (1957); *William Whyte, *Street Corner Society* (1943).

In the 1890's the Reverend Dr. Charles Parkhurst, shocked at the open police protection afforded New York's bordellos, demanded a state inquiry. In the Lexow investigation that followed, the young and dashing William Travers Jerome staged a set of public hearings that created sensation after sensation. He badgered "Clubber" Williams, First Inspector of the Police Department, to account for wealth and property far greater than could have been saved on his salary; it was earned, the Clubber explained laconically, through land speculation "in Japan." Heavy-set Captain Schmittberger, the "collector" for the "Tenderloin precincts"—Broadway's fabulous concentration of hotels, theaters, restaurants, gaming houses, and saloons—related in

Antioch Review, XIII, No. 2 (Summer 1953), 131–154. Reprinted by permission of the author and *Antioch Review*.

detail how protection money was distributed among the police force. Crooks, police-men, public officials, businessmen, all paraded across the stage, each adding his chapter to a sordid story of corruption and crime. The upshot of these revelations was reform—the election of William L. Strong, a stalwart businessman, as mayor, and the naming of Theodore Roosevelt as police commissioner.

It did not last, of course, just as previous reform victories had not lasted. Yet the ritual drama was re-enacted. Thirty years ago the Seabury investigation in New York uncovered the tin-box brigade and the thirty-three little McQuades. Jimmy Walker was ousted as Mayor and in came Fiorello LaGuardia. Tom Dewey became district attorney, broke the industrial rackets, sent Lucky Luciano to jail, and went to the governor's chair in Albany. Then reform was again swallowed up in the insatiable maw of corruption until in 1950 Kefauver and his committee counsel Rudolph Halley threw a new beam of light into the seemingly bottomless pit.

How explain this repetitive cycle? Obviously the simple moralistic distinction between "good guys" and "bad guys," so deep at the root of the reform impulse, bears little relation to the role of organized crime in American society. What, then, does?

THE QUEER LADDER

Americans have had an extraordinary talent for compromise in politics and ex-tremism in morality. The most shameless political deals (and "steals") have been rationalized as expedient and realistically necessary. Yet in no other country have there been such spectacular attempts to curb human appetites and brand them as illicit, and nowhere else such glaring failures. From the start America was at one and the same time a frontier community where "everything goes," and the fair country of the Blue Laws. At the turn of the century the cleavage developed between the Big City and the small-town conscience. Crime as a growing business was fed by the revenues from prostitution, liquor, and gambling that a wide-open urban society encouraged and that a middle-class Protestant ethos tried to suppress with a ferocity unmatched in any other civilized country. Catholic cultures have rarely imposed such restrictions and have rarely suffered such excesses. Even in prim and proper Anglican England, prostitution is a commonplace of Piccadilly night life, and gambling is one of the largest and most popular industries. In America the enforce-ment of public morals has been a continuing feature of our history.

Some truth may lie in Max Scheler's generalization that moral indignation is a peculiar fact of middle-class psychology and represents a disguised form of repressed envy. The larger truth lies perhaps in the brawling nature of American development and in the social character of crime. Crime, in many ways, is a Coney Island mirror, caricaturing the morals and manners of a society. The jungle quality of the American business community, particularly at the turn of the century, was reflected in the mode of "business" practiced by the coarse gangster elements, most of them from new immigrant families, who were "getting ahead," just as Horatio Alger had urged. In the older, Protestant tradition the intensive acquisitiveness, such as that of Daniel Drew, was rationalized by a compulsive moral fervor. But the formal obeisance of the ruthless businessman in the workday world to the church-going pieties of the Sabbath was one that the gangster could not make. Moreover, for the young criminal, hunting in the asphalt jungle of the crowded city, it was not the businessman with his wily manipulation of numbers but the "man with the gun" who was the American hero. "No amount of commercial prosperity," once wrote Teddy Roosevelt, "can supply the lack of the heroic virtues." The American was "the hunter, cowboy, frontiersman, the soldier, the naval hero"—and in the crowded slums, the gangster. He was a man with a gun, acquiring by personal merit what was denied him by complex orderings of stratified society. And the duel with the law was the morality play par excellence: the gangster, with whom ride our own illicit desires, and the prosecutor, representing final judgment and the force of the law.

Yet all this was acted out in a wider context. The desires satisfied in extra-legal fashion were more than a hunger for the "forbidden fruits" of conventional morality. They also involved, in the complex and ever shifting structure of group, class, and ethnic stratification, which is the warp and woof of America's "open" society, such "normal" goals as independence through a business of one's own, and such "moral" aspirations as the desire for social advancement and social prestige. For crime, in the language of the sociologists, has a "functional" role in the society, and the urban rackets—the illicit activity organized for continuing profit, rather than individual illegal acts—is one of the queer ladders of social mobility in American life. Indeed, it is not too much to say that the whole question of organized crime in America cannot be understood unless one appreciates (1) the distinctive role of organized gambling as a function of a mass-consumption economy; (2) the specific role of various immigrant groups as they, one after another, became involved in marginal business and crime; and (3) the relation of crime to the changing character of the urban political machines.

GATSBY'S MODEL

As a society changes, so does, in lagging fashion, its type of crime. As American society became more "organized," as the American businessman became more "civilized" and less "buccaneering," so did the American racketeer. And just as there were important changes in the structure of business enterprise, so the "institutionalized" criminal enterprise was transformed too.

In the America of the last fifty years the main drift of society has been toward the rationalization of industry, the domestication of the crude self-made captain of industry into the respectable man of manners, and the emergence of a mass-consumption economy. The most significant transformation in the field of "institutionalized" crime in the 1940's was the increasing importance of gambling as against other kinds of illegal activity. And, as a multi-billion-dollar business, gambling underwent a transition parallel to the changes in American enterprise as a whole. This parallel was exemplified in many ways: in gambling's industrial organization (e.g., the growth of a complex technology such as the national racing-wire service and the minimization of risks by such techniques as lay-off betting); in its respectability, as was evidenced in the opening of smart and popular gambling casinos in resort towns and in "satellite" adjuncts to metropolitan areas; in its functional role in a mass-consumption economy (for sheer volume of money changing hands, nothing has ever surpassed this feverish activity of fifty million American adults); in the social acceptance of the gamblers in the important status world of sport and entertainment, i.e., "café society."

In seeking to "legitimize" itself, gambling had quite often actually become a force against older and more vicious forms of illegal activity. In 1946, for example, when a Chicago mobster, Pat Manno, went down to Dallas, Texas, to take over gambling in the area for the Accardo-Guzik combine, he reassured the sheriff as follows: "Something I'm against, that's dope peddlers, pickpockets, hired killers. That's one thing I can't stomach, and that's one thing the fellows up there—the group won't stand for, things like that. They discourage it, they even go to headquarters and ask them why they don't do something about it."

Jimmy Cannon once reported that when the gambling raids started in Chicago the "combine" protested that, in upsetting existing stable relations, the police were only opening the way for ambitious young punks and hoodlums to start trouble. Nor is there today, as there was twenty or even forty years ago, prostitution of major organized scope in the United States. Aside from the fact that manners and morals have changed, prostitution *as an industry* doesn't pay as well as gambling. Besides, its existence threatened the tacit moral acceptance and quasi-respectability that gamblers and gambling have secured in the American way of life. It was, as any operator in the field might tell you, "bad for business."

The criminal world of the 1940's, its tone set by the captains of the gambling industry, is in startling contrast to the state of affairs in the decade before. If a Kefauver report had been written then, the main "names" would have been Lepke and Gurrah, Dutch Schultz, Jack "Legs" Diamond, Lucky Luciano, and, reaching back a little further, Arnold Rothstein, the czar of the underworld. These men (with the exception of Luciano, who was involved in narcotics and prostitution) were in the main "industrial racketeers." Rothstein, the model for Wolfsheim the gambler in F. Scott Fitzgerald's *The Great Gatsby*, had a larger function: he was, as Frank Costello became later, the financier of the underworld, the pioneer big businessman of crime who, understanding the logic of coordination, sought to *organize* crime as a source of regular income. His main interest in this direction was in industrial racketeering, and his entry was through labor disputes. At one time, employers in the garment trades hired Legs Diamond and his sluggers to break strikes, and the Communists, then in control of the cloakmakers union, hired one Little Orgie to protect the pickets and beat up the scabs; only later did both sides learn that Legs Diamond and Little Orgie were working for the same man, Rothstein.

Rothstein's chief successors, Lepke Buchalter and Gurrah Shapiro, were able, in the early thirties, to dominate sections of the men's and women's clothing industries, of painting, fur dressing, flour trucking, and other fields. In a highly chaotic and cutthroat industry such as clothing, the racketeer, paradoxically, played a stabilizing role by regulating competition and fixing prices. When the NRA came in and assumed this function, the businessman found that what had once been a quasi-economic service was now pure extortion, and he began to demand police action. In other types of racketeering, such as the trucking of perishable foods and waterfront loading, where the racketeers entrenched themselves as middlemen—taking up, by default, a service that neither shippers nor truckers wanted to assume—a pattern of accommodation was roughly worked out, and the rackets assumed a quasi-legal veneer. On the waterfront, old-time racketeers perform the necessary function of loading—but at an exorbitant price—and this monopoly was recognized by both the union and the shippers, and tacitly by the government.

But in the last decade and a half, industrial racketeering has not offered much in the way of opportunity. *Like American capitalism itself, crime shifted its emphasis from production to consumption.* The focus of crime became the direct exploitation of the citizen as consumer, largely through gambling. And while the protection of these huge revenues was inextricably linked to politics, the relation between gambling and "the mobs" became more complicated.

BIG-BUSINESS BOOKIES

Although it never showed up in the gross national product, gambling in the last decade was one of the largest industries in the United States. The Kefauver Committee estimated it as a $20 billion business. This figure has been picked up and widely quoted, but in truth no one knows what the gambling "turnover" and "take" actually is, nor how much is bet legally (parimutuel, etc.) and how much illegally. In fact, the figure cited by the committee was arbitrary and was arrived at quite sloppily. As one staff member said: "We had no real idea of the money spent. . . . The California crime commission said twelve billion. Virgil Peterson of Chicago estimated thirty billion. We picked twenty billion as a balance between the two."

If comprehensive data are not available, we do know, from specific instances, the magnitude of many of the operations. Some indication can be seen from these items called at random:

James Carroll and the M & G syndicate did a $20 million annual business in St. Louis. This was one of the two large books in the city.

The S & G syndicate in Miami did a $26 million volume yearly; the total for all books in the Florida resort reached $40 million.

Slot machines were present in 69,786 establishments in 1951 (each paid $100 for a license to the Bureau of Internal Revenue); the usual average is three machines to a license, which would add up to 210,000 slot machines in operation in the United States. In legalized areas, where the betting is higher and more regular, the average gross "take" per machine is $50 a week.

The largest policy wheel (i.e., "numbers") in Chicago's "Black Belt" reported taxable net profits for the four-year period from 1946 through 1949, after sizable deductions for "overhead," of $3,656,968. One of the large "white" wheels reported in 1947 a gross income of $2,317,000 and a net profit of $205,000. One CIO official estimated that perhaps 15 per cent of his union's lower-echelon officials are involved in the numbers racket (a steward, free to roam a plant, is in a perfect situation for organizing bets).

If one considers the amount of dollars bet on sports alone—an estimated six billion on baseball, a billion on football pools, another billion on basketball, six billion on horse racing—then Elmo Roper's judgment that "only the food, steel, auto, chemical, and machine-tool industries have a greater volume of business" does not seem too farfetched.

While gambling has long flourished in the United States, the influx of the big mobsters into the industry—and its expansion—started in the thirties, when repeal of Prohibition forced them to look about for new avenues of enterprise. (The change, one might say crudely, was in the "democratization" of gambling. In New York of the 1860's, 1870's, and 1880's one found elegant establishments where the wealthy men of the city, bankers and sportsmen gambled. The saloon was the home of the worker. The middle class of the time did not gamble. In the changing mores of America, the rise of gambling in the 1930's and 1940's meant the introduction of the middle class to gambling and casinos as a way of life.) Gambling, which had begun to flower under the nourishment of rising incomes, was the most lucrative field in sight. To a large extent the shift from bootlegging to gambling was a mere transfer of business operations. In the East, Frank Costello went into slot machines and the operation of a number of ritzy gambling casinos. He also became the "banker" for the Erickson "book," which "laid off" bets for other bookies. Joe Adonis, similarly, opened up a number of casinos, principally in New Jersey. Across the country, many other mobsters went into bookmaking. As other rackets diminished and gambling, particularly horse-race betting, flourished in the forties, a struggle erupted over the control of racing information.

Horse-race betting requires a peculiar industrial organization. The essential component is time. A bookie can operate only if he can get information on odds up to the very last minute before the race, so that he can "hedge" or "lay off" bets. With racing going on simultaneously on many tracks throughout the country, this information has to be obtained speedily and accurately. Thus, the racing wire is the nerve ganglion of race betting.

The racing-wire news service got started in the twenties through the genius of the late Moe Annenberg, who had made a fearful reputation for himself as Hearst's circulation manager in the rough-and-tough Chicago newspaper wars. Annenberg conceived the idea of a telegraphic news service which would gather information from tracks and shoot it immediately to scratch sheets, horse parlors, and bookie joints. In some instances, track owners gave Annenberg the right to send news from tracks; more often, the news was simply "stolen" by crews operating inside or near the tracks. So efficient did this news distribution system become, that in 1942, when a plane knocked out a vital telegraph circuit which served an Air Force field as well as the gamblers, the Continental Press managed to get its racing wire service for gamblers resumed in fifteen minutes, while it took the Fourth Army, which was responsible for the defense of the entire West Coast, something like three hours.

Annenberg built up a nationwide racing information chain that not only distributed wire news but controlled sub-outlets as well. In 1939, harassed by the Internal Revenue Bureau on income tax and chivvied by the Justice Department for "monopolistic" control of the wire service, the tired and aging Annenberg simply walked out of the business. He did not sell his interest or even seek to salvage some profit; he simply gave up. Yet, like any established and thriving institution, the enterprise continued, though on a decentralized basis. James Ragen, Annenberg's operation manager and likewise a veteran of the old Chicago circulation wars, took over the national wire service through a dummy friend and renamed it the Continental Press Service.

The salient fact is that in the operation of the Annenberg and Ragen wire service, formally illegal as many of its subsidiary operations may have been (i.e., in "stealing" news, supplying information to bookies, etc.), gangsters played no part. It was a business, illicit, true, but primarily a business. The distinction between gamblers and gangsters, as we shall see, is a relevant one.

In 1946, the Chicago mob, whose main interest was in bookmaking rather than in gambling casinos, began to move in on the wire monopoly. Following repeal, the Capone lieutenants had turned, like Lepke, to labor racketeering. Murray ("The Camel") Humphries muscled in on the teamsters, the operating engineers, and the cleaning-and-dyeing, laundry, and linen-supply industries. Through a small-time punk, Willie Bioff, and union official George Browne, Capone's chief successors, Frank ("The Enforcer") Nitti and Paul Ricca, came into control of the motion-picture union and proceeded to shake down the movie industry for fabulous sums in order to "avert strikes." In 1943, when the government moved in and smashed the industrial rackets, the remaining big shots, Charley Fischetti, Jake Guzik, and Tony Accardo, decided to concentrate on gambling, and in particular began a drive to take over the racing wire.

In Chicago, the Guzik-Accardo gang, controlling a subdistributor of the racing-news service, began tapping Continental's wires. In Los Angeles, the head of the local distribution agency for Continental was beaten up by hoodlums working for Mickey Cohen and Joe Sica. Out of the blue appeared a new and competitive nationwide racing information and distribution service, known as Trans-American Publishing, the money for which was advanced by the Chicago mobs and Bugsy Siegel, who, at the time, held a monopoly of the bookmaking and wire-news service in Las Vegas. Many books pulled out of Continental and bought information from the new outfit; many hedged by buying from both. At the end of a year, however, the Capone mob's wire had lost about $200,000. Ragen felt that violence would erupt and went to the Cook County district attorney and told him that his life had been threatened by his rivals. Ragen knew his competitors. In June, 1946, he was killed by a blast from a shotgun.

Thereafter, the Capone mob abandoned Trans-American and got a "piece" of Continental. Through their new control of the national racing-wire monopoly, the Capone mob began to muscle in on the lucrative Miami gambling business run by the so-called S & G syndicate. For a long time S & G's monopoly over bookmaking had been so complete that when New York gambler Frank Erickson bought a three months' bookmaking concession at the expensive Roney Plaza Hotel, for $45,000, the local police, in a highly publicized raid, swooped down on the hotel; the next year the Roney Plaza was again using local talent. The Capone group, however, was tougher. They demanded an interest in Miami bookmaking and, when refused, began organizing a syndicate of their own, persuading some bookies at the big hotels to join them. Florida Governor Warren's crime investigator appeared—a friend, it seemed, of old Chicago dog-track operator William Johnston, who had contributed $100,000 to the Governor's campaign fund—and began raiding bookie joints, but only those that were affiliated with S & G. Then S & G, which had been buying its racing news from the local distributor of Continental Press, found its service abruptly shut off. For a few days the syndicate sought to bootleg information from New Orleans, but found itself limping along. After ten days' war of attrition, the five S & G partners found themselves with a sixth partner, who, for a token "investment" of $20,000, entered a Miami business that grossed $26,000,000 in one year.

GAMBLERS AND GUYS

While Americans made gambling illegal, they did not in their hearts think of it as wicked—even the churches benefited from the Bingo and lottery crazes. So they gambled—and gamblers flourished. Against this open canvas, the indignant tones of Senator Wiley and the shocked righteousness of Senator Tobey during the Kefauver investigation rang oddly. Yet it was probably this very tone of surprise that gave the activity of the Kefauver Committee its piquant quality. Here were some senators who seemingly did not know the facts of life, as most Americans did. Here, in the person of Senator Tobey, was the old New England Puritan conscience poking around in industrial America, in a world it had made but never seen. Here was old-fashioned moral indignation, at a time when cynicism was rampant in public life.

Commendable as such moralistic fervor was, it did not make for intelligent discrimination of fact. Throughout the Kefauver hearings, for example, there ran the presumption that all gamblers were invariably gangsters. This was true of Chicago's Accardo-Guzik combine, which in the past had its fingers in many kinds of rackets. It was not nearly so true of many of the large gamblers is America, most of whom had the feeling that they were satisfying a basic American urge for sport and looked upon their calling with no greater sense of guilt than did many bootleggers. After all, Sherman Billingsley did start out as a speakeasy proprietor, as did the Kriendlers of the "21" Club; and today the Stork Club and the former Jack and Charlie's are the most fashionable night and dining spots in America (one prominent patron of the Stork Club: J. Edgar Hoover).

The S & G syndicate in Miami, for example (led by Harold Salvey, Jules Levitt, Charles Friedman, Sam Cohen, and Edward [Eddie Luckey] Rosenbaum), was simply a master pool of some two hundred bookies that arranged for telephone service, handled "protection," acted as bankers for those who needed ready cash on hard-hit books, and, in short, functioned somewhat analogously to the large factoring corporations in the textile field or the credit companies in the auto industry. Yet to Kefauver, the S & G men were "slippery and arrogant characters. . . . Salvey, for instance, was an old-time bookie who told us he had done nothing except engage in bookmaking or finance other bookmakers for twenty years." When, as a result of committee publicity and the newly found purity of the Miami police, the S & G syndicate went out of business, it was, as the combine's lawyer told Kefauver, because the "boys" were weary of being painted "the worst monsters in the world." "It is true," Cohen acknowledged, "that they had been law violators." But they had never done anything worse than gambling, and "to fight the world isn't worth it."

Most intriguing of all were the opinions of James J. Carroll, the St. Louis "betting commissioner," who for years had been widely quoted on the sports pages of the country as setting odds on the Kentucky Derby winter book and the baseball pennant races. Senator Wiley, speaking like the prosecutor in Camus's novel, *The Stranger*, became the voice of official morality:

> SENATOR WILEY: Have you any children?
> MR. CARROLL: Yes, I have a boy.
> SENATOR WILEY: How old is he?

> MR. CARROLL: Thirty-three.
> SENATOR WILEY: Does he gamble?
> MR. CARROLL: No.
> SENATOR WILEY: Would you like to see him grow up and become a gambler, either professional or amateur?
> MR. CARROLL: No. . . .
> SENATOR WILEY: All right. Is your son interested in your business?
> MR. CARROLL: No, he is a manufacturer.
> SENATOR WILEY: Why do you not get him into the business?
> MR. CARROLL: Well, psychologically a great many people are unsuited for gambling.

Retreating from this gambit, the Senator sought to pin Carroll down on his contributions to political campaigns:

> SENATOR WILEY: Now this morning I asked you whether you contributed any money for political candidates or parties, and you said not more than $200 at one time. I presume that does not indicate the total of your contributions in any one campaign, does it?
> MR. CARROLL: Well, it might, might not, Senator. I have been an "againster" in many instances. I am a reader of *The Nation* for fifty years and they have advertisements calling for contributions for different candidates, different causes. . . . They carried an advertisement for George Norris; I contributed, I think, to that, and to the elder LaFollette.

Carroll, who admitted to having been in the betting business since 1899, was the sophisticated—but not immoral!—counterpoint to moralist Wiley. Here was a man without the stigmata of the underworld or underground; he was worldly, cynical of official rhetoric, jaundiced about people's motives; he was an "againster" who believed that "all gambling legislation originates or stems from some group or some individual seeking special interests for himself or his cause."

Asked why people gamble, Carroll distilled his experiences of fifty years with a remark that deserves a place in American social history: "I really don't know how to answer the question," he said, "I think gambling is a biological necessity for certain types. I think it is the quality that gives substance to their daydreams."

In a sense, the entire Kefauver materials, unintentionally, seem to document that remark. For what the committee revealed time and time again was a picture of gambling as a basic institution in American life, flourishing openly and accepted widely. In many of the small towns, the gambling joint is as open as a liquor establishment. The town of Havana, in Mason County, Illinois, felt miffed when Governor Adlai Stevenson intervened against local gambling. In 1950, the town had raised $15,000 of its $50,000 budget by making friendly raids on the gambling houses every month and having the owners pay fines. "With the gambling fines cut off," grumbled Mayor Clarence Chester, "the next year is going to be tough."

Apart from the gamblers, there were the mobsters. But what Senator Kefauver and company failed to understand was that the mobsters, like the gamblers, and like the entire gangdom generally, were seeking to become quasi-respectable and establish a place for themselves in American life. For the mobsters, by and large, had immigrant roots, and crime, as the pattern showed, was a route of social ascent and place in American life.

THE MYTH OF THE MAFIA

The mobsters were able, where they wished, to "muscle in" on the gambling business because the established gamblers were wholly vulnerable, not being able to call on the law for protection. The senators, however, refusing to make any distinction between a gambler and a gangster, found it convenient to talk loosely of a nationwide conspiracy of "illegal" elements. Senator Kefauver asserted that a "nationwide crime syndicate does exist in the United States, despite the prótestations of a strangely assorted company of criminals, self-serving politicans, plain blind fools, and others who may be honestly misguided, that there is no such combine." The Senate committee report states the matter more dogmatically: "There is a nationwide crime syndicate known as the Mafia. . . . Its leaders are usually found in control of the most lucrative rackets in their cities. There are indications of a centralized direction and control of these rackets. . . . The Mafia is the cement that helps to bind the Costello-Adonis-Lansky syndicate of New York and the Accardo-Guzik-Fischetti syndicate of Chicago. . . . These groups have kept in touch with Luciano since his deportation from the country."

Unfortunately for a good story—and the existence of the Mafia would be a whale of a story—neither the Senate Crime Committee in its testimony, nor Kefauver in his book, presented any real evidence that the Mafia exists as a functioning organization. One finds police officials asserting before the Kefauver committee their *belief* in the Mafia: the Narcotics Bureau *thinks* that a world-wide dope ring allegedly run by Luciano is part of the Mafia; but the only other "evidence" presented—aside from the incredulous responses both of Senator Kefauver and Rudolph Halley when nearly all the Italian gangsters asserted that they didn't know about the Mafia—is that certain crimes bear "the earmarks of the Mafia."

The legend of the Mafia has been fostered in recent years largely by the peephole writing team of Jack Lait and Lee Mortimer. In their *Chicago Confidential*, they rattled off a series of names and titles that made the organization sound like a rival to an Amos and Andy Kingfish society. Few serious reporters, however, give it much credence. Burton Turkus, the Brooklyn prosecutor who broke up the "Murder, Inc." ring, denies the existence of the Mafia. Nor could Senator Kefauver even make out much of a case for his picture of a national crime syndicate. He is forced to admit that "as it exists today [it] is an elusive and furtive but nonetheless tangible thing," and that "its organization and machinations are not always easy to pinpoint." [1] His

[1] The accidental police discovery of a conference of Italian figures, most of them with underworld and police records, in Apalachin, New York, in November 1957, revived the talk of a Mafia. *Time* magazine assigned a reporter, Serrell Hillman, to check the story, and this is what he reported: "I spent some two weeks in New York, Washington and Chicago running down every clue to the so-called Mafia that I could find. I talked to a large number of Federal, state and local law enforcement authorities; to police, reporters, attorneys, detectives, non-profit civic groups such as the Chicago Crime Commission. Nobody from the F.B.I. and Justice Department officials on down, with the exception of a couple of Hearst crime reporters—always happy for the sake of a street sale to associate the 'Mafia' with the most routine barroom shooting— and the Narcotics Bureau believed that a Mafia exists as such. The Narcotics Bureau, which has to contend with a big problem in dope-trafficking, contends that a working alliance operates between an organized Mafia in Italy and Sicily and a U.S. Mafia. But the Bureau has never been able to submit proof of this, and the F.B.I. is skeptical. The generally held belief is that there is

"evidence" that many gangsters congregate at certain times of the year in such places as Hot Springs, Arkansas, in itself does not prove much; people "in the trade" usually do, and as the loquacious late Willie Moretti of New Jersey said, in explaining how he had met the late Al Capone at a race track, "Listen, well-charactered people you don't need introductions to; you just meet automatically."

Why did the Senate Crime Committee plumb so hard for its theory of a Mafia and a national crime syndicate? In part, they may have been misled by their own hearsay. The Senate committee was not in the position to do original research, and its staff, both legal and investigative, was incredibly small. Senator Kefauver had begun the investigation with the attitude that with so much smoke there must be a raging fire. But smoke can also mean a smoke screen. Mob activities is a field in which busy gossip and exaggeration flourish even more readily than in a radical political sect.

There is, as well, in the American temper, a feeling that "somewhere," "somebody" is pulling all the complicated strings to which this jumbled world dances. In politics the labor image is "Wall Street" or "Big Business"; while the business stereotype was the "New Dealers." In the field of crime, the side-of-the-mouth lowdown was "Costello."

The salient reason, perhaps, why the Kefauver Committee was taken in by its own myth of an omnipotent Mafia and a despotic Costello was its failure to assimilate and understand three of the more relevant sociological facts about institutionalized crime in its relation to the political life of large urban communities in America, namely: (1) the rise of the American Italian community, as part of the inevitable process of ethnic succession, to positions of importance in politics, a process that has been occurring independently but also simultaneously in most cities with large Italian constituencies—New York, Chicago, Kansas City, Los Angeles; (2) the fact that there are individual Italians who play prominent, often leading roles today in gambling and in the mobs; and (3) the fact that Italian gamblers and mobsters often possessed "status" within the Italian community itself and a "pull" in city politics. These three items are indeed related—but not so as to form a "plot."

THE JEWS . . . THE IRISH . . . THE ITALIANS

The Italian community has achieved wealth and political influence much later and in a harder way than previous immigrant groups. Early Jewish wealth, that of the German Jews of the late nineteenth century, was made largely in banking and mer-

---

no tightly knit syndicate, but instead a loose "trade association" of criminals in various cities and areas, who run their own shows in their own fields but have matters of mutual interest to take up (as at the Apalachin conference). At any rate, nobody has ever been able to produce specific evidence that a Mafia is functioning."

In early 1959, Fredric Sondern, Jr., an editor of the Reader's Digest, published a best-selling book on the Mafia, Brotherhood of Evil, but a close reading of Mr. Sondern's text indicates that his sources are largely the files of the Narcotics Bureau, and his findings little more than a rehash of previously published material. (For a devastating review of the book, see the Times Literary Supplement, London, June 12, 1959, p. 351.) Interestingly enough, in May, 1959, Alvin Goldstein, a former assistant district attorney in New York, who had prosecuted racketeer Johnny Dio, conducted a crime survey of California for Governor Pat Brown and reported that he found no evidence of the existence of a Mafia in California.

chandising. To that extent, the dominant group in the Jewish community was outside of, and independent of, the urban political machines. Later Jewish wealth, among the East European immigrants, was built in the garment trades, though with some involvement with the Jewish gangster, who was typically an industrial racketeer (Arnold Rothstein, Lepke and Gurrah, etc.). Among Jewish lawyers, a small minority, such as the "Tammany lawyer" (like the protagonist of Sam Ornitz's *Haunch, Paunch and Jowl*), rose through politics and occasionally touched the fringes of crime. Most of the Jewish lawyers, by and large the communal leaders, climbed rapidly, however, in the opportunities that established and legitimate Jewish wealth provided. Irish immigrant wealth in the northern urban centers, concentrated largely in construction, trucking, and the waterfront, has, to a substantial extent, been wealth accumulated in and through political alliance, e.g., favoritism in city contracts.

Control of the politics of the city thus has been crucial for the continuance of Irish political wealth. This alliance of Irish immigrant wealth and politics has been reciprocal; many noted Irish political figures lent their names as important window-dressing for business corporations (Al Smith, for example, who helped form the U.S. Trucking Corporation, whose executive head for many years was William J. Mc-Cormack, the alleged "Mr. Big" of the New York waterfront), while Irish business-men have lent their wealth to further the careers of Irish politicians. Irish mobsters have rarely achieved status in the Irish community, but have served as integral arms of the politicians, as strong-arm men on election day.

The Italians found the more obvious big-city paths from rags to riches preempted. In part this was due to the character of the early Italian immigrant. Most of them were unskilled and from rural stock. Jacob Riis could remark on the nineties, "the Italian comes in at the bottom and stays there." These dispossessed agricultural labor-ers found jobs as ditch-diggers, on the railroads as section hands, along the docks, in the service occupations, as shoemakers, barbers, garment workers, and stayed there. Many were fleeced by the "padrone" system; a few achieved wealth from truck farm-ing, wine growing, and marketing produce, but this "marginal wealth" was not the source of coherent and stable political power.

Significantly, although the number of Italians in the United States is about a third as high as the number of Irish, and of the thirty million Catholic communicants in the United States, about half are of Irish descent and a sixth of Italian, there is not one Italian bishop among the hundred Catholic bishops in this country or one Italian archbishop among the 21 archbishops. The Irish have a virtual monopoly. This is a factor related to the politics of the American church; but the condition also is possible because there is not significant or sufficient wealth among Italian Amer-icans to force some parity.

The children of the immigrants, the second and third generations, became wise in the ways of urban slums. Excluded from the political ladder—in the early thirties there were almost no Italians on the city payroll in top jobs, nor in books of the period can one find discussion of Italian political leaders—and finding few open routes to wealth, some turned to illicit ways. In the children's court statistics of the 1930's, the largest group of delinquents were the Italian; nor were there any Italian communal or social agencies to cope with these problems. Yet it was oddly enough, the quondam racketeer, seeking to become respectable, who provided one of the major supports for the drive to win a political voice for Italians in the power structure of the urban political machines.

This rise of the Italian political bloc was connected, at least in the major northern urban centers, with another important development which tended to make the traditional relation between the politician and the protected or tolerated illicit operator more close than it had been in the past. This is the fact that the urban political machines had to evolve new forms of fund-raising, since the big business contributions, which once went heavily into municipal politics, now—with the shift in the locus of power—go largely into national affairs. (The ensuing corruption in national politics, as recent Congressional investigations show, is no petty matter; the scruples of businessmen do not seem much superior to those of the gamblers.) One way that urban political machines raised their money resembled that of the large corporations which are no longer dependent on Wall Street: by self-financing—that is, by "taxing" the large number of municipal employees who bargain collectively with City Hall for their wage increases. So the firemen's union contributed money to O'Dwyer's campaign.

A second method was taxing the gamblers. The classic example, as *Life* reported, was Jersey City, where a top lieutenant of the Hague machine spent his full time screening applicants for unofficial bookmaking licenses. If found acceptable, the applicant was given a "location," usually the house or store of a loyal precinct worker, who kicked into the machine treasury a high proportion of the large rent exacted. The one thousand bookies and their one thousand landlords in Jersey City formed the hard core of the political machine that sweated and bled to get out the votes for Hague.

A third source for the financing of these machines was the new, and often illegally earned, Italian wealth. This is well illustrated by the career of Costello and his emergence as a political power in New York. Here the ruling motive has been the search for an entree—for oneself and one's ethnic group—into the ruling circles of the big city.

Frank Costello made his money originally in bootlegging. After repeal, his big break came when Huey Long, desperate for ready cash to fight the old-line political machines, invited Costello to install slot machines in Louisiana. Costello did, and he flourished. Together with Dandy Phil Kastel, he also opened the Beverly Club, an elegant gambling establishment just outside New Orleans, at which have appeared some of the top entertainers in America. Subsequently, Costello invested his money in New York real estate (including 79 Wall Street, which he later sold), the Copacabana night club, and a leading brand of Scotch whiskey.

Costello's political opportunity came when a money-hungry Tammany, starved by lack of patronage from Roosevelt and LaGuardia, turned to him for financial support. The Italian community in New York has for years nursed a grievance against the Irish and, to a lesser extent, the Jewish political groups for monopolizing political power. They complained about the lack of judicial jobs, the small number—usually one—of Italian congressmen, the lack of representation on the state tickets. But the Italians lacked the means to make their ambition a reality. Although they formed a large voting bloc, there was rarely sufficient wealth to finance political clubs. Italian immigrants, largely poor peasants from southern Italy and Sicily, lacked the mercantile experience of the Jews and the political experience gained in the seventy-five-year history of Irish immigration.

During the Prohibition years, the Italian racketeers had made certain political contracts in order to gain protection. Costello, always the compromiser and fixer rather than the muscle-man, was the first to establish relations with Jimmy Hines, the powerful leader of the West Side in Tammany Hall. But his rival, Lucky Luciano, suspicious of the Irish and seeking more direct power, backed and elected Al Marinelli for district leader of the Lower West Side. Marinelli in 1932 was the only Italian leader inside Tammany Hall. Later, he was joined by Dr. Paul Sarubbi, a partner of gangster Johnny Torrio in a large, legitimate liquor concern. Certainly, Costello and Luciano represented no "unified" move by the Italians as a whole for power; within the Italian community there are as many divisions as in any other group. What is significant is that different Italians, for different reasons and in various fashions, were achieving influence for the first time. Marinelli became county clerk of New York and a leading power in Tammany. In 1937, after being blasted by Tom Dewey, then running for district attorney, as a "political ally of thieves . . . and big-shot racketeers," Marinelli was removed from office by Governor Lehman. The subsequent conviction by Dewey of Luciano and Hines, and the election of LaGuardia, left most of the Tammany clubs financially weak and foundering. This was the moment Costello made his move. In a few years, by judicious financing, he controlled a bloc of "Italian" leaders in the Hall—as well as some Irish on the upper West Side and some Jewish leaders on the East Side—and was able to influence the selection of a number of Italian judges. The most notable incident, revealed by a wire tap on Costello's phone, was the "Thank you, Francisco" call in 1943 by Supreme Court judge nominee Thomas Aurelio, who gave Costello full credit for his nomination.

It was not only Tammany that was eager to accept campaign contributions from newly rich Italians, even though some of these *nouveaux riches* had "arrived" through bootlegging and gambling. Fiorello LaGuardia, the wiliest mind that melting-pot politics has ever produced, understood in the early thirties where much of his covert support came from. (So too, did Vito Marcantonio, an apt pupil of the master: Marcantonio has consistently made deals with the Italian leaders of Tammany Hall— in 1943 he supported Aurelio and refused to repudiate him even when the Democratic party formally did.) Joe Adonis, who had built a political following during the late twenties, when he ran a popular speakeasy, aided LaGuardia financially to a considerable extent in 1933. "The Democrats haven't recognized the Italians," Adonis told a friend. "There is no reason for the Italians to support anybody but LaGuardia; the Jews have played ball with the Democrats and haven't gotten much out of it. They know it now. They will vote for LaGuardia. So will the Italians."

Adonis played his cards shrewdly. He supported LaGuardia, but also a number of Democrats for local and judicial posts, and became a power in the Brooklyn area. His restaurant was frequented by Kenny Sutherland, the Coney Island Democratic leader; Irwin Steingut, the Democratic minority leader in Albany; Anthony DiGiovanni, later a councilman; William O'Dwyer, and Jim Moran. But, in 1937, Adonis made the mistake of supporting Royal Copeland against LaGuardia, and the irate Fiorello finally drove Adonis out of New York.

LaGuardia later turned his ire against Costello, too. Yet Costello survived and reached the peak of his influence in 1942, when he was instrumental in electing Michael Kennedy leader of Tammany Hall. Despite the Aurelio fiasco, which brought Costello into notoriety, he still had sufficient power in the Hall to swing votes for

Hugo Rogers as Tammany leader in 1948. In those years many a Tammany leader came hat-in-hand to Costello's apartment or sought him out on the golf links to obtain the nomination for a judicial post.

During this period, other Italian political leaders were also coming to the fore. Generoso Pope, whose Colonial Sand and Stone Company began to prosper through political contacts, became an important political figure, especially when his purchase of the two largest Italian-language dailies (later merged into one), and of a radio station, gave him almost a monopoly of channels to Italian-speaking opinion of the city. Through Generoso Pope, and through Costello, the Italians became a major political force in New York.

That the urban machines, largely Democratic, have financed their heavy campaign costs in this fashion rather than having to turn to the "moneyed interests" explains in some part why these machines were able, in part, to support the New and Fair Deals without suffering the pressures they might have been subjected to had their source of money supply been the business groups.[2] Although he has never publicly revealed his political convictions, it is likely that Frank Costello was a fervent admirer of Franklin D. Roosevelt and his efforts to aid the common man. The basic measures of the New Deal, which most Americans today agree were necessary for the public good, would not have been possible without the support of the "corrupt" big-city machines.

THE "NEW" MONEY—AND THE OLD

There is little question that men of Italian origin appeared in most of the leading roles in the high drama of gambling and mobs, just as twenty years ago the children of East European Jews were the most prominent figures in organized crime, and before that individuals of Irish descent were similarly prominent. To some extent statistical accident and the tendency of newspapers to emphasize the few sensational figures give a greater illusion about the domination of illicit activities by a single ethnic group than all the facts warrant. In many cities, particularly in the South and on the West Coast, the mob and gambling fraternity consisted of many other groups, and often, predominantly, of native white Protestants. Yet it is clear that in the major northern urban centers there was a distinct ethnic sequence in the modes of obtaining illicit wealth and that, uniquely in the case of the recent Italian elements, the former bootleggers and gamblers provided considerable leverage for the growth of political influence as well. A substantial number of Italian judges sitting on the bench in New York today are indebted in one fashion or another to Costello; so too are many Italian district leaders—as well as some Jewish and Irish politicians. And the motive in establishing Italian political prestige in New York was generous rather than scheming for personal advantage. For Costello it was largely a case of ethnic pride. As in earlier American eras, organized illegality became a stepladder of social ascent.

[2] This is an old story in American politics. Theodore Allen, a gambler and saloon keeper, whose American Mabille was an elegant music hall and bordello (he once told a Congressional investigating committee that he was the wickedest man in New York), gave Republican Boss Thurlow Weed a campaign contribution of $25,000 for the re-election of Abraham Lincoln in 1864.

To the world at large, the news and pictures of Frank Sinatra, for example, mingled with former Italian mobsters could come somewhat as a shock. Yet to Sinatra, and to many Italians, these were men who had grown up in their neighborhoods and who were, in some instances, by-words in the community for their helpfulness and their charities. The early Italian gangsters were hoodlums—rough, unlettered, and young (Al Capone was only twenty-nine at the height of his power). Those who survived learned to adapt. By now they are men of middle age or older. They learned to dress conservatively. Their homes are in respectable suburbs. They sent their children to good schools and sought to avoid publicity.[3] Costello even went to a psychiatrist in his efforts to overcome a painful feeling of inferiority in the world of manners.

As happens with all "new" money in American society, the rough and ready contractors, the construction people, trucking entrepreneurs, as well as racketeers, polished up their manners and sought recognition and respectability in their own ethnic as well as in the general community. The "shanty" Irish became the "lace curtain" Irish, and then moved out for wider recognition. Sometimes acceptance came first in established "American" society, and this was a certificate for later recognition by the ethnic community, a process well illustrated by the belated acceptance in established Negro society of such figures as Sugar Ray Robinson and Joe Louis, as well as leading popular entertainers.

Yet, after all, the foundation of many a distinguished older American fortune was laid by sharp practices and morally reprehensible methods. The pioneers of American capitalism were not graduated from Harvard's School of Business Administration. The early settlers and founding fathers, as well as those who "won the West" and built up cattle, mining, and other fortunes, often did so by shady speculations and a not inconsiderable amount of violence. They ignored, circumvented, or stretched the law when it stood in the way of America's destiny and their own—or were themselves the law when it served their purposes. This has not prevented them and their descendants from feeling proper moral outrage when, under the changed circumstances of the crowded urban environments, latecomers pursued equally ruthless tactics.

THE EMBOURGEOISEMENT OF CRIME

Ironically, the social development which made possible the rise to political influence sounds, too, the knell of the rough Italian gangster. For it is the growing number of Italians with professional training and legitimate business success that both prompts and permits the Italian group to wield increasing political influence; and increasingly it is the professionals and businessmen who provide models for Italian youth today, models that hardly existed twenty years ago. Ironically, the headlines and exposés of "crime" of the Italian "gangsters" came years after the fact. Many of the top "crime" figures had long ago forsworn violence, and even their income, in

[3] Except at times by being overly neighborly, like Tony Accardo, who, at Yuletide 1949, in his elegant River Forest home, decorated a 40-foot tree on his lawn and beneath it set a wooden Santa and reindeer, while around the yard, on tracks, electrically operated skating figures zipped merrily around while a loudspeaker poured out Christmas carols. The next Christmas, the Accardo lawn was darkened; Tony was on the lam from Kefauver.

large part, was derived from legitimate investments (real estate in the case of Costello, motor haulage and auto dealer franchises in the case of Adonis) or from such quasi-legitimate but socially respectable sources as gambling casinos. Hence society's "retribution" in the jail sentences for Costello and Adonis was little more than a trumped-up morality that disguised a social hypocrisy.

Apart from these considerations, what of the larger context of crime and the American way of life? The passing of the Fair Deal signalizes, oddly, the passing of an older pattern of illicit activities. The gambling fever of the past decade and a half was part of the flush and exuberance of rising incomes, and was characteristic largely of new upper-middle-class rich having a first fling at conspicuous consumption. These upper-middle-class rich, a significant new stratum in American life (not rich in the nineteenth-century sense of enormous wealth, but largely middle-sized businessmen and entrepreneurs of the service and luxury trades—the "tertiary economy" in Colin Clark's phrase—who by the tax laws have achieved sizable incomes often much higher than the managers of the super-giant corporations), were the chief patrons of the munificent gambling casinos. During the war decade when travel was difficult, gambling and the lush resorts provided important outlets for this social class. Now they are settling down, learning about Europe and culture. The petty gambling, the betting and bingo which relieve the tedium of small-town life, or the expectation among the urban slum dwellers of winning a sizable sum by a "lucky number" or a "lucky horse," goes on. To quote Bernard Baruch: "You can't stop people from gambling on horses. And why should you prohibit a man from backing his own judgment? It's another form of personal initiative." But the lush profits are passing from gambling as the costs of coordination rise. And in the future it is likely that gambling, like prostitution, winning tacit acceptance as a necessary fact, will continue on a decentralized, small entrepreneur basis.

But passing, too, is a political pattern, the system of political "bosses" which in its reciprocal relation provided "protection" for, was fed revenue from, crime. The collapse of the "boss" system was a product of the Roosevelt era. Twenty years ago Jim Farley's task was simple; he had to work only on some key state bosses. Now there is no longer such an animal. New Jersey Democracy was once ruled by Frank Hague; now there are five or six men, each "top dog," for the moment, in his part of the state or faction of the party. Within the urban centers, the old Irish-dominated political machines in New York, Boston, Newark, and Chicago, have fallen apart. The decentralization of the metropolitan centers, the growth of suburbs and satellite towns, the breakup of the old ecological patterns of slum and transient belts, the rise of functional groups, the increasing middle-class character of American life, all contribute to this decline.

With the rationalization and absorption of some illicit activities into the structure of the economy, the passing of an older generation that had established a hegemony over crime, the general rise of minority groups to social position, and the breakup of the urban boss system, the pattern of crime we have discussed is passing as well. Crime, of course, remains as long as passion and the desire for gain remain. But the kind of big, organized city crime, as we have known it for the past seventy-five years, was based on more than these universal motives. It was based on certain characteristics of the American economy, American ethnic groups, and American politics. The changes in all these areas mean that, in the form we have known it, it too will change.

Eight / Mobility

20 / Managerial Employees in Anthracite, 1902: A Study in Occupational Mobility

Ray Ginger

Throughout their history, most Americans have believed that they lived in a land of boundless opportunity for those who seized it. One's background was no barrier in the ascent from rags to riches. As one proponent of this belief put it: "Neither birth nor education, neither nationality nor religion, neither heredity nor environment are passports or obstacles to the highest success in this land of democracy."

Studies of the social origins of business, and to a lesser extent, of political elites indicate that this creed was largely a myth, as the following essay by Ray Ginger suggests. Even in the supposed golden age of opportunity, the nineteenth century, the rags to riches success story in business was exceptional. Most of those at the top came from privileged backgrounds.

Recently, several historians have examined the mobility patterns of the largely unskilled and uneducated working class groups. The results confirm the studies of the social origins of elites, and add important new insights into social mobility.

The following essays (essays 20 and 21) point out that social mobility for the working class was extremely limited; usually workers moved only one step ahead of the occupations of their fathers. Although few moved from rags to riches, those who persevered in a particular industry or struggled long enough in one place advanced modestly. As a result, these individuals could see changes and improvements in their lives. Moreover, since many of these workers were poor immigrants accustomed to deprivation in Europe, conditions in the United States, although not ideal, at least were better. Mobility thus was a relative concept.

Finally, as Stephan Thernstrom demonstrates in the selection from his study of working class groups in Newburyport, Massachusetts (1850 to 1880), workers who did not move up the rungs of the occupational ladder could, after years of struggle, accumulate a small bank account and purchase their own homes. The resulting sense of tangible achievement may explain why neither socialism nor bitter class consciousness ever took root in the American soil.

Journal of Economic History, XIV (Spring 1954), 146–157. Footnotes have been omitted.

For further reading: William Miller, "American Historians and the Business Elite," *Journal of Economic History,* IX (1949); Stephan Thernstrom, "Urbanization, Migration, and Social Mobility in Late Nineteenth Century America," in Barton J. Bernstein (ed.), *Towards a New Past: Dissenting Essays in American History* (1968); Pitirim Sorokin, *Social Mobility* (1927).

I

A considerable literature has now accumulated on the topic of occupational mobility, both horizontal and vertical: its degree, forms, and possible significance. Most of the research has consisted of field studies of the contemporary situation. Historians have remained largely aloof, even though the articles by William Miller and his associates have shown the vulnerability of many generalizations on the subject imbedded in recent historiography. The present paper is offered as a contribution to the empirical study of this problem. It deals specifically with the social origins and career patterns of sixty-five managerial employees in the anthracite industry in 1902, from corporation presidents down to foremen. It is based largely on the autobiographical testimony given by these persons before the Anthracite Coal Strike Commission of 1902–1903.

Since Mr. Miller and his associates were concerned with the backgrounds of top-level business executives, they could employ a fairly scientific sampling technique, which they have described in detail. Even so, they were frequently unable to find the required information about individuals in their samples. In the present investigation, which reaches further down in the occupational hierarchy, this difficulty became insuperable. The evidence that follows is not derived from an exhaustive study of all managerial employees in 1902, nor is it based on a random sample. The sample used should perhaps be called haphazard. The writer has no reason to think that it is highly biased for purposes of this inquiry, but he would be surprised if it was perfectly representative. Therefore, for each occupational category discussed below, the size of the sample is given in relation to the size of the statistical universe.

These limitations of the source materials will be obvious. But it is also important to ask what factors should be controlled in an investigation of this problem. Although a definitive answer must await the prosecution of several empirical studies, the following considerations may prove to be relevant. This paper suggests that the upward mobility of native-born workers was greater than the upward mobility of foreign-born workers in the anthracite industry. The degree of upward mobility might also vary between different regions of the country, between cities and rural areas, between periods of war and peace, between prosperity and depression, between industries, and between large and small firms in the same industry. And there might well be long-term trends in the degree of mobility operative in the American economy as a whole.

During the period with which this article is concerned, roughly from the Civil War to 1902, the anthracite industry was expanding rapidly, with interruptions in 1873–1879, in 1884, in 1893–1899. Production of anthracite was about 12 million net tons in 1865, about 57 million in 1900. Although, without doubt, production expanded more rapidly than employment, it seems certain that employment in 1902 was at least three times as great as in 1865. Conclusions about the degree of mobility reached from study of the anthracite industry in a period of growth obviously should not be applied to other industries that were growing less rapidly or declining, such as the cotton textile industry of New England.

The general structure of management in the anthracite industry can be understood by reference to the Philadelphia and Reading Coal and Iron Company, the largest producer in the industry, with 26,000 employees and 37 collieries. Since this company, like the other major firms, was a railroad subsidiary, its president knew little about the technical aspects of mining. The chief operating executive was the general superintendent. Next in the hierarchy came four division superintendents; then ten district superintendents, each of whom had jurisdiction over two to six collieries. Each mine had an inside foreman in charge of work underground, an outside foreman in charge of work above ground, and usually assistant foremen. Foremen and assistant foremen were recruited from among the fire bosses, who were charged with making an inspection of the entire mine each day for dangerous gases. Since the entire industry was conducted by a system of inside contracting, some managerial functions were discharged by the contract miners themselves. Each chamber (or "breast") was contracted to a miner on terms specified by the inside foreman, and the miner then hired his own laborers to load the coal. In a breast the miner ordinarily employed one or two laborers, but on larger contracts he might use as many as a dozen. These laborers were regarded by most companies as employees of the miner, so that their names did not appear on the payroll of the company. They were compensated by a percentage of the miner's earnings, and the miner was responsible for the safety of his laborers. Contract miners, fire bosses, and foremen had to pass an examination before they were licensed by the state of Pennsylvania.

At a conservative estimate, immigrants from eastern and southern Europe comprised 15 per cent of the anthracite labor force by 1890 and 33 per cent by 1902. Although a man could become a "good miner," according to the general superintendent of the Reading, in three or four years, these new immigrants in 1902 were still excluded from the managerial and clerical jobs. They were referred to contemptuously by several company officials and attorneys in the proceedings before the Commission of 1902–1903. The English-speaking miners allegedly used their control of the Miners' Examining Boards to exclude Slavs and Italians from the trade of contract miner. During the 1902 strike, a foreign-language document was circulated through the strike zone which purported to show that the Irish miners were monopolizing the union offices, favoring other Irishmen in their disbursement of strike benefits, and exploiting the union's members for their own profit.

The remainder of this paper will consist of an examination of the occupational backgrounds and career lines of persons at four levels of management: (a) inside foremen, (b) district and division superintendents, (c) general superintendents, (d) company presidents.

II

For the anthracite industry as a whole, there was one inside foreman for every 200 inside employees. Since the collieries of a company were geographically separated from each other, the inside foreman was the chief authority on the premises and he was free from close supervision. He had "charge of ventilation and everything pertaining to the safety of the men at the colliery as well as looking after the interests of his employer." He directly controlled the hiring for all inside jobs except the miners' laborers, and indirectly he could control that, too. The chief peculiarity in the functions of a foreman in the anthracite industry was his enormous influence on rates of pay and therefore on labor costs. The operating executives of the companies insisted that it was impossible to fix a standard daily wage for miners. Except for a small minority of employees, the industry was conducted on the basis of individual contracts between the contract miner and the foreman. This amounted to a system of payment by the piece, computed either (a) by the car of coal, (b) by the ton, or (c) by the linear yard. In the third method, the price per linear yard was set individually for each chamber. In the first two, there was a general rate per car or per ton, but each contract also stipulated certain allowances; such as, so much per ton for timbering, so much for rock and other waste, so much for installing brattices, etc. For one major company, about a third of the total pay of contract miners (and their laborers) in 1901 came from these allowances. An inside foreman, in setting and adjusting allowances, had constantly to balance the conflicting objectives of low unit costs and high employee morale. The participation of higher management was necessarily limited to a review of decisions made by the inside foremen.

The backgrounds of the men exercising these crucial functions of hiring and firing, safety control, and wage determination can be described tentatively on the basis of autobiographical testimony by twenty-two inside foremen before the commission. This constitutes only about a 5 per cent sample of the 454 inside foremen in the industry, and it was not chosen scientifically. Specific questions could not be addressed to the persons included. Obviously, therefore, the data relating to inside foremen is quite loose from a statistical viewpoint.

Four of these twenty-two men had been born abroad. But all four had been born in the British Isles; all of them had worked in the mines in the United States at least twenty years; all of them had worked in British mines before emigrating to the United States. Taking the entire group of twenty-two inside foremen, it is possible to state the tenure in the anthracite industry of fifteen:

Tenure in Years	Number of Foremen
10 and under 20	3
20 and under 30	4
30 and under 40	2
More than 40	6

The tenure in the industry before becoming a foreman is known for twelve, of whom eight had worked from ten to twenty years and four had worked more than twenty years. In view of these facts, it is perhaps not strange that the Slavs and Italians, who had entered the anthracite industry only after 1880, had not reached the managerial ranks by 1902. These new immigrants were not yet qualified in terms of seniority, however well they might fill the other requirements.

Eight of the twenty-two men testified that they had begun working full time in the mines when they were less than twelve years old, so they could hardly have had much formal education. One gets the definite impression that the foremen as a group were semieducated. So far as is known, not one of the twenty-two had gone to high school.

Their training was narrow and practical, and it had been secured by working up through the ranks in the industry. There were, however, several night schools in the anthracite region which taught grammar, mechanical drawing, mining, and other technical subjects. Also some companies had a rather formalized method of on-the-job training, in that a foreman might spend considerable time giving personal instruction to a miner who seemed willing to learn but who had not mastered the required techniques of mining.

It would be difficult to say that the background of any specific foreman was typical of the group, but the two following do not seem untypical. Theodore Hogan began working as a doorboy in 1879, when he was eleven years old. He became a driver, then a miner's laborer. After a few years as a company miner (working for a daily wage), he became a fire boss, then an assistant foreman. When he was promoted to foreman at the age of twenty-eight, he had already worked seventeen years in the anthracite industry. George O. Thomas was the son of a man who had worked forty years in the mines. Thomas himself began working as a breaker boy in his youth. He was then successively a doorboy, a driver, a miner's laborer, a contract miner, a fire boss, and an assistant foreman. Finally, after twenty years in the mines, he became a foreman in 1894.

The case histories of these twenty-two foremen also suggest that they had not moved much during their careers. The four who were born abroad had all worked in anthracite more than twenty years; several of the others had lived all their lives in the anthracite region. Only two men testified that they had worked in some other industry, both in bituminous coal. Several of these foremen had worked for only one firm, and some at only one mine. This impression is substantiated by direct testimony before the commission. The general superintendent of the Delaware and Hudson Company, a major operator, said that, except for ordinary unskilled manual labor, the employees of the company tended to stay put. Even when a colliery went out of operation temporarily because of a fire or breakdown, it was impossible to get most employees to work at another mine of the company; they simply remained idle at their homes until the mine was repaired and went back into production. Of the 13,000 employees of this firm in 1902, about 2,000 had worked for it fifteen years or more. The degree of horizontal mobility seems to have been greater at the higher levels of management.

III

This section deals with those managerial employees who had charge of more than one colliery, but who were below the general superintendents. Men at this middle level of management will be called "supervisors" in the remainder of this paper. The sample used here consists of twenty men. This is probably at least a 20 per cent sample, and it is well distributed among those companies in which this level of management existed. Therefore the results obtained should be more reliable than those given above for inside foremen.

Five of these twenty men had been born abroad: two in Scotland, one in Wales, one in Ireland, and one in Switzerland. All five had emigrated to the United States before they were eighteen years old and had begun working in the anthracite industry before they were twenty years old. Of the twenty men, the tenure in the industry is known for eighteen:

Tenure in Years	Number of Men
10 and under 20	3
20 and under 30	2
30 and under 40	8
More than 40	5

The tenure in the industry before reaching their present position is known for fourteen of the twenty:

Tenure in Years	Number of Men
Less than 10	1
10 and under 20	2
20 and under 30	4
30 and under 40	5
More than 40	2

Eleven of these twenty men had begun working full time in the mines when they were less than twelve years old. As in the case of the foremen, these supervisors seem to have had little formal education and to have secured their training by long experience in the industry. They too had spent their entire working careers in the anthracite fields, although one of them testified that he had worked as a youth in the lead mines of Illinois. They too had shown little horizontal mobility, having tended to remain with the same company and even at the same colliery.

Two case studies might be enlightening. R. S. Mercur, division superintendent for the Lehigh Valley Coal Company, had an unusual history. He began working for this company in 1890 in the engineer corps. By 1895 he was division engineer, and by 1897 he was promoted to division superintendent. It therefore seems likely that Mercur had an exceptional amount of formal or even technical education, although there is no direct evidence that any of the twenty men in our sample had ever attended high school. The career of John McGuire was more typical of the group. In 1856, when he was ten years old, he began working in the breaker, and two years later he became a driver boy in the mine. He worked as a miner's laborer and then as a contract miner. During the Civil War he served two years in the Army. After his release from military service, he went back to the anthracite industry. He worked a while at shaft-sinking, then successively as a contract miner, fire boss, assistant inside foreman, and inside foreman. In 1882, when he was thirty-six years old, he became a district superintendent for the Reading company. He held this job for ten years. From 1894 to 1902 he was a mine inspector for the state of Pennsylvania. In May 1902, he went back to the Reading company as one of its four division superintendents.

IV

The general superintendent was the chief operating executive in each company. The sample used here includes sixteen men. Of the seven who worked for small companies, three had begun working in the anthracite mines before they were twelve years old. Two of the seven had acquired some formal training in mining engineering, usually by studying at night; the other five evidently had no training at all beyond what they had gained by working up through the ranks in the industry. These seven men could be considered foremen as well as superintendents, since their responsibilities in some cases were not so great as those of an inside foreman at any important colliery of one of the big companies.

The remaining nine general superintendents worked for the major operators, and include all but one of the men holding this position in such companies. The background of these men is strikingly different from the career lines of men at the lower levels of management. Only one of the nine had begun working in the anthracite industry when he was less than twelve years old. Five of them had received a formal education in civil or mining engineering; two others had served for extended periods in the engineering corps of their companies. They had shown appreciably more horizontal mobility than had the managerial employees at the lower levels; two had worked as civil engineers for railroads, and another had been employed in the iron mines of Virginia and the copper mines of Michigan. At least three of them were still less than forty years old. These nine men as a group show that formal education could be substituted for seniority as a basis for promotion.

But the career of John Veith shows that, even at this highest level, formal education was not essential. Veith represents what might be called the "old-style" manager. From 1851 to 1863 he worked in several anthracite mines around Schuylkill County. He became the boss for a company in 1863, transferred to another company in 1869, and again transferred three months later to the Emanuel Bast Company at Ashland. In 1872 this company was bought out by the newly formed Philadelphia and Reading Coal and Iron Company, and Veith was given charge of two collieries. In 1873 he was promoted to district superintendent over nine collieries. He was made assistant general superintendent in 1877. A year later, his superior died, and Veith, at forty-six, became general superintendent of the largest firm in the industry. In 1903, when he was seventy, he still held the job.

Contrast the career of Sidney Williams. Following his graduation from M.I.T., he was employed by the Santa Fe Railroad. He then became general manager of the Philadelphia Belt Line. In 1896, when he was about thirty years old, he became controller for the Pennsylvania Coal Company and five years later was promoted to general superintendent of that firm. In October 1902, he transferred to a similar job at G. B. Markle and Company, one of the largest independent operators in the industry, with 2,500 employees. Williams was a "new-style" manager.

V

The sample of chief executives includes the presidents (one chairman) of the six big captive companies, and the president of G. B. Markle and Company. John Markle was the only one of them who had knowledge of anthracite production, but he knew it by virtue of both formal education and practical experience. He was born at Hazleton, Pennsylvania, in 1858, son of the founder of G. B. Markle and Company. Following his graduation from a mining engineering course at Lafayette College in 1880, he immediately became general superintendent of the company. When his

254 ESSAYS IN MODERN SOCIAL HISTORY

father retired, he became managing partner and president. Markle was also by far the youngest of these seven men—a fact which suggests that the way to reach the top quickly was to be born into the right family.

Of the six chief executives of the big captive companies, three had come up through the managerial ranks in the railroad industry. Two others were corporation lawyers. The sixth was a member of a prominent family of New York merchants and investors. Although he was the younger brother of a former president of the railroad firm, his only experience up to his fiftieth year had been in merchandising. In regard to formal training, one of the six was an engineer, two were attorneys, another had been associated for two years with a law firm specializing in railroad matters. Two of the six had degrees from Columbia University, and another had attended Franklin and Marshall College for a year.

Just as Sidney Williams was a new-style manager, so George F. Baer might be called a "new-style executive." Baer, born in Pennsylvania in 1842, began working at the Somerset *Democrat* in 1855. Six years later, he and his brother became co-owners of this paper. Baer then began reading law with his brother, and George was admitted to the bar in 1864. He quickly attracted attention as a lawyer in Reading. In 1870 he became counsel for the Philadelphia and Reading Railroad, and later he was made a director. He played a prominent part in reorganizing the firm in 1893. In 1901 he became president of the Reading Railroad and its subsidiaries, including the Coal and Iron Company. Baer himself stated candidly the key to his success: "For years confidential legal adviser in Pa. of J. Pierpont Morgan."

VI

What does all this mean? What does it show about the occupational mobility, both horizontal and vertical, of managerial employees in the anthracite industry in 1900? The following propositions, although not conclusively demonstrated at all points by the data given above, seem fairly secure. The writer doubts that more complete evidence would necessitate substantial modification of any of them.

1. Immigrants from eastern and southern Europe, although they had been numerically significant in the anthracite industry since before 1890, had not begun to reach the managerial levels by 1902, and few of them had become contract miners by that time.

2. Promotion was determined by specific attributes. In the absence of contrary evidence, such matters as personal ability and ambition may be assumed. But this paper points up the importance of seniority and formal training in engineering. Seniority was especially important at the lower and middle levels of management; formal education at the highest level. In this group of sixty-five managerial employees, every man who had finished a college course in engineering had become general superintendent of a major company, and the majority of the general superintendents had received such training. A few supervisors had learned some engineering in night school. But formal education in engineering had only begun to penetrate the industry, and it had not reached down below the highest level of management.

3. A large percentage, perhaps a majority, of the foremen and supervisors had begun

working in the anthracite industry before they were twelve years old. This strongly suggests that they were the sons of wage earners and were forced to work at an early age for economic reasons. If this be true, they had reached a socioeconomic stratum substantially higher than the one in which they had started life. But the persons who could afford more formal education had a better chance to reach the middle and highest managerial levels.

4. The chief executives of the anthracite companies had little or no knowledge of mining. Their training was as corporation lawyers or railroad executives. Their chief responsibility was still the administration of railroads. In regard to anthracite, they were concerned chiefly with finance and market strategy rather than with production.

5. A majority of the managerial employees had spent their entire careers in the industry. Horizontal mobility was greatest at the bottom and at the top of the labor force; that is, among the unskilled laborers and the general superintendents.

6. The general superintendent of the Delaware and Hudson Company testified before the Commission of 1902–1903: "We generally promoted our own men where we could possibly do it." Similar testimony was given by the general manager of the Pennsylvania and Hillside Coal Companies: ". . . my effort has been to recruit our managing force from our employees themselves." The evidence shows that the companies were actually guided by this declared policy.

7. The position held by a man at the end of his career was likely to be related to his initial status. A man who started his working career as a half-educated, untrained boy might become a supervisor, but a person with a college degree in engineering could reasonably expect to become general superintendent of a major company.

8. Nor should we overlook another field for advancement. The anthracite region grew along with the anthracite industry. New towns and cities were created, increasing the demand for professional and business services. Before 1875, the mine workers were English, Scotch, Welsh, Irish, and German. Many of the sons of these men worked in the mines in their youth, but later left the industry. Going to the larger towns in the area, they entered business or a profession. In 1903, a majority of the members of the Wilkes-Barre bar were allegedly sons of Irish miners; and some judges in the coal counties, according to a long-time resident of the region, had begun their careers picking slate on a breaker.

A crude model of occupational mobility in the anthracite industry in this period can now be constructed. Assume a representative group of 200 mine workers, aged twenty years, in 1865. In 1902, three of them are inside foremen. There is a fifty-fifty chance that another man has advanced even further up the managerial hierarchy. What has happened to the remaining 196 men? Here we are left to vague conjecture. Perhaps 100 have died from natural causes. Another fifteen have died from occupational injuries suffered in the anthracite industry. Some have left the region for jobs elsewhere, and some are now working in other industries in the anthracite area, such as the steel-fabricating plants of Scranton and Reading, the railroads, and the construction industry. A few are now small businessmen or lawyers or politicians in the anthracite counties. A handful have become clerical employees of the anthracite companies. The remainder are still contract miners, but they are probably getting the most lucrative contracts.

Clearly a man who began life on the lowest socioeconomic level had negligible chances of reaching the highest one. But many men were able to climb far enough to satisfy their own standards of success. The supervisor of 1902 had been, not uncommonly, a child laborer in 1860. And the child laborer of 1860, if he was still alive in 1902, had almost certainly climbed above the socioeconomic level of his father, either by leaving the anthracite industry, by reaching the managerial ranks, or by becoming one of the more favored and prosperous contract miners.

21 / The Process of Mobility

Stephan Thernstrom

THE MEANING OF MOBILITY: A TRIAL BALANCE

If nineteenth century Newburyport was to develop a permanent proletarian class, the families dealt with in this study should have formed it. These unskilled workmen began at the very bottom of the community occupational ladder in the 1850–1880 period. Their situation seemed anything but promising. They lacked both vocational skills and financial resources. Many were illiterate, and few had the means to see that their children received more than a primitive education. Most were relative strangers in the city, migrants from New England farms or Irish villages. Few inhabitants of Newburyport at mid-century were more likely candidates for membership in a permanently depressed caste.

That these working class families did not remain in a uniformly degraded social position throughout the 1850–1880 period is by now abundantly clear. If the Newburyport laboring class gave birth to no self-made millionaires during these years, the social advances registered by many of its members were nonetheless impressive. A brief review of the findings on geographical, occupational, and property mobility will clarify the significance of these social gains and provide a fresh perspective on social stratification in the nineteenth century city.

By 1880 the undifferentiated mass of poverty-stricken laboring families, the "lack-alls" who seemed at mid-century to be forming a permanent class, had separated into three layers. On top was a small but significant elite of laboring families who had gained a foothold in the lower fringes of the middle class occupational world. Below them was the large body of families who had attained property mobility while remaining in manual occupations, most often of the unskilled or semiskilled variety; these families constituted the stable, respectable, home-owning stratum of the Newburyport working class. At the very bottom of the social ladder was the impoverished, floating lower class, large in number but so transient as to be formless and powerless.

The composition of the Newburyport manual labor force in the latter half of the nineteenth century, we have seen, was extraordinarily volatile. A minority of the laboring families who came to the city in those years settled for as long as a decade. Most did not, and it was these floating families whose depressed position most resembled the classic European proletariat. Recurrently unemployed, often on relief, they rarely accumulated property or advanced themselves occupationally. Substantial numbers of these impoverished unskilled workmen, men who "had no interest in the country except the interest of breathing," were always to be found in Newburyport during this period, but this stratum had remarkably little continuity of membership. Members of this floating group naturally had no capacity to act in concert against an employer or to assert themselves politically; stable organization based on a consciousness of common grievances was obviously impossible. The pressure to migrate operated selectively to remove the least successful from the community; a mere 5 per-cent of the laboring families present in Newburyport throughout this entire thirty-year period found both occupational mobility and property mobility beyond their grasp.

The floating laborers who made up this large, ever renewed transient class occupied the lowest social stratum in nineteenth century Newburyport. A notch above it was the settled, property-owning sector of the working class; above that was the lower middle class, the highest social level attained by members of any of these laboring families. To obtain middle class status required entry into a nonmanual occupation and the adoption of a new style of life; this was an uncommon feat for either unskilled laborers or their children. Five sixths of the laboring families resident in Newburyport for a decade or more during this period found the middle class occupational world completely closed to them. And among the remaining sixth, the high mobility families, were many which remained partially dependent on manual employment for their support. It is doubtful that many of the elite high mobility families developed the attitudes and behavior patterns associated with the middle class style of life. This seems particularly unlikely in the case of laborers who became the operators of small farms, whose sons rarely entered middle class occupations. Nor did a marginal business or a menial clerkship necessarily provide the economic security and inspire the commitment to education needed to insure the transmission of middle class status to the next generation. The importance of the small group of laborers and laborers' sons who purchased shops and farms or found white collar jobs should not be minimized: these men did provide proof to their less successful brethren that class barriers could be hurdled by men of talent, however lowly their origin. But it should be emphasized that many of these upwardly mobile workmen obtained only a precarious hold on middle class status, and that their social milieu often differed little from the milieu of the propertied sector of the working class.

By far the most common form of social advance for members of laboring families in Newburyport in this period was upward movement *within* the working class, mobility into the stratum between the lower middle class and the floating group of destitute unskilled families. A few men from these intermediate mobility families became skilled craftsmen; this was extremely rare for the older generation but less unusual as an inter-generational move. Most often, however, these families advanced themselves by accumulating significant amounts of property while remaining in unskilled or semiskilled occupations. Here were men who offered the market little more than two hands and a strong back, but who succeeded in becoming respectable home owners and savings bank depositors.

What was the social significance of these modest advances? Nineteenth century propagandists took a simple view. The property-owning laborer was "a capitalist." If there was a working class in America, as soon as "a man has saved something he ceases to belong to this class"; "the laborers have become the capitalists in this new world." Accumulated funds, however small, were capital, and the possession of capital determined the psychological orientation of the workman. It was the nature of capital to multiply itself; he who possessed capital necessarily hungered for further expansion of his holdings. To save and to invest was the first step in the process of mobility; investment inspired a risk-taking, speculative mentality conducive to further mobility. The distinction between the "petty capitalist" workman and the rich merchant was one of degree. To move from the former status to the latter was natural; it happened "every day." Similar assumptions lie behind the still-popular view that "the typical American worker" has been "an expectant entrepreneur."

This was sheer fantasy. A mere handful of the property-owning laborers of Newburyport ventured into business for themselves. More surprising, the property mobility of a laboring man did not even heighten his children's prospects for mobility into a business or professional calling. Indeed, the working class family which abided by the injunction "spend less than you earn" could usually do so only by sacrificing the children's education for an extra paycheck, and thereby restricting their opportunities for inter-generational occupational mobility.

Furthermore, the use these laborers made of their savings testifies to their search for maximum security rather than for mobility out of the working class. An economically rational investor in nineteenth century Newburyport would not have let his precious stock of capital languish in a savings bank for long, and he certainly would not have tied it up in the kind of real estate purchased by these laborers. The social environment of the middle class American encouraged such investment for rising profits, but the working class social milieu did not. The earning capacity of the merchant, professional, or entrepreneur rose steadily as his career unfolded—the very term "career" connotes this. The middle class family head was ordinarily its sole source of support, and the family was able both to accumulate wealth and to improve its standard of living out of normal increments in the salary (or net profits) accruing to him over the years.

Ordinary workmen did not have "careers" in this sense. Their earning capacity did not increase with age; in unskilled and semiskilled occupations a forty-year-old man was paid no more than a boy of 17. Substantial saving by a working class family thus tended to be confined to the years when the children were old enough to bring in a supplementary income but too young to have married and established households of their own.

The tiny lots, the humble homes, and the painfully accumulated savings accounts were the fruits of those years. They gave a man dignity, and a slender margin of security against unpredictable, uncontrollable economic forces which could deprive him of his job at any time. Once the mortgage was finally discharged, home ownership reduced the family's necessary expenses by $60 to $100 a year, and a few hundred dollars in the savings bank meant some protection against illness, old age, or a sluggish labor market. A cynical observer would have noted the possibility that home ownership served also to confine the workman to the local labor market and to strengthen the hand of local employers, who were thus assured of a docile permanent work force, but few laborers of nineteenth century Newburyport were disposed to think in these terms.

Families belonging to the propertied stratum of the working class, in short, were socially mobile in the sense that they had climbed a rung higher on the social ladder, and had established themselves as decent, respectable, hard-working, churchgoing members of the community. They had not, however, set their feet upon an escalator which was to draw them up into the class of merchants, professionals, and entrepreneurs.

The contrast between the literal claims of the rags-to-riches mythology and the actual social experience of these families thus appears glaring. A few dozen farmers, small shopkeepers, and clerks, a large body of home-owning families unable to escape a grinding regimen of manual labor: this was the sum of the social mobility achieved by Newburyport's unskilled laborers by 1880. Could men like these have felt that the mobility ideology was at all relevant to their lives?

I think so. True, many of the optimistic assertions of popular writers and speakers were demonstrably false. Class differences in opportunities were deep and pervasive; a large majority of the unskilled laborers in Newburyport and a large majority of their sons remained in the working class throughout the 1850–1880 period. Not one rose from rags to genuine riches. Whoever seeks a Newburyport version of Andrew Carnegie must settle for Joseph Greenough, keeper of a livery stable worth $15,000, and Stephen Fowle, proprietor of a small newsstand. But we err if we take the mobility creed too literally. The rapt attention nineteenth century Americans gave Russell Conwell did not mean that his listeners literally believed that they soon would acquire riches equivalent to "an acre of diamonds." One ingredient of the appeal of mobility literature and oratory was that pleasant fantasies of sudden wealth and a vicarious sharing in the spectacular successes of other ordinary men provided a means of escaping the tedious realities of daily existence. Fantasies of this sort are not likely to flourish among men who have no hope at all of individual economic or social betterment. And indeed the laborers of Newburyport had abundant evidence that self-improvement was possible. To practice the virtues exalted by the mobility creed rarely brought middle class status to the laborer, or even to his children. But hard work and incessant economy did bring tangible rewards—money in the bank, a house to call his own, a new sense of security and dignity. "The man who owns the roof that is over his head and the earth under his dwelling can't help thinking that he's more of a man than though he had nothing, with poverty upon his back and want at home; and if he don't think so, other people will."

The ordinary workmen of Newburyport, in short, could view America as a land of opportunity despite the fact that the class realities which governed their life chances confined most of them to the working class. These newcomers to urban life arrived with a low horizon of expectations, it seems likely. If it is true that "in the last analysis the status of the worker is not a physical but a mental one, and is affected as much by comparisons with past conditions and with the status of other groups in the community as by the facts in themselves," the typical unskilled laborer who settled in Newburyport could feel proud of his achievements and optimistic about the future. Most of the social gains registered by laborers and their sons during these years were decidedly modest—a move one notch up the occupational scale, the acquisition of a small amount of property. Yet *in their eyes* these accomplishments must have loomed large. The contradiction between an ideology of limitless opportunity and the realities of working class existence is unlikely to have dismayed men whose aspirations and expectations were shaped in the Irish village or the New England subsistence farm. The "dream of success" certainly affected these laboring families, but the personal measure of success was modest. By this measure, the great majority of them had indeed "gotten ahead."

22 / Is America Still the Land of Opportunity?

William Petersen

In the following essay, William Petersen examines whether social mobility has decreased or increased in contemporary America. Until recently it was commonly believed that social mobility was greater in the nineteenth century than in the twentieth, but recent studies have challenged this view. Many now reach the top through the growing corporate bureaucracies rather than through their own businesses, and opportunities for most Americans are greater today than they were in the nineteenth century, the century of the self-made man. Education has become an increasingly important means of advancement in a complex bureaucratic society. The great expansion of higher education in America since 1945 has made educational opportunity more widely available than ever before. Moreover, the growing affluence of American society, especially in the last 25 years, has made possible greater income mobility. If one of the measures of mobility is the accumulation of goods, then the opportunities for achievement are greater today than ever before.

Nevertheless, Petersen notes that many believe the myth of declining mobility because it has limited validity. Although Americans have prized mobility as a distinctive characteristic of their society, uncertainty of status in the social order has generated anxieties among those striving to rise and in others fearful of displacement.

For further reading: Ely Chinoy, "Social Mobility Trends in the United States," *American Journal of Sociology*, XX (April 1955), 180–186; *Seymour Lipset and Reinhard Bendix, *Social Mobility in Industrial Society* (1963); *James C. Abegglen and W. Lloyd Warner, *Big Business Leaders in America* (1955); Mabel Newcomer, *The Big Business Executive* (1955).

A popular cliché has it that it is harder nowadays for a young man to get ahead in this country than it was, say, fifty or seventy-five years ago. Both the public and

Reprinted from *Commentary*, XVI (November 1953), 477–486, by permission; copyright © 1953 by the American Jewish Committee.

social scientists tend to agree that opportunities for advancement are now more limited, that class lines have become more rigid, that what sociologists term "social mobility" has been slowing down, that our society is becoming frozen. This consensus is remarkable in that it lacks the support of any really convincing facts. If anyone has questioned it—and hardly anyone has since the depression—this very lack of relevant data has permitted scholars and laymen to shrug the questioner off and continue holding on to their assumption that the Horatio Alger pattern is now obsolete.

Quite suddenly, the past two years have produced some authoritative material on the true situation. Only since then have the first reliable studies of social mobility in the United States been made, and these studies, whatever their faults and limitations, now make available for the first time data on which to base a serious judgment as to how fluid the American class structure is.

There are two rather different ways in which you can study social mobility: you can compare the occupations of sons with those of their fathers, and see whether they are lower or higher on the social scale; or you can trace the movements of individuals through their various occupations, and determine whether they have been going up or down on that scale.[1] Let us begin with the first.

The most important of these studies was conducted by Natalie Rogoff, and is about to appear in book form (*Recent Trends in Occupational Mobility*, The Free Press, Glencoe, Illinois). Applications for marriage licenses in Marion County, Indiana, which includes the city of Indianapolis and its suburbs, ask the prospective groom to give his father's as well as his own occupation, and this made an invaluable mine of data on social mobility available. Miss Rogoff analyzed all the Marion County marriage licenses for each of two periods, 1905–12 and 1938–41 (there were about 10,000 in each period), and could thus compare mobility before the First World War with that just before the Second World War. By a special device she also distinguished between two types of mobility—that resulting from changes in occupational structure (for example, if there is an increase in the percentage of white-collar positions and a decrease in the percentage of farm jobs one may expect fewer sons than fathers to be farmers, and more to be white-collar workers); and that resulting from the openness of opportunity in general. From her study, therefore, we can see whether there has been more or less social mobility than can be accounted for by changes in the country's occupational structure.

[1] In almost all the studies that we mention, social mobility is defined in terms of the movement from one occupational group to another. Of course, the kind of work a man does is not the only factor determining his social class; his income, his prestige, and his authority are also very important. But social scientists agree that occupation is the best index of class, for two reasons. It is very much more definite than other indices: a man is much more likely to be able to tell us, for example, that his father was a carpenter than what his father's status and standard of life were. Secondly, while all the factors that define a man's station in life interact, in most cases his occupation is the most important one; the work he does is more likely to affect his income or status than vice versa.

But it is well to be aware of some of the shortcomings of the occupational index. First of all, a good deal of mobility is possible *within* a single occupation, as when a physician rises from interne to small-town doctor to metropolitan specialist, or a businessman who begins with a single establishment develops it into a chain. Secondly, occupational groups are usually rather heterogeneous: "own business" ranges from push-cart peddlers to partnerships large enough to compete with major corporations; "farm" from migrant pickers to ranch-owners; and similarly for other groups.

Apart from these changes—in themselves enormous, and leading to a decline in the number of low-status occupations and an increase in the number of high-status occupations—Rogoff found overall social mobility to be essentially *the same in 1940 as it was in 1910*. There were some differences, however, as regards individual occupational groups; in particular, mobility into the "professionals," the highest group, had increased by about a quarter over the thirty-year period (that is to say, apart from the increase in professional positions, the number of sons in the professions who did not have fathers in the professions increased by one-quarter). In both periods, the rate of mobility was higher between white-collar occupational groups, as well as between manual groups, than between the two broad classes. The major barrier to both upward and downward mobility was found to lie between skilled workers and lower white-collar employees, between manual jobs and non-manual positions, between "hand" and "head" work.

The second study of social mobility over more than one generation was made in quite a different kind of community—Oakland, an industrial town across the bay from San Francisco—by Seymour M. Lipset, Reinhard Bendix, and F. Theodore Malm.[2] They interviewed the principal wage-earner in a random sample of 955 Oakland households (excluding the very highest and lowest socio-economic neighborhoods). Analysis was concentrated on a comparison of the sons of fathers who had spent most of their lives as manual workers with the sons of fathers who had spent most of their lives in non-manual work.

The results were startling. Of the sons of fathers who had spent most of their lives as manual workers, 47 per cent were working in non-manual occupations, as compared with 68 per cent of the sons of fathers who had spent most of their lives in non-manual occupations. The 21 per cent difference between these two figures measures the sum of all the obstacles, hereditary or cultural, that face the working-class boy who tries to cross the widest gap in the American class structure. In addition, almost half the sons of fathers who had done mostly manual work, and who at the time of this study were themselves doing manual work, had spent some parts of their careers in non-manual occupations.

These two studies are based on only two American communities, but their general conclusions are supported by two nationwide surveys of the occupations of sons and fathers. One of these surveys was made by the Office of Public Opinion Research of Princeton University in 1945, the other by the National Opinion Research Center in 1947. According to both these studies, about a third of the respondents were in the same occupational group as their fathers; somewhat more than a third were in a higher group; and a bit less than a third in a lower group. This rather high rate of *downward* mobility was in part a reflection of the fact that many of the respondents were still quite young, and some could be expected to rise later to a higher group.

What about social mobility as measured within an individual's occupational career, rather than in relation to his father's occupation? The Oakland survey is the only major study of this kind of mobility, and while this fast-growing city (its population increased by more than a quarter between 1940 and 1950) cannot be taken as typical

[2] "Social Mobility and Occupational Career Patterns: I. Stability of Jobholding" and "II. Social Mobility," in the *American Journal of Sociology*, Volume 57 (January 1952 and March 1952 respectively).

of the country as a whole, it does offer an index to the degree of social mobility in places where the American economy is expanding most rapidly.

When the Oakland respondents were classified according to the occupational groups (in addition to their present ones) in which they had worked, the data showed a variety of job experience that the authors term "staggering." A man who had begun in one occupational group and had remained there, without ever holding a job in another, was definitely atypical. On the other hand, most of this mobility was limited in range. Thus those who now had manual jobs had spent 80 per cent of their working careers in the manual class, and those now holding non-manual positions had spent 75 per cent of their careers in the non-manual class. Since in agreement with Rogoff the authors stress that the gap between manual and non-manual work is the widest in the American class structure, the converse of these figures is also relevant: manual workers had spent one-fifth of their occupational careers in non-manual positions, and white-collar workers one-quarter of theirs in manual jobs. Or, even more startling, 47 per cent of the manual workers had done white-collar work at some time, and 62 per cent of the white-collar workers had worked with their hands at some time.

Lipset and Bendix made a special analysis of the manner in which the gap between manual and non-manual work was crossed. Most workers who moved into the white-collar class had either set up their own small businesses or got low-status jobs, most often as salesmen. One reason for this is obvious: small business and selling are the two activities in which a person with a limited education tends to be least handicapped. More generally, education is one of the most important of the factors that shape the seemingly chaotic picture of social mobility. Thus, farmers' sons migrating to town are typically handicapped by their inferior schooling and tend to enter the urban labor market at or near the bottom. At the other extreme, professionals typically require a long period of rather specialized education and apprenticeship. Nevertheless, Rogoff's study showed that mobility into the professional group has increased fastest over the past generation; and virtually all professionals, according to Lipset and Bendix, have spent part of their working careers in other occupations, in many cases probably while they were attending school.

All these studies assume that change in occupation is an index to social mobility but, as we have pointed out, this is only an approximate measure. Yet if we use income as the index, the results turn out the same. It is generally recognized that the national income of the United States has risen and is continuing to rise, with per capita income regularly increasing at a well-nigh incredible rate of over 2 per cent annually. It has been repeatedly stated, however, that, while average income has risen, this trend has been largely countered by one toward polarization, which drains the middle-income group off into the groups above and below it. "The rich get richer, and the poor poorer." So far as the long-term perspective is concerned, this view can be founded on nothing but ideological preconceptions, for it has no data to support it.

After a diligent search, I was able to find only one study of income distribution that went back into the 19th century. In this unique work, the economist Rufus Tucker ("The Distribution of Income among Income Taxpayers in the United States, 1863–1935," *Quarterly Journal of Economics*, Vol. 52, August 1938) used government statistics on income-tax payments, which are available, with interruptions, from 1863 on. He converted the designated incomes into 1929 dollars, and calculated the percentage of the population that fell into various income groups in each of the years for which data were available. While the method itself was too rough to delineate any but gross differences, Tucker's general conclusions seem to be well based:

> Income is now [1935] much less concentrated in the United States than it was during and just after the Civil War. Although very wealthy persons are more numerous now than then, the number of persons of moderate incomes has increased more than the number of very wealthy persons, [and] the average purchasing power of wage-earners has increased greatly. . . . The members of the upper-income classes are a constantly shifting lot. The income-tax statistics as they stand give very little support to the idea of a hereditary plutocracy. . . . It is very difficult to maintain fortunes intact."

For the more recent period the best impression of income distribution can be got from a book by Simon Kuznets published only several months ago: *Shares of Upper Income Groups in Income and Savings* (National Bureau of Economic Research, 1953). For the greater part of his professional career Simon Kuznets has been directing the National Bureau of Economic Research's analysis of American national income, and his findings have been published in several scores of volumes. In this latest book he traces the percentage of the country's income that went, respectively, to the top 1 per cent and the top 5 per cent. The top 1 per cent were, for example, a family of three with an income of more than $6,300 in 1933, or $12,600 in 1929, or $16,800 in 1946, while the minimum income of the top 5 per cent ranged from $1,250 in 1933 to $2,300 in 1946. During the period between the First World War and the end of the depression, the proportion of the total income that these upper groups received varied little from year to year, only to fall sharply in the most recent period:

	Top 1%	Top 5%
Average, 1919–1938	13 %	25%
Average, 1947–1948	8.5%	18%

"The recent decline in upper group shares," Kuznets writes, "which for its magnitude and persistence is unmatched in the record, obviously has various causes. The most prominent are the reduction of unemployment and the marked increase in total income flowing to lower income groups (particularly farmers and wage earners); shifts in the saving and investment habits of upper income groups which may have curtailed their chances of getting large receipts from successful venture capital and equity investments; lower interest rates; and steeper income taxes. . . ."

In summary, it can be said that social mobility, whether measured from one generation to the next or within the job careers of individuals, whether by occupation or income, is high. Its range, however, tends to be limited: that is, farmers may become workmen; workers may rise to a higher level of skill or become small businessmen or lower white-collar employees; lower employees may rise to executive positions; and professional positions tend to be filled from upper white-collar or business groups. Many of the shifts are temporary, and there is a smaller but nonetheless significant rate of downward mobility. These tendencies, finally, while definite enough to fix a pattern, also encompass many individual exceptions.

What then is the basis for the notion, still generally held in learned as well as lay circles, that it is harder to get ahead than it was a generation ago?

Two scholarly myths have played an enormous role in maintaining this illusion. The first is that of "the closing of the American frontier." A generation ago, Frederick Jackson Turner stated his famous thesis that "the existence of an area of free land, its continuous recession, and the advance of American settlement westward, explain American development." A large number of his students, teaching American history in colleges throughout the country, have made of this assertion a dogma. As Frederic L. Paxson, a leading disciple, put it, "The frontier hypothesis presents the most attractive single explanation of the distinctive trends of American history." Even if it were the most attractive *single* explanation, it would still have the faults of any monolithic theory, and no more than any other can it encompass in one narrow concept the complexity of American society. In an oft-quoted passage, the Superintendent of the Census for 1890 declared that the frontier "cannot any longer have a place in the census reports." If this is what is meant by the closing of the frontier, it has not had a markedly adverse effect on the American economy, which has grown fastest since 1890. And if this is not what is meant, then the phrase becomes—what it does become in many discussions—hardly more than a metaphor, convenient because of its very vagueness.

Often the phrase "the closing of the frontier" has been a way of joining Turner's monolithism to that of Marx. Certainly, this is not the occasion to discuss the adequacy of the Marxist theory of capitalist development; but the recurrent issue of "American exceptionalism," as it is termed in Comintern jargon, would indicate that Marxism suffered its greatest reverse in the attempt made to apply it to America. Leading Russian theorists from Lenin to Voznesensky, American Communists from Jay Lovestone to Earl Browder, have not been sure that the breakdown of capitalism was proceeding according to schedule in the United States. A century after the *Communist Manifesto* was written many of its dire prophecies have been fulfilled —in Europe; but the center of world capitalism continues to grow in wealth and strength. In Communist terms, the United States is, indeed, "a riddle wrapped in a mystery inside an enigma." The rate of social mobility slowed down appreciably during the great depression of the 1930's, and a definitive evaluation of current trends would have to be based on some theory of economic development. But those who think some variant of Marxian theory will serve, and who consequently believe that another depression is just around the corner, seem to me to show a faith as touching—and unwarranted—as ex-President Hoover's.

If neither "the closing of the frontier" nor "the maturity of American capitalism" was relevant to social mobility, there were other structural changes in American society that were. In a stimulating article written in 1942,[3] the sociologist Elbridge Sibley presented the hypothesis that social mobility in the past had depended on two fundamental population trends. Typically, the average family size in the upper classes had been small, creating a social vacuum that the more numerous sons of the lower classes rushed in to fill. More recently, this class difference in fertility has

[3] Elbridge Sibley, "Some Demographic Clues to Stratification," *American Sociological Review*, Vol. 7, June 1942.

become smaller, for now the average family size of the upper classes has increased and that of the lower classes has decreased. Thus when professional or executive posts, say, are vacated by retirement or death, they can be filled by sons or nephews of the same social class. Secondly, the rapid upward mobility of the past had been in large part a consequence of immigration. Most of the million immigrants who came to this country yearly from 1900 to 1914 were peasants who spoke little or no English. Inevitably, they entered the American labor market at the bottom, and pushed native-born workers up at least one rung. But immigration is now restricted to a fraction of its pre-1914 numbers, and American society can no longer depend on this semi-automatic process to insure the continuance of its open-class structure. Moreover, Sibley might have added, some of the more recent immigrants, who came for political rather than economic reasons, have been urban professionals and other white-collar types who enter the labor market above its midpoint. Before 1914, in summary, both the differential fertility and the large immigration favored a high rate of upward mobility, but since then both of these underlying demographic trends have changed markedly.

Why, then, has the rate of mobility not fallen, contrary to Sibley's expectations? Very tentatively, four reasons can be suggested to explain this:

(1) The development of the economy continues to favor upward mobility. Sibley noted that between 1870 and 1930 an estimated nine million workers had shifted from manual to white-collar work; but that since 1930 technical progress had resulted in technological unemployment. His assumption, however, that the depression set a permanent downward trend has not proved to be correct.[4]

(2) Since the immigration law was passed in the 1920's, there seems to have been a compensatory increase in the immigration of unskilled laborers from the Western Hemisphere—French Canadians, Mexicans, and Puerto Ricans. While the total number has never approached the previous average of a million a year, it has been a significant factor for certain regions.

(3) Internal migration may serve some of the same functions as the former large overseas immigration. According to Census Bureau statistics, during the period 1934–39, 13.1 per cent of the population fourteen years and over moved from the county in which they were living; during the fiscal year 1940–1941, 20.8 per cent of the total population, including children, moved to another county; and for the fiscal year 1948–1949, this figure was about 6 per cent. True, these migrants do not typically take the lowest jobs as the pre-1914 immigrants used to do; the Oakland study, for example, showed a high correlation between geographical movement and upward mobility. But they do upset the social structure of the communities into which they move, as well as affecting that of the communities they leave.

(4) It may be that the continued movement of women into the labor force is a factor in promoting social mobility. While women take many of the white-collar jobs that become available, and thus absorb a portion of the social mobility implicit

[4] Indeed, from 1910 to 1953 the proportion of the labor force employed in white-collar occupations has almost doubled, increasing from 21 per cent in 1910 to 39 per cent in 1953, and the rate of increase has been highest in the last decade. The increase, moreover, was approximately the same in each of the occupational groups within the white-collar class, professional and executive as well as clerical. And within the working class, the major trend has been a marked decrease in the proportion of unskilled, from 15 per cent in 1910 to 6 per cent in 1953 (though this may be the consequence partly of changes in census classification). Farmers and farm workers have fallen from more than half of those occupied in 1870 to less than a tenth today.

in the structural change of the economy, within any occupational group they are usually bunched at the bottom, thus possibly helping the men in that group to rise.

However, it is not illusion or error alone that supports the idea that the rate of social mobility has declined. It does have a certain limited validity. Even today, with full employment, certain of the once typical paths up the social scale are much more difficult to climb. In particular, with the growing complexity of large industry, more and more firms have filled openings in the lower managerial ranks with graduates of engineering schools rather than by promoting skilled workers. But, while education has become the major barrier to upward social mobility, it has also become so widely distributed that it acts as a barrier through which more and more people can pass.

Over the past sixty years, the proportion of the population aged fourteen to seventeen years that was enrolled in secondary school has increased:

1890	7%
1910	15%
1930	51%
1950	84%

Thus, in half a century, the high school has changed from a preparatory school for a small elite to something almost as universally attended in this country as elementary school. Over the same period college enrollment has grown even faster, with college graduates increasing steadily from 9,371 in 1870 to 432,058 in 1950. At the present time, in proportion to the population of the two countries, there are as many college *teachers* in the United States as there are college *students* in Britain.

But the person who does not get on this educational bandwagon young is excluded from the highest positions pretty effectively: one may become a salesman or a small proprietor, as we have seen, but is not likely to go higher. And the chances of getting this valuable higher education are still much smaller for the children of workers or farmers than for the children of white-collar workers. A study in New York State showed that in 1940 whether high school graduates went on to college depended in part on their grades, but also on their fathers' incomes. The proportion of the best students that entered college varied from 41 per cent for the lowest income group to almost double that for the highest income group.

	Family Income			
Scholastic Standing	Less than $2,500	$2,500 to $4,999	$5,000 to $8,999	$9,000 and Over
Highest quarter	41%	41%	60%	76%
Second quarter	19%	26%	27%	56%
Lower half	11%	13%	27%	44%

This table indicates two things: that a young person's class has a definite influence on whether or not he attends college, but does not decide it. *Fully* four-tenths of those in the highest scholastic group and lowest income group went on to college in 1940, and *only* four-tenths of those in the lowest scholastic group and highest income group.

Whenever a conclusion is based on isolated facts torn from their social context, we do well to suspect that the choice of these facts was not haphazard but in line with some prejudice or ideology. In this case, two ideologies that seem to have little in common—nostalgic Americanism and Marxism—have cooperated to create and maintain "enlightened" illusions about the American class structure.

The prime representative of the first school is the anthropologist William Lloyd Warner. He began with a survey in Newburyport, Massachusetts, reported at length in the "Yankee City" series of books, and he and his disciples have carried out dozens of similar surveys throughout the country. These studies can be criticized on several grounds, but only one of these is relevant here. Warner made a virtue of the fact that he started his study without a conscious theoretical framework—without "distorting preconceptions," as the phrase goes. He went to Newburyport, looked around, and "discovered" class there; and the clear implication in all of the works of this school is that this is a new phenomenon to be viewed against the golden backdrop of America's heroic classless past. For example, in a book about "Jonesville," a small Midwestern town he has studied, he writes:

"The workers' 'stairway to the stars' in Jonesville and America is no longer an open highway. Climbing step by step to bigger and better jobs for most workers and their sons is a story of the past. . . . The Lincoln myth and the American dream of striving to win and getting to the top do not fit the mill worker. To start today in youth as a mill worker in the Jonesvilles of America is usually to end there in old age." [5] When present reality is contrasted with a stairway to the stars, an open highway, the Lincoln myth, the American Dream, is it any wonder that these analysts find it a bit grubby?

The vinegary review that C. Wright Mills wrote of one of Warner's earlier books achieved a certain fame in sociological circles, if only because of its contrast with the usually staid language of the learned journals. And yet Mills's own book, *White Collar*, is a perfect example of what might be called the Warner method of analysis. The drab picture he paints of the *"lumpen* bourgeoisie"* is made up in equal parts of carefully selected statistics, flamboyant prose, and American Dream background music. According to Mills's analysis, the independent farmer, for example, continues to exist only by grace of government largess, and he contrasts this—not with the railroads that grew fat on public lands, nor with the manufacturers who pushed tariff bills through Congress, nor with 19th-century farmers who took their largess in the form of cheap or free land—but with some fanciful image of a free-enterpriser who disdained any proffer of federal assistance and haughtily refused to manipulate state legislatures. Or: the independent storekeeper is under pressure from the chains and must work hard and long hours; but the precise working conditions of the crackerbox philosopher who kept a general store in the country a generation ago are left vague. As social scientists of opposed schools, Warner and Mills have cooperated in proving in this matter that reality and ideology are not in accord. If there is a difference between them, it may be that Warner is naive and that Mills hopes that his readers are.

As so often in social science, the difficulty in the case of social mobility is that we have no scale against which to measure our findings. Once we know that social mobility exists at a certain rate, how can we say whether it is "high" or "low" or whatever, unless we are able to say that it is "high" or "low" with respect to something else? As the Lipset-Bendix-Malm article puts it, "We are unable to interpret

[5] W. Lloyd Warner, et al., *Democracy in Jonesville: A Study in Quality and Inequality* (Harper, 1949).

a finding according to which 75 per cent of the manual workers have always done manual labor, while 25 per cent have also had jobs in the non-manual occupations. Such evidence is evidence neither for rigidity (75%) nor for mobility (25%), since we lack the comparative data necessary to make such assertions meaningful." Lacking such a scale, most analysts, either explicitly or by implication, have measured the social mobility they found against the absolute of "classless society," as found either in the mythical American past or in the utopian Marxian future. No concept in the study of society is so confused and abused as the "classless society."

Taken literally, a "classless society" is a contradiction in terms. In all of the dozen variants of the definition of "society," the main element is always a structured group; and one of the main planes of this structure is determined by the division of labor. What, then, is "classless society" in an industrialized country? Neither Marx's *Critique of the Gotha Program,* Lenin's *State and Revolution,* nor Bukharin's *Historical Materialism* gives us much enlightenment. Lenin tells us that the term means that "there is no difference between the members of society in their relation to the social means of production," or, in other words, that "classless society" signifies no more than the abolition of private property. Bukharin writes that it is "a question that has been but little discussed in Marxian literature," and he himself disposes of it in some three pages, which form the most detailed exposition of the idea that I know of in Marxist literature. Classes, he tells us, developed out of the division of labor, and from the differentiation resulting from technically necessary organizational functions. Why then will the abolition of private property lead to the disappearance of classes? Why is Robert Michels not correct when he says that socialists may be victorious, but not socialism?

"An example will show Michels' error," writes Bukharin. "When the bourgeoisie is in power, it is by reason of the power—as we know—not of all the members of the class, but of its leaders. Yet it is evident that this condition does not result in a class stratification *within* the bourgeoisie. The landlords in Russia ruled [through] their high officials . . . but this stratum did not set itself up as a class against the other landlords. The reason was that these other landlords did not have a lower standard of living than that of the former; furthermore, their cultural level was about the same, on the whole, and the rulers were constantly recruited from this class. . . .

"[During] the *transition period* from capitalism to socialism, i.e., the period of the proletarian dictatorship . . . there will inevitably result a *tendency* to 'degeneration,' i.e., the excretion of a leading stratum in the form of a class-germ. This tendency will be retarded by two opposing tendencies: first, by the growth of the productive forces; second, by the abolition of the *educational monopoly.* . . . The outcome of the struggle will depend on which tendencies turn out to be the stronger."

Thus, a "classless society" apparently means not a society without classes but rather one in which the class differences in income and culture are "on the whole" not very great. It is a society in which education is not a class monopoly, so that positions in the ruling "stratum" become open to all persons of competence. Moreover, the development of the economy is a decisive factor, for only with the sharply increased production that full industrialization affords will general cultural democratization be possible. In short, once "classless society" in its Marxian sense becomes more concrete than a mere slogan, it proves to be not an absolute against which to measure social mobility but actually something very like present-day American society.

On analysis, the "classless society" of the mythical American past turns out to be one, simply, in which social mobility was high. Once we attempt to analyze the slogan of the "American Dream," once we try to get behind the "tradition"—as Robert Lynd put it in his *Middletown in Transition*—that any "enterprising man with an idea and a shoestring of capital" could start his own business, we find a society with a quite definite class structure. Social mobility in the United States during the 19th century was very high compared with that in Europe, but whether it was higher than in present-day America no one can really say. So much is true: since the whole economy was different, the routes to higher status were not the same, but probably no greater proportion of the population achieved such status, nor was it easier to achieve.

Without going into details, it is necessary furthermore to indicate the long-term shift in class power that has taken place. Property qualifications for voting, present in twelve of the original thirteen states and persisting until well into the 19th century, have disappeared. The abolition of slavery was followed, but only after the First World War, by a painfully slow but real improvement in the Negro's status. Industrial laws replaced the common law under which employer-worker relations had been regulated by master-servant norms. The trade union movement grew to its present impressive size and strength and, perhaps even more important, its authority was made legitimate to the point where most middle-class persons recognize the right of the trade union movement to function as a class organization. The urban concentration of wealth has been counterbalanced by various "artificial" measures designed to raise the farmers' standard of living. The income tax has become a permanent feature of American society.

No matter how we try to analyze the long-term trend in social mobility—whether we look at the distribution of occupations, income, education, wealth or power—the sparse data we do have would indicate that the class structure has become more fluid rather than rigid.

In any society, the jobs to be done vary in degree of pleasantness, difficulty, and importance. To get the work done requires, first of all, a differentiation of authority; and jobs that are especially important and those requiring especially long training tend to be rewarded with a higher amount of material goods or by symbolic marks of prestige. In short, class differentiation serves a function. That is not to say, of course, that the class structure of any particular society serves its function perfectly, or even well. The point is rather that the class division in every society of which we have any knowledge exists not only because of the psychological differences among humans but because of the social function that class serves. In the abstract, one can conceive of other social institutions that might serve the same function—for example, a feeling of identity with the group intense enough to motivate all to work without supervision and to motivate some persons to do the less pleasant or more difficult work without special reward. On the basis of efficiency and other values, it is possible to choose (still in the abstract) between class division and some such alternative—bearing in mind, however, that the function class division serves is important and that there is no historical precedent for its complete replacement by other institutions.

Class structures may be compared by ranging them along a continuum from the caste society, in which the family a person is born into completely determines his life's chances, to the open-class society, in which birth has *no* effect on the individual's class and status. Neither of these ideal types has ever existed in pure form. In particular, so long as the family as we know it persists, each person's attitudes and aptitudes will continue to be formed in large part by his parents. Thus, it is completely logical that strongly egalitarian societies, such as the Soviet Union immediately after 1917, or Israeli *kibbutzim,* have tended to replace the family by public crèches. Such societies have also reacted against the social division of labor, the second principal determinant of class position. Sometimes, as in the various utopian communities of 19th-century America or, again, in the *kibbutzim,* the group has concentrated on agriculture and left it to the profane world outside to provide industrial products. Sometimes, though more in theory than in practice, the circulation of the entire labor force among the various occupations has been proclaimed. Thus, Lenin declared that "every cook" should become an administrator; and in the society that Edward Bellamy described in *Looking Backward* all young men and women were drafted for a period into a civilian service corps to which such menial tasks as waiting on tables were assigned.

Those who have advocated scrapping fundamental institutions have seldom indicated that their programs were based on a choice between competing values. The influence of the family is not wholly bad, by any criterion. And in our complex society a professional, for example, is likely to be thirty years old before he finishes his special schooling, his apprenticeship as interne or law clerk, and his starting practice. From the point of view of social efficiency, it is disadvantageous to force such a man to postpone his productive life, as such writers as Bellamy suggest, for, say, another two, or to shift him to a different occupation once he has learned his own.

A very high rate of social mobility may have harmful consequences, of which we can conveniently distinguish three kinds.

First, even in a rapidly growing economy, a high rate of upward mobility entails some downward mobility; and the consequent *nouveaux pauvres* are a liability in any social system. Typically, declassed people will seek to retain their status by irrational means: it is they who foster race hatred, who give demagogues their first support, who form the vanguard of totalitarian parties. So long as their number is relatively small they constitute a nuisance that can be controlled; but any social program that leads to an appreciable increase in declassed *"lumpen"* ought to include measures to reabsorb them into the social fabric as quickly as possible.

Secondly, a class system that fosters a very wide diffusion of cultural values may well sacrifice some of these values. While a very much higher percentage of young people attend college in the United States than in Britain—as we have noted in our discussion of education—the level of education at American colleges is, on the whole, decidedly lower. Just recently, for example, Dr. Minard Stout, president of the University of Nevada, has advocated that it admit any graduate of a Nevada high school, regardless of his academic rating or the kind of courses he had taken in high school. Opening the doors that wide is a first step toward closing them altogether.

Thirdly, rapid social mobility often results in personal maladjustment, if not actual neurosis. This is true both for those who try to climb up the social scale and fail, and for those who succeed. Middle-class Americans are not nearly as happy as their fantastically high standard of living would seem to warrant, for their aspirations are always higher. Instead of enjoying their ample possessions, they strive for higher positions, or gather more gadgets, as new symbols of higher status. The pattern is both to own more and to belittle what one has as hardly comparable with what one *will* have.

The disparity between boundless aspirations and the opportunities to fulfill them undoubtedly does much to create the restlessness typical of American civilization. In a more rigidly stratified society people get a sense of security from "knowing their place," but Americans have no place that endures from one generation to another, or even from year to year. They push upward, and if one avenue fails them they seek another. The result is a very active economy, full of ingenious new ideas and products and services such as were never dreamt of in any other society. On the other hand, criminologists agree that a fundamental cause of juvenile delinquency and crime is that the equal opportunities that slum children learn to expect as their right are not really given them. If this theory is correct, then the "cause" of the relatively high crime rate may not be so much the American slums, which are not worse on the whole than those in other countries, but the promissory note in the American democratic credo, inevitably unpayable to so many.

And there is also a price to be paid by the successful. Even if a person is able to climb the social ladder so fast that he catches up with his aspirations, this does not mean that in general he is content. For changing one's class means changing one's way of life. The son of a worker who becomes a lawyer has only begun the move that the shift in occupation implies. To complete it, he must forsake one set of friends and find another, forget pinochle and bowling and learn bridge and skiing, leave the Baptists and join the Episcopalians, and so on. He is of course gratified by his success, but he may feel too anxious to be very happy. He may become a prime example of that modern species, the marginal man, on the edge of several groups without belonging to any. The standards that he learned as a child are not those he is trying to learn now, and he may suffer from what sociologists term *anomie*—literally, normlessness; more generally, an inability to choose amid the confusion of conflicting standards. *Anomie,* a sense of not belonging, is typical of highly mobile societies; for in rigidly structured societies, by definition, a man knows where his place is and what behavior is expected of him.

The confusions frequently to be found in discussions of the American class system derive in part from the fact that they are conducted against the background of an egregious paradox: the United States, that arch representative of world capitalism, is becoming a socialist society, insofar as that term has any concrete meaning.

The American economy is no longer predominantly a laissez-faire one. Competitive production has been supplanted in crucial areas by controlled and subsidized production, especially for military uses. The increasing role of war production has speeded up long-range structural changes, and has markedly increased the role of government in the whole economy. The new principle is to grant, through government action, profits to those socially desirable enterprises that cannot obtain them in the open market—for example, defense items and agriculture. On the other hand, some of the idyllic virtues of the laissez-faire system have been retained, for it is still remarkably easy to set up a small business. The mortality rate among such small enterprises is indeed high, as Mills, and Lipset and Bendix, and others point out, but is it higher than it used to be? And, more important, is it higher than it ought to be? It is precisely the virtue of such a fluid system that it provides for a good deal of trial-and-error experiment, and to complain that a man starting his business has no guarantee of success is to demand the best of all possible worlds.

The American economy is mixed, but American culture is, in effect, socialist. It is based on the same essential factors—the enormous industrial production, the high and widely distributed income, the general distribution of equalitarian cultural values—that any socialist culture would rest on. The very high proportion of low-grade cultural products is related to the large number of people with purchasing power but without tradition—that is, to the fact that the society is highly mobile. That this low-grade culture is distributed commercially is true, but not as important as many have made it. The American economy can meet any reasonable demand, and in other types of consumers' products, where the demand has been for quality goods, the quality of production has been high.

The social structure, finally, is what Bukharin called a "classless society." Not indeed what orthodox Marxists look for in the ultimate phase of "communism" but what they expect during the transitional period of the "dictatorship of the proletariat." Differences in the income and culture of the entire population of the United States are great, but these differences tend to be less "on the whole" than in any advanced society we know of. Moreover, the two forces that will prevent, in Bukharin's terms, the United States from degenerating into a class society—"the growth of the productive forces" and "the abolition of the education monopoly"— are very much in evidence. But the clearest criterion is the rate of social mobility— the fact that the highest "stratum" is regularly recruited from the rest of the society.

23 / Our Invisible Poor

Dwight Macdonald

Although the United States is the richest nation in the world and has a high degree of social mobility, poverty has always existed for many Americans. The prosperity of the 1920's left great numbers of Americans still living in want. The New Deal programs helped millions, but largely neglected the very poor. Well over half the nation lived below the poverty line in the Great Depression. Not even the extraordinary increase in living standards after World War II eliminated poverty. Poor health, broken families, racial discrimination, old age, and lack of education and training lie at the root of poverty.

In the following essay Dwight Macdonald discusses these and other factors and some of the recent examinations of poverty. Some observers have concluded that poverty is inevitable and is structurally built into the American economy and society. If so, it will be increasingly difficult for the poor to escape from their poverty. Americans may not be able to count on traditional patterns of social mobility to eliminate poverty as they have for so many people in the past. A hard core of poor people seems immovable, although others have advanced. Poverty, however, is difficult to define and is a relative conception. Thus, the poor today are materially better off than the poor at the turn of the century, but they are surrounded by an increasingly affluent majority. Finally, poverty has become an embarrassing anomaly in a society rich enough to abolish it. Since poverty no longer seems inevitable, many Americans have come to regard it as an intolerable blight.

For further reading: *Michael Harrington, *The Other America* (1962); *Gabriel Kolko, *Wealth and Power in America* (1962); *Ben Seligman (ed.), *Poverty as a Public Issue* (1965); *Margaret S. Gordon (ed.), *Poverty in America* (1965); *Robert Bremner, *From the Depths: The Discovery of Poverty in the United States* (1956); Herman Miller, *Rich Man, Poor Man* (1964); *David Potter, *People of Plenty* (1954); *John Kenneth Galbraith, *The Affluent Society* (1958); *Louis Ferman, Joyce Kornbluh, and Alan Haber (eds.), *Poverty in America* (1965).

In his significantly titled "The Affluent Society" (1958) Professor J. K. Galbraith states that poverty in this country is no longer "a massive affliction [but] more nearly an afterthought." Dr. Galbraith is a humane critic of the American capitalist system, and he is generously indignant about the continued existence of even this nonmassive and afterthoughtish poverty. But the interesting thing about his pronouncement, aside from the fact that it is inaccurate, is that it was generally accepted as obvious. For a long time now, almost everybody has assumed that, because of the New Deal's social legislation and—more important—the prosperity we have enjoyed since 1940, mass poverty no longer exists in this country.

Dr. Galbraith states that our poor have dwindled to two hard-core categories. One is the "insular poverty" of those who live in the rural South or in depressed areas like West Virginia. The other category is "case poverty," which he says is "commonly and properly related to [such] characteristics of the individuals so afflicted [as] mental deficiency, bad health, inability to adapt to the discipline of modern economic life, excessive procreation, alcohol, insufficient education." He reasons that such poverty must be due to individual defects, since "nearly everyone else has mastered his environment; this proves that it is not intractable." Without pressing the similarity of this concept to the "Social Darwinism" whose fallacies Dr. Galbraith easily disposes of elsewhere in his book, one may observe that most of these characteristics are as much the result of poverty as its cause.

Dr. Galbraith's error is understandable, and common. Last April the newpapers reported some exhilarating statistics in a Department of Commerce study: the average family income increased from $2,340 in 1929 to $7,020 in 1961. (These figures are calculated in current dollars, as are all the others I shall cite.) But the papers did not report the fine type, so to speak, which showed that almost all the recent gain was made by families with incomes of over $7,500, and that the rate at which poverty is being eliminated has slowed down alarmingly since 1953. Only the specialists and the statisticians read the fine type, which is why illusions continue to exist about American poverty.

Now Michael Harrington, an alumnus of the *Catholic Worker* and the Fund for the Republic who is at present a contributing editor of *Dissent* and the chief editor of the Socialist Party biweekly, *New America,* has written "The Other America: Poverty in the United States" (Macmillan). In the admirably short space of under two hundred pages, he outlines the problem, describes in imaginative detail what it means to be poor in this country today, summarizes the findings of recent studies by economists and sociologists, and analyzes the reasons for the persistence of mass poverty in the midst of general prosperity. It is an excellent book—and a most important one.

My only serious criticism is that Mr. Harrington has popularized the treatment a bit too much. Not in the writing, which is on a decent level, but in a certain vagueness. There are no index, no bibliography, no reference footnotes. In our overspecialized culture, books like this tend to fall into two categories: Popular (no scholarly "apparatus") and Academic (too much). I favor something intermediate— why should the academics have *all* the footnotes? The lack of references means that the book is of limited use to future researchers and writers. A pity, since the author has brought together a great range of material.

I must also object that Mr. Harrington's treatment of statistics is more than a little impressionistic. His appendix, which he calls a coming to grips with the professional material, doesn't live up to its billing. "If my interpretation is bleak and grim," he writes, "and even if it overstates the case slightly, that is intentional. My moral point of departure is a sense of outrage. . . . In such a discussion it is inevitable that one gets mixed up with dry, graceless, technical matters. That should not conceal the crucial fact that these numbers represent people and that any tendency toward understatement is an intellectual way of acquiescing in suffering." But a fact is a fact, and Mr. Harrington confuses the issue when he writes that "these numbers represent people." They do—and one virtue of his book is that he never forgets it—but in dealing with statistics, this truism must be firmly repressed lest one begin to think from the heart rather than from the head, as he seems to do when he charges those statisticians who "understate" the numbers of the poor with having found "an intellectual way of acquiescing in suffering." This is moral bullying, and it reminds me, *toutes proportions gardées,* of the habitual confusion in Communist thinking between facts and political inferences from them. "A sense of outrage" is proper for a "moral point of departure," but statistics are the appropriate *factual* point of departure, as in the writings of Marx and Engels on the agony of the nineteenth-century English working class—writings that are by no means lacking in a sense of moral outrage, either.

These objections, however, do not affect Mr. Harrington's two main contentions: that mass poverty still exists in the United States, and that it is disappearing more slowly than is commonly thought. Two recent dry, graceless, and technical reports bear him out. One is that Commerce Department study, already mentioned. More important is "Poverty and Deprivation in the U.S.," a bulky pamphlet issued by the Conference on Economic Progress, in Washington, whose national committee includes Thurman Arnold, Leon H. Keyserling (said to be the principal author of the pamphlet), and Walter P. Reuther.

In the last year we seem to have suddenly awakened, rubbing our eyes like Rip van Winkle, to the fact that mass poverty persists, and that it is one of our two gravest social problems. (The other is related: While only eleven per cent of our population is non-white, twenty-five per cent of our poor are.) Two other current books confirm Mr. Harrington's thesis: "Wealth and Power in America" (Praeger), by Dr. Gabriel Kolko, a social historian who has recently been at Harvard and the University of Melbourne, Australia, and "Income and Welfare in the United States" (McGraw-Hill), compiled by an imposing battery of four socio-economists headed by Dr. James N. Morgan, who rejoices in the title of Program Director of the Survey Research Center of the Institute for Social Research at the University of Michigan.

Dr. Kolko's book resembles Mr. Harrington's in several ways: It is short, it is based on earlier studies, and it is liberally inclined. It is less readable, because it is written in an academic jargon that is merely a vehicle for the clinching Statistic. Although it is impossible to write seriously about poverty without a copious use of statistics—as this review will demonstrate—it *is* possible to bring thought and feeling to bear on such raw material. Mr. Harrington does this more successfully than Dr. Kolko, whose prose is afflicted not only with academic blight but also with creeping ideology. Dr. Kolko leans so far to the socialist side that he sometimes falls on his nose, as when he clinches the inequality of wealth in the United States with a statistic: "In 1959, 23% of those earning less than $1,000 [a year] owned a car, compared to 95% of those earning more than $10,000." The real point is just the opposite, as any citizen of Iran, Ghana, Yemen, or the U.S.S.R. would appreciate—not that the rich have cars but that almost a quarter of the extremely poor do. Similarly, although Dr. Kolko has two chapters on poverty that confirm Mr. Harrington's argument, his main point is a different and more vulnerable one: "The basic distribution of income and wealth in the United States is essentially the same now as it was in 1939, or even 1910." This is a half fact. The rich are almost as rich as ever and the poor are even poorer, in the percentage of the national income they receive. Yet, as will become apparent later, there have been major changes in the distribution of wealth, and there has been a general improvement in living standards, so that the poor are much fewer today than they were in 1939. "Most low-income groups live substantially better today," Dr. Kolko admits. "But even though their real wages have mounted, their percentage of the national income has not changed." That in the last half century the rich have kept their riches and the poor their poverty is indeed a scandal. But it is theoretically possible, assuming enough general increase in wealth, that the relatively poor might by now have achieved a decent standard of living, no matter how inferior to that of the rich. As the books under consideration show, however, this theoretical possibility has not been realized.

Inequality of wealth is not necessarily a major social problem per se. Poverty is. The late French philosopher Charles Péguy remarks, in his classic essay on poverty, "The duty of tearing the destitute from their destitution and the duty of distributing goods equitably are not of the same order. The first is an urgent duty, the second is a duty of convenience. . . . When all men are provided with the necessities . . . what do we care about the distribution of luxury?" What indeed? Envy and emulation are the motives—and not very good ones—for the equalization of wealth. The problem of poverty goes much deeper.

"Income and Welfare in the United States" differs from the other works reviewed here in length (531 big pages) and in being the result of original research; 2,800 families were interviewed "in depth." I must confess that, aside from a few interesting bits of data, I got almost nothing out of it. I assume the authors think poverty is still an important social problem, else why would they have gone to all this labor, but I'm not at all sure what their general conclusions are; maybe there aren't supposed to be any, in the best tradition of American scholarship. Their book is one of those behemoths of collective research financed by a foundation (in this case, largely by Ford) that daunt the stoutest-hearted lay reader (in this case, me). Based on "a multi-stage area probability sample that gives equal chance of selection to all non-institutional dwelling units in the conterminous United States [and that] was clustered geographically at each stage and stratified with interlaced controls," it is a specimen of what Charles Lamb called *biblia abiblia*—things that have the outward appearance of books but are not books, since they cannot be read. Methodologically, it employs something called the "multivariate analysis," which is explained in Appendix E. Typographically, Appendix E looks like language, but it turns out to be strewn with booby traps, all doubtless well known in the trade, like "dummy variables," "F ratios," "regression coefficients," "beta coefficients" (and "partial beta coefficients"), and two kinds of "standard deviations"—"of explanatory variable A" and "of the dependent variable."

My experience with such works may be summarized as follows: (alpha) the coefficient of comprehensibility decreases in direct ratio to the increase in length, or the longer the incomprehensibler, a notion that is illustrated here by the fact that Dr. Kolko's short work is more understandable than Dr. Morgan et al.'s long one; (beta) the standard deviation from truism is inversely related to the magnitude of the generalization, or the bigger the statement the more obvious. (Beta) is illustrated by the authors' five general proposals for action ("Implications for Public Policy"). The second of these is: "Fuller employment and the elimination of discrimination based on prejudice would contribute greatly to the independence of non-white persons, women, teen-agers, and some of the aged." That is, if Negroes and the rest had jobs and were not discriminated against, they would be better off—a point that doesn't need to be argued or, for that matter, stated. The authors have achieved such a mastery of truism that they sometimes achieve the same monumental effect even in non-magnitudinous statements, as: "Table 28–1 shows that the proportion of parents who indicated that their children will attend private colleges is approximately twice as large for those with incomes over $10,000 as for those with incomes under $3,000." Could be.

What is "poverty"? It is a historically relative concept, first of all. "There are new definitions [in America] of what man can achieve, of what a human standard of life should be," Mr. Harrington writes. "Those who suffer levels of life well below those that are possible, even though they live better than medieval knights or Asian peasants, are poor. . . . Poverty should be defined in terms of those who are denied the minimal levels of health, housing, food, and education that our present stage of scientific knowledge specifies as necessary for life as it is now lived in the United States." His dividing line follows that proposed in recent studies by the United States Bureau of Labor Statistics: $4,000 a year for a family of four and $2,000 for an individual living alone. (All kinds of income are included, such as food grown and consumed on farms.) This is the cutoff line generally drawn today.

Mr. Harrington estimates that between forty and fifty million Americans, or about a fourth of the population, are now living in poverty. Not just below the level of comfortable living, but real poverty, in the old-fashioned sense of the word—that they are hard put to it to get the mere necessities, beginning with enough to eat. This is difficult to believe in the United States of 1963, but one has to make the effort, and it is now being made. The extent of our poverty has suddenly become visible. The same thing has happened in England, where working-class gains as a result of the Labour Party's post-1945 welfare state blinded almost everybody to the continued existence of mass poverty. It was not until Professor Richard M. Titmuss, of the London School of Economics, published a series of articles in the *New Statesman* last fall, based on his new book, "Income Distribution and Social Change" (Allen & Unwin), that even the liberal public in England became aware that the problem still persists on a scale that is "statistically significant," as the economists put it.

Statistics on poverty are even trickier than most. For example, age and geography make a difference. There is a distinction, which cannot be rendered arithmetically, between poverty and low income. A childless young couple with $3,000 a year is not poor in the way an elderly couple might be with the same income. The young couple's statistical poverty may be a temporary inconvenience; if the husband is a graduate student or a skilled worker, there are prospects of latter affluence or at least comfort. But the old couple can look forward only to diminishing earnings and increasing medical expenses. So also geographically: A family of four in a small town with $4,000 a year may be better off than a like family in a city—lower rent, no bus fares to get to work, fewer occasions (or temptations) to spend money. Even more so with a rural family. Although allowance is made for the value of the vegetables they may raise to feed themselves, it is impossible to calculate how much money they *don't* spend on clothes, say, or furniture, because they don't have to keep up with the Joneses. Lurking in the crevices of a city, like piranha fish in a Brazilian stream, are numerous tempting opportunities for expenditure, small but voracious, which can strip a budget to its bones in a surprisingly short time. The subtlety and complexity of poverty statistics may be discovered by a look at Dr. Kolko's statement that in 1959 "23% of those earning less than $1,000 owned a car." Does this include college students, or are they included in their families' statistics? If the first is true, then Dr. Kolko's figure loses much of its meaning. If the second is, then it is almost *too* meaningful, since it says that one-fourth of those earning less than twenty dollars a week are able to afford a car. Which it is, deponent sayeth not.

It is not, therefore, surprising to find that there is some disagreement about just how many millions of Americans are poor. The point is that all these recent studies agree that American poverty is still a mass phenomenon. One of the lowest estimates appears in the University of Michigan's "Income and Welfare," which states, "Poor families comprise one-fifth of the nation's families." The authors do not develop this large and crucial statement, or even give sources for it, despite their meticulous pedantry in all unimportant matters. So one can only murmur that the other experts put the number of poor much higher. (Though even a fifth is still over 35,000,000 people.) The lowness of the Michigan estimate is especially puzzling since its cutoff figure for poverty is $4,330, which is slightly higher than the commonly accepted one. The tendentious Dr. Kolko is also unconvincing, in the opposite direction. "Since 1947," he writes, "one-half of the nation's families and unattached individuals have had an income too small to provide them with a maintenance standard of living," which he sets at $4,500 a year for a family. He does give a table, with a long supporting footnote that failed to make clear to me how he could have possibly decided that 90,000,000 Americans are now living on less than $4,500 a year; I suspect some confusion between a "maintenance" and a "minimum-comfort" budget.

More persuasive estimates appear in the Conference on Economic Progress pamphlet, "Poverty and Deprivation." Using the $4,000 cutoff, the authors conclude that 38,000,000 persons are now living in poverty, which is slightly less than Mr. Harrington's lowest estimate. One reason may be that the pamphlet discriminates, as most studies don't, between "multiple-person families" and "unattached individuals," rating the latter as poor only if they have less than $2,000 a year. But there is more to it than that, including a few things I don't feel competent to judge. Income statistics are never compiled on exactly the same bases and there are all kinds of refinements, which vary from one study to another. Thus the Commerce Department's April report estimates there are 17,500,000 families *and* "unattached individuals" with incomes of less than $4,000. How many of the latter are there? "Poverty and Deprivation" puts the number of single persons with under $2,000 at 4,000,000. Let us say that in the 17,500,000 under $4,000 there are 6,500,000 single persons—the proportion of unattached individuals tends to go down as income rises. This homemade estimate gives us 11,000,000 families with incomes of under $4,000. Figuring the average American family at three and a half persons—which it is—this makes 38,500,000 individuals in families, or a grand total, if we add in the 4,000,000 "unattached individuals" with under $2,000 a year, of 42,500,000 Americans now living in poverty, which is close to a fourth of the total population.

The reason Dr. Galbraith was able to see poverty as no longer "a massive affliction" is that he used a cutoff of $1,000, which even in 1949, when it was adopted in a

Congressional study, was probably too low (the C.I.O. argued for $2,000) and in 1958 when "The Affluent Society" appeared, was simply fantastic.

The model postwar budgets drawn up in 1951 by the Bureau of Labor Statistics to "maintain a level of adequate living" give a concrete idea of what poverty means in this country—or would mean if poor families lived within their income and spent it wisely, which they don't. Dr. Kolko summarizes the kind of living these budgets provide:

> Three members of the family see a movie once every three weeks, and one member sees a movie once every two weeks. There is no telephone in the house, but the family makes three pay calls a week. They buy one book a year and write one letter a week.
>
> The father buys one heavy wool suit every two years and a light wool suit every three years; the wife, one suit every ten years or one skirt every five years. Every three or four years, depending on the distance and time involved, the family takes a vacation outside their own city. In 1950, the family spent a total of $80 to $90 on all types of home furnishings, electrical appliances, and laundry equipment. . . . The family eats cheaper cuts of meat several times a week, but has more expensive cuts on holidays. The entire family consumes a total of two five-cent ice cream cones, one five-cent candy bar, two bottles of soda, and one bottle of beer a week. The family owes no money, but has no savings except for a small insurance policy.

One other item is included in the B.L.S. "maintenance" budget: a new car every twelve to eighteen years.

This is an ideal picture, drawn up by social workers, of how a poor family *should* spend its money. But the poor are much less provident—installment debts take up a lot of their cash, and only a statistician could expect an actual live woman, however poor, to buy new clothes at intervals of five or ten years. Also, one suspects that a lot more movies are seen and ice cream cones and bottles of beer are consumed than in the Spartan ideal. But these necessary luxuries are had only at the cost of displacing other items—necessary necessities, so to speak—in the B.L.S. budget.

The Conference on Economic Progress's "Poverty and Deprivation" deals not only with the poor but also with another large section of the "underprivileged," which is an American euphemism almost as good as "senior citizen"; namely, the 37,000,000 persons whose family income is between $4,000 and $5,999 and the 2,000,000 singles who have from $2,000 to $2,999. The authors define "deprivation" as "above poverty but short of minimum requirements for a modestly comfortable level of living." They claim that 77,000,000 Americans, or *almost half the population,* live in poverty or deprivation. One recalls the furor Roosevelt aroused with his "one-third of a nation—ill-housed, ill-clad, ill-nourished." But the political climate was different then.

The distinction between a family income of $3,500 ("poverty") and $4,500 ("deprivation") is not vivid to those who run things—the 31 per cent whose incomes are between $7,500 and $14,999 and the 7 per cent of the topmost top dogs, who get $15,000 or more. These two minorities, sizable enough to feel they *are* the nation, have been as unaware of the continued existence of mass poverty as this reviewer was until he read Mr. Harrington's book. They are businessmen, congressmen, judges, government officials, politicians, lawyers, doctors, engineers, scientists, editors, journalists, and administrators in colleges, churches, and foundations. Since their education, income, and social status are superior, they, if anybody, might be expected to accept responsibility for what the Constitution calls "the general welfare." They have not done so in the case of the poor. And they have a good excuse. It is becoming harder and harder simply to *see* the one-fourth of our fellow-citizens who live below the poverty line.

> The poor are increasingly slipping out of the very experience and consciousness of the nation [Mr. Harrington writes]. If the middle class never did like ugliness and poverty, it was at least aware of them. "Across the tracks" was not a very long way to go. . . . Now the American city has been transformed. The poor still inhabit the miserable housing in the central area, but they are increasingly isolated from contact with, or sight of, anybody else. . . . Living out in the suburbs, it is easy to assume that ours is, indeed, an affluent society. . . .
>
> Clothes make the poor invisible too: America has the best-dressed poverty the world has ever known. . . . It is much easier in the United States to be decently dressed than it is to be decently housed, fed, or doctored. . . .
>
> Many of the poor are the wrong age to be seen. A good number of them are sixty-five years of age or better; an even larger number are under eighteen. . . .
>
> And finally, the poor are politically invisible. . . . They are without lobbies of their own; they put forward no legislative program. As a group, they are atomized. They have no face; they have no voice. . . . Only the social agencies have a really direct involvement with the other America, and they are without any great political power. . . .
>
> Forty to fifty million people are becoming increasingly invisible.

The invisible people fall mostly into the following categories, some of them overlapping: poor farmers, who operate 40 per cent of the farms and get 7 per cent of the farm cash income; migratory farm workers; unskilled, unorganized workers in offices, hotels, restaurants, hospitals, laundries, and other service jobs; inhabitants of areas where poverty is either endemic ("peculiar to a people or district"), as in the rural South, or epidemic ("prevalent among a community at a special time and produced by some special causes"), as in West Virginia, where the special cause was the closing of coal mines and steel plants; Negroes and Puerto Ricans, who are a fourth of the total poor; the alcoholic derelicts in the big-city skid rows; the hillbillies from Kentucky, Tennessee, and Oklahoma who have migrated to Midwestern cities in search of better jobs. And, finally, almost half our "senior citizens."

The only pages in "Poverty and Deprivation" that can be read are the statistical tables. The rest is a jungle of inchoate data that seems deliberately to eschew, like other collective research projects, such human qualities as reason (the reader has to do most of the work of ordering the material) and feeling (if Mr. Harrington sometimes has too much, it is a venial sin compared to the bleakness of this prose). My hypothesis is that "Poverty and Deprivation" was composed on that TX-o "electronic brain" at M.I.T. This would account both for the vitality of the tables and for the deadness of the text.

And what shall one say about the University of Michigan's "Income and Welfare in the United States"? Even its *tables* are not readable. And its text makes "Poverty and Deprivation" look like the Federalist Papers. On the first page, the authors unloose a generalization of stupefying generality: "The United States has arrived at the point where poverty could be abolished easily and simply by a stroke of the pen. [Where have we heard *that* before?] To raise every individual and family in the nation now below a subsistence income to the subsistence level would cost about

$10 billion a year. This is less than 2 per cent of the gross national product. It is less than 10 per cent of tax revenues. [They mean, but forgot to say so, *federal* taxes, since if state and local taxes were added, the total would be much higher than $100 billion.] It is about one-fifth of the cost of national defense." (They might have added that it is slightly more than three times the $3 billion Americans spend on their dogs and cats and canaries every year.) This got big headlines in the press, as must have been expected: "'STROKE OF PEN' COULD ELIMINATE POVERTY IN U.S., 4 SCIENTISTS SAY." But the authors, having dropped the $10 billion figure on the first page, never explain its meaning—is it a seedbed operation or a permanent dole? They are not clear even on how they arrived at it. At their own estimate of 35,000,000 poor, $10 billion would work out to slightly less than $300 per person. This seems too little to abolish poverty "easily and simply by a stroke of the pen."

There are other vaguenesses: "A careful analysis of the characteristics of families whose incomes are inadequate reveals that they should earn considerably more than they do on the basis of their education and other characteristics. The multivariate analysis . . . indicates that heads of poor families should average $2,204 in earnings. In fact heads of poor families earned an average of only $932 in 1959." I have already confessed my inability to understand the multivariate analysis, but the compilers seem to be saying that according to the variables in their study (race, age, sex, education, physical disabilities, and locale), heads of poor families should now be making twice as much as they are. And why don't they? "The discrepancy may arise from psychological dependency, lack of motivation, lack of intelligence, and a variety of other factors that were not studied." One wonders why they were not studied—and what those "other factors" were, exactly. Also, whether such a discrepancy—the earnings the researchers expected to find were actually less than half those they *did* find—may not indicate some ghastly flaw in that "multivariate analysis." There is, of course, no suggestion in the book that Dr. Morgan and his team are in any way worried.

The most obvious citizens of the Other America are those whose skins are the wrong color. The folk slogans are realistic: "Last to be hired, first to be fired" and "If you're black, stay back." There has been some progress. In 1939, the non-white worker's wage averaged 41.4 per cent of the white worker's; by 1958 it had climbed to 58 per cent. A famous victory, but the non-whites still average only slightly more than half as much as the whites. Even this modest gain was due not to any Rooseveltian or Trumanian social reform but merely to the fact that for some years there was a war on and workers were in demand, whether black, white, or violet. By 1947, the non-whites had achieved most of their advance—to 54 per cent of white earnings, which means they have gained, in the last fifteen years, just 4 per cent.

The least obvious poverty affects our "senior citizens"—those over sixty-five. Mr. Harrington estimates that half of them—8,000,000—live in poverty, and he thinks they are even more atomized and politically helpless than the rest of the Other America. He estimates that one-fourth of the "unrelated individuals" among them, or a million persons, have less than $580 a year, which is about what is allotted *for food alone* in the Department of Agriculture's minimum-subsistence budget. (The average American family now spends only 20 per cent of its income for food—an indication of the remarkable prosperity we are all enjoying, except for one-quarter of us.) One can imagine, or perhaps one can't, what it would be like to live on $580 a year, or $11 a week. It is only fair to note that most of our senior citizens do better:

The average per-capita income of those over sixty-five is now estimated to be slightly over $20 a week. That is, about $1,000 a year.

The aged poor have two sources of income besides their earnings or savings. One is contributions by relatives. A 1961 White House Conference Report put this at 10 per cent of income, which works out to $8 a week for an income of $4,000—and the 8,000,000 aged poor all have less than that. The other is Social Security, whose benefits in 1959 averaged $18 a week. Even this modest sum is more than any of the under-$4,000 got, since payments are proportionate to earnings and the poor, of course, earned less than the rest. A quarter of them, and those in general the neediest, are not covered by Social Security. The last resort is relief, and Mr. Harrington describes most vividly the humiliations the poor often have to put up with to get that.

The problem of the aged poor is aggravated by the fact that, unlike the Italians or the English, we seem to have little respect for or interest in our "senior citizens," beyond giving them that honorific title, and we don't include them in family life. If we can afford it, we are likely to send them to nursing homes—"a storage-bin philosophy," a Senate report calls it—and if we can't, which is the case with the poor, they must make do with the resources noted above. The Michigan study has a depressing chapter on "The Economics of Living with Relatives." Nearly two-thirds of the heads of families queried were opposed to having their aged parents live with their children. "The old do not understand the young, and the young do not understand the old or the young," observed one respondent, who must have had a sense of humor. Other replies were "Old people are pretty hard to get along with" and "The parents and the children try to boss each other and when they live with you there's always fighting." The minority in favor gave practical reasons, like "It's a good thing to have them with you so you can see after them" and "The old folks might get a pension or something, so they could help you out." Hardly anyone expressed any particular respect for the old, or a feeling that their experience might enrich family life. The most depressing finding was "People most able to provide support for relatives are most opposed to it. Older people with some college education are eleven to one against it." The most favorable toward including older people in the home were Negroes, and even they were mostly against it.

The whole problem of poverty and the aged is especially serious today because Americans are living longer. In the first half of this century, life expectancy increased 17.6 years for men and 20.3 years for women. And between 1950 and 1960 the over-sixty-five group increased twice as fast as the population as a whole.

The worst part of being old and poor in this country is the loneliness. Mr. Harrington notes that we have not only racial ghettos but geriatric ones, in the cheap rooming-house districts of large cities. He gives one peculiarly disturbing statistic: "One-third of the aged in the United States, some 5,000,000 or more human beings, have no phone in their place of residence. They are literally cut off from the rest of America."

Ernest Hemingway's celebrated deflation of Scott Fitzgerald's romantic notion that the rich are "different" somehow—"Yes, they have money"—doesn't apply to the poor. They are different in more important ways than their lack of money, as Mr. Harrington demonstrates:

> Emotional upset is one of the main forms of the vicious circle of impoverishment. The structure of the society is hostile to these people. The poor tend to

become pessimistic and depressed; they seek immediate gratification instead of saving; they act out.

Once this mood, this unarticulated philosophy becomes a fact, society can change, the recession can end, and yet there is no motive for movement. The depression has become internalized. The middle class looks upon this process and sees "lazy" people who "just don't want to get ahead." People who are much too sensitive to demand of cripples that they run races ask of the poor that they get up and act just like everyone else in the society.

The poor are not like everyone else. . . . They think and feel differently; they look upon a different America than the middle class looks upon.

The poor are also different in a physical sense: they are much less healthy. According to "Poverty and Deprivation," the proportion of those "disabled or limited in their major activity by chronic ill health" rises sharply as income sinks. In reasonably well-off families ($7,000 and up), 4.3 per cent are so disabled; in reasonably poor families ($2,000 to $3,999), the proportion doubles, to 8 per cent; and in unreasonably poor families (under $2,000), it doubles again, to 16.5 per cent. An obvious cause, among others, for the very poor being four times as much disabled by "chronic ill health" as the well-to-do is that they have much less money to spend for medical care—in fact, almost nothing. This weighs with special heaviness on the aged poor. During the fifties, Mr. Harrington notes, "all costs on the Consumer Price Index went up by 12 per cent. But medical costs, that terrible staple of the aged, went up by 36 per cent, hospitalization rose by 65 per cent, and group hospitalization costs (Blue Cross premiums) were up by 83 per cent."

This last figure is particularly interesting, since Blue Cross and such plans are the A.M.A.'s alternative to socialized medicine, or, rather, to the timid fumblings toward it that even our most liberal politicians have dared to propose. Such figures throw an unpleasant light on the Senate's rejection of Medicare. The defeat was all the more bitter because, in the usual effort to appease the conservatives (with the usual lack of success—only five Republicans and only four Southern Democrats voted pro), the bill was watered down in advance. Not until he had spent $90 of his own money —which is 10 per cent of the annual income of some 3,000,000 aged poor—would a patient have been eligible. And the original program included only people already covered by Social Security or Railroad Retirement pensions and excluded the neediest of all—the 2,500,000 aged poor who are left out of both these systems. These untouchables were finally included in order to placate five liberal Republican senators, led by Javits of New York. They did vote for Medicare, but they were the only Republicans who did.

Mental as well as physical illness is much greater among the poor, even though our complacent cliché is that nervous breakdowns are a prerogative of the rich because the poor "can't afford" them. (They can't, but they have them anyway.) This bit of middle-class folklore should be laid to rest by a study made in New Haven: "Social Class and Mental Illness," by August B. Hollingshead and Frederick C. Redlich (Wiley). They found that the rate of "treated psychiatric illness" is about the same from the rich down through decently paid workers—an average of 573 per 100,000. But in the bottom fifth it shoots up to 1,659 per 100,000. There is an even more striking difference in the *kind* of mental illness. Of those in the four top income groups who had undergone psychiatric treatment, 65 per cent had been treated for neurotic problems and 35 per cent for psychotic disturbances. In the bottom fifth, the treated illnesses were almost all psychotic (90 per cent). This shows there is something to the notion that the poor "can't afford" nervous breakdowns—the milder kind, that is—since the reason the proportion of *treated* neuroses among the poor is only 10 per cent is that a neurotic can keep going, after a fashion. But the argument cuts deeper the other way. The poor go to a psychiatrist (or, more commonly, are committed to a mental institution) only when they are completely unable to function because of psychotic symptoms. Therefore, even that nearly threefold increase in mental disorders among the poor is probably an underestimate.

The poor are different, then, both physically and psychologically. During the fifties, a team of psychiatrists from Cornell studied "Midtown," a residential area in this city that contained 170,000 people, of all social classes. The area was 99 per cent white, so the findings may be presumed to understate the problem of poverty. The description of the poor—the "low social economic status individual"—is blunt: "[They are] rigid, suspicious, and have a fatalistic outlook on life. They do not plan ahead. . . . They are prone to depression, have feelings of futility, lack of belongingness, friendliness, and a lack of trust in others." Only a Dr. Pangloss would expect anything else. As Mr. Harrington points out, such characteristics are "a realistic adaptation to a socially perverse situation."

As for the isolation that is the lot of the American poor, that is a point on which Mr. Harrington is very good:

> America has a self-image of itself as a nation of joiners and doers. There are social clubs, charities, community drives, and the like. [One might add organizations like the Elks and Masons, Rotary and Kiwanis, cultural groups like our women's clubs, also alumni associations and professional organizations.] And yet this entire structure is a phenomenon of the middle class. Some time ago, a study in Franklin, Indiana [this vagueness of reference is all too typical of "The Other America"], reported that the percentage of people in the bottom class who were without affiliations of any kind was eight times as great as the percentage in the high-income class.
>
> Paradoxically, one of the factors that intensifies the social isolation of the poor is that America thinks of itself as a nation without social classes. As a result, there are few social or civic organizations that are separated on the basis of income and class. The "working-class culture" that sociologists have described in a country like England does not exist here. . . . The poor person who might want to join an organization is afraid. Because he or she will have less education, less money, less competence to articulate ideas than anyone else in the group, they stay away.

One reason our society is a comparatively violent one is that the French and Italian and British poor have a communal life and culture that the American poor lack. As one reads "The Other America," one wonders why there is not even more violence than there is.

The richest city of all, New York, has been steadily growing poorer, if one looks beyond Park Avenue and Wall Street. Of its 2,080,000 families, just under half (49 per cent) had incomes in 1959 of less than $6,000; for the city's non-white families, the percentage was 71. And a fourth of all New York families in 1959 were below the poverty line of $4,000. These percentages are at present slightly higher than the national average—an ominous reversal of the city's earlier position. In 1932, the average national weekly wage was only 67 per cent of the New York City average.

In 1960, it was 108 per cent. The city's manufacturing workers in 1946 earned $11 more a week than the national average; in 1960 they earned $6.55 a week less. The two chief reasons are probably the postwar influx of Puerto Ricans and the exodus to the suburbs of the well-to-do. But whatever the reasons, the city seems to be turning into an economically backward area, like Arkansas or New Hampshire. Even the bankers—the "non-supervisory" ones, that is—are modestly paid: 54 per cent of the males and 78 per cent of the females make less than $80 a week. All these statistics come from John O'Rourke, president of Joint Council 16, International Brotherhood of Teamsters, which has 168,000 members in the area. Mr. O'Rourke has been campaigning to persuade Mayor Wagner to raise the city's minimum hourly wage to $1.50. (The Mayor has gone as far as $1.25.) The New York teamsters are motivated by enlightened self-interest: the more other wages stagnate, the harder it will be to maintain their own comparatively high level of pay. They complain especially about the low wages in the highly organized garment trade, to which Mr. Dubinsky's International Ladies' Garment Workers' Union replies that if it presses for higher wages the manufacturers will simply move to low-wage, non-union areas, mostly in the South, as the New England textile manufacturers did many years ago—a riposte that is as realistic as it is uncheering. However, Mr. O'Rourke has an enterprising research staff, plenty of persistence, and a sharp tongue. "New Yorkers," he says, "are accustomed to thinking of themselves as pacesetters in an allegedly affluent society [but] at the rate we are going, we will soon qualify for the title 'Sweatshop Capital of the Nation.'"

The main reason the American poor have become invisible is that since 1936 their numbers have been reduced by two-thirds. Astounding as it may seem, the fact is that President Roosevelt's "one-third of a nation" was a considerable understatement; over two-thirds of us then lived below the poverty line, as is shown by the tables that follow. But today the poor are a minority, and minorities can be ignored if they are so heterogeneous that they cannot be organized. When the poor were a majority, they simply could not be overlooked. Poverty is also hard to see today because the middle class ($6,000 to $14,999) has vastly increased—from 13 per cent of all families in 1936 to a near-majority (47 per cent) today. That mass poverty can persist despite this rise to affluence is hard to believe, or see, especially if one is among those who have risen.

Two tables in "Poverty and Deprivation" summarize what has been happening in the last thirty years. They cover only multiple-person families; all figures are converted to 1960 dollars; and the income is before taxes. I have omitted, for clarity, all fractions.

The first table is the percentage of families with a given income:

	1935–36	1947	1953	1960
Under $ 4,000	68%	37%	28%	23%
$4,000 to $ 5,999	17	29	28	23
$6,000 to $ 7,499	6	12	17	16
$7,500 to $14,999	7	17	23	31
Over $15,000	2	4	5	7

The second table is the share each group had in the family income of the nation:

	1935–36	1947	1953	1960
Under $ 4,000	35%	16%	11%	7%
$4,000 to $ 5,999	21	24	21	15
$6,000 to $ 7,499	10	14	17	14
$7,500 to $14,999	16	28	33	40
Over $15,000	18	18	19	24

Several interesting conclusions can be drawn from these tables:

(1) The New Deal didn't do anything about poverty: The under-$4,000 families in 1936 were 68 per cent of the total population, which was slightly *more* than the 1929 figure of 65 per cent.

(2) The war economy (hot and cold) did do something about poverty: Between 1936 and 1960 the proportion of all families who were poor was reduced from 68 per cent to 23 per cent.

(3) If the percentage of under-$4,000 families decreased by two-thirds between 1936 and 1960, their share of the national income dropped a great deal more—from 35 per cent to 7 per cent.

(4) The well-to-do ($7,500 to $14,999) have enormously increased, from 7 per cent of all families in 1936 to 31 per cent today. The rich ($15,000 and over) have also multiplied—from 2 to 7 per cent. But it should be noted that the very rich, according to another new study, "The Share of Top Wealth-Holders in National Wealth, 1922–1956," by Robert J. Lampman (Princeton), have experienced a decline. He finds that the top 1 per cent of wealth-holders owned 38 per cent of the national wealth in 1929 and own only 28 per cent today. (Though let's not get sentimental over that "only.") Thus, *pace* Dr. Kolko, there has in fact been a redistribution of wealth—in favor of the well-to-do and the rich at the expense of the poor and the very rich.

(5) The reduction of poverty has slowed down. In the six years 1947–53, the number of poor families declined 9 per cent, but in the following seven years only 5 per cent. The economic stasis that set in with Eisenhower and that still persists under Kennedy was responsible. (This stagnation, however, did not affect the over-$7,500 families, who increased from 28 per cent to 38 per cent between 1953 and 1960.) In the New York *Times Magazine* for last November 11th, Herman P. Miller, of the Bureau of the Census, wrote, "During the forties, the lower-paid occupations made the greatest relative gains in average income. Laborers and service workers . . . had increases of about 180% . . . and professional and managerial workers, the highest paid workers of all, had the lowest relative gains—96%." But in the last decade the trend has been reversed; laborers and service workers have gained 39% while professional-managerial workers have gained 68%. This is because in the wartime forties the unskilled were in great demand, while now they are being replaced by machines. Automation is today the same kind of menace to the unskilled —that is, the poor—that the enclosure movement was to the British agricultural population centuries ago. "The facts show that our 'social revolution' ended nearly twenty years ago," Mr. Miller concludes, "yet important segments of the American public, many of them highly placed Government officials and prominent educators, think and act as though it were a continuing process."

"A reduction of about 19% [in the under-$6,000 families] in more than thirty years, or at a rate of about 0.7% per year, is no ground for complacency," the authors of "Poverty and Deprivation" justly observe. There is even less ground for complacency in the recent figures on *extreme* poverty. The authors estimate the number of families in 1929 with incomes of under $2,000 (in current dollars) at 7,500,000. By 1947 there were less than 4,000,000, not because of any philanthropic effort by their more prosperous fellow-citizens but entirely because of those first glorious years of a war economy. Six years later, in 1953, when the economy had begun to slow down, there were still 3,300,000 of these families with incomes of less than $2,000, and seven years later, in 1960, "there had been no further reduction." Thus in the last fifteen years the bottom dogs have remained on the bottom, sharing hardly at all in the advances that the income groups above them have made in an ascending scale that is exquisitely adjusted, by the automatic workings of capitalism, so that it is inversely proportionate to need.

There are, finally, the bottomest bottom dogs; i.e., *families* with incomes of *under $1,000*. I apologize for the italics, but some facts insist on them. According to "Poverty and Deprivation," the numbers of these families "appear to have risen slightly" of late (1953–60), from 800,000 to about 1,000,000. It is only fair, and patriotic, to add that according to the Commerce Department study, about 10,000,000 of our families and unattached individuals now enjoy incomes of $10,000 a year and up. So while some 3,500,000 Americans are in under-$1,000 families, ten times as many are in over-$10,000 families. Not bad at all—in a way.

The post-1940 decrease in poverty was not due to the policies or actions of those who are not poor, those in positions of power and responsibility. The war economy needed workers, wages went up, and the poor became less poor. When economic stasis set in, the rate of decrease in poverty slowed down proportionately, and it is still slow. Kennedy's efforts to "get the country moving again" have been unsuccessful, possibly because he has, despite the suggestions of many of his economic advisers, not yet advocated the one big step that might push the economy off dead center: a massive increase in government spending. This would be politically courageous, perhaps even dangerous, because of the superstitious fear of "deficit spending" and an "unbalanced" federal budget. American folklore insists that a government's budget must be arranged like a private family's. Walter Lippmann wrote, after the collapse of the stock market last spring:

> There is mounting evidence that those economists were right who told the Administration last winter that it was making the mistake of trying to balance the budget too soon. It will be said that the budget is not balanced: it shows a deficit in fiscal 1962 of $7 billion. . . . But . . . the budget that matters is the Department of Commerce's income and product accounts budget. Nobody looks at it except the economists [but] while the Administrative budget is necessary for administration and is like a man's checkbook, the income budget tells the real story. . . .
>
> [It] shows that at the end of 1962 the outgo and ingo accounts will be virtually in balance, with a deficit of only about half a billion dollars. Thus, in reality, the Kennedy administration is no longer stimulating the economy, and the economy is stagnating for lack of stimulation. We have one of the lowest rates of growth among the advanced industrial nations of the world.

One shouldn't be hard on the President. Franklin Roosevelt, a more daring and experimental politician, at least in his domestic policy, listened to the American disciples of J. M. Keynes in the early New Deal years and unbalanced his budgets, with splendid results. But by 1936 he had lost his nerve. He cut back government spending and there ensued the 1937 recession, from which the economy recovered only when war orders began to make up for the deficiency in domestic buying power. "Poverty and Deprivation" estimates that between 1953 and 1961 the annual growth rate of our economy was "only 2.5 per cent per annum contrasted with an estimated 4.2 per cent required to maintain utilization of manpower and other productive resources." The poor, who always experience the worst the first, understand quite personally the meaning of that dry statistic, as they understand Kipling's "The toad beneath the harrow knows / Exactly where each toothpoint goes." They are also most intimately acquainted with another set of statistics: the steady postwar rise in the unemployment rate, from 3.1 per cent in 1949 to 4.3 per cent in 1954 to 5.1 per cent in 1958 to over 7 per cent in 1961. (The Tory Government is worried because British unemployment is now at its highest point for the last three years. This point is 2.1 per cent, which is less than our lowest rate in the last fifteen years.)

Some of the post-1940 gains of the poor have been their own doing. "Moonlighting"—or holding two or more jobs at once—was practiced by about 3 per cent of the employed in 1950; today this percentage has almost doubled. Far more important is what might be called "wife-flitting": Between 1940 and 1957, the percentage of wives with jobs outside the home doubled, from 15 per cent to 30 per cent. The head of the United States Children's Bureau, Mrs. Katherine B. Oettinger, announced last summer, not at all triumphantly, that there are now two-thirds more working mothers than there were ten years ago and that these mothers have about 15,000,000 children under eighteen—of whom 4,000,000 are under six. This kind of economic enterprise ought to impress Senator Goldwater and the ideologues of the *National Review*, whose reaction to the poor, when they think about such an uninspiring subject, is "Why don't they *do* something about it?" The poor have done something about it and the family pay check is bigger and the statistics on poverty look better. But the effects on family life and on those 4,000,000 pre-school children is something else. Mrs. Oettinger quoted a roadside sign, "IRONING, DAY CARE AND WORMS FOR FISHING BAIT," and mentioned a baby-sitter who pacified her charge with sleeping pills and another who met the problem of a cold apartment by putting the baby in the oven. "The situation has become a 'national disgrace,' with many unfortunate conditions that do not come to public attention until a crisis arises," the *Times* summed up her conclusion. This crisis has finally penetrated to public attention. The President recently signed a law that might be called Day-care. It provides $5,000,000 for such facilities this fiscal year, which works out to $1.25 for each of the 4,000,000 under-six children with working mothers. Next year, the program will provide all of $2.50 per child. This is a free, democratic society's notion of an adequate response. Almost a century ago, Bismarck instituted in Germany state-financed social benefits far beyond anything we have yet ventured. Granted that he did it merely to take the play way from the Social Democratic Party founded by Marx and Engels. Still, one imagines that Count Bismarck must be amused—in the circle of Hell reserved for reactionaries—by that $2.50 a child.

It's not that Public Opinion doesn't become Aroused every now and then. But the arousement never leads to much. It was aroused twenty-four years ago when John Steinbeck published "The Grapes of Wrath," but Mr. Harrington reports that things in the Imperial Valley are still much the same: low wages, bad housing, no effective union. Public Opinion is too public—that is, too general; of its very nature, it can have no sustained interest in California agriculture. The only groups with such a continuing interest are the workers and the farmers who hire them. Once Public Opinion ceased to be Aroused, the battle was again between the two antagonists with a real, personal stake in the outcome, and there was no question about which was stronger. So with the rural poor in general. In the late fifties, the average annual wage for white male American farm workers was slightly over $1,000; women, children, Negroes, and Mexicans got less. One recalls Edward R. Murrow's celebrated television program about these people, "Harvest of Shame." Once more everybody was shocked, but the harvest is still shameful. One also recalls that Mr. Murrow, after President Kennedy had appointed him head of the United States Information Agency, tried to persuade the B.B.C. not to show "Harvest of Shame." His argument was that it would give an undesirable "image" of America to foreign audiences.

There is a monotony about the injustices suffered by the poor that perhaps accounts for the lack of interest the rest of society shows in them. Everything seems to go wrong with them. They never win. It's just boring.

Public housing turns out not to be for them. The 1949 Housing Act authorized 810,000 new units of low-cost housing in the following four years. Twelve years later, in 1961, the A.F.L.-C.I.O. proposed 400,000 units to complete the lagging 1949 program. The Kennedy administration ventured to recommend 100,000 to Congress. Thus, instead of 810,000 low-cost units by 1953, the poor will get, if they are lucky, 500,000 by 1963. And they are more likely to be injured than helped by slum clearance, since the new projects usually have higher rents than the displaced slum-dwellers can afford. (There has been no dearth of government-financed *middle-income* housing since 1949.) These refugees from the bulldozers for the most part simply emigrate to other slums. They also become invisible; Mr. Harrington notes that half of them are recorded as "address unknown." Several years ago, Charles Abrams, who was New York State Rent Administrator under Harriman and who is now president of the National Committee Against Discrimination in Housing, summed up what he had learned in two decades in public housing: "Once social reforms have won tonal appeal in the public mind, their slogans and goal-symbols may degenerate into tools of the dominant class for beleaguering the minority and often for defeating the very aims which the original sponsors had intended for their reforms." Mr. Abrams was probably thinking, in part, of the Title I adventures of Robert Moses in dealing with New York housing. There is a Moses or two in every American city, determined to lead us away from the promised land.

And this is not the end of tribulation. The poor, who can least afford to lose pay because of ill health, lose the most. A National Health Survey, made a few years ago, found that workers earning under $2,000 a year had twice as many "restricted-activity days" as those earning over $4,000.

The poor are even fatter than the rich. (The cartoonists will have to revise their clichés.) "Obesity is seven times more frequent among women of the lowest socio-economic level than it is among those of the highest level," state Drs. Moore, Stunkard, and Srole in a recent issue of the *Journal of the American Medical Association*. (The proportion is almost the same for men.) They also found that overweight associated with poverty is related to mental disease. Fatness used to be a sign of wealth, as it still is in some parts of Africa, but in more advanced societies it is now a stigma of poverty, since it means too many cheap carbohydrates and too little exercise—which has changed from a necessity for the poor into a luxury for the rich, as may be confirmed by a glance at the models in any fashion magazine.

Although they are the most in need of hospital insurance, the poor have the least, since they can't afford the premiums; only 40 per cent of poor families have it, as against 63 per cent of all families. (It should be noted, however, that the poor who are war veterans can get free treatment, at government expense, in Veterans Administration Hospitals.)

The poor actually pay more taxes, in proportion to their income, than the rich. A recent study by the Tax Foundation estimates that 28 per cent of incomes under $2,000 goes for taxes, as against 24 per cent of the incomes of families earning five to seven times as much. Sales and other excise taxes are largely responsible for this curious statistic. It is true that such taxes fall impartially on all, like the blessed rain from heaven, but it is a form of egalitarianism that perhaps only Senator Goldwater can fully appreciate.

The final irony is that the Welfare State, which Roosevelt erected and which Eisenhower, no matter how strongly he felt about it, didn't attempt to pull down, is not for the poor, either. Agricultural workers are not covered by Social Security, nor are many of the desperately poor among the aged, such as "unrelated individuals" with incomes of less than $1,000, of whom only 37 per cent are covered, which is just half the percentage of coverage among the aged in general. Of the Welfare State, Mr. Harrington says, "Its creation had been stimulated by mass impoverishment and misery, yet it helped the poor least of all. Laws like unemployment compensation, the Wagner Act, the various farm programs, all these were designed for the middle third in the cities, for the organized workers, and for the . . . big market farmers. . . . [It] benefits those least who need help most." The industrial workers, led by John L. Lewis, mobilized enough political force to put through Section 7(a) of the National Industrial Recovery Act, which, with the Wagner Act, made the C.I.O. possible. The big farmers put enough pressure on Henry Wallace, Roosevelt's first Secretary of Agriculture—who talked a good fight for liberal principles but was a Hamlet when it came to action—to establish the two basic propositions of Welfare State agriculture: subsidies that now cost $3 billion a year and that chiefly benefit the big farmers; and the exclusion of sharecroppers, tenant farmers, and migratory workers from the protection of minimum-wage and Social Security laws.

No doubt the Kennedy administration would like to do more for the poor than it has, but it is hampered by the cabal of Republicans and Southern Democrats in Congress. The 1961 revision of the Fair Labor Standards Act, which raised the national minimum wage to the not exorbitant figure of $1.15 an hour, was a slight improvement over the previous act. For instance, it increased coverage of retail-trade workers from 3 per cent to 33 per cent. (But one-fourth of the retail workers still excluded earn less than $1 an hour.) There was also a considerable amount of shadowboxing involved: Of the 3,600,000 workers newly covered, only 663,000 were making less than $1 an hour. And there was the exclusion of a particularly ill-paid group of workers. Nobody had anything against the laundry workers *personally*. It was just that they were weak, unorganized, and politically expendable. To appease the conservatives in Congress, whose votes were needed to get the revision through, they were therefore expended. The result is that of the 500,000 workers in the laundry, dry-cleaning, and dyeing industries, just 17,000 are now protected by the Fair Labor Standards Act.

In short, one reaches the unstartling conclusion that rewards in class societies, including Communist ones, are according to power rather than need. A recent illustration is the campaign of an obscure organization called Veterans of World War I of the U.S.A. to get a bill through Congress for pensions of about $25 a week. It was formed by older men who think other veterans' organizations (such as the American Legion, which claims 2,500,000 members to their 200,000) are dominated by the relatively young. It asks for pensions for veterans of the First World War with incomes of under $2,400 (if single) or $3,600 (if married)—that is, only for *poor* veterans. The editorials have been violent: "STOP THIS VETERANS' GRAB," implored the *Herald Tribune;* "WORLD WAR I PENSION GRAB," echoed the *Saturday Evening Post.* Their objection was, in part, that many of the beneficiaries would not be bonafide poor, since pensions, annuities, and Social Security benefits were excluded from the maximum income needed to qualify. Considering that the average Social Security payment is about $1,000 a year, this would not put any potential beneficiary into the rich or even the comfortably-off class, even if one assumes another $1,000, which is surely too high, from annuities and pensions. It's all very confusing. The one clear aspect is that the minuscule Veterans of World War I of the U.S.A. came very near to bringing it off. Although their bill was opposed by both the White House and by the chairman of the House Committee on Veterans' Affairs, two hundred and one members of the House signed a petition to bring the measure to a vote, only eighteen less than needed "to accomplish this unusual parliamentary strategy," as the *Times* put it. These congressmen were motivated by politics rather than charity, one may assume. Many were up for reëlection last November, and the two hundred thousand Veterans of World War I had two advantages over the fifty million poor: They were organized, and they had a patriotic appeal only a wink away from the demagogic. Their "unusual parliamentary strategy" failed by eighteen votes in the Congress. But there will be another Congress.

It seems likely that mass poverty will continue in this country for a long time. The more it is reduced, the harder it is to keep on reducing it. The poor, having dwindled from two-thirds of the population in 1936 to one-quarter today, no longer are a significant political force, as is shown by the Senate's rejection of Medicare and by the Democrats' dropping it as an issue in the elections last year. Also, as poverty decreases, those left behind tend more and more to be the ones who have for so long accepted poverty as their destiny that they need outside help to climb out of it. This new minority mass poverty, so much more isolated and hopeless than the old majority poverty, shows signs of becoming chronic. "The permanence of low incomes is inferred from a variety of findings," write the authors of the Michigan survey. "In many poor families the head has never earned enough to cover the family's present needs." They give a vignette of what the statistics mean in human terms:

> For most families, however, the problem of chronic poverty is serious. One such family is headed by a thirty-two-year-old man who is employed as a dishwasher. Though he works steadily and more than full time, he earned slightly over $2,000 in 1959. His wife earned $300 more, but their combined incomes are not enough to support themselves and their three children. Although the head of the family is only thirty-two, he feels that he has no chance of advancement partly

because he finished only seven grades of school. . . . The possibility of such families leaving the ranks of the poor is not high.

Children born into poor families today have less chance of "improving themselves" than the children of the pre-1940 poor. Rags to riches is now more likely to be rags to rags. "Indeed," the Michigan surveyors conclude, "it appears that a number of the heads of poor families have moved into less skilled jobs than their fathers had." Over a third of the children of the poor, according to the survey, don't go beyond the eighth grade and "will probably perpetuate the poverty of their parents." There are a great many of these children. In an important study of poverty, made for a Congressional committee in 1959, Dr. Robert J. Lampman estimated that eleven million of the poor were under eighteen. "A considerable number of younger persons are starting life in a condition of 'inherited poverty,'" he observed. To which Mr. Harrington adds, "The character of poverty has changed, and it has become more deadly for the young. It is no longer associated with immigrant groups with high aspirations; it is now identified with those whose social existence makes it more and more difficult to break out into the larger society." Even when children from poor families show intellectual promise, there is nothing in the values of their friends or families to encourage them to make use of it. Dr. Kolko, citing impressive sources, states that of the top 16 per cent of high-school students—those scoring 120 and over in I.Q. tests—only half go on to college. The explanation for this amazing—and alarming—situation is as much cultural as economic. The children of the poor now tend to lack what the sociologists call "motivation." At least one foundation is working on the problem of why so many bright children from poor families don't ever try to go beyond high school.

Mr. Raymond M. Hilliard, at present director of the Cook County (i.e., Chicago) Department of Public Aid and formerly Commissioner of Welfare for New York City, recently directed a "representative-sample" investigation, which showed that more than half of the 225,000 able-bodied Cook County residents who were on relief were "functionally illiterate." One reason Cook County has to spend $16,500,000 a month on relief is "the lack of basic educational skills of relief recipients which are essential to compete in our modern society." An interesting footnote, apropos of recent happenings at "Ole Miss," is that the illiteracy rate of the relief recipients who were educated in Chicago is 33 per cent, while among those who were educated in Mississippi and later moved to Chicago it is 77 per cent.

The problem of educating the poor has changed since 1900. Then it was the language and cultural difficulties of immigrants from foreign countries; now it is the subtler but more intractable problems of internal migration from backward regions, mostly in the South. The old immigrants wanted to Better Themselves and to Get Ahead. The new migrants are less ambitious, and they come into a less ambitious atmosphere. "When they arrive in the city," wrote Christopher Jencks in an excellent two-part survey, "Slums and Schools," in the New Republic last fall, "they join others equally unprepared for urban life in the slums—a milieu which is in many ways utterly dissociated from the rest of America. Often this milieu is self-perpetuating. I have been unable to find any statistics on how many of these migrants' children and grandchildren have become middle-class, but it is probably not too inaccurate to estimate that about 30,000,000 people live in urban slums, and that about half are second-generation residents." The immigrants of 1890–1910 also arrived in a milieu that was "in many ways utterly dissociated from the rest of America," yet they had a vision—a rather materialistic one, but still a vision—of what life in America could be if they worked hard enough; and they did work, and they did aspire to something more than they had; and they did get out of the slums. The disturbing thing about the poor today is that so many of them seem to lack any such vision. Mr. Jencks remarks:

> While the economy is changing in a way which makes the eventual liquidation of the slums at least conceivable, young people are not seizing the opportunities this change presents. Too many are dropping out of school before graduation (more than half in many slums); too few are going to college. . . . As a result there are serious shortages of teachers, nurses, doctors, technicians, and scientifically trained executives, but 4,500,000 unemployables.

"Poverty is the parent of revolution and crime," Aristotle wrote. This is now a half truth—the last half. Our poor are alienated; they don't consider themselves part of society. But precisely because they don't they are not politically dangerous. It is people with "a stake in the country" who make revolutions. The best—though by no means the only—reason for worrying about the Other America is that its existence should make us feel uncomfortable.

The federal government is the only purposeful force—I assume wars are not purposeful—that can reduce the numbers of the poor and make their lives more bearable. The authors of "Poverty and Deprivation" take a dim view of the Kennedy administration's efforts to date:

> The Federal Budget is the most important single instrument available to us as a free people to induce satisfactory economic performance, and to reduce poverty and deprivation. . . .
> Projected Federal outlays in the fiscal 1963 Budget are too small. The items in this Budget covering programs directly related to human improvement and the reduction of mass poverty and deprivation allocate far too small a portion of our total national production to these great purposes.

The effect of government policy on poverty has two quite distinct aspects. One is the indirect effect of the stimulation of the economy by federal spending. Such stimulation—though by war-time demands rather than government policy—has in the past produced a prosperity that did cut down American poverty by almost two-thirds. But I am inclined to agree with Dr. Galbraith that it would not have a comparable effect on present-day poverty:

> It is assumed that with increasing output poverty must disappear [he writes]. Increased output eliminated the general poverty of all who worked. Accordingly it must, sooner or later, eliminate the special poverty that still remains. . . . Yet just as the arithmetic of modern politics makes it tempting to overlook the very poor, so the supposition that increasing output will remedy their case has made it easy to do so too.

He underestimates the massiveness of American poverty, but he is right when he says there is now a hard core of the specially disadvantaged—because of age, race, environment, physical or mental defects, etc.—that would not be significantly reduced by general prosperity. (Although I think the majority of our present poor *would* benefit, if only by a reduction in the present high rate of unemployment.)

To do something about this hard core, a second line of government policy would be required; namely, direct intervention to help the poor. We have had this since the New Deal, but it has always been grudging and miserly, and we have never accepted the principle that every citizen should be provided, at state expense, with a reasonable minimum standard of living regardless of any other considerations. It should not depend on earnings, as does Social Security, which continues the inequalities and inequities and so tends to keep the poor forever poor. Nor should it exclude millions of our poorest citizens because they lack the political pressure to force their way into the Welfare State. The governmental obligation to provide, out of taxes, such a minimum living standard for all who need it should be taken as much for granted as free public schools have always been in our history.

It may be objected that the economy cannot bear the cost, and certainly costs must be calculated. But the point is not the calculation but the principle. Statistics— and especially statistical forecasts—can be pushed one way or the other. Who can determine in advance to what extent the extra expense of giving our 40,000,000 poor enough income to rise above the poverty line would be offset by the lift to the economy from their increased purchasing power? We really don't know. Nor did we know what the budgetary effects would be when we established the principle of free public education. The rationale then was that all citizens should have an equal chance of competing for a better status. The rationale now is different: that every citizen has a right to become or remain part of our society because if this right is denied, as it is in the case of at least one-fourth of our citizens, it impoverishes us all. Since 1932, "the government"—local, state, and federal—has recognized a responsibility to provide its citizens with a subsistence living. Apples will never again be sold on the street by jobless accountants, it seems safe to predict, nor will any serious political leader ever again suggest that share-the-work and local charity can solve the problem of unemployment. "Nobody starves" in this country any more, but, like every social statistic, this is a tricky business. Nobody starves, but who can measure the starvation, not to be calculated by daily intake of proteins and calories, that reduces life for many of our poor to a long vestibule to death? Nobody starves, but every fourth citizen rubs along on a standard of living that is below what Mr. Harrington defines as "the minimal levels of health, housing, food, and education that our present stage of scientific knowledge specifies as necessary for life as it is now lived in the United States." Nobody starves, but a fourth of us are excluded from the common social existence. Not to be able to afford a movie or a glass of beer is a kind of starvation—if everybody else can.

The problem is obvious: the persistence of mass poverty in a prosperous country. The solution is also obvious: to provide, out of taxes, the kind of subsidies that have always been given to the public schools (not to mention the police and fire departments and the post office)—subsidies that would raise incomes above the poverty level, so that every citizen could feel he is indeed such. "Civis Romanus sum!" cried St. Paul when he was threatened with flogging—and he was not flogged. Until our poor can be proud to say "Civis Americanus sum!," until the act of justice that would make this possible has been performed by the three-quarters of Americans who are not poor—until then the shame of the Other America will continue.

Nine / Values and Beliefs

24 / The Power Within

Irvin G. Wyllie

Throughout much of their history, Americans have extolled business success. The preachers of success and the gospel of wealth argued that not everyone could achieve material wealth, but only those with certain virtues. One's social status, education, race, religion, or nationality were not the important attributes; rather industry, sobriety, perseverance, honesty, and similar virtues were the keys to material salvation. These were virtues that came from within, that made one a self-made man. Each individual had a responsibility to choose the right path and stick to it.

Irvin G. Wyllie in the following selection discusses the virtues stressed in the nineteenth-century success literature. However, not all Americans accepted these preachments of success; some questioned both the desirability of material success and the notion that one's social background played no role in determining one's fortunes. Moreover, the Horatio Alger stories emphasized that luck often made the man, and increasingly the unethical and illegal methods of business leaders cast a shadow over the gospel of wealth. To poor immigrants, poor farm boys, and the urban working classes laboring 10 to 12 hours per day, 6 to 7 days per week, success must have seemed remote and irrelevant. Yet the myth must have reached beyond the middle classes; for the working classes did achieve some mobility and clung to the dream of success, however imperfect.

For further reading: *Moses Rischin, *The American Gospel of Success* (1965); *Sigmund Diamond, *The Reputation of the American Businessman* (1955); John Cawelti, *Apostles of the Self Made Man* (1965); John Tebbel, *From Rags to Riches: Horatio Alger, Jr., and the American Dream* (1963); *David Potter, *People of Plenty* (1954).

I

He who is interested in the relation of business methods to business success will find little elucidation in the rags-to-riches literature of the nineteenth century. Most

Irvin G. Wyllie, *The Self-Made Man in America* (New Brunswick, New Jersey: Rutgers University Press, 1954), 34–53. Without footnotes.

of these self-help handbooks offer little practical advice on advertising methods, ac-counting systems, investment procedures, production techniques, and other such mundane matters. Technical considerations are quite remote from their main dis-cussion which revolves around private character and morality. What profited it a man to master all the skills of trade if he had not first mastered himself? At best, successful methods were merely by-products of successful character. The businessman who had the right personal qualities would have little difficulty in developing the necessary managerial skills, but the possession of no amount of skill could com-pensate for lack of character or other essential personal traits. So ran the argument.

In considering the inner qualities that make for success self-help theorists min-imized the importance of talents that were inherited rather than cultivated. Eco-nomic salvation, like spiritual salvation, was not reserved for men of superior physique and intellect, but could be attained by all men of good character. In respect to char-acter, presumably, all started as equals. It was not the boast of the self-made man that nature had made him stronger and more intelligent than his fellows, it was that through the cultivation of good character he had managed his own elevation. As Theodore Roosevelt remarked, in explaining success, "no brilliancy of intellect, no perfection of bodily development will count when weighed in the balance against that assemblage of virtues . . . which we group together under the name of char-acter."

To the great majority not endowed with genius the success gospel offered the comforting assurance that no high order of intelligence was required of the business-man. This assurance was heard with special frequency before 1890, in the years when opportunity seemed limitless, and there were few giant corporations to restrict chances for the average man. The genius, like the college man, was usually described as lazy, vain, impatient, and undisciplined, a man who sought a conspicuous place, a short work, and a large reward. Henry Ward Beecher, notorious for his dullness as a boy, touched on a common theme when he analyzed the genius for an audience of young men at Indianapolis in 1844. "So far as my observations have ascertained the species," he said, "they abound in academies, colleges, and Thespian societies; in village debating clubs; in coteries of young artists, and young professional aspirants. They are to be known by a reserved air, excessive sensitiveness, and utter indolence; by very long hair, and very open shirt collars; by the reading of much wretched poetry, and the writing of much, yet more wretched; by being very conceited, very affected, very disagreeable, and very useless:—beings whom no man wants for friend, pupil, or companion." Beecher did not stand alone in this estimate. In 1878 Albert Rhodes, the American consul at Rouen, France, writing in defense of the "successful mediocrity" for the International Review, asserted that geniuses were irregular in the performance of duty, imprudent in word and deed, poorly married, and worst of all, poor of purse. William Holmes McGuffey tried to explain to his youthful readers that the trouble with the genius was that he relied too much on his natural powers, and too little on the cultivated qualities that win success:

> Thus, plain, plodding people, we often shall find,
>   Will leave hasty, confident people behind:
> Like the tortoise and hare, though together they start,
>   We soon clearly see they are widely apart.

While one trusts the gifts Dame Nature bestows,
    And relying on these, calmly stops for repose,
The other holds slowly and surely his way,
    And thus wins the race, ere the close of the day.

From Ralph Waldo Emerson to Orison Marden experts on moneymaking agreed that genius was not only not required; it was not even desirable. Emerson's observations led him to believe that the right man for business was that just-average man who had an abundance of common sense. The business community itself echoed this sentiment. "There is no genius required," said James D. Mills, a New York merchant. "And if there were, some great men have said that genius is no more than common-sense intensified." Presumably the businessman needed an orderly and methodical mind, an affinity for facts, a sound memory, good judgment, and mathematical skill. Theodore Parker summarized the necessary requirements when he analyzed Amos Lawrence as a careful, methodical, diligent man, and one of very ordinary intellect. "He had no uncommon culture of the understanding or the imagination," Parker observed, "and of the higher reason still less. But in respect of the greater faculties—in respect of conscience, affection, the religious element—he was well born, well bred, eminently well disciplined by himself." Others who reflected on these matters argued that in the business world, at least, perseverance and industry could accomplish far more than genius. "The genius which has accomplished great things in the world, as a rule, is the genius for downright hard work, persistent drudgery," Orison Marden declared. "This is the genius that has transformed the world, and led civilization from the rude devices of the Hottentots to the glorious achievements of our own century."

If self-help advocates deprecated genius, they thought better of other gifts of nature, particularly the specialized talents or aptitudes. In keeping with the dominant faculty psychology of the nineteenth century most success theorists assumed that the human mind consisted of many separate faculties, each of which could be improved through conscious effort. Presumably every man had special faculties which, if properly cultivated, would help him win outstanding success in his chosen field. According to Orison Marden, God organized man's whole anatomy for the purpose of achievement. Every cell, nerve, and fiber had its special role to play. "The Creator made man a success-machine," he declared, "and failure is as abnormal to him as discord is to harmony." God did not intend all men for business, of course, or for any other single vocation. Provision had to be made for all useful occupations and was accomplished through the distribution of diverse faculties among men. The discovery, development, and application of these faculties added up to the success of the individual and the welfare of the world.

The special faculty of the businessman equipped him to make money, for he was peculiarly endowed with what a Chicago financial editor described as "the organ of acquisitiveness." Sooner or later he would feel the faculty of business stirring within him and know that he had been called to a lifetime of accumulation. Once called, it was a sin for him to turn aside from the career for which God had prepared him. Authorities on success warned continually against misinterpreting, resisting, or ignoring one's natural bent respecting a vocation. Those who erred in this respect invited failure, for "Unless a man enters upon a vocation intended for him by nature, and best suited to his peculiar genius, he cannot succeed . . . we see many who have mistaken their calling, from the blacksmith up (or down) to the clergy-man. You will see, for instance, the 'learned blacksmith,' who ought to have been a teacher of languages; and you may have seen lawyers, doctors, and clergymen who were better fitted by nature for the anvil or the lapstone."

In this, as in all other matters, the ambitious youth was supposed to be self-reliant, for no one could know him as well as he knew himself. Every young man was sup-posed to study his interests and abilities in relation to the requirements of the various vocations, and on this basis make a decision regarding his life's work. If after much self-analysis the issue was still in doubt, the nineteenth-century youth was some-times advised to turn to a phrenologist for counsel. In 1873 a New York medical doctor, Joseph Simms, urged ambitious boys to "seek the counsel of a professional physiognomist," on the ground that phrenologists could predict "with complete scientific accuracy" the vocation in which a youth would prosper. By writing guide-books to success, nationally known phrenologists such as Samuel Wells and Nelson Sizer extended their knowledge to those who could not visit their parlors for personal readings. It is doubtful, however, that their advice differed very extensively from the counsel of clergymen, journalists, and businessmen.

Self-help theorists generally agreed that self-analysis did not end with the discovery of one's general calling. Within each calling there were specialties, and the man who aimed for the highest success had to cultivate one of these. Rural America had honored versatility, cherishing the Jack-of-all-trades above the expert, but the de-mands of urban life reversed this system of values. As businesses grew in size and complexity in the years after the Civil War the highly specialized man became the darling of the success cult. "Silly men may cry out against one-idea men," an ad-viser wrote in 1878, "but very seldom have men with two ideas accomplished any creditable work." Competition was so severe, time so short, and human energy so limited, that no man could win fortune if he divided his efforts among several enter-prises. "Knowledge is now so various, so extensive, and so minute," said Andrew Carnegie, "that it is impossible for any man to know thoroughly more than one small branch." Carnegie spoke for the entire school of success experts when he ad-vised young men to put all their eggs in one basket, and then watch the basket.

Advice on specialization, like all other advice offered by success counselors, was meaningless if considered apart from the all-powerful human will, the most im-portant of God's gifts to man. What use to advise if man had no power to remodel himself along profitable lines? Behind the success cult's exhortations lay the assump-tion that every man could make himself over in the image of success, if he would only determine to do so. Through willpower sloth could be transformed into indus-try, wastefulness into frugality, and intemperance into sobriety. "To the man of vigorous will, there are few impossibilities," said a clerical adviser. "Obstructions melt before his fiat like spring snowflakes." It mattered little whether the obstruc-tions consisted of defects of character or defects of circumstance, for a strong will could conquer all. "*Will* it, and it is thine," said a typical self-help handbook. "No longer grovel as though the hand of fate were upon thee. Stand erect. Thou art a man, and thy mission is a noble one." The eternal boast of the self-made man was that he had overcome every limiting circumstance, and in so doing had won a higher station in life than fate had intended for him.

II

Of the cultivated qualities that helped men to rise, industry was the one most often prescribed and most elaborately justified by self-help advisers. The standard justification started with an assault on idleness, emphasizing at the outset that a lazy man forfeited his claim to humanity and violated all the higher requirements of his nature. According to William A. Alcott, a Connecticut schoolmaster, the idle man was scarcely human: "he is half quadruped, and of the most stupid species too." Alcott could not conceive how a rational being could squander the precious gift of life through unproductive idleness. Nor could Andrew Carnegie conceive of such a course. When only a boy he revealed an appreciation of this commonplace of the success cult by confiding to his diary that labor was the universal law of life. Other experts, observing that many men sought relief from boredom through work, argued therefrom that idleness was repugnant to man's physical and spiritual nature. "To any healthy nature idleness is an intolerable burden," a clergyman declared, "and its enforced endurance a more painful penance than the hardest labors."

The case against idleness also included the material argument that laziness doomed men to obscurity and failure. Franklin's Poor Richard was not the last to suggest that the sleeping fox catches no poultry, or that laziness travels so slowly that poverty soon overtakes him. For generation after generation Franklin's successors denounced indolence as the principal obstacle which blocked the road to fame and fortune. "More young men are hindered from arriving at positions of honor and usefulness, by indolence and want of order, than from any other causes," a typical handbook declared.

Condemnation of idleness proceeded on social as well as personal grounds, for most authorities agreed that the well-being of society depended on the exertions of the individual. "To live in idleness, even if you have the means, is not only injurious to yourself, but a species of fraud upon the community," said William A. Alcott. From society's point of view the idler could not justify his existence, for "He cannot engage himself in any employment or profession, because he will never have diligence enough to follow it; he can succeed in no undertaking, for he will never pursue it. He must be a bad husband, father, and relation, for he will not take the least pains to preserve his wife, children, and family from starving; and he must be a worthless friend, for he would not draw his hand from his bosom, though to prevent the destruction of the universe." Was it any wonder that society condemned idlers to poverty and disgrace?

Nor was it any more surprising that those who commanded wealth and honor were the industrious men who had been trained to believe that energetic labor could accomplish anything. "Let those who would leave their mark in the world pull off their coats, roll up their sleeves, and set manfully to work," said one authority; ". . . hosts of successful men have risen from the humbler walks of life, brushing away, by industry and force of character, the social impediments to their upward flight, with which the peculiarity of their birth essayed to fetter them." Since this was a lesson best learned in childhood, homilies on industry had a prominent place in school textbooks. The famous McGuffey readers, for example, extolled the glories of labor to several generations of American youth:

> *Work, work, my boy, be not afraid;*
> *Look labor boldly in the face;*
> *Take up the hammer or the spade,*
> *And blush not for your humble place.*

However poor or unfortunate, no boy had any reason to despair as long as he was willing to work. "Persevering industry will enable one to accomplish almost anything," said a New England common school textbook. "It makes the smallest man equal to the greatest labors. By it Lilliputians can bind a Gulliver, or a mouse can release a lion from captivity."

Successful businessmen frequently claimed that they owed everything to superior industry. When a Brooklyn clergyman questioned some five hundred prominent men in 1883, three out of four attributed their success to the work habits they cultivated in youth. Russell Sage, writing for the Hearst syndicate in 1903, testified that he, like other prominent businessmen of his generation, so loved work he even despised holidays. "Work has been the chief, and, you might say, the only source of pleasure in my life," Sage asserted; "it has become the strongest habit that I have and the only habit that I would find it impossible to break." When Frank W. Taussig and C. S. Joslyn questioned twentieth-century business leaders they discovered that many still attributed their triumphs to superior industry. Typical comments ran as follows:

> Just an average man, but I work at it harder than the average man.

> Hard knocks, hard work, long hours, and constant plugging produced results.

> Success comes from honesty and industry. . . . On the farm I learned to work and no matter how hard I had to work afterwards it was comparatively easy.

> I was brought up in a small town where I learned that work was the normal lot of man, not a misfortune, as is taught now.

To what degree successful businessmen actually did work, or what the relation of industry actually was to success is almost impossible to determine. One can easily discount their own testimonies on the basis of bias, but it is more difficult to write off the observations of those whose personal careers were not concerned. Matthew H. Smith, a journalist who had firsthand knowledge of the failings and virtues of New York's post-Civil-War business leaders, reported that most of these men worked like galley slaves. Men like A. T. Stewart and William B. Astor, for example, put in more hours than any of their employees, and never sought relief from work except on Sunday. Foreign observers sometimes commented that this intense work psychology extended beyond the business community to include the entire nation. America seemed to be the only country where a man felt ashamed if he had nothing to do. In 1904 a British observer reported that in the American business community idling was not only despised but dull: there were no interesting men with whom to do nothing. The American man of affairs, he averred, took his work along with him to dinner, theater, and bed, and when he won success at last, he thought not of retiring, but of expanding his operations. "Study the lives of successful men," said the self-made journalist, Edward Bok, "and the story will be found in each case exactly the same. The methods vary, as they must, but the actual basis of every successful life is the persistent, hard, hard work of years, and many a personal sacrifice." After studying the careers of American millionaires Sorokin came to the same conclusion, for he believed it would have been difficult to find a busier, more energetic, harder-working group than America's leading moneymakers. However useful Thorstein Veblen's "conspicuous leisure" concept might be in describing the activities of the descendants of wealthy men, Sorokin thought it of little value in approaching the careers of the moneymakers themselves. Despite such expert testimony, the industry attributed to business leaders as a distinct group was undoubtedly overestimated; common sense suggests that no one trait could have been so generally characteristic. "Name me any manner of man you care to," said one thoughtful writer, "and I will name you a millionaire to correspond." Precisely the same objection can be raised against the other virtues imputed to self-made men in order to explain their triumphs.

Perseverance followed close behind industry in the success cult's catalogue of virtues. The persevering man would not admit defeat or even discouragement, and fortunately so, for even the most optimistic self-help advisers admitted that in the upward climb he was bound to have to face both. It was only the man who would plod on, regardless of temporary setbacks, who could win the ultimate victory. "All that I have accomplished, or expect or hope to accomplish," said one self-made man, "has been or will be by that plodding, patient, persevering process of accretion which builds the antheap—particle by particle, thought by thought, fact by fact." This was also a lesson of the McGuffey readers:

TRY, TRY AGAIN

If you find your task is hard
 Try, try again;
Time will bring you your reward,
 Try, try again;
All that other folks can do,
 Why, with patience, should not you?
Only keep this rule in view:
 Try, try again.

"Perseverance is the great thing," said John D. Rockefeller, in deducing the rules of success from his own career. "The young man who sticks is the one who succeeds."

In the year 1786 Thomas Jefferson told a friend that he would welcome the appearance of any missionary who would make frugality the basis of his religious system, and who would go about the country preaching it as the only way to salvation. Had Jefferson lived into the last half of the nineteenth century he would have witnessed hundreds of such missionaries at work, preaching that very gospel. It was a poor success philosopher who did not urge young men to emulate the bee in storing up reserves against the winter of want. The art of making income exceed expenditures was hailed as one of the noblest private virtues, and a sure foundation for personal fortune. The man who husbanded his receipts, guarded against needless expenditures, and placed his savings at interest was certain to become a man of wealth. He who neglected this duty would suffer a reverse fortune. As Horace Greeley warned an audience of young men at the Cooper Union in 1867, the spendthrift was certain to "die a poor man, and, if he lives in this city, he will probably be buried at the public cost." Beyond its importance to the security of private fortune frugality was also important to society as a whole. Capital was scarce in nineteenth-century America, and sorely needed for the development of railroads, factories, mines, and other vital industrial projects. The man who made it a practice to save money became a public benefactor in his ability to provide capital for such purposes. "Man must exercise thrift and save before he can produce anything material of great value," Andrew Carnegie reasoned. Capitalists always sought saving young men as their partners, according to Carnegie, because savings offered proof that the beginner possessed the inner virtues necessary for the creation of capital.

In seeking partners or employees capitalists also looked for the quality of sobriety, if the gospel of success can be believed. Sobriety meant the total moral deportment of the young man, not just control of his drinking habits; and moral deportment was important because he who had no reputation allegedly had no credit. Drinking, smoking, and the keeping of late hours and fast company were all vigorously condemned by self-help theorists, for such practices cost heavily in time and money, and jeopardized the health and reputation of the practitioner.

One mid-nineteenth-century moralist estimated that the drinking man consumed twenty-five thousand dollars in a fifty-year period. No businessman could afford to squander his capital in this way. Bankers and financiers, men who professed to have firsthand knowledge in this field, were especially vehement in denouncing drink. In 1856 Wesley Smead, a Cincinnati banker, asserted that the liquor habit inevitably dragged a businessman down to failure: "It ruins his credit, wastes his property, destroys his health, and brings him to a premature grave." Russell Sage, a more eminent financier, was equally convinced on this point. "I have never used any intoxicating liquor or wine of any kind in my long life," Sage declared in 1903, "and it is my honest belief that if it was not for that I should not have retained my health until now." Tobacco suffered the same criticism. According to one estimate the habitual smoker puffed away eight thousand dollars in fifty years, while the "vile masticator of the filthy weed" chewed up five thousand over a similar period. Russell Sage attacked smoking as a terrible time-waster, pointing out that smokers usually enjoyed themselves best while reclining in easy chairs, a practice shunned by men intent upon success.

Toward the middle of the century success advisers also warned ambitious youth against the pleasures of bad company and the theater. Wealth did not come to those who wasted their time "on the pavements of Broadway, in ladies' drawing rooms, in cafes, and in theaters." Arthur Tappan, the prominent New York merchant, forbade his employees to attend the theater, or even to associate with entertainers. Tappan may have had in mind the warning of William Van Doren, a New York clergyman, who called attention to the possible double meaning of the familiar theater sign ENTRANCE TO THE PIT. If the young businessman did not ruin his prospects by theater-going, he certainly did not improve them either. "The fast young man, who with his sweet-heart, visits the theatre on the average of three times a week, spends in fifty years a fortune of near $50,000," declared one moralist who had an interest in the money cost of this vice; the moral cost, of course, was incalculable.

Thanks to the relaxation of moral standards in the urban centers, and to the growth of big businesses in which it was impossible for the employer to supervise the morals of all his employees, prohibitions against drinking, smoking, and theater-going did not survive the century. In 1885 when Andrew Carnegie warned a group of business college students against drunkenness and the frequenting of bars he insisted that he was no temperance lecturer in disguise. To prove his point he told his audience that a drink at mealtime would not adversely affect their business careers.

Carnegie and others emphasized moderation rather than abstinence. "I do not preach total abstinence of any habits to which human nature is prone," said Edward Bok. "Every man ought to know what is good for him and what is injurious to his best interests. But an excess of anything is injurious, and a young man on the threshold of a business career cannot afford to be excessive in a single direction." Any pleasure was dangerous if it befuddled the mind or fatigued the body, making it unfit for the work of the morrow. The responsible young man was the one who knew that his obligations to his employer extended through his off-duty hours as well as through his working day.

III

When a young man had mastered these major virtues he had taken a long step forward on the path to success. But the road was long and the obstacles many; he would need other virtues to sustain him along the way. Above all he would need to develop those qualities which most impressed employers. Since the employee who came to work on time was the one who caught his master's eye, the cultivation of habits of punctuality became a prime necessity. "Holding punctuality among the major virtues, he is ever true to the appointed hour," said Horace Mann, "and as he goes and comes, men set their watches by him, as though he were a clock-face of the sun, and moved by solar machinery." According to experts on success this robotlike quality always impressed employers, and always won rewards.

The wise employee would also strive to be both reliable and indispensable. "Let your eye light up at his request, and your feet be nimble," said one guide to wealth; "be the arch upon which your employer may rest with safety; let him feel that he may intrust you with uncounted gold." At all times an employee who wished to get ahead placed his employer's interests above his own. "Eliminate your personal self," one authority advised, "endeavor to become to your employer a thoughtful machine, and the meed of respect and confidence that will be yours will amply compensate." Naturally, the youth who thought first of his employer's interest would not run off and leave him when superior opportunities beckoned. Instead he followed the example of the wise young man of the McGuffey reader who testified that "When I had a good place and was getting on well, I was not willing to leave it and spend some days or weeks in trying to find a better place. When other young men said, 'Come with us, and we will find you something better to do,' I shook my head, and stuck to my bush. After a while my employers took me into partnership with them in their business." Too often the desire for a new job was born of the deluded idea that other men worked under better conditions. The sensible man never wavered in his loyalties. "Remember, you have passed through espousals, and are new wedded," said a clergyman who favored sticking it out in one job. "Preserve your chastity with it; and when you are blessed with its profits and joys, welcome them as a legitimate posterity."

Nor did the correct employee ever disobey his master's commands. As long as the employer required no dishonorable service, every command, no matter how personally repugnant, was to be cheerfully fulfilled. "Be willing to undertake whatever task is assigned to you, pleasant or not," a speaker told an audience of young men at Chautauqua in 1892. "If it comes in the regular course of duty . . . don't hesitate, step right up and go through with it." Employees were paid to obey, not to command. "Let a young man in business show that he is capable of carrying out the wishes of his employer," said Edward Bok, "and he demonstrates a most valuable quality. To do a thing precisely as one is told to do it is the first step to success." "Always obey instructions," John D. Rockefeller advised; "you must learn to obey orders before you can hope to give them."

Not only must an employee cheerfully accept the tasks required of him, he must also be sure to execute each and every one, giving particular attention to little details. A trail of half-done or badly done jobs never led to success. "Many a man acquires a fortune by doing his business thoroughly," said P. T. Barnum, "while his neighbor remains poor for life, because he only half does it." "It is the surest key to success in business," Edward Bok declared, "thoroughness in everything a man does; thoroughness, especially in little things."

The valuable employee also demonstrated initiative. This was an especially useful virtue in the years following 1890, when corporate arrangements made it impossible for owners to know and direct the work of their employees. "Spare no effort to get acquainted with the entire business," said one adviser, "bearing in mind the important but often overlooked fact that men who can enlarge their employer's interests . . . are always more valuable than those who simply . . . follow the same dull routine year after year without progressing as the world moves forward." The employee who merely filled his position deserved but a small payment; the man who knew how to do more than was required of him, however, was a man of executive genius who could expect commensurate reward. In large businesses underlings were especially fortunate in that they often knew more about their specialized departments than owners could possibly know, and thus had greater opportunities to act independently and beyond the exact requirements of their jobs. This was the fact behind Andrew Carnegie's rule that employees should break orders to save owners.

According to the rules of the game no special recognition or pay should be expected for extra services; appreciation for initiative should be taken for granted. "This is where so many young people make a fatal mistake," said Orison Marden, "in begrudging over-services which they render and for which they get no recognition or pay." It was only the man who earned more than he was paid who was worthy of the advancements that were sure to come. President Charles R. Van Hise of the University of Wisconsin warned the university's graduating class of 1907 to remember that if they wished for success "Each of you should appreciate that the only possible way in which promotion can come to you is by earning more than you are receiving. . . . No other basis will be recognized. All who are worthy of the places they occupy, whether janitors or heads of divisions, are earning more than they are receiving. These only may hope for advancement." Charles M. Schwab had the same thought in mind when he advised employees not to be afraid of imperiling their health by working extra hours for the company that paid their salary. The man who counted his hours and complained about his pay was destined to be a self-elected failure. "If more persons would get so enthused over their day's work that some one would have to remind them to go out to lunch there would be more happiness in the world and less indigestion," Schwab proclaimed. "If you must be a glutton, be a glutton for work."

Behind all these exhortations to economic virtue lay the idea that the drama of economic salvation paralleled that of spiritual salvation in every particular. The god of the business universe was the employer, who, like the true deity, was just, providing for all a way unto salvation. Those who willed salvation and diligently cultivated industry, frugality, sobriety, perseverance, punctuality, loyalty, obedience, initiative, and a host of kindred virtues, would find their reward in success. Those who willed damnation on the other hand and cultivated the virtues conducive thereto, would sin their way to economic hell. The employer-god knew the ways of the just and the unjust; no secret could be hid from his prying eye, for "Employers are not blind to what is going on around them, and though they may often seem unobservant, they are always watching those under them. They know who shirks, who watches the clock, who clips a few minutes here and there from his employer's time, who comes a little late in the morning and goes a little earlier in the evening; in other words, they keep thoroughly posted in regard to the work and general conduct of their employees." The employer-god recorded the sins and good works of every man in his book of judgment and on the day of reckoning knew who deserved poverty and who wealth. Among the damned many cried out against poverty's torments, but in their hearts they knew they had earned their fate.

25 / The Tradition of Opportunity
and the Aspirations of Automobile Workers

Ely Chinoy

In a study of a selected group of automobile workers, Ely Chinoy examined their aspirations and compared them to the American belief in opportunity. He found that few actually believed they could rise from rags to riches or even achieve substantial occupational mobility. Yet these men still retained a belief in America as the land of opportunity, although they redefined opportunity to mean limited job mobility and the accumulation of material goods as a tangible sign of success. The data would seem to support the findings of Stephan Thernstrom's study of Newburyport, Massachusetts, in the nineteenth century. There, workers achieved little occupational mobility but did acquire some property. Perhaps, like Chinoy's workers, they transferred their aspirations to their children for whom there were better prospects of advancing up the occupational hierarchy than there had been for themselves.

Chinoy did not study immigrants or black workers, nor do we know to what extent other white workers shared the aspirations of the auto workers. Since Chinoy's study appeared, the American economy has rapidly expanded and the standard of living for most Americans has substantially improved. In a society oriented toward consumption, it is likely that opportunity and aspirations are increasingly viewed in terms of the accumulation of goods and greater leisure rather than of dramatic jumps from rags to riches.

For further reading: *Ely Chinoy, *Automobile Workers and the American Dream* (1955); Joseph A. Kahl, "Educational and Occupational Aspirations of 'Common Man' Boys," *Harvard Educational Review*, XXIII (1953), 186–203; *David Riesman, *The Lonely Crowd* (1950); Arthur B. Shostak and William Gomberg (eds.), *Blue-Collar World* (1964); Eli Ginzberg and Hyman Berman, *The American Worker in the Twentieth Century* (1963); C. Wright Mills, *New Men of Power* (1948).

The United States is widely pictured as the "land of promise," where golden opportunities beckon to everyone without regard to his original station in life. The

American Journal of Sociology, LXVII (March 1952), 453–459.

Horatio Alger sagas of "little tykes who grow into big tycoons," it is asserted, "truly express a commonplace of American experience." School children learn early of humble Americans whose careers fulfilled the promise, and the occasional new arrival at the top of the success ladder is publicly acclaimed as a fresh illustration that opportunity is open to all.

Based on some concrete facts plus a substantial admixture of myth and optimism, the tradition of opportunity which has been a sprawled folk gospel deeply imbedded in the American character has now also become a consciously manipulated dream only partially related to the changing conditions of American life. Large corporations, rendered defensive by the events of the post-1929 decades, and the conservative press have tried to bolster their version of free enterprise by energetically fostering the belief that, to quote one newspaper advertisement, "There are more opportunities in this country than ever before."

The American experience has indeed been distinctive in the opportunities it offered to able and ambitious men. The expansion across a rich unpeopled continent of a population that roughly doubled every twenty-five years between 1790 and 1914 enabled farm boys, bookkeepers, prospectors, peddlers, clerks, and mechanics to rise significantly in the world, to become in some cases captains of industry and titans of finance.

But, with the closing of the frontier, the leveling of the rate of population growth, and the concentration of industry, upward mobility by men starting at the bottom has become more difficult. In this era of big business, with its heavy capital requirements for independent enterprise and its demands for specialized managerial and technical skills in industry, factory workers, with whom we are centrally concerned, are severely handicapped. "It is widely recognized," declared the authors of a report prepared for the Temporary National Economic Committee in 1940, "that substantial opportunity does not exist for a large proportion of workers in either small or large corporations. . . . Most of them, therefore, must look forward to remaining more or less at the same levels, despite the havoc this might visit upon the tradition of 'getting ahead.' "

Industrial workers, therefore, face in their occupational lives a palpable disparity between the exhortations of the tradition and the realities of their own experience. On the one hand, they are encouraged to pursue ambitious goals by the assurance that anyone with ability and determination can, by his own efforts, "get ahead in the world"; on the other hand, only limited opportunities are open to them.

This selection, which is a partial summary of a larger investigation, is an attempt to explore what opportunity looks like to a group of automobile workers in a middle-sized midwestern city. What are the goals of men who are caught between the promises of the culture and the exigencies of their workaday world? What, if anything, does "getting ahead" mean to them?

Automobile workers were chosen for this investigation because they work in an industry which poses sharply the problems related to opportunity. Automobile manufacturing is a glamorous, relatively new industry whose spectacular growth dramatized and gave new substance to the American success story but whose present characteristics—giant plants, an extremely high degree of mechanization, and specialized corporate bureaucracies—make it difficult for the men who operate its machines to rise from the industrial ranks.

The research for the study was done over a period of fourteen months, from

August, 1946, to July, 1947, plus the summer months of 1948. The bulk of the data was secured in seventy-eight prolonged interviews with sixty-two men employed in one large automobile plant. Since the problem of aspirations takes a somewhat different form among Negroes and, perhaps, among immigrants and second-generation Americans, interviews were confined to white workers who, with few exceptions, were at least third-generation citizens. All but six were married. In age they ranged from twenty to sixty-three, with no marked concentration at any age level and a mean age of thirty-eight. Thirty-five men had been employed in the plant prior to the outbreak of the war, fifteen had been hired during the war, and the rest were postwar employees. The group included fifteen skilled workers, ten machine operators, nine assembly-line tenders, and twenty-eight others who held various semiskilled jobs. Most types of work in the plant were represented. The data drawn from interviews were supplemented by several weeks of work in the factory by the investigator, by reports from informants, and by innumerable hours of casual conversation and informal social participation with men from the plant.

The aspirations of the automobile workers who were thus studied represent a constant balancing of hope and desire against the objective circumstances in which they find themselves. Recent research has tended to picture industrial workers as creatures of feeling and sentiment whose "social logic" contrasts sharply with the "rational logic" of managers and engineers. But, as our data clearly show, the aspirations of these men are controlled by a reasonably objective appraisal of the opportunities available to them. Given the unreliable picture presented by the culture, they are remarkably rational in their selection of goals. By and large they confine their aims to those limited alternatives which seem possible for men with their skills and resources.

With few exceptions, they see little chance of ever rising into salaried positions in the large corporation in which they work. To them the admonition to "think of the corporation as a pyramid of opportunities from the bottom toward the top with thousands of chances for advancement" has little meaning. They are clearly aware that engineering and management have become so highly selective as to exclude them almost completely. Not one of these workers ever suggested the possibility of moving into the top-salaried ranks. Only foremanship, which itself rarely leads to better managerial posts, remains as an obvious escape hatch from wage labor on the factory floor. And even this seemed to hold little promise for most of the workers who were interviewed.

In normal times only eight or ten openings on the supervisory level occur each year in this plant of almost six thousand workers. To many of them, therefore, it seems as though, in the words of one disillusioned toolmaker with fifteen years' seniority: "They'll have to die off in my department before anybody could get to be a foreman." Since forty of the sixty-two men interviewed had not completed high school, their chances of gaining promotion were further contracted, as they can readily see, by management's increasing preference for men with substantial educational qualifications.

Even in these circumstances, however, a few workers with only limited education still manage to become foremen, and their example might provoke a good deal of hope and effort, were it not for uncertainties in the selection process. Since new foremen are chosen on the basis of recommendations by foremen, the crucial question for workers seeking advancement is: What qualities and actions will bring us to the favorable attention of our supervisors? According to management, only merit and ability are taken into account when considering men for promotion. But, because the criteria used to define merit and ability remain unspecified, workers tend to stress "pull," "connections," and various personal techniques for gaining favor—"buddying up to the foreman," "running around squealing on everybody," sending the foreman a Christmas card, or getting one's name in the union paper. The rich variety of invidious terms applied to many of these techniques, however—"bootlicking," "brown-nosing," "sucking around"—indicates how workers feel about them. And in any case there was no consensus as to which methods were effective, no guide lines to direct men's efforts.

It is not surprising, therefore, that only five of the sixty-two men interviewed expressed any real hope of ever becoming foremen. While seven others had given up the hopes they had once had, fifty said that they would not want to be foremen or that they had never thought of the possibility. Given the obstacles to advancement into supervision, it is easy to imagine the build-up of verbal objections to foremanship as a rationalization against the likely disappointment of any hopes men might secretly entertain. Or, alternatively, men may protect themselves against the prospect of failure by disclaiming any interest in the goal.

Yet it is not unlikely that the disparagement of foremanship and the lack of interest are in many cases genuine. There are those who, for various reasons, are unwilling to assume responsibility. And the difficulties in the foreman's position which have been documented by numerous academic investigators are clearly evident to the men in the shop.

It is interesting to note that the five men who had hopes of becoming foremen were all still relatively young and that they had done fairly well for themselves in the plant. One was thirty-five, the others between twenty-nine and thirty-two. Three were skilled workers, two of whom had moved up from semiskilled labor during the war. One was a former line tender who had become an inspector, a more pleasant if not a better-paying job; one was a group leader in the shipping department, who had started there as an unskilled laborer. The seven men who had given up hope were, on the average, older and had not moved ahead in the shop. Only two were under thirty-five, while the others were thirty-eight or older. Only one had gained any personal advancement, a toolmaker who had finally become a group leader—after thirteen years in the plant. Two had been moved down after the war from skilled to semiskilled work, and the others were all on about the same level on which they had begun in the plant anywhere from five to sixteen years earlier. These facts suggest the possibility that, unless industrial workers gain some evidence while still young that advancement is possible, they are likely to confine their aspirations to modest objectives.

But the advancement which might encourage hope for foremanship or other substantial objectives is hard for these men to secure. Constant mechanization of automobile production has left most automobile workers as semiskilled operatives who can be moved about easily from one job to another. There were relatively few unskilled workers in the work force of almost 6,000, while only 300 were skilled craftsmen.

For the semiskilled workers who constitute the great majority in the plant, the obvious line of advancement would be into the few remaining skilled jobs, which represent the top of the wage hierarchy. But the leveling of skill makes it impossible for the plant to provide any sequence of progressively more demanding tasks which might lead toward the skilled occupations.

In the years before recognition of the union it was sometimes possible to learn enough as a helper to be able to pass one's self off as skilled. Now that the union insists that men work only within their job classifications, this possibility has been virtually eliminated; a helper cannot try to do the work of a journeyman, even under the latter's guidance. With this informal route closed—at least in this plant— apprentice training has become the only way to acquire a trade. Admission to apprentice training, however, is limited to high-school graduates not over twenty-one years old, stipulations which exclude most of the workers studied. Only during the war, when there was an acute shortage of skilled labor, were semiskilled men— "upgraders," as they were called—trained by journeymen to do at least part of a skilled job.

Thus to practically all the semiskilled workers interviewed entry to the skilled trades seemed to be completely closed. Only two veterans whose war service exempted them from the age limitation on apprentice training were planning to enter the trade through this route. And one former upgrader who had been returned to semiskilled work after the war still had hopes that he might some day be recalled to a skilled job.

With both foremanship and skilled work out of reach, the best that most workers can see for themselves in the factory is a series of isolated small gains—transfer to a job that pays a few cents more per hour or to one that is easier, steadier, or more interesting. Substantial wage increases for individual workers are almost out of the question, however, since wage rates for semiskilled jobs are highly compressed. In 1947, in the production, inspection, and material-handling divisions of the plant, for example, maximum wage rates for 240 of 280 job classifications fell within a 9-cent range, from $1.41 to $1.50 per hour, while only seven classifications brought as much as $1.64 per hour.

The achievement of even those small monetary gains which are possible has been taken out of the hand of individual workers by the impersonal seniority rule which provides that promotion to better-paying jobs should go to the men with the longest service. For the most part, therefore, higher wages and other economic benefits are now achieved through gaining and holding standardized agreements, a collective effort in which the union rather than the individual plays the central role.

As a result, the factory is not a place where men can do much as individuals to gain personal advancement. If they have worked in the plant long enough to "know the ropes," they may be able to secure a transfer to an easier, steadier, or more interesting job; otherwise they are exposed to the chance job shifts occasioned by constant changes in technology. The traditional imperatives for success—hard work and inventiveness—play an insignificant role in the context of carefully timed jobs and organized scientific research. Nor are "character" and "personality"—the other important traditional requisites for advancement—of much value to men who work with things rather than with people.

Despite the fact that they saw few opportunities for advancement in the factory, most of the workers studied could see no other future for themselves. Although forty-eight of the sixty-two answered "Yes" to the question: "Have you ever thought of getting out of the shop?" only eight had gone past wishful thinking or escapist dreams. Five of these were planning to buy a small farm or to go into some kind of small business. One had applied for a position on the local police force. And the other two—one a twenty-year-old single man, the other a twenty-nine-year-old veteran who could receive governmental assistance—were planning to go to college. The other forty who answered "Yes" quickly qualified their desire to leave with reasons why they could not do so or confessed that they had only vague, unfocused desires. Much as many of these men would like to gain independence and to escape from the factory, they soon recognize that they have neither the financial resources nor, in some cases, the educational and personal qualifications that are needed.

Nevertheless, the possibility of leaving the shop forms a staple topic of conversation on the job. A dozen men spontaneously observed that "everybody" or "almost everybody" talks about getting out of the shop. This endless discussion, though unrelated in most cases to feasible plans or substantial hopes, serves an important psychological function. As one assembly-line tender put it: "It makes the time go quicker and easier if I keep thinking about that turkey farm I'd like to buy." A few minutes later he admitted that he could never hope to save enough money to buy the farm. Even though hopes shrivel when put to the test of reality, however, the talk and daydreams they generate soften the harsh reality of the moment.

To summarize our findings thus far: Of the sixty-two men interviewed, only eight felt that they had a promising future outside the factory. Within the factory, five men had real hope that they might some day become foremen, while only three semi-skilled workers felt that it might be possible to move into the ranks of skilled labor. The remaining forty-six, both skilled and non-skilled, could see little room for personal advancement and hence restricted their ambitions to small goals.

Despite their limited aspirations and their pessimism regarding opportunity for themselves, these men have not given up the success values of American society. "Everybody wants to get ahead," said a machine operator, and none of his fellows would contradict him. But if they accept the success values and yet see little opportunity for themselves, how do they explain their failure to move up in the economic order? How do they reconcile their limited aspirations with the cultural admonition to aim high and to persevere relentlessly?

The tradition of opportunity itself provides a ready-made explanation for failure which is accepted by some of these workers. Responsibility is placed squarely upon each individual. Failure cannot result from lack of opportunity but only from lack of ambition or ability, from unwillingness to make the necessary sacrifices, or from defects in one's character and personality. "I guess I'm just not smart enough," said one worker. "It's my own fault," said another. "Sometimes," he went on, "I look at myself in the mirror and I say to myself, 'Pat, you dumb so-and-so, you could have been somebody if you'd only set your mind to it.'" By thus focusing criticism upon the individual rather than upon its institutions, society protects itself against the reactions of those who fail.

But the self-blame thus engendered is obviously painful, and men therefore seek other ways of reconciling their small ambitions with their acceptance of success values. This they do primarily by redefining the meaning of advancement in terms closer to the realities of their own experience, and to a lesser degree by fostering ambitious hopes for their children and by verbally retaining the illusion of out-of-the-shop ambitions.

By labeling the small goals they pursue in the shop as "getting ahead," these workers maintain for themselves the appearance of sustained effort and ambition.

Then, if they manage to secure a job that pays 5 cents an hour more or one that is less exacting or more interesting, they seem to be advancing. "I'll be getting ahead all right," said a discontented line tender, "if I can just get off the line." But, as men reach the low ceiling imposed on this kind of advancement or as they come to the conclusion that they are in dead-end jobs, they must turn to other meanings if they are to avoid admission of failure.

Since there are few opportunities for occupational advancement, they shift their attention toward security, on the one hand, and toward the acquisition of material possessions, on the other, identifying both as "getting ahead." Security, which has always been a crucial concern for automobile workers because of the erratic employment pattern in the industry, is now equated with advancement. Questions which tried to elicit from these workers the relative importance assigned to security as over against opportunities for advancement proved to be virtually meaningless. They could see no difference between the two. "If you're secure, then you're getting ahead," explained one worker with many years of seniority.

As with wages, security has taken on a collective character. Protection against arbitrary layoffs and assurance of recall after a shutdown are provided by the seniority rule incorporated in the union contract. In 1950 pensions were gained via collective bargaining, and the union has now set its sights on a guaranteed annual wage. Only in the accumulation of personal savings, which is itself defined as advancement, does security retain an individual character. "If you can put away a couple of hundred dollars, then you're getting ahead," said a worker struggling to make ends meet. If one can pay one's bills and meet the installments on the house, the car, or a new refrigerator and still save a little money, then one is moving forward.

The visible evidence of advancement in this world of anonymous jobs and standardized wage rates, however, is the acquisition of material possessions. With their wants constantly stimulated by high-powered advertising, they measure their success by what they are able to buy. A new car standing in front of one's own home—this is the prevailing symbol of advancement, with a new washing machine, living-room furniture, and now probably a television set as further confirmation that one is "getting ahead." This shift in the context of advancement from the occupational to the consumption sphere is justified whenever possible by stressing the potential economic returns from a large purchase, particularly in the case of a home and a car.

Even if men can see little hope for personal advancement in the present, they may still maintain their identification with the tradition of opportunity by focusing their aspirations upon their children's future, a practice strongly encouraged by the culture. "What sustains us as a nation . . . ," wrote Eleanor Roosevelt in one of her daily columns, "[is] the feeling that if you are poor . . . you still see visions of your children having the opportunities you missed." "I never had much of a chance," said a semiskilled laborer whose entire working life had been spent in this one large plant, "but I want my kid to go to college and do something better than work in a factory." All of the twenty-six men with sons not yet old enough to work felt that their children could do better than factory work; none of them wanted their sons to go into the factory, except perhaps as skilled workers. But, with their limited income and lack of knowledge, these fathers can provide little financial assistance or occupational guidance. Yet they all felt that, if their sons would exert the necessary effort and make the requisite sacrifices, they could move up in the economic order. By thus placing responsibility upon their sons, however, they protect themselves against the disappointment they are likely to experience.

Finally, men seek to maintain the illusion that they themselves are still striving by constantly talking about their intention to leave the shop, even though, as we have seen, they admit when pressed that they would probably never do so. Stimulated both by the still lively small-business tradition and by their urgent desire to escape from factory jobs, many of these workers continue to believe that at least modest success as a small entrepreneur is possible for the hardworking, personable man with ideas and initiative. They therefore verbally entertain, in usually disorderly succession, various business ambitions which are critically scrutinized and rejected as impractical or are mulled over, dreamed about, vaguely examined, and eventually permitted to fade away because there is little likelihood of their immediate realization.

From our analysis it seems evident that these automobile workers have to a large extent retained the form but lost the substance of the American tradition of opportunity. It is, of course, difficult to gauge how often and under what conditions these men see through their fabric of rationalization and self-justification to the fact that they are confined to their working-class status despite the promises of the culture. But as long as they can "get ahead," even on their own terms, they are unlikely to question seriously the validity of the tradition of opportunity.

Ten / Cities and Farms

26 / Revolution on the Farm

Albert Britt

Between 1820 and 1920 the nation changed from a predominantly rural to a predominantly urban society. Millions poured into the mushrooming cities in search of employment in factories and offices. There the pressures of urban life altered social institutions and values. For those who remained on the farms, technological changes also dramatically altered living patterns. Machine power replaced manpower and the capital investment and size of farms grew immensely. The actual number of farmers has decreased in recent years as increased productivity from new technology and scientific advances enable a few million to feed 200 million Americans. Many farmers have become managers, or agricultural businessmen, supervising their large investments and farm laborers who often resemble factory hands. Other farmers have become part-time farmers who supplement their income by working in nearby industries.

The independent yeoman farmer with his 160 acres has become a relic of the past. Modern communications have ended rural isolation, and the lines dividing rural from urban America have become blurred. Radio, television, and copies of Dr. Spock reach into farm as well as city households. Farm wives have the same kitchen appliances as city wives. Transportation and educational reform destroyed the old one-room country school house.

In the following essay Albert Britt discusses these and other changes in a reminiscence of rural childhood in late nineteenth-century Illinois. The trends toward an increasing use of machinery and fertilizers, requiring more capital and knowledge and managerial skills, and the sprawling urban complexes that reach into the countryside will continue to bring about the "revolution on the farm."

For further reading: *Fred Shannon, *The Farmer's Last Frontier* (1945); Carl C. Taylor *et al.*, *Rural Life in the United States* (1949); *Arthur Raper, *Preface to Peasantry* (1936); *James West, *Plainville, U.S.A.* (1945); *Arthur J. Vidich and Joseph Bensman, *Small Town in Mass Society* (1958); Art Gallaher, *Plainville Fifteen Years Later* (1961); Otis

The Yale Review, LVI (December 1960), 234–246. Copyright 1960 by Yale University Press.

Duncan and Albert Reiss, *Social Characteristics of Urban and Rural Communities, 1950* (1956).

I was born on a farm in Illinois a good few years ago, eighty-five to be explicit. School and college and then a job in New York weaned me away from the fields and ways of my youth. After twenty-five years I returned to that rural scene as president of the college that had graduated me. By that time motors had moved in and horses had moved out. That much I knew of course. But was that all that had happened? What had the old life been like beneath the surface? And what was the new life like?

The world that I had been born into was a world of horses, horse-power and horse-speed. I grew up among horses, riding them, driving them, working them in the field. I have been kicked, bitten, run over by and away with, and generally maltreated by these gentle, kind, and devoted friends of man. I had no illusions about horses. I never liked or trusted them, but they were indispensable. Most of the time they were docile creatures, going about their business steadily if without enthusiasm, then without reason or warning something—a windblown leaf perhaps —would send the dull plodder into panic-stricken rout. All that this means is that I never gave "horse-sense" a very high rating. Faithful servant or potential thunderbolt, the horse was the most important factor in our economy. In 1850 horses provided 79 percent of the power we used, men 15 percent, machines 6 percent. In 1960, today that is, the proportions run: machines 96 percent, men 3 percent, horses 1 percent. Percentage figures are often lifeless things, but not these.

In that distant time the horse not only did our work (with our help of course) but he also chose our acquaintances for us. Ten miles of dusty or muddy road was a good full day's work, going and coming; less than half of that for friendly visitation. What is it today? Call it two hundred and fifty, with minimum time for lunch; make it fifty for dinner and an evening of bridge.

Horses and men were inseparable; when our draft animals worked men worked with them, generally in the ratio of one man to two horses. On the typical family-size farm of a hundred and sixty acres, a quarter section, there was work for three men and at least six horses through the busy planting and harvesting season from sowing oats in early April to cornhusking in late November. When Gottfried Daimler in faroff Germany hitched a small gasoline motor to his bicycle in 1887 he triggered the most profound revolution that agriculture has ever known.

Consider some of the ways in which this revolution has changed American life. We went to a country school as did all other country children. The little red school house of sacred tradition was an institution about which a great deal of sentimental nonsense has been uttered by people who don't know what they're talking about. When I appeared at Science Hall—the name for our school in District Number Four, perhaps because no science was taught there—McGuffey's readers and Webster's spelling book, the blue-backed little volume of sacred memory, held the center of the stage; I remember also Ray's arithmetic. All the country schools were one-room, ungraded affairs, with a single teacher. Some of the teachers were good, some were lazy and incompetent, a few were petty tyrants, bigoted and terrifying to the children. All were underpaid, eighteen to twenty dollars a month. A member of the local school board once asserted without fear of contradiction that no woman teacher was worth more than that. Pay of course was for only the eight or nine months of the school year, a magnificent salary of a hundred and eighty dollars a year at most.

Instruction was largely by rote, especially in American history—we were taught no other—repeating the text of Barnes' *History of the United States* if possible word for word. This was easy enough for those with a flypaper memory—such as my own —but it produced little understanding of the matters dealt with. The study of arithmetic, in our school at least, was a highly individualistic affair, each pupil going at his own pace, slow or swift, usually the former. The result sometimes was that pupil A, aged ten, was still entangled in the multiplication table while pupil B, same age, was probing the complexities of decimal fractions.

Geography, which might have been a fascinating consideration of man's relation to his physical environment, preferably beginning with District Number Four, was only another dull exercise in memorizing obvious facts: What were Russia or Italy or India bounded by? Principal cities, rivers, mountains? Chief products? What was India to us or we to India? We lived in District Number Four of Kelly Township, Warren County, State of Illinois. Why not start where we stood and work out from there? But we didn't; we committed the text to memory, and sometimes it stuck overnight.

Penmanship as taught in that old school was at least definite and personal. The method taught was the Spencerian devised by Platt Rogers Spencer, who died ten years before I was born but was still hanging around teaching me how to write. It didn't work in my case.

The strongest point in the old country school routine was spelling. Here was a competitive element that some of us at least found challenging and sometimes satisfying. A popular game was "spelling down." We stood in line while the teacher gave out words from Mr. Webster's spelling book. As the game progressed a miss sent the unhappy loser, dragging or swaggering as his mood dictated, back to his seat until only one was left, the champion of the day. One of my achievements that is still remembered with pride was the mastering of *phthisic*. That time the teacher, J. C. Wright, the bigoted-tyrant type generally, unbent sufficiently to give me a congratulatory tap on the shoulder. Incidentally the following week he gave me a sound thrashing for fighting on the playground at recess, but even that couldn't alter the fact that I had licked *phthisic*.

Was the Little Red School House good or bad? It was surely better than nothing, which was the alternative. In spelling the method was at least thorough, more than could be said of most of the other subjects. Did the children of that day spell better than children do now? How can I tell? Spelling is at best an acquired art, and not the most important.

The praise of the "three R's" of the older days is largely nearsighted nostalgia for a time that never quite existed. My memory of the golden school days is of long sessions of unmitigated dullness from nine to four, relieved by fifteen-minute breaks at ten-thirty and two-thirty, with an hour for lunch. Life was real and life was earnest; it was also filled with wearying routine. If the children disliked it, so much the better. Their dislike proved that it was good for them. Teachers were expected to instruct, not to entertain. A teacher whom the pupils praised was obviously a slacker, one not to be considered for another term.

When an old school friend told me that the doors of Science Hall had closed for the last time it seemed incredible. The deed conveying the land where the school stood had asserted that it was to be used for school purposes "forever." I had known it in its heyday and I had outlived it. I had not supposed that forever was such a short time.

How come? In my time the district had sent twenty or more pupils into Science Hall. I learned that attendance had been shrinking for some time, but nobody paid any particular attention until a check had revealed the embarrassing fact that the whole district contained only one boy of elementary school age and he could be cared for at the new union school in a nearby small town. The change had come gradually and imperceptibly, but it had come. Our first census in 1790 had shown 94.9 percent of us living in rural areas and we had taken it for granted that it would always be like that. But it wasn't, and the old school was closed forever. Here was something that could be charged to the account of Herr Daimler. Motordriven machinery that had sent horses off the land had also drawn the boys and girls out of the little red school houses.

Later I drove with an older brother around this neighborhood that I had once known so well and was saddened by the sight of weed-grown depressions and occasional remains of a chimney showing where a family had built a home from which had come the children for the old school. Here was eloquent reminder of the human cost of mechanical progress. One man with a tractor was equal to six men or more with a dozen or fifteen horses. No horses, no men; no men, no homes; no homes, no children in the country school. The district produced more and better corn than ever, but with fewer men and no horses to plow and plant. Gasoline set the yellow school buses rolling over concrete or gravel roads to call the children into union schools with better equipment and well-trained teachers who were decently paid. Is the net result an asset or a liability in our social ledger? That's for better accountants than this one; perhaps something of both. The old school served its time when there was no other way and it deserves remembrance, not deification.

Another cherished institution that has been ground under by the iron wheels of progress is the country church, in our neighborhood Methodist or Campbellite, the latter with naive arrogance calling itself "Christian." Ours was of the Methodist persuasion. In both denominations the services were simple and the theology primitive, with strong emphasis on the perfervid type of pulpit oratory deriving from campmeeting days. The choice of denominations, if more than one was offered, was largely one of chance plus distance. The latter was important, especially in the mud or snow of winter. The case of my own family was rather special, both of my parents having been born in the Church of England. Why my father chose to be a Methodist I shall never know, except that he seemed to take it for granted that membership in a church, any church, was a matter of course like naturalization, voting, and ownership of land, an attribute of citizenship. It was hunger for land of his own that had drawn him away from the pleasant countryside of Sussex back of Hastings. England was a green and pleasant land, but there was none of it for the son of a laborer born on the wrong side of the thick hedges that shut in the parks and estates of which there were plenty in Sussex. So this little man landed in America to be a landowner, a church member, and a citizen.

As with the country schoolhouses, country churches, many of them at least, stand idle or are opened only occasionally for a special service, usually a funeral of some older resident. A few in especially prosperous neighborhoods where a high percentage of the local farmers own the land on which they live still hang on, but they are pitifully few. Automobiles and hard roads take some of the country people to larger churches in nearby towns, but for them there is little sense of belonging. These city churches with pipe organs, vested choirs, and gowned ministers are far from the farmer and his life.

A fundamental difference between that day and this is that we of the country thought of ourselves as country people and so set apart from dwellers in the towns. We wore different clothes, had different manners, thought different thoughts. Town boys were cocky, glib, and knew their way about, but it was our fixed belief that they were sissies at heart and that any one of us could lick any town boy in fair fight, age for age, and maybe two or three. The men and women of the town were well dressed, businesslike, and sophisticated, but we consoled ourselves with the thought that we were real Americans, no matter where our parents were born. We were of the breed that had driven out the Indians and we could ride and shoot in our turn if the need came. Now the machine has made the countryman indistinguishable from the townsman.

Among the things that our isolation forced us to provide for ourselves was entertainment, and we did it not too badly. We organized a debating society that met in the country school and contested over such weighty questions as "Resolved, that the pen is mightier than the sword." Another time it was "Resolved, that the love of money is the root of all evil." On this highly moot point the affirmative had the edge in our God-fearing church-going neighborhood, but in a room full of hardworking farmers there was more than one good word for money, especially as the first of March, the date for the payment of interest on the inevitable mortgage, drew near. We held spelling contests in the same school, giving my retentive memory a chance to shine in the presence of my elders.

Winter was the time for parties, usually with icecream and cake—if we could find the ice to operate a rickety old White Mountain freezer. Dancing was taboo but kissing games were common. Some of these were played to a musical accompaniment, producing a close imitation of a dance. The reasons for blacklisting the dance were obscure, but all our churches agreed that dancing was of the devil. Curiously enough the fiddle did not fall under the ban, except of course in church. Older members of our church could well remember when the congregation was split from top to bottom over the vexing question of the purchase of a small cabinet organ for the Sunday services. In general local fiddlers were in great demand, obliging with such old-time dance tunes as "Money Musk," "Irish Washerwoman," "Arkansaw Traveler," "Oh, Susanna," melodies that had enlivened evenings around the campfire in the long trek across the plains to Oregon. Waltzing was frowned upon as especially sinful, "hugging to music" we called it. Either hugging or music by itself was permissible and agreeable; apparently it was the combination that constituted the sin.

Summer had picnics of various kinds: Fourth of July, Old Settlers', Sunday School, occasionally political, in our neighborhood usually of the Republican persuasion. The shadow of the Civil War still hovered over us and Democrats were suspected of uncertain loyalty. Whatever the occasion, a picnic on a warm summer day was a notable event, a chance to meet old friends for the adults and a feast of fried chicken, pie, and cake for us younger fry. There are still picnics in that old neighborhood in spite of the diabolic machinations of Herr Daimler, but there are fewer people to enjoy them.

If the modern observer of the rural scene wishes to gauge the extent of the change that has taken place he has only to visit Main Street, any Main Street, on a pleasant Saturday night. He will see the sidewalks packed with slow moving throngs window-shopping or just sauntering. The pavement is filled with cars also moving slowly, the occupants doing nothing, going nowhere. These are the country boys and girls of this machine age in the act of entertaining themselves. We played kissing games; they sit in parked cars on Main Street or crowd into already overcrowded moving picture houses to see overrated pictures.

The modern farmer is a capitalist and he has need to be. Tractor-drawn machinery costs money, lots of it, and so does gasoline. We bought good horses for less than a hundred dollars apiece or raised them ourselves. The machine dictates the size of the farm today. An eighty-acre holding once common can hardly carry the overhead cost of even a few pieces of equipment. Big machines call for big farms and disc plows, two-row cultivators, and four-row cornplanters. In the rush of planting, a headlight and operators working in shifts can push the daily acreage planted beyond the imagination of the old-timer. Horses worked twelve hours at a pinch and then insisted on food and rest; tractors require only gas and oil.

The hardest work that I recall from my farm boy days was cornhusking. The time was November, the weather always disagreeable, the days long. We dragged ourselves out of warm beds before daylight, flexed chapped fingers, fed, curried, and harnessed the horses by lantern light, gulped down abundant hot breakfasts, and were in the field before the sun came up. A crack hand could husk a hundred bushels a day and shovel it into a high crib to boot. Now the mechanical husker can do a thousand to fifteen hundred bushels in the same time. The really up-to-date operator has a mechanical elevator that hoists the corn from wagon to crib without benefit of shovel. Cornhusking by hand has become a competitive sport with county, state, and national champions. Hundreds of people, and not farmers only, drive miles to see them and old men in comfortable chairs can get it by radio. That's a perfect way to pick corn.

Turn where you will the tale is the same, more machines, fewer men, no horses. Being a capitalist has its disadvantages. The old farmer kept few books and needed few. His chief cost was labor, his own and that of his sons. The high cost of today's machines must be paid by the farm. Most of the farms in the corn belt were settled by young men who brought all their worldly goods, including a baby or two, in a Conestoga wagon. Their farming tools were few and simple, basically an axe, a spade, a plow, in earlier days a long rifle just in case. Plow horses pulled the wagon and a milch cow was towed meekly behind. That was America on its westward wandering. These men had no money or credit, only youth, strength, and hope. The government price for raw land was a dollar and a quarter an acre—after the Homestead Act of 1862 only the small fee for recording the claim. By the time my own family appeared on the scene the price had risen to twenty-five dollars an acre but local banks and moneylenders were available to lend the money necessary, taking a discreet mortgage of course. The price of good land now is two hundred dollars an acre or more, in boom times double that. As costs rise the farm must work harder to carry the load.

Ours was a moneyless economy. Except for taxes and the payments on the mortgage we lived by barter. One of my earliest memories is of the dealing with the groceryman in a nearby town, trading eggs, butter, apples, potatoes, all of which the farm produced in abundance, for the goods the farm could not provide. Our cash crop was corn plus hogs, but our orchard and garden flourished and our cellar was full of canned fruit, preserves, barrels of apples, bins of potatoes for the winter. Given hams and bacon in the smokehouse and homemade sausage savored with sage of our own growing and we were well buttressed against the onslaughts of cold and snow. Good years and bad alike we lived well and periods of depression that sent city workers into breadlines failed to touch us.

The last time I drove past the old farm to have a look, one look was enough. Only a few stumps and straggling branches marked the site of the orchard whose trees had once filled the air with fragrance and the barrels with ripe fruit. Where flowers had once bloomed bravely there was nothing but ragged grass and tall weeds. The house seemed ashamed, and perhaps it was. This may not be a good example, but it has its meaning. Orchards and gardens are the fruit of hard manual work and lame backs and the farmer who lives by the machine has lost the aptitude and willingness for the use of the hoe and the spading fork. I did not need to inquire how many men and horses found work on this farm now; one man on the seat of a tractor and no horses.

The need for extra labor in harvest and threshing time in the old days was met by the simple expedient of "trading work" with neighbors. The basic unit of value in this exchange was a man and a team for one day. I found myself involved in this network at the early age of twelve. I rated as half a man, not much but it gave me a place and a price. Threshing was a major job calling for ten or a dozen men and a corresponding number of teams. Then I found myself standing alongside the "feeder," cutting the twine bands on the bundles of grain thrown down on the feeding board. It was a tough spot; the butts of the bundles scratched my face, chaff sifted through my clothes, and the footing on a narrow board was none too sure, but I was at least half a man.

Dinner for threshers was a feast—roast beef or pork, sometimes chicken, mounds of potatoes, turnips, parsnips, bowls of rich gravy, all topped off with two or three kinds of pie and cake. The table manners of threshing crews were not Chesterfieldian. Pie was eaten with a knife as a matter of course, and conversation only interfered with the concern of the moment. When they were gorged to the limit the men lay in the shade talking idly about nothing much, telling stories, usually offcolor, dozing, then back to feed the hungry machine till the job was done. A day for each farm was about the average. The next day another farm, usually with the same workers, until the neighborhood was cleaned up.

How is it now? In grain country an ingenious machine known as a combine does the whole sequence of cutting, threshing, weighing in one continuous process. Only the bonanza farms that count their acres by the thousand can stand the cost of a combine. For the run of the mine farmer the work is done by itinerant outfits, starting in the South, Texas and Oklahoma, as soon as the wheat is ripe, working up to the Canadian border, Kansas, Nebraska, Montana, the Dakotas, as the days grow shorter and the time of frost draws nearer. Whether in Texas or the Dakotas the threshing crew of the old days is a thing of the past. Combines carry their own sleeping tents and commissary, presumably their own bawdy stories. There is no more trading of work, neighbor with neighbor. The traveling machines do their work, the farmer pays the bill—in cash or check—and the combine goes on down the road.

A great wheat farm with a combine working, sometimes more than one, is an impressive sight, especially to one who remembers the early McCormick reapers with hand binders following close behind and the crude threshing machine driven by horse power and usually owned by a neighboring farmer with a turn for mechanics, but the bonanza method is possible only in a highly organized, well capitalized economy. Today nearly 60 percent of us live in urban areas and look to a handful of the farms to provide the makings of our daily bread; of that handful only a small fraction count for anything in the markets. The rest of the farmers are marginal, getting little beyond their own board and keep. That was what happened to the farm that had once been ours.

It was of the tradition of the small colleges that dotted the map of the Middle West early in our history that their mission was to light the lamp of learning in the country homes round about. They did a good job of it too. Two of our near neighbors, prosperous working farmers, were college graduates. Several others had had a year or two of college before settling into the groove of farm work. Many more from our neighborhood found college the doorway through which they might pass into professional or business life as lawyers, ministers, doctors, teachers, many of them winning distinction in their careers. We were a distinct group on the campus, wearing rougher clothing than the town boys, seldom shining as social lights, useful on the football team sometimes, occasionally coming off with academic honors, but winning no prizes on the dance floor. Farm incomes were low but so were college charges. Two hundred dollars a year would see us through and if there was need, jobs for room and board were plentiful. Summer work on the farm or a whirl as a book agent or an aluminum salesman would put a bit of jam on the prosaic bread and butter.

Has the country boy completely disappeared from the campus? Not entirely. His disappearance is in part illusory, a result of his merging into the campus population so that country boy and girl become indistinguishable from their urban companions, but there is evidence that the farm product is dwindling. Recently a college president, weary of the routine of administration, resigned to launch a project in which he had interested a large foundation; the purpose was to make a study of the academic performance of farm boys and girls in college today. The institution chosen was a coeducational college with excellent standing in a small town in the midst of a prosperous farming area, with a tradition of service to the surrounding agrarian environment, a perfect example for the proposed study. Unfortunately inquiry from the college brought out the disconcerting fact that there were no farm boys and girls on that campus that had once known many.

It would be unfair to charge this change entirely to the account of Herr Daimler, but it is quite fair to call attention to the shrinkage of farm population brought about by the introduction of power-driven machinery and the consequent reduction of the mass from which college material may be drawn. It is reasonable to look also at the effect on the whole economy of the increased weight of our expanding capital structure. This is more than the inflation that Washington discusses with trepidation and ignorance. It is a raising of the whole level on which we live, with an accompanying elevation of the price level all along the line. Solely by way of illustration the tuition charges of the small college sixty years ago were in the neighborhood of fifty dollars a year, perhaps twenty or twenty-five in the preparatory departments. In most cases boys made their own arrangements for room and board. Five dollars a month for two boys was a fair average for a furnished room, and board could be secured in a boarding club coöperatively run by the students for as little as two dollars a week. Sometimes boys lived together and did their own catering, bringing the costs even lower, perhaps a dollar and a half a week with occasional boxes from home.

As our level of living has lifted, college dormitories and dining halls have increased in numbers and in cost and the requirement that all students must live on campus has come into vogue. This has brought also the comprehensive fee covering tuition, laboratory charges, activities fees, and board and room. At present fifteen hundred dollars a year is a low estimate, and tomorrow it will be higher.

Have net farm incomes risen in like proportion? Probably not. How otherwise account for the disappearance of the farm boy from the liberal arts campus? It must be admitted that he has lasted longer in the agricultural schools. Is all this a part of the price we must pay for our "improved" standard of living? Probably.

In outward seeming the old farmhouse appears little changed today except for the shabby neglect of orchards and gardens. The pressing demand for a cash crop to put money in the bank account keeps the farmer in his fields of corn and beans that bring in the cash. I did not look inside our old house on the day of my last visit, but I had been in many others like it and I knew what I would have found. First of all electricity, with the companion blessings of inside plumbing, plenty of hot water, probably a refrigerator, possibly a real bathroom. These and other kitchen appliances are a vast improvement over the woman-killing stoves, hand pumps, and washtubs of the earlier day. The kitchen is the bright side of the revolution on the farm. Electricity has lifted a grievous burden from the shoulders of the farm wife and endowed her with a leisure that her mother never knew. Now she has time to look around, for church work, a neighborhood women's club, perhaps a spot of bridge; even an afternoon of poor bridge is better than endless hours and days of cooking, washing, scrubbing, mending.

I wonder what I would have seen if I had ventured down cellar in our old house. Would there have been rows of canned fruit and vegetables, jellies, jams, preserves, bins of apples and potatoes, hams and sides of bacon hanging from the rafters of the smokehouse? Or would I have found in the pantry a few tins flaunting commercial brands, a loaf of widely advertised bread, a few slices of premium bacon?

I remembered our running account with I. R. Green & Sons, Grocers, in our nearby market town, net balance due of debit or credit at the end of the year to be carried over to the next year. We had paid for our necessary commercial staples with goods of our own producing. The farmer of today pays by check drawn on the account that his cash crop struggles to support. That's what the revolution on the farm has done to an important segment of the farm economy. Good or bad? Take your choice. The old farmer at least paid his way without benefit of parity payments.

The early settlers had built grist mills as a matter of course. The small streams that fed the great Mississippi had plenty of water year round to drive the wheels. The revolution had not yet produced the tile drains and drainage districts with their levees and pumps—and bond issues—to carry the growing load of capital investment. Most of the early mills had disappeared before I came along, leaving a few mounds and hollows to show where mills and millraces and dams had been, but one remained, "Pete's Mill" we called it. Pete ground our corn, taking his pay from the "middlins" with which he fed his fat pigs. Now Pete has gone along with the little streams and the catfish, and the monster operators of Minneapolis and Fargo and Bismarck are turning out the flour with which the monster bakers make the bread the jolly farmer eats.

The old days are gone and the old ways, and with them the country blacksmith shop, the crossroads store that was the social center of the neighborhood, the combination locksmith and gunsmith that was once to be found in every country town. Add the old shoemaker to the obituary column. My father had his boots made to order, paying for each pair a cord of hickory wood. As a boy I writhed inwardly at thought of that primitive arrangement. It seemed somehow unworthy of an independent, self-respecting farmer, but for all my pride and my larger income I cannot afford to have even one shoe made to order or of leather half as good.

I have called this a *farm* revolution. It is more than that. We are all involved in it, whether we know it or not. We are all changed because of it. If there has been a hint of censure or of praise in this attempt to recapture some of the color of a time so near and at the same time so remote it is unintended. This was an America that I knew.

27 / The Changing Economic Function of the Central City

Raymond Vernon

The most common form of mobility in American history has been geographic. In the midtwentieth century, nearly one American in five moves each year. From the beginning the direction of movement has been westward. After 1820 an increasingly important direction of migration was to the cities, a process still occurring in the South and West. But the most striking development in recent years has been decentralization, the movement to the suburbs.

In the following essay, Raymond Vernon discusses the shift of jobs as well as people from the central city to the suburbs. Some commentators think that suburbia is shaping a new social type in much the same way that the large city altered traditional agrarian ways. However, the differences between the city and its suburbs have been highly exaggerated. The suburban employment opportunities have brought blue-collar as well as white-collar organization men to the suburbs, and these workers have not automatically changed their ways when they changed residence. Not only have jobs and people moved out of the city, but many urban problems have followed them. Thus, the suburbs are becoming an extension of the central city. Yet crucial differences do exist. The movement from the city has been mainly of whites; the black population continues to live and grow within the city. As job opportunities decline in the central city, and the poor, mostly black, multiply, the problems of the nation's cities have outdistanced their ability to solve them.

For further reading: Blake McKelvey, *The Emergence of Metropolitan America, 1915–1966* (1968); Blake McKelvey, *The Urbanization of America, 1860–1915* (1963); *Charles N. Glaab and A. Theodore Brown, *A History of Urban America* (1967); *Jean Gottman, *Megalopolis: The Urbanized Northeastern Seaboard of the United States* (1961); Constance McL. Green, *American Cities in the Growth of the Nation* (1957).

The Changing Economic Function of the Central City (New York: The Committee for Economic Development, 1959), 40–62. Reprinted with the permission of The Committee for Economic Development and the author. Footnotes have been omitted.

By almost any objective standard, the major central cities of our nation, over the past fifty years or more, have been developing more slowly than the suburban areas that surround them. By many such standards, this *relative* decline has lately begun to appear as an *absolute* decline as well.

Neither the relative nor the absolute decline, considered by itself, is conclusively a sign of deterioration in the central city's economic or social life. But the signs of an absolute decline do raise questions which the relative decline did not. They suggest the possibility of a flight from an environment whose deterioration might conceivably be arrested. They suggest the abandonment of public and private capital which might conceivably still have economic use. They suggest also the possibility that precious space may be available in the central city for conversion to new uses, if only the processes of abandonment were understood and the new uses defined. Our job here is to try to understand the forces which lie behind these trends.

POPULATION MOVEMENT

The placement of American cities has typically been dominated by problems of transportation—problems of servicing the movement of goods and people across oceans, down rivers, and through mountain passes. Sheer chance also played a part, no doubt, in their original placement: sheer chance reflected in the sequence by which various land areas were explored and settled or by the special enterprise of some individual or group.

At any event, almost from the moment the first house was erected, the first street laid, and the first drainage ditch dug in any of these embryo cities, a process of obsolescence took hold which dominated the pattern of subsequent development. This obsolescence, one should note, developed not only in the private structures but also in the public domain. It was not only that the first dwellings soon became inadequate by the standards of the people who lived in the city, but also that the street layouts, the sewage systems, and the water supply systems also became obsolescent. Almost from the first, then, there was rebuilding as well as building: a tearing down and reordering of structures and public facilities. "New York will be a great city," a visiting Englishman remarked a century ago, "when it gets built."

In the course of this building and rebuilding, however, the general tendency was to add to the ossification of the structure: to surface the public streets more permanently and to cram their sub-surface with more and more cables, mains, and transit conveyances; to replace wood dwellings with stone, and one-story structures with three- and four-story dwellings and factories. Each rebuilding, therefore, tended to make the next one a little more difficult than the last.

But the obsolescence process went on. In middle income homes, sanitary facilities and water supplies were brought into the home; gas mantles were replaced by electricity; the servant's bedroom gave way to the utility closet and the dishwasher; the private automobile supplemented shank's mare, the bicycle, the horse trolley and the subway.

The response of families who could afford it, at one stage or another in most central cities, was to abandon the original residential neighborhoods and to build new neighborhoods elsewhere at points further removed from the city center. Step by step,

Bostonians retreated from the Common, Philadelphians from Independence Hall, New Yorkers from Astor Place. By 1881, Henry James—speaking through one of his fictional characters—was saying:

> . . . At the end of three or four years we'll move. That's the way to live in New York—to move every three or four years. Then you always get the last thing. . . . So you see we'll always have a new house; you get all the latest improvements. . . .

By the beginning of the twentieth century, the electric trolley and the suburban railway were quickening the moving process. By the 1930's, the automobile and the bus had speeded the movement even more.

This tendency produced a typical growth pattern around our central cities. At any stage, one could discern points outside the older areas—points where the rail lines and public conveyances ran—where new residential construction was at a peak and populations were increasing at a rapid rate. As time went on, these points where maximum growth rates were being registered were further and further removed from the center of the city, and when the automobile came they were no longer isolated points but a continuous band of maximum growth ringing the central city.

Thus, during the decade of 1900 to 1910, the most rapidly growing parts of metropolitan areas were the central cities themselves. In 1910 to 1920, the maximum growth rates occurred in a five-mile wide ring surrounding the edges of the central cities. In the next three decades, the high growth rates had moved outward still further to a ring 5 to 10 miles from the central city. By 1956, the outward tendency was so marked that over three-quarters of the major metropolitan areas' new dwelling units, measured by number or value, were scheduled for construction outside the central cities.

The result of this pattern of development is suggested by Table I. In every case, it will be noted, populations in the central city depicted in the table tended to decline in relation to the metropolitan area of which it was a part. This, of course, reflects relative rather than absolute decline. After 1950, however, New York City's populations declined in absolute terms. The odds are high that a few others may also have done so.

To account for the absolute decline in New York City's populations and to appreciate why other cities are likely to experience a similar pattern, one must return to a consideration of the process of growth and structural obsolescence which dominates the central cities. Earlier, we carried the story to the point at which the middle-income groups moved to new neighborhoods further removed from the city's center. But this was not typically the end of the economic life of the structures vacated by them.

The next stage was the familiar one, almost universally observed in the nation's central cities. Most of the structures abandoned by one income group were filled by another group several rungs lower on the income ladder. The new tenants crowded the old structures much more than their predecessors had done. Maintenance and repair standards deteriorated. Ultimately, the middle class areas became slums.

But a careful observation of the neighborhood patterns within central cities indicates that the slums, in turn, are having a population cycle of their own. An initial heavy crowding is eventually followed by a tapering off of populations in the slum areas. The ring of slum population growth crawls outward from the center of the city in a belated imitation of the middle-income group that preceded.

The pattern is illustrated by developments in Philadelphia in recent years. The greatest concentration of old dilapidated structures in that city is found in its south-

TABLE I

CENTRAL CITIES' PROPORTION OF POPULATION IN THIRTEEN STANDARD METROPOLITAN AREAS, 1900–1950

Central Cities as % of Corresponding Standard Metropolitan Areas

Central Cities	1900	1910	1920	1930	1940	1950
Baltimore	79.6	77.5	86.1	81.7	79.3	71.0
Boston, Lowell, Lawrence[a]	42.6	42.6	41.3	37.0	36.0	34.0
Buffalo	69.3	68.2	67.3	62.9	60.1	53.3
Chicago	81.2	79.4	76.7	72.2	70.4	65.9
Cincinnati	61.8	61.6	63.8	59.7	57.9	55.7
Cleveland	82.8	84.9	82.0	72.4	69.3	62.4
Detroit	66.9	75.9	76.1	72.0	68.3	61.3
Los Angeles	53.9	59.3	57.8	53.2	51.6	45.1
N.Y. City, Jersey City, Newark	77.0	76.4	74.6	70.8	70.2	66.8
Philadelphia	68.4	68.3	67.2	62.2	60.4	56.4
Pittsburgh	41.7	36.3	33.4	33.1	32.3	30.6
St. Louis	71.8	68.4	67.8	60.5	57.0	51.0
San Francisco, Oakland	75.5	73.3	71.6	68.1	64.1	51.8
Total, Listed Central Cities	69.1	68.6	67.7	63.7	62.1	57.2

Source: Donald J. Bogue, *Population Growth in Standard Metropolitan Areas 1900–1950*, Appendix.

[a] As percentage of area consisting of the counties of Essex, Middlesex, Norfolk, and Suffolk in Massachusetts. The sum of the four counties differs slightly from the corresponding town-delimited standard metropolitan areas.

east section, bounded by the Sckuylkill and Delaware rivers. Seven out of eight of the one-family dwelling units in this area had been built before 1919 and 26 per cent of the dwelling units in the area were substandard by 1950. In the rest of the city, such dwelling units were much less aged and less dilapidated on the average. The differences were reflected in population changes during the 1940–1950 decade. While the southeast area's population declined by 3 per cent, that of the rest of the city rose by 10 per cent.

The same pattern appeared in Manhattan's lower East Side, at an even earlier date. Here, about two-thirds of the dwelling units had been erected before 1919 and about half of the dwelling units were classified as substandard in the 1940 census. From 1930 to 1940, population on the lower East Side declined 19 per cent while that in the rest of the borough rose 3 per cent. To be sure, some razing of slum structures has occurred in these old areas and elsewhere, a fact which has either hastened the population decline of deteriorated areas or tended to reclaim depopulated areas for other uses. On the whole, however, such razing has commonly failed to match the population decline in the slum districts where it occurred. The picture is one of the reduced use of old slum dwellings and the development of new slums to replace them.

RETAIL JOB MOVEMENT

Inevitably, the number of retail jobs in central cities has changed with the changing pattern of their populations. As households have shifted outward toward the suburbs, the neighborhood retail trade has gone along. This is illustrated by Table II, which

TABLE II

CENTRAL CITIES' PROPORTION OF RETAIL TRADE [a] EMPLOYMENT
IN THIRTEEN STANDARD METROPOLITAN AREAS, 1929–1954
(PAID EMPLOYEES ONLY)

Central Cities as % of Corresponding Standard Metropolitan Areas

Central Cities	1929	1939	1948	1954
Baltimore	94.8	91.4	88.3	81.9
Boston, Lowell, Lawrence[b]	61.3	54.5	52.4	48.7
Buffalo	78.9	73.2	70.3	64.5
Chicago	81.7	78.3	75.6	69.1
Cincinnati	79.8	76.8	73.8	69.6
Cleveland	87.7	83.4	80.6	73.5
Detroit	82.2	77.9	72.6	63.3
Los Angeles	70.0	61.7	54.4	48.3
N.Y. City, Jersey City, Newark	79.8	76.1	74.6	67.8
Philadelphia	79.2	70.4	67.8	61.1
Pittsburgh	61.0	55.3	52.5	45.7
St. Louis	79.9	73.1	67.6	61.3
San Francisco, Oakland	85.2	80.7	72.3	63.5
Total, Listed Central Cities	78.0	72.8	69.4	62.7

Sources: U. S. Census of Business, 1929, 1939, 1948, 1954.

[a] Coverage varies for the several years. 1948 & 1954 data exclude "Milk Dealers" which are included in the 1929 & 1939 figures. 1929 data also include "automobile garage, repair services" which are covered by the census of Selected Services for the later years. 1929 data are based on full-time employees only.

[b] As percentage of area consisting of the counties of Essex, Middlesex, Norfolk, and Suffolk in Massachusetts. The sum of the four counties differs slightly from the corresponding town-delimited standard metropolitan areas.

shows how the central cities' proportion of retail trade in their respective metropolitan areas has changed in the past quarter century.

But something more than a simple proportionate shift in retail trade has occurred, as evidenced by trends in retail trade in the central business districts of these cities. These districts, as delineated by the United States Bureau of the Census, typically embrace the main city shopping centers and typically drawn their trade from all corners of their respective metropolitan areas. From 1948 to 1954—while the central cities as a whole were slipping in relative positions as retail trade centers—the central business districts of these cities were slipping even faster. Whereas 13 central cities registered a decline of one-tenth in their share of the 13 metropolitan areas' retail trade employment in which they were located, the 13 central business districts' share fell by one-quarter. Indeed in seven of these central business districts, there was not only a relative decline in retail sales but an absolute decline as well, a decline all the more remarkable because it occurred during a period when retail sales in the nation were growing prodigiously.

Behind this decline in the central business district's role as a retail shopping center, there lie three main forces. One of these already has been mentioned—the fact that populations in the oldest portions of the central city have tended to grow more slowly than for the city in total or have actually declined in absolute number in some neighborhoods. Another force has been the relatively slower rate of growth of the number of jobs of all kinds in the central cities, a tendency which has reduced the number of prospective "downtown" shoppers; we shall have more to say about this tendency at a later point. Finally—perhaps most importantly—there has been the almost universal preference of the shopper to use the automobile instead of mass transit facilities in the journey from home to bargain counter.

There is not much need to labor the point that a revolutionary shift in transportation preferences has been occurring. The shift has been documented copiously in other sources. The implications of the shift are pointed up by the experience recorded in New York City's central business district. Between 1940 and 1956, the number of persons entering the district on a typical business day had barely changed; it was 3,271,000 on the earlier date and 3,316,000 on the later. Yet during this same period, the number of motor vehicles entering the district had risen from 351,200 to 519,300 daily, a rise of 48 per cent. One can also be reasonably certain that the number of cars circulating entirely within the central business district rose by something like the same magnitude during the 16-year period.

This rise, one need hardly point out, has taxed the obsolescent street system of the area almost beyond endurance. Congestion has always been characteristic of some obsolescent sections in most central cities; Boston's narrow crooked street system in the neighborhoods of Scollay Square and the Washington Street area, New York's street system in the Greenwich Village district, and the narrow north-south streets of Philadelphia's and Baltimore's downtown grids were never designed for the automobile and could scarcely accommodate the horse-drawn dray. But the revolutionary shift away from mass transit has made congestion throughout these and other central city areas widespread and endemic; and some of the results are seen in the decline of shopping in the central city.

WHOLESALE JOB MOVEMENT

From the ancient days when central cities were principally market towns, wholesaling has been a significant feature of city activity. Goods carried overseas by ships to Atlantic or Pacific ports; articles floated on rivers and lakes or dragged overland to St. Louis, Chicago, Pittsburgh and Denver; these formed the nucleus for the wholesaling function in the towns which were to become our great central cities. Here, the goods were weighed, inspected and bought on the spot.

The ties between wholesaling and the institutions of the city grew more and more firm with the passage of time. In the 19th century, the city was the mecca where the wholesaler from distant markets arranged his financing, indulged his more exotic appetites, and acquired his trade intelligence. Reminiscing about that period in New York, Jacob Knickerbocker says:

In the 50's [the 1850's], the wholesale business was located in the lower sections of the city. . . . The position and activities of the salesmen were rather unique. Each had his list of customers from the various sections of the country. When they came to New York to purchase most of them also expected to have a "good time" and looked to the salesmen to provide it for them. Sometimes the entertainment graded the extent of the purchases. . . .

So dominant was the central city in this type of activity that even as late as 1929, the central cities in 13 metropolitan areas accounted for over 93 per cent of the wholesaling jobs in those areas. From that date on, however, there was a rapid decline in the relative importance of wholesaling jobs in all these cities, as Table III shows.

TABLE III

CENTRAL CITIES' PROPORTION OF WHOLESALE EMPLOYMENT [a]
IN THIRTEEN STANDARD METROPOLITAN AREAS, 1929–1954
(PAID EMPLOYEES ONLY)

Central Cities as % of Corresponding Standard Metropolitan Areas

Central Cities	1929	1939	1948	1954
Baltimore	99.5	97.4	94.7	94.2
Boston, Lowell, Lawrence[b]	82.9	79.7	75.1	66.6
Buffalo	93.4	91.0	90.0	85.4
Chicago	96.9	94.1	91.6	86.6
Cincinnati	96.2	92.7	87.8	86.5
Cleveland	97.1	97.9	96.4	93.5
Detroit	94.8	92.0	90.1	76.8
Los Angeles	80.7	70.1	71.9	66.3
N.Y. City, Jersey City, Newark	95.1	93.1	90.4	84.6
Philadelphia	93.6	91.0	88.3	81.8
Pittsburgh	88.6	83.6	82.9	75.6
St. Louis	89.7	92.7	90.7	85.5
San Francisco, Oakland	96.1	95.0	94.4	85.1
Total, Listed Central Cities	93.1	90.3	88.1	81.7

Sources: U. S. Census of Business, 1929, 1939, 1948, 1954.
[a] Data for the several years are not strictly comparable due to the various changes in coverage.
[b] As percentage of area consisting of the counties of Essex, Middlesex, Norfolk, and Suffolk in Massachusetts. The sum of the four counties differs slightly from the corresponding town-delimited standard metropolitan areas.

Once again, the forces which lie behind this shift can be traced in part to transportation changes and to the advanced state of obsolescence of the central city. On the transport side, the shift in goods movement from rail to truck has freed wholesalers from the compelling need to be on a rail line and has weakened the advantage of being close to a rail junction. As long as wholesalers relied principally on the rail lines in our principal central cities, the fact that the point of convergence of different lines was typically within the central city acted as an attractive force. Once the truck began to be used, however, the attraction of the central city as the preferred distribution point for wholesalers was weakened.

Yet it should not be assumed that the shift from rail to truck is the only transportation force which is pushing wholesalers with stocks from locations in the central city. As we indicated earlier, the best location for distribution to local markets is not necessarily at the center of the market. As the proportion of the total market outside the congested center grows, and as the relative level of congestion in the center area increases, the case for locating outside the center progressively improves. This is one of the elements which has produced the trend shown in Table III.

Some of the forces which have pushed wholesaling and distribution from the city centers, however, stem from changes within the warehouse. Goods-handling has been undergoing a technological revolution in recent decades. In some instances, the city-style multi-story warehouse has been readily adaptable to these changes. But for the most part, the palletizing of goods and the use of fork-lift trucks and drag lines have created a substantial demand for horizontal warehousing space, with wide bays and high ceilings. These are developments which have not yet spent their full force.

MANUFACTURING JOB MOVEMENT

For as long as the record can be constructed, the major central cities of the nation have been declining in importance as manufacturing centers relative to their suburban hinterlands. As Table IV shows, virtually every one of the 13 metropolitan areas depicted there experienced this relative decline of the central city.

Once again, it is well to make a distinction between a *relative* decline and an *absolute* decline in the jobs contained in the central city limits. In recent years—from 1947 to 1954, for example—the cities of Boston, Chicago, Detroit, Pittsburgh, St. Louis, and San Francisco recorded not only a *relative* decline but also an *absolute* decline in the number of these jobs.

Manufacturing enterprises can differ so much from one another in their locational needs that one hesitates to generalize about the movement of these jobs out of the central cities. Some industries have been quite invulnerable to the creeping obsolescence of the central city's environment; others have been highly sensitive to it. Some have departed from their central city location at a precipitate rate; a few are still as highly concentrated in central city locations as they were a quarter century ago. Nevertheless, there are a few generalizations which apply in some degree to most of the manufacturing economy found in large metropolitan areas.

To understand the forces which determined industrial location in our major central cities a century or two ago, one has to turn once again to the overwhelming restraints imposed by problems of transportation. When these cities were in their embryo state, such industry as existed—the mills and metal-working shops, and even the tanneries and abattoirs—necessarily lay inside or close by the city. For the city itself typically sat athwart the natural transportation routes of the area, such as the rivers, lakes and mountain passes. And the city typically provided much of the market and all the labor which the factory employed.

By the middle of the 19th century, however, the problem of industrial location had grown rather more complex. By this time, large manufacturing plants were no longer a rarity and the development of the railroad and the horse trolley were offering them a little more latitude in the choice of a site suitable for the construction of substantial factory structures. Still, these plants were as reliant as ever on rail or water for their transport needs. And since the major rail junctures had commonly developed within the limits of the larger cities, special advantages still existed in remaining in the vicinity of the cities. What is more, homes and factories still could not be too

TABLE IV

CENTRAL CITIES' PROPORTION OF MANUFACTURING
PRODUCTION WORKERS [a] IN THIRTEEN METROPOLITAN AREAS, 1899–1954

Central Cities as % of Corresponding Metropolitan Areas

Central Cities	BASED ON INDUSTRIAL AREAS[b]				BASED ON STANDARD METROPOLITAN AREAS[c]			
	1899	1909	1919	1929	1929	1939	1947	1954
Baltimore	91.8	87.1	88.0	86.0	85.5	72.0	70.4	62.9
Boston, Lowell, Lawrence	22.3	22.3	23.9	26.6[d]	40.6[d]	40.4	40.5	34.7
Buffalo	74.7	68.7	65.1	59.8	59.8	49.8	47.9	43.1
Chicago	88.0	82.0	77.7	73.6	73.6	71.9	70.4	65.2
Cincinnati	75.4	65.9	61.8	56.1[e]	67.7[e]	72.6	71.3	59.8
Cleveland	91.0	82.5	85.3	83.1[e]	89.1[e]	86.3	83.0	69.5
Detroit	83.6	88.1	63.2	75.6	75.2	57.7	60.3	53.5
Los Angeles	83.4	80.2	70.5	66.4[d]	66.6[d]	55.4	46.9	42.3
N.Y. City, Jersey City, Newark	69.9	67.5	61.7	61.3[d]	69.8[d]	67.9	66.3	63.0
Philadelphia	78.4	74.1	60.4	65.7	65.7	61.0	61.3	56.0
Pittsburgh	53.1	35.4	34.0	27.1	27.1	22.6	23.0	22.6
St. Louis	80.6	72.7	70.6	70.6	69.9	69.7	70.6	63.9
San Francisco, Oakland	81.2	60.5	46.1	48.5[d]	68.2[d]	62.3	55.9	50.4
Total, Listed Central Cities[f]	69.3	64.8	60.4	61.7	66.1	61.9	60.8	55.5
Total, 48[g] Central Cities					66.5	62.3	62.1	57.5

Sources: Based on the manufacturing censuses of the U.S. Bureau of the Census. The 1899–1929 series of central cities as percentages of their corresponding industrial areas were taken from Glenn E. McLaughlin, *Growth of American Manufacturing Areas* (Pittsburgh, 1938), pp. 98, 129. The 1929–1939 series of central cities as percentages of their corresponding standard metropolitan areas were based on data given in Evelyn M. Kitagawa and Donald J. Bogue, *Suburbanization of Manufacturing Activity within Standard Metropolitan Areas* (Oxford, Ohio, 1955), pp. 132–139. The 1947 and 1954 data are those reported in the State Bulletins of the *1954 Census of Manufactures*.

[a] The coverage of industries is not strictly comparable from year to year due to the various changes in industry classifications and definitions of the several censuses. No adjustment other than those made by McLaughlin and Kitagawa and Bogue has been attempted. For details, see McLaughlin, p. 99, footnote, and Kitagawa and Bogue, pp. 4–5.

[b] For definition of the industrial areas, see U.S. Bureau of the Census, *15th Census of the U.S., Manufactures, 1929*, Vol. III, p. 11, and McLaughlin, p. 11.

[c] For definition and area covered by the various standard metropolitan areas (S.M.A.), see Kitagawa and Bogue, p. 13, and U.S. Bureau of the Census, *Census of Manufactures, 1947*, Vol. III, p. 32. The Boston area given here is based on whole counties while the census since 1939 has delimited the New England areas along town boundaries. (See Kitagawa and Bogue, pp. 13, 139, 140.)

[d] For the central cities of Boston, New York, and San Francisco, more than one city is considered as the central city in the 1929–1954 S.M.A. series. According to the 1899–1929 industrial area series, only one single city is taken as the central city. For the central city of Los Angeles, the discrepancy between the two 1929 figures is due to the fact that the S.M.A. series is based on the 1932 expanded boundaries of the city of Los Angeles.

[e] In general, for the 13 areas given here, with the exception of Cincinnati and Cleveland, the various S.M.A.'s are either identical with or larger than the corresponding industrial areas. The industrial area of Cincinnati includes one more county, namely, Butler County, Ohio, than the Cincinnati S.M.A. The Cleveland S.M.A. is substituting Lake County (Ohio) for the industrial area's Lorain County (Ohio). In terms of manufacturing, Lorain County was more important than Lake County in 1929.

[f] These are the 13 large areas selected by McLaughlin. See McLaughlin, pp. 13–15.

[g] These are the S.M.A.'s with at least 40,000 manufacturing employees in 1947. The 1947 census reports listed 53 S.M.A.'s with this qualification. For three of the 53, 1954 data are not complete. 1954 census also combined four of the New England S.M.A.'s into two.

far apart—no further than an hour's journey by foot, ferry or trolley. This, too, contributed to the cohesive development of the city.

In the course of time, however, some of the more noisome industries began to feel the pressures to locate in less constricted spaces. Abattoirs, smelters, and other unsocial industries began to look for sites where no inhibitions would exist to polluting the air or water. Industries of this sort accordingly began to locate in what was then regarded as the far outskirts of the growing cities.

Nevertheless, though the sites which they selected in the late 19th century often seemed remote from the city limits at the time, the cities' growth over the next several decades soon engulfed them. Today, these industries often sit in little enclaves surrounded by urban development; within these enclaves they share a blight perpetuated by the sometimes unavoidable by-products of their operations. Yet in many cases, these industries have little apparent choice but to remain where they are. For their next move—overleaping and locating beyond the urban development which surrounds them —would frequently carry them into territory well removed from their markets or their labor force.

Most of the movement from the central city, however, came later and was spurred by other factors. As time went on, manufacturing structures, like residential structures, became obsolescent. The process of obsolescence was greatly accelerated by the introduction of assembly line techniques in manufacture and by revolutionary developments in materials handling to which we earlier referred. As a result of these changes, as we now all know, the old multi-story mill-style building became increasingly inappropriate for many operations which it had previously housed. The preferred type of structure became the elongated one-story building, laid out on large sites with the easy possibility of expansion in any direction. The advent of trucking was of course of considerable importance in this development. No longer confined to railside or waterside locations, manufacturers were free to look for sites over much more extensive areas.

There were times, to be sure, when the manufacturer replaced his obsolescent old structure on the very site where his original plant had stood or on a site nearby. There were numerous advantages in such a course: Some of the sunk capital in the old site could be salvaged by such a process; some of the old labor force could be retained; some of the neighborhood contacts in the central city, such as repair services and supply sources, could still be utilized.

By and large, the possibility of carving out a new site or greatly enlarging an old site in the central city became increasingly difficult with the passage of time. Zoning regulations were a part of the problem; these regulations, which first appeared in American cities to any extent in the 1920's, often inhibited the expansion of manufacturing in neighborhoods where some manufacturing already existed. To be sure, such restraints ordinarily did not apply to plants in existence prior to the adoption of the zoning requirements. But they did operate to discourage the radical expansion or total replacement of plants in many city areas.

Even where zoning ordinances played no role, however, the assembly of a city site was a formidable operation. As the city developed, most of its land was cut up in small parcels and covered with durable structures of one kind or another. The problem of assembling these sites, in the absence of some type of condemnation power, required a planning horizon of many years and a willingness to risk the possibility of price gouging by the last holdout. Moreover, once a site was acquired, razing costs alone could easily run on the order of $50,000 an acre in current dollar terms. All told, the value of the site could amount to 20 or 30 times more than that of an equivalent area in a developed suburban location. In these circumstances, it was small wonder that many manufacturing establishments chose a suburban location in replacing their obsolescent structures.

Other factors were also operating to push manufacturing into the suburbs. Some of the main forces which previously had drawn manufacturing plants to the centers of the old cities were being weakened by technological change. We have already observed how the truck and the automobile were providing a new mobility to goods and to the labor force, allowing manufacturers to locate at greater distances from existing clusters of homes and factories. In addition, some of the other features unique to the old cities—some of the "external economies" of such cities—were being found over increasingly wider areas. Special power facilities, special transportation services, a variety of repair services, all of these were being extended in the course of time to an increasing number of points outside the older industrial districts.

In tracing the outward movement of manufacturing plants for the central city, one must not overlook the special problems of the plant which operates from industrial lofts and other multi-tenanted quarters. Plants of this sort, anxious to avoid any investment in bricks and mortar, typically have had to take their space where they found it. Accordingly, they have been limited in their locational choices either to industrial buildings constructed for multiple tenancy or to obsolete factory buildings abandoned by their original users.

Establishments of this sort also have tended to move outward from the central city. For with the passage of time, factory buildings have become available to an increasing extent for subdivision and rental in suburban industrial areas. And the scale of existing rentals for such space has been sufficiently low to prevent the construction of new industrial loft structures either in the central cities' confines or elsewhere. Besides, the fact that some of the "external economies" unique to the old cities were appearing on the outskirts as well, removed a major obstacle to suburban locations for many small firms.

The net effect of these outward tendencies has been to delineate more sharply the special characteristics of the central city as a site for manufacturing operations. More and more, the central city has come to specialize in the "communications-oriented" segment of manufacturing. More and more, too, the emphasis has been on the "unstandardized," the uncertain, and the exotic type of manufacturing specialization. And there is every reason to expect that, to the extent that manufacturing remains in the central city, these forms of specialization will grow more pronounced still.

OFFICE JOB MOVEMENT

Those who are concerned with analyzing the economic future of central cities are dogged at the outset with special problems of data gathering. For enough has been written here to underline the point that the business of cities is of a kind which tends to evade the census-taker and which, once detected, resists statistical classification— namely, the new, shifting, different, "unstandardized" operation.

The problem reaches new intensity with respect to the activities which go on in the offices of the nation's great central cities. Whereas manufacturing, transportation, retail trade, and wholesale trade are economic activities whose existence is easily recognized and catalogued, many aspects of office activity are more difficult to classify. Where the work of a firm or an institution is such that all of it is performed in an office setting—as is the case with banks, insurance companies, securities dealers, and related institutions—the problem is not so difficult. But most office activities—most record-keeping, data-processing, purchasing, routing, billing, controlling, expediting, designing, scheduling, and researching—have developed as adjuncts of producing, transporting, and selling and are not ordinarily identified and enumerated as an independent operation. Yet because the central cities are coming more and more to be reliant for their economic existence upon office activity, it is indispensable to probe into this amorphous group of operations and to draw what generalizations can be pulled out of the unstructured and unsatisfying data.

The financial institutions, we have observed, were among the more easily recognized office activities. From their earliest beginnings, these activities sought out central city locations. We have dwelt upon the forces conducive to central city growth enough by this time to have indicated why banks and security markets should have gravitated toward the very heart of the old cities. "Information" was the greatest stock-in-trade of the security dealer and the banker—information about the credit of an individual, the affairs of an enterprise, the condition of a trade, the politics of a nation; in the ordinary course, such information could best be acquired at the points where ships arrived and departed, where travelers congregated, where news was gathered, and where the posts were swiftest and most frequent.

Besides, the most critical business of these financial entities ordinarily was that of negotiation—the subtle jockeying between buyer and seller, borrower and lender. This is a type of activity which one could scarcely leave to the mails, to the telegraph, or even to the telephone, except where the negotiations were perfunctory, routinized and repetitive.

The pull of the big cities was not due solely to these factors, however. Some aspects of the financial community's activities were indeed sufficiently routinized and standardized that a central city location would not have been absolutely compelling. Insurance company activities, for instance, are largely of a routine and repetitive character. Where such companies chose to centralize their record keeping activities in a single office, the problem was to find a large enough pool of literate clerks to handle the volume of work generated by such an office. In general, women did better than men at this sort of work. Accordingly, the problem became one of locating at a point where a large number of literate women would be assembled daily. The obvious location indicated was a large city, where literacy rates were high, at a point in the city close by mass transit facilities.

The affinity of the financial institutions for the central city was so marked in 1947 that in eight metropolitan areas every major branch of the financial community—banking, insurance, and securities dealers—had more than four-fifths of its employment in the central cities.

As the nation's larger manufacturing, transport, and utility companies developed central offices sufficiently large to make a separate establishment feasible, they too were pulled to the downtown areas of the cities, reacting to much the same forces as had drawn the financial institutions to such locations. One of the functions of these central offices as they developed was to be close to the trade currents—to know what was going on in markets, in technology, in finance. Another was the subtle business of negotiation. Besides, like the insurance companies, their labor requirements were large quantities of literate clerks and stenographers. Their indicated locations, therefore, were the downtown sections of the nation's great cities.

In the end, this use of the central business district tended to elbow out competing uses. The capacity of the office to preempt the downtown area stemmed in part from the relative intensity of its need for central locations. It arose in part also from the special insensitivity of many office activities to the cost of space. Office space costs constitute an incidental fraction of the total costs of manufacturing companies; they involve the prestige center of the enterprise; they affect the daily surroundings and contacts of the firm's elite; accordingly, their location is less prone to determination on a dry-as-dust least-cost calculation than a manufacturing facility or than a warehousing location would be.

As a major fount of employment for a variety of related services, the central offices and the financial institutions managed to draw to the downtown portions of central cities a considerable variety of appended activities. Advertising agencies, employment agencies, management advisory services, addressing and mailing services, all were drawn to the area, where they might provide the type of service which their customers demanded. In 1948, the 13 central cities covered earlier accounted for 94 per cent of the employment in their metropolitan areas' business services.

Nevertheless, although all of these activities have grown in the central city, they have also shared to some degree in the general outward redistribution of population and jobs. In the first place, a considerable proportion of the financial community's activities has come to be oriented to residential neighborhoods. With the much more widespread ownership of personal savings and checking accounts and with the growing use of consumer credit, a considerable segment of banking activity has taken on the locational attributes of any consumer-oriented service. The outward shift of residences, coupled with that of manufacturing, wholesaling and retail trade, has accordingly led to a redistribution of the financial facilities which service them. In the brief period from 1947 to 1956, for eight selected metropolitan areas, there was a modest outward shift in each category of financial facilities except insurance carriers.

This still leaves a significant nub of office employment, located in the central city, which has no obvious reason for dispersal to the suburbs. Just how large this cluster may be is quite unclear, since the statistics seem hopelessly incomplete on this score. But many central offices, business service offices, insurance companies, and "downtown" financial institutions must probably be counted in this category.

By all the signs, the activities of this sector of the nation's economy should continue to grow, perhaps at a rate much faster than of the economy as a whole. Yet even here—even in this stronghold of big city employment—there are certain factors to be taken into account in appraising the future ties to the central city.

One of these is the fact that as central cities decline in population, and as Negroes and other groups with more restricted job opportunities constitute a larger proportion of the population that remains, the young women who have constituted so large a proportion of the labor force of these office installations will become more and more remote from the downtown portions of the central cities. With commuting distances lengthening and mass transit facilities deteriorating in most cities, the question is raised whether the downtown area will continue to be the optimum point at which to collect the preferred office labor force.

A second factor which could affect the growth of central city office employment is the impact of new data-processing and communication techniques on employment. One must be careful not to exaggerate the speed or extent of the shifts which these developments will produce. The introduction of new data-processing systems is a slow and costly business. Besides, its introduction often stimulates the demand for new and timelier data in the firm, thus blunting its labor-displacing effects. Yet there is no denying that such innovations can suppress the growth in office manpower, change the nature of required office skills, and shift the preferred location of some office functions out of the central city. The repetitive, standardized processes of the office are likely to be most amenable to an out-of-city location, while the elite functions are unlikely to be much affected.

The introduction of mass-data processing equipment has another implication for location. It opens up the possibility of central data-handling for the multi-plant or multi-warehouse firm which previously had been performing many of its office functions on a regional or local basis. This in turn creates the possibility of a redelegation of decisions to the central office—decisions on inventories, shipments, production schedules and the like. To the extent that the office function grows, therefore, the growth may well occur to a disproportionate extent in the office districts of the larger central cities, at the expense of the regional centers.

The possibility that only the largest cities may be the principal beneficiaries of continued office growth—indeed, the possibility that they may be the only beneficiaries —is raised also by the increased use of air travel by business executives. All of the locational implications of such travel are not yet clear. But one of the consequences of the use of such travel is that far-flung plants, warehouses and sales offices are no longer so remote from headquarters as they used to be. Accordingly, the risks of operating through absentee management and the need to delegate decision-making to the field may seem somewhat reduced.

Of course the development of air travel may be read two ways. For the availability of such air travel opens up the possibility of stationing key corporate offices in the field, yet being able to summon them to headquarters on a few hours' notice. But the odds seem heavy that the increased mobility among executives will not be exploited by dispersing them to the field but rather by gathering them in to central points; that in the rival pulls for more face-to-face contact among top executives and more face-to-face contact with plant managers, the former pull will be the stronger. This, too, suggests that "central office cities" may grow more so, at the expense of the lesser regional office centers. But it would be comforting if hard data could be brought to bear to test these conjectures.

SUMMARY

As one fits these various trends into a coherent whole, they suggest the possibility that we may have entered upon a new phase in the development of the large central cities of the nation. At the very center of such cities—more so in the larger than in the smaller ones—there is every reason to expect continued vitality. Office activities in the nation are expanding and will continue to expand. The central cities may not capture quite as high a proportion of such activity as they have in the past, but there is not much doubt that absolute increases in such employment will occur. Nor is there much doubt that, to the extent that they occur, they will offer a continued stimulus to some central business districts.

This activity aside, one sees only a growing obsolescence in the rest of the central city beyond its central business district. There is nothing in view calculated to interrupt the cycle so far evident in the old cities. When middle-income structures reach an advanced stage of obsolescence, they will be converted to intensive low-income use. The ancient slums will be partially abandoned, as they have been in the past, for the newer ones; populations will thin out in the former and rise in the latter, in a wave which moves gradually outward to the edges of the city and into the older portions of the suburban towns.

The outward movement of people will be matched by an outward movement of jobs. Retail trade will follow the populations. Manufacturing and wholesaling establishments will continue to respond to obsolescence by looking for new quarters and by renting in structures in the suburban industrial areas where obsolescence is less advanced. The movement of jobs will reinforce the movement of residences.

Beyond the central business district, therefore, but within the confines of the central city, there is likely to be a long-run decline in the intensive use of space as sites for jobs and homes. Will such space be converted to other uses? It is difficult to detect any actual or incipient private demand for city space which is of a magnitude calculated to replace such prior uses. Modern factory space is ruled out by the high costs of recapturing the site; new multi-story lofts face a poor market, since they will be competing with obsolescent factories vacated by their prior owners; office space, however greatly it expands, can scarcely be expected to fill more than a minuscule area, largely concentrated toward the city center; high-income renters may fill a little more space, but not much.

This leaves two possibilities: that middle-income families may decide to return to the cities in great numbers; or that subsidized governmental intervention, such as low-income housing or open-space projects, may be expanded to such levels as to constitute a significant space-using force. The first possibility would fly in the face of deep-seated historical trends, based on powerful sociological forces. The latter demands a scale of intervention much larger than any which heretofore has been contemplated.

Eleven / Race and Nationality

28 / Assimilation in America: Theory and Reality

Milton Gordon

Over 40 million immigrants have come to the United States since the founding of the colonies. Although immigration was sharply curtailed by the restrictive acts of the 1920's and by the Great Depression and World War II that followed, an average of over 300,000 immigrants have come to the United States each year since 1945.

The first settlers, who were largely English and Protestant, initially shaped the country's values and institutions, but waves of immigrants of different backgrounds have altered these values and institutions. Some historians have studied the immigrant experience and have assessed the impact of American culture on the newcomers and their children. Other scholars have focussed on the nativist hostility to immigration.

In the following essay, sociologist Milton Gordon briefly examines this literature, discusses the history of immigration, and proceeds to examine the extent to which assimilation has taken place in American life. It is important to note his definition of assimilation. He argues that the melting pot has had limited success. Several subcultures still exist, based on race, religion, and national background. To what extent are new forces breaking down these subcultures? Can an ethnically pluralistic society survive the impact of the mass media, the use of English and the loss of the old world language, intermarriage, the movement away from the old nationality neighborhoods to the suburbs, the decline of religious sectarianism, and the unifying consequences of increased education?

For further reading: *Oscar Handlin, *The Uprooted* (1952); *Nathan Glazer and Daniel P. Moynihan, *Beyond the Melting Pot* (1963); *John Higham, *Strangers in the Land* (1955); *Maldwyn Allen Jones, *American Immigration* (1960); W. Lloyd Warner and Leo Strole, *The Social Systems of American Ethnic Groups* (1956); Judith Kramer and Samuel Leventman, *Children of the Gilded Ghetto* (1961).

Daedalus, XC (Spring 1961), 263–285. Reprinted by permission of *Daedalus,* Journal of the American Academy of Arts and Sciences, Boston, Mass. Footnotes have been omitted.

Three ideologies or conceptual models have competed for attention on the American scene as explanations of the way in which a nation, in the beginning largely white, Anglo-Saxon, and Protestant, has absorbed over 41 million immigrants and their descendants from variegated sources and welded them into the contemporary American people. These ideologies are Anglo-conformity, the melting pot, and cultural pluralism. They have served at various times, and often simultaneously, as explanations of what has happened—descriptive models—and of what should happen—goal models. Not infrequently they have been used in such a fashion that it is difficult to tell which of these two usages the writer has had in mind. In fact, one of the more remarkable omissions in the history of American intellectual thought is the relative lack of close analytical attention given to the theory of immigrant adjustment in the United States by its social scientists.

The result has been that this field of discussion—an overridingly important one since it has significant implications for the more familiar problems of prejudice, discrimination, and majority-minority group relations generally—has been largely preempted by laymen, representatives of belles lettres, philosophers, and apologists of various persuasions. Even from these sources the amount of attention devoted to ideologies of assimilation is hardly extensive. Consequently, the work of improving intergroup relations in America is carried out by dedicated professional agencies and individuals who deal as best they can with day-to-day problems of discriminatory behavior, but who for the most part are unable to relate their efforts to an adequate conceptual apparatus. Such an apparatus would, at one and the same time, accurately describe the present structure of American society with respect to its ethnic groups (I shall use the term "ethnic group" to refer to any racial, religious, or national-origins collectivity), and allow for a considered formulation of its assimilation or integration goals for the foreseeable future. One is reminded of Alice's distraught question in her travels in Wonderland: "Would you tell me, please, which way I ought to go from here?" "That depends a good deal," replied the Cat with irrefutable logic, "on where you want to get to."

The story of America's immigration can be quickly told for our present purposes. The white American population at the time of the Revolution was largely English and Protestant in origin, but had already absorbed substantial groups of Germans and Scotch-Irish and smaller contingents of Frenchmen, Dutchmen, Swedes, Swiss, South Irish, Poles, and a handful of migrants from other European nations. Catholics were represented in modest numbers, particularly in the middle colonies, and a small number of Jews were residents of the incipient nation. With the exception of the Quakers and a few missionaries, the colonists had generally treated the Indians and their cultures with contempt and hostility, driving them from the coastal plains and making the western frontier a bloody battleground where eternal vigilance was the price of survival.

Although the Negro at that time made up nearly one-fifth of the total population, his predominantly slave status, together with racial and cultural prejudice, barred him from serious consideration as an assimilable element of the society. And while many groups of European origin started out as determined ethnic enclaves, eventually, most historians believe, considerable ethnic intermixture within the white population took place. "People of different blood" [sic]—write two American historians about the colonial period, "English, Irish, German, Huguenot, Dutch, Swedish—mingled and intermarried with little thought of any difference." In such a society, its people predominantly English, its white immigrants of other ethnic origins either English-speaking or derived largely from countries of northern and western Europe whose cultural divergences from the English were not great, and its dominant white population excluding by fiat the claims and considerations of welfare of the non-Caucasian minorities, the problem of assimilation understandably did not loom unduly large or complex.

The unfolding events of the next century and a half with increasing momentum dispelled the complacency which rested upon the relative simplicity of colonial and immediate post-Revolutionary conditions. The large-scale immigration to America of the famine-fleeing Irish, the Germans, and later the Scandinavians (along with additional Englishmen and other peoples of northern and western Europe) in the middle of the nineteenth century (the so-called "old immigration"), the emancipation of the Negro slaves and the problems created by post-Civil War reconstruction, the placing of the conquered Indian with his broken culture on government reservations, the arrival of the Oriental, first attracted by the discovery of gold and other opportunities in the West, and finally, beginning in the last quarter of the nineteenth century and continuing to the early 1920's, the swelling to proportions hitherto unimagined of the tide of immigration from the peasantries and "pales" of southern and eastern Europe—the Italians, Jews, and Slavs of the so-called "new immigration," fleeing the persecutions and industrial dislocations of the day—all these events constitute the background against which we may consider the rise of the theories of assimilation mentioned above. After a necessarily foreshortened description of each of these theories and their historical emergence, we shall suggest analytical distinctions designed to aid in clarifying the nature of the assimilation process, and then conclude by focusing on the American scene.

ANGLO-CONFORMITY

"Anglo-conformity" is a broad term used to cover a variety of viewpoints about assimilation and immigration; they all assume the desirability of maintaining English institutions (as modified by the American Revolution), the English language, and English-oriented cultural patterns as dominant and standard in American life. However, bound up with this assumption are related attitudes. These may range from discredited notions about race and "Nordic" and "Aryan" racial superiority, together with the nativist political programs and exclusionist immigration policies which such notions entail, through an intermediate position of favoring immigration from northern and western Europe on amorphous, unreflective grounds ("They are more like us"), to a lack of opposition to any source of immigration, as long as these immigrants and their descendants duly adopt the standard Anglo-Saxon cultural patterns. There is by no means any necessary equation between Anglo-conformity and racist attitudes.

It is quite likely that "Anglo-conformity" in its more moderate aspects, however explicit its formulation, has been the most prevalent ideology of assimilation goals in America throughout the nation's history. As far back as colonial times, Benjamin Franklin recorded concern about the clannishness of the Germans in Pennsylvania, their slowness in learning English, and the establishment of their own native-language press. Others of the founding fathers had similar reservations about large-scale immigration from Europe. In the context of their times they were unable to foresee the role such immigration was to play in creating the later greatness of the nation. They were not at all men of unthinking prejudices. The disestablishment of religion and the separation of church and state (so that no religious group—whether New England Congregationalists, Virginian Anglicans, or even all Protestants combined— could call upon the federal government for special favors or support, and so that man's religious conscience should be free) were cardinal points of the new national policy they fostered. "The Government of the United States," George Washington had written to the Jewish congregation of Newport during his first term as president, "gives to bigotry no sanction, to persecution no assistance."

Political differences with ancestral England had just been written in blood; but there is no reason to suppose that these men looked upon their fledgling country as an impartial melting pot for the merging of the various cultures of Europe, or as a new "nation of nations," or as anything but a society in which, with important political modifications, Anglo-Saxon speech and institutional forms would be standard. Indeed, their newly won victory for democracy and republicanism made them especially anxious that these still precarious fruits of revolution should not be threatened by a large influx of European peoples whose life experiences had accustomed them to the bonds of despotic monarchy. Thus, although they explicitly conceived of the new United States of America as a haven for those unfortunates of Europe who were persecuted and oppressed, they had characteristic reservations about the effects of too free a policy. "My opinion, with respect to immigration," Washington wrote to John Adams in 1794, "is that except of useful mechanics and some particular descriptions of men or professions, there is no need of encouragement, while the policy or advantage of its taking place in a body (I mean the settling of them in a body) may be much questioned; for, by so doing, they retain the language, habits and principles (good or bad) which they bring with them." Thomas Jefferson, whose views on race and attitudes towards slavery were notably liberal and advanced for his time, had similar doubts concerning the effects of mass immigration on American institutions, while conceding that immigrants, "if they come of themselves . . . are entitled to all the rights of citizenship."

The attitudes of Americans toward foreign immigration in the first three-quarters of the nineteenth century may correctly be described as ambiguous. On the one hand, immigrants were much desired, so as to swell the population and importance of states and territories, to man the farms of expanding prairie settlement, to work the mines, build the railroads and canals, and take their place in expanding industry. This was a period in which no federal legislation of any consequence prevented the entry of aliens, and such state legislation as existed attempted to bar on an individual basis only those who were likely to become a burden on the community, such as convicts and paupers. On the other hand, the arrival in an overwhelmingly Protestant society of large numbers of poverty-stricken Irish Catholics, who settled in groups in the slums of Eastern cities, roused dormant fears of "Popery" and Rome. Another source of anxiety was the substantial influx of Germans, who made their way to the cities and farms of the mid-West and whose different language, separate communal life, and freer ideas on temperance and sabbath observance brought them into conflict with the Anglo-Saxon bearers of the Puritan and Evangelical traditions. Fear of foreign "radicals" and suspicion of the economic demands of the occasionally aroused workingmen added fuel to the nativist fires. In their extreme form these fears resulted in the Native-American movement of the 1830's and 1840's and the

"American" or "Know-Nothing" party of the 1850's, with their anti-Catholic campaigns and their demands for restrictive laws on naturalization procedures and for keeping the foreign-born out of political office. While these movements scored local political successes and their turbulences so rent the national social fabric that the patches are not yet entirely invisible, they failed to influence national legislative policy on immigration and immigrants; and their fulminations inevitably provoked the expected reactions from thoughtful observers.

The flood of newcomers to the westward expanding nation grew larger, reaching over one and two-thirds million between 1841 and 1850 and over two and one-half million in the decade before the Civil War. Throughout the entire period, quite apart from the excesses of the Know-Nothings, the predominant (though not exclusive) conception of what the ideal immigrant adjustment should be was probably summed up in a letter written in 1818 by John Quincy Adams, then Secretary of State, in answer to the inquiries of the Baron von Fürstenwaerther. If not the earliest, it is certainly the most elegant version of the sentiment, "If they don't like it here, they can go back where they came from." Adams declared:

> They [immigrants to America] come to a life of independence, but to a life of labor—and, if they cannot accommodate themselves to the character, moral, political and physical, of this country with all its compensating balances of good and evil, the Atlantic is always open to them to return to the land of their nativity and their fathers. To one thing they must make up their minds, or they will be disappointed in every expectation of happiness as Americans. They must cast off the European skin, never to resume it. They must look forward to their posterity rather than backward to their ancestors; they must be sure that whatever their own feelings may be, those of their children will cling to the prejudices of this country.

The events that followed the Civil War created their own ambiguities in attitude toward the immigrant. A nation undergoing wholesale industrial expansion and not yet finished with the march of westward settlement could make good use of the never faltering waves of newcomers. But sporadic bursts of labor unrest, attributed to foreign radicals, the growth of Catholic institutions and the rise of Catholics to municipal political power, and the continuing association of immigrant settlement with urban slums revived familiar fears. The first federal selective law restricting immigration was passed in 1882, and Chinese immigration was cut off in the same year. The most significant development of all, barely recognized at first, was the change in the source of European migrants. Beginning in the 1880's, the countries of southern and eastern Europe began to be represented in substantial numbers for the first time, and in the next decade immigrants from these sources became numerically dominant. Now the notes of a new, or at least hitherto unemphasized, chord from the nativist lyre began to sound—the ugly chord, or discord, of racism. Previously vague and romantic notions of Anglo-Saxon peoplehood, combined with general ethnocentrism, rudimentary wisps of genetics, selected tidbits of evolutionary theory, and naive assumptions from an early and crude imported anthropology produced the doctrine that the English, Germans, and others of the "old immigration" constituted a superior race of tall, blonde, blue-eyed "Nordics" or "Aryans," whereas the peoples of eastern and southern Europe made up the darker Alpines or Mediterraneans—both "inferior" breeds whose presence in America threatened, either by intermixture or supplementation, the traditional American stock and culture. The obvious corollary to this doctrine was to exclude the allegedly inferior breeds; but if the new type of immigrant could not be excluded, then everything must be done to instill Anglo-Saxon virtues in these benighted creatures. Thus, one educator writing in 1909 could state:

> These southern and eastern Europeans are of a very different type from the north Europeans who preceded them. Illiterate, docile, lacking in self-reliance and initiative, and not possessing the Anglo-Teutonic conceptions of law, order, and government, their coming has served to dilute tremendously our national stock, and to corrupt our civic life. . . . Everywhere these people tend to settle in groups or settlements, and to set up here their national manners, customs, and observances. Our task is to break up these groups or settlements, to assimilate and amalgamate these people as a part of our American race, and to implant in their children, so far as can be done, the Anglo-Saxon conception of righteousness, law and order, and popular government, and to awaken in them a reverence for our democratic institutions and for those things in our national life which we as a people hold to be of abiding worth.

Anglo-conformity received its fullest expression in the so-called Americanization movement which gripped the nation during World War I. While "Americanization" in its various stages had more than one emphasis, it was essentially a consciously articulated movement to strip the immigrant of his native culture and attachments and make him over into an American along Anglo-Saxon lines—all this to be accomplished with great rapidity. To use an image of a later day, it was an attempt at "pressure-cooking assimilation." It had prewar antecedents, but it was during the height of the world conflict that federal agencies, state governments, municipalities, and a host of private organizations joined in the effort to persuade the immigrant to learn English, take out naturalization papers, buy war bonds, forget his former origins and culture, and give himself over to patriotic hysteria.

After the war and the "Red scare" which followed, the excesses of the Americanization movement subsided. In its place, however, came the restriction of immigration through federal law. Foiled at first by presidential vetoes, and later by the failure of the 1917 literacy test to halt the immigrant tide, the proponents of restriction finally put through in the early 1920's a series of acts culminating in the well-known national-origins formula for immigrant quotas which went into effect in 1929. Whatever the merits of a quantitative limit on the number of immigrants to be admitted to the United States, the provisions of the formula, which discriminated sharply against the countries of southern and eastern Europe, in effect institutionalized the assumptions of the rightful dominance of Anglo-Saxon patterns in the land. Reaffirmed with only slight modifications in the McCarran-Walter Act of 1952, these laws, then, stand as a legal monument to the creed of Anglo-conformity and a telling reminder that this ideological system still has numerous and powerful adherents on the American scene.

THE MELTING POT

While Anglo-conformity in various guises has probably been the most prevalent ideology of assimilation in the American historical experience, a competing viewpoint with more generous and idealistic overtones has had its adherents and exponents from the eighteenth century onward. Conditions in the virgin continent, it was clear, were modifying the institutions which the English colonists brought with them from the mother country. Arrivals from non-English homelands such as Germany, Sweden, and France were similarly exposed to this fresh environment. Was it not possible, then, to think of the evolving American society not as a slightly modified England but rather as a totally new blend, culturally and biologically, in which the stocks and folkways of Europe, figuratively speaking, were indiscriminately mixed in the political pot of the emerging nation and fused by the fires of American influence and interaction into a distinctly new type?

Such, at any rate, was the conception of the new society which motivated that eighteenth-century French-born writer and agriculturalist, J. Hector St. John Crève-coeur, who, after many years of American residence, published his reflections and observations in *Letters from an American Farmer*. Who, he asks, is the American?

> He is either an European, or the descendant of an European, hence that strange mixture of blood, which you will find in no other country. I could point out to you a family whose grandfather was an Englishman, whose wife was Dutch, whose son married a French woman, and whose present four sons have now four wives of different nations. *He* is an American, who leaving behind him all his ancient prejudices and manners, receives new ones from the new mode of life he has embraced, the new government he obeys, and the new rank he holds. He becomes an American by being received in the broad lap of our great *Alma Mater*. Here individuals of all nations are melted into a new race of men, whose labours and posterity will one day cause great changes in the world.

Some observers have interpreted the open-door policy on immigration of the first three-quarters of the nineteenth century as reflecting an underlying faith in the effectiveness of the American melting pot, in the belief "that all could be absorbed and that all could contribute to an emerging national character." No doubt many who observed with dismay the nativist agitation of the times felt as did Ralph Waldo Emerson that such conformity-demanding and immigrant-hating forces represented a perversion of the best American ideals. In 1845, Emerson wrote in his Journal:

> I hate the narrowness of the Native American Party. It is the dog in the manger. It is precisely opposite to all the dictates of love and magnanimity; and therefore, of course, opposite to true wisdom. . . . Man is the most composite of all creatures. . . . Well, as in the old burning of the Temple at Corinth, by the melting and intermixture of silver and gold and other metals a new compound more precious than any, called Corinthian brass, was formed; so in this continent,—asylum of all nations,—the energy of Irish, Germans, Swedes, Poles, and Cossacks, and all the European tribes,—of the Africans, and of the Polynesians,—will construct a new race, a new religion, a new state, a new literature, which will be as vigorous as the new Europe which came out of the smelting-pot of the Dark Ages, or that which earlier emerged from the Pelasgic and Etruscan barbarism. *La Nature aime les croisements.*

Eventually, the melting-pot hypothesis found its way into historical scholarship and interpretation. While many American historians of the late nineteenth century, some fresh from graduate study at German universities, tended to adopt the view that American institutions derived in essence from Anglo-Saxon (and ultimately Teutonic) sources, others were not so sure. One of these was Frederick Jackson

Turner, a young historian from Wisconsin, not long emerged from his graduate training at Johns Hopkins. Turner presented a paper to the American Historical Association, meeting in Chicago in 1893. Called "The Significance of the Frontier in American History," this paper proved to be one of the most influential essays in the history of American scholarship, and its point of view, supported by Turner's subsequent writings and his teaching, pervaded the field of American historical interpretation for at least a generation. Turner's thesis was that the dominant influence in the shaping of American institutions and American democracy was not this nation's European heritage in any of its forms, nor the forces emanating from the eastern seaboard cities, but rather the experiences created by a moving and variegated western frontier. Among the many effects attributed to the frontier environment and the challenges it presented was that it acted as a solvent for the national heritages and the separatist tendencies of the many nationality groups which had joined the trek westward, including the Germans and Scotch-Irish of the eighteenth century and the Scandinavians and Germans of the nineteenth. "The frontier," asserted Turner, "promoted the formation of a composite nationality for the American people. . . . In the crucible of the frontier the immigrants were Americanized, liberated, and fused into a mixed race, English in neither nationality nor characteristics. The process has gone on from the early days to our own." And later, in an essay on the role of the Mississippi Valley, he refers to "the tide of foreign immigration which has risen so steadily that it has made a composite American people whose amalgamation is destined to produce a new national stock."

Thus far, the proponents of the melting pot idea had dealt largely with the diversity produced by the sizeable immigration from the countries of northern and western Europe alone—the "old immigration," consisting of peoples with cultures and physical appearance not greatly different from those of the Anglo-Saxon stock. Emerson, it is true, had impartially included Africans, Polynesians, and Cossacks in his conception of the mixture; but it was only in the last two decades of the nineteenth century that a large-scale influx of peoples from the countries of southern and eastern Europe imperatively posed the question of whether these uprooted newcomers who were crowding into the large cities of the nation and the industrial sector of the economy could also be successfully "melted." Would the "urban melting pot" work as well as the "frontier melting pot" of an essentially rural society was alleged to have done?

It remained for an English-Jewish writer with strong social convictions, moved by his observation of the role of the United States as a haven for the poor and oppressed of Europe, to give utterance to the broader view of the American melting pot in a way which attracted public attention. In 1908, Israel Zangwill's drama, *The Melting Pot*, was produced in this country and became a popular success. It is a play dominated by the dream of its protagonist, a young Russian-Jewish immigrant to America, a composer, whose goal is the completion of a vast "American" symphony which will express his deeply felt conception of his adopted country as a divinely appointed crucible in which all the ethnic divisions of mankind will divest themselves of their ancient animosities and differences and become fused into one group, signifying the brotherhood of man. In the process he falls in love with a beautiful and cultured Gentile girl. The play ends with the performance of the symphony and, after numerous vicissitudes and traditional family opposition from both sides, with the approaching marriage of David Quixano and his beloved. During the course of these developments, David, in the rhetoric of the time, delivers himself of such sentiments as these:

> America is God's crucible, the great Melting Pot where all the races of Europe are melting and re-forming! Here you stand, good folk, think I, when I see them at Ellis Island, here you stand in your fifty groups, with your fifty languages and histories, and your fifty hatreds and rivalries. But you won't be long like that, brothers, for these are the fires of God you've come to—these are the fires of God. A fig for your feuds and vendettas! Germans and Frenchmen, Irishmen and Englishmen, Jews and Russians—into the Crucible with you all! God is making the American.

Here we have a conception of a melting pot which admits of no exceptions or qualifications with regard to the ethnic stocks which will fuse in the great crucible. Englishmen, Germans, Frenchmen, Slavs, Greeks, Syrians, Jews, Gentiles, even the black and yellow races, were specifically mentioned in Zangwill's rhapsodic enumeration. And this pot patently was to boil in the great cities of America.

Thus around the turn of the century the melting-pot idea became embedded in the ideals of the age as one response to the immigrant receiving experience of the nation. Soon to be challenged by a new philosophy of group adjustment (to be discussed below) and always competing with the more pervasive adherence to Anglo-conformity, the melting-pot image, however, continued to draw a portion of the attention consciously directed toward this aspect of the American scene in the first half of the twentieth century. In the mid-1940's a sociologist who had carried out an investigation of intermarriage trends in New Haven, Connecticut, described a revised conception of the melting process in that city and suggested a basic modification of the theory of that process. In New Haven, Ruby Jo Reeves Kennedy reported from a study of intermarriages from 1870 to 1940 that there was a distinct tendency for the British-Americans, Germans, and Scandinavians to marry among themselves— that is, within a Protestant "pool"; for the Irish, Italians, and Poles to marry among themselves—a Catholic "pool"; and for the Jews to marry other Jews. In other words, intermarriage was taking place across lines of nationality background, but there was a strong tendency for it to stay confined within one or the other of the three major religious groups, Protestants, Catholics, and Jews. Thus, declared Mrs. Kennedy, the picture in New Haven resembled a "triple melting pot" based on religious divisions, rather than a "single melting pot." Her study indicated, she stated, that "while strict endogamy is loosening, religious endogamy is persisting and the future cleavages will be along religious lines rather than along nationality lines as in the past. If this is the case, then the traditional 'single-melting-pot' idea must be abandoned, and a new conception, which we term the 'triple-melting-pot' theory of American assimilation, will take its place as the true expression of what is happening to the various nationality groups in the United States." The triple melting-pot thesis was later taken up by the theologian, Will Herberg, and formed an important sociological frame of reference for his analysis of religious trends in American society, *Protestant-Catholic-Jew*. But the triple melting-pot hypothesis patently takes us into the realm of a society pluralistically conceived. We turn now to the rise of an ideology which attempts to justify such a conception.

CULTURAL PLURALISM

Probably all the non-English immigrants who came to American shores in any significant numbers from colonial times onward—settling either in the forbidding wilderness, the lonely prairie, or in some accessible urban slum—created ethnic enclaves and looked forward to the preservation of at least some of their native cultural patterns. Such a development, natural as breathing, was supported by the later accretion of friends, relatives, and countrymen seeking out oases of familiarity in a strange land, by the desire of the settlers to rebuild (necessarily in miniature) a society in which they could communicate in the familiar tongue and maintain familiar institutions, and, finally, by the necessity to band together for mutual aid and mutual protection against the uncertainties of a strange and frequently hostile environment. This was as true of the "old" immigrants as of the "new." In fact, some of the liberal intellectuals who fled to America from an inhospitable political climate in Germany in the 1830's, 1840's, and 1850's looked forward to the creation of an all-German state within the union, or, even more hopefully, to the eventual formation of a separate German nation, as soon as the expected dissolution of the union under the impact of the slavery controversy should have taken place. Oscar Handlin, writing of the sons of Erin in mid-nineteenth-century Boston, recent refugees from famine and economic degradation in their homeland, points out: "Unable to participate in the normal associational affairs of the community, the Irish felt obliged to erect a society within a society, to act together in their own way. In every contact therefore the group, acting apart from other sections of the community, became intensely aware of its peculiar and exclusive identity." Thus cultural pluralism was a fact in American society before it became a theory—a theory with explicit relevance for the nation as a whole, and articulated and discussed in the English-speaking circles of American intellectual life.

Eventually, the cultural enclaves of the Germans (and the later arriving Scandinavians) were to decline in scope and significance as succeeding generations of their native-born attended public schools, left the farms and villages to strike out as individuals for the Americanizing city, and generally became subject to the influences of a standardizing industrial civilization. The German-American community, too, was struck a powerful blow by the accumulated passions generated by World War I —a blow from which it never fully recovered. The Irish were to be the dominant and pervasive element in the gradual emergence of a pan-Catholic group in America, but these developments would reveal themselves only in the twentieth century. In the meantime, in the last two decades of the nineteenth, the influx of immigrants from southern and eastern Europe had begun. These groups were all the more sociologically visible because the closing of the frontier, the occupational demands of an expanding industrial economy, and their own poverty made it inevitable that they would remain in the urban areas of the nation. In the swirling fires of controversy and the steadier flame of experience created by these new events, the ideology of cultural pluralism as a philosophy for the nation was forged.

The first manifestations of an ideological counterattack against draconic Americanization came not from the beleaguered newcomers (who were, after all, more concerned with survival than with theories of adjustment), but from those idealistic members of the middle class who, in the decade or so before the turn of the century, had followed the example of their English predecessors and "settled" in the slums to "learn to sup sorrow with the poor." Immediately, these workers in the "settlement houses" were forced to come to grips with the realities of immigrant life and adjustment. Not all reacted in the same way, but on the whole the settlements developed an approach to the immigrant which was sympathetic to his native cultural heritage and to his newly created ethnic institutions. For one thing, their workers, necessarily in intimate contact with the lives of these often pathetic and bewildered newcomers and their daily problems, could see how unfortunate were the effects of those forces which impelled rapid Americanization in their impact on the immigrants' children, who not infrequently became alienated from their parents and the restraining influence of family authority. Were not their parents ignorant and uneducated "Hunkies," "Sheenies," or "Dagoes," as that limited portion of the American environment in which they moved defined the matter? Ethnic "self-hatred" with its debilitating psychological consequences, family disorganization, and juvenile delinquency, were not unusual results of this state of affairs. Furthermore, the immigrants themselves were adversely affected by the incessant attacks on their culture, their language, their institutions, their very conception of themselves. How were they to maintain their self-respect when all that they knew, felt, and dreamed, beyond their sheer capacity for manual labor—in other words, all that they *were*—was despised or scoffed at in America? And—unkindest cut of all—their own children had begun to adopt the contemptuous attitude of the "Americans." Jane Addams relates in a moving chapter of her *Twenty Years at Hull House* how, after coming to have some conception of the extent and depth of these problems, she created at the settlement a "Labor Museum," in which the immigrant women of the various nationalities crowded together in the slums of Chicago could illustrate their native methods of spinning and weaving, and in which the relation of these earlier techniques to contemporary factory methods could be graphically shown. For the first time these peasant women were made to feel by some part of their American environment that they possessed valuable and interesting skills—that they too had something to offer—and for the first time, the daughters of these women who, after a long day's work at their dank "needletrade" sweatshops, came to Hull House to observe, began to appreciate the fact that their mothers, too, had a "culture," that this culture possessed its own merit, and that it was related to their own contemporary lives. How aptly Jane Addams concludes her chapter with the hope that "our American citizenship might be built without disturbing these foundations which were laid of old time."

This appreciative view of the immigrant's cultural heritage and of its distinctive usefulness both to himself and his adopted country received additional sustenance from another source: those intellectual currents of the day which, however overborne by their currently more powerful opposites, emphasized liberalism, internationalism, and tolerance. From time to time, an occasional educator or publicist protested the demands of the "Americanizers," arguing that the immigrant, too, had an ancient and honorable culture, and that this culture had much to offer an America whose character and destiny were still in the process of formation, an America which must serve as an example of the harmonious cooperation of various heritages to a world inflamed by nationalism and war. In 1916 John Dewey, Norman Hapgood, and the young literary critic, Randolph Bourne, published articles or addresses elaborating various aspects of this theme.

The classic statement of the cultural pluralist position, however, had been made over a year before. Early in 1915 there appeared in the pages of *The Nation* two articles under the title "Democracy *versus* the Melting-Pot." Their author was Horace Kallen, a Harvard-educated philosopher with a concern for the application of philosophy to societal affairs, and, as an American Jew, himself derivative of an ethnic background which was subject to the contemporary pressures for dissolution implicit in the "Americanization," or Anglo-conformity, and the melting-pot theories. In these articles Kallen vigorously rejected the usefulness of these theories as models of what was actually transpiring in American life or as ideals for the future. Rather he was impressed by the way in which the various ethnic groups in America were coincident with particular areas and regions, and with the tendency for each group to preserve its own language, religion, communal institutions, and ancestral culture. All the while, he pointed out, the immigrant has been learning to speak English as the language of general communication, and has participated in the over-all economic and political life of the nation. These developments in which "the United States are in the process of becoming a federal state not merely as a union of geographical and administrative unities, but also as a cooperation of cultural diversities, as a federation or commonwealth of national cultures," the author argued, far from constituting a violation of historic American political principles, as the "Americanizers" claimed, actually represented the inevitable consequences of democratic ideals, since individuals are implicated in groups, and since democracy for the individual must by extension also mean democracy for his group.

The processes just described, however, as Kallen develops his argument, are far from having been thoroughly realized. They are menaced by "Americanization" programs, assumptions of Anglo-Saxon superiority, and misguided attempts to promote "racial" amalgamation. Thus America stands at a kind of cultural crossroads. It can attempt to impose by force an artificial, Anglo-Saxon oriented uniformity on its peoples, or it can consciously allow and encourage its ethnic groups to develop democratically, each emphasizing its particular cultural heritage. If the latter course is followed, as Kallen puts it at the close of his essay, then,

> The outlines of a possible great and truly democratic commonwealth become discernible. Its form would be that of the federal republic; its substance a democracy of nationalities, cooperating voluntarily and autonomously through common institutions in the enterprise of self-realization through the perfection of men according to their kind. The common language of the commonwealth, the language of its great tradition, would be English, but each nationality would have for its emotional and involuntary life its own peculiar dialect or speech, its own individual and inevitable esthetic and intellectual forms. The political and economic life of the commonwealth is a single unit and serves as the foundation and background for the realization of the distinctive individuality of each *natio* that composes it and of the pooling of these in a harmony above them all. Thus "American civilization" may come to mean the perfection of the cooperative harmonies of "European civilization"—the waste, the squalor and the distress of Europe being eliminated—a multiplicity in a unity, an orchestration of mankind.

Within the next decade Kallen published more essays dealing with the theme of American multiple-group life, later collected in a volume. In the introductory note to this book he used for the first time the term "cultural pluralism" to refer to his position. These essays reflect both his increasingly sharp rejection of the onslaughts on the immigrant and his culture which the coming of World War I and its attendant fears, the "Red scare," the projection of themes of racial superiority, the continued exploitation of the newcomers, and the rise of the Ku Klux Klan all served to increase in intensity, and also his emphasis on cultural pluralism as the democratic antidote to these ills. He has since published other essays elaborating or annotating the theme of cultural pluralism. Thus, for at least forty-five years, most of them spent teaching at the New School for Social Research, Kallen has been acknowledged as the originator and leading philosophical exponent of the idea of cultural pluralism.

In the late 1930's and early 1940's the late Louis Adamic, the Yugoslav immigrant who had become an American writer, took up the theme of America's multicultural heritage and the role of these groups in forging the country's national character. Borrowing Walt Whitman's phrase, he described America as "a nation of nations," and while his ultimate goal was closer to the melting-pot idea than to cultural pluralism, he saw the immediate task as that of making America conscious of what it owed to all its ethnic groups, not just to the Anglo-Saxons. The children and grandchildren of immigrants of non-English origins, he was convinced, must be taught to be proud of the cultural heritage of their ancestral ethnic group and of its role in building the American nation; otherwise, they would not lose their sense of ethnic inferiority and the feeling of rootlessness he claimed to find in them.

Thus in the twentieth century, particularly since World War II, "cultural pluralism" has become a concept which has worked its way into the vocabulary and imagery of specialists in intergroup relations and leaders of ethnic communal groups. In view of this new pluralistic emphasis, some writers now prefer to speak of the "integration" of immigrants rather than of their "assimilation." However, with a few exceptions, no close analytical attention has been given either by social scientists or practitioners of intergroup relations to the meaning of cultural pluralism, its nature and relevance for a modern industrialized society, and its implications for problems of prejudice and discrimination—a point to which we referred at the outset of this discussion.

CONCLUSIONS

In the remaining pages I can make only a few analytical comments which I shall apply in context to the American scene, historical and current. My view of the American situation will not be documented here, but may be considered as a series of hypotheses in which I shall attempt to outline the American assimilation process.

First of all, it must be realized that "assimilation" is a blanket term which in reality covers a multitude of subprocesses. The most crucial distinction is one often ignored—the distinction between what I have elsewhere called "behavioral assimilation" and "structural assimilation." The first refers to the absorption of the cultural behavior patterns of the "host" society. (At the same time, there is frequently some modification of the cultural patterns of the immigrant-receiving country, as well.) There is a special term for this process of cultural modification or "behavioral assimilation"—namely, "acculturation." "Structural assimilation," on the other hand, refers to the entrance of the immigrants and their descendants into the social cliques, organizations, institutional activities, and general civic life of the receiving society. If this process takes place on a large enough scale, then a high frequency of intermarriage must result. A further distinction must be made between, on the one hand, those activities of the general civic life which involve earning a living, carrying out political responsibilities, and engaging in the instrumental affairs of the larger community, and, on the other hand, activities which create personal friendship patterns, frequent home intervisiting, communal worship, and communal recreation. The first type usually develops so-called "secondary relationships," which tend to be relatively impersonal and segmental; the latter type leads to "primary relationships," which are warm, intimate, and personal.

With these various distinctions in mind, we may then proceed.

Built on the base of the original immigrant "colony" but frequently extending into the life of successive generations, the characteristic ethnic group experience is this: within the ethnic group there develops a network of organizations and informal social relationships which permits and encourages the members of the ethnic group to remain within the confines of the group for all of their primary relationships and some of their secondary relationships throughout all the stages of the life cycle. From the cradle in the sectarian hospital to the child's play group, the social clique in high school, the fraternity and religious center in college, the dating group within which he searches for a spouse, the marriage partner, the neighborhood of his residence, the church affiliation and the church clubs, the men's and the women's social and service organizations, the adult clique of "marrieds," the vacation resort, and then, as the age cycle nears completion, the rest home for the elderly and, finally, the sectarian cemetery—in all these activities and relationships which are close to the core of personality and selfhood—the member of the ethnic group may if he wishes follow a path which never takes him across the boundaries of his ethnic structural network.

The picture is made more complex by the existence of social class divisions which cut across ethnic group lines just as they do those of the white Protestant population in America. As each ethnic group which has been here for the requisite time has developed second, third, or in some cases, succeeding generations, it has produced a college-educated group which composes an upper middle class (and sometimes upper class, as well) segment of the larger groups. Such class divisions tend to restrict primary group relations even further, for although the ethnic-group member feels a general sense of identification with all the bearers of his ethnic heritage, he feels comfortable in intimate social relations only with those who also share his own class background or attainment.

In short, my point is that, while *behavioral assimilation* or acculturation has taken place in America to a considerable degree, *structural assimilation*, with some important exceptions, has not been extensive. The exceptions are of two types. The first brings us back to the "triple melting pot" thesis of Ruby Jo Reeves Kennedy and Will Herberg. The "nationality" ethnic groups have tended to merge within each of the three major religious groups. This has been particularly true of the Protestant and Jewish communities. Those descendants of the "old" immigration of the nineteenth century, who were Protestant (many of the Germans and all the Scandinavians), have in considerable part gradually merged into the white Protestant "subsociety." Jews of Sephardic, German, and Eastern-European origins have similarly tended to come together in their communal life. The process of absorbing the various Catholic nationalities, such as the Italians, Poles, and French Canadians, into an American Catholic community hitherto dominated by the Irish has begun, although I do not believe that it is by any means close to completion. Racial and quasi-racial groups such as the Negroes, Indians, Mexican-Americans, and Puerto Ricans still retain their separate sociological structures. The outcome of all this in contemporary American life is thus pluralism—but it is more than "triple" and it is more accurately described as *structural pluralism* than as cultural pluralism, although some of the latter also remains.

My second exception refers to the social structures which implicate intellectuals. There is no space to develop the issue here, but I would argue that there is a social world or subsociety of the intellectuals in America in which true structural inter-mixture among persons of various ethnic backgrounds, including the religious, has markedly taken place.

My final point deals with the reasons for these developments. If structural as-similation has been retarded in America by religious and racial lines, we must ask why. The answer lies in the attitudes of both the majority and the minority groups and in the way these attitudes have interacted. A saying of the current day is, "It takes two to tango." To apply the analogy, there is no good reason to believe that white Protestant America has ever extended a firm and cordial invitation to its minorities to dance. Furthermore, the attitudes of the minority-group members themselves on the matter have been divided and ambiguous. Particularly for the minority religious groups, there is a certain logic in ethnic communality, since there is a commitment to the perpetuation of the religious ideology and since structural intermixture leads to intermarriage and the possible loss to the group of the inter-married family. Let us, then, examine the situation serially for various types of minorities.

With regard to the immigrant, in his characteristic numbers and socioeconomic background, structural assimilation was out of the question. He did not want it, and he had a positive need for the comfort of his own communal institutions. The native American, moreover, whatever the implications of his public pronouncements, had no intention of opening up his primary group life to entrance by these hordes of alien newcomers. The situation was a functionally complementary standoff.

The second generation found a much more complex situation. Many believed they heard the siren call of welcome to the social cliques, clubs, and institutions of white Protestant America. After all, it was simply a matter of learning American ways, was it not? Had they not grown up as Americans, and were they not culturally different from their parents, the "greenhorns?" Or perhaps an especially eager one reasoned (like the Jewish protagonist of Myron Kaufmann's novel, *Remember Me To God*, aspiring to membership in the prestigious club system of Harvard under-graduate social life) "If only I can go the last few steps in Ivy League manners and behavior, they will surely recognize that I am one of them and take me in." But, alas, Brooks Brothers suit notwithstanding, the doors of the fraternity house, the city men's club, and the country club were slammed in the face of the immigrant's offspring. That invitation was not really there in the first place; or, to the extent it was, in Joshua Fishman's phrase, it was a " 'look me over but don't touch me' invitation to the American minority group child." And so the rebuffed one returned to the homelier but dependable comfort of the communal institutions of his ancestral group. There he found his fellows of the same generation who had never stirred from the home fires. Some of these had been too timid to stray; others were ethnic ideologists committed to the group's survival; still others had never really believed in the authenticity of the siren call or were simply too passive to do more than go along the familiar way. All could now join in the task that was well within the realm of the sociologically possible—the build-up of social institutions and organizations within the ethnic enclave, manned increasingly by members of the second generation and suitably separated by social class.

Those who had for a time ventured out gingerly or confidently, as the case might be, had been lured by the vision of an "American" social structure that was somehow larger than all subgroups and was ethnically neutral. Were they, too, not Americans? But they found to their dismay that at the primary group level a neutral American social structure was a mirage. What at a distance seemed to be a quasi-public edifice flying only the all-inclusive flag of American nationality turned out on closer inspection to be the clubhouse of a particular ethnic group—the white Anglo-Saxon Protestants, its operation shot through with the premises and expectations of its parental ethnicity. In these terms, the desirability of whatever invitation was grudgingly extended to those of other ethnic backgrounds could only become a considerably attenuated one.

With the racial minorities, there was not even the pretense of an invitation. Negroes, to take the most salient example, have for the most part been determinedly barred from the cliques, social clubs, and churches of white America. Consequently, with due allowance for internal class differences, they have constructed their own network of organizations and institutions, their own "social world." There are now many vested interests served by the preservation of this separate communal life, and doubtless many Negroes are psychologically comfortable in it, even though at the same time they keenly desire that discrimination in such areas as employment, education, housing, and public accommodations be eliminated. However, the ideological attachment of Negroes to their communal separation is not conspicuous. Their sense of identification with ancestral African national cultures is virtually nonexistent, although Pan-Africanism engages the interest of some intellectuals and although "black nationalist" and "black racist" fringe groups have recently made an appearance at the other end of the communal spectrum. As for their religion, they are either Protestant or Catholic (overwhelmingly the former). Thus, there are no "logical" ideological reasons for their separate communality; dual social structures are created solely by the dynamics of prejudice and discrimination, rather than being reinforced by the ideological commitments of the minority itself.

Structural assimilation, then, has turned out to be the rock on which the ships of Anglo-conformity and the melting pot have foundered. To understand that behavioral assimilation (or acculturation) without massive structural intermingling in primary relationships has been the dominant motif in the American experience of creating and developing a nation out of diverse peoples is to comprehend the most essential sociological fact of that experience. It is against the background of "structural pluralism" that strategies of strengthening intergroup harmony, reducing ethnic discrimination and prejudice, and maintaining the rights of both those who stay within and those who venture beyond their ethnic boundaries must be thoughtfully devised.

29 / The Formation of Racial Ghettos and Conditions of Life in the Ghettos

Report of the National Advisory Commission on Civil Disorders

For most of their history, black Americans have lived in two environments: the southern plantation and the urban ghetto, north and south. After the destruction of slavery, most blacks ended up on plantations as sharecroppers and tenants, although some did live in cities and small towns and others managed to become independent farmers. In the late nineteenth century a steady migration of blacks to the cities began, but the Great Migration did not begin until the second decade of the twentieth century. As a result the vast majority of blacks now live in cities and roughly half live outside the South.

The appalling conditions of the ghettos have led to many frustrations and to eruptions of violence. Following the violence in the cities during the summer of 1967, President Lyndon B. Johnson created a Commission on Civil Disorders. The Commission concluded that America was moving in the direction of two separate societies: one black, one white. Actually blacks and whites had always lived apart in many ways; the ghetto intensified this separation. The report also contended that the crux of the problem was white racism and made modest proposals for social change, which have not been implemented thus far. Whether or not America can achieve a peaceful and just multiracial society remains unclear.

For further reading: *Gilbert Osofsky, *Harlem: The Making of a Ghetto* (1965); *Allan Spear, *Black Chicago* (1967); *Kenneth Clark, *Dark Ghetto* (1965); *St. Clair Drake and Horace R. Cayton, *Black Metropolis* (1962); *W. E. B. DuBois, *The Philadelphia Negro* (1899).

MAJOR TRENDS IN NEGRO POPULATION

Throughout the 20th century, and particularly in the last three decades, the Negro population of the United States has been steadily moving—from rural areas to urban, from South to North and West.

Report of the National Advisory Commission on Civil Disorders (Washington: U.S. Government Printing Office, 1968), 115–121, 133–141.

In 1910, 2.7 million Negroes lived in American cities—27 percent of the nation's Negro population of 9.8 million. Today, about 15 million Negro Americans live in metropolitan areas, or 69 percent of the Negro population of 21.5 million. In 1910, 885,000 Negroes—9 percent—lived outside the South. Now, almost 10 million, about 45 percent, live in the North or West.

These shifts in population have resulted from three basic trends:

> A rapid increase in the size of the Negro population.
> A continuous flow of Negroes from Southern rural areas, partly to large cities in the South, but primarily to large cities in the North and West.
> An increasing concentration of Negroes in large metropolitan areas within racially segregated neighborhoods.

Taken together, these trends have produced large and constantly growing concentrations of Negro population within big cities in all parts of the nation. Because most major civil disorders of recent years occurred in predominantly Negro neighborhoods, we have examined the causes of this concentration.

THE GROWTH RATE OF THE NEGRO POPULATION

During the first half of this century, the white population of the United States grew at a slightly faster rate than the Negro population. Because fertility rates[1] among Negro women were more than offset by death rates among Negroes and large-scale immigration of whites from Europe, the proportion of Negroes in the country declined from 12 percent in 1900 to 10 percent in 1940.

By the end of World War II—and increasingly since then—major advances in medicine and medical care, together with the increasing youth of the Negro population resulting from higher fertility rates, caused death rates among Negroes to fall much faster than among whites. This is shown in the following table:

DEATH RATE/1,000 POPULATION

Year	Whites	Nonwhites	Ratio of Nonwhite Rate to White Rate
1900	17.0	25.0	1.47
1940	10.4	13.8	1.33
1965	9.4	9.6	1.02

In addition, white immigration from outside the United States dropped dramatically after stringent restrictions were adopted in the 1920's.

20-year Period	Total Immigration (Millions)
1901–20	14.5
1921–40	4.6
1941–60	3.6

---

[1] The "fertility rate" is the number of live births per year per 1,000 women age 15 to 44 in the group concerned.

Thus, by mid-century, both factors which had previously offset higher fertility rates among Negro women no longer were in effect.

While Negro fertility rates, after rising rapidly to 1957, have declined sharply in the past decade, white fertility rates have dropped even more, leaving Negro rates much higher in comparison.

LIVE BIRTHS PER 1,000 WOMEN AGED 15–44

Year	White	Nonwhite	Ratio of Nonwhite to White
1940	77.1	102.4	1.33
1957	117.4	163.4	1.39
1965	91.4	133.9	1.46

The result is that Negro population is now growing significantly faster than white population. From 1940 to 1960, the white population rose 34.0 percent, but the Negro population rose 46.6 percent. From 1960 to 1966, the white population grew 7.6 percent, whereas Negro population rose 14.4 percent, almost twice as much.

Consequently, the proportion of Negroes in the total population has risen from 10.0 percent in 1950 to 10.5 percent in 1960, and 11.1 percent in 1966.[2]

In 1950, at least one of every ten Americans was Negro; in 1966, one of nine. If this trend continues, one of every eight Americans will be Negro by 1972.

Another consequence of higher birth rates among Negroes is that the Negro population is considerably younger than the white population. In 1966, the median age among whites was 29.1 years, as compared to 21.1 among Negroes. About 35 percent of the white population was under 18 years of age, compared with 45 percent for Negroes. About one of every six children under five and one of every six new babies are Negro.

Negro-white fertility rates bear an interesting relationship to educational experience. Negro women with low levels of education have more children than white women with similar schooling, while Negro women with four years or more of college education have fewer children than white women similarly educated. The following table illustrates this:

Education Level Attained	Number of Children Ever Born to All Women Married or Unmarried) 35–39 Years Old, by Level of Education (Based on 1960 Census)	
	Nonwhite	White
Completed elementary school	3.0	2.8
Four years of high school	2.3	2.3
Four years of college	1.7	2.2
Five years or more of college	1.2	1.6

This suggests that the difference between Negro and white fertility rates may decline in the future if Negro educational attainment compares more closely with that of whites, and if a rising proportion of members of both groups complete college.

[2] These proportions are undoubtedly too low because the Census Bureau has consistently undercounted the number of Negroes in the U.S. by as much as 10 percent.

THE MIGRATION
OF NEGROES FROM THE SOUTH

The Magnitude of This Migration

In 1910, 91 percent of the Nation's 9.8 million Negroes lived in the South. Twenty-seven percent of American Negroes lived in cities of 2,500 persons or more, as compared to 49 percent of the Nation's white population.

By 1966, the Negro population had increased to 21.5 million, and two significant geographic shifts had taken place. The proportion of Negroes living in the South had dropped to 55 percent, and about 69 percent of all Negroes lived in metropolitan areas compared to 64 percent for whites. While the total Negro population more than doubled from 1910 to 1966, the number living in cities rose over fivefold (from 2.7 million to 14.8 million) and the number outside the South rose elevenfold (from 885,000 to 9.7 million).

Negro migration from the South began after the Civil War. By the turn of the century, sizeable Negro populations lived in many large Northern cities—Philadelphia, for example, had 63,400 Negro residents in 1900. The movement of Negroes out of the rural South accelerated during World War I, when floods and boll weevils hurt farming in the South and the industrial demands of the war created thousands of new jobs for unskilled workers in the North. After the war, the shift to mechanized farming spurred the continuing movement of Negroes from rural Southern areas.

The Depression slowed this migratory flow, but World War II set it in motion again. More recently, continuing mechanization of agriculture and the expansion of industrial employment in Northern and Western cities have served to sustain the movement of Negroes out of the South, although at a slightly lower rate.

Period	Net Negro Out-migration from the South	Annual Average Rate
1910–20	454,000	45,400
1920–30	749,000	74,900
1930–40	348,000	34,800
1940–50	1,597,000	159,700
1950–60	1,457,000	145,700
1960–66	613,000	102,500

From 1960 to 1963, annual Negro out-migration actually dropped to 78,000 but then rose to over 125,000 from 1963 to 1966.

Important Characteristics
of This Migration

It is useful to recall that even the latest scale of Negro migration is relatively small when compared to the earlier waves of European immigrants. A total of 8.8 million immigrants entered the United States between 1901 and 1911, and another 5.7 million arrived during the following decade. Even during the years from 1960 through 1966, the 1.8 million immigrants from abroad were almost three times the

613,000 Negroes who departed the South. In these same 6 years, California alone gained over 1.5 million new residents from internal shifts of American population.

Three major routes of Negro migration from the South have developed. One runs north along the Atlantic Seaboard toward Boston, another north from Mississippi toward Chicago, and the third west from Texas and Louisiana toward California. Between 1955 and 1960, 50 percent of the nonwhite migrants to the New York metropolitan area came from North Carolina, South Carolina, Virginia, Georgia, and Alabama; North Carolina alone supplied 20 percent of all New York's nonwhite immigrants. During the same period, almost 60 percent of the nonwhite migrants to Chicago came from Mississippi, Tennessee, Arkansas, Alabama, and Louisiana; Mississippi accounted for almost one-third. During these years, three-fourths of the nonwhite migrants to Los Angeles came from Texas, Louisiana, Mississippi, Arkansas, and Alabama.

The flow of Negroes from the South has caused the Negro population to grow more rapidly in the North and West, as indicated below.

Period	Total Negro Population Gains (Millions)		Percent of Gain In North and West
	North and West	South	
1940–50	1.859	0.321	85.2
1950–60	2.741	1.086	71.6
1960–66	2.119	0.517	80.4

As a result, although a much higher proportion of Negroes still reside in the South, the distribution of Negroes throughout the United States is beginning to approximate that of whites, as the following tables show.

PERCENT DISTRIBUTION OF THE POPULATION BY REGION—
1950, 1960, AND 1966

	Negro			White		
	1950	1960	1966	1950	1960 [a]	1966
United States	100	100	100	100	100	100
South	68	60	55	27	27	28
North	28	34	37	59	56	55
Northeast	13	16	17	28	26	26
Northcentral	15	18	20	31	30	29
West	4	6	8	14	16	17

[a] Rounds to 99.

NEGROES AS A PERCENTAGE OF THE TOTAL POPULATION IN THE UNITED STATES AND EACH REGION, 1950, 1960, AND 1966

	1950	1960	1966
United States	10	11	11
South	22	21	20
North	5	7	8
West	3	4	5

Negroes in the North and West are now so numerous that natural increase rather than migration provides the greater part of Negro population gains there. And even though Negro migration has continued at a high level, it comprises a constantly declining proportion of Negro growth in these regions.

Period	Percentage of Total North and West Negro Gain from Southern In-mi- gration
1940–50	85.9
1950–60	53.1
1960–66	28.9

In other words, we have reached the point where the Negro populations of the North and West will continue to expand significantly even if migration from the South drops substantially.

Future Migration

Despite accelerating Negro migration from the South, the Negro population there has continued to rise.

Date	Negro Population in the South (Millions)	Change from Preceding Date	
		Total	Annual Average
1940	9.9		
1950	10.2	321,000	32,100
1960	11.3	1,086,000	108,600
1966	11.8	517,000	86,200

Nor is it likely to halt. Negro birth rates in the South, as elsewhere, have fallen sharply since 1957, but so far this decline has been offset by the rising Negro population base remaining in the South. From 1950 to 1960, southern Negro births generated an average net increase of 254,000 per year and, from 1960 to 1966, an average of 188,000 per year. Even if Negro birth rates continue to fall they are likely to remain high enough to support significant migration to other regions for some time to come.

The Negro population in the South is becoming increasingly urbanized. In 1950, there were 5.4 million southern rural Negroes; by 1960, 4.8 million. But this decline has been more than offset by increases in the urban population. A rising proportion of interregional migration now consists of persons moving from one city to another. From 1960 to 1966, rural Negro population in the South was far below its peak, but the annual average migration of Negroes from the South was still substantial.

These facts demonstrate that Negro migration from the South, which has maintained a high rate for the past 60 years, will continue unless economic conditions change dramatically in either the South or the North and West. This conclusion is reinforced by the fact that most Southern states in recent decades have also experienced outflows of white population. From 1950 to 1960, 11 of the 17 Southern states (including the District of Columbia) "exported" white population—as compared to 13 which "exported" Negro population. Excluding Florida's net gain by migration of 1.5 million, the other 16 Southern states together had a net loss by migration of 1.46 million whites.

THE CONCENTRATION
OF NEGRO POPULATION IN LARGE CITIES

Where Negro Urbanization Has Occurred

Statistically, the Negro population in America has become more urbanized, and more metropolitan, than the white population. According to Census Bureau estimates, almost 70 percent of all Negroes in 1966 lived in metropolitan areas, compared to 64 percent of all whites. In the South, more than half the Negro population now lives in cities. Rural Negroes outnumber urban Negroes in only four states: Arkansas, Mississippi, North Carolina, and South Carolina.

Basic data concerning Negro urbanization trends, presented in tables [on page 377], indicate that:

> Almost all Negro population growth is occurring within metropolitan areas, primarily within central cities. From 1950 to 1966, the U.S. Negro population rose 6.5 million. Over 98 percent of that increase took place in metropolitan areas —86 percent within central cities, 12 percent in the urban fringe.

> The vast majority of white population growth is occurring in suburban portions of metropolitan areas. From 1950 to 1966, 77.8 percent of the white population increase of 35.6 million took place in the suburbs. Central cities received only 2.5 percent of this total white increase. Since 1960, white central-city population has actually declined by 1.3 million.

> As a result, central cities are steadily becoming more heavily Negro, while the urban fringes around them remain almost entirely white. The proportion of Negroes in all central cities rose steadily from 12 percent in 1950, to 17 percent in 1960, to 20 percent in 1966. Meanwhile, metropolitan areas outside of central cities remained 95 percent white from 1950 to 1960 and became 96 percent white by 1966.

> The Negro population is growing faster, both absolutely and relatively, in the larger metropolitan areas than in the smaller ones. From 1950 to 1966, the proportion of nonwhites in the central cities of metropolitan areas with 1 million or more persons doubled, reaching 26 percent, as compared with 20 percent in the central cities of metropolitan areas containing from 250,000 to 1 million persons and 12 percent in the central cities of metropolitan areas containing under 250,000 persons.

> The 12 largest central cities—New York, Chicago, Los Angeles, Philadelphia, Detroit, Baltimore, Houston, Cleveland, Washington, D.C., St. Louis, Milwaukee, and San Francisco—now contain over two-thirds of the Negro population outside the South and almost one-third of the total in the United States. All these cities have experienced rapid increases in Negro population since 1950. In six—Chicago, Detroit, Cleveland, St. Louis, Milwaukee, and San Francisco—the proportion of Negroes at least doubled. In two others—New York and Los Angeles—it

probably doubled. In 1968, seven of these cities are over 30 percent Negro, and one, Washington, D.C., is two-thirds Negro.

Factors Causing Residential Segregation in Metropolitan Areas

The early pattern of Negro settlement within each metropolitan area followed that of immigrant groups. Migrants converged on the older sections of the central city because the lowest cost housing was located there, friends and relatives were likely to be living there, and the older neighborhoods then often had good public transportation.

But the later phases of Negro settlement and expansion in metropolitan areas diverge sharply from those typical of white immigrants. As the whites were absorbed by the larger society, many left their predominantly ethnic neighborhoods and moved to outlying areas to obtain newer housing and better schools. Some scattered randomly over the suburban area. Others established new ethnic clusters in the suburbs, but even these rarely contained solely members of a single ethnic group. As a result, most middle-class neighborhoods—both in the suburbs and within central cities—have no distinctive ethnic character, except that they are white.

Nowhere has the expansion of America's urban Negro population followed this pattern of dispersal. Thousands of Negro families have attained incomes, living standards, and cultural levels matching or surpassing those of whites who have "upgraded" themselves from distinctly ethnic neighborhoods. Yet most Negro families have remained within predominantly Negro neighborhoods, primarily because they have been effectively excluded from white residential areas.

Their exclusion has been accomplished through various discriminatory practices, some obvious and overt, others subtle and hidden. Deliberate efforts are sometimes made to discourage Negro families from purchasing or renting homes in all-white neighborhoods. Intimidation and threats of violence have ranged from throwing garbage on lawns and making threatening phone calls to burning crosses in yards and even dynamiting property. More often, real estate agents simply refuse to show homes to Negro buyers.

Many middle-class Negro families, therefore, cease looking for homes beyond all-Negro areas or nearby "changing" neighborhoods. For them, trying to move into all-white neighborhoods is not worth the psychological efforts and costs required.

Another form of discrimination just as significant is white withdrawal from, or refusal to enter, neighborhoods where large numbers of Negroes are moving or already residing. Normal population turnover causes about 20 percent of the residents of average U.S. neighborhoods to move out every year because of income changes, job transfers, shifts in life-cycle position or deaths. This normal turnover rate is even higher in apartment areas. The refusal of whites to move into changing areas when vacancies occur there from normal turnover means that most of these vacancies are eventually occupied by Negroes. An inexorable shift toward heavy Negro occupancy results.

Once this happens, the remaining whites seek to leave, thus confirming the existing belief among whites that complete transformation of a neighborhood is inevitable once Negroes begin to enter. Since the belief itself is one of the major causes of the transformation, it becomes a self-fulfilling prophecy which inhibits the development of racially integrated neighborhoods.

As a result, Negro settlements expand almost entirely through "massive racial transition" at the edges of existing all-Negro neighborhoods, rather than by a gradual dispersion of population throughout the metropolitan area.

Two points are particularly important:

> "Massive transition" requires no panic or flight by the original white residents of a neighborhood into which Negroes begin moving. All it requires is the failure or refusal of other whites to fill the vacancies resulting from normal turnover.
>
> Thus, efforts to stop massive transition by persuading present white residents to remain will ultimately fail unless whites outside the neighborhood can be persuaded to move in.

It is obviously true that some residential separation of whites and Negroes would occur even without discriminatory practices by whites. This would result from the desires of some Negroes to live in predominantly Negro neighborhoods and from differences in meaningful social variables, such as income and educational levels. But these factors alone would not lead to the almost complete segregation of whites and Negroes which has developed in our metropolitan areas.

The Exodus of Whites from Central Cities

The process of racial transition in central-city neighborhoods has been only one factor among many others causing millions of whites to move out of central cities as the Negro populations there expanded. More basic perhaps have been the rising mobility and affluence of middle-class families and the more attractive living conditions—particularly better schools—in the suburbs.

Whatever the reason, the result is clear. In 1950, 45.5 million whites lived in central cities. If this population had grown from 1950 to 1960 at the same rate as the Nation's white population as a whole, it would have increased by 8 million. It actually rose only 2.2 million, indicating an outflow of 5.8 million.[3]

From 1960 to 1966, the white outflow appears to have been even more rapid. White population of central cities declined 1.3 million instead of rising 3.6 million—as it would if it had grown at the same rate as the entire white population. In theory, therefore, 4.9 million whites left central cities during these 6 years.

Statistics for all central cities as a group understate the relationship between Negro population growth and white outflow in individual central cities. The fact is, many cities with relatively few Negroes experienced rapid white-population growth, thereby obscuring the size of white out-migration that took place in cities having large increases in Negro population. For example, from 1950 to 1960, the 10 largest cities in the United States had a total Negro population increase of 1.6 million, or 55 percent, while the white population there declined 1.4 million. If the two cities where the white population increased (Los Angeles and Houston) are excluded, the nonwhite population in the remaining eight rose 1.4 million, whereas their white population declined 2.1 million. If the white population in these cities had increased at only half the rate of the white population in the United States as a

---

[3] The outflow of whites may be somewhat smaller than the 5.8 million difference between these figures, because the ages of the whites in many central cities are higher than in the Nation as a whole, and therefore the population would have grown somewhat more slowly.

whole from 1950 to 1960, it would have risen by 1.4 million. Thus, these eight cities actually experienced a white out-migration of at least 3.5 million, while gaining 1.4 million nonwhites.

The Extent of Residential Segregation

The rapid expansion of all-Negro residential areas and large-scale white withdrawal have continued a pattern of residential segregation that has existed in American cities for decades. A recent study[4] reveals that this pattern is present to a high degree in every large city in America. The authors devised an index to measure the degree of residential segregation. The index indicates for each city the percentage of Negroes who would have to move from the blocks where they now live to other blocks in order to provide a perfectly proportional, unsegregated distribution of population.

PROPORTION OF NEGROES IN EACH OF THE 30 LARGEST CITIES, 1950, 1960, AND ESTIMATED 1965

	1950	1960	Estimate,[a] 1965
New York, N.Y.	10	14	18
Chicago, Ill.	14	23	28
Los Angeles, Calif.	9	14	17
Philadelphia, Pa.	18	26	31
Detroit, Mich.	16	29	34
Baltimore, Md.	24	35	38
Houston, Tex.	21	23	23
Cleveland, Ohio	16	29	34
Washington, D.C.	35	54	66
St. Louis, Mo.	18	29	36
Milwaukee, Wis.	3	8	11
San Francisco, Calif.	6	10	12
Boston, Mass.	5	9	13
Dallas, Tex.	13	19	21
New Orleans, La.	32	37	41
Pittsburgh, Pa.	12	17	20
San Antonio, Tex.	7	7	8
San Diego, Calif.	5	6	7
Seattle, Wash.	3	5	7
Buffalo, N.Y.	6	13	17
Cincinnati, Ohio	16	22	24
Memphis, Tenn.	37	37	40
Denver, Colo.	4	6	9
Atlanta, Ga.	37	38	44
Minneapolis, Minn.	1	2	4
Indianapolis, Ind.	15	21	23
Kansas City, Mo.	12	18	22
Columbus, Ohio	12	16	18
Phoenix, Ariz.	5	5	5
Newark, N.J.	17	34	47

[a] Except for Cleveland, Buffalo, Memphis, and Phoenix, for which a special census has been made in recent years, these are very rough estimations computed on the basis of the change in relative proportions of Negro births and deaths since 1960.

Source: U.S. Department of Commerce, Bureau of the Census, BLS Report No. 332, p. 11.

[4] "Negroes in Cities," Karl and Alma Taeuber, Aldine Publishing Co., Chicago (1965).

According to their findings, the average segregation index for 207 of the largest U.S. cities was 86.2 in 1960. This means that an average of over 86 percent of all Negroes would have had to change blocks to create an unsegregated population distribution. Southern cities had a higher average index (90.9) than cities in the Northeast (79.2), the North Central (87.7), or the West (79.3). Only eight cities had index values below 70, whereas over 50 had values above 91.7.

The degree of residential segregation for all 207 cities has been relatively stable, averaging 85.2 in 1940, 87.3 in 1950, and 86.2 in 1960. Variations within individual regions were only slightly larger. However, a recent Census Bureau study shows that in most of the 12 large cities where special censuses were taken in the mid-1960's, the proportions of Negroes living in neighborhoods of greatest Negro concentration had increased since 1960.

Residential segregation is generally more prevalent with respect to Negroes than for any other minority group, including Puerto Ricans, Orientals, and Mexican-Americans. Moreover, it varies little between central city and suburb. This nearly universal pattern cannot be explained in terms of economic discrimination against all low-income groups. Analysis of 15 representative cities indicates that white upper- and middle-income households are far more segregated from Negro upper- and middle-income households than from white lower-income households.

In summary, the concentration of Negroes in central cities results from a combination of forces. Some of these forces, such as migration and initial settlement patterns in older neighborhoods, are similar to those which affected previous ethnic minorities. Others—particularly discrimination in employment and segregation in housing and schools—are a result of white attitudes based on race and color. These forces continue to shape the future of the central city.

The conditions of life in the racial ghetto are strikingly different from those to which most Americans are accustomed—especially white, middle-class Americans. We believe it important to describe these conditions and their effect on the lives of people who cannot escape from the ghetto.[5]

CRIME AND INSECURITY

Nothing is more fundamental to the quality of life in any area than the sense of personal security of its residents, and nothing affects this more than crime.

In general, crime rates in large cities are much higher than in other areas of our country. Within such cities, crime rates are higher in disadvantaged Negro areas than anywhere else.

The most widely used measure of crime is the number of "index crimes" (homicide, forcible rape, aggravated assault, robbery, burglary, grand larceny, and auto theft) in relation to population. In 1966, 1,754 such crimes were reported to police for every 100,000 Americans. In cities over 250,000, the rate was 3,153, and in cities over 1 million, it was 3,630—or more than double the national average. In suburban areas alone, including suburban cities, the rate was only 1,300, or just over one-third the rate in the largest cities.

[5] We have not attempted here to describe conditions relating to the fundamental problems of housing, education, and welfare, which are treated in detail later in the report.

Within larger cities, personal and property insecurity has consistently been highest in the older neighborhoods encircling the downtown business district. In most cities, crime rates for many decades have been higher in these inner areas than anywhere, except in downtown areas themselves, where they are inflated by the small number of residents.

High crime rates have persisted in these inner areas even though the ethnic character of their residents continually changed. Poor immigrants used these areas as "entry ports," then usually moved on to more desirable neighborhoods as soon as they acquired enough resources. Many "entry port" areas have now become racial ghettos.

The difference between crime rates in these disadvantaged neighborhoods and in other parts of the city is usually startling, as a comparison of crime rates in five police districts in Chicago for 1965 illustrates. These five include one high-income, all-white district at the periphery of the city, two very low-income, virtually all-Negro districts near the city core with numerous public housing projects, and two predominantly white districts, one with mainly lower middle-income families, the other containing a mixture of very high-income and relatively low-income households. The table shows crime rates against persons and against property in these five districts, plus the number of patrolmen assigned to them per 100,000 residents, as follows:

INCIDENCE OF INDEX CRIMES AND PATROLMEN ASSIGNMENTS PER 100,000 RESIDENTS IN 5 CHICAGO POLICE DISTRICTS, 1965

Number	High-Income White District	Low Middle-Income White District	Mixed High- and Low-Income White District	Very Low Income Negro District No. 1	Very Low Income Negro District No. 2
Index crimes against persons	80	440	338	1,615	2,820
Index crimes against property	1,038	1,750	2,080	2,508	2,630
Patrolmen assigned	93	133	115	243	291

These data indicate that:

Variations in the crime rate against persons within the city are extremely large. One very low income Negro district had 35 times as many serious crimes against persons per 100,000 residents as did the high-income white district.

Variations in the crime rate against property are much smaller. The highest rate was only 2.5 times larger than the lowest.

The lower the income in an area, the higher the crime rate there. Yet low-income Negro areas have significantly higher crime rates than low-income white areas. This reflects the high degree of social disorganization in Negro areas described previously, as well as the fact that poor Negroes as a group have lower incomes than poor whites as a group.

The presence of more police patrolmen per 100,000 residents does not necessarily offset high crime in certain parts of the city. Although the Chicago Police Department had assigned over three times as many patrolmen per 100,000 resi-

dents to the highest crime areas shown as to the lowest, crime rates in the highest crime area for offenses against both persons and property combined were 4.9
times as high as in the lowest crime area.

Because most middle-class Americans live in neighborhoods similar to the more
crime-free district described above, they have little comprehension of the sense of
insecurity that characterizes the ghetto resident. Moreover, official statistics normally
greatly understate actual crime rates because the vast majority of crimes are not
reported to the police. For example, studies conducted for the President's Crime
Commission in Washington, D.C., Boston, and Chicago, showed that three to six
times as many crimes were actually committed against persons and homes as were
reported to the police.

Two facts are crucial to an understanding of the effects of high crime rates in racial
ghettos; most of these crimes are committed by a small minority of the residents,
and the principal victims are the residents themselves. Throughout the United
States, the great majority of crimes committed by Negroes involve other Negroes as
victims. A special tabulation made by the Chicago Police Department for the
President's Crime Commission indicated that over 85 percent of the crimes committed against persons by Negroes between September, 1965, and March, 1966,
involved Negro victims.

As a result, the majority of law-abiding citizens who live in disadvantaged Negro
areas face much higher probabilities of being victimized than residents of most
higher income areas, including almost all suburbs. For nonwhites, the probability of
suffering from any index crime except larceny is 78 percent higher than for whites.
The probability of being raped is 3.7 times higher among nonwhite women, and
the probability of being robbed is 3.5 times higher for nonwhites in general.

The problems associated with high crime rates generate widespread hostility toward
the police in these neighborhoods for reasons described elsewhere in this report.
Thus, crime not only creates an atmosphere of insecurity and fear throughout Negro
neighborhoods but also causes continuing attrition of the relationship between Negro
residents and police. This bears a direct relationship to civil disorder.

There are reasons to expect the crime situation in these areas to become worse in
the future. First, crime rates throughout the United States have been rising rapidly
in recent years. The rate of index crimes against persons rose 37 percent from 1960
to 1966, and the rate of index crimes against property rose 50 percent. In the first
9 months of 1967, the number of index crimes was up 16 percent over the same
period in 1966, whereas the U.S. population rose about 1 percent. In cities of
250,000 to 1 million, index crime rose by over 20 percent, whereas it increased 4
percent in cities of over 1 million.[6]

Second, the number of police available to combat crime is rising much more
slowly than the amount of crime. In 1966, there were about 20 percent more police
employees in the United States than in 1960, and per capita expenditures for police
rose from $15.29 in 1960 to $20.99 in 1966, a gain of 37 percent. But over the
6-year period, the number of reported index crimes had jumped 62 percent. In
spite of significant improvements in police efficiency, it is clear that police will be

[6] The problem of interpreting and evaluating "rising" crime rates is complicated by the
changing age distribution of the population, improvements in reporting methods, and the increasing willingness of victims to report crimes. Despite these complications, there is general agreement on the serious increase in the incidence of crime in the United States.

unable to cope with their expanding workload unless there is a dramatic increase in the resources allocated by society to this task.

Third, in the next decade, the number of young Negroes aged 14 to 24 will increase rapidly, particularly in central cities. This group is responsible for a disproportionately high share of crimes in all parts of the Nation. In 1966, persons under 25 years of age comprised the following proportions of those arrested for various major crimes: murder, 37 percent; forcible rape, 64 percent; robbery, 71 percent; burglary, 81 percent; larceny, about 77 percent; and auto theft, 89 percent. For all index crimes together, the arrest rate for Negroes is about four times higher than that for whites. Yet the number of young Negroes aged 14 to 24 in central cities will rise about 63 percent from 1966 to 1975, as compared to only 32 percent for the total Negro population of central cities.[7]

HEALTH AND SANITATION CONDITIONS

The residents of the racial ghetto are significantly less healthy than most other Americans. They suffer from higher mortality rates, higher incidence of major diseases, and lower availability and utilization of medical services. They also experience higher admission rates to mental hospitals.

These conditions result from a number of factors.

Poverty

From the standpoint of health, poverty means deficient diets, lack of medical care, inadequate shelter and clothing and often lack of awareness of potential health needs. As a result, almost 30 percent of all persons with family incomes less than $2,000 per year suffer from chronic health conditions that adversely affect their employment—as compared with less than 8 percent of the families with incomes of $7,000 or more.

Poor families have the greatest need for financial assistance in meeting medical expenses. Only about 34 percent of families with incomes of less than $2,000 per year use health insurance benefits, as compared to nearly 90 percent of those with incomes of $7,000 or more.[8]

These factors are aggravated for Negroes when compared to whites for the simple reason that the proportion of persons in the United States who are poor is 3.5 times as high among Negroes (41 percent in 1966) as among whites (12 percent in 1966).

---

[7] Assuming those cities will experience the same proportion of total United States Negro population growth that they did from 1960 to 1966. The calculations are derived from population projections in Bureau of the Census, *Population Estimates,* Current Population Reports, Series P–25, No. 381. Dec. 18, 1967, p. 63.

[8] Public programs of various kinds have been providing significant financial assistance for medical care in recent years. In 1964, over $1.1 billion was paid out by various governments for such aid. About 52 percent of medical vendor payments came from Federal Government agencies, 33 percent from states, and 12 percent from local governments. The biggest contributions were made by the Old Age Assistance Program and the Medical Assistance for the Aged Program. The enactment of Medicare in 1965 has significantly added to this flow of public assistance for medical aid. However, it is too early to evaluate the results upon health conditions among the poor.

Maternal Mortality

Mortality rates for nonwhite mothers are four times as high as those for white mothers. There has been a sharp decline in such rates since 1940, when 774 nonwhite and 320 white mothers died for each 100,000 live births. In 1965, only 84 nonwhite and 21 white mothers died per 100,000 live births—but the gap between nonwhites and whites actually increased.

Infant Mortality

Mortality rates among nonwhite babies are 58 percent higher than among whites for those under 1 month old and almost three times as high among those from 1 month to 1 year old. This is true in spite of a large drop in infant mortality rates in both groups since 1940.

NUMBER OF INFANTS WHO DIED PER 1,000 LIVE BIRTHS

	Less than 1 month old		1 month to 1 year old	
Year	White	Nonwhite	White	Nonwhite
1940	27.2	39.7	16.0	34.1
1950	19.4	27.5	7.4	17.0
1960	17.2	26.9	5.7	16.4
1965	16.1	25.4	5.4	14.9

Life Expectancy

To some extent because of infant mortality rates, life expectancy at birth was 6.9 years longer for whites (71.0 years) than for nonwhites (64.1 years) in 1965. Even in the prime working ages, life expectancy is significantly lower among nonwhites than among whites. In 1965, white persons 25 years old could expect to live an average of 48.6 more years, whereas nonwhites 25 years old could expect to live another 43.3 years, or 11 percent less. Similar but smaller discrepancies existed at all ages from 25 through 55; some actually increased slightly between 1960 and 1965.

Lower Utilization of Health Services

A fact that also contributes to poorer health conditions in the ghetto is that Negro families with incomes similar to those of whites spend less on medical services and visit medical specialists less often.

PERCENT OF FAMILY EXPENDITURES SPENT FOR MEDICAL CARE, 1960–61

Income group	White	Nonwhite	Ratio, White to Nonwhite
Under $3,000	9	5	1.8:1
$3,000 to $7,499	7	5	1.4:1
$7,500 and over	6	4	1.5:1

Since the lowest income group contains a much larger proportion of nonwhite families than white families, the overall discrepancy in medical care spending between these two groups is very significant, as shown by the following table:

HEALTH EXPENSES PER PERSON PER YEAR FOR
THE PERIOD FROM JULY TO DECEMBER 1962

| Income by Racial Group | Expenses | | | | | |
| | Medical | | | | | |
	Total	Hospital	Doctor	Dental	Medicine	Other
Under $2,000 per family per year:						
White	$130	$33	$41	$11	$32	$13
Nonwhite	63	15	23	5	16	5
$10,000 and more per family per year:						
White	179	34	61	37	31	16
Nonwhite	133	34	50	19	23	8

These data indicate that nonwhite families in the lower income group spent less than half as much per person on medical services as white families with similar incomes. This discrepancy sharply declines but is still significant in the higher income group, where total nonwhite medical expenditures per person equal, on the average, 74.3 percent of white expenditures.

Negroes spend less on medical care for several reasons. Negro households generally are larger, requiring greater nonmedical expenses for each household and leaving less money for meeting medical expenses. Thus, lower expenditures per person would result even if expenditures per household were the same. Negroes also often pay more for other basic necessities such as food and consumer durables, as discussed in the next part of this chapter. In addition, fewer doctors, dentists, and medical facilities are conveniently available to Negroes than to most whites—a result both of geographic concentration of doctors in higher income areas in large cities and of discrimination against Negroes by doctors and hospitals. A survey in Cleveland indicated that there were 0.45 physicians per 1,000 people in poor neighborhoods, compared to 1.13 per 1,000 in nonpoverty areas. The result nationally is fewer visits to physicians and dentists.

PERCENT OF POPULATION MAKING ONE OR MORE VISITS TO INDICATED
TYPE OF MEDICAL SPECIALIST FROM JULY 1963 TO JUNE 1964

| Type of Medical Specialist | Family Incomes of $2,000–$3,999 | | Family Incomes of $7,000–$9,999 | |
	White	Nonwhite	White	Nonwhite
Physician	64	56	70	64
Dentist	31	20	52	33

Although widespread use of health insurance has led many hospitals to adopt nondiscriminatory policies, some private hospitals still refuse to admit Negro patients or to accept doctors with Negro patients. And many individual doctors still discriminate against Negro patients. As a result, Negroes are more likely to be treated in hospital clinics than whites and they are less likely to receive personalized service. This conclusion is confirmed by the following data:

PERCENT OF ALL VISITS TO PHYSICIANS FROM JULY 1963 TO JUNE 1964, MADE IN INDICATED WAYS

Type of Visit to Physician	Family Incomes of $2,000–$3,000		Family Incomes of $7,000–$9,999	
	White	Nonwhite	White	Nonwhite
In physician's office	68	56	73	66
Hospital clinic	17	35	7	16
Other (mainly telephone)	15	9	20	18
Total	100	100	100	100

Environmental Factors

Environmental conditions in disadvantaged Negro neighborhoods create further reasons for poor health conditions there. The level of sanitation is strikingly below that which is prevalent in most higher income areas. One simple reason is that residents often lack proper storage facilities for food—adequate refrigerators, freezers, even garbage cans, which are sometimes stolen as fast as landlords can replace them.

In areas where garbage collection and other sanitation services are grossly inadequate—commonly in the poorer parts of our large cities—rats proliferate. It is estimated that in 1965, there were over 14,000 cases of ratbite in the United States, mostly in such neighborhoods.

The importance of these conditions was outlined for the Commission as follows[9]:

> Sanitation Commissioners of New York City and Chicago both feel this [sanitation] to be an important community problem and report themselves as being under substantial pressure to improve conditions. *It must be concluded that slum sanitation is a serious problem in the minds of the urban poor and well merits, at least on that ground, the attention of the Commission.* A related problem, according to one Sanitation Commissioner, is the fact that residents of areas bordering on slums feel that sanitation and neighborhood cleanliness is a crucial issue, relating to the stability of their blocks and constituting an important psychological index of "how far gone" their area is.
>
> * * * There is no known study comparing sanitation services between slum and non-slum areas. The experts agree, however, that there are more services in the slums on a quantitative basis, although perhaps not on a per capita basis. In New York, for example, garbage pickups are supposedly scheduled for about six times a week in slums, compared to three times a week in other areas of the city; the comparable figures in Chicago are two to three times a week versus once a week.
>
> The point, therefore, is not the relative quantitative level of services but the peculiarly intense needs of ghetto areas for sanitation services. This high demand is the product of numerous factors including: (1) higher population density; (2) lack of well managed buildings and adequate garbage services provided by landlords, numbers of receptacles, carrying to curbside, number of electric garbage disposals; (3) high relocation rates of tenants and businesses, producing heavy volume of bulk refuse left on streets and in buildings; (4) different uses of the streets—as outdoor living rooms in summer, recreation areas—producing high visibility and sensitivity to garbage problems; (5) large numbers of abandoned cars; (6) severe rodent and pest problems; (7) traffic congestion blocking garbage collection; and (8) obstructed street cleaning and snow removal on crowded, car-

[9] Memorandum to the Commission dated Nov. 16, 1967, from Robert Patricelli, minority counsel, Subcommittee on Employment Manpower and Poverty, U.S. Senate.

choked streets. Each of these elements adds to the problem and suggests a different possible line of attack.

EXPLOITATION OF DISADVANTAGED CONSUMERS BY RETAIL MERCHANTS

Much of the violence in recent civil disorders has been directed at stores and other commercial establishments in disadvantaged Negro areas. In some cases, rioters focused on stores operated by white merchants who, they apparently believed, had been charging exorbitant prices or selling inferior goods. Not all the violence against these stores can be attributed to "revenge" for such practices. Yet it is clear that many residents of disadvantaged Negro neighborhoods believe they suffer constant abuses by local merchants.

Significant grievances concerning unfair commercial practices affecting Negro consumers were found in 11 of the 20 cities studied by the Commission. The fact that most of the merchants who operate stores in Negro areas are white undoubtedly contributes to the conclusion among Negroes that they are exploited by white society.

It is difficult to assess the precise degree and extent of exploitation. No systematic and reliable survey comparing consumer pricing and credit practices in all-Negro and other neighborhoods has ever been conducted on a nationwide basis. Differences in prices and credit practices between white middle-income areas and Negro low-income areas to some extent reflect differences in the real costs of serving these two markets (such as differential losses from pilferage in supermarkets), but the exact extent of these cost differences has never been estimated accurately. Finally, an examination of exploitative consumer practices must consider the particular structure and functions of the low-income consumer durables market.

Installment Buying

This complex situation can best be understood by first considering certain basic facts:

> Various cultural factors generate constant pressure on low-income families to buy many relatively expensive durable goods and display them in their homes. This pressure comes in part from continuous exposure to commercial advertising, especially on television. In January, 1967, over 88 percent of all Negro households had TV sets. A 1961 study of 464 low-income families in New York City showed that 95 percent of these relatively poor families had TV sets.
>
> Many poor families have extremely low incomes, bad previous credit records, unstable sources of income or other attributes which make it virtually impossible for them to buy merchandise from established large national or local retail firms. These families lack enough savings to pay cash, and they cannot meet the standard credit requirements of established general merchants because they are too likely to fall behind in their payments.
>
> Poor families in urban areas are far less mobile than others. A 1967 Chicago study of low-income Negro households indicated their low automobile ownership compelled them to patronize neighborhood merchants. These merchants typically provided smaller selection, poorer services and higher prices than big national out-

lets. The 1961 New York study also indicated that families who shopped outside their own neighborhoods were far less likely to pay exorbitant prices.

Most low-income families are uneducated concerning the nature of credit purchase contracts, the legal rights and obligations of both buyers and sellers, sources of advice for consumers who are having difficulties with merchants and the operation of the courts concerned with these matters. In contrast, merchants engaged in selling goods to them are very well informed.

In most states, the laws governing relations between consumers and merchants in effect offer protection only to informed, sophisticated parties with understanding of each other's rights and obligations. Consequently, these laws are little suited to protect the rights of most low-income consumers.

In this situation, exploitative practices flourish. Ghetto residents who want to buy relatively expensive goods cannot do so from standard retail outlets and are thus restricted to local stores. Forced to use credit, they have little understanding of the pitfalls of credit buying. But because they have unstable incomes and frequently fail to make payments, the cost to the merchants of serving them is significantly above that of serving middle-income consumers. Consequently, a special kind of merchant appears to sell them goods on terms designed to cover the high cost of doing business in ghetto neighborhoods.

Whether they actually gain higher profits, these merchants charge higher prices than those in other parts of the city to cover the greater credit risks and other higher operating costs inherent in neighborhood outlets. A recent study conducted by the Federal Trade Commission in Washington, D.C., illustrates this conclusion dramatically. The FTC identified a number of stores specializing in selling furniture and appliances to low-income households. About 92 percent of the sales of these stores were credit sales involving installment purchases, as compared to 27 percent of the sales in general retail outlets handling the same merchandise.

The median income annually of a sample of 486 customers of these stores was about $4,200, but one-third had annual incomes below $3,600, about 6 percent were receiving welfare payments, and another 76 percent were employed in the lowest paying occupations (service workers, operatives, laborers and domestics), as compared to 36 percent of the total labor force in Washington in those occupations.

Definitely catering to a low-income group, these stores charged significantly higher prices than general merchandise outlets in the Washington area. According to testimony by Paul Rand Dixon, Chairman of the FTC, an item selling wholesale at $100 would retail on the average for $165 in a general merchandise store and for $250 in a low-income specialty store. Thus, the customers of these outlets were paying an average price premium of about 52 percent.

While higher prices are not necessarily exploitative in themselves, many merchants in ghetto neighborhoods take advantage of their superior knowledge of credit buying by engaging in various exploitative tactics—high-pressure salesmanship, "bait advertising," misrepresentation of prices, substitution of used goods for promised new ones, failure to notify consumers of legal actions against them, refusal to repair or replace substandard goods, exorbitant prices or credit charges, and use of shoddy merchandise. Such tactics affect a great many low-income consumers. In the New York study 60 percent of all households had suffered from consumer problems (some of which were purely their own fault). About 23 percent had experienced serious exploitation. Another 20 percent, many of whom were also exploited, had experienced repossession, garnishment, or threat of garnishment.

Garnishment

Garnishment practices in many states allow creditors to deprive individuals of their wages through court action, without hearing or trial. In about 20 states, the wages of an employee can be diverted to a creditor merely upon the latter's deposition, with no advance hearing where the employee can defend himself. He often receives no prior notice of such action and is usually unaware of the law's operation and too poor to hire legal defense. Moreover, consumers may find themselves still owing money on a sales contract even after the creditor has repossessed the goods. The New York study cited earlier in this chapter indicated that 20 percent of a sample of low-income families had been subjected to legal action regarding consumer purchases. And the Federal Trade Commission study in Washington, D.C., showed that, on the average, retailers specializing in credit sales of furniture and appliances to low-income consumers resorted to court action once for every $2,200 of sales. Since their average sale was for $207, this amounted to using the courts to collect from one of every 11 customers. In contrast, department stores in the same area used court action against approximately one of every 14,500 customers.[10]

Variations in Food Prices

Residents of low-income Negro neighborhoods frequently claim that they pay higher prices for food in local markets than wealthier white suburbanites and receive inferior quality meat and produce. Statistically reliable information comparing prices and quality in these two kinds of areas is generally unavailable. The U.S. Bureau of Labor Statistics, studying food prices in six cities in 1966, compared prices of a standard list of 18 items in low-income areas and higher income areas in each city. In a total of 180 stores, including independent and chain stores, and for items of the same type sold in the same types of stores, there were no significant differences in prices between low-income and high-income areas. However, stores in low-income areas were more likely to be small independents (which had somewhat higher prices), to sell low-quality produce and meat at any given price, and to be patronized by people who typically bought smaller sized packages which are more expensive per unit of measure. In other words, many low-income consumers in fact pay higher prices, although the situation varies greatly from place to place.

Although these findings must be considered inconclusive, there are significant reasons to believe that poor households generally pay higher prices for the food they buy and receive lower quality food. Low-income consumers buy more food at local groceries because they are less mobile. Prices in these small stores are significantly higher than in major supermarkets because they cannot achieve economies of scale and because real operating costs are higher in low-income Negro areas than in outlying suburbs. For instance, inventory "shrinkage" from pilfering and other causes is normally under 2 percent of sales but can run twice as much in high-crime areas. Managers seek to make up for these added costs by charging higher prices for food or by substituting lower grades.

These practices do not necessarily involve exploitation, but they are often per-

---

[10] Assuming their sales also averaged $207 per customer.

ceived as exploitative and unfair by those who are aware of the price and quality differences involved but unaware of operating costs. In addition, it is probable that genuinely exploitative pricing practices exist in some areas. In either case, differential food prices constitute another factor convincing urban Negroes in low-income neighborhoods that whites discriminate against them.

30 / The Negro Family: The Case for National Action

The Moynihan Report

The publication of *The Negro Family: The Case for National Action* (the Moynihan report) in 1965 was greeted by a storm of protest. Some critics pointed to methodological faults in the study, noting that high illegitimacy rates for blacks could partly be accounted for by the fact that whites used contraceptives and abortion more frequently, maintaining that birth control and abortion were more closely related to class than race. Others questioned the report on the grounds that it did not consider changes in welfare regulations that invalidated some of its conclusions. Still others suggested that by emphasizing the instability of black families, the report shifted attention away from the real source of the race problem. They contended that the fundamental weakness of the black community was not the deterioration of the black family but, rather, white racism. Some attackers of the report said that by establishing white middle-class families as a norm, the report subtly supported racist ideology. In reading this document, it is essential to consider these criticisms as well as the main assumptions of the report: that social mobility is highly desirable and closely related to family stability. Apart from the criticism, it does raise several important historical problems. To what extent has the black family evolved differently from the white because of the black experience in slavery and the urban ghetto? The experiences of the black family should prompt one to consider to what extent the transition from slavery to freedom really altered the condition of black people in America. Slavery ended, but white racism hardly did, and its results have continued to brutalize black Americans, whether in families or as individuals.

For further reading: *E. Franklin Frazier, *The Negro Family in the United States* (1966); John Hope Franklin, *From Slavery to Freedom* (1967); *Elliott Rudwick and August Meier, *From Plantation to Ghetto* (1966); *Gunnar Myrdal, *An American Dilemma* (1944); *Lee Rainwater and William Yancey (eds.), *The Moynihan Report and the Politics*

The Negro Family: The Case for National Action (Washington: Office of Policy Planning and Research, U.S. Dept. of Labor, 1965). Tables and footnotes have been omitted.

of *Controversy* (1967); *Thomas Pettigrew, *Profile of the Negro American* (1964); Talcott Parsons and Kenneth B. Clark (eds.), *The Negro American* (1966); *Andrew Billingsley, *Black Families in White America* (1968).

THE NEGRO AMERICAN FAMILY

At the heart of the deterioration of the fabric of Negro society is the deterioration of the Negro family.

It is the fundamental source of the weakness of the Negro community at the present time.

There is probably no single fact of Negro American life so little understood by whites. The Negro situation is commonly perceived by whites in terms of the visible manifestations of discrimination and poverty, in part because Negro protest is directed against such obstacles, and in part, no doubt, because these are facts which involve the actions and attitudes of the white community as well. It is more difficult, however, for whites to perceive the effect that three centuries of exploitation have had on the fabric of Negro society itself. Here the consequences of the historic injustices done to Negro Americans are silent and hidden from view. But here is where the true injury has occurred: unless this damage is repaired, all the effort to end discrimination and poverty and injustice will come to little.

The role of the family in shaping character and ability is so pervasive as to be easily overlooked. The family is the basic social unit of American life; it is the basic socializing unit. By and large, adult conduct in society is learned as a child.

A fundamental insight of psychoanalytic theory, for example, is that the child learns a way of looking at life in his early years through which all later experience is viewed and which profoundly shapes his adult conduct.

It may be hazarded that the reason family structure does not loom larger in public discussion of social issues is that people tend to assume that the nature of family life is about the same throughout American society. The mass media and the development of suburbia have created an image of the American family as a highly standardized phenomenon. It is therefore easy to assume that whatever it is that makes for differences among individuals or groups of individuals, it is not a different family structure.

There is much truth to this; as with any other nation, Americans are producing a recognizable family system. But that process is not completed by any means. There are still, for example, important differences in family patterns surviving from the age of the great European migration to the United States, and these variations account for notable differences in the progress and assimilation of various ethnic and religious groups. A number of immigrant groups were characterized by unusually strong family bonds; these groups have characteristically progressed more rapidly than others.

But there is one truly great discontinuity in family structure in the United States at the present time: that between the white world in general and that of the Negro American.

The white family has achieved a high degree of stability and is maintaining that stability.

By contrast, the family structure of lower class Negroes is highly unstable, and in many urban centers is approaching complete breakdown.

N.B. There is considerable evidence that the Negro community is in fact dividing between a stable middle-class group that is steadily growing stronger and more successful, and an increasingly disorganized and disadvantaged lower-class group. There are indications, for example, that the middle-class Negro family puts a higher premium on family stability and the conserving of family resources than does the white middle-class family. The discussion of this paper is not, obviously, directed to the first group excepting as it is affected by the experiences of the second—an important exception.

There are two points to be noted in this context.

First, the emergence and increasing visibility of a Negro middle class may beguile the nation into supposing that the circumstances of the remainder of the Negro community are equally prosperous, whereas just the opposite is true at present, and is likely to continue so.

Second, the lumping of all Negroes together in one statistical measurement very probably conceals the extent of the disorganization among the lower-class group. If conditions are improving for one and deteriorating for the other, the resultant statistical averages might show no change. Further, the statistics on the Negro family and most other subjects treated in this paper refer only to a specific point in time. They are a vertical measure of the situation at a given moment. They do not measure the experience of individuals over time. Thus the average monthly unemployment rate for Negro males for 1964 is recorded as 9 percent. But *during* 1964, some 29 percent of Negro males were unemployed at one time or another. Similarly, for example, if 36 percent of Negro children are living in broken homes *at any specific moment*, it is likely that a far higher proportion of Negro children find themselves in that situation *at one time or another* in their lives.

Nearly a Quarter of Urban
Negro Marriages Are Dissolved

Nearly a quarter of Negro women living in cities who have ever married are divorced, separated, or are living apart from their husbands.

The rates are highest in the urban Northeast where 26 percent of Negro women ever married are either divorced, separated, or have their husbands absent.

On the urban frontier, the proportion of husbands absent is even higher. In New York City in 1960, it was 30.2 percent, *not* including divorces.

Among ever-married nonwhite women in the nation, the proportion with husbands present *declined* in *every* age group over the decade 1950–60, as follows:

	Percent with Husbands Present	
Age	*1950*	*1960*
15–19 years	77.8	72.5
20–24 years	76.7	74.2
25–29 years	76.1	73.4
30–34 years	74.9	72.0
35–39 years	73.1	70.7
40–44 years	68.9	68.2

Although similar declines occurred among white females, the proportion of white husbands present never dropped below 90 percent except for the first and last age groups.

Nearly One-Quarter of Negro Births Are Now Illegitimate

Both white and Negro illegitimacy rates have been increasing, although from dramatically different bases. The white rate was 2 percent in 1940; it was 3.07 percent in 1963. In that period, the Negro rate went from 16.8 percent to 23.6 percent.

The number of illegitimate children per 1,000 live births increased by 11 among whites in the period 1940–63, but by 68 among non-whites. There are, of course, limits to the dependability of these statistics. There are almost certainly a considerable number of Negro children who, although technically illegitimate, are in fact the offspring of stable unions. On the other hand, it may be assumed that many births that are in fact illegitimate are recorded otherwise. Probably the two opposite effects cancel each other out.

On the urban frontier, the nonwhite illegitimacy rates are usually higher than the national average, and the increase of late has been drastic.

In the District of Columbia, the illegitimacy rate for nonwhites grew from 21.8 percent in 1950, to 29.5 percent in 1964.

A similar picture of disintegrating Negro marriages emerges from the divorce statistics. Divorces have increased of late for both whites and nonwhites, but at a much greater rate for the latter. In 1940 both groups had a divorce rate of 2.2 percent. By 1964 the white rate had risen to 3.6 percent, but the nonwhite rate had reached 5.1 percent—40 percent greater than the formerly equal white rate.

Almost One-Fourth of Negro Families Are Headed by Females

As a direct result of this high rate of divorce, separation, and desertion, a very large percent of Negro families are headed by females. While the percentage of such families among whites has been dropping since 1940, it has been rising among Negroes.

The percent of nonwhite families headed by a female is more than double the percent for whites. Fatherless nonwhite families increased by a sixth between 1950 and 1960, but held constant for white families.

It has been estimated that only a minority of Negro children reach the age of 18 having lived all their lives with both their parents.

Once again, this measure of family disorganization is found to be diminishing among white families and increasing among Negro families.

The Breakdown of the Negro Family Has Led to a Startling Increase in Welfare Dependency

The majority of Negro children receive public assistance under the AFDC program at one point or another in their childhood.

At present, 14 percent of Negro children are receiving AFDC assistance, as against 2 percent of white children. Eight percent of white children receive such assistance at some time, as against 56 percent of nonwhites, according to an extrapolation based on HEW data. (Let it be noted, however, that out of a total of 1.8 million non-white illegitimate children in the nation in 1961, 1.3 million were *not* receiving aid under the AFDC program, although a substantial number have, or will, receive aid at some time in their lives.)

Again, the situation may be said to be worsening. The AFDC program, deriving from the long established Mothers' Aid programs, was established in 1935 principally to care for widows and orphans, although the legislation covered all children in homes deprived of parental support because one or both of their parents are absent or incapacitated.

In the beginning, the number of AFDC families in which the father was absent because of desertion was less than a third of the total. Today it is two-thirds. HEW estimates "that between two-thirds and three-fourths of the 50 percent increase from 1948 to 1955 in the number of absent-father families receiving ADC may be explained by an increase in broken homes in the population."

A 1960 study of Aid to Dependent Children in Cook County, Ill., stated:

> The "typical" ADC mother in Cook County was married and had children by her husband, who deserted; his whereabouts are unknown, and he does not contribute to the support of his children. She is not free to remarry and has had an illegitimate child since her husband left. (Almost 90 percent of the ADC families are Negro.)

The steady expansion of this welfare program, as of public assistance programs in general, can be taken as a measure of the steady disintegration of the Negro family structure over the past generation in the United States.

THE ROOTS OF THE PROBLEM

Slavery

The most perplexing question about American slavery, which has never been altogether explained, and which indeed most Americans hardly know exists, has been stated by Nathan Glazer as follows: "Why was American slavery the most awful the world has ever known?" The only thing that can be said with certainty is that this is true: it was.

American slavery was profoundly different from, and in its lasting effects on individuals and their children, indescribably worse than, any recorded servitude, ancient or modern. The peculiar nature of American slavery was noted by Alexis de Tocqueville and others, but it was not until 1948 that Frank Tannenbaum, a South American specialist, pointed to the striking differences between Brazilian and American slavery. The feudal, Catholic society of Brazil had a legal and religious tradition which accorded the slave a place as a human being in the hierarchy of society—a luckless, miserable place, to be sure, but a place withal. In contrast, there was nothing in the tradition of English law or Protestant theology which could accommodate to the fact of human bondage—the slaves were therefore reduced to the status of chattels—often, no doubt, well cared for, even privileged chattels, but chattels nevertheless.

Glazer, also focusing on the Brazil-United States comparison, continues.

In Brazil, the slave had many more rights than in the United States: he could legally marry, he could, indeed had to, be baptized and become a member of the Catholic Church, his family could not be broken up for sale, and he had many days on which he could either rest or earn money to buy his freedom. The Government encouraged manumission, and the freedom of infants could often be purchased for a small sum at the baptismal fount. In short: the Brazilian slave knew he was a man, and that he differed in degree, not in kind, from his master.

[In the United States,] the slave was totally removed from the protection of organized society (compare the elaborate provisions for the protection of slaves in the Bible), his existence as a human being was given no recognition by any religious or secular agency, he was totally ignorant of and completely cut off from his past, and he was offered absolutely no hope for the future. His children could be sold, his marriage was not recognized, his wife could be violated or sold (there was something comic about calling the woman with whom the master permitted him to live a "wife"), and he could also be subject, without redress, to frightful barbarities—there were presumably as many sadists among slaveowners, men and women, as there are in other groups. The slave could not, by law, be taught to read or write; he could not practice any religion without the permission of his master, and could never meet with his fellows, for religious or any other purposes, except in the presence of a white; and finally, if a master wished to free him, every legal obstacle was used to thwart such action. This was not what slavery meant in the ancient world, in medieval and early modern Europe, or in Brazil and the West Indies.

More important, American slavery was also awful in its effects. If we compared the present situation of the American Negro with that of, let us say, Brazilian Negroes (who were slaves 20 years longer), we begin to suspect that the differences are the result of very different patterns of slavery. Today the Brazilian Negroes are Brazilians; though most are poor and do the hard and dirty work of the country, as Negroes do in the United States, they are not cut off from society. They reach into its highest strata, merging there—in smaller and smaller numbers, it is true, but with complete acceptance—with other Brazilians of all kinds. The relations between Negroes and whites in Brazil show nothing of the mass irrationality that prevails in this country.

Stanley M. Elkins, drawing on the aberrant behavior of the prisoners in Nazi concentration camps, drew an elaborate parallel between the two institutions. This thesis has been summarized as follows by Thomas F. Pettigrew:

Both were closed systems, with little chance of manumission, emphasis on survival, and a single, omnipresent authority. The profound personality change created by Nazi internment, as independently reported by a number of psychologists and psychiatrists who survived, was toward childishness and total acceptance of the SS guards as father figures—a syndrome strikingly similar to the "Sambo" caricature of the Southern slave. Nineteenth-century racists readily believed that the "Sambo" personality was simply an inborn racial type. Yet no African anthropological data have ever shown any personality type resembling Sambo; and the concentration camps molded the equivalent personality pattern in a wide variety of Caucasian prisoners. Nor was Sambo merely a product of "slavery" in the abstract, for the less devastating Latin American system never developed such a type.

Extending this line of reasoning, psychologists point out that slavery in all its forms sharply lowered the need for achievement in slaves. . . . Negroes in bondage, stripped of their African heritage, were placed in a completely dependent role. All of their rewards came, not from individual initiative and enterprise, but from absolute obedience—a situation that severely depresses the need for achievement among all peoples. Most important of all, slavery vitiated family life. . . . Since many slaveowners neither fostered Christian marriage among their slave couples nor hesitated to separate them on the auction block, the slave household often developed a fatherless matrifocal (mother-centered) pattern.

The Reconstruction

With the emancipation of the slaves, the Negro American family began to form in the United States on a widespread scale. But it did so in an atmosphere markedly different from that which has produced the white American family.

The Negro was given liberty, but not equality. Life remained hazardous and marginal. Of the greatest importance, the Negro male, particularly in the South, became an object of intense hostility, an attitude unquestionably based in some measure on fear.

When Jim Crow made its appearance towards the end of the 19th century, it may be speculated that it was the Negro male who was most humiliated thereby; the male was more likely to use public facilities, which rapidly became segregated once the process began, and just as important, segregation, and the submissiveness it exacts, is surely more destructive to the male than to the female personality. Keeping the Negro "in his place" can be translated as keeping the Negro male in his place: the female was not a threat to anyone.

Unquestionably, these events worked against the emergence of a strong father figure. The very essence of the male animal, from the bantam rooster to the four-star general, is to strut. Indeed, in 19th century America, a particular type of exaggerated male boastfulness became almost a national style. Not for the Negro male. The "sassy nigger" was lynched.

In this situation, the Negro family made but little progress toward the middle-class pattern of the present time. Margaret Mead has pointed out that while "In every known human society, everywhere in the world, the young male learns that when he grows up one of the things which he must do in order to be a full member of society is to provide food for some female and her young." This pattern is not immutable, however: it can be broken, even though it has always eventually reasserted itself.

> Within the family, each new generation of young males learn the appropriate nurturing behavior and superimpose upon their biologically given maleness this learned parental role. When the family breaks down—as it does under slavery, under certain forms of indentured labor and serfdom, in periods of extreme social unrest during wars, revolutions, famines, and epidemics, or in periods of abrupt transition from one type of economy to another—this delicate line of transmission is broken. Men may flounder badly in these periods, during which the primary unit may again become mother and child, the biologically given, and the special conditions under which man has held his social traditions in trust are violated and distorted.

E. Franklin Frazier makes clear that at the time of emancipation Negro women were already "accustomed to playing the dominant role in family and marriage relations" and that this role persisted in the decades of rural life that followed.

Urbanization

Country life and city life are profoundly different. The gradual shift of American society from a rural to an urban basis over the past century and a half has caused abundant strains, many of which are still much in evidence. When this shift occurs suddenly, drastically, in one or two generations, the effect is immensely disruptive of traditional social patterns.

It was this abrupt transition that produced the wild Irish slums of the 19th Century Northeast. Drunkenness, crime, corruption, discrimination, family disorganization, juvenile delinquency were the routine of that era. In our own time, the same sudden transition has produced the Negro slum—different from, but hardly better than its predecessors, and fundamentally the result of the same process.

Negroes are now more urbanized than whites.

Negro families in the cities are more frequently headed by a woman than those in the country. The difference between the white and Negro proportions of families headed by a woman is greater in the city than in the country.

The promise of the city has so far been denied the majority of the Negro migrants, and most particularly the Negro family.

In 1939, E. Franklin Frazier described its plight movingly in that part of *The Negro Family* entitled "In the City of Destruction":

> The impact of hundreds of thousands of rural southern Negroes upon northern metropolitan communities presents a bewildering spectacle. Striking contrasts in levels of civilization and economic well-being among these newcomers to modern civilization seem to baffle any attempt to discover order and direction in their mode of life.
>
> In many cases, of course, the dissolution of the simple family organization has begun before the family reaches the northern city. But, if these families have managed to preserve their integrity until they reach the northern city, poverty, ignorance, and color force them to seek homes in deteriorated slum areas from which practically all institutional life has disappeared. Hence, at the same time that these simple rural families are losing their internal cohesion, they are being freed from the controlling force of public opinion and communal institutions. Family desertion among Negroes in cities appears, then, to be one of the inevitable consequences of the impact of urban life on the simple family organization and folk culture which the Negro has evolved in the rural South. The distribution of desertions in relation to the general economic and cultural organization of Negro communities that have grown up in our American cities shows in a striking manner the influence of selective factors in the process of adjustment to the urban environment.

Frazier concluded his classic study, *The Negro Family*, with the prophesy that the "travail of civilization is not yet ended."

> First, it appears that the family which evolved within the isolated world of the Negro folk will become increasingly disorganized. Modern means of communication will break down the isolation of the world of the black folk, and, as long as the bankrupt system of southern agriculture exists, Negro families will continue to seek a living in the towns and cities of the country. They will crowd the slum areas of southern cities or make their way to northern cities where their family life will become disrupted and their poverty will force them to depend upon charity.

In every index of family pathology—divorce, separation, and desertion, female family head, children in broken homes, and illegitimacy—the contrast between the urban and rural environment for Negro families is unmistakable.

Harlem, into which Negroes began to move early in this century, is the center and symbol of the urban life of the Negro American. Conditions in Harlem are not worse, they are probably better than in most Negro ghettos. The social disorganization of central Harlem, comprising ten health areas, was thoroughly documented by the HARYOU report, save for the illegitimacy rates. These have now been made available to the Labor Department by the New York City Department of Health. There could hardly be a more dramatic demonstration of the crumbling—the breaking—of the family structure on the urban frontier.

Unemployment and Poverty

The impact of unemployment on the Negro family, and particularly on the Negro male, is the least understood of all the developments that have contributed to the present crisis. There is little analysis because there has been almost no inquiry. Unemployment, for whites and nonwhites alike, has on the whole been treated as an economic phenomenon, with almost no attention paid for at least a quarter-century to social and personal consequences.

In 1940, Edward Wight Bakke described the effects of unemployment on family structure in terms of six stages of adjustment. Although the families studied were white, the pattern would clearly seem to be a general one, and apply to Negro families as well.

The first two stages end with the exhaustion of credit and the entry of the wife into the labor force. The father is no longer the provider and the elder children become resentful.

The third stage is the critical one of commencing a new day-to-day existence. At this point two women are in charge:

> Consider the fact that relief investigators or case workers are normally women and deal with the housewife. Already suffering a loss in prestige and authority in the family because of his failure to be the chief bread winner, the male head of the family feels deeply this obvious transfer of planning for the family's well-being to two women, one of them an outsider. His role is reduced to that of errand boy to and from the relief office.

If the family makes it through this stage Bakke finds that it is likely to survive, and the rest of the process is one of adjustment. *The critical element of adjustment was not welfare payments, but work.*

> Having observed our families under conditions of unemployment with no public help, or with that help coming from direct [sic] and from work relief, we are convinced that after the exhaustion of self-produced resources, work relief is the only type of assistance which can restore the strained bonds of family relationship in a way which promises the continued functioning of that family in meeting the responsibilities imposed upon it by our culture.

Work is precisely the one thing the Negro family head in such circumstances has not received over the past generation.[1]

[1] An exception is the rather small impact of the ADC-U program since 1961, now expanded by Title V of the Economic Opportunity Act.

The fundamental, overwhelming fact is that *Negro unemployment*, with the exception of a few years during World War II and the Korean War, *has continued at disaster levels for 35 years.*

Once again, this is particularly the case in the northern urban areas to which the Negro population has been moving.

The 1930 Census (taken in the spring, before the depression was in full swing) showed Negro unemployment at 6.1 percent, as against 6.6 percent for whites. But taking out the South reversed the relationship: white 7.4 percent, nonwhite 11.5 percent.

By 1940, the 2 to 1 white-Negro unemployment relationship that persists to this day had clearly emerged. Taking out the South again, whites were 14.8 percent, nonwhites 29.7 percent.

Since 1929, the Negro worker has been tremendously affected by the movements of the business cycle and of employment. He has been hit worse by declines than whites, and proportionately helped more by recoveries.

From 1951 to 1963, the level of Negro male unemployment was on a long-run rising trend, while at the same time following the short-run ups and downs of the business cycle. During the same period, the number of broken families in the Negro world was also on a long-run rise, with intermediate ups and downs.

[The statistics reveal] that the series move in the same directions—up and down together, with a long-run rising trend—but that the peaks and troughs are 1 year out of phase. Thus unemployment peaks 1 year before broken families, and so on. By plotting these series in terms of deviation from trend, and moving the unemployment curve *1 year ahead,* we [can] see the clear relation of the two otherwise seemingly unrelated series of events; the cyclical swings in unemployment have their counterpart in increases and decreases in separations.

The effect of recession unemployment on divorces further illustrates the economic roots of the problem. The nonwhite divorce rates dipped slightly in high unemployment years like 1954–55, 1958, 1961–62. . . .

Divorce is expensive: those without money resort to separation or desertion. While divorce is not a desirable goal for a society, it recognizes the importance of marriage and family, and for children some family continuity and support is more likely when the institution of the family has been so recognized.

The conclusion from these and similar data is difficult to avoid: During times when jobs were reasonably plentiful (although at no time during this period, save perhaps the first 2 years, did the unemployment rate for Negro males drop to anything like a reasonable level) the Negro family became stronger and more stable. As jobs became more and more difficult to find, the stability of the family became more and more difficult to maintain.

This relation is clearly seen in terms of the illegitimacy rates of census tracts in the District of Columbia compared with male unemployment rates in the same neighborhoods.

In 1963, a prosperous year, 29.2 percent of all Negro men in the labor force were unemployed at some time during the year. Almost half of these men were out of work 15 weeks or more.

The impact of poverty on Negro family structure is no less obvious, although again it may not be widely acknowledged. There would seem to be an American tradition, agrarian in its origins but reinforced by attitudes of urban immigrant groups, to the effect that family morality and stability decline as income and social position rise. Over the years this may have provided some consolation to the poor, but there is little evidence that it is true. On the contrary, higher family incomes are unmistakably associated with greater family stability—which comes first may be a matter for conjecture, but the conjunction of the two characteristics is unmistakable.

The Negro family is no exception. In the District of Columbia, for example, census tracts with median incomes over $8,000 had an illegitimacy rate one-third that of tracts in the category under $4,000.

The Wage System

The American wage system is conspicuous in the degree to which it provides high incomes for individuals, but is rarely adjusted to insure that family, as well as individual needs are met. Almost without exception, the social welfare and social insurance systems of other industrial democracies provide for some adjustment or supplement of a worker's income to provide for the extra expenses of those with families. American arrangements do not, save for income tax deductions.

The Federal minimum wage of $1.25 per hour provides a basic income for an individual, but an income well below the poverty line for a couple, much less a family with children.

The 1965 Economic Report of the President revised the data on the number of persons living in poverty in the United States to take account of the varying needs of families of different sizes, rather than using a flat cut off at the $3,000 income level. The resulting revision illustrates the significance of family size. Using these criteria, the number of poor families is smaller, but the number of large families who are poor increases, and the number of children in poverty rises by more than one-third—from 11 million to 15 million. This means that one-fourth of the Nation's children live in families that are poor.

A third of these children belong to families in which the father was not only present, but was employed the year round. In overall terms, median family income is lower for large families than for small families. Families of six or more children have median incomes 24 percent below families with three. (It may be added that 47 percent of young men who fail the Selective Service education test come from families of six or more.)

During the 1950–60 decade of heavy Negro migration to the cities of the North and West, the ratio of nonwhite to white family income in cities increased from 57 to 63 percent. Corresponding declines in the ratio in the rural nonfarm and farm areas kept the national ratio virtually unchanged. But between 1960 and 1963, median nonwhite family income slipped from 55 percent to 53 percent of white income. The drop occurred in three regions, with only the South, where a larger proportion of Negro families have more than one earner, showing a slight improvement.

This population growth must inevitably lead to an unconcealable crisis in Negro unemployment. The most conspicuous failure of the American social system in the past 10 years has been its inadequacy in providing jobs for Negro youth. Thus, in January 1965 the unemployment rate for Negro teenagers stood at 29 percent. This problem will now become steadily more serious.

Because in general terms Negro families have the largest number of children and the lowest incomes, many Negro fathers literally cannot support their families. Because the father is either not present, is unemployed, or makes such a low wage, the Negro woman goes to work. Fifty-six percent of Negro women, age 25 to 64, are in the work force, against 42 percent of white women. This dependence on the mother's income undermines the position of the father and deprives the children of the kind of attention, particularly in school matters, which is now a standard feature of middle-class upbringing.

The Dimensions Grow

The dimensions of the problems of Negro Americans are compounded by the present extraordinary growth in Negro population. At the founding of the nation, and into the first decade of the 19th century, 1 American in 5 was a Negro. The proportion declined steadily until it was only 1 in 10 by 1920, where it held until the 1950's, when it began to rise. Since 1950, the Negro population has grown at a rate of 2.4 percent per year compared with 1.7 percent for the total population. If this rate continues, in seven years 1 American in 8 will be nonwhite.

These changes are the result of a declining Negro death rate, now approaching that of the nation generally, and a fertility rate that grew steadily during the postwar period. By 1959, the ratio of white to nonwhite fertility rates reached 1:1.42. Both the white and nonwhite fertility rates have declined since 1959, but the differential has not narrowed.

Family size increased among nonwhite families between 1950 and 1960—as much for those without fathers as for those with fathers. Average family size changed little among white families, with a slight increase in the size of husband-wife families balanced by a decline in the size of families without fathers.

Negro women not only have more children, but have them earlier. Thus in 1960, there were 1,247 children ever born per thousand ever-married nonwhite women 15 to 19 years of age, as against only 725 among white women, a ratio of 1.7:1. The Negro fertility rate overall is now 1.4 times the white, but what might be called the generation rate is 1.7 times the white.

During the rest of the 1960's the nonwhite civilian population 14 years of age and over will increase by 20 percent—more than double the white rate. The nonwhite labor force will correspondingly increase 20 percent in the next 6 years, double the rate of increase in the nonwhite labor force of the past decade.

As with the population as a whole, there is much evidence that children are being born most rapidly in those Negro families with the least financial resources. This is an ancient pattern, but because the needs of children are greater today it is very possible that the education and opportunity gap between the offspring of these families and those of stable middle-class unions is not closing, but is growing wider.

A cycle is at work; too many children too early make it most difficult for the parents to finish school. (In February, 1963, 38 percent of the white girls who dropped out of school did so because of marriage or pregnancy, as against 49 percent of nonwhite girls.) An Urban League study in New York reported that 44 percent of girl dropouts left school because of pregnancy.

Low education levels in turn produce low income levels, which deprive children of many opportunities, and so the cycle repeats itself.

THE TANGLE OF PATHOLOGY

That the Negro American has survived at all is extraordinary—a lesser people might simply have died out, as indeed others have. That the Negro community has not only survived, but in this political generation has entered national affairs as a moderate, humane, and constructive national force is the highest testament to the healing powers of the democratic ideal and the creative vitality of the Negro people.

But it may not be supposed that the Negro American community has not paid a fearful price for the incredible mistreatment to which it has been subjected over the past three centuries.

In essence, the Negro community has been forced into a matriarchal structure which, because it is so out of line with the rest of the American society, seriously retards the progress of the group as a whole, and imposes a crushing burden on the Negro male and, in consequence, on a great many Negro women as well.

There is, presumably, no special reason why a society in which males are dominant in family relationships is to be preferred to a matriarchal arrangement. However, it is clearly a disadvantage for a minority group to be operating on one principle, while the great majority of the population, and the one with the most advantages to begin with, is operating on another. This is the present situation of the Negro. Ours is a society which presumes male leadership in private and public affairs. The arrangements of society facilitate such leadership and reward it. A subculture, such as that of the Negro American, in which this is not the pattern, is placed at a distinct disadvantage.

Here an earlier word of caution should be repeated. There is much evidence that a considerable number of Negro families have managed to break out of the tangle of pathology and to establish themselves as stable, effective units, living according to patterns of American society in general. E. Franklin Frazier has suggested that the middle-class Negro American family is, if anything, more patriarchal and protective of its children than the general run of such families. Given equal opportunities, the children of these families will perform as well or better than their white peers. They need no help from anyone, and ask none.

While this phenomenon is not easily measured, one index is that middle-class Negroes have even fewer children than middle-class whites, indicating a desire to conserve the advances they have made and to insure that their children do as well or better. Negro women who marry early to uneducated laborers have more children than white women in the same situation; Negro women who marry at the common age for the middle class to educated men doing technical or professional work have only four-fifths as many children as their white counterparts.

It might be estimated that as much as half of the Negro community falls into the middle class. However, the remaining half is in desperate and deteriorating circumstances. Moreover, because of housing segregation it is immensely difficult for the stable half to escape from the cultural influences of the unstable one. The children of middle-class Negroes often as not must grow up in, or next to the slums, an experience almost unknown to white middle-class children. They are therefore constantly exposed to the pathology of the disturbed group and constantly in danger of being drawn into it. It is for this reason that the propositions put forth in this study may be thought of as having a more or less general application.

In a word, most Negro youth are in *danger* of being caught up in the tangle of pathology that affects their world, and probably a majority are so entrapped. Many of those who escape do so for one generation only: as things now are, their children may have to run the gauntlet all over again. That is not the least vicious aspect of the world that white America has made for the Negro.

Obviously, not every instance of social pathology afflicting the Negro community can be traced to the weakness of family structure. If, for example, organized crime in the Negro community were not largely controlled by whites, there would be more capital accumulation among Negroes, and therefore probably more Negro business enterprises. If it were not for the hostility and fear many whites exhibit towards Negroes, they in turn would be less afflicted by hostility and fear and so on. There is no one Negro community. There is no one Negro problem. There is no one solution. Nonetheless, at the center of the tangle of pathology is the weakness of the family structure. Once or twice removed, it will be found to be the principal source of most of the aberrant, inadequate, or anti-social behavior that did not establish, but now serves to perpetuate the cycle of poverty and deprivation.

It was by destroying the Negro family under slavery that white America broke the will of the Negro people. Although that will has reasserted itself in our time, it is a resurgence doomed to frustration unless the viability of the Negro family is restored.

Matriarchy

A fundamental fact of Negro American family life is the often reversed roles of husband and wife.

Robert O. Blood, Jr., and Donald M. Wolfe, in a study of Detroit families, note that "Negro husbands have unusually low power," and while this is characteristic of all low income families, the pattern pervades the Negro social structure: "the cumulative result of discrimination in jobs . . . , the segregated housing, and the poor schooling of Negro men." In 44 percent of the Negro families studied, the wife was dominant, as against 20 percent of white wives. "Whereas the majority of white families are equalitarian, the largest percentage of Negro families are dominated by the wife."

The matriarchal pattern of so many Negro families reinforces itself over the generations. This process begins with education. Although the gap appears to be closing at the moment, for a long while, Negro females were better educated than Negro males, and this remains true today for the Negro population as a whole.

The difference in educational attainment between nonwhite men and women in the labor force is even greater; men lag 1.1 years behind women.

The disparity in educational attainment of male and female youth age 16 to 21 who were out of school in February, 1963, is striking. Among the nonwhite males, 66.3 percent were not high school graduates, compared with 55.0 percent of the females. A similar difference existed at the college level, with 4.5 percent of the males having completed 1 to 3 years of college compared with 7.3 percent of the females.

The poorer performance of the male in school exists from the very beginning, and the magnitude of the difference was documented by the 1960 Census in statistics on the number of children who have fallen one or more grades below the typical grade for children of the same age. The boys have more frequently fallen behind at every age level. (White boys also lag behind white girls, but at a differential of 1 to 6 percentage points.)

In 1960, 39 percent of all white persons 25 years of age and over who had completed 4 or more years of college were women. Fifty-three percent of the nonwhites who had attained this level were women.

However, the gap is closing. By October 1963, there were slightly more Negro men in college than women. Among whites there were almost twice as many men as women enrolled.

There is much evidence that Negro females are better students than their male counterparts.

Daniel Thompson of Dillard University, in a private communication on January 9, 1965, writes:

> As low as is the aspirational level among lower class Negro girls, it is considerably higher than among the boys. For example, I have examined the honor rolls in Negro high schools for about 10 years. As a rule, from 75 to 90 percent of all Negro honor students are girls.

Dr. Thompson reports that 70 percent of all applications for the National Achievement Scholarship Program financed by the Ford Foundation for outstanding Negro high school graduates are girls, despite special efforts by high school principals to submit the names of boys.

The finalists for this new program for outstanding Negro students were recently announced. Based on an inspection of the names, only about 43 percent of all the 639 finalists were male. (However, in the regular National Merit Scholarship program, males received 67 percent of the 1964 scholarship awards.)

Inevitably, these disparities have carried over to the area of employment and income.

In 1 out of 4 Negro families where the husband is present, is an earner, and someone else in the family works, the husband is not the principal earner. The comparable figure for whites is 18 percent.

More important, it is clear that Negro females have established a strong position for themselves in white collar and professional employment, precisely the areas of the economy which are growing most rapidly, and to which the highest prestige is accorded.

The President's Committee on Equal Employment Opportunity, making a preliminary report on employment in 1964 of over 16,000 companies with nearly 5 million employees, revealed this pattern with dramatic emphasis.

> In this work force, Negro males outnumber Negro females by a ratio of 4 to 1. Yet Negro males represent only 1.2 percent of all males in white collar occupations, while Negro females represent 3.1 percent of the total female white collar work force. Negro males represent 1.1 percent of all male professionals, whereas Negro females represent roughly 6 percent of all female professionals. Again, in technician occupations, Negro males represent 2.1 percent of all male technicians while Negro females represent roughly 10 percent of all female technicians. It would appear therefore that there are proportionately 4 times as many Negro females in significant white collar jobs [as] Negro males.

Although it is evident that office and clerical jobs account for approximately 50 percent of all Negro female white collar workers, it is significant that 6 out of every 100 Negro females are in professional jobs. This is substantially similar to the rate of all females in such jobs. Approximately 7 out of every 100 Negro females are in technician jobs. This exceeds the proportion of all females in technician jobs—approximately 5 out of every 100.

Negro females in skilled jobs are almost the same as that of all females in such jobs. Nine out of every 100 Negro males are in skilled occupations while 21 out of 100 of all males are in such jobs.

This pattern is to be seen in the Federal government, where special efforts have been made recently to insure equal employment opportunity for Negroes. These efforts have been notably successful in Departments such as Labor, where some 19 percent of employees are now Negro. (A not disproportionate percentage, given the composition of the work force in the areas where the main Department offices are located.) However, it may well be that these efforts have redounded mostly to the benefit of Negro women, and may even have accentuated the comparative disadvantage of Negro men. Seventy percent of the Negro employees of the Department of Labor are women, as contrasted with only 42 percent of the white employees.

Among nonprofessional Labor Department employees—where the most employment opportunities exist for all groups—Negro women outnumber Negro men 4 to 1, and average almost one grade higher in classification.

The testimony to the effects of these patterns in Negro family structure is widespread, and hardly to be doubted.

Only 57 percent of Negro adults reported themselves as married—spouse present, as compared with 78 percent of native white American gentiles, 91 percent of Italian-American, and 96 percent of Jewish informants. Of the 93 unmarried Negro youths interviewed, 22 percent did not have their mother living in the home with them, and 42 percent reported that their father was not living in their home. One-third of the youths did not know their father's present occupation, and two-thirds of a sample of 150 Negro adults did not know what the occupation of their father's father had been. Forty percent of the youths said that they had brothers and sisters living in other communities: another 40 percent reported relatives living in their home who were not parents, siblings, or grandparents.[2]

The Failure of Youth

Williams' account of Negro youth growing up with little knowledge of their fathers, less of their fathers' occupations, still less of family occupational traditions, is in sharp contrast to the experience of the white child. The white family, despite many variants, remains a powerful agency not only for transmitting property from one generation to the next, but also for transmitting no less valuable contracts with the world of education and work. In an earlier age, the Carpenters, Wainwrights, Weavers, Mercers, Farmers, Smiths acquired their names as well as their trades from their fathers and grandfathers. Children today still learn the patterns of work from their fathers even though they may no longer go into the same jobs.

White children without fathers at least perceive all about them the pattern of men working.

Negro children without fathers flounder—and fail.

[2] Robin M. Williams, Jr., in a Study of Elmira, New York.

Not always, to be sure. The Negro community produces its share, very possibly more than its share, of young people who have the something extra that carries them over the worst obstacles. But such persons are always a minority. The common run of young people in a group facing serious obstacles to success do not succeed.

A prime index of the disadvantage of Negro youth in the United States is their consistently poor performance on the mental tests that are a standard means of measuring ability and performance in the present generation.

There is absolutely no question of any genetic differential: Intelligence potential is distributed among Negro infants in the same proportion and pattern as among Icelanders or Chinese or any other group. American society, however, impairs the Negro potential. The statement of the HARYOU report that "there is no basic disagreement over the fact that central Harlem students are performing poorly in school" may be taken as true of Negro slum children throughout the United States.

Delinquency and Crime

The combined impact of poverty, failure, and isolation among Negro youth has had the predictable outcome in a disastrous delinquency and crime rate.

In a typical pattern of discrimination, Negro children in all public and private orphanages are a smaller proportion of all children than their proportion of the population although their needs are clearly greater.

On the other hand Negroes represent a third of all youth in training schools for juvenile delinquents.

It is probable that at present, a majority of the crimes against the person, such as rape, murder, and aggravated assault are committed by Negroes. There is, of course, no absolute evidence; inference can only be made from arrest and prison population statistics. The data that follow unquestionably are biased against Negroes, who are arraigned much more casually than are whites, but it may be doubted that the bias is great enough to affect the general proportions.

Again on the urban frontier the ratio is worse: 3 out of every 5 arrests for these crimes were of Negroes.

In Chicago in 1963, three-quarters of the persons arrested for such crimes were Negro; in Detroit, the same proportions held.

In 1960, 37 percent of all persons in Federal and State prisons were Negro. In that year, 56 percent of the homicide and 57 percent of the assault offenders committed to State institutions were Negro.

The overwhelming number of offenses committed by Negroes are directed toward other Negroes: the cost of crime to the Negro community is a combination of that to the criminal and to the victim.

Some of the research on the effects of broken homes on delinquent behavior recently surveyed by Thomas F. Pettigrew in *A Profile of the Negro American* is summarized below, along with several other studies of the question.

Mary Diggs found that three-fourths—twice the expected ratio—of Philadelphia's Negro delinquents who came before the law during 1948 did not live with both their natural parents.

In predicting juvenile crime, Eleanor and Sheldon Glueck also found that a higher proportion of delinquent than nondelinquent boys came from broken homes. They identified five critical factors in the home environment that made a difference in whether boys would become delinquents: discipline of boy by father, supervision of boy by mother, affection of father for boy, affection of mother for boy, and cohesiveness of family.

In 1952, when the New York City Youth Board set out to test the validity of these five factors as predictors of delinquency, a problem quickly emerged. The Glueck sample consisted of white boys of mainly Irish, Italian, Lithuanian, and English descent. However, the Youth Board group was 44 percent Negro and 14 percent Puerto Rican, and the frequency of broken homes within these groups was out of proportion to the total number of delinquents in the population.

> In the majority of these cases, the father was usually never in the home at all, absent for the major proportion of the boy's life, or was present only on occasion.

(The final prediction table was reduced to three factors: supervision of boy by mother, discipline of boy by mother, and family cohesiveness within what family, in fact, existed, but was, nonetheless, 85 percent accurate in predicting delinquents and 96 percent accurate in predicting nondelinquents.)

Researchers who have focused upon the "good" boy in high delinquency neighborhoods noted that they typically come from exceptionally stable, intact families.

Recent psychological research demonstrates the personality effects of being reared in a disorganized home without a father. One study showed that children from fatherless homes seek immediate gratification of their desires far more than children with fathers present. Others revealed that children who hunger for immediate gratification are more prone to delinquency, along with other less social behavior. Two psychologists, Pettigrew says, maintain that inability to delay gratification is a critical factor in immature, criminal, and neurotic behavior.

Finally, Pettigrew discussed the evidence that a stable home is a crucial factor in counteracting the effects of racism upon Negro personality.

> A warm, supportive home can effectively compensate for many of the restrictions the Negro child faces outside of the ghetto; consequently, the type of home life a Negro enjoys as a child may be far more crucial for governing the influence of segregation upon his personality than the form the segregation takes—legal or informal, Southern or Northern.

A Yale University study of youth in the lowest socioeconomic class in New Haven in 1950 whose behavior was followed through their 18th year revealed that among the delinquents in the group, 38 percent came from broken homes, compared with 24 percent of nondelinquents.

The President's Task Force on Manpower Conservation in 1963 found that of young men rejected for the draft for failure to pass the mental tests, 42 percent of those with a court record came from broken homes, compared with 30 percent of those without a court record. Half of all the nonwhite rejectees in the study with a court record came from broken homes.

An examination of the family background of 44,448 delinquency cases in Philadelphia between 1949 and 1954 documents the frequency of broken homes among delinquents. Sixty-two percent of the Negro delinquents and 36 percent of white delinquents were not living with both parents. In 1950, 33 percent of nonwhite children and 7 percent of white children in Philadelphia were living in homes without both parents. Repeaters were even more likely to be from broken homes than first offenders.

Alienation

The term alienation may by now have been used in too many ways to retain a clear meaning, but it will serve to sum up the equally numerous ways in which large numbers of Negro youth appear to be withdrawing from American society.

One startling way in which this occurs is that the men are just not there when the Census enumerator comes around.

According to Bureau of Census population estimates for 1963, there are only 87 nonwhite males for every 100 females in the 30-to-34-year age group. The ratio does not exceed 90 to 100 throughout the 25-to-44-year age bracket. In the urban Northeast, there are only 76 males per 100 females 20-to-24-years of age, and males as a percent of females are below 90 percent throughout all ages after 14.

There are not really fewer men than women in the 20-to-40 age bracket. What obviously is involved is an error in counting: the surveyors simply do not find the Negro man. Donald J. Bogue and his associates, who have studied the Federal count of the Negro man, place the error as high as 19.8 percent at age 28; a typical error of around 15 percent is estimated from age 19 through 43. Preliminary research in the Bureau of the Census on the 1960 enumeration has resulted in similar conclusions, although not necessarily the same estimates of the extent of the error. The Negro male *can* be found at age 17 and 18. On the basis of birth records and mortality records, the conclusion must be that he is there at age 19 as well.

When the enumerators do find him, his answers to the standard questions asked in the monthly unemployment survey often result in counting him as "not in the labor force." In other words, Negro male unemployment may in truth be somewhat greater than reported.

The labor force participation rates of nonwhite men have been falling since the beginning of the century and for the past decade have been lower than the rates for white men. In 1964, the participation rates were 78.0 percent for white men and 75.8 percent for nonwhite men. Almost one percentage point of this difference was due to a higher proportion of nonwhite men unable to work because of long-term physical or mental illness; it seems reasonable to assume that the rest of the difference is due to discouragement about finding a job.

If nonwhite male labor force participation rates were as high as the white rates, there would have been 140,000 more nonwhite males in the labor force in 1964. If we further assume that the 140,000 would have been unemployed, the unemployment rate for nonwhite men would have been 11.5 percent instead of the recorded rate of 9 percent, and the ratio between the nonwhite rate and the white rate would have jumped from 2:1 to 2.4:1.

Understated or not, the official unemployment rates for Negroes are almost unbelievable.

The unemployment statistics for Negro teenagers—29 percent in January 1965—reflect lack of training and opportunity in the greatest measure, but it may not be doubted that they also reflect a certain failure of nerve.

"Are you looking for a job?" Secretary of Labor Wirtz asked a young man on a Harlem street corner. "Why?" was the reply.

Richard A. Cloward and Robert Ontell have commented on this withdrawal in a discussion of the Mobilization for Youth project on the lower East Side of New York.

What contemporary slum and minority youth probably lack that similar children in earlier periods possessed is not motivation but some minimal sense of competence.

We are plagued, in work with these youth, by what appears to be a low tolerance for frustration. They are not able to absorb setbacks. Minor irritants and rebuffs are magnified out of all proportion to reality. Perhaps they react as they do because they are not equal to the world that confronts them, and they know it. And it is the knowing that is devastating. Had the occupational structure remained intact, or had the education provided to them kept pace with occupational changes, the situation would be a different one. But it is not, and that is what we and they have to contend with.

Narcotic addiction is a characteristic form of withdrawal. In 1963, Negroes made up 54 percent of the addict population of the United States. Although the Federal Bureau of Narcotics reports a decline in the Negro proportion of new addicts, HARYOU reports the addiction rate in central Harlem rose from 22.1 per 10,000 in 1955 to 40.4 in 1961.

There is a larger fact about the alienation of Negro youth than the tangle of pathology described by these statistics. It is a fact particularly difficult to grasp by white persons who have in recent years shown increasing awareness of Negro problems.

The present generation of Negro youth growing up in the urban ghettos has probably less personal contact with the white world than any generation in the history of the Negro American.

Until World War II it could be said that in general the Negro and white worlds lived if not together, at least side by side. Certainly they did, and do, in the South.

Since World War II, however, the two worlds have drawn physically apart. The symbol of this development was the construction in the 1940's and 1950's of the vast white, middle- and lower-middle class suburbs around all of the Nation's cities. Increasingly the inner cities have been left to Negroes—who now share almost no community life with whites.

In turn, because of this new housing pattern—most of which has been financially assisted by the Federal government—it is probable that the American school system has become *more*, rather than less segregated in the past two decades.

School integration has not occurred in the South, where a decade after *Brown v. Board of Education* only 1 Negro in 9 is attending school with white children.

And in the North, despite strenuous official efforts, neighborhoods and therefore schools are becoming more and more of one class and one color.

In New York City, in the school year 1957–58 there were 64 schools that were 90 percent or more Negro or Puerto Rican. Six years later there were 134 such schools.

Along with the diminution of white middle-class contacts for a large percentage of Negroes, observers report that the Negro churches have all but lost contact with men in the Northern cities as well. This may be a normal condition of urban life, but it is probably a changed condition for the Negro American and cannot be a socially desirable development.

The only religious movement that appears to have enlisted a considerable number of lower class Negro males in Northern cities of late is that of the Black Muslims: a movement based on total rejection of white society, even though it emulates whites more.

In a word: the tangle of pathology is tightening.